QPB Anthology of Women's Writing

By Susan Cahill

— Nonfiction —

For the Love of Ireland
A Literary Companion for Readers and Travelers

Desiring Italy
Women Writers Celebrate a Country

A Literary Guide to Ireland
(with Thomas Cahill)

— Anthologies —

Wise Women
Two Thousand Years of Spiritual Writing by Women

Writing Women's Lives
Autobiographical Narratives by 20th-Century American Women Writers

Growing Up Female
Stories by Women Writers from the American Mosaic

Women and Fiction
Short Stories by and About Women

— Fiction —

Earth Angels

QPB Anthology of

Women's Writing

FROM THE 14TH CENTURY TO THE PRESENT

EDITED BY SUSAN CAHILL

Quality Paperback Book Club
New York

Book design by Irene Lipton

QPB Anthology of Women's Writing is a publication of Quality Paperback Book Club, 1271 Avenue of the Americas, New York, NY 10020

Printed in the United States of America

for Tillie Olsen

Contents

Introduction

As the editor of this book, I've had the pleasure of sifting through the almost seven-hundred-year-old territory of writing by women from the United States, Canada, England, Ireland, and South Africa. It's a landscape of imagination and language that is compelling, diverse, and charged with revelation. My overall impression, and I hope yours, is of a "mosaic beauty," to use author Dorothy Canfield Fisher's phrase. It's a hard place to pull back from.

But the editorial process means you must at some point stop reading and get practical. Choices must be made: of this writer over that writer, of this poem rather than another, of a long story that will take up the number of pages on which two stories could easily run. One never forgets the writings not chosen.

In the end, though, there comes a certain confidence. First, that you've chosen with delight. Then, that the selections in this book represent a solid portion of the best writing by women on both sides of the Atlantic (and beyond) since it was first recorded in the fourteenth century. And most of all, that in each fiction, essay, poem, memoir, or letter, there's a voice that comes through, a voice you remember clearly even after reading thousands more pages since first hearing it. The collective voices of this book are hardly soothing, but the writers, to a woman, have a perfect ear, and that is always invigorating. From their distinctive angles, they urge the contemplation of the world and the ways women and men live and die in it. Some writers challenge readers to change, or at least to reread their lives under the bright light of an original or perhaps subversive vision.

I haven't travelled this territory solo. I've worked under the influence of other editors, critics, writers, readers, and the students with whom I've read much of this literature since I assembled my first anthology of writing by women in 1975. Together, we've respected certain writings as classics, certain writers as "among the best." Most of these established favorites—Jane Austen, the Brontës, Alice Munro, Maya Angelou, to name a few—are included here. In a book like this one, these names are quite simply *musts*.

I've also included writing that, though esteemed by critics and other writers, still deserves a larger popular audience. The legendary editor and novelist William Maxwell called Maeve Brennan's story "The Springs of

Affection" one of the great short stories of the twentieth century, but Brennan's fiction still comes as a surprise to many readers. (A few wrote to me after another story of hers appeared in an earlier collection, asking questions, wanting more of the mysterious Maeve.)

To make space for other lesser knowns, I've left out some of the most widely anthologized works, for example, Charlotte Perkins Gilman's "The Yellow Wallpaper" and Shirley Jackson's "The Lottery." Some writers who are best known for their fiction (Toni Morrison, Edna O'Brien) are represented here by their formidable nonfiction. A few writers (Grace Paley, Virginia Woolf, Cynthia Ozick, Elizabeth Bishop) can be heard in both forms of prose, fictional and nonfictional. Choosing between them—well, some choices simply can't be done.

Writers who are primarily novelists are not here, though I could easily have used a short story to represent most of them. But what's the point of misrepresenting them with work that is not what they do best? Still, it's the limitations of space more than anything else that explain the absence of Elizabeth Bowen, Margaret Atwood, Jeanette Winterson, Hilary Mantel, Mary McCarthy, Carson McCullers, Mary Gordon, Margaret Drabble, Maxine Hong Kingston, Ursula Le Guin, as well as the Hannah Green of *The Dead of the House* ("evocation at the level of magic," in the words of Wallace Stegner). Also omitted in the interest of a book that does not weigh in as a doorstopper: Catharine Sedgwick, Dorothy Canfield Fisher, H.D., Christina Rossetti—her best poetry, "Goblin Market" ("as original a creation as Mary Shelley's *Frankenstein*," according to Ellen Moers's *Literary Women*) and her sonnet sequence *Monna Innominata*, are too long for a book of modest length; this anthology was never meant to be another *Norton Anthology of Literature by Women*. And even academic anthologies must exclude as often as they include; the field of writing by women in English is simply too vast to be covered completely in any one volume. But a strong selection of highlights such as this book offers can stimulate an appetite for the whole wide world of it.

Surveying this bounty as the twentieth century turned into the twenty-first, I've found the received wisdom of literary feminism less compelling than it was when its *ur* text, Virginia Woolf's *A Room of One's Own*, was published in 1929. As we readers encounter in books by men and women the particulars of women's lives, their racial and ethnic identifications, their heterosexuality and lesbianism, their poverty and privilege played out in every role and religion under the sun, we feel that Woolf's complaint about the obscurity of women's lives—she calls them "vanished" and "unrecorded"— well, that part of the complaint has lost its edge. By the end of the century in which Woolf wrote, readers have taken many journeys of consciousness far beyond our limited and solitary selfhoods into every possible configuration of women's experience. These inquiries and discoveries, often acts of catalysis, enabled by editors, publishers, and above all, by the writers themselves, were simply not available to the Bloomsbury of 1929. Woolf's once revolutionary challenge to reclaim the lives of women from silence has now become more of a core insight of women's literary history than an existential urgency. And though today's mainstream publishing and reviewing industry continues to underrepresent the work of women writers—for evidence, you can track their numbers as both writers and reviewers in *The New York Times Book Review* over a month of Sundays—things are still better for women in the literary marketplace and the academic curriculum than they were in Woolf's generation. In 1935, for instance, *Major American Writers*, the standard college textbook and anthology adopted by English departments into the 1960s, included no women writers at all.

There's also room for optimism in the material circumstances of contemporary women writers' lives. Researching through centuries of biography about the writers in this book, I found again and again life stories of poverty and difficult if not impossible conditions cutting into the writers' opportunities to do their work. That the Brontës and Harriet Jacobs and Harriet Beecher Stowe persisted in the face of their respective disasters—their mettle leaves you speechless, then grateful for their willpower.

By mid-twentieth century, the material lives of many women writers began to change. The causes of these socioeconomic shifts are both well-known and beside the point. Reading the life stories of and the interviews with women writers since World War II, I found many of the usual difficulties—how to earn a living and keep on writing, how to balance the responsibilities of family and work—but these difficulties were clearly less dire than their eighteenth- and nineteenth-century versions. There have also been some good endings after bad times. The Great Depression that diminished the youth of Tillie Olsen, for instance, was not her final chapter. Sandra Cisneros survived a hand-to-mouth childhood in a large family of immigrants to become a voice and celebrant of her Chicana culture. With more money of their own and more academic scholarships and foundation grants available, the material worlds of women do look easier for those who write. Difficult circumstances are no longer if they ever were an inevitable dead end. Women have learned to escape, to move on, to reread and discard the cultural scripts that sap the spirit. This bit of progress turns up in fiction in the heroines whom novelist Diane Johnson describes as "interpretive consciousnesses," reliable female narrators who are, in her words, "a modern innovation perhaps, for whom we are unprepared by a tradition of heroines who were only acted upon."

And yet. Natalie Angier, the author of *Woman: An Intimate Geography*, heard the following assessment in an interview with a professional woman which Angier published as "Exploring the Gender Gap and the Absence of Equality" in *The New York Times*:

> Q: What about your own life? Do you feel that you have been discriminated against as a woman in academia?
>
> A: I don't like to talk about my own situation. Nobody wants to feel like a victim—it's too depressing. But what I think is wrong is for people to deal with not wanting to be a victim by denying there's any undervaluation of women in the first place. It's necessary to see things as they are if we're ever to devise effective ways of doing something about them.

In some professional arenas, even ones that acknowledge the imperatives of justice and fairness, the emotional colors of women's experience remain as opaque as ever. The economic facts of women's lives as workers remain depressingly unfair: there is still not equal pay for equal work; many women over the age of sixty-five, despite lifetimes of unending work in the service of others, live close to the bone or in statistical poverty. But mentioning in the same breath victimhood and women is considered about as irrelevant as you can get in these times of crisis politics.

Literature sees things the way they are, in the wide and deep and mysteriously paradoxical dimensions of human experience. It takes us to the dark places of women's lives, to the wastelands and dead ends of feeling and hope. Is there a more tragic story in modern American literature than Willa Cather's "A Wagner Matinée"? When a particular work of literature is conceived in a generous or visionary imagination, it may give us some light, as in the poetry of Mary Oliver or in Mary Lavin's fiction; Lorrie Moore's is a quickening art, as indefinable as music. There's good social comedy running through Jane Austen and Edith Wharton; there's the sensual delight of June Jordan's imagery. In some writers we hear both hope and despair. In the poetry of Denise Levertov, and in the fiction of Nadine Gordimer, there's a bold resistance to the social and political forces that crush people, who are sometimes women.

Writing that is undertaken as a simultaneous act of resistance and of a determined self-affirmation is not just a modern phenomenon. The contents of this anthology begin with the medieval English mystic Julian of Norwich (c. 1342–c. 1423). Starting off with Julian is not only chronologically accurate from the point of view of recorded literary history. Her writing also underscores the fact that despite the patriarchal structures of established religious institutions, spiritual experience, as the historian Gerda Lerner documents so fully, has often acted as a catalyst in liberating women's consciousness and creativity. It can also awaken the courage to confront the forces that diminish them as persons. You can feel the reverberations of this experience particularly in the work of African American women writers of the last two centuries. What novelist A. S. Byatt says of Toni Morrison, that the religious imagination of the community empowers her writing, is also true of Maya Angelou, Lucille Clifton, and Rita Dove.

We the readers are the partners of these writers as they imagine their rich understandings about our particular female identities and our common humanity in the many different layers of time and place embodied in these contents. In their laments and celebrations you won't find every variety of experience. You won't necessarily discern your own point of view on the bitterness and the grace of women's experience as it is transformed into poetry and prose. What you will find is a lively selection of the best writing in English that has been done by women in the course of almost seven centuries. As readers we're invited to collaborate with these artists on our mutual projects of self-formation. That's a theme you hear recurring in this book—how important reading has been in the formation of these writers' identities as women and as writers.

About the mutually creative interactions of writers and readers, Joyce Carol Oates has written beautifully:

> All of us who write work out of a conviction that we are partici-
> pating in some sort of communal activity. Whether my role is
> writing, or reading and responding, might not be very important.
> I take seriously Flaubert's statement that we must love one anoth-
> er in our art as the mystics love one another in God. By honoring
> one another's creation we honor something that deeply connects
> us all, and goes beyond us.

This notion of a community of the word sustains the mind of any civilization worthy of the name. Literature is the polyphonic voice of this
community. This book presents the pleasures of the women's voices. In
their elegant harmonies and in their dissonance, they are at once serious
and thrilling.

While editing this book, I was also orchestrating my first and only daughter's wedding. Something came back to me as both productions headed
into the homestretch. It was while I was engaged in a harrowingly long
labor with this child—she gave her first serious nudge at 12:45 A.M. on a
Tuesday, then went by turns sluggish and hyperactive, finally joining a
grand push for freedom at 6:16 P.M. on a Thursday—well, during this
marathon of puffing, blowing, and hellish bowls of Jell-O, I finished up
the manuscript of the long-lived anthology *Women and Fiction* (1975). That
book was followed by a novel and then by a number of collections by
women that I edited in the course of my daughter's first twenty-five years
of life. She, like me, grew up to be a reader, taking especially to women
writers' testimonies. At Berkeley she wrote her senior thesis about
Thomas Hardy's Tess, a character after her own un-Puritan heart; as a
high school English teacher in Oakland, she helps her students enter the
free world of Zora Neale Hurston's *Their Eyes Were Watching God*.
   This personal story, about a coincidence of mother-daughter tastes bred
literally—at least according to the stopwatch—in the birth canal, repeats
itself in the cultural history of the last part of the twentieth century. What
Elaine Showalter has called the midcentury's "renaissance" of women's literary history has been a renaissance come down to earth, open to everyone.
For the good and bad news of women's lives as told by women has now
become part of the consciousness of younger generations. Among the many

students I've known as a teacher of literature in college classrooms, there are the young men who love Grace Paley, her irreverent wit and profound humanity; the young women who respond with sympathy to Tillie Olsen's "I Stand Here Ironing," some reflecting in their papers that they've lived that story, both as daughters and as mothers. Year after year many of these men and women say their favorite story of the semester is Eudora Welty's "A Worn Path." (This from a generation which, according to the pundits, has the attention span of a tired toddler.) These same readers regard listening to the tape of Toni Morrison's Nobel Lecture as a treat, not complaining about the enigmatic parts they don't get. They are mesmerized by her voice, prophetic and kind, as they first came to feel the spell of her books back in high school. Their readings of these women writers have, I think, helped both women and men to desire—and imagine—more generous alternatives to some of the closed worlds they were born into. Their reading has enlarged their sympathy with what—and who—is beyond the self. However inarticulate, this sympathy is as real as it makes us new. My own experience, as teacher, mother, and editor of this book—this most choice feast—grounds my hope for all of us.

—Susan Neunzig Cahill, Ph.D.
New York City, 2001

QPB Anthology of Women's Writing

Julian of Norwich

(c. 1342–c. 1423)

Julian, who lived alone in a cavelike cell adjoining a church in Norwich, England, was a mystic who believed she had a divine commission to record her visions. *Showings* (also called *Revelations*) describes her experience of God's presence in the course of one day, May 13, 1373. Julian's passionate though difficult theology has inspired a strong interest among modern readers. Like the Hebrew prophet Isaiah and various Christian saints, she imagines the feminine side of God: she conceives of each of the three persons in God—Father, Son, and Holy Spirit—as a nursing mother; as mothers they reveal their "lovingness" and wisdom. Interpreting her claim of illiteracy as an expression of her sense of herself as a weak writer, medieval scholars and modern translators have praised her rhetorical style and called the substance of her narrative "the most profound . . . of all medieval English spiritual writings."

FROM *Showings*

As truly as God is our Father, so truly is God our Mother, and he revealed that in everything, and especially in these sweet words where he says: I am he; that is to say: I am he, the power and goodness of fatherhood; I am he, the wisdom and the lovingness of motherhood; I am he, the light and the grace which is all blessed love; I am he, the Trinity; I am he, the unity; I am he, the great supreme goodness of every kind of thing; I am he who makes you to love; I am he who makes you to long; I am he, the endless fulfilling of all true desires. For where the soul is highest, noblest, most honourable, still it is lowest, meekest and mildest.

And from this foundation in substance we have all the powers of our sensuality by the gift of nature, and by the help and the furthering of mercy and grace, without which we cannot profit. Our great Father, almighty God, who is being, knows us and loved us before time began. Out of this knowledge, in his most wonderful deep love, by the prescient eternal counsel of all the blessed Trinity, he wanted the second person to become our Mother, our brother and our savior. From this it follows that as truly as God is our Father, so truly is God our Mother. Our Father wills, our Mother works, our good Lord the Holy Spirit confirms. And therefore it is our part to love our God in whom we have our being, reverently thanking and praising him for our creation, mightily praying to our Mother for mercy and pity, and to our Lord the Holy Spirit for help and grace. For in these three is all our life: nature, mercy and grace, of which we have mildness, patience and pity, and hatred of sin and wickedness; for the virtues must of themselves hate sin and wickedness.

And so Jesus is our true Mother in nature by our first creation, and he is our true Mother in grace by his taking our created nature. All the lovely works and all the sweet loving offices of beloved motherhood are appropriated to the second person, for in him we have this godly will, whole and safe forever, both in nature and in grace, from his own goodness proper to him.

I understand three ways of contemplating motherhood in God. The first is the foundation of our nature's creation; the second is his taking of our nature, where the motherhood of grace begins; the third is the motherhood at work. And in that, by the same grace, everything is penetrated, in length and in breadth, in height and in depth without end; and it is all one love.

But now I should say a little more about this penetration, as I understood our Lord to mean: How we are brought back by the motherhood of mercy and grace into our natural place, in which we were created by the motherhood of love, a mother's love which never leaves us.

Our Mother in nature, our Mother in grace, because he wanted altogether to become our Mother in all things, made the foundation of his work most humbly and most mildly in the maiden's womb. And he revealed that in the first revelation, when he brought the meek maiden before the eye of my understanding in the simple stature which she had when she conceived; that is to say that our great God, the supreme wisdom of all things, arrayed and prepared himself in this humble place, all ready in our poor flesh, himself to do the service and the office of motherhood in everything. The mother's service is nearest, readiest and surest: nearest because it is most natural, readiest because it is most loving, and surest because it is truest. No one ever might or could perform this office fully, except only him. We know that all our mothers bear us for pain and for death. O, what is that? But our true Mother Jesus, he alone bears us for joy and for endless life, blessed may he be. So he carries us within him in love and travail, until the full time when he wanted to suffer the sharpest thorns and cruel pains that ever were or will be, and at the last he died. And when he had finished, and had borne us so for bliss, still all this could not satisfy his wonderful love. And he revealed this in these great surpassing words of love: If I could suffer more, I would suffer more. He could not die any more, but he did not want to cease working; therefore he must needs nourish us, for the precious love of motherhood has made him our debtor.

The mother can give her child the suck of her milk, but our precious Mother Jesus can feed us with himself, and does, most courteously and most tenderly, with the blessed sacrament, which is the precious food of true life; and with all the sweet sacraments he sustains us most mercifully and graciously, and so he meant in these blessed words, where he said: I am he whom Holy Church preaches and teaches to you. That is to say: All the health and the life of the sacraments, all the power and grace of my word, all the goodness which is ordained in Holy Church for you, I am he.

The mother can lay her child tenderly to her breast, but our tender Mother Jesus can lead us easily into his blessed breast through his sweet open side, and show us there a part of the godhead and the joys of heaven, with inner certainty of endless bliss. And that he revealed in the tenth revelation, giving us the same understanding in these sweet words which he says: See, how I love you, looking into his blessed side, rejoicing.

This fair lovely word "mother" is so sweet and so kind in itself that it cannot truly be said of anyone or to anyone except of him and to him who is the true Mother of life and of all things. To the property of motherhood belong nature, love, wisdom and knowledge, and this is God. For though it may be so that our bodily bringing to birth is only little, humble and simple in comparison with our spiritual bringing to birth, still it is he who does it in the creatures by whom it is done. The kind, loving mother who knows and sees the need of her child guards it very tenderly, as the nature and condition of motherhood will have. And always as the child grows in age and in stature, she acts differently, but she does not change her love.

This book is begun by God's gift and his grace, but it is not yet performed, as

I see it. For charity, let us all join with God's working in prayer, thanking, trusting, rejoicing, for so will our good Lord be entreated, by the understanding which I took in all his own intention, and in the sweet words where he says most happily: I am the foundation of your beseeching. For truly I saw and understood in our Lord's meaning that he revealed it because he wants to have it better known than it is. In which knowledge he wants to give us grace to love him and to cleave to him, for he beholds his heavenly treasure with so great love on earth that he will give us more light and solace in heavenly joy, by drawing our hearts from the sorrow and the darkness which we are in.

And from the time that it was revealed, I desired many times to know in what was our Lord's meaning. And fifteen years after and more, I was answered in spiritual understanding, and it was said: What, do you wish to know your Lord's meaning in this thing? Know it well, love was his meaning. Who reveals it to you? Love. What did he reveal to you? Love. Why does he reveal it to you? For love. Remain in this, and you will know more of the same. But you will never know different, without end.

So I was taught that love is our Lord's meaning. And I saw very certainly in this and in everything that before God made us he loved us, which love was never abated and never will be. And in this love he has done all his works, and in this love he has made all things profitable to us, and in this love our life everlasting. In our creation we had beginning, but the love in which he created us was in him from without beginning. In this love we have our beginning, and all this shall we see in God without end.

Thanks be to God. Here ends the book of revelations of Julian the anchorite of Norwich, on whose soul may God have mercy.

Anne Bradstreet

(1612–1672)

Leaving behind a leisured life and a good library in Lincolnshire, Anne Bradstreet, an educated and well-read woman, followed her father and husband into the Puritan wilderness of the Massachusetts Bay Colony. While bearing and raising eight children in this strange new world where sickness, savage weather, and fire destroyed life and homes on a regular basis, she wrote poetry. When her brother-in-law made a trip back to London, he brought along her manuscripts, which were published as *The Tenth Muse, Lately Sprung Up in America* (1650), making Bradstreet the author of the first collection of original poems produced in America. Its dominant theme is her devotion to her marriage and children and her interior struggle to remain faithful to the letter and spirit of Puritan Christianity. But despite her arduous religious and domestic trials—she describes the difficulties of pregnancy and child care in the new colony—her poetic voice is sure and direct, like a prophet's.

To My Dear and Loving Husband

If ever two were one, then surely we.
If ever man were lov'd by wife, then thee;
If ever wife was happy in a man,
Compare with me ye women if you can.
I prize thy love more then whole Mines of gold,
Or all the riches that the East doth hold.
My love is such that Rivers cannot quench,
Nor ought but love from thee, give recompence.
Thy love is such I can no way repay,
The heavens reward thee manifold I pray.
Then while we live, in love lets so persever,
That when we live no more, we may live ever.

In Reference to Her Children, 23 June 1659

Here Bradstreet refers to her children who've grown up and left Andover, Massachusetts, where she was then living, to study in England, or to marry, or to study at Harvard. In 1659 Hannah, Mercy, and John were still living at home.

I had eight birds hatch in one nest,
Four cocks there were, and hens the rest.
I nursed them up with pain and care,
Nor cost, nor labor did I spare,
Till at the last they felt their wing,
Mounted the trees, and learned to sing.
Chief of the brood then took his flight
To regions far, and left me quite:
My mournful chirps I after send,
Till he return, or I do end:
Leave not thy nest, thy dam and sire,
Fly back and sing amidst this choir.
My second bird did take her flight,
And with her mate flew out of sight;
Southward they both their course did bend,
And seasons twain they there did spend:
Till after blown by southern gales,
They norward steered with filled sails.
A prettier bird was nowhere seen,
Along the beach among the treen.
I have a third of color white,
On whom I placed no small delight;
Coupled with mate loving and true,
Hath also bid her dam adieu:
And where Aurora first appears,
She now hath perched to spend her years;
One to the academy flew
To chat among that learned crew:
Ambition moves still in his breast
That he might chant above the rest,

Striving for more than to do well,
That nightingales he might excel.
My fifth, whose down is yet scarce gone,
Is 'mongst the shrubs and bushes flown,
And as his wings increase in strength,
On higher boughs he'll perch at length.
My other three still with me nest,
Until they're grown; then as the rest,
Or here or there they'll take their flight,
As is ordained, so shall they light.
If birds could weep, then would my tears
Let others know what are my fears
Lest this my brood some harm should catch,
And be surprized for want of watch,
Whilst pecking corn and void of care,
They fall un'wares in fowler's snare:
Or whilst on trees they sit and sing,
Some untoward boy at them do fling.
Or whilst allured with bell and glass,
The net be spread, and caught alas.
Or lest by lime-twigs they be foiled,
Or by some greedy hawks be spoiled.
O would my young, ye saw my breast,
And knew what thoughts there sadly rest;
Great was my pain when I you bred,
Great was my care when I you fed,
Long did I keep you soft and warm,
And with my wings kept off all harm;
My cares are more, and fears than ever,
My throbs such now as 'fore were never:
Alas, my birds, you wisdom want,
Of perils you are ignorant;
Oft times in grass, on trees, in flight,
Sore accidents on you may light.
O to your safety have an eye,
So happy may you live and die:

Meanwhile my days in tunes I'll spend,
Till my weak lays with me shall end;
In shady woods I'll sit and sing,
And things that passed to mind I'll bring.
Once young and pleasant, as are you,
But former toys (no joys), adieu.
My age I will not once lament,
But sing, my time so near is spent.
And from the top bough take my flight
Into a country beyond sight,
Where old ones instantly grow young,
And there with seraphims set song:
No seasons cold, nor storms they see;
But spring lasts to eternity.
When each of you shall in your nest
Among your young ones take your rest,
In chirping language, oft them tell,
You had a dam that loved you well,
That did what could be done for young,
And nursed you up till you were strong,
And 'fore she once would let you fly,
She showed you joy and misery;
Taught what was good and what was ill,
What would save life, and what would kill.
Thus gone, amongst you I may live,
And dead, yet speak, and counsel give:
Farewell, my birds; farewell, adieu,
I happy am, if well with you.

Margaret Cavendish
Duchess of Newcastle

(1623–1674)

"Mad Margaret" was scorned as a child for the shyness that kept her tongue-tied and as a woman for her unconventional outfits, hairdos, and having the nerve to write books. In his diary Samuel Pepys called her husband, who encouraged her writing, an "ass" for "suffering" his wife's habit. She produced at a furious rate: letters, poems, plays, philosophical studies in which she denounced the trivialization of women's lives, and a biography of the husband she loved. In an essay in praise of Cavendish's wit, Virginia Woolf ridiculed her dull-minded critics. "The Hunting of the Hare," the poet's protest against the tyranny of blood sports, can also be read as a sexual allegory about power and powerlessness. In the words of the old English folk song "The Hares on the Mountain":

> Young women they'll run like hares on the mountain
> Young women they'll run like hares on the mountain
> If I was but a young man I'd soon go a-hunting . . .

The Claspe

Give *Mee* the *Free*, and *Noble Stile,*
Which seems *uncurb'd,* though it be *wild*:
Though *It* runs wild about, *It* cares not where;
It shewes more *Courage,* then *It* doth of *Feare.*
Give me a *Stile* that *Nature* frames, not *Art*:
For *Art* doth seem to take the *Pedants* part.
And that seemes *Noble,* which is *Easie, Free,*
Not to be bound with ore-nice *Pedantry.*

The Hunting of the Hare

Betwixt two *Ridges* of *Plowd-land*, lay *Wat*,★
Pressing his *Body* close to the *Earth* lay squat.
His *Nose* upon his two *Fore-feet* close lies,
Glaring obliquely with his *great gray Eyes*
His *Head* he alwaies sets against the *Wind*;
If turne his *Taile*, his *Haires* blow up behind:
Which *he* too cold will grow, but *he* is wise,
And keepes his *Coat* still downe, so warm *he* lies.
Thus resting all the *day*, till *Sun* doth set,
Then riseth up, his *Reliefe* for to get.
Walking about until the *Sun* doth rise,
Then back returnes, downe in his *Forme he* lyes.
At last, *Poore Wat* was found, as *he* there lay,
By *Hunts-men*, with their *Dogs* which came that way.
Seeing, gets up, and fast begins to run,
Hoping some waies the *Cruell Dogs* to shun.
But they by *Nature* have so quick a *Sent*,
That by their *Nose* they trace, what way *he* went.
And with their deep, wide *Mouths* set forth a *Cry*,
Which answer'd was by *Ecchoes* in the *Skie*.
Then *Wat* was struck with *Terrour*, and with *Feare*,
Thinkes every *Shadow* still the *Dogs* they were.
And running out some distance from the *noise,*
To hide himselfe, his *Thoughts* he new imploies.
Under a *Clod* of *Earth* in *Sand-pit* wide,
Poore *Wat* sat close, hoping himselfe to hide.
There long he had not sat, but strait his *Eares*
The *Winding Hornes*, and crying *Dogs* he heares:
Starting with *Feare*, up leapes, then doth he run,
And with such speed, the *Ground* scarce treades upon.
Into a great thick *Wood he* strait way gets,
Where underneath a *broken bough he* sits.
At every *Leafe* that with the *wind* did shake,

★ "Wat" is a dialect word for hare.

Did bring such *terrour*, made his *Heart* to ake.
That *Place he* left, to *Champian Plaines he* went,
Winding about, for to deceive their *Sent*.
And while they *snuffling* were, to find his *Track*,
Poore Wat, being weary, his swift pace did slack.
On his two *hinder* legs for ease did sit,
His *Fore-feet* rub'd his *Face* from *Dust,* and *Sweat.*
Licking his *Feet, he* wip'd *Eares* so cleane,
That none could tell that *Wat* had hunted been.
But casting round about his *faire great Eyes,*
The *Hounds* in full *Careere he* neere him 'spies:
To *Wat* it was so terrible a *Sight,*
Feare gave him *Wings,* and made his *Body* light.
Though weary was before, by running long,
Yet now his *Breath* he never felt more strong.
Like those that *dying* are, think *Health* returnes,
When tis but a *faint Blast,* which *Life* out burnes.
For *Spirits* seek to guard the *Heart* about,
Striving with *Death,* but *Death* doth quench them out.
Thus they so fast came on, with such loud *Cries,*
That *he* no hopes hath left, nor *help* espies.
With that the *Winds* did pity *poore Wats* case,
And with their *Breath* the *Sent* blew from the *Place.*
Then every *Nose* is busily imployed,
And every *Nostrill* is set open wide:
And every *Head* doth seek a severall way,
To find what *Grasse,* or *Track,* the *Sent* on lay.
Thus quick Industry, that is not slack,
Is like to Witchery, brings lost things back.
For though the *Wind* had tied the *Sent* up close,
A *Busie Dog* thrust in his *Snuffling Nose*:
And drew it out, with it did foremost run,
Then *Hornes* blew loud, for th' rest to follow on.
The *great slow-Hounds,* their throats did set a *Base,*
The *Fleet swift Hounds,* as *Tenours* next in place;
The little *Beagles* they a *Trebble* sing,
And through the *Aire* their *Voice* a round did ring?

Which made a *Consort*, as they ran along;
If they but *words* could speak, might sing a *Song*,
The *Horses* kept time, the *Hunters* shout for *Joy*,
And valiant seeme, *poore Wat* for to destroy:
Spurring their *Horses* to a full *Careere*,
Swim Rivers deep, leap Ditches without feare;
Indanger *Life*, and *Limbes*, so fast will ride,
Onely to see how patiently *Wat* died.
For why, the *Dogs* so neere his *Heeles* did get,
That they their sharp *Teeth* in his *Breech* did set.
Then tumbling downe, did fall with *weeping Eyes*,
Gives up his *Ghost*, and thus poore *Wat he* dies.
Men hooping loud, such *Acclamations* make,
As if the *Devill* they did *Prisoner* take.
When they do but a *shiftlesse Creature* kill;
To hunt, there needs no *Valiant Souldiers* skill.
But *Man* doth think that *Exercise,* and *Toile*,
To keep their *Health*, is best, which makes most spoile.
Thinking that *Food*, and *Nourishment* so good,
And *Appetite*, that feeds on *Flesh*, and *blood*.
When they do *Lions, Wolves, Beares, Tigers* see,
To kill poore *Sheep*, strait say, they cruell be.
But for themselves all *Creatures* think too few,
For *Luxury* wish *God* would make them new.
As if that *God* made *Creatures* for *Mans meat*,
To give them *Life*, and *Sense*, for *Man* to eat;
Or else for *Sport*, or *Recreations* sake,
Destroy those *Lifes* that *God* saw good to make:
Making their *Stomacks, Graves*, which full they fill
With *Murther'd Bodies*, that in sport they kill.
Yet *Man* doth think himselfe so gentle, mild,
When *he* of *Creatures* is most cruell wild.
And is so *Proud*, thinks onely he shall live,
That *God* a *God*-like *Nature* did him give.
And that all *Creatures* for his sake alone,
Was made for him, to *Tyrannize* upon.

Aphra Behn

(1640-1689)

A widow, Mrs. Behn supported herself by writing and working for the English government. A staunch supporter of the Stuarts, she was a spy for Charles II in Antwerp (where Margaret Cavendish and her husband waited out the Cromwellian occupation), did time in debtor's prison, and in the annals of literary history earned the title of England's first professional woman writer. She was the best known of the literary women of the Restoration. Her poems and plays were frankly erotic, a commonplace among male writers for the Restoration stage; one of her "novels"—an early prose fiction titled *Oroonoko* (1688)—is a passionate protest against the institution of slavery, which she observed firsthand on a visit to the West Indies. Author Ellen Moers's comment on the women writers of the Restoration—"they were sexually experienced, highly literate, short of money, and indifferent to respectability"—points up how much things changed for women who would publish over the next centuries. Though Behn's comic sexual frankness provoked lampoons—she was "the lewd harlot" who deserved her poverty and illness—she was given the honor of burial in Westminster Abbey under the name of Astrea Behn.

The Willing Mistress

This is a song from Behn's play The Dutch Lover.

Amyntas led me to a grove,
    Where all the trees did shade us;
The sun itself, though it had strove,
    It could not have betrayed us.

The place secured from human eyes
    No other fear allows
But when the winds that gently rise
    Do kiss the yielding boughs.

Down there we sat upon the moss,
    And did begin to play
A thousand amorous tricks, to pass
    The heat of all the day.
A many kisses did he give
    And I returned the same,
Which made me willing to receive
    That which I dare not name.

His charming eyes no aid required
    To tell their softening tale;
On her that was already fired.
    'Twas easy to prevail.
He did but kiss and clasp me round,
    Whilst those his thoughts expressed:
And laid me gently on the ground;
    Ah who can guess the rest?

The Adventure of the Black Lady

About the beginning of last June (as near as I can remember) Bellamora came to town from Hampshire, and was obliged to lodge the first night at the same inn where the stage coach set up. The next day she took coach for Covent Garden, where she thought to find Madam Brightly, a relation of hers, with whom she designed to continue for about half a year undiscovered, if possible, by her friends in the country; and ordered therefore her trunk, with her clothes, and most of her money and jewels, to be brought after her to Madam Brightly's by a strange porter, whom she spoke to in the street as she was taking coach, being utterly unacquainted with the neat practices of this fine city. When she came to Bridges Street, where indeed her cousin had lodged near three or four years since, she was strangely surprised that she could not learn anything of her; no, nor so much as meet with anyone that had ever heard of her cousin's name; till, at last, describing Madam Brightly to one of the housekeepers in that place, he told her, that there was such a kind of lady, whom he had sometimes seen there about a year and a half ago, but that he believed she was married and removed towards Soho. In this perplexity she quite forgot her trunk and money, etc, and wandered in her hackney coach all over St. Ann's parish, inquiring for Madam Brightly, still describing her person, but in vain, for no soul could give her any tale or tidings of such a lady. After she had thus fruitlessly rambled, till she, the coachman, and the very horses were even tired, by good fortune for her, she happened on a private house where lived a good, discreet, ancient gentlewoman, who was fallen to decay, and forced to let lodgings for the best part of her livelihood; from whom she understood, that there was such a kind of lady, who had lain there somewhat more than a twelvemonth, being near three months after she was married; but that she was now gone abroad with the gentleman her husband, either to the play, or to take the fresh air; and she believed would not return till night. This discourse of the good gentlewoman's so elevated Bellamora's drooping spirits that after she had begged the liberty of staying there till they came home, she discharged the coachman in all haste, still forgetting her trunk, and the more valuable furniture of it.

When they were alone, Bellamora desired she might be permitted the freedom to send for a pint of sack, which, with some little difficulty, was at last allowed her. They began then to chat for a matter of half an hour of things indifferent; and at length the ancient gentlewoman asked the fair innocent (I must not say foolish) one, of what country, and what her name was: to both which she answered directly and truly, though it might have proved not discreetly. She then enquired of Bellamora if her parents were living, and the occasion of her coming to town. The fair unthinking creature replied, that her father and mother were both dead, and that she had escaped from her uncle, under the pretence of making a visit to a young lady, her cousin, who was lately married, and lived above twenty miles from her uncle's, in the road to London, and that the cause of her quitting the country was to avoid the hated importunities of a gentleman, whose pretended love to her she feared had been her eternal ruin. At which she wept and

sighed most extravagantly. The discreet gentlewoman endeavoured to comfort her by all the softest and most powerful arguments in her capacity,
promising her all the friendly assistance that she could expect from her, during Bellamora's stay in town; which she did with so much earnestness, and
visible integrity, that the pretty innocent creature was going to make her a
full and real discovery of her imaginary insupportable misfortunes; and
(doubtless) had done it, had she not been prevented by the return of the
lady, whom she hoped to have found her cousin Brightly. The gentleman,
her husband, just saw her within doors, and ordered the coach to drive to
some of his bottle companions, which gave the women the better opportunity of entertaining one another, which happened to be with some surprise
on all sides. As the lady was going up into her apartment, the gentlewoman
of the house told her there was a young lady in the parlour, who came out
of the country that very day on purpose to visit her; the lady stepped immediately to see who it was, and Bellamora approaching to receive her hoped-
for cousin, stopped on the sudden just as she came to her, and sighed out
aloud, "Ah, madam! I am lost—it is not your ladyship I seek." "No, madam,"
returned the other, "I am apt to think you did not intend me this honour.
But you are as welcome to me, as you could be to the dearest of your
acquaintance. Have you forgot me, Madam Bellamora?" continued she.
That name startled the other. However, it was with a kind of joy. "Alas!
Madam," replied the young one, "I now remember that I have been so
happy to have seen you, but where and when, my memory can't tell me."
"'Tis indeed some years since," return'd the lady, "but of that another time.
Meanwhile, if you are unprovided of a lodging, I dare undertake, you shall
be welcome to this gentlewoman." The unfortunate returned her thanks;
and whilst a chamber was preparing for her, the lady entertained her in her
own. About ten o'clock they parted, Bellamora being conducted to her lodging by the mistress of the house, who then left her to take what rest she
could amidst her so many misfortunes, returning to the other lady, who
desired her to search into the cause of Bellamora's retreat to town.

   The next morning the good gentlewoman of the house, coming up to
her, found Bellamora almost drowned in tears, which by many kind and
sweet words she at last stopped; and, asking whence so great signs of sorrow
should proceed, vowed a most profound secrecy if she would discover to her
their occasion; which, after some little reluctancy, she did, in this manner.

"I was courted," said she, "above three years ago, when my mother was yet living, by one Mr. Fondlove, a gentleman of good estate, and true worth; and one who, I dare believe, did then really love me. He continued his passion for me, with all the earnest and honest solicitations imaginable, till some months before my mother's death, who, at that time, was most desirous to see me disposed of in marriage to another gentleman, of much better estate than Mr. Fondlove, but one whose person and humour did by no means hit with my inclinations; and this gave Fondlove the unhappy advantage over me. For, finding me one day all alone in my chamber, and lying on my bed, in as mournful and wretched a condition to my then foolish apprehension, as now I am, he urged his passion with such violence and accursed success for me, with reiterated promises of marriage whensoever I pleased to challenge them, which he bound with the most sacred oaths, and most dreadful execrations that, partly with my aversion to the other, and partly with my inclinations to pity him, I ruined myself." Here she relapsed into a greater extravagance of grief than before, which was so extreme that it did not continue long. When therefore she was pretty well come to herself, the ancient gentlewoman asked her, why she imagined herself ruined. To which she answered, "I am great with child by him, madam, and wonder you did not perceive it last night. Alas! I have not a month to go. I am ashamed, ruined, and damned, I fear, for ever lost." "Oh! fie, madam, think not so," said the other, "for the gentleman may yet prove true, and marry you." "Ay, madam," replied Bellamora, "I doubt not that he would marry me; for soon after my mother's death, when I came to be at my own disposal, which happened about two months after, he offered, nay most earnestly solicited me to it, which still he perseveres to do." "This is strange!" returned the other, "and it appears to me to be your own fault that you are yet miserable. Why did you not or why will you not consent to your own happiness?" "Alas!" cried Bellamora, "'tis the only thing I dread in this world. For, I am certain, he can never love me after. Besides, ever since I have abhorred the sight of him, and this is the only cause that obliges me to forsake my uncle, and all my friends and relations in the country, hoping in this populous and public place to be most private, especially, madam, in your house, and in your fidelity and discretion." "Of the last you may assure yourself, madam," said the other, "but what provision have you made for the reception of the young stranger that you carry about you?" "Ah, madam!" cried Bellamora, "you have brought to my mind another misfortune." Then she acquainted her with the supposed loss of her money and jewels, telling her withal, that she had but three guineas and some silver left, and the rings she wore, in her present possession. The good gentlewoman of the house told her she would send to enquire at the inn where she lay the first night she came to town; for, haply, they might give some account of the porter to whom she had entrusted her trunk; and withal repeated her promise of all the help in her power, and for that time left her much more composed than she found her. The good gentlewoman went directly to the other lady, her lodger, to whom she recounted Bellamora's mournful confession; at which the lady appeared mightily concerned: and at last she told her landlady, that she would take care that Bellamora should lie in according to her quality. "For," she added, "the child, it seems, is my own brother's."

As soon as she had dined, she went to the Exchange, and brought childbed linen, but desired that Bellamora might not have the least notice of it. And at her return dispatched a letter to her brother Fondlove in Hampshire, with an account of every particular; which soon brought him up to town, without satisfying any of his or her friends with the reason of his sudden departure. Meanwhile, the good gentlewoman of the house had sent to the Star Inn on Fish Street Hill, to demand the trunk, which she rightly supposed to have been carried back thither. For, by good luck, it was a fellow that plied thereabouts who brought it to Bellamora's lodgings that very night, but unknown to her. Fondlove no sooner got to London, but he posts to his sister's lodgings, where he was advised not to be seen of Bellamora till they had worked farther upon her, which the landlady began in this manner. She told her that her things were miscarried and, she feared, lost; that she had but a little money herself, and if the overseers of the poor (justly so called from their over-looking them) should have the least suspicion of a stranger and unmarried person who was entertained in her house big with child, and so near her time as Bellamora was, she should be troubled, if they could not give security to the parish of twenty or thirty pounds that they should not suffer by her, which she could not; or otherwise she must be sent to the house of correction, and her child to a parish nurse. This discourse, one may imagine, was very dreadful to a person of her youth, beauty, education, family and estate. However, she resolutely protested that she had rather undergo all this than be exposed to the scorn of her friends and relations in the country. The other told her then that she must write down to her uncle a farewell letter, as if she were just going aboard the packet-boat for Holland, that he might not send to enquire for her in town, when he should understand she was not at her new-married cousin's in the country; which accordingly she did, keeping herself close prisoner to her chamber, where she was daily visited by Fondlove's sister and the landlady, but by no soul else, the first dissembling the knowledge she had of her misfortunes.

Thus she continued for above three weeks, not a servant being suffered to enter her chamber, so much as to make her bed, lest they should take notice of her great belly; but for all this caution, the secret had taken wind, by the means of an attendant of the other lady below, who had overheard her speaking of it to her husband. This soon got out of doors, and spread abroad, till it reached the long ears of the wolves of the parish, who, next day, designed to pay her a visit. But Fondlove, by good providence, prevented it; who, the night before, was ushered in Bellamora's chamber by his sister, his brother-in-law, and the landlady. At the sight of him she had like to have swooned away, but he, taking her in his arms, began again, as he was wont to do, with tears in his eyes, to beg that she would marry him ere she was delivered; if not for his, nor her own, yet for the child's sake, which she hourly expected, that it might not be born out of wedlock, and so be made uncapable of inheriting either of their estates; with a great many more pressing arguments on all sides, to which at last she consented; and an honest officious gentleman, whom they had before provided, was called up, who made an end of the dispute. So to bed they went together that night; next day to the Exchange, for several pretty businesses that ladies in her condition want. Whilst they were abroad, came the vermin of the parish (I mean, the overseers of the poor, who eat the bread from them) to search for a young black-haired lady (for so was Bellamora) who was either brought to bed, or just ready to lie down. The landlady showed them all the rooms in her house, but no such lady could be found. At last she bethought herself, and led them into her parlour, where she opened a little closet door, and showed them a black cat that had just kittened, assuring them that she should never trouble the parish as long as she had rats or mice in the house; and so dismissed them like loggerheads as they came.

Lady Mary Wortley Montagu

(1689–1762)

When she was twenty, Lady Mary declared, "I believe more follies are committed out of complaisance to the world than in following our own inclinations. I am amazed to see that people of good sense in other things can make their happiness consist in the opinion of others." Impulsively, she eloped with Mr. Montagu, and after years of following him to Turkey, where he was ambassador, she left him to live in Brescia, Italy. A woman in possession of her own mind, an essayist, dramatist, and journalist whose correspondence fills three volumes, her letters were published a year after her death, against the wishes of her family (her daughter, Lady Bute, who was not cut from the same cloth, burned her mother's journal). They drew a hugely enthusiastic audience and had to be reprinted again and again. Voltaire rated them superior to Madame de Sévigné's; Tobias Smollett, Dr. Johnson, and later, Lord Byron praised their brilliance. "Her wit," said Lytton Strachey, "has that quality which is the best of all preservatives against dullness—it goes straight to the point."

FROM *The Letters of Lady Mary Wortley Montagu*

To Mr. Wortley Montagu

[Indorsed "24th November," 1714]

I have taken up and laid down my pen several times, very much unresolved in what stile I ought to write you: for once I suffer my inclination to get the better of my reason. I have not oft opportunities of indulging myself, and I will do it in this one letter. I know very well that nobody was ever teized into a liking: and 'tis perhaps harder to revive a past one, than to overcome an aversion; but I cannot forbear any longer telling you, I think you use me very unkindly. I don't say so much of your absence, as I should do if you was in

the country and I in London; because I would not have you believe I am
impatient to be in town, when I say I am impatient to be with you; but I am
very sensible I parted with you in July and 'tis now the middle of November.
As if this was not hardship enough, you do not tell me you are sorry for it.
You write seldom, and wish so much indifference as shews you hardly think
of me at all. I complain of ill health, and you only say you hope 'tis not so bad
as I make it. You never enquire after your child. I would fain flatter myself
you have more kindness for me and him than you express: but I reflect with
grief a man that is ashamed of passions that are natural and reasonable, is generally proud of those that [are] shameful and silly.

You should consider solitude, and spleen the consequence of solitude, is
apt to give the most melancholy ideas, and there needs at least tender letters
and kind expressions to hinder uneasinesses almost inseparable from absence.
I am very sensible, how far I ought to be contented when your affairs oblige
you to be without me. I would not have you do them any prejudice; but a little kindness will cost you nothing. I do not bid you lose any thing by hasting
to see me, but I would have you think it a misfortune when we are asunder.
Instead of that, you seem perfectly pleased with our separation, and indifferent how long it continues. When I reflect on all your behaviour, I am ashamed
of my own: I think I am playing the part of my Lady Winchester. At least be
as generous as my lord; and as he made her an early confession of his aversion,
own to me your inconstancy, and upon my word I will give you no more trouble about it. I have concealed as long as I can, the uneasiness the nothingness
of your letters has given me, under an affected indifference; but dissimulation
always sits awkwardly upon me; I am weary of it; and must beg you to write
to me no more, if you cannot bring yourself to write otherwise. Multiplicity
of business or diversions may have engaged you, but all people find time to do
what they have a mind to. If your inclination is gone, I had rather never receive
a letter from you, than one which, in lieu of comfort for your absence, gives
me a pain even beyond it. For my part, as 'tis my first, this is my last complaint,
and your next of the kind shall go back enclosed to you in blank paper.

To Lady ———

Adrianople, 1 April 1717

I am now got into a new world where everything I see appears to me a change of scene, and I write to your Ladyship with some content of mind, hoping at least that you will find the charm of novelty in my letters and no longer reproach me that I tell you nothing extraordinary. I won't trouble you with a relation of our tedious journey, but I must not omit what I saw remarkable at Sophia, one of the most beautiful towns in the Turkish Empire and famous for its hot baths that are resorted to both for diversion and health. I stopped here one day on purpose to see them. Designing to go incognito, I hired a Turkish coach. These *voitures* are not at all like ours, but much more convenient for the country, the heat being so great that glasses would be very troublesome. They are made a good deal in the manner of the Dutch coaches, having wooden lattices painted and gilded, the inside being painted with baskets and nosegays of flowers, intermixed commonly with little poetical mottoes. They are covered all over with scarlet cloth, lined with silk and very often richly embroidered and fringed. This covering entirely hides the person in them, but may be thrown back at pleasure and the ladies peep through the lattices. They hold four people very conveniently, seated on cushions, but not raised.

In one of these covered wagons I went to the bagnio about ten o'clock. It was already full of women. It is built of stone in the shape of a dome with no windows but in the roof, which gives light enough. There was five of these domes joined together, the outmost being less than the rest and serving only as a hall where the porteress stood at the door. Ladies of quality generally give this woman the value of a crown or ten shillings, and I did not forget that ceremony. The next room is a very large one, paved with marble, and all round it raised two sofas of marble, one above another. There were four fountains of cold water in this room, falling first into marble basins and then running on the floor in little channels made for that purpose, which carried the streams into the next room, something less than this, with the same sort of marble sofas, but so hot with steams of sulphur proceeding from the baths joining to it, 'twas impossible to stay there with one's clothes on. The two other domes were the hot baths, one of which had cocks of cold water turning into it to temper it to what degree of warmth the bathers have a mind to.

I was in my travelling habit, which is a riding dress, and certainly appeared very extraordinary to them, yet there was not one of 'em that showed the least surprise or impertinent curiosity, but received me with all the obliging civility possible. I know no European court where the ladies would have behaved themselves in so polite a manner to a stranger. I believe in the whole there were two hundred women and yet none of those disdainful smiles or satiric whispers that never fail in our assemblies when anybody appears that is not dressed exactly in fashion. They repeated over and over to me, "Uzelle, pek uzelle," which is nothing but, "Charming, very charming." The first sofas were covered with cushions and rich carpets, on which sat the ladies, and on the second their slaves behind 'em, but without any distinction of rank by their dress, all being in the state of nature, that is, in plain English, stark naked, without any beauty or defect concealed, yet there was not the least wanton smile or immodest gesture amongst 'em. They walked and moved with the same majestic grace which Milton describes of our General Mother. There were many amongst them as exactly proportioned as ever any goddess was drawn by the pencil of Guido or Titian, and most of their skins shiningly white, only adorned by their beautiful hair divided into many tresses hanging on their shoulders, braided either with pearl or riband, perfectly representing the figures of the Graces.

I was here convinced of the truth of a reflection that I had often made, that if 'twas the fashion to go naked the face would hardly be observed. I perceived that the ladies with the finest skins and most delicate shapes had the greatest share of my admiration, though their faces were sometimes less beautiful than those of their companions. To tell you the truth, I had wickedness enough to wish secretly that Mr. Jervas could have been there invisible. I fancy it would have very much improved his art to see so many fine women naked in different postures, some in conversation, some working, others drinking coffee or sherbet, and many negligently lying on their cushions while their slaves (generally pretty girls of seventeen or eighteen) were employed in braiding their hair in several pretty manners. In short, 'tis the women's coffee-house, where all the news of the town is told, scandal invented, etc. They generally take this diversion once a week, and stay there at least four or five hours without getting cold by immediate coming out of the hot bath into the cool room, which was very surprising to me. The lady that seemed the most considerable amongst them entreated me to sit by her and would fain have undressed me for the bath. I excused myself with some difficulty, they being all so earnest in persuading me. I was at last forced to open my skirt and show them my stays, which satisfied 'em very well, for I saw they believed I was so locked up in that machine that it was not in my own power to open it, which contrivance they attributed to my husband. I was charmed with their civility and beauty and should have been very glad to pass more time with them, but Mr. Wortley resolving to pursue his journey the next morning early I was in haste to see the ruins of Justinian's church, which did not afford me so agreeable a prospect as I had left, being little more than a heap of stones.

Adieu, madam. I am sure I have now entertained you with an account of such a sight as you never saw in your life and what no book of travels could inform you of. 'Tis no less than death for a man to be found in one of these places.

—

To Lady Bute [Lady Mary's daughter]

Gottolengo, January 1750

My Dear Child,

I am extremely concerned to hear you complain of ill health at a time of life when you ought to be in the flower of your strength. I hope I need not recommend to you the care of it. The tenderness you have for your children is sufficient to enforce you to the utmost regard for the preservation of a life so necessary to their well-being. I do not doubt your prudence in their education; neither can I say anything particular relating to it at this distance, different tempers requiring different management. In general, never attempt to govern them (as most people do) by deceit. If they find themselves cheated (even in trifles) it will so far lessen the authority of their instructor as to make them neglect all their future admonitions. And (if possible) breed them free from prejudices; those contracted in the nursery often influence the whole life after, of which I have seen many melancholy examples.

I shall say no more of this subject, nor would have said this little if you had not asked my advice. 'Tis much easier to give rules than to practise them. I am sensible my own natural temper is too indulgent. I think it the least dangerous error, yet still it is an error. I can only say with truth that I do not know in my whole life having ever endeavoured to impose on you or give a false colour to anything that I represented to you. If your daughters are inclined to love reading, do not check their inclination by hindering them of the diverting part of it. It is as necessary for the amusement of women as the reputation of men; but teach them not to expect or desire any applause from it. Let their brothers shine, and let them content themselves with making their lives easier by it, which I experimentally know is more efficiently done by study than any other way. Ignorance is as much the fountain of vice as idleness, and indeed generally produces it. People that do not read or work for a livelihood have many hours they know not how to employ, especially women, who commonly fall into vapours or something worse. I am afraid you'll think this letter very tedious. Forgive it as coming from your most affectionate mother,

M. W.

My compliments to Lord Bute and blessing to my grandchildren.

—

To Lady Bute

Gottolengo, 28 January 1753

Dear Child,

You have given me a great deal of satisfaction by your account of your eldest daughter. I am particularly pleased to hear she is a good arithmetician; it is the best proof of understanding. The knowledge of numbers is one of the chief distinctions between us and brutes. If there is anything in blood you may reasonably expect your children should be endowed with an uncommon share of good sense. Mr. Wortley's family and mine have both produced some of the greatest men that have been born in England. I mean Admiral Sandwich, and my great-grandfather who was distinguished by the name of Wise William. I have heard Lord Bute's father mentioned as an extraordinary genius (though he had not many opportunities of showing it), and his uncle the present Duke of Argyle has one of the best heads I ever knew.

I will therefore speak to you as supposing Lady Mary not only capable but desirous of learning. In that case, by all means let her be indulged in it. You will tell me, I did not make it a part of your education. Your prospect was very different from hers, as you had no defect either in mind or person to hinder, and much in your circumstances to attract, the highest offers. It seemed your business to learn how to live in the world, as it is hers to know how to be easy out of it. It is the common error of builders and parents to follow some plan they think beautiful (and perhaps is so) without considering that nothing is beautiful that is misplaced. Hence we see so many edifices raised that the raisers can never inhabit, being too large for their fortunes. Vistas are laid open over barren heaths, and apartments contrived for a coolness very agreeable in Italy but killing in the north of Britain. Thus every woman endeavours to breed her daughter a fine lady, qualifying her for a station in which she will never appear, and at the same time incapacitating her for that retirement to which she is destined. Learning (if she has a real taste for it) will not only make her contented but happy in it. No entertainment is so cheap as reading, nor any pleasure so lasting. She will not want new fashions nor regret the loss of expensive diversions or variety of company if she can be amused with an author in her closet. To render this amusement extensive, she should be permitted to learn the languages. I have heard it lamented that boys lose so many years in mere learning of words. This is no objection to a girl, whose time is not so precious. She cannot advance herself in any profession, and has therefore more hours to spare; and as you say her memory is good she will be very agreeably employed this way.

There are two cautions to be given on this subject: first, not to think herself learned when she can read Latin or even Greek. Languages are more properly to be called vehicles of learning than learning itself, as may be observed in many schoolmasters, who though perhaps critics in grammar are the most ignorant fellows upon earth. True knowledge consists in knowing things, not words. I would wish her no further a linguist than to enable her to read books in their originals, that are often corrupted and always injured by translations. Two hours application every morning will bring this about much sooner than you can imagine, and she will have leisure enough beside to run over the English poetry, which is a more important part of a woman's education than is generally supposed. Many a young damsel has been ruined by a fine copy of verses, which she would have laughed at if she had known it had been stolen from Mr. Waller. I remember when I was a girl I saved one of my companions from destruction, who communicated to me an epistle she was quite charmed with. As she had a natural good taste she observed the lines were not so smooth as Prior's or Pope's, but had more thought and spirit than any of theirs. She was wonderfully delighted with such a demonstration of her lover's sense and passion, and not a little pleased with her own charms, that had force enough to inspire such elegancies. In the midst of this triumph I showed her they were taken from Randolph's *Poems*, and the unfortunate transcriber was dismissed with the scorn he deserved. To say truth, the poor plagiary was very unlucky to fall into my hands; that author, being no longer in fashion, would have escaped anyone of less universal reading than myself. You should encourage your daughter to talk over with you what she reads, and as you are very capable of distinguishing, take care she does not mistake pert folly for wit and humour, or rhyme for poetry, which are the common errors of young people, and have a train of ill consequences.

The second caution to be given her (and which is most absolutely necessary) is to conceal whatever learning she attains, with as much solicitude as she would hide crookedness or lameness. The parade of it can only serve to draw on her the envy, and consequently the most inveterate hatred of all he and she fools, which will certainly be at least three parts in four of all her acquaintance. The use of knowledge in our sex (beside the amusement of solitude) is to moderate the passions and learn to be contented with a small expense, which are the certain effects of a studious life and, it may be, preferable even to that fame which men have engrossed to themselves and will not suffer us to share. You will tell me I have not observed this rule myself, but you are mistaken; it is only inevitable accident that has given me any reputation that way. I have always carefully avoided it, and ever thought it a misfortune.

The explanation of this paragraph would occasion a long digression, which I will not trouble you with, it being my present design only to say what I think useful for the instruction of my granddaughter, which I have much at heart. If she has the same inclination (I should say passion) for learning that I was born with, history, geography, and philosophy will furnish her with materials to pass away cheerfully a longer life than is allotted to mortals. I believe there are few heads capable of making Sir Isaac Newton's calculations, but the result of them is not difficult to be understood by a moderate capacity. Do not fear this should make her affect the character of Lady ——, or Lady ——, or Mrs. ——. Those women are ridiculous not because they have learning but because they have it not. One thinks herself a complete historian after reading Echard's *Roman History*, another a profound philosopher having got by heart some of Pope's unintelligible essays and a third an able divine on the strength of Whitefield's sermons. Thus you hear them screaming politics and controversy. It is a saying of Thucydides: Ignorance is bold, and knowledge reserved. Indeed it is impossible to be far advanced in it without being more humbled by a conviction of human ignorance than elated by learning.

At the same time I recommend books I neither exclude work nor drawing. I think it as scandalous for a woman not to know how to use a needle, as for a man not to know how to use a sword. I was once extremely fond of my pencil, and it was a great mortification to me when my father turned off my master, having made a considerable progress for the short time I learned. My over-eagerness in the pursuit of it had brought a weakness on my eyes that made it necessary to leave it off, and all the advantage I got was the improvement of my hand. I see by hers that practice will make her a ready writer. She may attain it by serving you for a secretary when your health or affairs make it troublesome to you to write yourself, and custom will make it an agreeable amusement to her. She cannot have too many for that station of life which will probably be her fate. The ultimate end of your education was to make you a good wife (and I have the comfort to hear that you are one); hers ought to be, to make her happy in a virgin state. I will not say it is happier, but it is undoubtedly safer than any marriage. In a lottery where there is (at the lowest computation) ten thousand blanks to a prize it is the most prudent choice not to venture.

I have always been so thoroughly persuaded of this truth that notwithstanding the flattering views I had for you (as I never intended you a sacrifice to my vanity) I thought I owed you the justice to lay before you all the hazards attending matrimony. You may recollect I did so in the strongest manner. Perhaps you may have more success in the instructing of your daughter. She has so much company at home she will not need seeking it abroad, and will more readily take the notions you think fit to give her. As you were alone in my family, it would have been thought a great cruelty to suffer you no companions of your own age, especially having so many near relations, and I do not wonder their opinions influenced yours. I was not sorry to see you not determined on a single life, knowing it was not your father's intention, and contented myself with endeavoring to make your home so easy that you might not be in haste to leave it.

I am afraid you will think this a very long and insignificant letter. I hope the kindness of the design will excuse it, being willing to give you every proof in my power that I am your most affectionate mother,

M. Wortley

To Lady Bute

Gottolengo, 6 March 1753

I cannot help writing a sort of apology for my last letter, foreseeing that you will think it wrong, or at least Lord Bute will be extremely shocked at the proposal of a learned education for daughters, which the generality of men believe as great a profanation as the clergy would do if the laity should presume to exercise the functions of the priesthood. I desire you would take notice I would not have learning enjoined them as a task, but permitted as a pleasure if their genius leads them naturally to it. I look upon my granddaughters as a sort of lay nuns. Destiny may have laid up other things for them, but they have no reason to expect to pass their time otherwise than their aunts do at present, and I know by experience it is in the power of study not only to make solitude tolerable but agreeable. I have now lived almost seven years in a stricter retirement than yours in the Isle of Bute, and can assure you I have never had half an hour heavy on my hands for want of something to do.

Whoever will cultivate their own mind will find full employment. Every virtue does not only require great care in the planting, but as much daily solicitude in cherishing as exotic fruits and flowers; the vices and passions (which I am afraid are the natural product of the soil) demand perpetual weeding. Add to this the search after knowledge (every branch of which is entertaining), and the longest life is too short for the pursuit of it, which, though in some regards confined to very strait limits, leaves still a vast variety of amusements to those capable of tasting them, which is utterly impossible for those that are blinded by prejudices, which are the certain effect of an ignorant education. My own was one of the worst in the world, being exactly the same as Clarissa Harlowe's, her pious Mrs. Norton so perfectly resembling my governess (who had been nurse to my mother) I could almost fancy the author was acquainted with her. She took so much pains from my infancy to fill my head with superstitious tales and false notions, it was none of her fault I am not at this day afraid of witches and hobgoblins, or turned Methodist.

Almost all girls are bred after this manner. I believe you are the only woman (perhaps I might say person) that never was either frighted or cheated into anything by your parents. I can truly affirm I never deceived anybody in my life excepting (which I confess has often happened undesignedly) by speaking plainly. As Earl Stanhope used to say (during his ministry), he always imposed on the foreign ministers by telling them the naked truth, which, as they thought impossible to come from the mouth of a statesman, they never failed to write informations to their respective courts directly contrary to the assurances he gave them, most people confounding the ideas of sense and cunning, though there are really no two things in nature more opposite. It is in part from this false reasoning, the unjust custom prevails of debarring our sex from the advantages of learning, the men fancying the improvement of our understandings would only furnish us with more art to deceive them, which is directly contrary to the truth. Fools are always enterprising, not seeing the difficulties of deceit or the ill consequences of detection. I could give many examples of ladies whose ill conduct has been very notorious, which has been owing to that ignorance which has exposed them to idleness, which is justly called the mother of mischief.

There is nothing so like the education of a woman of quality as that of a prince. They are taught to dance and the exterior part of what is called good breeding, which if they attain they are extraordinary creatures in their kind, and have all the accomplishments required by their directors. The same characters are formed by the same lessons, which inclines me to think (if I dare say it) that nature has not placed us in an inferior rank to men, no more than the females of other animals, where we see no distinction of capacity, though I am persuaded if there was a commonwealth of rational horses (as Doctor Swift has supposed) it would be an established maxim amongst them that a mare could not be taught to pace. I could add a great deal on this subject, but I am not now endeavouring to remove the prejudices of mankind. My only design is to point out to my granddaughters the method of being contented with that retreat to which probably their circumstances will oblige them, and which is perhaps preferable to all the show of public life. It has always been my inclination. Lady Stafford (who knew me better than anybody else in the world, both from her own just discernment, and my heart being ever as open to her as myself) used to tell me my true vocation was a monastery, and I now find by experience more sincere pleasures with my books and garden than all the flutter of a court could give me.

If you follow my advice in relation to Lady Mary, my correspondence may be of use to her, and I shall very willingly give her those instructions that may be necessary in the pursuit of her studies. Before her age I was in the most regular commerce with my grandmother, though the difference of our time of life was much greater, she being past forty-five when she married my grandfather. She died at ninety-six, retaining to the last the vivacity and clearness of her understanding, which was very uncommon. You cannot remember her, being then in your nurse's arms. I conclude with repeating to you, I only recommend but am far from commanding, which I think I have no right to do. I tell you my sentiments because you desired to know them, and hope you will receive them with some partiality as coming from your most affectionate mother,

M. Wortley

Mary Wollstonecraft

(1759-1797)

When *A Vindication of the Rights of Woman* was published in 1792, it created a furor. Widely read and heatedly argued, it may even, according to biographer Claire Tomalin, have influenced Jane Austen's conception of the character of Marianne in *Sense and Sensibility*. Independent of mind, free of the habits of social hypocrisy, yet romantically vulnerable—there is a kind of suicide attempt following an infatuation with an unworthy man— Marianne suggests aspects of Wollstonecraft's life. Her feminism came out of her childhood: she spent it protecting her submissive mother from an alcoholic and violent father. Leaving home at seventeen, she supported herself as a maid, a governess, a teacher, and finally as a writer whose books in defense of a new order of equity between men and women—argued against a background of the actual oppressive circumstances of women's lives—made hers the voice of revolution. She died after giving birth to Mary Wollstonecraft Godwin Shelley, who in her own youth read her mother's books while sitting next to her grave.

FROM *A Vindication of the Rights of Woman*

Women are, therefore, to be considered either as moral beings, or so weak that they must be entirely subjected to the superior faculties of men.

Let us examine this question. Rousseau declares, that a woman should never, for a moment feel herself independent, that she should be governed by fear to exercise her *natural* cunning, and made a coquetish slave in order to render her a more alluring object of desire, a *sweeter* companion to man, whenever he chooses to relax himself. He carries the arguments, which he pretends to draw from the indications of nature, still further, and insinuates that truth and fortitude the corner stones of all human virtue, shall be cultivated with certain restrictions, because with respect to the female character, obedience is the grand lesson which ought to be impressed with unrelenting rigour.

What nonsense! when will a great man arise with sufficient strength of mind to puff away the fumes which pride and sensuality have thus spread over the subject! If women are by nature inferior to men, their virtues must be the same in quality, if not in degree, or virtue is a relative idea; consequently, their conduct should be founded on the same principles and have the same aim.

Connected with man as daughters, wives, and mothers, their moral character may be estimated by their manner of fulfilling those simple duties; but the end, the grand end of their exertions should be to unfold their own faculties, and acquire the dignity of conscious virtue. They may try to render their road pleasant; but ought never to forget, in common with man, that life yields not the felicity which can satisfy an immortal soul. I do not mean to insinuate, that either sex should be so lost, in abstract reflections or distant views, as to forget the affections and duties that lie before them, and are in truth, the means appointed to produce the fruit of life: on the contrary, I would warmly recommend them, even while I assert, that they afford most satisfaction when they are considered in their true subordinate light.

Probably the prevailing opinion, that woman was created for man, may have taken its rise from Moses's poetical story; yet, as very few it is presumed, who have bestowed any serious thought on the subject, ever supposed that Eve was, literally speaking, one of Adam's ribs, the deduction must be allowed to fall to the ground; or only be so far admitted as it proves that man, from the remotest antiquity, found it convenient to exert his strength to subjugate his companion, and his invention to show that she ought to have her neck bent under the yoke; because she as well as the brute creation, was created to do his pleasure.

Let it not be concluded, that I wish to invert the order of things; I have already granted, that, from the constitution of their bodies, men seem to be designed by Providence to attain a greater degree of virtue. I speak collectively of the whole sex; but I see not the shadow of a reason to conclude that their virtues should differ in respect to their nature. In fact, how can they, if virtue has only one eternal standard? I must, therefore, if I reason consequentially, as strenuously maintain, that they have the same simple direction, as that there is a God.

It follows then, that cunning should not be opposed to wisdom, little cares to great exertions, nor insipid softness, varnished over with the name of gentleness, to that fortitude which grand views alone can inspire.

I shall be told, that woman would then lose many of her peculiar graces, and the opinion of a well known poet might be quoted to refute my unqualified assertions. For Pope has said, in the name of the whole male sex,

> Yet ne'er so sure our passions to create,
> As when she touch'd the brink of all we hate.

In what light this sally places men and women, I shall leave to the judicious to determine; meanwhile I shall content myself with observing, that I cannot discover why, unless they are mortal, females should always be degraded by being made subservient to love or lust.

To speak disrespectfully of love is, I know, high treason against sentiment and fine feelings; but I wish to speak the simple language of truth, and rather to address the head than the heart. To endeavour to reason love out of the world, would be to out Quixote Cervantes, and equally offend against common sense; but an endeavour to restrain this tumultuous passion, and to prove that it should not be allowed to dethrone superior powers, or to usurp the sceptre which the understanding should ever coolly wield, appears less wild.

Youth is the season for love in both sexes; but in those days of thoughtless enjoyment, provision should be made for the more important years of life, when reflection takes place of sensation. But Rousseau, and most of the male writers who have followed his steps, have warmly inculcated that the whole tendency of female education ought to be directed to one point to render them pleasing.

Let me reason with the supporters of this opinion, who have any knowledge of human nature, do they imagine that marriage can eradicate the habitude of life? The woman who has only been taught to please, will soon find that her charms are oblique sun-beams, and that they cannot have much effect on her husband's heart when they are seen every day, when the summer is past and gone. Will she then have sufficient native energy to look into herself for comfort and cultivate her dormant faculties? or, is it not more rational to expect, that she will try to please other men; and, in the emotions raised by the expectation of new conquests, endeavour to forget the mortification her love or pride has received? When the husband ceases to be a lover—and the time will inevitably come, her desire of pleasing will then grow languid, or become a spring of bitterness; and love, perhaps, the most evanescent of all passions, gives place to jealousy or vanity.

I now speak of women who are restrained by principle or prejudice; such women though they would shrink from an intrigue with real abhorrence, yet, nevertheless, wish to be convinced by the homage of gallantry, that they are cruelly neglected by their husbands; or, days and weeks are spent in dreaming of the happiness enjoyed by congenial souls, till the health is undermined and the spirits broken by discontent. How then can the great art of pleasing be such a necessary study? it is only useful to a mistress; the chaste wife, and serious mother, should only consider her power to please as the polish of her virtues, and the affection of her husband as one of the comforts that render her task less difficult, and her life happier. But, whether she be loved or neglected, her first wish should be to make herself respectable, and not rely for all her happiness on a being subject to like infirmities with herself.

Jane Austen

(1775–1817)

In *Jane Austen: A Life* (1997), biographer Claire Tomalin devotes a full chapter to the letter that follows here, pursuing an angle on Austen that to date scholars have ignored. Twenty-one-year-old Jane, writing to her sister Cassandra, describes the ball where she met Tom Lefroy—"my Irish friend"—a good-looking, charming young man with whom she danced and talked about the novel *Tom Jones*. Both Jane and Tom enjoyed that bawdy story, with its plots of sex, fornication, bastards, the hypocrisy of clergy; implicit is Jane and Tom's endorsement of the novel's theme: "the sins of the flesh are of little account, and much to be preferred to the meanness of spirit of sober, prudent people." In Tomalin's words, "It is the only surviving letter in which Jane is clearly writing as the heroine of her own youthful story, living for herself the short period of power, excitement and adventure that might come to a young woman when she was thinking of choosing a husband; just for a brief time she is enacting instead of imagining."

When he was an old man, Tom Lefroy told a nephew that he had been in love with Jane Austen. But his Hampshire relatives sent him packing back to Ireland before anything came of it. She, after all, was the penniless daughter of a clergyman; Tom was also dependent on the fortune of others. He went on to become the Lord Chief Justice of Ireland, she to write some of the greatest novels in the English language. *Pride and Prejudice* she called her "darling child." Its plot of the inviolable bond between money and marriage she knew from her own experience of a mutual attraction cut dead by pragmatic families. The fact of women's economic dependence would always figure as the dark hard ground beneath her bright surfaces.

FROM *The Letters of Jane Austen*

To Cassandra Austen

Steventon: Saturday, 9 January 1796

In the first place I hope you will live twenty-three years longer. Mr. Tom Lefroy's birthday was yesterday, so that you are very near of an age.

After this necessary preamble I shall proceed to inform you that we had an exceeding good ball last night, and that I was very much disappointed at not seeing Charles Fowle of the party, as I had previously heard of his being invited. In addition to our set at the Harwoods' ball, we had the Grants, St. Johns, Lady Rivers, her three daughters and a son, Mr. and Miss Heathcote, Mrs. Lefevre, two Mr. Watkins, Mr. J. Portal, Miss Deanes, two Miss Ledgers, and a tall clergyman who came with them, whose name Mary would never have guessed.

We were so terribly good as to take James in our carriage, though there were three of us before; but indeed he deserves encouragement for the very great improvement which has lately taken place in his dancing. Miss Heathcote is pretty, but not near so handsome as I expected. Mr. H. began with Elizabeth, and afterwards danced with her again; but *they* do not know how *to be particular*. I flatter myself, however, that they will profit by the three successive lessons which I have given them.

You scold me so much in the nice long letter which I have this moment received from you, that I am almost afraid to tell you how my Irish friend and I behaved. Imagine to yourself everything most profligate and shocking in the way of dancing and sitting down together. I *can* expose myself, however, only *once more*, because he leaves the country soon after next Friday, on which day we *are* to have a dance at Ashe after all. He is a very gentlemanlike, good-looking, pleasant young man, I assure you. But as to our having ever met, except at the last three balls, I cannot say much; for he is excessively laughed at about me at Ashe, that he is ashamed of coming to Steventon, and ran away when we called on Mrs. Lefroy a few days ago.

We left Warren at Dean Gate, on our way home last night, and he is now on his road to town. He left his love, &c., to you, and I will deliver it when we meet. Henry goes to Harden to-day on his way to his Master's degree. We shall feel the loss of these two most agreeable young men exceedingly, and shall have nothing to console us till the arrival of the Coopers on Tuesday. As they will stay here till the Monday following, perhaps Caroline will go to the Ashe ball with me, though I dare say she will not.

I danced twice with Warren last night, and once with Mr. Charles Watkins, and, to my inexpressible astonishment, I entirely escaped John Lyford. I was forced to fight hard for it, however. We had a very good supper, and the greenhouse was illuminated in a very elegant manner.

We had a visit yesterday morning from Mr. Benjamin Portal, whose eyes are as handsome as ever. Everybody is extremely anxious for your return, but as you cannot come home by the Ashe ball, I am glad that I have not fed them with false hopes. James danced with Alithea, and cut up the turkey last night with great perseverance. You say nothing of the silk stockings; I flatter myself, therefore, that Charles has not purchased any, as I cannot very well afford to pay for them; all my money is spent in buying white gloves and pink persian. I wish Charles had been at Manydown, because he would have given you some description of my friend, and I think you must be impatient to hear something about him.

Henry is still hankering after the Regulars, and as his project of purchasing the adjutancy of the Oxfordshire is now over, he has got a scheme in his head about getting a lieutenancy and adjutancy in the 86th, a new-raised regiment, which he fancies will be ordered to the Cape of Good Hope. I heartily hope that he will, as usual, be disappointed in this scheme. We have trimmed up and given away all the old paper hats of Mamma's manufacture; I hope you will not regret the loss of yours.

After I had written the above, we received a visit from Mr. Tom Lefroy and his cousin George. The latter is really very well-behaved now; and as for the other, he has but *one* fault, which time will, I trust, entirely remove—it is that his morning coat is a great deal too light. He is a very great admirer of Tom Jones, and therefore wears the same colored clothes, I imagine, which *he* did when he was wounded.

Sunday.— By not returning till the 19th, you will exactly contrive to miss seeing the Coopers, which I suppose it is your wish to do. We have heard nothing from Charles for some time. One would suppose they must have sailed by this time, as the wind is so favourable. What a funny name Tom has got for his vessel! But he has no taste in names, as we well know, and I dare say he christened it himself. I am sorry for the Beaches' loss of their little girl, especially as it is the one so much like me.

I condole with Miss M. on her losses and with Eliza on her gains, and am ever yours,

J. A.

FROM *Pride and Prejudice*

CHAPTER I

It is a truth universally acknowledged, that a single man in possession of a good fortune must be in want of a wife.

However little known of the feelings or views of such a man may be on his first entering a neighbourhood, this truth is so well fixed in the minds of the surrounding families, that he is considered as the rightful property of some one or other of their daughters.

"My dear Mr. Bennet," said his lady to him one day, "have you heard that Netherfield Park is let at last?"

Mr. Bennet replied that he had not.

"But it is," returned she; "for Mrs. Long has just been here, and she told me all about it."

Mr. Bennet made no answer.

"Do not you want to know who has taken it?" cried his wife impatiently.

"*You* want to tell me, and I have no objection to hearing it."

This was invitation enough.

"Why, my dear, you must know, Mrs. Long says that Netherfield is taken by a young man of large fortune from the north of England; that he came down on Monday in a chaise and four to see the place, and was so much delighted with it that he agreed with Mr. Morris immediately; that he is to take possession before Michaelmas, and some of his servants are to be in the house by the end of next week."

"What is his name?"

"Bingley."

"Is he married or single?"

"Oh! single, my dear, to be sure! A single man of large fortune; four or five thousand a-year. What a fine thing for our girls!"

"How so? how can it affect them?"

"My dear Mr. Bennet," replied his wife, "how can you be so tiresome! You must know that I am thinking of his marrying one of them."

"Is that his design in settling here?"

"Design! nonsense, how can you talk so! But it is very likely that he *may* fall in love with one of them, and therefore you must visit him as soon as he comes."

"I see no occasion for that. You and the girls may go, or you may send them by themselves, which perhaps will be still better, for as you are as handsome as any of them, Mr. Bingley might like you the best of the party."

"My dear, you flatter me. I certainly *have* had my share of beauty, but I do not pretend to be any thing extraordinary now. When a woman has five grown up daughters, she ought to give over thinking of her own beauty."

"In such cases, a woman has not often much beauty to think of."

"But, my dear, you must indeed go and see Mr. Bingley when he comes into the neighbourhood."

"It is more than I engage for, I assure you."

"But consider your daughters. Only think what an establishment it would be for one of them. Sir William and Lady Lucas are determined to go, merely on that account, for in general you know they visit no new comers. Indeed you must go, for it will be impossible for *us* to visit him if you do not."

"You are over scrupulous, surely. I dare say Mr. Bingley will be very glad to see you; and I will send a few lines by you to assure him of my hearty consent to his marrying which ever he chuses of the girls; though I must throw in a good word for my little Lizzy."

"I desire you will do no such thing. Lizzy is not a bit better than the others; and I am sure she is not half so handsome as Jane, nor half so good humoured as Lydia. But you are always giving *her* the preference."

"They have none of them much to recommend them," replied he; "they are all silly and ignorant, like other girls; but Lizzy has something more of quickness than her sisters."

"Mr. Bennet, how can you abuse your own children in such a way? You take delight in vexing me. You have no compassion on my poor nerves."

"You mistake me, my dear. I have a high respect for your nerves. They are my old friends. I have heard you mention them with consideration these twenty years at least."

"Ah! you do not know what I suffer."

"But I hope you will get over it, and live to see many young men of four thousand a year come into the neighbourhood."

"It will be no use to us, if twenty such should come, since you will not visit them."

"Depend upon it, my dear, that when there are twenty, I will visit them all."

Mr. Bennet was so odd a mixture of quick parts, sarcastic humour, reserve, and caprice, that the experience of three and twenty years had been insufficient to make his wife understand his character. *Her* mind was less difficult to develope. She was a woman of mean understanding, little information, and uncertain temper. When she was discontented, she fancied herself nervous. The business of her life was to get her daughters married; its solace was visiting and news.

Mary Shelley

(1797–1851)

The journal of Mary Shelley records a seemingly endless cycle of suffering and loss in the voice of a woman determined to survive her own despair. The daughter of Mary Wollstonecraft (see page 33) and philosopher William Godwin, Mary Shelley ran away with the poet Percy Bysshe Shelley when she was seventeen, bore four children, only one of whom lived, wrote *Frankenstein*—the most famous work of science fiction in the English language—when she was nineteen, and, after Shelley drowned off the coast of Italy in 1821, came back to England alone and poor, having herself and her child to support. Muriel Spark's biography, *Mary Shelley: Child of Light*, recounts the nastiness Mary was dealt in her widowhood by literary London and Shelley's father, who made the single mother pay for her irresponsible youth. She continued to publish newspaper articles, short stories, and novels—Spark compares *Valperga* (1823), a novel of medieval Italy, with George Eliot's *Romola*—but was always in need of money and often depressed. In the 1840s, she returned to Italy with her son, by this time a university student, and wrote a travel book, *Rambles in Germany and Italy* (1844), which was well received. Italy restored her to happiness: "The name of Italy has magic in its very syllables," she wrote in the preface. "At the name of Italy I grow young again."

FROM *Mary Shelley's Journal*

ALBARO, ITALY, 1822

Oct. 2—On the 8th of July I finished my journal. This is a curious coincidence. The date still remains—the fatal 8th—a monument to show that all ended then. And I began again? Oh, never! But several motives induce me, when the day has gone down, and all is silent around me, steeped in sleep, to pen as occasion wills, my reflections and feelings. First, I have no friend. For eight years I communicated, with unlimited freedom, with one whose genius, far transcending mine, awakened and guided my thoughts. I conversed with him: rectified my errors of judgment; obtained new lights from him; and my mind was satisfied. Now I am alone—oh, how alone! The stars may behold my tears, and the winds drink my sighs; but my thoughts are a sealed treasure, which I can confide to none. But can I express all I feel? Can I give words to thoughts and feelings that, as a tempest, hurry me along? Is this the sand that the ever-flowing sea of thought would impress indelibly? Alas! I am alone. No eye answers mine; my voice can with none assume its natural modulation. What a change! O my beloved Shelley! how often during those happy days— happy, though chequered—I thought how superiorly gifted I had been in being united to one to whom I could unveil myself, and who could under- stand me! Well, then, now I am reduced to these white pages, which I am to blot with dark imagery. As I write, let me think what he would have said if, speaking thus to him, he could have answered me. Yes, my own heart, I would fain know what to think of my desolate state: what you think I ought to do, what to think. I guess you would answer thus:—"Seek to know your own heart, and, learning what it best loves, try to enjoy that." Well, I cast my eyes around, and, look forward to the bounded prospect in view: I ask myself what pleases me there? My child;—so many feelings arise when I think of him, that I turn aside to think no more. Those I most loved are gone for ever; those who held the second rank are absent; and among those near me as yet, I trust to the disinterested kindness of one alone. Beneath all this, my imagination never flags. Literary labours, the improvement of my mind, and the enlargement of my ideas, are the only occupations that elevate me from my lethargy; all events seem to lead me to that one point, and the courses of destiny having dragged me to that single resting-place, have left me. Father, mother, friend, husband, children—all made, as it were, the team that conducted me here; and now all, except you, my poor boy (and you are necessary to the continuance of my life), all are gone, and I am left to fulfil my task. So be it. . . .

1823

May 31—The lanes are filled with fireflies: they dart between the trunks of the trees, and people the land with earth-stars. I walked among them to-night, and descended towards the sea. I passed by the ruined church, and stood on the platform that overlooks the beach. The black rocks were stretched out among the blue waters, which dashed with no impetuous motion against them. The dark boats, with their white sails, glided gently over its surface, and the star-enlightened promontories closed in the bay: below, amid the crags, I heard the monotonous but harmonious, voices of the fishermen.

How beautiful these shores, and this sea! Such is the scene—such the waves within which my beloved vanished from mortality.

The time is drawing near when I must quit this country. It is true that, in the situation I now am, Italy is but the corpse of the enchantress that she was. Besides, if I had stayed here, the state of things would have been different. The idea of our Child's advantage alone enables me to keep fixed in my resolution to return to England. It is best for him—and I go.

Four years ago, we lost our darling William; four years ago, in excessive agony, I called for death to free me from all I felt that I should suffer here. I continue to live, and *thou* art gone. I leave Italy and the few that still remain to me. That, I regret less; for our intercourse is [so] much chequered with all of dross that this earth so delights to blend with kindness and sympathy, that I long for solitude, with the exercise of such affections as still remain to me. Away, I shall be conscious that these friends love me, and none can then gainsay the pure attachment which chiefly clings to them, because they knew and loved you—because I knew them when with you, and I cannot think of them without feeling your spirit beside me.

I cannot grieve for you, beloved Shelley; I grieve for thy friends—for the world—for thy Child—most for myself, enthroned in thy love, growing wiser and better beneath thy gentle influence, taught by you the highest philosophy—your pupil, friend, lover, wife, mother of your children! The glory of the dream is gone. I am a cloud from which the light of sunset has passed. Give me patience in the present struggle. *Meum cordium cor!* Good night!

> I would give
> All that I am to be as thou now art:
> But I am chain'd to time, and cannot thence depart[*]

[*] *Adonais.* XXVI.

LONDON, ENGLAND, 1824★

Jan. 18—I have now been nearly four months in England and if I am to judge of the future by the past and the present, I have small delight in looking forward. I even regret those days and weeks of intense melancholy that composed my life at Genoa. Yes, solitary and unbeloved as I was there, I enjoyed a more pleasurable state of being than I do here. I was still in Italy, and my heart and imagination were both gratified by that circumstance. I awoke with the light and beheld the theatre of nature from my window: the trees spread their green beauty before me, the resplendent sky was above me, the mountains were invested with enchanting colours. I had even begun to contemplate painlessly the blue expanse of the tranquil sea, speckled by the snow-white sails, gazed upon by the unclouded stars. There was morning and its balmy air, noon and its exhilarating heat, evening and its wondrous sunset, night and its starry pageant. Then, my studies; my drawing, which soothed me; my Greek, which I studied with greater complacency as I stole every now and then a look on the scene near me; my metaphysics, that strengthened and elevated my mind. Then my solitary walks and my reveries; they were magnificent, deep, pathetic, wild, and exalted. I sounded the depths of my own nature; I appealed to the nature around me to corroborate the testimony that my own heart bore to its purity. I thought of *him* with hope; my grief was active, striving, expectant. I was worth something then in the catalogue of beings. I could have written something, been something. Now, I am exiled from these beloved scenes; its language is becoming a stranger to mine ears; my Child is forgetting it. I am imprisoned in a dreary town; I see neither fields, nor hills, nor trees, nor sky; the exhilaration of enrapt contemplation is no more felt by me; aspirations agonising, yet grand, from which the soul reposed in peace, have ceased to ascend from the quenched altar of my mind. Writing has become a task; my studies irksome; my life dreary. In this prison it is only in human intercourse that I can pretend to find consolation; and woe, woe, and triple woe, to whoever seeks pleasure in human intercourse when that pleasure is not founded on deep and intense affection; as for the rest—

> The bubble floats before,
> The shadow stalks behind.

★ Mary left Albaro for England on July 22, 1823. On January 14, 1824, she was living at 14 Speldhurst Street, Brunswick Square, London.

My father's situation, his cares and debts, prevent my enjoying his society.

I love Jane [Williams] better than any other human being, but I am pressed upon by the knowledge that she but slightly returns this affection. I love her, and my purest pleasure is derived from that source—a capacious basin, and but a small rill flows into it. I love some one or two more, "with a degree of love," but I see them seldom. I am excited while with them, but the reaction of this feeling is dreadfully painful, but while in London I cannot forego this excitement. I know some clever men, in whose conversation I delight, but this is rare, like angels' visits. Alas! having lived day by day with one of the wisest, best, and most affectionate of spirits, how void, bare, and drear is the scene of life!

Oh, Shelley, dear, lamented, beloved! help me, raise me, support me: let me not feel ever thus fallen and degraded! My imagination is dead, my genius lost, my energies sleep. Why am I not beneath that weedgrown tower?★ Seeing Coleridge last night reminded me forcibly of past times: his beautiful descriptions reminded me of Shelley's conversations. Such was the intercourse I once daily enjoyed, added to supreme and active goodness, sympathy, and affection, and a wild, picturesque mode of living that suited my active spirit and satisfied its craving for novelty of impression.

I will go into the country and philosophise: some gleams of past entrancement may visit me there.

May 14—This, then, is my English life: and thus I am to drag on existence; confined in my small room, friendless. Each day I string me to the task. I endeavour to read and write; my ideas stagnate and my understanding refuses to follow the words I read: day after day passes while torrents fall from the dark clouds, and my mind is as gloomy as this odious day. Without human friends I must attach myself to natural objects; but though I talk of the country, what difference shall I find in this miserable climate. Italy, dear Italy, murderess of those I love and of all my happiness, one word of your soft language coming unawares upon me, has made me shed bitter tears. When shall I hear it again spoken, when see your skies, your trees, your streams? The imprisonment attendant on a succession of rainy days has quite overcome me. God knows I strive to be content, but in vain. Amidst all the depressing circumstances that weigh on me, none sinks deeper than the failure of my intellec-

★ Shelley's grave is at the foot of a tower in the Protestant cemetery in Rome.

tual powers; nothing I write pleases me. Whether I am just in this, or whether the want of Shelley's (oh, my loved Shelley, it is some alleviation only to write your name!) encouragement, I can hardly tell, but it seems to me as if the lovely and sublime objects of nature had been my best inspirers, and wanting these I am lost. Although so utterly miserable at Genoa, yet what reveries were mine as I looked on the aspect of the ravine—the sunny deep and its boats—the promontories clothed in purple light—the starry heavens—the fireflies—the uprising of Spring! Then I could think, and my imagination could invent and combine, and self became absorbed in the grandeur of the universe I created. Now, my mind is a blank, a gulf filled with formless mist.

The last man!* Yes, I may well describe that solitary being's feelings, feeling myself as the last relic of a beloved race, my companions extinct before me.

And thus has the accumulating sorrows of days and weeks been forced to find a voice, because the word *lucena* met my eyes, and the idea of lost Italy sprang in my mind. What graceful lamps those are, though of bare construction and vulgar use; I thought of bringing one with me; I am glad I did not. I will go back only to have a *lucena*. If I told people so they would think me mad, and yet not madder than they seem to be now, when I say that the blue skies and verdure-clad earth of that dear land are necessary to my existence.

If there be a kind spirit attendant on me, in compensation for these miserable days, let me only dream to-night that I am in Italy! Mine own Shelley, what a horror you had (fully sympathised in by me) of returning to this miserable country! To be here without you is to be doubly exiled, to be away from Italy is to lose you twice. Dearest, why is my spirit thus losing all energy? Indeed, indeed. I must go back, or your poor utterly lost Mary will never dare think herself worthy to visit you beyond the grave. . . .

1824

Sept. 3—With what hopes did I come to England? I pictured little of what was pleasurable; the feeling I had, could not be called hope; it was expectation. Yet, at that time, now a year ago, what should I have said if a prophet had told me, that after the whole revolution of the year, I should be as poor in all estimable treasures as when I arrived. . . .

---

* Her novel *The Last Man* was published in 1826.

I have just completed my 27th year; at such a time hope and youth are still in their prime, and the pains I feel, therefore, are ever alive and vivid within me. What shall I do? Nothing! I study, that passes the time. I write, at times that pleases me; though double sorrow comes when I feel that Shelley no longer reads and approves of what I write; besides, I have no great faith in my success. Composition is delightful, but if you do not expect the sympathy of your fellow creatures in what you write, the pleasure of writing is of short duration.

I have my lovely Boy, without him I could not live. I have Jane, in her society I forget time, but the idea of it does not cheer me in my griefful moods. It is strange that the religious feeling that exalted my emotions in happiness deserts me in my misery. I have little enjoyment, no hope. I have given myself ten years more of life. God grant that they may not be augmented. I should be glad that they were curtailed. Loveless beings surround me; they talk of my personal attractions, of my talents, my manners.

The wisest and best have loved me. The beautiful, and glorious, and noble have looked on me with the divine expression of love, till Death, the reaper, carried to his over-stocked barns my lamented harvest.

But now I am not loved! Never, oh, never more shall I love. Synonymous to such words are, never more shall I be happy, never more feel life sit triumphant in my frame. I am a wreck. By what do the fragments cling together? Why do they not part, to be borne away by the tide to the boundless ocean, where those are whom day and night I pray that I may rejoin?

I shall be happier, perhaps, in Italy; yet, when I sometimes think that she is the murderess, I tremble for my Boy. We shall see: if no change comes, I shall be unable to support the burthen of time, and no change, if it hurt not his dear head, can be for the worse.

Oct. 26.—Time rolls on, and what does it bring? What can I do? How change my destiny? Months change their names, years their cyphers. My brow is sadly trenched, the blossom of youth faded. My mind gathers wrinkles. What will become of me?

How long it is since an emotion of joy filled my once exulting heart, or beamed from my once bright eyes. I am young still, though age creeps on apace; but I may not love any but the dead. I think that an emotion of joy would destroy me, so new, so strange would it be to my widowed heart. . . .

LONDON, ENGLAND, 1838

Sunday, Oct. 21—I have been so often abused by pretended friends for my lukewarmness in "the good cause," that, though I disdain to answer them, I shall put down here a few thoughts on this subject. I am much of a self-examiner. Vanity is not my fault, I think; if it is, it is uncomfortable vanity, for I have none that teaches me to be satisfied with myself; far otherwise, —and, if I use the word disdain, it is that I think my qualities (such as they are) not appreciated from unworthy causes.

In the first place, with regard to "the good cause"—the cause of the advancement of freedom and knowledge, of the rights of women, &c.—I am not a person of opinions. I have said elsewhere that human beings differ greatly in this. Some have a passion for reforming the world; others do not cling to particular opinions. That my parents and Shelley were of the former class, makes me respect it. I respect such when joined to real disinterestedness, toleration, and a clear understanding. My accusers, after such as these, appear to me mere drivellers. For myself, I earnestly desire the good and enlightenment of my fellow-creatures, and see all, in the present course, tending to the same, and rejoice; but I am not for violent extremes, which only bring on an injurious reaction. I have never written a word in disfavour of liberalism; that I have not supported it openly in writing, arises from the following causes, as far as I know:—

That I have not argumentative powers: I see things pretty clearly, but cannot demonstrate them. Besides, I feel the counter-arguments too strongly. I do not feel that I could say ought to support the cause efficiently: besides that, on some topics (especially with regard to my own sex), I am far from making up my mind. I believe we are sent here to educate ourselves, and that self-denial, and disappointment, and self-control, are a part of our education; that it is not by taking away all restraining law that our improvement is to be achieved: and, though many things need great amendment, I can by no means go so far as my friends would have me. When I feel that I can say what will benefit my fellow-creatures, I will speak: not before.

Then, I recoil from the vulgar abuse of the inimical press. I do more than recoil: proud and sensitive, I act on the defensive—an inglorious position.

To hang back, as I do, brings a penalty. I was nursed and fed with a love of glory. To be something great and good was the precept given me by my Father: Shelley reiterated it. Alone and poor, I could only be something by joining a party; and there was much in me—the woman's love of looking up, and being guided, and being willing to do anything if any one supported and brought me forward—which would have made me a good partisan. But Shelley died, and I was alone. My Father, from age and domestic circumstances, could not "*me faire valoir.*" My total friendlessness, my horror of pushing, and inability to put myself forward unless led, cherished and supported,—all this has sunk me in a state of loneliness no other human being ever before, I believe, endured—except Robinson Crusoe. How many tears and spasms of anguish this solitude has cost me, lies buried in my memory.

If I had raved and ranted about what I did not understand: had I adopted a set of opinions, and propagated them with enthusiasm; had I been careless of attack, and eager for notoriety; then the party to which I belonged had gathered round me, and I had not been alone. But since I had lost Shelley I have no wish to ally myself to the Radicals—they are full of repulsion to me—violent without any sense of Justice—selfish in the extreme—talking without knowledge—rude, envious and insolent—I wish to have nothing to do with them.

It has been the fashion with these same friends to accuse me of worldliness. There, indeed, in my own heart and conscience, I take a high ground. I may distrust my own judgment too much—be too indolent and too timid; but in conduct I am above merited blame.

I like society; I believe all persons who have any talent (who are in good health) do. The soil that gives forth nothing, may lie ever fallow; but that which produces—however humble its product—needs cultivation, change of harvest, refreshing dews, and ripening sun. Books do much; but the living intercourse is the vital heat. Debarred from that, how have I pined and died!

My early friends chose the position of enemies. When I first discovered that a trusted friend had acted falsely by me, I was nearly destroyed. My health was shaken. I remembered thinking, with a burst of agonizing tears, that I should prefer a bed of torture to the unutterable anguish a friend's falsehood engendered. There is no resentment; but the world can never be to me what it was before. Trust, and confidence, and the heart's sincere devotion, are gone.

I sought at that time to make acquaintances—to divert my mind from this anguish. I got entangled in various ways through my ready sympathy and too eager heart; but I never crouched to society—never sought it unworthily. If I have never written to vindicate the rights of women, I have ever befriended women when oppressed. At every risk I have befriended and supported victims to the social system; but I make no boast, for in truth it is simple justice I perform; and so I am still reviled for being worldly.

God grant a happier and better day is near! Percy—my all-in-all—will, I trust, by his excellent understanding, his clear, bright, sincere spirit and affectionate heart, repay me for sad long years of desolation. His career may lead me into the thick of life or only gild a quiet home. I am content with either, and, as I grow older I grow more fearless for myself—I become firmer in my opinions. The experienced, the suffering, the thoughtful may at last speak unrebuked. If it be the will of God that I live, I may ally my name yet to "the good cause," though I do not expect to please my accusers.

Thus have I put down my thoughts. I may have deceived myself; I may be in the wrong; I try to examine myself; and such as I have written appears to me the exact truth.

Enough of this! The great work of life goes on.

Elizabeth Barrett Browning

(1806-1861)

The mythic Elizabeth Barrett lies year after year on a couch in the shadowy drawing room of her autocratic father's house in Wimpole Street, London. With the appearance of the messianic Robert Browning, she swoons. Somehow she rouses herself to show up for a secret marriage at St. Marylebone's and then to run away with her romantic poet husband to the resurrecting sunshine of far-off Italy. In fact, Miss Barrett was stronger than she looked. She eloped at forty (Robert was thirty-four), had her first child at forty-three, and published prolifically after she set up house on little money in Florence: *Sonnets from the Portuguese* (1850); *Casa Guidi Windows* (1851); and the "epic novel" *Aurora Leigh* (1856). Speaking for the poet, Aurora declares, "I too have my vocation—work to do . . . most serious work." Dedicated to international human rights, Barrett Browning advocated republicanism in Italy, abolition in the United States, child welfare laws in England, and full humanity for women. Though her voice is sometimes cloying, she writes as a serious humanitarian committed to social justice. And in the sonnets, the ethereal world of dreams is for children and angels; the woman celebrates the here-and-now of human passions.

FROM *Sonnets from the Portuguese*

XXII

When our two souls stand up erect and strong,
Face to face, silent, drawing nigh and nigher,
Until the lengthening wings break into fire
At either curvèd point,—what bitter wrong
Can the earth do to us, that we should not long
Be here contented? Think. In mounting higher,

The angels would press on us and aspire
To drop some golden orb of perfect song
Into our deep, dear silence. Let us stay
Rather on earth, Belovèd,—where the unfit
Contrarious moods of men recoil away
And isolate pure spirits, and permit
A place to stand and love in for a day,
With darkness and the death-hour rounding it.

XXVI

I lived with visions for my company
Instead of men and women, years ago,
And found them gentle mates, nor thought to know
A sweeter music than they played to me.
But soon their trailing purple was not free
Of this world's dust, their lutes did silent grow,
And I myself grew faint and blind below
Their vanishing eyes. Then THOU didst
come—to be,
Belovèd, what they seemed. Their shining fronts,
Their songs, their splendors (better, yet the same,
As river-water hallowed into fonts),
Met in thee, and from out thee overcame
My soul with satisfaction of all wants:
Because God's gifts put man's best dreams to shame.

XXVII

My own Belovèd, who has lifted me
From this drear flat of earth where I was thrown,
And, in betwixt the languid ringlets, blown
A life-breath, till the forehead hopefully
Shines out again, as all the angels see,

Before thy saving kiss! My own, my own,
Who camest to me when the world was gone,
And I who looked for only God, found *thee*!
I find thee; I am safe, and strong, and glad.
As one who stands in dewless asphodel
Looks backward on the tedious time he had
In the upper life,—so I, with bosom-swell,
Make witness, here, between the good and bad,
That Love, as strong as Death, retrieves as well.

XLIII

How do I love thee? Let me count the ways.
I love thee to the depth and breadth and height
My soul can reach, when feeling out of sight
For the ends of Being and ideal Grace.
I love thee to the level of every day's
Most quiet need, by sun and candlelight.
I love thee freely, as men strive for Right;
I love thee purely, as they turn from Praise;
I love thee with the passion put to use
In my old griefs, and with my childhood's faith.
I love thee with a love I seemed to lose
With my lost saints—I love thee with the breath,
Smiles, tears of all my life!—and, if God choose,
I shall but love thee better after death.

Margaret Fuller

(1810–1850)

The way she used to be remembered—as the bluestocking disciple of Ralph Waldo Emerson and the model for the joyless Xenobia in Nathaniel Hawthorne's *The Blithedale Romance*—misses the point of Margaret Fuller entirely. A passionate and original woman, who was patronized by Emerson and ridiculed by Hawthorne, the best move she ever made was to leave the New England Oversoul behind and go to work as a reporter for a newspaper in New York, becoming the first self-supporting woman journalist in America. The *New York Tribune* sent her to Italy, where she covered the war for the Roman Republic. (She arrived in Europe to find she was admired as the author of the highly regarded and widely read *Woman in the Nineteenth Century*.) The articles she sent back to America, collected under the title *Dispatches from Europe to the New York Tribune, 1846–1850*, are now considered the best writing she ever did. She said Italy brought her back to life. "Once I was almost all intellect; now I am almost all feeling," she wrote in her journal. "Nature vindicates her rights, and I feel all Italy glowing beneath the Saxon crust." She had a baby with her Italian lover, Giovanni Angelo Ossoli, whom she may have married, became a good friend of the patriots Mazzini and Garibaldi, and in her columns introduced the poetry of her friends the Brownings to an American audience. Returning to America after the defeat of the Italian republican army and carrying with her her manuscript about the history of the short-lived Roman Republic, she and her family drowned in a shipwreck a mile off the coast of Fire Island. (Marie Ponsot's poem "Foreign Correspondent"—see page 409—evokes this tragedy.) In commemoration of her service in support of Italian independence—the soldiers she nursed spoke with fervor of her compassion—the city of Rome named a park after her on the Janiculum Hill.

FROM *Woman in the Nineteenth Century*

Male and female represent the two sides of the great radical dualism. But, in fact, they are perpetually passing into one another. Fluid hardens to solid, solid rushes to fluid. There is no wholly masculine man, no purely feminine woman. . . .

—

Let us be wise, and not impede the soul. Let her work as she will. Let us have one creative energy, one incessant revelation. Let it take what form it will, and let us not bind it by the past to man or woman, black or white. Jove sprang from Rhea, Pallas from Jove. So let it be.

If it has been the tendency of these remarks to call Woman rather to the Minerva side,—if I, unlike the more generous writer, have spoken from society no less than the soul,—let it be pardoned! It is love that has caused this,— love for many incarcerated souls, that might be freed, could the idea of religious self-dependence be established in them, could the weakening habit of dependence on others be broken up. . . .

—

Women must leave off asking [men] and being influenced by them, but retire within themselves, and explore the ground-work of life till they find their peculiar secret. Then, when they come forth again, renovated and baptized, they will know how to turn all dross to gold, and will be rich and free though they live in a hut, tranquil if in a crowd. Then their sweet singing shall not be from passionate impulse, but the lyrical overflow of a divine rapture, and a new music shall be evolved from this many-chorded world.

Grant her, then, for a while, the armor and the javelin. Let her put from her the press of other minds, and meditate in virgin loneliness. . . .

—

I have urged on Woman independence of Man, not that I do not think the sexes mutually needed by one another, but because in Woman this fact has led to an excessive devotion, which has cooled love, degraded marriage, and prevented either sex from being what it should be to itself or the other.

I wish Woman to live, *first* for God's sake. Then she will not make an imperfect man her god, and thus sink to idolatry. Then she will not take what is not fit for her from a sense of weakness and poverty. Then, if she finds what she needs in Man embodied, she will know how to love, and be worthy of being loved.

By being more a soul, she will not be less Woman, for nature is perfected through spirit.

Now there is no woman, only an overgrown child.

That her hand may be given with dignity, she must be able to stand alone. I wish to see men and women capable of such relations as are depicted by Landor in his Pericles and Aspasia, where grace is the natural garb of strength, and the affections are calm, because deep. The softness is that of a firm tissue, as when

> The gods approve
> The depth, but not the tumult of the soul,
> A fervent, not ungovernable love.

A profound thinker has said, "No married woman can represent the female world, for she belongs to her husband. The idea of Woman must be represented by a virgin."

But that is the very fault of marriage, and of the present relation between the sexes, that the woman *does* belong to the man, instead of forming a whole with him. Were it otherwise, there would be no such limitation to the thought.

Woman, self-centred, would never be absorbed by any relation; it would only be an experience to her as to man. It is a vulgar error that love, *a* love, to Woman is her whole existence; she also is born for Truth and Love in their universal energy.

FROM *Dispatches from Europe to the New York Tribune, 1846–1850*

Dispatch 14   ROME, MAY 1847

There is very little that I can like to write about Italy. Italy is beautiful, worthy to be loved and embraced, not talked about. Yet I remember well that when afar I liked to read what was written about her; now all thought of it is very tedious.

The traveler passing along the beaten track, vetturinoed from inn to inn, ciceroned from gallery to gallery, thrown, through indolence, want of tact, or ignorance of the language, too much into the society of his compatriots, sees the least possible of the country; fortunately, it is impossible to avoid seeing a great deal. The great features of the past pursue and fill the eye.

Yet I find that it is quite out of the question to know Italy; to say anything of her that is full and sweet, so as to convey any idea of her spirit, without long residence, and residence in the districts untouched by the scorch and dust of foreign invasion, (the invasion of the dilettanti I mean,) and without an intimacy of feeling, an abandonment to the spirit of the place, impossible to most Americans; they retain too much of their English blood; and the traveling English, as a tribe, seem to me the most unseeing of all possible animals. There are exceptions; for instance, the perceptions and pictures of Browning seem as delicate and just here on the spot as they did at a distance; but, take them as a tribe, they have the vulgar familiarity of Mrs. Trollope without her vivacity, the cockneyism of Dickens without his graphic power and love of the odd corners of human nature. I admired the English at home in their island; I admired their honor, truth, practical intelligence, persistent power. But they do not look well in Italy; they are not the figures for this landscape. I am indignant at the contempt they have presumed to express for the faults of our semi-barbarous state. What is the vulgarity expressed in our tobacco-chewing, and way of eating eggs, compared to that which elbows the Greek marbles, guide-book in hand—chatters and sneers through the Miserere of the Sistine Chapel, beneath the very glance of Michel Angelo's Sibyls,—praises St. Peter's as "*nice*," talks of "*managing*" the Colosseum by moonlight,—and snatches "*bits*" for a "*sketch*" from the sublime silence of the Campagna. . . .

I have heard owls hoot in the Colosseum by moonlight, and they spoke more to the purpose than I ever heard any other voice upon that subject. I have seen all the pomps and shows of Holy Week in the Church of St. Peter, and found them less imposing than an habitual acquaintance with the place with processions of monks and nuns stealing in now and then, or the swell of vespers from some side chapel. I have ascended the dome and seen thence Rome and its Campagna, its villas with their cypresses and pines serenely sad as is nothing else in the world, and the fountains of the Vatican Garden gushing hard by. I have been in the Subterranean to see a poor little boy introduced, much to his surprise, to the bosom of the Church; and then I have seen by torchlight the stone Popes where they lie on their tombs, and the old mosaics, and Virgins with gilt caps. It is all rich and full,—very impressive in its way. St. Peter's must be to each one a separate poem. . . .

To Ralph Waldo Emerson   JUNE 10, 1849

. . . I received your letter amid the round of cannonade and musketry. It was a terrible battle fought here from the first to the last light of day. I could see all its progress from my balcony. The Italians fought like lions. It is a truly heroic spirit that animates them. They make a stand here for honor and their rights, with little ground for hope that they can resist, now they are betrayed by France.

Since the 30th of April, I go almost daily to the hospitals, and though I have suffered, for I had no idea before how terrible gunshot wounds and wound-fevers are, yet I have taken pleasure, and great pleasure, in being with the men. There is scarcely one who is not moved by a noble spirit. Many, especially among the Lombards, are the flower of the Italian youth. When they begin to get better, I carry them books and flowers; they read, and we talk.

The palace of the Pope, on the Quirinal, is now used for convalescents. In those beautiful gardens I walk with them, one with his sling, another with his crutch. The gardener plays off all his water-works for the defenders of the country, and gathers flowers for me, their friend.

A day or two since, we sat in the Pope's little pavilion, where he used to give private audience. The sun was going gloriously down over Monte Mario,* where gleamed the white tents of the French light-horse among the trees. The cannonade was heard at intervals. Two bright-eyed boys sat at our feet, and gathered up eagerly every word said by the heroes of the day. It was a beautiful hour, stolen from the midst of ruin and sorrow, and tales were told as full of grace and pathos as in the gardens of Boccaccio, only in a very different spirit,—with noble hope for man, and reverence for woman. . . .

Should I never return, and sometimes I despair of doing so, it seems so far off,—so difficult, I am caught in such a net of ties here,—if ever you know of my life here, I think you will only wonder at the constancy with which I have sustained myself,—the degree of profit to which, amid great difficulties, I have

---

* Beautifully visible from the Gallery of Pius IV in Castel Sant' Angelo, Monte Mario rises above the Tiber on the northwest outskirts of the city.

put the time,—at least in the way of observation. Meanwhile, love me all you can. Let me feel that, amid the fearful agitations of the world, there are pure hands, with healthful, even pulse, stretched out toward me, if I claim their grasp.

I feel profoundly for Mazzini. At moments I am tempted to say, "Cursed with every granted prayer,"—so cunning is the demon. Mazzini has become the inspiring soul of his people. He saw Rome, to which all his hopes through life tended, for the first time as a Roman citizen, and to become in a few days its ruler. He has animated, he sustains her to a glorious effort, which, if it fails this time, will not in the age. His country will be free. Yet to me it would be so dreadful to cause all this bloodshed,—to dig the graves of martyrs!

Then, Rome is being destroyed; her glorious oaks,—her villas, haunts of sacred beauty, that seemed the possession of the world for ever,—the villa of Raphael, the villa of Albani, home of Winckelmann and the best expression of the ideal of modern Rome, and so many other sanctuaries of beauty,—all must perish, lest a fool should level his musket from their shelter. I could not, could not!

I know not, dear friend, whether I shall ever get home across that great ocean, but here in Rome I shall no longer wish to live. Oh Rome, *my* country! could I imagine that the triumph of what I held dear was to heap such desolation on thy head!

Speaking of the republic, you say, "Do you not wish Italy had a great man?" Mazzini is a great man. In mind, a great, poetic statesman; in heart, a lover; in action, decisive and full of resource as Caesar. Dearly I love Mazzini. He came in, just as I had finished the first letter to you. His soft, radiant look makes melancholy music in my soul; it consecrates my present life, that, like Magdalen, I may, at that important hour, shed all consecrated ointment on his head. . . .

Harriet Beecher Stowe

(1811-1896)

No doubt the leader of the pack that Nathaniel Hawthorne dismissed as "that damn'd mob of scribbling women" was the author of *Uncle Tom's Cabin* (1851–52), an overnight bestseller in America and Europe, selling into the millions. Mrs. Stowe's novel, though banned in the South, was admired by Charles Dickens, George Eliot, and George Sand, and, according to many, contributed more than any one thing to slavery's abolition. When Lincoln greeted her at the White House during the Civil War with the legendary words "So this is the little lady who wrote the book that made this great war" (neither the remark nor the meeting can be documented), he was only saying what her friends, fans, and enemies believed. The book, however, was conceived as much in Stowe's personal sorrow as in her outrage over slavery and the Fugitive Slave Law of 1850, which forbade all citizens, including those in northern states where slavery had been abolished, to help fugitive slaves. When her seventh and last baby died in a cholera epidemic in 1850, she later said, "It was at Charley's dying bed and at his grave that I learned what a poor slave mother may feel when her child is torn away from her." Knowing maternal love and loss in her own life, she wrote the separations of slave mothers and their children as the serial tragedies of the novel. She believed that if women in particular felt the slave women's suffering, they would provide the moral and political force needed to abolish the "peculiar institution." In the idealized figure of Rachel Halliday, the good Quaker mother on the underground railroad at the center of "The Quaker Settlement"—the chapter that follows here—Stowe embodies the domestic politics that she believed could overcome the evil of the world. Reviled by southerners as fanatical, malignant, and pharisaical, patronized by critics for its sentimentality and the abject character of Uncle Tom, Stowe's masterpiece continues to make a powerful impression on contemporary readers.

FROM *Uncle Tom's Cabin*

THE QUAKER SETTLEMENT

A quiet scene now rises before us. A large, roomy, neatly-painted kitchen, its yellow floor glossy and smooth, and without a particle of dust; a neat, well-blacked cooking stove; rows of shining tin, suggestive of unmentionable good things to the appetite; glossy green wood chairs, old and firm; a small flag-bottomed rocking-chair, with a patch-work cushion in it, neatly contrived out of small pieces of different colored woolen goods, and a larger sized one, motherly and old, whose wide arms breathed hospitable invitation, seconded by the solicitation of its feather cushions,—a real comfortable, persuasive old chair, and worth, in the way of honest, homely enjoyment, a dozen of your plush or brocatelle drawing-room gentry; and in the chair, gently swaying back and forward, her eyes bent on some fine sewing, sat our old friend Eliza.* Yes, there she is, paler and thinner than in her Kentucky home, with a world of quiet sorrow lying under the shadow of her long eyelashes, and marking the outline of her gentle mouth! It was plain to see how old and firm the girlish heart was grown under the discipline of heavy sorrow; and when, anon, her large dark eyes were raised to follow the gambols of her little Harry, who was sporting, like some tropical butterfly, hither and thither over the floor, she showed a depth of firmness and steady resolve that was never there in her earlier and happier days.

By her side sat a woman with a bright tin pan in her lap, into which she was carefully sorting some dried peaches. She might be fifty-five or sixty; but hers was one of those faces that time seems to touch only to brighten and adorn. The snowy lisse crape cap, made after the strait Quaker pattern,—the plain white muslin handkerchief, lying in placid folds across her bosom,—the drab shawl and dress,—showed at once the community to which she belonged. Her face was round and rosy, with a healthful downy softness, suggestive of a ripe peach. Her hair, partially silvered by age, was parted smoothly back from a high placed forehead, on which time had written no inscription, except peace on earth, good will to men, and beneath shone a large pair of clear, honest, loving brown eyes; you only needed to look straight into them, to feel that you saw to the bottom of a heart as good

---

* Eliza Harris, the runaway slave, subject of much American fiction and painting.

and true as ever throbbed in a woman's bosom. So much has been said and sung of beautiful young girls, why doesn't somebody wake up to the beauty of old women? If any want to get up an inspiration under this head, we refer them to our good friend Rachel Halliday, just as she sits there in her little rocking-chair. It had a turn for quacking and squeaking,—that chair had,— either from having taken cold in early life, or from some asthmatic infection, or perhaps from nervous derangement; but, as she gently swung backward and forward, the chair kept up a kind of subdued "creechy crawchy," that would have been intolerable in any other chair. But old Simeon Halliday often declared it was as good as any music to him, and the children all avowed that they wouldn't miss of hearing mother's chair for anything in the world. For why? for twenty years or more, nothing but loving words, and gentle moralities, and motherly loving kindness, had come from that chair;—head-aches and heart-aches innumerable had been cured there,— difficulties spiritual and temporal solved there,—all by one good, loving woman, God bless her!

"And so thee still thinks of going to Canada, Eliza?" she said, as she was quietly looking over her peaches.

"Yes, ma'am," said Eliza, firmly. "I must go onward, I dare not stop."

"And what'll thee do, when thee gets there? Thee must think about that, my daughter."

"My daughter" came naturally from the lips of Rachel Halliday; for hers was just the face and form that made "mother" seem the most natural in the world.

Eliza's hands trembled, and some tears fell on her fine work; but she answered, firmly,

"I shall do—anything I can find. I hope I can find something."

"Thee knows thee can stay here, as long as thee pleases," said Rachel.

"O, thank you," said Eliza, "but"—she pointed to Harry—"I can't sleep nights; I can't rest. Last night I dreamed I saw the man coming into the yard," she said, shuddering.

"Poor child!" said Rachel, wiping her eyes; "but thee mustn't feel so. The Lord hath ordered it so that never hath a fugitive been stolen from our village. I trust thine will not be the first."

The door here opened, and a little short, round, pin-cushiony woman stood at the door, with a cheery, blooming face, like a ripe apple. She was dressed, like Rachel, in sober gray, with the muslin folded neatly across her round, plump little chest.

"Ruth Stedman," said Rachel, coming joyfully forward; "how is thee, Ruth?" she said, heartily taking both her hands.

"Nicely," said Ruth, taking off her little drab bonnet, and dusting it with her handkerchief, displaying, as she did so, a round little head, on which the Quaker cap sat with a sort of jaunty air, despite all the stroking and patting of the small fat hands, which were busily applied to arranging it. Certain stray locks of decidedly curly hair, too, had escaped here and there, and had to be coaxed and cajoled into their place again; and then the new comer, who might have been five-and-twenty, turned from the small looking-glass, before which she had been making these arrangements, and looked well pleased,—as most people who looked at her might have been,—for she was decidedly a wholesome, whole-hearted, chirruping little woman, as ever gladdened man's heart withal.

"Ruth, this friend is Eliza Harris; and this is the little boy I told thee of."

"I am glad to see thee, Eliza,—very," said Ruth, shaking hands, as if Eliza were an old friend she had long been expecting; "and this is thy dear boy,—I brought a cake for him," she said, holding out a little heart to the boy, who came up, gazing through his curls, and accepted it shyly.

"Where's thy baby, Ruth?" said Rachel.

"O, he's coming; but thy Mary caught him as I came in, and ran off with him to the barn, to show him to the children."

At this moment, the door opened, and Mary, an honest, rosy-looking girl, with large brown eyes, like her mother's, came in with the baby.

"Ah! ha!" said Rachel coming up, and taking the great, white, fat fellow in her arms; "how good he looks, and how he does grow!"

"To be sure, he does," said little bustling Ruth, as she took the child, and began taking off a little blue silk hood, and various layers and wrappers of outer garments; and having given a twitch here, and a pull there, and variously adjusted and arranged him, and kissed him heartily, she set him on the floor to collect his thoughts. Baby seemed quite used to this mode of proceeding, for he put his thumb in his mouth (as if it were quite a thing of course), and seemed soon absorbed in his own reflections, while the mother seated herself, and taking out a long stocking of mixed blue and white yarn, began to knit with briskness.

"Mary, thee'd better fill the kettle, hadn't thee?" gently suggested the mother.

Mary took the kettle to the well, and soon reappearing, placed it over the stove, where it was soon purring and steaming, a sort of censer of hospitality and good cheer. The peaches, moreover, in obedience to a few gentle whispers from Rachel, were soon deposited, by the same hand, in a stew-pan over the fire.

Rachel now took down a snowy moulding-board, and, tying on an apron, proceeded quietly to making up some biscuits, first saying to Mary,— "Mary, hadn't thee better tell John to get a chicken ready?" and Mary disappeared accordingly.

"And how is Abigail Peters?" said Rachel, as she went on with her biscuits.

"O, she's better," said Ruth; "I was in, this morning; made the bed, tidied up the house. Leah Hills went in, this afternoon, and baked bread and pies enough to last some days; and I engaged to go back to get her up, this evening."

"I will go in to-morrow, and do any cleaning there may be, and look over the mending," said Rachel.

"Ah! that is well," said Ruth. "I've heard," she added, "that Hannah Stanwood is sick. John was up there, last night,—I must go there to-morrow."

"John can come in here to his meals, if thee needs to stay all day," suggested Rachel.

"Thank thee, Rachel; will see, to-morrow; but, here comes Simeon."

Simeon Halliday, a tall, straight, muscular man, in drab coat and pantaloons, and broad-brimmed hat, now entered.

"How is thee, Ruth?" he said, warmly, as he spread his broad hand for her little fat palm; "and how is John?"

"O! John is well, and all the rest of our folks," said Ruth, cheerily.

"Any news, father?" said Rachel, as she was putting her biscuits into the oven.

"Peter Stebbins told me that they should be along tonight, with *friends*," said Simeon, significantly, as he was washing his hands at a neat sink, in a little back porch.

"Indeed!" said Rachel, looking thoughtfully, and glancing at Eliza.

"Did thee say thy name was Harris?" said Simeon to Eliza, as he re-entered.

Rachel glanced quickly at her husband, as Eliza tremulously answered "yes;" her fears, ever uppermost, suggesting that possibly there might be advertisements out for her.

"Mother!" said Simeon, standing in the porch, and calling Rachel out.

"What does thee want, father?" said Rachel, rubbing her floury hands, as she went into the porch.

"This child's husband is in the settlement, and will be here to-night," said Simeon.

"Now, thee doesn't say that, father?" said Rachel, all her face radiant with joy.

"It's really true. Peter was down yesterday, with the wagon, to the other stand, and there he found an old woman and two men; and one said his name was George Harris; and, from what he told of his history, I am certain who he is. He is a bright, likely fellow, too."

"Shall we tell her now?" said Simeon.

"Let's tell Ruth," said Rachel. "Here, Ruth,—come here."

Ruth laid down her knitting-work, and was in the back porch in a moment.

"Ruth, what does thee think?" said Rachel. "Father says Eliza's husband is in the last company, and will be here to-night."

A burst of joy from the little Quakeress interrupted the speech. She gave such a bound from the floor, as she clapped her little hands, that two stray curls fell from under her Quaker cap, and lay brightly on her white neckerchief.

"Hush thee, dear!" said Rachel, gently; "hush, Ruth! Tell us, shall we tell her now?"

"Now! to be sure,—this very minute. Why, now, suppose 'twas my John, how should I feel? Do tell her, right off."

"Thee uses thyself only to learn how to love thy neighbor, Ruth," said Simeon, looking, with a beaming face, on Ruth.

"To be sure. Isn't it what we are made for? If I didn't love John and the baby, I should not know how to feel for her. Come, now, do tell her,—do!" and she laid her hands persuasively on Rachel's arm. "Take her into thy bed-room, there, and let me fry the chicken while thee does it."

Rachel came out into the kitchen, where Eliza was sewing, and opening the door of a small bed-room, said, gently, "Come in here with me, my daughter; I have news to tell thee."

The blood flushed in Eliza's pale face; she rose, trembling with nervous anxiety, and looked towards her boy.

"No, no," said little Ruth, darting up, and seizing her hands. "Never thee fear; it's good news, Eliza,—go in, go in!" And she gently pushed her to the door, which closed after her; and then, turning round, she caught little Harry in her arms, and began kissing him.

"Thee'll see thy father, little one. Does thee know it? Thy father is coming," she said, over and over again, as the boy looked wonderingly at her.

Meanwhile, within the door, another scene was going on. Rachel Halliday drew Eliza toward her, and said, "The Lord hath had mercy on thee, daughter; thy husband hath escaped from the house of bondage."

The blood flushed to Eliza's cheek in a sudden glow, and went back to her heart with as sudden a rush. She sat down, pale and faint.

"Have courage, child," said Rachel, laying her hand on her head. "He is among friends, who will bring him here to-night."

"To-night!" Eliza repeated, "to-night!" The words lost all meaning to her; her head was dreamy and confused; all was mist for a moment.

When she awoke, she found herself snugly tucked up on the bed, with a blanket over her, and little Ruth rubbing her hands with camphor. She opened her eyes in a state of dreamy, delicious languor, such as one has who has long been bearing a heavy load, and now feels it gone, and would rest. The tension of the nerves, which had never ceased a moment since the first hour of her flight, had given way, and a strange feeling of security and rest came over her; and, as she lay, with her large, dark eyes open, she followed, as in a quiet dream, the motions of those about her. She saw the door open into the other room; saw the supper table with its snowy cloth, heard the dreamy murmur of the singing tea-kettle; saw Ruth tripping backward and forward, with plates of cake and saucers of preserves, and ever and anon stopping to put a cake into Harry's hand, or pat his head, or twine his long curls round her snowy fingers. She saw the ample, motherly form of Rachel, as she ever and anon came to the bed-side, and smoothed and arranged something about the bed-clothes, and gave a tuck here and there, by way of expressing her good-will; and was conscious of a kind of sunshine beaming down upon her from her large, clear, brown eyes. She saw Ruth's husband come in,—saw her fly up to him, and commence whispering very earnestly, ever and anon, with impressive gesture, pointing her little finger toward the room. She saw her, with the baby in her arms, sitting down to tea; she saw them all at table, and little Harry in a high chair, under the shadow of Rachel's ample wing; there were low murmurs of talk, gentle tinkling of tea-spoons, and musical clatter of cups and saucers, and all mingled in a delightful dream of rest; and Eliza slept, as she had not slept before, since the fearful midnight hour when she had taken her child and fled through the frosty starlight.

She dreamed of a beautiful country,—a land, it seemed to her, of rest,—green shores, pleasant islands, and beautifully glittering water; and there, in a house which kind voices told her was a home, she saw her boy playing, a free and happy child. She heard her husband's footsteps; she felt him coming nearer; his arms were around her, his tears falling on her face, and she awoke! It was no dream. The daylight had long faded; her child lay calmly sleeping by her side; a candle was burning dimly on the stand, and her husband was sobbing by her pillow.

Harriet A. Jacobs

(1813–1897)

Harriet A. Jacobs, the most-read African American woman of the nineteenth century, was born a slave in North Carolina and became a fugitive in the 1830s. In 1861, under the pseudonym of Linda Brent, she published *Incidents in the Life of a Slave Girl*, her autobiographical account of her run to freedom. As she wrote to a friend, "God . . . gave me a soul that burned for freedom and a heart nerved with determination to suffer even unto death in pursuit of . . . liberty." In the voice of Linda Brent, the book's narrator, Jacobs tells the history of her family; most vivid is her indomitable grandmother who hid her in an attic for seven years. She describes the sexual oppression she knew as a young slave in the home of her master, Dr. Flint, and in moving detail the black and white communities who helped her on her long and dangerous flight to the north, before and after the Fugitive Slave Law of 1850. Along with Frederick Douglass's autobiography, *Incidents in the Life of a Slave Girl* is one of the two archetypes in the genre of the slave narrative; it is studied today as a classic of American history and literature, of women's writing, and of the African American experience.

FROM *Incidents in the Life of a Slave Girl*

CHILDHOOD

I was born a slave; but I never knew it till six years of happy childhood had passed away. My father was a carpenter, and considered so intelligent and skilful in his trade, that, when buildings out of the common line were to be erected, he was sent for from long distances, to be head workman. On condition of paying his mistress two hundred dollars a year, and supporting himself, he was allowed to work at his trade, and manage his own affairs. His strongest wish was to purchase his children; but, though he several times offered his hard earnings for that purpose, he never succeeded. In complexion my parents were a light shade of brownish yellow, and were termed mulattoes. They lived together in a comfortable home; and, though we were all slaves, I was so fondly shielded that I never dreamed I was a piece of merchandise, trusted to them for safe keeping, and liable to be demanded of them at any moment. I had one brother, William, who was two years younger than myself—a bright, affectionate child. I had also a great treasure in my maternal grandmother, who was a remarkable woman in many respects. She was the daughter of a planter in South Carolina, who, at his death, left her mother and his three children free, with money to go to St. Augustine, where they had relatives. It was during the Revolutionary War; and they were captured on their passage, carried back, and sold to different purchasers. Such was the story my grandmother used to tell me; but I do not remember all the particulars. She was a little girl when she was captured and sold to the keeper of a large hotel. I have often heard her tell how hard she fared during childhood. But as she grew older she evinced so much intelligence, and was so faithful, that her master and mistress could not help seeing it was for their interest to take care of such a valuable piece of property.

She became an indispensable personage in the household, officiating in all capacities, from cook and wet nurse to seamstress. She was much praised for her cooking; and her nice crackers became so famous in the neighborhood that many people were desirous of obtaining them. In consequence of numerous requests of this kind, she asked permission of her mistress to bake crackers at night, after all the household work was done; and she obtained leave to do it, provided she would clothe herself and her children from the profits. Upon these terms, after working hard all day for her mistress, she began her midnight bakings, assisted by her two oldest children. The business proved profitable; and each year she laid by a little, which was saved for a fund to purchase her children. Her master died, and the property was divided among his heirs. The widow had her dower in the hotel, which she continued to keep open. My grandmother remained in her service as a slave; but her children were divided among her master's children. As she had five, Benjamin, the youngest one, was sold, in order that each heir might have an equal portion of dollars and cents. There was so little difference in our ages that he seemed more like my brother than my uncle. He was a bright, handsome lad, nearly white; for he inherited the complexion my grandmother had derived from Anglo-Saxon ancestors. Though only ten years old, seven hundred and twenty dollars were paid for him. His sale was a terrible blow to my grandmother; but she was naturally hopeful, and she went to work with renewed energy, trusting in time to be able to purchase some of her children. She had laid up three hundred dollars, which her mistress one day begged as a loan, promising to pay her soon. The reader probably knows that no promise or writing given to a slave is legally binding; for, according to Southern laws, a slave, *being* property, can *hold* no property. When my grandmother lent her hard earnings to her mistress, she trusted solely to her honor. The honor of a slaveholder to a slave!

To this good grandmother I was indebted for many comforts. My brother Willie and I often received portions of the crackers, cakes, and preserves, she made to sell; and after we ceased to be children we were indebted to her for many more important services.

Such were the unusually fortunate circumstances of my early childhood. When I was six years old, my mother died; and then, for the first time, I learned, by the talk around me, that I was a slave. My mother's mistress was the daughter of my grandmother's mistress. She was the foster sister of my mother; they were both nourished at my grandmother's breast. In fact, my mother had been weaned at three months old, that the babe of the mistress might obtain sufficient food. They played together as children; and, when they became women, my mother was a most faithful servant to her whiter foster sister. On her death-bed her mistress promised that her children should never suffer for any thing; and during her lifetime she kept her word. They all spoke kindly of my dead mother, who had been a slave merely in name, but in nature was noble and womanly. I grieved for her, and my young mind was troubled with the thought who would now take care of me and my little brother. I was told that my home was now to be with her mistress; and I found it a happy one. No toilsome or disagreeable duties were imposed upon me. My mistress was so kind to me that I was always glad to do her bidding, and proud to labor for her as much as my young years would permit. I would sit by her side for hours, sewing diligently, with a heart as free from care as that of any free-born white child. When she thought I was tired, she would send me out to run and jump; and away I bounded, to gather berries or flowers to decorate her room. Those were happy days—too happy to last. The slave child had no thought for the morrow; but there came that blight, which too surely waits on every human being born to be a chattel.

When I was nearly twelve years old, my kind mistress sickened and died. As I saw the cheek grow paler, and the eye more glassy, how earnestly I prayed in my heart that she might live! I loved her; for she had been almost like a mother to me. My prayers were not answered. She died, and they buried her in the little churchyard where, day after day, my tears fell upon her grave.

I was sent to spend a week with my grandmother. I was now old enough to begin to think of the future; and again and again I asked myself what they would do with me. I felt sure I should never find another mistress so kind as the one who was gone. She had promised my dying mother that her children should never suffer for any thing; and when I remembered that, and recalled her many proofs of attachment to me, I could not help having some hopes that she had left me free. My friends were almost certain it would be so. They thought she would be sure to do it, on account of my mother's love and faithful service. But, alas! we all know that the memory of a faithful slave does not avail much to save her children from the auction block.

After a brief period of suspense, the will of my mistress was read, and we learned that she had bequeathed me to her sister's daughter, a child of five years old. So vanished our hopes. My mistress had taught me the precepts of God's Word: "Thou shalt love thy neighbor as thyself." "Whatsoever ye would that men should do unto you, do ye even so unto them." But I was her slave, and I suppose she did not recognize me as her neighbor. I would give much to blot out from my memory that one great wrong. As a child, I loved my mistress; and, looking back on the happy days I spent with her, I try to think with less bitterness of this act of injustice. While I was with her, she taught me to read and spell; and for this privilege, which so rarely falls to the lot of a slave, I bless her memory.

She possessed but few slaves; and at her death those were all distributed among her relatives. Five of them were my grandmother's children, and had shared the same milk that nourished her mother's children. Notwithstanding my grandmother's long and faithful service to her owners, not one of her children escaped the auction block. These God-breathing machines are no more, in the sight of their masters, than the cotton they plant, or the horses they tend.

THE NEW MASTER AND MISTRESS

Dr. Flint, a physician in the neighborhood, had married the sister of my mistress, and I was now the property of their little daughter. It was not without murmuring that I prepared for my new home; and what added to my unhappiness, was the fact that my brother William was purchased by the same family. My father, by his nature, as well as by the habit of transacting business as a skilful mechanic, had more of the feelings of a freeman than is common among slaves. My brother was a spirited boy; and being brought up under such influences, he early detested the name of master and mistress. One day, when his father and his mistress had happened to call him at the same time, he hesitated between the two; being perplexed to know which had the strongest claim upon his obedience. He finally concluded to go to his mistress. When my father reproved him for it, he said, "You both called me, and I didn't know which I ought to go to first."

"You are *my* child," replied our father, "and when I call you, you should come immediately, if you have to pass through fire and water."

Poor Willie! He was now to learn his first lesson of obedience to a master. Grandmother tried to cheer us with hopeful words, and they found an echo in the credulous hearts of youth.

When we entered our new home we encountered cold looks, cold words, and cold treatment. We were glad when the night came. On my narrow bed I moaned and wept, I felt so desolate and alone.

I had been there nearly a year, when a dear little friend of mine was buried. I heard her mother sob, as the clods fell on the coffin of her only child, and I turned away from the grave, feeling thankful that I still had something left to love. I met my grandmother, who said, "Come with me, Linda;" and from her tone I knew that something sad had happened. She led me apart from the people, and then said, "My child, your father is dead." Dead! How could I believe it? He had died so suddenly I had not even heard that he was sick. I went home with my grandmother. My heart rebelled against God, who had taken from me mother, father, mistress, and friend. The good grandmother tried to comfort me. "Who knows the ways of God?" said she. "Perhaps they have been kindly taken from the evil days to come." Years afterwards I often thought of this. She promised to be a mother to her grandchildren, so far as she might be permitted to do so; and strengthened by her love, I returned to my master's. I thought I should be allowed to go to my father's house the next morning; but I was ordered to go for flowers, that my mistress's house might be decorated for an evening party. I spent the day gathering flowers and weaving them into festoons, while the dead body of my father was lying within a mile of me. What cared my owners for that? he was merely a piece of property. Moreover, they thought he had spoiled his children, by teaching them to feel that they were human beings. This was blasphemous doctrine for a slave to teach; presumptuous in him, and dangerous to the masters.

The next day I followed his remains to a humble grave beside that of my dear mother. There were those who knew my father's worth, and respected his memory.

My home now seemed more dreary than ever. The laugh of the little slave-children sounded harsh and cruel. It was selfish to feel so about the joy of others. My brother moved about with a very grave face. I tried to comfort him, by saying, "Take courage, Willie; brighter days will come by and by."

"You don't know any thing about it, Linda," he replied. "We shall have to stay here all our days; we shall never be free."

I argued that we were growing older and stronger, and that perhaps we might, before long, be allowed to hire our own time, and then we could earn money to buy our freedom. William declared this was much easier to say than to do; moreover, he did not intend to *buy* his freedom. We held daily controversies upon this subject.

Little attention was paid to the slaves' meals in Dr. Flint's house. If they could catch a bit of food while it was going, well and good. I gave myself no trouble on that score, for on my various errands I passed my grandmother's house, where there was always something to spare for me. I was frequently threatened with punishment if I stopped there; and my grandmother, to avoid detaining me, often stood at the gate with something for my breakfast or dinner. I was indebted to *her* for all my comforts, spiritual or temporal. It was *her* labor that supplied my scanty wardrobe. I have a vivid recollection of the linsey-woolsey dress given me every winter by Mrs. Flint. How I hated it! It was one of the badges of slavery.

While my grandmother was thus helping to support me from her hard earnings, the three hundred dollars she had lent her mistress were never repaid. When her mistress died, her son-in-law, Dr. Flint, was appointed executor. When grandmother applied to him for payment, he said the estate was insolvent, and the law prohibited payment. It did not, however, prohibit him from retaining the silver candelabra, which had been purchased with that money. I presume they will be handed down in the family, from generation to generation.

My grandmother's mistress had always promised her that, at her death, she should be free; and it was said that in her will she made good the promise. But when the estate was settled, Dr. Flint told the faithful old servant that, under existing circumstances, it was necessary she should be sold.

On the appointed day, the customary advertisement was posted up, proclaiming that there would be a "public sale of negroes, horses, &c." Dr. Flint called to tell my grandmother that he was unwilling to wound her feelings by putting her up at auction, and that he would prefer to dispose of her at private sale. My grandmother saw through this hypocrisy; she understood very well that he was ashamed of the job. She was a very spirited woman, and if he was base enough to sell her, when her mistress intended she should be free, she was determined the public should know it. She had for a long time supplied many families with crackers and preserves; consequently, "Aunt Marthy," as she was called, was generally known, and every body who knew her respected her intelligence and good character. Her long and faithful service in the family was also well known, and the intention of her mistress to leave her free. When the day of sale came, she took her place among the chattels, and at the first call she sprang upon the auction-block. Many voices called out, "Shame! Shame! Who is going to sell *you*, aunt Marthy? Don't stand there! That is no place for *you*." Without saying a word, she quietly awaited her fate. No one bid for her. At last, a feeble voice said, "Fifty dollars." It came from a maiden lady, seventy years old, the sister of my grandmother's deceased mistress. She had lived forty years under the same roof with my grandmother; she knew how faithfully she had served her owners, and how cruelly she had been defrauded of her rights; and she resolved to protect her. The auctioneer waited for a higher bid; but her wishes were respected; no one bid above her. She could neither read nor write; and when the bill of sale was made out, she signed it with a cross. But what consequence was that, when she had a big heart overflowing with human kindness? She gave the old servant her freedom.

At that time, my grandmother was just fifty years old. Laborious years had passed since then; and now my brother and I were slaves to the man who had defrauded her of her money, and tried to defraud her of her freedom. One of my mother's sisters, called Aunt Nancy, was also a slave in his family. She was a kind, good aunt to me; and supplied the place of both housekeeper and waiting maid to her mistress. She was, in fact, at the beginning and end of every thing.

Mrs. Flint, like many southern women, was totally deficient in energy. She had not strength to superintend her household affairs; but her nerves were so strong, that she could sit in her easy chair and see a woman whipped, till the blood trickled from every stroke of the lash. She was a member of the church; but partaking of the Lord's supper did not seem to put her in a Christian frame of mind. If dinner was not served at the exact time on that particular Sunday, she would station herself in the kitchen, and wait till it was dished, and then spit in all the kettles and pans that had been used for cooking. She did this to prevent the cook and her children from eking out their meagre fare with the remains of the gravy and other scrapings. The slaves could get nothing to eat except what she chose to give them. Provisions were weighed out by the pound and ounce, three times a day. I can assure you she gave them no chance to eat wheat bread from her flour barrel. She knew how many biscuits a quart of flour would make, and exactly what size they ought to be.

Dr. Flint was an epicure. The cook never sent a dinner to his table without fear and trembling; for if there happened to be a dish not to his liking, he would either order her to be whipped, or compel her to eat every mouthful of it in his presence. The poor, hungry creature might not have objected to eating it; but she did object to having her master cram it down her throat till she choked.

They had a pet dog, that was a nuisance in the house. The cook was ordered to make some Indian mush for him. He refused to eat, and when his head was held over it, the froth flowed from his mouth into the basin. He died a few minutes after. When Dr. Flint came in, he said the mush had not been well cooked, and that was the reason the animal would not eat it. He sent for the cook, and compelled her to eat it. He thought that the woman's stomach was stronger than the dog's; but her sufferings afterwards proved that he was mistaken. This poor woman endured many cruelties from her master and mistress; sometimes she was locked up, away from her nursing baby, for a whole day and night.

When I had been in the family a few weeks, one of the plantation slaves was brought to town, by order of his master. It was near night when he arrived, and Dr. Flint ordered him to be taken to the work house, and tied up to the joist, so that his feet would just escape the ground. In that situation he was to wait till the doctor had taken his tea. I shall never forget that night. Never before, in my life, had I heard hundreds of blows fall, in succession, on a human being. His piteous groans, and his "O, pray don't, massa," rang in my ear for months afterwards. There were many conjectures as to the cause of this terrible punishment. Some said master accused him of stealing corn; others said the slave had quarrelled with his wife, in presence of the overseer, and had accused his master of being the father of her child. They were both black, and the child was very fair.

I went into the work house next morning, and saw the cowhide still wet with blood, and the boards all covered with gore. The poor man lived, and continued to quarrel with his wife. A few months afterwards Dr. Flint handed them both over to a slavetrader. The guilty man put their value into his pocket, and had the satisfaction of knowing that they were out of sight and hearing. When the mother was delivered into the trader's hands, she said, "You *promised* to treat me well." To which he replied, "You have let your tongue run too far; damn you!" She had forgotten that it was a crime for a slave to tell who was the father of her child.

From others than the master persecution also comes in such cases. I once saw a young slave girl dying soon after the birth of a child nearly white. In her agony she cried out, "O Lord, come and take me!" Her mistress stood by, and mocked at her like an incarnate fiend. "You suffer, do you?" she exclaimed. "I'm glad of it. You deserve it all, and more too."

The girl's mother said, "The baby is dead, thank God; and I hope my poor child will soon be in heaven, too."

THE SLAVES' NEW YEAR'S DAY

Dr. Flint owned a fine residence in town, several farms, and about fifty slaves, besides hiring a number by the year.

Hiring-day at the south takes place on the 1st of January. On the 2d, the slaves are expected to go to their new masters. On a farm, they work until the corn and cotton are laid. They then have two holidays. Some masters give them a good dinner under the trees. This over, they work until Christmas eve. If no heavy charges are meantime brought against them, they are given four or five holidays, whichever the master or overseer may think proper. Then comes New Year's eve; and they gather together their little alls, or more properly speaking, their little nothings, and wait anxiously for the dawning of day. At the appointed hour the grounds are thronged with men, women, and children, waiting, like criminals, to hear their doom pronounced. The slave is sure to know who is the most humane, or cruel master, within forty miles of him.

It is easy to find out, on that day, who clothes and feeds his slaves well; for he is surrounded by a crowd, begging, "Please, massa, hire me this year. I will work *very* hard, massa."

If a slave is unwilling to go with his new master, he is whipped, or locked up in jail, until he consents to go, and promises not to run away during the year. Should he chance to change his mind, thinking it justifiable to violate an extorted promise, woe unto him if he is caught! The whip is used till the blood flows at his feet; and his stiffened limbs are put in chains, to be dragged in the field for days and days!

If he lives until the next year, perhaps the same man will hire him again, without even giving him an opportunity of going to the hiring-ground. After those for hire are disposed of, those for sale are called up.

O, you happy free women, contrast *your* New Year's day with that of the poor bond-woman! With you it is a pleasant season, and the light of the day is blessed. Friendly wishes meet you every where, and gifts are showered upon you. Even hearts that have been estranged from you soften at this season, and lips that have been silent echo back, "I wish you a happy New Year." Children bring their little offerings, and raise their rosy lips for a caress. They are your own, and no hand but death can take them from you.

But to the slave mother New Year's day comes laden with peculiar sorrows. She sits on her cold cabin floor, watching the children who may all be torn from her the next morning; and often does she wish that she and they might die before the day dawns. She may be an ignorant creature, degraded by the system that has brutalized her from childhood; but she has a mother's instincts, and is capable of feeling a mother's agonies.

On one of these sale days, I saw a mother lead seven children to the auction-block. She knew that *some* of them would be taken from her; but they took *all*. The children were sold to a slave-trader, and their mother was bought by a man in her own town. Before night her children were all far away. She begged the trader to tell her where he intended to take them; this he refused to do. How *could* he, when he knew he would sell them, one by one, wherever he could command the highest price? I met that mother in the street, and her wild, haggard face lives to-day in my mind. She wrung her hands in anguish, and exclaimed, "Gone! All gone! Why *don't* God kill me?" I had no words wherewith to comfort her. Instances of this kind are of daily, yea, of hourly occurrence.

Charlotte Brontë

(1816–1855)

The letters of Charlotte Brontë, like her novels, express a woman of firm conviction. Reading them, you wonder at the popular image of her as a modest Victorian authoress, a slave to duty in the shadow of tombstones, the temperamental opposite of the "unregenerate and undisciplined spirit" (in the words of one reviewer) of the heroine of *Jane Eyre*. A portrait of the oldest of the Brontë children, the letters show Charlotte's father, the Reverend Patrick Brontë, born in County Down, Ireland, educated and married in England, at the center of her first and longest loyalty. She comes across as a woman with a generous capacity for friendship. The letters also reflect her determination on behalf of herself as a professional writer; the condescension of laureate Robert Southey and critic George Lewes was no match for her. The moody disequilibrium of the letters—elation and dejection move through them like the tempestuous weather of her native Yorkshire (and her father's native Ireland)—may account for her husband Arthur Nicholls' fear of them. As Brontë wrote to her friend Ellen Nussey, "Men don't seem to understand making letters a vehicle of communication—they always seem to think us incautious. I'm sure I don't think I have said anything rash—however you must *burn* it when read. Arthur says such letters as mine never ought to be kept—they are dangerous as lucifer matches."

FROM *The Letters of Charlotte Brontë*

Edited by Margaret Smith

Years before she published Jane Eyre *(1847), Brontë sent some of her poetry and a letter about her desire to write to poet laureate Robert Southey. His reply—and hers to him—follow.*

Robert Southey to Charlotte Brontë   12 March 1837
                                                              Keswick

Madam,

You will probably ere this have given up all expectation of receiving an answer
to your letter of Decr. 29. I was on the borders of Cornwall when that letter
was written. It found me a fortnight afterwards in Hampshire. During my
subsequent movements in different parts of the country, & a tarriance of 3
busy weeks in London, I had no leisure for replying to it. And now that I am
once more at home & am clearing the arrears of business wh[ich] had accu-
mulated during a long absence, it has lain unanswered till the last of a numerous pile—not from disrespect or indifference to its contents, but in truth,
because it is not an easy task to answer it, nor a pleasant one to cast a damp
over the high spirits & the generous desires of youth.

What you are I can only infer from your letter, wh[ich] appears to be written in sincerity, tho' I may suspect you have used a fictitious signature. Be that
as it may, the letter & the verse bear the same stamp, & I can well understand
the state of mind wh[ich] they indicate. What I am, you might have learnt by
such of my publications as have come into your hands: but you live in a visionary world & seem to imagine that this is my case also, when you speak of my
"stooping from a throne of light & glory." Had you happened to be acquainted
with me, a little personal knowledge [would] have tempered your enthusiasm.
You who so ardently desire "to be for ever known" as a poetess, might have had
your ardour in some degree abated, by seeing a poet in the decline of life, &
witnessing the effect wh[ich] age produces upon our hopes & aspirations. Yet I
am neither [a] disappointed man, nor a discontented one, & you [would] never
have heard from me any chilling sermonisings upon the text that all is vanity.

It is not my advice that you have asked as to the direction of your talents,
but my opinion of them. Yet the opinion may be worth little, & the advice much.
You evidently possess & in no inconsiderable degree what Wordsworth calls "the
faculty of Verse." I am not depreciating it when I say that in these times it is not
rare. Many volumes of poems are now published every year without attracting
public attention, any one of wh[ich], if it had appeared half a century ago,
[would] have obtained a high reputation for its author. Whoever therefore is
ambitious of distinction in this way, ought to be prepared for disappointment.

But it is not with a view to distinction that you [should] cultivate this talent, if you consult your own happiness. I who have made literature my profession, & devoted my life to it, & have never for a moment repented of the deliberate choice, think myself nevertheless bound in duty to caution every young man who applies as an aspirant [to me] for encouragement & advice, against taking so perilous a course. You will say that a woman has no need of such a caution, there can be no peril in it for her: & in a certain sense this is true. But there is a danger of wh[ich] I [would] with all kindness & all earnestness warn you. The daydreams in wh[ich] you habitually indulge are likely to induce a distempered state of mind, & in proportion as all the "ordinary uses of the world" seem to you "flat & unprofitable," you will be unfitted for them, without becoming fitted for anything else. Literature cannot be the business of a woman's life: & it ought not to be. The more she is engaged in her proper duties, the less leisure will she have for it, even as an accomplishment & a recreation. To those duties you have not yet been called, & when you are you will be less eager for celebrity. You will then not seek in imagination for excitement, of wh[ich] the vicissitudes of this life & the anxieties, from wh[ich] you must not hope to be exempted (be your station what it may) will bring [with] them but too much.

But do not suppose that I disparage the gift wh[ich] you possess, nor that I [would] discourage you from exercising it, I only exhort you so to think of it & so to use it, as to render it conducive to your own permanent good. Write poetry for its own sake, not in a spirit of emulation, & not with a view to celebrity: the less you aim at <u>that,</u> the more likely you will be to deserve, & finally to obtain it. So written, it is wholesome both for the heart & soul. It may be made next to religion the surest means of soothing the mind & elevating it. You may embody in it your best thoughts & your wisest feelings, & in so doing discipline & strengthen them.

Farewell Madam! It is not because I have forgotten that I was once young myself that I write to you in this strain—but because I remember it. You will neither doubt my sincerity, nor my good will. And however ill what has been said may accord with your present views & temper, the longer you live the more reasonable it will appear to you. Tho' I may be but an ungracious adviser, you will allow me therefore to subscribe myself,

With the best wishes for your happiness, here & hereafter,

Your true friend
(Sd) Robert Southey

To Robert Southey   16 March 1837
                                                        [?Roe Head]

Sir,

I cannot rest till I have answered your letter, even though by addressing you
a second time I should appear a little intrusive; but I must thank you for the
kind & wise advice you have condescended to give me. I had not ventured to
hope for such a reply; so considerate in its tone, so noble in its spirit. I must
suppress what I feel, or you will think me foolishly enthusiastic.

At the first perusal of your letter I felt only shame, and regret that I had
ever ventured to trouble you with my crude rhapsody;—I felt a painful heat
rise to my face, when I thought of the quires of paper I had covered with
what once gave me so much delight, but which now was only a source of
confusion; but, after I had thought a little and read it again and again, the
prospect seemed to clear. You do not forbid me to write; you do not say that
what I write is utterly destitute of merit. You only warn me against the folly
of neglecting real duties, for the sake of imaginative pleasures; of writing for
the love of fame; for the selfish excitement of emulation. You kindly allow
me to write poetry for its own sake, provided I leave undone nothing which
I ought to do, in order to pursue that single absorbing exquisite gratifica-
tion. I am afraid, Sir, you think me very foolish. I know the first letter I
wrote to you was senseless trash from beginning to end; but I am not altogether the idle dreaming being it would seem to denote. My father is a clergyman of limited, though competent, income, and I am the eldest of his
children. He expended quite as much in my education as he could afford
in justice to the rest. I thought it therefore my duty, when I left school, to
become a governess. In that capacity, I find enough to occupy my thoughts
all day long, and my head & hands too, without having a moment's time for
one dream of the imagination. In the evenings, I confess, I do think, but I
never trouble any one else with my thoughts. I carefully avoid any appearance of pre-occupation, and eccentricity, which might lead those I live
amongst to suspect the nature of my pursuits. Following my Father's
advice,—who from my childhood has counselled me just in the wise and
friendly tone of your letter—I have endeavoured not only attentively to
observe all the duties a woman ought to fulfil, but to feel deeply interested
in them. I don't always succeed, for sometimes when I'm teaching or

sewing I would rather be reading or writing; but I try to deny myself; and my Father's approbation amply rewarded me for the privation. Once more allow me to thank you with sincere gratitude. I trust I shall never more feel ambitious to see my name in print; if the wish should rise, I'll look at Southey's letter, and suppress it. It is honour enough for me that I have written to him, and received an answer. That letter is consecrated; no one shall ever see it, but Papa and my brother and sisters. Again I thank you. This incident I suppose will be renewed no more; if I live to be an old woman I shall remember it thirty years hence as a bright dream. The signature which you suspected of being fictitious is my real name. Again, therefore, I must sign myself,

C. Brontë

P.S.—Pray, Sir, excuse me for writing you a second time; I could not help writing, partly to tell you how thankful I am for your kindness, and partly to let you know that your advice shall not be wasted; however sorrowfully and reluctantly it may be at first followed. C.B.

Robert Southey to Charlotte Brontë   22 March 1837
Keswick

Dear Madam,

Your letter has given me great pleasure, & I should not forgive myself if I did not tell you so. You have received admonition as considerately & kindly as it was given. Let me now request that if you ever should come to these Lakes while I am living here, you will let me see you. You will then think of me afterwards with more good will, for you will then perceive that there is neither severity nor moroseness in the state of mind to which years & observation have brought me.

It is, by God's mercy, in our power to attain a degree of self-government which is essential to our own happiness, & contributes greatly to that of those around us.—Take care of over-excitement, & endeavour to keep a quiet mind; [even for your health it is the best advice that can be given you.] Your moral & spiritual improvement will then keep pace with the culture of your intellectual powers.

And now Miss Brontë, God bless you! Farewell,
& believe me to be
Your sincere friend
Robert Southey[*]

⌐

Correspondence about the publication of Jane Eyre *from "C Bell"—Currer Bell—the male pseudonym Charlotte Brontë adopted.*

To Messrs Smith Elder & Co.   24 August 1847
Haworth

Gentlemen,

I now send you per. Rail—a M.S. entitled "Jane Eyre," a novel, in 3 vols. by Currer Bell.

I find I cannot pre-pay the carriage of the parcel as money for that purpose is not received at the small Station-house where it is left.

If, when you acknowledge the receipt of the M.S. you will have the goodness to mention the amount charged on delivery—I will immediately transmit it in postage stamps.

It is better in future to address Mr. Currer Bell—under cover to Miss Brontë—Haworth—Bradford Yorks—as there is a risk of letters otherwise directed, not reaching me at present—

To save trouble I enclose an envelope—

I am Gentlemen
Yours respectfully
C Bell

To Messrs Smith Elder & Co.   19 October 1847
[Haworth]

Gentlemen

The six copies of "Jane Eyre" reached me this morning. You have given the

---

[*] Of his correspondence with Charlotte Brontë, Southey wrote to a friend in late March 1837: "I sent a dose of cooling admonition to the poor girl whose flighty letter reached me at Buckland. It was well taken, and she thanked me for it . . . probably she will think kindly of me as long as she lives."

work every advantage which good paper, clear type and a seemly outside can supply—if it fails—the fault will lie with the author—you are exempt.

I now await the judgment of the press and the public.

I am Gentlemen
Yrs. respectfully
C Bell

To Messrs Smith Elder & Co. 26 October 1847
[Haworth]

Gentlemen
I have received the newspapers. They speak quite favourably of "Jane Eyre" as I expected them to do. The notice in the Literary Gazette seems certainly to have been indited in rather a flat mood, and the Athenaeum has a style of its own which I respect, but cannot exactly relish; Still when one considers that journals of that standing have a dignity to maintain which would be deranged by a too cordial recognition of the claims of an obscure author—I suppose there is every reason to be satisfied.

Meantime a brisk sale would be an effectual support under the hauteur of lofty critics—

I am Gentlemen
respe[c]tfully yours
C Bell

To W. S. Williams 28 October 1847
[Haworth]

Dear Sir
Your last letter was very pleasant to me to read, and is very cheering to reflect on. I feel honoured in being approved by Mr. Thackeray because I approve Mr. Thackeray. This may sound presumptuous perhaps, but I mean that I have long recognized in his writings genuine talent such as I admired, such

as I wondered at and delighted in. No author seems to distinguish so exquisitely as he does dross from ore, the real from the counterfeit. I believed too he had deep and true feelings under his seeming sternness—now I am sure he has. One good word from such a man is worth pages of praise from ordinary judges.

You are right in having faith in the reality of Helen Burns's character: she was real enough: I have exaggerated nothing there: I abstained from recording much that I remember respecting her, lest the narrative should sound incredible. Knowing this, I could not but smile at the quiet, self-complacent dogmatism with which one of the journals lays it down that "such creations as Helen Burns are very beautiful but very untrue."

The plot of "Jane Eyre" may be a hackneyed one; Mr. Thackeray remarks that it is familiar to him; but having read comparatively few novels, I never chanced to meet with it, and I thought it original—. The critic of the Athenaeum's work, I had not the good fortune to hear of. . . .

TO G. H. Lewes   6 November 1847
                                                          [Haworth]

Dear Sir

Your letter reached me yesterday; I beg to assure you that I appreciate fully the intention with which it was written, and I thank you sincerely both for its cheering commendation and valuable advice.

You warn me to beware of Melodrame and you exhort me to adhere to the real. When I first began to write, so impressed was I with the truth of the principles you advocate that I determined to take Nature and Truth as my sole guides and to follow in their very footprints; I restrained imagination, eschewed romance, repressed excitement: over-bright colouring too I avoided, and sought to produce something which should be soft, grave and true.

My work (a tale in I vol.) being completed, I offered it to a publisher. He said it was original, faithful to Nature, but he did not feel warranted in accepting it, such a work would not sell. I tried six publishers in succession; they all told me it was deficient in "startling incident" and "thrilling excitement," that it would never suit the circulating libraries, and as it was on those libraries the success of works of fiction mainly depended they could not undertake to publish what would be overlooked there—"Jane Eyre" was rather objected to at first [on] the same grounds—but finally found acceptance.

I mention this to you, not with a view of pleading exemption from censure, but in order to direct your attention to the root of certain literary evils—if in your forthcoming article in "Frazer" you would bestow a few words of enlightenment on the public who support the circulating libraries, you might, with your powers, do some good.

You advise me too, not to stray far from the ground of experience as I become weak when I enter the region of fiction; and you say "real experience is perennially interesting and to all men . . ."

I feel that this also is true, but, dear Sir, is not the real experience of each individual very limited? and if a writer dwells upon that solely or principally is he not in danger of repeating himself, and also of becoming an egotist?

Then too, Imagination is a strong, restless faculty which claims to be heard and exercised, are we to be quite deaf to her cry and insensate to her struggles? When she shews us bright pictures are we never to look at them and try to reproduce them?—And when she is eloquent and speaks rapidly and urgently in our ear are we not to write to her dictation[?]

I shall anxiously search the next number of "Frazer" for your opinions on these points.

Believe me, dear Sir,
Yours gratefully
C Bell

Emily Brontë

(1818-1848)

The fifth of Maria and Patrick Brontë's six children, Emily Brontë was the most private. She grew up in Yorkshire, in her father's Haworth parsonage, the daughter of a clergyman (like Jane Austen, George Eliot, and Harriet Beecher Stowe). With her sisters Charlotte and Anne and brother, Branwell, she created fantastic plays and stories; she roamed the countryside but didn't talk to the neighbors. Charlotte described her as "a native and nursling of the moors," and the wild lonely freedom of those heather deserts resonates through her masterpiece, *Wuthering Heights* (1847), one of the greatest love stories ever written. Though it has received far less attention, Emily Brontë's poetry is equally intense, a mystical vision of the divine presence she felt within nature; she defines suffering as the alienation of the individual from the divinity that animates creation. It was her older sister Charlotte who persuaded Emily to publish. She came upon the poems accidentally and heard at once their "peculiar music—wild, melancholy, and elevating."

Remembrance

Cold in the earth, and the deep snow piled above thee!
Far, far removed, cold in the dreary grave!
Have I forgot, my Only Love, to love thee,
Severed at last by Time's all-wearing wave?

Now, when alone, do my thoughts no longer hover
Over the mountains on Angora's shore;
Resting their wings where heath and fern-leaves cover
That noble heart for ever, ever more?

Cold in the earth, and fifteen wild Decembers
From those brown hills have melted into spring—
Faithful indeed is the spirit that remembers
After such years of change and suffering!

Sweet Love of youth, forgive if I forgot thee
While the World's tide is bearing me along:
Sterner desires and darker hopes beset me,
Hopes which obscure but cannot do thee wrong.

No other Sun has lightened up my heaven;
No other Star has ever shone for me;
All my life's bliss from thy dear life was given—
All my life's bliss in the grave with thee.

But when the days of golden dreams had perished
And even Despair was powerless to destroy,
Then did I learn how existence could be cherished,
Strengthened and fed without the aid of joy;

Then did I check the tears of useless passion,
Weaned my young soul from yearning after thine;
Sternly denied its burning wish to hasten
Down to that tomb already more than mine!

And even yet, I dare not let it languish,
Dare not indulge in Memory's rapturous pain;
Once drinking deep of that divinest anguish,
How could I seek the empty world again?

At Such a Time

At such a time, in such a spot
The world seems made of light;
Our blissful hearts remember not
How surely follows night.

I cannot, Alfred, dream of aught
That casts a shade of woe;
That heaven is reigning in my thought
Which wood and wave and earth have caught
From skies that overflow.

That heaven which my sweet lover's brow
Has won me to adore,
Which from his blue eyes beaming now
Reflects a still intenser glow
Than Nature's heaven can pour.

I know our souls are all divine;
I know that when we die,
What seems the vilest, even like thine
A part of God himself shall shine
In perfect purity.

But coldly breaks November's day;
Its changes charmless all
Unmarked, unloved, they pass away;
We do not wish one hour to stay
Nor sigh at evening's fall.

And glorious is the gladsome rise
Of June's rejoicing morn;
And who with unregretful eyes
Can watch the lustre leave its skies
To twilight's shade forlorn?

Then art thou not my golden June;
All mist and tempest-free?
As shines earth's sun in summer noon
So heaven's sun shines in thee.

Let others seek its beams divine
In cell and cloister drear;
But I have found a fairer shrine
And happier worship here.

By dismal rites they win their bliss—
By penance, fasts, and fears.
I have one rite—a gentle kiss;
One penance—tender tears.

O could it thus for ever be
That I might so adore;
I'd ask for all eternity
To make a paradise for me,
My love—and nothing more!

Come, Walk with Me

Come, walk with me,
There's only thee
To bless my spirit now—
We used to love on winter nights
To wander through the snow;
Can we not woo back old delights?
The clouds rush dark and wild,
They fleck with shade our mountain heights
The same as long ago
And on the horizon rest at last
In looming masses piled;
While moonbeams flash and fly so fast
We scarce can say they smiled.

Come walk with me—come, walk with me;
We were not once so few,
But Death has stolen our company
As sunshine steals the dew.
He took them one by one and we
Are left the only two;
So closer would my feelings twine
Because they have no stay but thine.

"Nay, call me not; it may not be—
Is human love so true?
Can Friendship's flower droop on for years
And then revive anew?
No, though the soil be wet with tears
How fair so'er it grew
The vital sap once perished
Will never flow again
And surer than that dwelling dread,
The narrow dungeon of the Dead,
Time parts the hearts of men."

The Night-Wind

In summer's mellow midnight,
A cloudless moon shone through
Our open parlor window
And rosetrees wet with dew.

I sat in silent musing,
The soft wind waved my hair:
It told me Heaven was glorious,
And sleeping Earth was fair.

I needed not its breathing
To bring such thoughts to me,
But still it whispered lowly,
"How dark the woods will be!

"The thick leaves in my murmur
Are rustling like a dream,
And all their myriad voices
Instinct with spirit seem."

I said, "Go, gentle singer,
Thy wooing voice is kind,
But do not think its music
Has power to reach my mind.

"Play with the scented flower,
The young tree's supple bough,
And leave my human feelings
In their own course to flow."

The wanderer would not leave me;
Its kiss grew warmer still—
"O come," it sighed so sweetly,
"I'll win thee 'gainst thy will.

"Have we not been from childhood friends?
Have I not loved thee long?
As long as thou hast loved the night
Whose silence wakes my song.

"And when thy heart is laid at rest
Beneath the church-yard stone
I shall have time enough to mourn
And thou to be alone."

George Eliot

(1819-1880)

George Eliot, the pseudonym of English novelist Mary Ann (Marian) Evans, was the daughter of a farmer and land agent in Warwickshire to whom she wrote the letter that follows here: an uncompromising declaration of conscience she later revised. A supporter of the Church of England and a culturally conservative Christian, Robert Evans was unmoved by his brilliant daughter's crisis of faith. Her rejection of Christianity, in particular the evangelicalism to which she had converted, became a wound between them that was never healed. After her father's death, the intellectually independent daughter went on to write novels that have made her reputation as the greatest English novelist. Of her masterpiece, *Middlemarch* (1871–72), Emily Dickinson said, "What do I think of *Middlemarch*? What do I think of glory?" Its heroine, Dorothea Brooke, is a nineteenth-century Protestant version of the sixteenth-century Catholic Saint Teresa of Avila who is evoked in the novel's prelude.

Letter to Robert Evans, 28 February 1842

When George Eliot refused to go to church, her family and friends argued with her. Her father didn't speak to her for nine weeks. Finally, the agnostic daughter wrote him a letter.

Foleshill Monday Morning

My dear Father,

As all my efforts in conversation have hitherto failed in making you aware of the real nature of my sentiments, I am induced to try if I can express myself more clearly on paper so that both I in writing and you in reading may have our judgements unobstructed by feeling, which they can hardly be when we are together. I wish entirely to remove from your mind the false notion that

I am inclined visibly to unite myself with any Christian community, or that I have any affinity in opinion with Unitarians more than with other classes of believers in the Divine authority of the books comprising the Jewish and Christian Scriptures. I regard these writings as histories consisting of mingled truth and fiction, and while I admire and cherish much of what I believe to have been the moral teaching of Jesus himself, I consider the system of doctrines built upon the facts of his life and drawn as to its materials from Jewish notions to be most dishonourable to God and most pernicious in its influence on individual and social happiness. In thus viewing this important subject I am in unison with some of the finest minds in Christendom in past ages, and with the majority of such in the present (as an instance more familiar to you than any I could name I may mention Dr. Franklin). Such being my very strong convictions, it cannot be a question with any mind of strict integrity, whatever judgement may be passed on their truth, that I could not without vile hypocrisy and a miserable truckling to the smile of the world for the sake of my supposed interests, profess to join in worship which I wholly disapprove. This and *this alone* I will not do even for your sake—anything else however painful I would cheerfully brave to give you a moment's joy.

I do not hope to convince any other member of our family and probably not yourself that I am really sincere, that my only desire is to walk in that path of rectitude which however rugged is the only path to peace, but the prospect of contempt and rejection shall not make me swerve from my determination so much as a hair's breadth until I feel that I *ought* to do so. From what my Brother more than insinuated and from what you have yourself intimated I perceive that your establishment at Foleshill is regarded as an unnecessary expence having no other object than to give me a centre in society—that since you now consider me to have placed an insurmountable barrier to my prosperity in life this one object of an expenditure held by the rest of the family to be disadvantageous to them is frustrated—I am glad at any rate this is made clear to me, for I could not be happy to remain as an incubus or an unjust absorber of your hardly earned gains which might be better applied among my Brothers and Sisters with their children.

I should be just as happy living with you at your cottage at Packington or any where else if I can thereby minister in the least to your comfort—of course unless that were the case I must prefer to rely on my own energies and resources feeble as they are—I fear nothing but voluntarily leaving you. I can cheerfully do it if you desire it and shall go with deep gratitude for all the tenderness and rich kindness you have never been tired of shewing me. So far from complaining I shall joyfully submit if as a proper punishment for the pain I have most unintentionally given you, you determine to appropriate any provision you may have intended to make for my future support to your other children whom you may consider more deserving. As a last vindication of herself from one who has no one to speak for her I may be permitted to say that if ever I loved you I do so now, if ever I sought to obey the laws of my Creator and to follow duty wherever it may lead me I have that determination now and the consciousness of this will support me though every being on earth were to frown upon me.   •

Your affectionate Daughter
Mary Ann

FROM *Middlemarch*

PRELUDE

Who that cares much to know the history of man, and how the mysterious mixture behaves under the varying experiments of Time, has not dwelt, at least briefly, on the life of Saint Theresa, has not smiled with some gentleness at the thought of the little girl walking forth one morning hand-in-hand with her still smaller brother, to go and seek martyrdom in the country of the Moors? Out they toddled from rugged Avila, wide-eyed and helpless-looking as two fawns, but with human hearts, already beating to a national idea; until domestic reality met them in the shape of uncles, and turned them back from their great resolve. That child-pilgrimage was a fit beginning. Theresa's passionate, ideal nature demanded an epic life: what were many-volumed romances of chivalry and the social conquests of a brilliant girl to her? Her flame quickly burned up that light fuel; and, fed from within, soared after some illimitable satisfaction, some object which would never justify weariness, which would reconcile self-despair with the rapturous consciousness of life beyond self. She found her epos in the reform of a religious order.

That Spanish woman who lived three hundred years ago, was certainly not the last of her kind. Many Theresas have been born who found for themselves no epic life wherein there was a constant unfolding of far-resonant action; perhaps only a life of mistakes, the offspring of a certain spiritual grandeur ill-matched with the meanness of opportunity; perhaps a tragic failure which found no sacred poet and sank unwept into oblivion. With dim lights and tangled circumstance they tried to shape their thought and deed in noble agreement; but after all, to common eyes their struggles seemed mere inconsistency and formlessness; for these later-born Theresas were helped by no coherent social faith and order which could perform the function of knowledge for the ardently willing soul. Their ardour alternated between a vague ideal and the common yearning of womanhood; so that the one was disapproved as extravagance, and the other condemned as a lapse.

Some have felt that these blundering lives are due to the inconvenient indefiniteness with which the Supreme Power has fashioned the natures of women: if there were one level of feminine incompetence as strict as the ability to count three and no more, the social lot of women might be treated with scientific certitude. Meanwhile the indefiniteness remains, and the limits of variation are really much wider than any one would imagine from the sameness of women's coiffure and the favourite love-stories in prose and verse. Here and there a cygnet is reared uneasily among the ducklings in the brown pond, and never finds the living stream in fellowship with its own oary-footed kind. Here and there is born a Saint Theresa, foundress of nothing, whose loving heartbeats and sobs after an unattained goodness tremble off and are dispersed among hindrances, instead of centring in some long-recognizable deed.

Frances E. W. Harper

(1825–1911)

African American writer F. E. W. Harper was born to free parents in Baltimore, Maryland, which was then a slave state. She received a good education at her uncle's school, became a teacher herself, but quit teaching to work in the antislavery movement. During the 1850s she broke the Fugitive Slave Law by accompanying runaway slaves on the Underground Railroad. Over a long career she published in every literary genre available—novels, essays, poetry, stories, letters—writing that is now said to have initiated the tradition of African American protest literature. A widow after 1864, she supported four children by returning to the lecture circuit, where she had worked as an abolitionist before the war. At the center of her poem "Eliza Harris" is the same fugitive slave who figures in Harriet Beecher Stowe's "The Quaker Settlement" (see page 64) in *Uncle Tom's Cabin*. Both writers based their character on an actual incident that occurred in Cincinnati, Ohio. Politically active on many often contentious fronts—for instance, the campaigns for suffrage for black men and white women—she often acted as mediator in these early battles of identity politics, reminding the antagonists: "We are all bound up together in one great bundle of humanity."

Eliza Harris

Like a fawn from the arrow, startled and wild,
A woman swept by us, bearing a child;
In her eye was the night of a settled despair,
And her brow was o'ershaded with anguish and care.

She was nearing the river—in reaching the brink,
She heeded no danger, she paused not to think!
For she is a mother—her child is a slave—
And she'll give him his freedom, or find him a grave!

It was a vision to haunt us, that innocent face—
So pale in its aspect, so fair in its grace;
As the tramp of the horse and the bay of the hound,
With the fetters that gall, were trailing the ground!

She was nerv'd by despair, and strengthened by woe,
As she leap'd o'er the chasms that yawn'd from below;
Death howl'd in the tempest, and rav'd in the blast,
But she heard not the sound till the danger was past.

Oh! how shall I speak of my proud country's shame?
Of the stains on her glory, how give them their name?
How say that her banner in mockery waves—
Her "star spangled banner"—o'er millions of slaves?

How say that the lawless may torture and chase
A woman whose crime is the hue of her face?
How the depths of the forest may echo around
With the shrieks of despair, and the bay of the hound?

With her step on the ice, and her arm on her child,
The danger was fearful, the pathway was wild;
But, aided by Heaven, she gained a free shore,
Where the friends of humanity open'd their door.

So fragile and lovely, so fearfully pale,
Like a lily that bends to the breath of the gale,
Save the heave of her breast, and the sway of her hair,
You'd have thought her a statue of fear and despair.

In agony close to her bosom she press'd
The life of her child, the child of her breast:—
Oh! love from its tenderness gathering might,
Had strengthen'd her soul for the dangers of flight.

But she's free—yes, free from the land where the slave
From the hand of oppression must rest in the grave;
Where bondage and torture, where scourges and chains,
Have plac'd on our banner indelible stains.

Did a fever e'er burning through bosom and brain,
Send a lava-like flood through every vein,
Till it suddenly cooled 'neath a healing spell,
And you knew, oh! the joy! you knew you were well?

So felt this young mother, as a sense of the rest
Stole gently and sweetly o'er *her* weary breast,
As her boy looked up, and, wondering, smiled
On the mother whose love had freed her child.

The bloodhounds have miss'd the scent of her way;
The hunter is rifled and foil'd of his prey;
Fierce jargon and cursing, with clanking of chains,
Make sounds of strange discord on Liberty's plains.

With the rapture love and fulness of bliss,
She plac'd on his brow a mother's fond kiss:—
Oh! poverty, danger and death she can brave,
For the child of her love is no longer a slave!

The Slave Mother

Heard you that shriek? It rose
    So wildly on the air,
It seemed as if a burden'd heart
    Was breaking in despair.

Saw you those hands so sadly clasped—
    The bowed and feeble head—
The shuddering of that fragile form—
    That look of grief and dread?

Saw you the sad, imploring eye?
    Its every glance was pain,
As if a storm of agony
    Were sweeping through the brain.

She is a mother, pale with fear,
    Her boy clings to her side,
And in her kirtle vainly tries
    His trembling form to hide.

He is not hers, although she bore
    For him a mother's pains;
He is not hers, although her blood
    Is coursing through his veins!

He is not hers, for cruel hands
    May rudely tear apart
The only wreath of household love
    That binds her breaking heart.

His love has been a joyous light
    That o'er her pathway smiled,
A fountain gushing ever new,
    Amid life's desert wild.

His lightest word has been a tone
    Of music round her heart,
Their lives a streamlet blent in one—
    Oh, Father! must they part?

They tear him from her circling arms,
    Her last and fond embrace.
Oh! never more may her sad eyes
    Gaze on his mournful face.

No marvel, then, these bitter shrieks
    Disturb the listening air:
She is a mother, and her heart
    Is breaking in despair.

Emily Dickinson

(1830–1886)

Emily Dickinson's poems, deceptively simple, are among the most enigmatic and innovative of the nineteenth century. Only eight were published in her lifetime. After her death, 1,776 others were found in her bedroom in her father's Amherst, Massachusetts, house, where she lived an increasingly reclusive life as she grew older. Her withdrawal from society is a subject of controversy. Did she insist on solitude as the only access to the ecstasies of art? Was her behavior a manifestation of agoraphobia, a fear of public places? Could her extreme self-protectiveness have had its origins in a traumatic event, perhaps a hopeless love affair? Many poems concern conflicts between ecstasy and terror, eroticism and renunciation, the power and limits of language, spiritual freedom and captivity, the presence of divinity in nature and the emptiness of social forms. Wendy Martin in *An American Triptych*, a study of the connection between Anne Bradstreet, Emily Dickinson, and Adrienne Rich and the Puritan tradition of New England, emphasizes Dickinson's independent mind. A rebel against orthodoxies, she was a mystical poet who conceived of her writing as a sacred calling, a countercultural liturgy of language in a theophanous universe. She read widely, especially the works of her favorite female precursors, Charlotte Brontë's *Jane Eyre*, Emily Brontë's *Wuthering Heights*, George Eliot's *Middlemarch*, and Elizabeth Barrett Browning's *Aurora Leigh*.

254

"Hope" is the thing with feathers—
That perches in the soul—
And sings the tune without the words—
And never stops—at all—

And sweetest—in the Gale—is heard—
And sore must be the storm—
That could abash the little Bird
That kept so many warm—

I've heard it in the chillest land—
And on the strangest Sea—
Yet, never, in Extremity,
It asked a crumb—of Me.

280

I felt a Funeral, in my Brain,
And Mourners to and fro
Kept treading—treading—till it seemed
That Sense was breaking through—

And when they all were seated,
A Service, like a Drum—
Kept beating—beating—till I thought
My Mind was going numb—

And then I heard them lift a Box
And creak across my Soul
With those same boots of Lead, again,
Then Space—began to toll,

As all the Heavens were a Bell,
And Being, but an Ear,
And I, and Silence, some strange Race
Wrecked, solitary, here—

And then a Plank in Reason, broke,
And I dropped down, and down—
And hit a World, at every plunge,
And Finished knowing—then—

292

If your Nerve, deny you—
Go above your Nerve—
He can lean against the Grave,
If he fear to swerve—

That's a steady posture—
Never any bend
Held of those Brass arms—
Best Giant made—

If your Soul seesaw—
Lift the Flesh door—
The Poltroon wants Oxygen—
Nothing more—

303

The Soul selects her own Society—
Then—shuts the Door—
To her divine Majority—
Present no more—

Unmoved—she notes the Chariots—pausing—
At her low Gate—
Unmoved—an Emperor be kneeling
Upon her Mat—

I've known her—from an ample nation—
Choose One—
Then—close the Valves of her attention—
Like Stone—

324

Some keep the Sabbath going to Church—
I keep it, staying at Home—
With a Bobolink for a Chorister—
And an Orchard, for a Dome—

Some keep the Sabbath in Surplice—
I just wear my Wings—
And instead of tolling the Bell, for Church,
Our little Sexton—sings.

God preaches, a noted Clergyman—
And the sermon is never long,
So instead of getting to Heaven, at last—
I'm going, all along.

479

She dealt her pretty words like Blades—
How glittering they shone—
And every One unbared a Nerve
Or wantoned with a Bone—

She never deemed—she hurt—
That—is not Steel's Affair—
A vulgar grimace in the Flesh—
How ill the Creatures bear—

To Ache is human—not polite—
The Film upon the eye
Mortality's old Custom—
Just locking up—to Die.

508

I'm ceded—I've stopped being Theirs—
The name They dropped upon my face
With water, in the country church
Is finished using, now,
And They can put it with my Dolls,
My childhood, and the string of spools,
I've finished threading—too—

Baptized, before, without the choice,
But this time, consciously, of Grace—
Unto supremest name—
Called to my Full—The Crescent dropped—
Existence's whole Arc, filled up,
With one small Diadem.

My second Rank—too small the first—
Crowned—Crowing—on my Father's breast—
A half unconscious Queen—
But this time—Adequate—Erect,
With Will to choose, or to reject,
And I choose, just a Crown—

613

They shut me up in Prose—
As when a little Girl
They put me in the Closet—
Because they liked me "still"—

Still! Could themself have peeped—
And seen my Brain—go round—
They might as wise have lodged a Bird
For Treason—in the Pound—

Himself has but to will
And easy as a Star
Abolish his Captivity—
And laugh—No more have I—

739

I many times thought Peace had come
When Peace was far away—
As Wrecked Men—deem they sight the Land—
At Centre of the Sea—

And struggle slacker—but to prove
As hopelessly as I—
How many the fictitious Shores—
Before the Harbor be—

829

Ample make this Bed—
Make this Bed with Awe—
In it wait till Judgment break
Excellent and Fair.

Be its Mattress straight—
Be its Pillow round—
Let no Sunrise' yellow noise
Interrupt this Ground—

917

Love—is anterior to Life—
Posterior—to Death—
Initial of Creation, and
The Exponent of Earth—

1075

The Sky is low—the Clouds are mean.
A Travelling Flake of Snow
Across a Barn or through a Rut
Debates if it will go—

A Narrow Wind complains all Day
How some one treated him
Nature, like Us is sometimes caught
Without her Diadem.

1718

Drowning is not so pitiful
As the attempt to rise.
Three times, 'tis said, a sinking man
Comes up to face the skies,
And then declines forever
To that abhorred abode,
Where hope and he part company—
For he is grasped of God.
The Maker's cordial visage,
However good to see,
Is shunned, we must admit it,
Like an adversity.

Louisa May Alcott

(1832–1888)

Maybe it was New England steeliness, but Louisa May Alcott kept the resolution she made at the age of eighteen: to become self-supporting and enable her mother's household to survive the chronic poverty that came with her father Bronson Alcott's failed experiments in educational reform. She took every job a decent girl could accept—maid, governess, teacher, Civil War nurse, travel companion on a trip to Europe—before she wrote *Little Women* (1868). After its success (it sold more than a million copies in her lifetime), she became the family breadwinner at Orchard House in Concord, Massachusetts, publishing a book a year until her death twenty years later. An active feminist—she was the first woman to cast a vote in Concord—her early gothic novels, now being rediscovered and compared with Poe's and Hawthorne's, show her anger at the economic and social powerlessness of nineteenth-century women. She was her mother's daughter. Abigail Alcott, an advocate of both abolition and woman's suffrage, confessed in *Little Women* in the voice of the long-suffering "Marmee": "I have been angry every day of my life." Many readers still find Alcott's most famous book irresistible for its main character, the smart and rebellious Jo, an autobiographical portrait of the writer as a young girl.

FROM *Little Women*

"Christmas won't be Christmas without any presents," grumbled Jo, lying on the rug.

"It's so dreadful to be poor!" sighed Meg, looking down at her old dress.

"I don't think it's fair for some girls to have plenty of pretty things, and other girls nothing at all," added little Amy, with an injured sniff.

"We've got father and mother and each other," said Beth contentedly, from her corner.

The four young faces on which the firelight shone brightened at the cheerful words, but darkened again as Jo said sadly,—"We haven't got father, and shall not have him for a long time." She didn't say "perhaps never," but each silently added it, thinking of father far away, where the fighting was.

Nobody spoke for a minute; then Meg said in an altered tone,—

"You know the reason mother proposed not having any presents this Christmas was because it is going to be a hard winter for everyone; and she thinks we ought not to spend money for pleasure, when our men are suffering so in the army. We can't do much, but we can make our little sacrifices, and ought to do it gladly. But I am afraid I don't;" and Meg shook her head, as she thought regretfully of all the pretty things she wanted.

"But I don't think the little we should spend would do any good. We've each got a dollar, and the army wouldn't be much helped by our giving that. I agree not to expect anything from mother or you, but I do want to buy Undine and Sintram for myself; I've wanted it *so* long," said Jo, who was a bookworm.

"I have planned to spend mine in new music," said Beth, with a little sigh, which no one heard but the hearth-brush and kettle-holder.

"I shall get a nice box of Faber's drawing-pencils; I really need them," said Amy decidedly.

"Mother didn't say anything about our money, and she won't wish us to give up everything. Let's each buy what we want, and have a little fun; I'm sure we work hard enough to earn it," cried Jo, examining the heels of her shoes in a gentlemanly manner.

"I know *I* do,—teaching those tiresome children nearly all day, when I'm longing to enjoy myself at home," began Meg, in the complaining tone again.

"You don't have half such a hard time as I do," said Jo. "How would you like to be shut up for hours with a nervous, fussy old lady, who keeps you trotting, is never satisfied, and worries you till you're ready to fly out of the window or cry?"

"It's naughty to fret; but I do think washing dishes and keeping things tidy is the worst work in the world. It makes me cross; and my hands get so stiff, I can't practise well at all"; and Beth looked at her rough hands with a sigh that any one could hear that time.

"I don't believe any of you suffer as I do," cried Amy; "for you don't have to go to school with impertinent girls, who plague you if you don't know your lessons, and laugh at your dresses, and label your father if he isn't rich, and insult you when your nose isn't nice."

"If you mean *libel*, I'd say so, and not talk about *labels,* as if papa was a pickle-bottle," advised Jo, laughing.

"I know what I mean, and you needn't be *statirical* about it. It's proper to use good words, and improve your *vocabilary*," returned Amy, with dignity.

"Don't peck at one another, children. Don't you wish we had the money papa lost when we were little, Jo? Dear me! how happy and good we'd be, if we had no worries!" said Meg, who could remember better times.

"You said, the other day, you thought we were a deal happier than the King children, for they were fighting and fretting all the time, in spite of their money."

"So I did, Beth. Well, I think we are; for, though we do have to work, we make fun for ourselves, and are a pretty jolly set, as Jo would say."

"Jo does use such slang words!" observed Amy, with a reproving look at the long figure stretched on the rug. Jo immediately sat up, put her hands in her pockets, and began to whistle.

"Don't, Jo; it's so boyish!"

"That's why I do it."

"I detest rude, unlady-like girls!"

"I hate affected, niminy-piminy chits!"

"'Birds in their little nests agree,'" sang Beth, the peacemaker, with such a funny face that both sharp voices softened to a laugh, and the "pecking" ended for that time.

"Really, girls, you are both to be blamed," said Meg, beginning to lecture in her elder-sisterly fashion. "You are old enough to leave off boyish tricks, and to behave better, Josephine. It didn't matter so much when you were a little girl; but now you are so tall, and turn up your hair, you should remember that you are a young lady."

"I'm not! and if turning up my hair makes me one, I'll wear it in two tails till I'm twenty," cried Jo, pulling off her net, and shaking down a chestnut mane. "I hate to think I've got to grow up, and be Miss March, and wear long gowns, and look as prim as a China-aster! It's bad enough to be a girl, anyway, when I like boys' games and work and manners! I can't get over my disappointment in not being a boy; and it's worse than ever now, for I'm dying to go and fight with papa, and I can only stay at home and knit, like a poky old woman!" And Jo shook the blue army-sock till the needles rattled like castanets, and her ball bounded across the room.

"Poor Jo! It's too bad, but it can't be helped; so you must try to be contented with making your name boyish, and playing brother to us girls," said Beth, stroking the rough head at her knee with a hand that all the dishwashing and dusting in the world could not make ungentle, in its touch.

"As for you, Amy," continued Meg, "you are altogether too particular and prim. Your airs are funny now; but you'll grow up an affected little goose, if you don't take care. I like your nice manners and refined ways of speaking, when you don't try to be elegant; but your absurd words are as bad as Jo's slang."

"If Jo is a tom-boy and Amy a goose, what am I, please?" asked Beth, ready to share the lecture.

"You're a dear, and nothing else," answered Meg warmly; and no one contradicted her, for the "Mouse" was the pet of the family.

As young readers like to know "how people look," we will take this moment to give them a little sketch of the four sisters, who sat knitting away in the twilight, while the December snow fell quietly without, and the fire crackled cheerfully within. It was a comfortable old room, though the carpet was faded and the furniture very plain; for a good picture or two hung on the walls, books filled the recesses, chrysanthemums and Christmas roses bloomed in the windows, and a pleasant atmosphere of home-peace pervaded it.

Margaret, the eldest of the four, was sixteen, and very pretty, being plump and fair, with large eyes, plenty of soft, brown hair, a sweet mouth, and white hands, of which she was rather vain. Fifteen-year-old Jo was very tall, thin, and brown, and reminded one of a colt; for she never seemed to know what to do with her long limbs, which were very much in her way. She had a decided mouth, a comical nose, and sharp, gray eyes, which appeared to see everything, and were by turns fierce, funny, or thoughtful. Her long, thick hair was her one beauty; but it was usually bundled into a net, to be out of her way. Round shoulders had Jo, big hands and feet, a fly-away look to her clothes, and the uncomfortable appearance of a girl who was rapidly shooting up into a woman, and didn't like it. Elizabeth—or Beth, as everyone called her—was a rosy, smooth-haired, bright-eyed girl of thirteen, with a shy manner, a timid voice, and a peaceful expression, which was seldom disturbed. Her father called her "Little Tranquillity," and the name suited her excellently; for she seemed to live in a happy world of her own, only venturing out to meet the few whom she trusted and loved. Amy, though the youngest, was a most important person,—in her own opinion at least. A regular snow-maiden, with blue eyes, and yellow hair, curling on her shoulders, pale and slender, and always carrying herself like a young lady mindful of her manners. What the characters of the four sisters were we will leave to be found out.

The clock struck six; and, having swept up the hearth, Beth put a pair of slippers down to warm. Somehow the sight of the old shoes had a good effect upon the girls; for mother was coming, and everyone brightened to welcome her. Meg stopped lecturing, and lighted the lamp, Amy got out of the easy-chair without being asked, and Jo forgot how tired she was as she sat up to hold the slippers nearer to the blaze.

"They are quite worn out; Marmee must have a new pair."

"I thought I'd get her some with my dollar," said Beth.

"No, I shall!" cried Amy.

"I'm the oldest," began Meg, but Jo cut in with a decided—

"I'm the man of the family now papa is away, and *I* shall provide the slippers, for he told me to take special care of mother while he was gone."

"I'll tell you what we'll do," said Beth; "let's each get her something for Christmas, and not get anything for ourselves."

"That's like you, dear! What will we get?" exclaimed Jo.

Everyone thought soberly for a minute; then Meg announced, as if the idea was suggested by the sight of her own pretty hands, "I shall give her a nice pair of gloves."

"Army shoes, best to be had," cried Jo.

"Some handkerchiefs, all hemmed," said Beth.

"I'll get a little bottle of cologne; she likes it, and it won't cost much, so I'll have some left to buy my pencils," added Amy.

"How will we give the things?" asked Meg.

"Put them on the table, and bring her in and see her open the bundles. Don't you remember how we used to do on our birthdays?" answered Jo.

"I used to be *so* frightened when it was my turn to sit in the big chair with the crown on, and see you all come marching round to give the presents, with a kiss. I liked the things and the kisses, but it was dreadful to have you sit looking at me while I opened the bundles," said Beth, who was toasting her face and the bread for tea, at the same time.

"Let Marmee think we are getting things for ourselves, and then surprise her. We must go shopping to-morrow afternoon, Meg; there is so much to do about the play for Christmas night," said Jo, marching up and down, with her hands behind her back and her nose in the air.

"I don't mean to act any more after this time; I'm getting too old for such things," observed Meg, who was as much a child as ever about "dressing-up" frolics.

"You won't stop, I know, as long as you can trail round in a white gown with your hair down, and wear gold-paper jewelry. You are the best actress we've got, and there'll be an end of everything if you quit the boards," said Jo. "We ought to rehearse to-night. Come here, Amy, and do the fainting scene, for you are as stiff as a poker in that."

"I can't help it; I never saw anyone faint, and I don't choose to make myself all black and blue, tumbling flat as you do. If I can go down easily, I'll drop; if I can't I shall fall into a chair and be graceful; I don't care if Hugo does come at me with a pistol," returned Amy, who was not gifted with dramatic power, but was chosen because she was small enough to be borne out shrieking by the villain of the piece.

"Do it this way: clasp your hands so, and stagger across the room, crying frantically, 'Roderigo! save me! save me!'" and away went Jo with a melodramatic scream which was truly thrilling.

Amy followed, but she poked her hands out stiffly before her, and jerked herself along as if she went by machinery; and her "Ow!" was more suggestive of pins being run into her than of fear and anguish. Jo gave a despairing groan, and Meg laughed outright, while Beth let her bread burn as she watched the fun, with interest.

"It's no use! Do the best you can when the time comes and if the audience laugh, don't blame me. Come on, Meg."

Then things went smoothly, for Don Pedro defied the world in a speech of two pages without a single break; Hagar, the witch, chanted an awful incantation over her kettleful of simmering toads, with weird effect; Roderigo rent his chains asunder manfully, and Hugo died in agonies of remorse and arsenic, with a wild "Ha! ha!"

"It's the best we've had yet," said Meg, as the dead villain sat up and rubbed his elbows.

"I don't see how you can write and act such splendid things, Jo. You're a regular Shakespeare!" exclaimed Beth, who firmly believed that her sisters were gifted with wonderful genius in all things.

"Not quite," replied Jo modestly. "I do think 'The Witch's Curse, an

Operatic Tragedy,' is rather a nice thing; but I'd like to try Macbeth, if we only had a trap-door for Banquo. I always wanted to do the killing part. 'Is that a dagger that I see before me?'" muttered Jo, rolling her eyes and clutching at the air, as she had seen a famous tragedian do.

"No, it's the toasting fork, with mother's shoe on it instead of the bread. Beth's stage-struck!" cried Meg, and the rehearsal ended in a general burst of laughter.

"Glad to find you so merry, my girls," said a cheery voice at the door, and actors and audience turned to welcome a tall, motherly lady, with a "can-I-help-you" look about her which was truly delightful. She was not elegantly dressed, but a noble-looking woman, and the girls thought the gray cloak and unfashionable bonnet covered the most splendid mother in the world.

"Well, dearies, how have you got on to-day? There was so much to do, getting the boxes ready to go to-morrow, that I didn't come home to dinner. Has anyone called, Beth? How is your cold, Meg? Jo, you look tired to death. Come and kiss me, baby."

While making these maternal inquiries Mrs. March got her wet things off, her warm slippers on, and sitting down in the easy chair, drew Amy to her lap, preparing to enjoy the happiest hour of her busy day. The girls flew about, trying to make things comfortable, each in her own way. Meg arranged the tea-table; Jo brought wood and set chairs, dropping, overturning, and clattering everything she touched; Beth trotted to and fro between parlor and kitchen, quiet and busy; while Amy gave directions to everyone, as she sat with her hands folded.

As they gathered about the table, Mrs. March said, with a particularly happy face, "I've got a treat for you after supper."

A quick, bright smile went round like a streak of sunshine. Beth clapped her hands, regardless of the biscuit she held, and Jo tossed up her napkin, crying, "A letter! a letter! Three cheers for father!"

"Yes, a nice long letter. He is well, and thinks he shall get through the cold season better than we feared. He sends all sorts of loving wishes for Christmas, and an especial message to you girls," said Mrs. March, patting her pocket as if she had got a treasure there.

"Hurry and get done! Don't stop to quirk your little finger, and simper over your plate, Amy," cried Jo, choking in her tea, and dropping her bread, butter side down, on the carpet, in her haste to get at the treat.

Beth ate no more, but crept away, to sit in her shadowy corner and brood over the delight to come, till the others were ready.

"I think it was so splendid in father to go as a chaplain when he was too old to be drafted, and not strong enough for a soldier," said Meg warmly.

"Don't I wish I could go as a drummer, a *vivan*—what's its name? or a nurse, so I could be near him and help him," exclaimed Jo, with a groan.

"It must be very disagreeable to sleep in a tent, and eat all sorts of bad-tasting things, and drink out of a tin mug," sighed Amy.

"When will he come home, Marmee?" asked Beth, with a little quiver in her voice.

"Not for many months, dear, unless he is sick. He will stay and do his work faithfully as long as he can, and we won't ask for him back a minute sooner than he can be spared. Now come and hear the letter."

They all drew to the fire, mother in the big chair with Beth at her feet, Meg and Amy perched on either arm of the chair, and Jo leaning on the back, where no one would see any sign of emotion if the letter should happen to be touching. Very few letters were written in those hard times that were not touching, especially those which fathers sent home. In this one little was said of the hardships endured, the dangers faced, or the homesickness conquered; it was a cheerful, hopeful letter, full of lively descriptions of camp life, marches, and military news; and only at the end did the writer's heart overflow with fatherly love and longing for the little girls at home.

"Give them all my dear love and a kiss. Tell them I think of them by day, pray for them by night, and find my best comfort in their affection at all times. A year seems very long to wait before I see them, but remind them that while we wait we may all work, so that these hard days need not be wasted. I know they will remember all I said to them, that they will be loving children to you, will do their duty faithfully, fight their bosom enemies bravely, and conquer themselves so beautifully, that when I come back to them I may be fonder and prouder than ever of my little women."

Everyone sniffed when they came to that part; Jo wasn't ashamed of the great tear that dropped off the end of her nose, and Amy never minded the rumpling of her curls as she hid her face on her mother's shoulder and sobbed out, "I *am* a selfish girl! but I'll truly try to be better, so he mayn't be disappointed in me by and by."

"We all will!" cried Meg. "I think too much of my looks, and hate to work, but won't any more, if I can help it."

"I'll try and be what he loves to call me, 'a little woman,' and not be rough and wild; but do my duty here instead of wanting to be somewhere else," said Jo, thinking that keeping her temper at home was a much harder task than facing a rebel or two down South.

Beth said nothing, but wiped away her tears with the blue army-sock, and began to knit with all her might, losing no time in doing the duty that lay nearest her, while she resolved in her quiet little soul to be all that father hoped to find her when the year brought round the happy coming home.

Mrs. March broke the silence that followed Jo's words, by saying in her cheery voice, "Do you remember how you used to play Pilgrim's Progress when you were little things? Nothing delighted you more than to have me tie my piece-bags on your backs for burdens, give you hats and sticks and rolls of paper, and let you travel through the house from the cellar, which was the City of Destruction, up, up, to the house-top, where you had all the lovely things you could collect to make a Celestial City."

"What fun it was, especially going by the lions, fighting Apollyon, and passing through the valley where the hobgoblins were!" said Jo.

"I liked the place where the bundles fell off and tumbled downstairs," said Meg.

"My favorite part was when we came out on the flat roof where our flowers and arbors and pretty things were, and all stood and sung for joy up there in the sunshine," said Beth, smiling, as if that pleasant moment had come back to her.

"I don't remember much about it, except that I was afraid of the cellar and the dark entry, and always liked the cake and milk we had up at the top. If I wasn't too old for such things, I'd rather like to play it over again," said Amy, who began to talk of renouncing childish things at the mature age of twelve.

"We never are too old for this, my dear, because it is a play we are playing all the time in one way or another. Our burdens are here, our road is before us, and the longing for goodness and happiness is the guide that leads us through many troubles and mistakes to the peace which is a true Celestial City. Now, my little pilgrims, suppose you begin again, not in play, but in earnest, and see how far on you can get before father comes home."

"Really, mother? Where are our bundles?" asked Amy, who was a quite literal young lady.

"Each of you told what your burden was just now, except Beth. I rather think she hasn't got any," said her mother.

"Yes, I have; mine is dishes and dusters, and envying girls with nice pianos, and being afraid of people."

Beth's bundle was such a funny one that everybody wanted to laugh; but nobody did, for it would have hurt her feelings very much.

"Let us do it," said Meg thoughtfully. "It is only another name for trying to be good, and the story may help us; for though we do want to be good, it's hard work, and we forget, and don't do our best."

"We were in the Slough of Despond to-night, and mother came and pulled us out as Help did in the book. We ought to have our roll of directions, like Christian. What shall we do about that?" asked Jo, delighted with the fancy which lent a little romance to the very dull task of doing her duty.

"Look under your pillows, Christmas morning, and you will find your guide-book," replied Mrs. March.

They talked over the new plan while old Hannah cleared the table; then out came the four little work-baskets, and the needles flew as the girls made sheets for Aunt March. It was uninteresting sewing, but to-night no one grumbled. They adopted Jo's plan of dividing the long seams into four parts, and calling the quarters Europe, Asia, Africa, and America, and in that way got on capitally, especially when they talked about the countries as they stitched their way through them.

At nine they stopped work, and sung, as usual, before they went to bed. No one but Beth could get much music out of the old piano; but she had a way of softly touching the yellow keys, and making a pleasant accompaniment to the simple songs they sung. Meg had a voice like a flute, and she and her mother led the little choir. Amy chirped like a cricket, and Jo wandered through the airs at her own sweet will, always coming out at the wrong place with a croak or a quaver that spoilt the most pensive tune. They had always done this from the time they could lisp, "Crinkle, crinkle, 'ittle 'tar," and it had become a household custom, for the mother was a born singer. The first sound in the morning was her voice, as she went about the house singing like a lark; and the last sound at night was the same cheery sound, for the girls never grew too old for that familiar lullaby.

Sarah Orne Jewett

(1849–1909)

In her lifetime, Sarah Orne Jewett's fiction—the collections *Deephaven* (1877), *A White Heron* (1886), and the novel *The Country of the Pointed Firs* (1896)—won her a reputation as a great regional colorist of her native South Maine coast. Editor William Dean Howells first published her "sketches" in the *Atlantic Monthly*; John Greenleaf Whittier, Rudyard Kipling, and Henry James praised her; James Russell Lowell liked the effect of her use of dialect, "for flavor, but not so oppressively as to suggest garlic." Willa Cather, to whom Jewett was an important mentor, dedicated *O Pioneers!* to her and wrote with loving insight about her work. In the last twenty years more attention has been paid to Jewett's biography and its reverberations in her fiction. She had as her own mentor, Annie Adams Fields (1834–1915), wife of the publisher and editor James T. Fields, and a literary hostess, novelist, poet, diarist, and memoirist. After the deaths of Fields's husband and Jewett's father, the two women became companions, their "Boston marriage" lasting until Jewett's death. Critic Josephine Donovan's reading of Jewett's fictional world as a community of matriarchal Christianity inspired by women's values reflects the centrality of same-sex friendships in Jewett's life.

Martha's Lady

One day, many years ago, the old Judge Pyne house wore an unwonted look of gayety and youthfulness. The high-fenced green garden was bright with June flowers. Under the elms in the large shady front yard you might see some chairs placed near together, as they often used to be when the family were all at home and life was going on gayly with eager talk and pleasure-making; when the elder judge, the grandfather, used to quote that great author, Dr. Johnson, and say to his girls, "Be brisk, be splendid, and be public."

One of the chairs had a crimson silk shawl thrown carelessly over its straight back, and a passer-by, who looked in through the latticed gate between the tall gate-posts with their white urns, might think that this piece of shining East Indian color was a huge red lily that had suddenly bloomed against the syringa bush. There were certain windows thrown wide open that were usually shut, and their curtains were blowing free in the light wind of a summer afternoon; it looked as if a large household had returned to the old house to fill the prim best rooms and find them full of cheer.

It was evident to everyone in town that Miss Harriet Pyne, to use the village phrase, had company. She was the last of her family, and was by no means old; but being the last, and wonted to live with people much older than herself, she had formed all the habits of a serious elderly person. Ladies of her age, something past thirty, often wore discreet caps in those days, especially if they were married, but being single, Miss Harriet clung to youth in this respect, making the one concession of keeping her waving chestnut hair as smooth and stiffly arranged as possible. She had been the dutiful companion of her father and mother in their latest years, all her elder brothers and sisters having married and gone, or died and gone, out of the old house. Now that she was left alone it seemed quite the best thing frankly to accept the fact of age, and to turn more resolutely than ever to the companionship of duty and serious books. She was more serious and given to routine than her elders themselves, as sometimes happened when the daughters of New England gentlefolks were brought up wholly in the society of their elders. At thirty-five she had more reluctance than her mother to face an unforeseen occasion, certainly more than her grandmother, who had preserved some cheerful inheritance of gayety and worldliness from colonial times.

There was something about the look of the crimson silk shawl in the front yard to make one suspect that the sober customs of the best house in a quiet New England village were all being set at defiance, and once when the mistress of the house came to stand in her own doorway, she wore the pleased but somewhat apprehensive look of a guest. In these days New England life held the necessity of much dignity and discretion of behavior; there was the truest hospitality and good cheer in all occasional festivities, but it was sometimes a self-conscious hospitality, followed by an inexorable return to asceticism both of diet and of behavior. Miss Harriet Pyne belonged to the very dullest days of New England, those which perhaps held the most priggishness for the learned professions, the most limited interpretation of the word "evangelical," and the pettiest indifference to large things. The outbreak of a desire for larger religious freedom caused at first a most determined reaction toward formalism, especially in small and quiet villages like Ashford, intently busy with their own concerns. It was high time for a little leaven to begin its work, in this moment when the great impulses of the war for liberty had died away and those of the coming war for patriotism and a new freedom had hardly yet begun.

The dull interior, the changed life of the old house, whose former activities seemed to have fallen sound asleep, really typified these larger conditions, and a little leaven had made its easily recognized appearance in the shape of a light-hearted girl. She was Miss Harriet's young Boston cousin, Helena Vernon, who, half-amused and half-impatient at the unnecessary sober-mindedness of her hostess and of Ashford in general, had set herself to the difficult task of gayety. Cousin Harriet looked on at a succession of ingenious and, on the whole, innocent attempts at pleasure, as she might have looked on at the frolics of a kitten who easily substitutes a ball of yarn for the uncertainties of a bird or a wind-blown leaf, and who may at any moment ravel the fringe of a sacred curtain-tassle in preference to either.

Helena, with her mischievous appealing eyes, with her enchanting old songs and her guitar, seemed the more delightful and even reasonable because she was so kind to everybody, and because she was a beauty. She had the gift of most charming manners. There was all the unconscious lovely ease and grace that had come with the good breeding of her city home, where many pleasant people came and went; she had no fear, one had almost said no respect, of the individual, and she did not need to think of herself. Cousin Harriet turned cold with apprehension when she saw the minister coming in at the front gate, and wondered in agony if Martha were properly attired to go to the door, and would by any chance hear the knocker; it was Helena who, delighted to have anything happen, ran to the door to welcome the Reverend Mr. Crofton as if he were a congenial friend of her own age. She could behave with more or less propriety during the stately first visit, and even contrive to lighten it with modest mirth, and to extort the confession that the guest had a tenor voice, though sadly out of practice; but when the minister departed a little flattered, and hoping that he had not expressed himself too strongly for a pastor upon the poems of Emerson, and feeling the unusual stir of gallantry in his proper heart, it was Helena who caught the honored hat of the late Judge Pyne from its last resting-place in the hall, and holding it securely in both hands, mimicked the minister's self-conscious entrance. She copied his pompous and anxious expression in the dim parlor in such delicious fashion that Miss Harriet, who could not always extinguish a ready spark of the original sin of humor, laughed aloud.

"My dear!" she exclaimed severely the next moment, "I am ashamed of your being so disrespectful!" and then laughed again, and took the affecting old hat and carried it back to its place.

"I would not have had anyone else see you for the world," she said sorrowfully as she returned, feeling quite self-possessed again, to the parlor doorway; but Helena still sat in the minister's chair, with her small feet placed as his stiff boots had been, and a copy of his solemn expression before they came to speaking of Emerson and of the guitar. "I wish I had asked him if he would be so kind as to climb the cherry-tree," said Helena, unbending a little at the discovery that her cousin would consent to laugh no more. "There are all those ripe cherries on the top branches. I can climb as high as he, but I can't reach far enough from the last branch that will bear me. The minister is so long and thin—"

"I don't know what Mr. Crofton would have thought of you; he is a very serious young man," said cousin Harriet, still ashamed of her laughter. "Martha will get the cherries for you, or one of the men. I should not like to have Mr. Crofton think you were frivolous, a young lady of your opportunities"—but Helena had escaped through the hall and out at the garden door at the mention of Martha's name. Miss Harriet Pyne sighed anxiously, and then smiled, in spite of her deep convictions, as she shut the blinds and tried to make the house look solemn again.

The front door might be shut, but the garden door at the other end of the broad hall was wide open upon the large sunshiny garden, where the last of the red and white peonies and the golden lilies, and the first of the tall blue larkspurs lent their colors in generous fashion. The straight box borders were all in fresh and shining green of their new leaves, and there was a fragrance of the old garden's inmost life and soul blowing from the honeysuckle blossoms on a long trellis. It was now late in the afternoon, and the sun was low behind great apple-trees at the garden's end, which threw their shadows over the short turf of the bleaching-green. The cherry-trees stood at one side in full sun-shine, and Miss Harriet, who presently came to the garden steps to watch like a hen at the water's edge, saw her cousin's pretty figure in its white dress of India muslin hurrying across the grass. She was accompanied by the tall, ungainly shape of Martha the new maid, who, dull and indifferent to every-one else, showed a surprising willingness and allegiance to the young guest.

"Martha ought to be in the dining-room, already, slow as she is; it wants but half an hour of tea-time," said Miss Harriet, as she turned and went into the shaded house. It was Martha's duty to wait at table, and there had been many trying scenes and defeated efforts toward her education. Martha was certainly very clumsy, and she seemed the clumsier because she had replaced her aunt, a most skillful person, who had but lately married a thriving farm and its prosperous owner. It must be confessed that Miss Harriet was a most bewildering instructor, and that her pupil's brain was easily confused and prone to blunders. The coming of Helena had been somewhat dreaded by reason of this incompetent service, but the guest took no notice of frowns or futile gestures at the first tea-table, except to establish friendly relations with Martha on her own account by a reassuring smile. They were about the same age, and next morning, before cousin Harriet came down, Helena showed by a word and a quick touch the right way to do something that had gone wrong and been impossible to understand the night before. A moment later the anx-ious mistress came in without suspicion, but Martha's eyes were as affec-tionate as a dog's, and there was a new look of hopefulness on her face; this dreaded guest was a friend after all, and not a foe come from proud Boston to confound her ignorance and patient efforts.

The two young creatures, mistress and maid, were hurrying across the bleaching-green.

"I can't reach the ripest cherries," explained Helena politely, "and I think Miss Pyne ought to send some to the minister. He has just made us a call. Why, Martha, you haven't been crying again!"

"Yes'm," said Martha sadly. "Miss Pyne always loves to send something to the minister," she acknowledged with interest, as if she did not wish to be asked to explain these latest tears.

"We'll arrange some of the best cherries in a pretty dish. I'll show you how, and you shall carry them over to the parsonage after tea," said Helena cheerfully, and Martha accepted the embassy with pleasure. Life was beginning to hold moments of something like delight in the last few days.

"You'll spoil your pretty dress, Miss Helena," Martha gave shy warning, and Miss Helena stood back and held up her skirts with unusual care while the country girl, in her heavy blue checked gingham, began to climb the cherry-tree like a boy.

Down came the scarlet fruit like bright rain into the green grass.

"Break some nice twigs with the cherries and leaves together; oh, you're a duck, Martha!" and Martha, flushed with delight, and looking far more like a thin and solemn blue heron, came rustling down to earth again, and gathered the spoils into her clean apron.

That night at tea, during her handmaiden's temporary absence, Miss Harriet announced, as if by way of apology, that she thought Martha was beginning to understand something about her work. "Her aunt was a treasure, she never had to be told anything twice; but Martha has been as clumsy as a calf," said the precise mistress of the house. "I have been afraid sometimes that I never could teach her anything. I was quite ashamed to have you come just now, and find me so unprepared to entertain a visitor."

"Oh, Martha will learn fast enough because she cares so much," said the visitor eagerly. "I think she is a dear good girl. I do hope that she will never go away. I think she does things better every day, cousin Harriet," added Helena pleadingly, with all her kind young heart. The china-closet door was open a little way, and Martha heard every word. From that moment, she not only knew what love was like, but she knew love's dear ambitions. To have come from a stony-hill farm and a bare small wooden house, was like a cave-dweller's coming to make a permanent home in an art museum, such had seemed the elaborateness and elegance of Miss Pyne's fashion of life; and Martha's simple brain was slow enough in its processes and recognitions. But with this sympathetic ally and defender, this exquisite Miss Helena who believed in her, all difficulties appeared to vanish.

Later that evening, no longer homesick or hopeless, Martha returned from her polite errand to the minister, and stood with a sort of triumph before the two ladies, who were sitting in the front doorway, as if they were waiting for visitors, Helena still in her white muslin and red ribbons, and Miss Harriet in a thin black silk. Being happily self-forgetful in the greatness of the moment, Martha's manners were perfect, and she looked for once almost pretty and quite as young as she was.

"The minister came to the door himself, and returned his thanks. He said that cherries were always his favorite fruit, and he was much obliged to both Miss Pyne and Miss Vernon. He kept me waiting a few minutes, while he got this book ready to send to you, Miss Helena."

"What are you saying, Martha? I have sent him nothing!" exclaimed Miss Pyne, much astonished. "What does she mean, Helena?"

"Only a few cherries," explained Helena. "I thought Mr. Crofton would like them after his afternoon of parish calls. Martha and I arranged them before tea, and I sent them with our compliments."

"Oh, I am very glad you did," said Miss Harriet, wondering, but much relieved. "I was afraid—"

"No, it was none of my mischief," answered Helena daringly. "I did not think that Martha would be ready to go so soon. I should have shown you how pretty they looked among their green leaves. We put them in one of your best white dishes with the openwork edge. Martha shall show you to-morrow; mamma always likes to have them so." Helena's fingers were busy with the hard knot of a parcel.

"See this, cousin Harriet!" she announced proudly, as Martha disappeared round the corner of the house, beaming with the pleasures of adventure and success. "Look! the minister has sent me a book: Sermons on *what?* Sermons—it is so dark that I can't quite see."

"It must be his 'Sermons on the Seriousness of Life'; they are the only ones he has printed, I believe," said Miss Harriet, with much pleasure. They are considered very fine discourses. He pays you a great compliment, my dear. I feared that he noticed your girlish levity."

"I behaved beautifully while he stayed," insisted Helena. "Ministers are only men," but she blushed with pleasure. It was certainly something to receive a book from its author, and such a tribute made her of more value to the whole reverent household. The minister was not only a man, but a bachelor, and Helena was at the age that best loves conquest; it was at any rate comfortable to be reinstated in cousin Harriet's good graces.

"Do ask the kind gentleman to tea! He needs a little cheering up," begged the siren in India muslin, as she laid the shiny black volume of sermons on the stone doorstep with an air of approval, but as if they had quite finished their mission.

"Perhaps I shall, if Martha improves as much as she has within the last day or two," Miss Harriet promised hopefully. "It is something I always dread a little when I am all alone, but I think Mr. Crofton likes to come. He converses so elegantly."

These were the days of long visits, before affectionate friends thought it quite worth while to take a hundred miles' journey merely to dine or to pass a night in one another's houses. Helena lingered through the pleasant weeks of early summer, and departed unwillingly at last to join her family at the White Hills, where they had gone, like other households of high social station, to pass the month of August out of town. The happy-hearted young guest left many lamenting friends behind her, and promised each that she would come back again next year. She left the minister a rejected lover, as well as the preceptor of the academy, but with their pride unwounded, and it may have been with wider outlooks upon the world and a less narrow sympathy both for their own work in life and for their neighbors' work and hindrances. Even Miss Harriet Pyne herself had lost some of the unnecessary provincialism and prejudice which had begun to harden a naturally good and open mind and affectionate heart. She was conscious of feeling younger and more free, and not so lonely. Nobody had ever been so gay, so fascinating, or so kind as Helena, so full of social resource, so simple and undemanding in her friendliness. The light of her young life cast no shadow on either young or old companions, her pretty clothes never seemed to make other girls look dull or out of fashion. When she went away up the street in Miss Harriet's carriage to take the slow train toward Boston and the gayeties of the new Profile House, where her mother waited impatiently with a group of Southern friends, it seemed as if there would never be any more picnics or parties in Ashford, and as if society had nothing left to do but to grow old and get ready for winter.

Martha came into Miss Helena's bedroom that last morning, and it was easy to see that she had been crying; she looked just as she did in that first sad week of homesickness and despair. All for love's sake she had been learning to do many things, and to do them exactly right; her eyes had grown quick to see the smallest chance for personal service. Nobody could be more humble and devoted; she looked years older than Helena, and wore already a touching air of caretaking.

"You spoil me, you dear Martha!" said Helena from the bed. "I don't know what they will say at home, I am so spoiled."

Martha went on opening the blinds to let in the brightness of the summer morning, but she did not speak.

"You are getting on splendidly, aren't you?" continued the little mistress. "You have tried so hard that you make me ashamed of myself. At first you crammed all the flowers together, and now you make them look beautiful. Last night cousin Harriet was so pleased when the table was so charming, and I told her that you did everything yourself, every bit. Won't you keep the flowers fresh and pretty in the house until I come back? It's so much pleasanter for Miss Pyne, and you'll feed my little sparrows, won't you? They're growing so tame."

"Oh, yes, Miss Helena!" and Martha looked almost angry for a moment, then she burst into tears and covered her face with her apron. "I couldn't understand a single thing when I first came. I never had been anywhere to see anything, and Miss Pyne frightened me when she talked. It was you made me think I could ever learn. I wanted to keep the place, 'count of mother and the little boys; we're dreadful hard pushed. Hepsy has been good in the kitchen; she said she ought to have patience with me, for she was awkward herself when she first came."

Helena laughed; she looked so pretty under the tasseled white curtains.

"I dare say Hepsy tells the truth," she said. "I wish you had told me about your mother. When I come again, some day we'll drive up country, as you call it, to see her. Martha I wish you would think of me sometimes after I go away. Won't you promise?" and the bright young face suddenly grew grave. "I have hard times myself; I don't always learn things that I ought to learn, I don't always put things straight. I wish you wouldn't forget me ever, and would just believe in me. I think it does help more than anything."

"I won't forget," said Martha slowly. "I shall think of you every day." She spoke almost with indifference, as if she had been asked to dust a room, but she turned aside quickly and pulled the little mat under the hot water jug quite out of its former straightness; then she hastened away down the long white entry, weeping as she went.

To lose out of sight the friend whom one has loved and lived to please is to lose joy out of life. But if love is true, there comes presently a higher joy of pleasing the ideal, that is to say, the perfect friend. The same old happiness is lifted to a higher level. As for Martha, the girl who stayed behind in Ashford, nobody's life could seem duller to those who could not understand; she was slow of step, and her eyes were almost always downcast as if intent upon incessant toil; but they startled you when she looked up, with their shining light. She was capable of the happiness of holding fast to a great sentiment, the ineffable satisfaction of trying to please one whom she truly loved. She never thought of trying to make other people pleased with herself; all she lived for was to do the best she could for others, and to conform to an ideal, which grew at last to be like a saint's vision, a heavenly figure painted upon the sky.

On Sunday afternoons in summer, Martha sat by the window of her chamber, a low-storied little room, which looked into the side yard and the great branches of an elm-tree. She never sat in the old wooden rocking-chair except on Sundays like this; it belonged to the day of rest and to happy meditation. She wore her plain black dress and a clean white apron, and held in her lap a little wooden box, with a brass ring on top for a handle. She was past sixty years of age and looked even older, but there was the same look on her face that it had sometimes worn in girlhood. She was the same Martha; her hands were old-looking and work-worn, but her face still shone. It seemed like yesterday that Helena Vernon had gone away, and it was more than forty years.

War and peace had brought their changes and great anxieties, the face of the earth was furrowed by floods and fire, the faces of mistress and maid were furrowed by smiles and tears, and in the sky the stars shone on as if nothing had happened. The village of Ashford added a few pages to its unexciting history, the minister preached, the people listened; now and then a funeral crept along the street, and now and then the bright face of a little child rose above the horizon of a family pew. Miss Harriet Pyne lived on in the large white house, which gained more and more distinction because it suffered no changes, save successive repaintings and a new railing about its stately roof. Miss Harriet herself had moved far beyond the uncertainties of an anxious youth. She had long ago made all her decisions, and settled all necessary questions; her scheme of life was as faultless as the miniature landscape of a Japanese garden, and as easily kept in order. The only important change she would ever be capable of making was the final change to another and a better world; and for that nature itself would gently provide, and her own innocent life.

Hardly any great social event had ruffled the easy current of life since Helena Vernon's marriage. To this Miss Pyne had gone, stately in appearance and carrying gifts of some old family silver which bore the Vernon crest, but not without some protest in her heart against the uncertainties of married life. Helena was so equal to a happy independence and even to the assistance of other lives grown strangely dependent upon her quick sympathies and instinctive decisions, that it was hard to let her sink her personality into the affairs of another. Yet a brilliant English match was not without its attractions to an old-fashioned gentlewoman like Miss Pyne, and Helena herself was amazingly happy; one day there had come a letter to Ashford, in which her very heart seemed to beat with love and self-forgetfulness, to tell cousin Harriet of such new happiness and high hope. "Tell Martha all that I say about my dear Jack," wrote the eager girl; "please show my letter to Martha, and tell her that I shall come home next summer and bring the handsomest and best man in the world to Ashford. I have told him all about the dear house and the dear garden; there never was such a lad to reach for cherries with his six-foot-two." Miss Pyne, wondering a little, gave the letter to Martha, who took it deliberately and as if she wondered too, and went away to read it slowly by herself. Martha cried over it, and felt a strange sense of loss and pain; it hurt her heart a little to read about the cherry-picking. Her idol seemed to be less her own since she had become the idol of a stranger. She never had taken such a letter in her hands before, but love at last prevailed, since Miss Helena was happy, and she kissed the last page where her name was written, feeling over-bold, and laid the envelope on Miss Pyne's secretary without a word.

The most generous love cannot but long for reassurance, and Martha had the joy of being remembered. She was not forgotten when the day of the wedding drew near, but she never knew that Miss Helena had asked if cousin Harriet would not bring Martha to town; she should like to have Martha there to see her married. "She would help about the flowers," wrote the happy girl; "I know she will like to come, and I'll ask mamma to plan to have someone take her all about Boston and make her have a pleasant time after the hurry of the great day is over."

Cousin Harriet thought it was very kind and exactly like Helena, but Martha would be out of her element; it was most imprudent and girlish to have thought of such a thing. Helena's mother would be far from wishing for any unnecessary guest just then, in the busiest part of her household, and it was best not to speak of the invitation. Some day Martha should go to Boston if she did well, but not now. Helena did not forget to ask if Martha had come, and was astonished by the indifference of the answer. It was the first thing which reminded her that she was not a fairy princess having everything her own way in that last day before the wedding. She knew that Martha would have loved to be near, for she could not help understanding in that moment of her own happiness the love that was hidden in another heart. Next day this happy young princess, the bride, cut a piece of a great cake and put it into a pretty box that had held one of her wedding presents. With eager voices calling her, and all her friends about her, and her mother's face growing more and more wistful at the thought of parting, she still lingered and ran to take one or two trifles from her dressing-table, a little mirror and some tiny scissors that Martha would remember, and one of the pretty handkerchiefs marked with her maiden name. These she put in the box too; it was half a girlish freak and fancy, but she could not help trying to share her happiness, and Martha's life was so plain and dull. She whispered a message, and put the little package into cousin Harriet's hand for Martha as she said good-bye. She was very fond of cousin Harriet. She smiled with a gleam of her old fun; Martha's puzzled look and tall awkward figure seemed to stand suddenly before her eyes, as she promised to come again to Ashford. Impatient voices called to Helena, her lover was at the door, and she hurried away, leaving her old home and girlhood gladly. If she had only known it, as she kissed cousin Harriet good-bye, they were never going to see each other again until they were old women. The first step that she took out of her father's house that day, married, and full of hope and joy, was a step that led her away from the green elms of Boston Common and away from her own country and those she loved best, to a brilliant, much-varied foreign life, and to nearly all the sorrows and nearly all the joys that the heart of one woman could hold or know.

On Sunday afternoons Martha used to sit by the window in Ashford and hold the wooden box which a favorite young brother, who afterward died at sea, had made for her, and she used to take out of it the pretty little box with a gilded cover that had held the piece of wedding-cake, and the small scissors, and the blurred bit of a mirror in its silver case; as for the handkerchief with the narrow lace edge, once in two or three years she sprinkled it as if it were a flower, and spread it out in the sun on the old bleaching-green, and sat near by in the shrubbery to watch lest some bold robin or cherry-bird should seize it and fly away.

Miss Harriet Pyne was often congratulated upon the good fortune of having such a helper and friend as Martha. As time went on this tall, gaunt woman, always thin, always slow, gained a dignity of behavior and simple affectionateness of look which suited the charm and dignity of the ancient house. She was unconsciously beautiful like a saint, like the picturesqueness of a lonely tree which lives to shelter unnumbered lives and to stand quietly in its place. There was such rustic homeliness and constancy belonging to her, such beautiful powers of apprehension, such reticence, such gentleness for those who were troubled or sick; all these gifts and graces Martha hid in her heart. She never joined the church because she thought she was not good enough, but life was such a passion and happiness of service that it was impossible not to be devout, and she was always in her humble place on Sundays, in the back pew next to the door. She had been educated by a remembrance; Helena's young eyes forever looked at her reassuringly from a gay girlish face. Helena's sweet patience in teaching her own awkwardness could never be forgotten.

"I owe everything to Miss Helena," said Martha, half aloud, as she sat alone by the window; she had said it to herself a thousand times. When she looked in the little keepsake mirror she always hoped to see some faint reflection of Helena Vernon, but there was only her own brown old New England face to look back at her wonderingly.

Miss Pyne went less and less often to pay visits to her friends in Boston; there were very few friends left to come to Ashford and make long visits in the summer, and life grew more and more monotonous. Now and then there came news from across the sea and messages of remembrance, letters that were closely written on thin sheets of paper, and that spoke of lords and ladies, of great journeys, of the death of little children and the proud successes of boys at school, of the wedding of Helena Dysart's only daughter; but even that had happened years ago. These things seemed far away and vague, as if they belonged to a story and not to life itself; the true links with the past were quite different. There was the unvarying flock of ground-sparrows that Helena had begun to feed; every morning Martha scattered crumbs for them from the side doorsteps while Miss Pyne watched from the dining-room window, and they were counted and cherished year by year.

Miss Pyne herself had many fixed habits, but little ideality or imagination, and so at last it was Martha who took thought for her mistress, and gave freedom to her own good taste. After a while, without anyone's observing the change, the every-day ways of doing things in the house came to be the stately ways that had once belonged only to the entertainment of guests. Happily both mistress and maid seized all possible chances for hospitality, yet Miss Harriet nearly always sat alone at her exquisitely served table with its fresh flowers, and the beautiful old china which Martha handled so lovingly that there was no good excuse for keeping it hidden on the closet shelves. Every year when the old cherry-trees were in fruit, Martha carried the round white old English dish with a fretwork edge, full of pointed green leaves and scarlet cherries, to the minister, and his wife never quite understood why every year he blushed and looked so conscious of the pleasure, and thanked Martha as if he had received a very particular attention. There was no pretty suggestion toward the pursuit of the fine art of housekeeping in Martha's limited acquaintance with newspapers that she did not adopt; there was no refined old custom of the Pyne housekeeping that she consented to let go. And every day, as she had promised, she thought of Miss Helena,—oh, many times in every day: whether this thing would please her, or that be likely to fall in with her fancy or ideas of fitness. As far as was possible the rare news that reached Ashford through an occasional letter or the talk of guests was made part of Martha's own life, the history of her own heart. A worn old geography often stood open at the map of Europe on the lightstand in her room, and a little old-fashioned gilt button, set with a bit of glass like a ruby, that had broken and fallen from the trimming of one of Helena's dresses, was used to mark the city of her dwelling-place. In the changes of a diplomatic life Martha followed her lady all about the map. Sometimes the button was at Paris, and sometimes at Madrid; once, to her great anxiety, it remained long at St. Petersburg. For such a slow scholar Martha was not unlearned at last, since everything about life in these foreign towns was of interest to her faithful heart. She satisfied her own mind as she threw crumbs to the tame sparrows; it was all part of the same thing and for the same affectionate reasons.

One Sunday afternoon in early summer Miss Harriet Pyne came hurrying along the entry that led to Martha's room and called two or three times before its inhabitant could reach the door. Miss Harriet looked unusually cheerful and excited, and she held something in her hand. "Where are you, Martha?" she called again. "Come quick, I have something to tell you!"

"Here I am, Miss Pyne," said Martha, who had only stopped to put her precious box in the drawer, and to shut the geography.

"Who do you think is coming this very night at half-past six? We must have everything as nice as we can; I must see Hannah at once. Do you remember my cousin Helena who has lived abroad so long? Miss Helena Vernon,—the Honorable Mrs. Dysart, she is now."

"Yes, I remember her," answered Martha, turning a little pale.

"I knew that she was in this country, and I had written to ask her to come for a long visit," continued Miss Harriet, who did not often explain things, even to Martha, though she was always conscientious about the kind messages that were sent back by grateful guests. "She telegraphs that she means to anticipate her visit by a few days and come to me at once. The heat is beginning in town, I suppose. I daresay, having been a foreigner so long, she does not mind traveling on Sunday. Do you think Hannah will be prepared? We must have tea a little later."

"Yes, Miss Harriet," said Martha. She wondered that she could speak as usual, there was such a ringing in her ears. "I shall have time to pick some fresh strawberries; Miss Helena is so fond of our strawberries."

"Why, I had forgotten," said Miss Pyne, a little puzzled by something quite unusual in Martha's face. "We must expect to find Mrs. Dysart a good deal changed, Martha; it is a great many years since she was here; I have not seen her since her wedding, and she has had a great deal of trouble, poor girl. You had better open the parlor chamber, and make it ready before you go down."

"It is all ready," said Martha. "I can carry some of those little sweet-brier roses upstairs before she comes."

"Yes, you are always thoughtful," said Miss Pyne, with unwonted feeling.

Martha did not answer. She glanced at the telegram wistfully. She had never really suspected before that Miss Pyne knew nothing of the love that had been in her heart all these years; it was half a pain and half a golden joy to keep such a secret; she could hardly bear this moment of surprise.

Presently the news gave wings to her willing feet. When Hannah, the cook, who had never known Miss Helena, went to the parlor an hour later on some errand to her old mistress, she discovered that this stranger guest must be a very important person. She had never seen the tea-table look exactly as it did that night, and in the parlor itself there were fresh blossoming boughs in the old East India jars, and lilies in the paneled hall, and flowers everywhere, as if there were some high festivity.

Miss Pyne sat by the window watching, in her best dress, looking stately and calm; she seldom went out now, and it was almost time for the carriage. Martha was just coming in from the garden with the strawberries, and with more flowers in her apron. It was a bright cool evening in June, the golden robins sang in the elms, and the sun was going down behind the apple-trees at the foot of the garden. The beautiful old house stood wide open to the long-expected guest.

"I think that I shall go down to the gate," said Miss Pyne, looking at Martha for approval, and Martha nodded and they went together slowly down the broad front walk.

There was a sound of horses and wheels on the roadside turf: Martha could not see at first; she stood back inside the gate behind the white lilac-bushes as the carriage came. Miss Pyne was there; she was holding out both arms and taking a tired, bent little figure in black to her heart. "Oh, my Miss Helena is an old woman like me!" and Martha gave a pitiful sob; she had never dreamed it would be like this; this was the one thing she could not bear.

"Where are you, Martha?" called Miss Pyne. "Martha will bring these in; you have not forgotten my good Martha, Helena?" Then Mrs. Dysart looked up and smiled just as she used to smile in the old days. The young eyes were there still in the changed face, and Miss Helena had come.

That night Martha waited in her lady's room just as she used to, humble and silent, and went through with the old unforgotten loving services. The long years seemed like days. At last she lingered a moment trying to think of something else that might be done, then she was going silently away, but Helena called her back. She suddenly knew the whole story and could hardly speak.

"Oh, my dear Martha!" she cried, "won't you kiss me good-night? Oh, Martha, have you remembered like this, all these long years!"

Edith Wharton

(1862-1937)

In fact and spirit, Edith Wharton led a double life. A child of snobbish, cold parents, she knew how to play her part in a cold and snobbish New York society. As a woman and an artist, she also imagined and lived the alternatives. She fled to Europe from what she called the ignorance and crassness of late nineteenth-century America and wrote novels (*The House of Mirth* [1905], *Ethan Frome* [1911], *The Age of Innocence* [1920]) and short stories exposing the myths of class—predominantly, their suffocating consequences for women—all the while cultivating and enjoying the world of money and privilege she knew from the cradle and dramatized as a moral wasteland in her fictions. She married a dunce (Henry James referred to Edward Wharton as the "cerebrally compromised Teddy"), and after trying to make the absurd marriage work for twelve years, she suffered a nervous breakdown. She resurrected as a committed, professional writer (who would publish fifty volumes of fiction and nonfiction), eventually finding the nerve to divorce Teddy, engage in a love affair, and in numerous plots and characters dramatize the power of sexual desire and the hypocrisy of the rich and respectable. Though she could be an intimidating presence—F. Scott Fitzgerald stuttered when introduced—she was, as "Souls Belated" makes clear, neither Puritan nor Victorian. Scrutinizing the rules governing marriage and divorce and how they insinuate themselves into a man and a woman's consciousness, in this story, as in her novels, she reveals herself as one of the great subversives of American literature.

Souls Belated

I

Their railway carriage had been full when the train left Bologna; but at the first station beyond Milan their only remaining companion—a courtly person who ate garlic out of a carpetbag—had left his crumb-strewn seat with a bow.

Lydia's eye regretfully followed the shiny broadcloth of his retreating back till it lost itself in the cloud of touts and cab drivers hanging about the station; then she glanced across at Gannett and caught the same regret in his look. They were both sorry to be alone.

"*Par-ten-za!*" shouted the guard. The train vibrated to a sudden slamming of doors; a waiter ran along the platform with a tray of fossilized sandwiches; a belated porter flung a bundle of shawls and bandboxes into a third-class carriage; the guard snapped out a brief *Partenza!* which indicated the purely ornamental nature of his first shout; and the train swung out of the station.

The direction of the road had changed, and a shaft of sunlight struck across the dusty red-velvet seats into Lydia's corner. Gannett did not notice it. He had returned to his *Revue de Paris*, and she had to rise and lower the shade of the farther window. Against the vast horizon of their leisure such incidents stood out sharply.

Having lowered the shade, Lydia sat down, leaving the length of the carriage between herself and Gannett. At length he missed her and looked up.

"I moved out of the sun," she hastily explained.

Her looked at her curiously: the sun was beating on her through the shade.

"Very well," he said pleasantly; adding, "You don't mind?" as he drew a cigarette case from his pocket.

It was a refreshing touch, relieving the tension of her spirit with the suggestion that, after all, if he could *smoke*—! The relief was only momentary. Her experience of smokers was limited (her husband had disapproved of the use of tobacco) but she knew from hearsay that men sometimes smoked to get away from things; that a cigar might be the masculine equivalent of darkened windows and a headache. Gannett, after a puff or two, returned to his review.

It was just as she had foreseen; he feared to speak as much as she did. It was one of the misfortunes of their situation that they were never busy enough to necessitate, or even to justify, the postponement of unpleasant discussions. If they avoided a question it was obviously, unconcealably because the question was disagreeable. They had unlimited leisure and an accumulation of mental energy to devote to any subject that presented itself; new topics were in fact at a premium. Lydia sometimes had premonitions of a famine-stricken period when there would be nothing left to talk about, and she had already caught herself doling out piecemeal what, in the first prodigality of their confidences, she would have flung to him in a breath. Their silence therefore might simply mean that they had nothing to say; but it was another disadvantage of their position that it allowed infinite opportunity for the classification of minute differences. Lydia had learned to distinguish between real and factitious silences; and under Gannett's she now detected a hum of speech to which her own thoughts made breathless answer.

How could it be otherwise, with that thing between them? She glanced up at the rack overhead. The *thing* was there, in her dressing bag, symbolically suspended over her head and his. He was thinking of it now; just as she was; they had been thinking of it in unison ever since they had entered the train. While the carriage had held other travelers they had screened her from his thoughts; but now that he and she were alone she knew exactly what was passing through his mind; she could almost hear him asking himself what he should say to her.

The thing had come that morning, brought up to her in an innocent-looking envelope with the rest of their letters, as they were leaving the hotel at Bologna. As she tore it open, she and Gannett were laughing over some ineptitude of the local guidebook—they had been driven, of late, to make the most of such incidental humors of travel. Even when she had unfolded the document she took it for some unimportant business paper sent abroad for her signature, and her eye traveled inattentively over the curly *Whereases* of the preamble until a word arrested her: Divorce. There it stood, an impassible barrier, between her husband's name and hers.

She had been prepared for it, of course, as healthy people are said to be prepared for death, in the sense of knowing it must come without in the least expecting that it will. She had known from the first that Tillotson meant to divorce her—but what did it matter? Nothing mattered, in those first days of supreme deliverance, but the fact that she was free; and not so much (she had begun to be aware) that freedom had released her from Tillotson as that it had given her to Gannett. This discovery had not been agreeable to her self-esteem. She had preferred to think that Tillotson had himself embodied all her reasons for leaving him; and those he represented had seemed cogent enough to stand in no need of reinforcement. Yet she had not left him till she met Gannett. It was her love for Gannett that had made life with Tillotson so poor and incomplete a business. If she had never, from the first, regarded her marriage as a full canceling of her claims upon life, she had at least, for a number of years, accepted it as a provisional compensation,—she had made it "do." Existence in the commodious Tillotson mansion in Fifth Avenue—with Mrs. Tillotson senior commanding the approaches from the second-story front windows—had been reduced to a series of purely automatic acts. The moral atmosphere of the Tillotson interior was as carefully screened and curtained as the house itself: Mrs. Tillotson senior dreaded ideas as much as a draft in her back. Prudent people liked an even temperature; and to do anything unexpected was as foolish as going out in the rain. One of the chief advantages of being rich was that one need not be exposed to unforeseen contingencies: by the use of ordinary firmness and common sense one could make sure of doing exactly the same thing every day at the same hour. These doctrines, reverentially imbibed with his mother's milk, Tillotson (a model son who had never given his parents an hour's anxiety) complacently expounded to his wife, testifying to his sense of their importance by the regularity with which he wore galoshes on damp days, his punctuality at meals, and his elaborate precautions against burglars and contagious diseases. Lydia, coming from a smaller town, and entering New York life through the portals of the Tillotson mansion, had mechanically accepted this point of view as inseparable from having a front pew in church and a parterre box at the opera. All the people who came to the house revolved in the same circle of prejudices. It was the kind of society in which, after dinner, the ladies compared the exorbitant charges of their children's teachers, and agreed that, even with the new duties on French clothes, it was cheaper in the end to get everything from Worth; while the husbands, over their cigars, lamented municipal corruption, and decided that the men to start a reform were those who had no private interests at stake.

To Lydia this view of life had become a matter of course, just as lumbering about in her mother-in-law's landau had come to seem the only possible means of locomotion, and listening every Sunday to a fashionable Presbyterian divine the inevitable atonement for having thought oneself bored on the other six days of the week. Before she met Gannett her life had seemed merely dull; his coming made it appear like one of those dismal Cruikshank prints in which the people are all ugly and all engaged in occupations that are either vulgar or stupid.

It was natural that Tillotson should be the chief sufferer from this read-justment of focus. Gannett's nearness had made her husband ridiculous, and a part of the ridicule had been reflected on herself. Her tolerance laid her open to a suspicion of obtuseness from which she must, at all costs, clear her-self in Gannett's eyes.

She did not understand this until afterwards. At the time she fancied that she had merely reached the limits of endurance. In so large a charter of liberties as the mere act of leaving Tillotson seemed to confer, the small question of divorce or no divorce did not count. It was when she saw that she had left her husband only to be with Gannett that she perceived the sig-nificance of anything affecting their relations. Her husband, in casting her off, had virtually flung her at Gannett: it was thus that the world viewed it. The measure of alacrity with which Gannett would receive her would be the subject of curious speculation over afternoon tea tables and in club corners. She knew what would be said—she had heard it so often of others! The rec-ollection bathed her in misery. The men would probably back Gannett to "do the decent thing"; but the ladies' eyebrows would emphasize the worth-lessness of such enforced fidelity; and after all, they would be right. She had put herself in a position where Gannett "owed" her something; where, as a gentleman, he was bound to "stand the damage." The idea of accepting such compensation had never crossed her mind; the so-called rehabilitation of such a marriage had always seemed to her the only real disgrace. What she dreaded was the necessity of having to explain herself; of having to combat his arguments; of calculating, in spite of herself, the exact measure of insis-tence with which he pressed them. She knew not whether she most shrank from his insisting too much or too little. In such a case the nicest sense of proportion might be at fault; and how easily to fall into the error of taking her resistance for a test of his sincerity! Whichever way she turned, an iron-ical implication confronted her: she had the exasperated sense of having walked into the trap of some stupid practical joke.

Beneath all these preoccupations lurked the dread of what he was think-ing. Sooner or later, of course, he would have to speak; but that, in the mean-time, he should think, even for a moment, that there was any use in speaking, seemed to her simply unendurable. Her sensitiveness on this point was aggravated by another fear, as yet barely on the level of consciousness; the fear of unwillingly involving Gannett in the trammels of her dependence. To look upon him as the instrument of her liberation; to resist in herself the least tendency to a wifely taking possession of his future; had seemed to Lydia the one way of maintaining the dignity of their relation. Her view had not changed, but she was aware of a growing inability to keep her thoughts fixed on the essential point—the point of parting with Gannett. It was easy to face as long as she kept it sufficiently far off: but what was this act of mental postponement but a gradual encroachment on his future? What was needful was the courage to recognize the moment when, by some word or look, their voluntary fellowship should be transformed into a bondage the more wearing that it was based on none of those common obligations which make the most imperfect marriage in some sort a center of gravity.

When the porter, at the next station, threw the door open, Lydia drew back, making way for the hoped-for intruder; but none came, and the train took up its leisurely progress through the spring wheat fields and budding copses. She now began to hope that Gannett would speak before the next station. She watched him furtively, half-disposed to return to the seat opposite his, but there was an artificiality about his absorption that restrained her. She had never before seen him read with so conspicuous an air of warding off interruption. What could he be thinking of? Why should he be afraid to speak? Or was it her answer that he dreaded?

The train paused for the passing of an express, and he put down his book and leaned out of the window. Presently he turned to her with a smile.

"There's a jolly old villa out here," he said.

His easy tone relieved her, and she smiled back at him as she crossed over to his corner.

Beyond the embankment, through the opening in a mossy wall, she caught sight of the villa, with its broken balustrades, its stagnant fountains, and the stone satyr closing the perspective of a dusky grass walk.

"How should you like to live there?" he asked as the train moved on.

"There?"

"In some such place, I mean. One might do worse, don't you think so? There must be at least two centuries of solitude under those yew trees. Shouldn't you like it?"

"I—I don't know," she faltered. She knew now that he meant to speak.

He lit another cigarette. "We shall have to live somewhere, you know," he said as he bent above the match.

Lydia tried to speak carelessly. *"Je n'en vois pas la nécessité!* Why not live everywhere, as we have been doing?"

"But we can't travel forever, can we?"

"Oh, forever's a long word," she objected, picking up the review he had thrown aside.

"For the rest of our lives then," he said, moving nearer.

She made a slight gesture which caused his hand to slip from hers.

"Why should we make plans? I thought you agreed with me that it's pleasanter to drift."

He looked at her hesitatingly. "It's been pleasant, certainly; but I suppose I shall have to get at my work again some day. You know I haven't written a line since—all this time," he hastily amended.

She flamed with sympathy and self-reproach. "Oh, if you mean *that*—if you want to write—of course we must settle down. How stupid of me not to have thought of it sooner! Where shall we go? Where do you think you could work best? We oughtn't to lose any more time."

He hesitated again. "I had thought of a villa in these parts. It's quiet; we shouldn't be bothered. Should you like it?"

"Of course I should like it." She paused and looked away. "But I thought—I remember your telling me once that your best work had been done in a crowd—in big cities. Why should you shut yourself up in a desert?"

Gannett, for a moment, made no reply. At length he said, avoiding her eye as carefully as she avoided his: "It might be different now; I can't tell, of course, till I try. A writer ought not to be dependent on his *milieu*; it's a mistake to humor oneself in that way; and I thought that just at first you might prefer to be—"

She faced him. "To be what?"

"Well—quiet. I mean—"

"What do you mean by 'at first'?" she interrupted.

He paused again. "I mean after we are married."

She thrust up her chin and turned toward the window. "Thank you!" she tossed back at him.

"Lydia!" he exclaimed blankly; and she felt it in every fiber of her averted person that he had made the inconceivable, the unpardonable mistake of anticipating her acquiescence.

The train rattled on and he groped for a third cigarette. Lydia remained silent.

"I haven't offended you?" he ventured at length, in the tone of a man who feels his way.

She shook her head with a sigh. "I thought you understood," she moaned. Their eyes met and she moved back to his side.

"Do you want to know how not to offend me? By taking it for granted, once for all, that you've said your say on the odious question and that I've said mine, and that we stand just where we did this morning before that—that hateful paper came to spoil everything between us!"

"To spoil everything between us? What on earth do you mean? Aren't you glad to be free?"

"I was free before."

"Not to marry me," he suggested.

"But I don't *want* to marry you!" she cried.

She saw that he turned pale. "I'm obtuse, I suppose," he said slowly. "I confess I don't see what you're driving at. Are you tired of the whole business? Or was I simply a—an excuse for getting away? Perhaps you didn't care to travel alone? Was that it? And now you want to chuck me?" His voice had grown harsh. "You owe me a straight answer, you know; don't be tenderhearted!"

Her eyes swam as she leaned to him. "Don't you see it's because I care—because I care so much? Oh, Ralph! Can't you see how it would humiliate me? Try to feel it as a woman would! Don't you see the misery of being made your wife in this way? If I'd known you as a girl—that would have been a real marriage! But now—this vulgar fraud upon society—and upon a society we despised and laughed at—this sneaking back into a position that we've voluntarily forfeited: don't you see what a cheap compromise it is? We neither of us believe in the abstract 'sacredness' of marriage; we both know that no ceremony is needed to consecrate our love for each other; what object can we have in marrying, except the secret fear of each that the other might escape, or the secret longing to work our way back gradually—oh, very gradually—into the esteem of the people whose conventional morality we have always ridiculed and hated? And the very fact that, after a decent interval, these same people would come and dine with us—the women who talk about the indissolubility of marriage, and who would let me die in a gutter today because I am 'leading a life of sin'—doesn't that disgust you more than their turning their backs on us now? I can stand being cut by them, but I couldn't stand their coming to call and asking what I meant to do about visiting that unfortunate Mrs. So-and-so!"

She paused, and Gannett maintained a perplexed silence.

"You judge things too theoretically," he said at length, slowly. "Life is made up of compromises."

"The life we ran away from—yes! If we had been willing to accept them"—she flushed—"we might have gone on meeting each other at Mrs. Tillotson's dinners."

He smiled slightly. "I didn't know that we ran away to found a new system of ethics. I supposed it was because we loved each other."

"Life is complex, of course; isn't it the very recognition of that fact that separates us from the people who see it *tout d'une pièce*? If *they* are right—if marriage is sacred in itself and the individual must always be sacrificed to the family—then there can be no real marriage between us, since our—our being together is a protest against the sacrifice of the individual to the family." She interrupted herself with a laugh. "You'll say now that I'm giving you a lecture on sociology! Of course one acts as one can—as one must, perhaps—pulled by all sorts of invisible threads; but at least one needn't pretend, for social advantages, to subscribe to a creed that ignores the complexity of human motives—that classifies people by arbitrary signs, and puts it in everybody's reach to be on Mrs. Tillotson's visiting list. It may be necessary that the world should be ruled by conventions—but if we believed in them, why did we break through them? And if we don't believe in them, is it honest to take advantage of the protection they afford?"

Gannett hesitated. "One may believe in them or not; but as long as they do rule the world it is only by taking advantage of their protection that one can find a *modus vivendi*."

"Do outlaws need a *modus vivendi*?"

He looked at her hopelessly. Nothing is more perplexing to man than the mental process of a woman who reasons her emotions.

She thought she had scored a point and followed it up passionately. "You do understand, don't you? You see how the very thought of the thing humiliates me! We are together today because we choose to be—don't let us look any farther than that!" She caught his hands. "*Promise* me you'll never speak of it again; promise me you'll never *think* of it even," she implored, with a tearful prodigality of italics.

Through what followed—his protests, his arguments, his final unconvinced submission to her wishes—she had a sense of his but half-discerning all that, for her, had made the moment so tumultuous. They had reached the memorable point in every heart history when, for the first time, the man seems obtuse and the woman irrational. It was the abundance of his intentions that consoled her, on reflection, for what they lacked in quality. After all, it would have been worse, incalculably worse, to have detected any over-readiness to understand her.

II

When the train at nightfall brought them to their journey's end at the edge of one of the lakes, Lydia was glad that they were not, as usual, to pass from one solitude to another. Their wanderings during the year had indeed been like the flight of the outlaws: through Sicily, Dalmatia, Transylvania and Southern Italy they had persisted in their tacit avoidance of their kind. Isolation, at first, had deepened the flavor of their happiness, as night intensifies the scent of certain flowers; but in the new phase on which they were entering, Lydia's chief wish was that they should be less abnormally exposed to the action of each other's thoughts.

She shrank, nevertheless, as the brightly-looming bulk of the fashionable Anglo-American hotel on the water's brink began to radiate toward their advancing boat its vivid suggestion of social order, visitors' lists, Church services, and the bland inquisition of the *table d'hôte*. The mere fact that in a moment or two she must take her place on the hotel register as Mrs. Gannett seemed to weaken the springs of her resistance.

They had meant to stay for a night only, on their way to a lofty village among the glaciers of Monte Rosa; but after the first plunge into publicity, when they entered the dining room, Lydia felt the relief of being lost in a crowd, of ceasing for a moment to be the center of Gannett's scrutiny; and in his face she caught the reflection of her feeling. After dinner, when she went upstairs, he strolled into the smoking room, and an hour or two later, sitting in the darkness of her window, she heard his voice below and saw him walking up and down the terrace with a companion cigar at his side. When he came he told her he had been talking to the hotel chaplain—a very good sort of fellow.

"Queer little microcosms, these hotels! Most of these people live here all summer and then migrate to Italy or the Riviera. The English are the only people who can lead that kind of life with dignity—those soft-voiced old ladies in Shetland shawls somehow carry the British Empire under their caps. *Civis Romanus sum*. It's a curious study—there might be some good things to work up here."

He stood before her with the vivid preoccupied stare of the novelist on the trail of a "subject." With a relief that was half painful she noticed that, for the first time since they had been together, he was hardly aware of her presence.

"Do you think you could write here?"

"Here? I don't know." His stare dropped. "After being out of things so long one's first impressions are bound to be tremendously vivid, you know. I see a dozen threads already that one might follow—"

He broke off with a touch of embarrassment.

"Then follow them. We'll stay," she said with sudden decision.

"Stay here?" He glanced at her in surprise, and then, walking to the window, looked out upon the dusky slumber of the garden.

"Why not?" she said at length, in a tone of veiled irritation.

"The place is full of old cats in caps who gossip with the chaplain. Shall you like—I mean, it would be different if—"

She flamed up.

"Do you suppose I care? It's none of their business."

"Of course not; but you won't get them to think so."

"They may think what they please."

He looked at her doubtfully.

"It's for you to decide."

"We'll stay," she repeated.

Gannett, before they met, had made himself known as a successful writer of short stories and of a novel which had achieved the distinction of being widely discussed. The reviewers called him "promising," and Lydia now accused herself of having too long interfered with the fulfillment of his promise. There was a special irony in the fact, since his passionate assurances that only the stimulus of her companionship could bring out his latent faculty had almost given the dignity of a "vocation" to her course: there had been moments when she had felt unable to assume, before posterity, the responsibility of thwarting his career. And, after all, he had not written a line since they had been together: his first desire to write had come from renewed contact with the world! Was it all a mistake then? Must the most intelligent choice work more disastrously than the blundering combinations of chance? Or was there a still more humiliating answer to her perplexities? His sudden impulse of activity so exactly coincided with her own wish to withdraw, for a time, from the range of his observation, that she wondered if he too were not seeking sanctuary from intolerable problems.

"You must begin tomorrow!" she cried, hiding a tremor under the laugh with which she added, "I wonder if there's any ink in the inkstand?"

Whatever else they had at the Hotel Bellosguardo, they had, as Miss Pinsent said, "a certain tone." It was to Lady Susan Condit that they owed this ines-timable benefit; an advantage ranking in Miss Pinsent's opinion above even the lawn tennis courts and the resident chaplain. It was the fact of Lady Susan's annual visit that made the hotel what it was. Miss Pinsent was certainly the last to underrate such a privilege: "It's so important, my dear, forming as we do a little family, that there should be someone to give *the tone*; and no one could do it better than Lady Susan—an earl's daughter and a person of such determina-tion. Dear Mrs. Ainger now—who really *ought*, you know, when Lady Susan's away—absolutely refuses to assert herself." Miss Pinsent sniffed derisively. "A bishop's niece!—my dear, I saw her once actually give in to some South Americans—and before us all. She gave up her seat at table to oblige them—such a lack of dignity! Lady Susan spoke to her very plainly about it afterwards."

Miss Pinsent glanced across the lake and adjusted her auburn front.

"But of course I don't deny that the stand Lady Susan takes is not always easy to live up to—for the rest of us, I mean. Monsieur Grossart, our good proprietor, finds it trying at times, I know—he has said as much, privately, to Mrs. Ainger and me. After all, the poor man is not to blame for wanting to fill his hotel, is he? And Lady Susan is so difficult—so very difficult—about new people. One might almost say that she disapproves of them beforehand, on principle. And yet she's had warnings—she very nearly made a dreadful mistake once with the Duchess of Levens, who dyed her hair and—well, swore and smoked. One would have thought that might have been a lesson to Lady Susan." Miss Pinsent resumed her knitting with a sigh. "There are exceptions, of course. She took at once to you and Mr. Gannett—it was quite remarkable, really. Oh, I don't mean that either—of course not! It was per-fectly natural—we *all* thought you so charming and interesting from the first day—we knew at once that Mr. Gannett was intellectual, by the magazines you took in; but you know what I mean. Lady Susan is so very—well, I won't say prejudiced, as Mrs. Ainger does—but so prepared *not* to like new people, that her taking to you in that way was a surprise to us all, I confess."

Miss Pinsent sent a significant glance down the long laurustinus alley from the other end of which two people—a lady and a gentleman—were strolling toward them through the smiling neglect of the garden.

"In this case, of course, it's very different; that I'm willing to admit. Their looks are against them; but, as Mrs. Ainger says, one can't exactly tell them so."

"She's very handsome," Lydia ventured, with her eyes on the lady, who showed, under the dome of a vivid sunshade, the hourglass figure and superlative coloring of a Christmas chromo.

"That's the worst of it. She's too handsome."

"Well, after all, she can't help that."

"Other people manage to," said Miss Pinsent skeptically.

"But isn't it rather unfair of Lady Susan—considering that nothing is known about them?"

"But, my dear, that's the very thing that's against them. It's infinitely worse than any actual knowledge."

Lydia mentally agreed that, in the case of Mrs. Linton, it possibly might be.

"I wonder why they came here?" she mused.

"That's against them too. It's always a bad sign when loud people come to a quiet place. And they've brought van loads of boxes—her maid told Mrs. Ainger's that they meant to stop indefinitely."

"And Lady Susan actually turned her back on her in the salon?"

"My dear, she said it was for our sakes: that makes it so unanswerable! But poor Grossart *is* in a way! The Lintons have taken his most expensive suite, you know—the yellow damask drawing room above the portico—and they have champagne with every meal!"

They were silent as Mr. and Mrs. Linton sauntered by; the lady with tempestuous brows and challenging chin; the gentleman, a blond stripling, trailing after her, head downward, like a reluctant child dragged by his nurse.

"What does your husband think of them, my dear?" Miss Pinsent whispered as they passed out of earshot.

Lydia stooped to pick a violet in the border.

"He hasn't told me."

"Of your speaking to them, I mean. Would he approve of that? I know how very particular nice Americans are. I think your action might make a difference; it would certainly carry weight with Lady Susan."

"Dear Miss Pinsent, you flatter me!"

Lydia rose and gathered up her book and sunshade.

"Well, if you're asked for an opinion—if Lady Susan asks you for one—I think you ought to be prepared," Miss Pinsent admonished her as she moved away.

III

Lady Susan held her own. She ignored the Lintons, and her little family, as Miss Pinsent phrased it, followed suit. Even Mrs. Ainger agreed that it was obligatory. If Lady Susan owed it to the others not to speak to the Lintons, the others clearly owed it to Lady Susan to back her up. It was generally found expedient, at the Hotel Bellosguardo, to adopt this form of reasoning.

Whatever effect this combined action may have had upon the Lintons, it did not at least have that of driving them away. Monsieur Grossart, after a few days of suspense, had the satisfaction of seeing them settle down in his yellow damask *premier* with what looked like a permanent installation of palm trees and silk cushions, and a gratifying continuance in the consumption of champagne. Mrs. Linton trailed her Doucet draperies up and down the garden with the same challenging air, while her husband, smoking innumerable cigarettes, dragged himself dejectedly in her wake; but neither of them, after the first encounter with Lady Susan, made any attempt to extend their acquaintance. They simply ignored their ignorers. As Miss Pinsent resentfully observed, they behaved exactly as though the hotel were empty.

It was therefore a matter of surprise, as well as of displeasure, to Lydia, to find, on glancing up one day from her seat in the garden, that the shadow which had fallen across her book was that of the enigmatic Mrs. Linton.

"I want to speak to you," that lady said, in a rich hard voice that seemed the audible expression of her gown and her complexion.

Lydia started. She certainly did not want to speak to Mrs. Linton.

"Shall I sit down here?" the latter continued, fixing her intensely-shaded eyes on Lydia's face, "or are you afraid of being seen with me?"

"Afraid?" Lydia colored. "Sit down, please. What is that you wish to say?"

Mrs. Linton, with a smile, drew up a garden chair and crossed one open-work ankle above the other.

"I want you to tell me what my husband said to your husband last night."

Lydia turned pale.

"My husband—to yours?" she faltered, staring at the other.

"Didn't you know they were closeted together for hours in the smoking room after you went upstairs? My man didn't get to bed until nearly two o'clock and when he did I couldn't get a word out of him. When he wants to be aggravating I'll back him against anybody living!" Her teeth and eyes flashed persuasively upon Lydia. "But you'll tell me what they were talking about, won't you? I know I can trust you—you look so awfully kind. And it's for his own good. He's such a precious donkey and I'm so afraid he's got into some beastly scrape or other. If he'd only trust his own old woman! But they're always writing to him and setting him against me. And I've got nobody to turn to." She laid her hand on Lydia's with a rattle of bracelets. "You'll help me, won't you?"

Lydia drew back from the smiling fierceness of her brows.

"I'm sorry—but I don't think I understand. My husband has said nothing to me of—of yours."

The great black crescents over Mrs. Linton's eyes met angrily.

"I say—is that true?" she demanded.

Lydia rose from her seat.

"Oh, look here, I didn't mean that, you know—you mustn't take one up so! Can't you see how rattled I am?"

Lydia saw that, in fact, her beautiful mouth was quivering beneath softened eyes.

"I'm beside myself!" the splendid creature wailed, dropping into her seat.

"I'm so sorry," Lydia repeated, forcing herself to speak kindly; "but how can I help you?"

Mrs. Linton raised her head sharply.

"By finding out—there's a darling!"

"Finding what out?"

"What Trevenna told him."

"Trevenna—?" Lydia echoed in bewilderment.

Mrs. Linton clapped her hand to her mouth.

"Oh, Lord—there, it's out! What a fool I am! But I supposed of course you knew; I supposed everybody knew." She dried her eyes and bridled.

"Didn't you know that he's Lord Trevenna? I'm Mrs. Cope."

Lydia recognized the names. They had figured in a flamboyant elopement which had thrilled fashionable London some six months earlier.

"Now you see how it is—you understand, don't you?" Mrs. Cope continued on a note of appeal. "I knew you would—that's the reason I came to you. I suppose *he* felt the same thing about your husband; he's not spoken to another soul in the place." Her face grew anxious again. "He's awfully sensitive, generally—he feels our position, he says—as if it were *my* place to feel that! But when he does get talking there's no knowing what he'll say. I know he's brooding over something lately, and I *must* find out what it is—it's to his interest that I should. I always tell him that I think only of his interest; if he'd only trust me! But he's been so odd lately—I can't think what he's plotting. You will help me, dear?"

Lydia, who had remained standing, looked away uncomfortably.

"If you mean by finding out what Lord Trevenna has told my husband, I'm afraid it's impossible."

"Why impossible?"

"Because I infer that it was told in confidence."

Mrs. Cope stared incredulously.

"Well, what of that? Your husband looks such a dear—anyone can see he's awfully gone on you. What's to prevent your getting it out of him?"

Lydia flushed.

"I'm not a spy!" she exclaimed.

"A spy—a spy? How dare you!" Mrs. Cope flamed out. "Oh, I don't mean that either! Don't be angry with me—I'm so miserable." She essayed a softer note. "Do you call that spying—for one woman to help out another? I do need help so dreadfully! I'm at my wits' end with Trevenna, I am indeed. He's such a boy—a mere baby, you know; he's only two-and-twenty." She dropped her orbed lids. "He's younger than me—only fancy, a few months younger. I tell him he ought to listen to me as if I was his mother; oughtn't he now? But he won't, he won't! All his people are at him, you see—oh, I know *their* little game! Trying to get him away from me before I can get my divorce—that's what they're up to. At first he wouldn't listen to them; he used to toss their letters over to me to read; but now he reads them himself, and answers 'em too, I fancy; he's always shut up in his room, writing. If I only knew what his plan is I could stop him fast enough—he's such a simpleton. But he's dreadfully deep too—at times I can't make him out. But I know he's told your husband everything—I knew that last night the minute I laid eyes on him. And I *must* find out—you must help me—I've got no one else to turn to!"

She caught Lydia's fingers in a stormy pressure.

"Say you'll help me—you and your husband."

Lydia tried to free herself.

"What you ask is impossible; you must see that it is. No one could interfere in—in the way you ask."

Mrs. Cope's clutch tightened.

"You won't, then? You won't?"

"Certainly not. Let me go, please."

Mrs. Cope released her with a laugh.

"Oh, go by all means—pray don't let me detain you! Shall you go and tell Lady Susan Condit that there's a pair of us—or shall I save you the trouble of enlightening her?"

Lydia stood still in the middle of the path, seeing her antagonist through a mist of terror. Mrs. Cope was still laughing.

"Oh, I'm not spiteful by nature, my dear; but you're a little more than flesh and blood can stand! It's impossible, is it? Let you go, indeed! You're too good to be mixed up in my affairs, are you? Why, you little fool, the first day I laid eyes on you I saw that you and I were both in the same box—that's the reason I spoke to you."

She stepped nearer, her smile dilating on Lydia like a lamp through a fog.

"You can take your choice, you know; I always play fair. If you'll tell I'll promise not to. Now then, which is it to be?"

Lydia, involuntarily, had begun to move away from the pelting storm of words; but at this she turned and sat down again.

"You may go," she said simply. "I shall stay here."

IV

She stayed there for a long time, in the hypnotized contemplation, not of Mrs. Cope's present, but of her own past. Gannett, early that morning, had gone off on a long walk—he had fallen into the habit of taking these mountain tramps with various fellow lodgers; but even had he been within reach she could not have gone to him just then. She had to deal with herself first. She was surprised to find how, in the last months, she had lost the habit of introspection. Since their coming to the Hotel Bellosguardo she and Gannett had tacitly avoided themselves and each other.

She was aroused by the whistle of the three o'clock steamboat as it neared the landing just beyond the hotel gates. Three o'clock! Then Gannett would soon be back—he had told her to expect him before four. She rose hurriedly, her face averted from the inquisitorial façade of the hotel. She could not see him just yet; she could not go indoors. She slipped through one of the overgrown garden alleys and climbed a steep path to the hills.

It was dark when she opened their sitting-room door. Gannett was sitting on the window ledge smoking a cigarette. Cigarettes were now his chief resource: he had not written a line during the two months they had spent at the Hotel Bellosguardo. In that respect, it had turned out not to be the right *milieu* after all.

He started up at Lydia's entrance.

"Where have you been? I was getting anxious."

She sat down in a chair near the door.

"Up the mountain," she said wearily.

"Alone?"

"Yes."

Gannett threw away his cigarette: the sound of her voice made him want to see her face.

"Shall we have a little light?" he suggested.

She made no answer and he lifted the globe from the lamp and put a match to the wick. Then he looked at her.

"Anything wrong? You look done up."

She sat glancing vaguely about the little sitting room, dimly lit by the pallid-globed lamp, which left in twilight the outlines of the furniture, of his writing table heaped with books and papers, of the tea roses and jasmine drooping on the mantelpiece. How like home it had all grown—how like home!

"Lydia, what is wrong?" he repeated.

She moved away from him, feeling for her hatpins and turning to lay her hat and sunshade on the table.

Suddenly she said: "That woman has been talking to me."

Gannett stared.

"That woman? What woman?"

"Mrs. Linton—Mrs. Cope."

He gave a start of annoyance, still, as she perceived, not grasping the full import of her words.

"The deuce! She told you—?"

"She told me everything."

Gannett looked at her anxiously.

"What impudence! I'm so sorry that you should have been exposed to this, dear."

"Exposed!" Lydia laughed.

Gannett's brow clouded and they looked away from each other.

"Do you know *why* she told me? She had the best of reasons. The first time she laid eyes on me she saw that we were both in the same box."

"Lydia!"

"So it was natural, of course, that she should turn to me in a difficulty."

"What difficulty?"

"It seems she has reason to think that Lord Trevenna's people are trying to get him away from her before she gets her divorce—"

"Well?"

"And she fancied he had been consulting with you last night as to—as to the best way of escaping from her."

Gannett stood up with an angry forehead.

"Well—what concern of yours was all this dirty business? Why should she go to you?"

"Don't you see? It's so simple. I was to wheedle his secret out of you."

"To oblige that woman?"

"Yes; or, if I was unwilling to oblige her, then to protect myself."

"To protect yourself? Against whom?"

"Against her telling everyone in the hotel that she and I are in the same box."

"She threatened that?"

"She left me the choice of telling it myself or of doing it for me."

"The beast!"

There was a long silence. Lydia had seated herself on the sofa, beyond the radius of the lamp, and he leaned against the window. His next question surprised her.

"When did this happen? At what time, I mean?"

She looked at him vaguely.

"I don't know—after luncheon, I think. Yes, I remember; it must have been about three o'clock."

He stepped into the middle of the room and as he approached the light she saw that his brow had cleared.

"Why do you ask?" she said.

"Because when I came in, at about half-past three, the mail was just being distributed, and Mrs. Cope was waiting as usual to pounce on her letters; you know she was always watching for the postman. She was standing so close to me that I couldn't help seeing a big official-looking envelope that was handed to her. She tore it open, gave one look at the inside, and rushed off upstairs like a whirlwind, with the director shouting after her that she had left all her other letters behind. I don't believe she ever thought of you again after that paper was put into her hand."

"Why?"

"Because she was too busy. I was sitting in the window, watching for you, when the five o'clock boat left, and who should go on board, bag and baggage, valet and maid, dressing bags and poodle, but Mrs. Cope and Trevenna. Just an hour and a half to pack up in! And you should have seen her when they started. She was radiant—shaking hands with everybody—waving her handkerchief from the deck—distributing bows and smiles like an empress. If ever a woman got what she wanted just in the nick of time that woman did. She'll be Lady Trevenna within a week, I'll wager."

"You think she has her divorce?"

"I'm sure of it. And she must have got it just after her talk with you."

Lydia was silent.

At length she said, with a kind of reluctance, "She was horribly angry when she left me. It wouldn't have taken long to tell Lady Susan Condit."

"Lady Susan Condit has not been told."

"How do you know?"

"Because when I went downstairs half an hour ago I met Lady Susan on the way—"

He stopped, half smiling.

"Well?"

"And she stopped to ask if I thought you would act as patroness to a charity concert she is getting up."

In spite of themselves they both broke into a laugh. Lydia's ended in sobs and she sank down with her face hidden. Gannett bent over her, seeking her hands.

"That vile woman—I ought to have warned you to keep away from her; I can't forgive myself! But he spoke to me in confidence; and I never dreamed—well, it's all over now."

Lydia lifted her head.

"Not for me. It's only just beginning."

"What do you mean?"

She put him gently aside and moved in her turn to the window. Then she went on, with her face turned toward the shimmering blackness of the lake, "You see of course that it might happen again at any moment."

"What?"

"This—this risk of being found out. And we could hardly count again on such a lucky combination of chances, could we?"

He sat down with a groan.

Still keeping her face toward the darkness, she said, "I want you to go and tell Lady Susan—and the others."

Gannett, who had moved towards her, paused a few feet off.

"Why do you wish me to do this?" he said at length, with less surprise in his voice than she had been prepared for.

"Because I've behaved basely, abominably, since we came here: letting these people believe we were married—lying with every breath I drew—"

"Yes, I've felt that too," Gannett exclaimed with sudden energy.

The words shook her like a tempest: all her thoughts seemed to fall about her in ruins.

"You—you've felt so?"

"Of course I have." He spoke with low-voiced vehemence. "Do you suppose I like playing the sneak any better than you do? It's damnable."

He had dropped on the arm of a chair, and they stared at each other like blind people who suddenly see.

"But you have liked it here," she faltered.

"Oh, I've liked it—I've liked it." He moved impatiently. "Haven't you?"

"Yes," she burst out; "that's the worst of it—that's what I can't bear. I fancied it was for your sake that I insisted on staying—because you thought you could write here; and perhaps just at first that really was the reason. But afterwards I wanted to stay here myself—I loved it." She broke into a laugh. "Oh, do you see the full derision of it? These people—the very prototypes of the bores you took me away from, with the same fenced-in view of life, the same keep-off-the-grass morality, the same little cautious virtues and the same little frightened vices—well, I've clung to them, I've delighted in them, I've done my best to please them. I've toadied Lady Susan, I've gossiped with Miss Pinsent, I've pretended to be shocked with Mrs. Ainger. Respectability! It was the one thing in life that I was sure I didn't care about, and it's grown so precious to me that I've stolen it because I couldn't get it in any other way."

She moved across the room and returned to his side with another laugh.

"I who used to fancy myself unconventional! I must have been born with a cardcase in my hand. You should have seen me with that poor woman in the garden. She came to me for help, poor creature, because she fancied that, having 'sinned,' as they call it, I might feel some pity for others who had been tempted in the same way. Not I! She didn't know me. Lady Susan would have been kinder, because Lady Susan wouldn't have been afraid. I hated the woman—my one thought was not to be seen with her—I could have killed her for guessing my secret. The one thing that mattered to me at that moment was my standing with Lady Susan!"

Gannett did not speak.

"And you—you've felt it too!" she broke out accusingly. "You've enjoyed being with these people as much as I have; you've let the chaplain talk to you by the hour about The Reign of Law and Professor Drummond. When they asked you to hand the plate in church I was watching you—*you wanted to accept.*"

She stepped close, laying her hand on his arm.

"Do you know, I begin to see what marriage is for. It's to keep people away from each other. Sometimes I think that two people who love each other can be saved from madness only by the things that come between them—children, duties, visits, bores, relations—the things that protect married people from each other. We've been too close together—that has been our sin. We've seen the nakedness of each other's souls."

She sank again on the sofa, hiding her face in her hands.

Gannett stood above her perplexedly: he felt as though she were being swept away by some implacable current while he stood helpless on its bank.

At length he said, "Lydia, don't think me a brute—but don't you see yourself that it won't do?"

"Yes, I see it won't do," she said without raising her head.

His face cleared.

"Then we'll go tomorrow."

"Go—where?"

"To Paris; to be married."

For a long time she made no answer; then she asked slowly, "Would they have us here if we were married?"

"Have us here?"

"I mean Lady Susan—and the others."

"Have us here? Of course they would."

"Not if they knew—at least, not unless they could pretend not to know."

He made an impatient gesture.

"We shouldn't come back here, of course; and other people needn't know—no one need know."

She sighed. "Then it's only another form of deception and a meaner one. Don't you see that?"

"I see that we're not accountable to any Lady Susans on earth!"

"Then why are you ashamed of what we are doing here?"

"Because I am sick of pretending that you're my wife when you're not— when you won't be."

She looked at him sadly.

"If I were your wife you'd have to go on pretending. You'd have to pretend that I'd never been—anything else. And our friends would have to pretend that they believed what you pretended."

Gannett pulled off the sofa tassel and flung it away.

"You're impossible," he groaned.

"It's not I—it's our being together that's impossible. I only want you to see that marriage won't help it."

"What will help it then?"

She raised her head.

"My leaving you."

"You're leaving me?" He sat motionless, staring at the tassel which lay at the other end of the room. At length some impulse of retaliation for the pain she was inflicting made him say deliberately:

"And where would you go if you left me?"

"Oh!" she cried.

He was at her side in an instant.

"Lydia—Lydia—you know I didn't mean it; I couldn't mean it! But you've driven me out of my senses; I don't know what I'm saying. Can't you get out of this labyrinth of self-torture? It's destroying us both."

"That's why I must leave you."

"How easily you say it!" He drew her hands down and made her face him. "You're very scrupulous about yourself—and others. But have you thought of me? You have no right to leave me unless you've ceased to care—"

"It's because I care—"

"Then I have a right to be heard. If you love me you can't leave me."

Her eyes defied him.

"Why not?"

He dropped her hands and rose from her side.

"Can you?" he said sadly.

The hour was late and the lamp flickered and sank. She stood up with a shiver and turned toward the door of her room.

V

At daylight a sound in Lydia's room woke Gannett from a troubled sleep. He sat up and listened. She was moving about softly, as though fearful of disturbing him. He heard her push back one of the creaking shutters; then there was a moment's silence, which seemed to indicate that she was waiting to see if the noise had roused him.

Presently she began to move again. She had spent a sleepless night, probably, and was dressing to go down to the garden for a breath of air. Gannett rose also; but some undefinable instinct made his movements as cautious as hers. He stole to his window and looked out through the slats of the shutter.

It had rained in the night and the dawn was gray and lifeless. The cloud-muffled hills across the lake were reflected in its surface as in a tarnished mirror. In the garden, the birds were beginning to shake the drops from the motionless laurustinus boughs.

An immense pity for Lydia filled Gannett's soul. Her seeming intellectual independence had blinded him for a time to the feminine cast of her mind. He had never thought of her as a woman who wept and clung: there was a lucidity in her intuitions that made them appear to be the result of reasoning. Now he saw the cruelty he had committed in detaching her from the normal conditions of life; he felt, too, the insight with which she had hit upon the real cause of their suffering. Their life was "impossible," as she had said—and its worst penalty was that it had made any other life impossible for them. Even had his love lessened, he was bound to her now by a hundred ties of pity and self-reproach; and she, poor child, must turn back to him as Latude returned to his cell.

A new sound startled him: it was the stealthy closing of Lydia's door. He crept to his own and heard her footsteps passing down the corridor. Then he went back to the window and looked out.

A minute or two later he saw her go down the steps of the porch and enter the garden. From his post of observation her face was invisible, but something about her appearance struck him. She wore a long traveling cloak and under its folds he detected the outline of a bag or bundle. He drew a deep breath and stood watching her.

She walked quickly down the laurustinus alley toward the gate; there she paused a moment, glancing about the little shady square. The stone benches under the trees were empty, and she seemed to gather resolution from the solitude about her, for she crossed the square to the steamboat landing, and he saw her pause before the ticket office at the head of the wharf. Now she was buying her ticket. Gannett turned his head a moment to look at the clock: the boat was due in five minutes. He had time to jump into his clothes and overtake her—

He made no attempt to move; an obscure reluctance restrained him. If any thought emerged from the tumult of his sensations, it was that he must let her go if she wished it. He had spoken last night of his rights: what were they? At the last issue, he and she were two separate beings, not made one by the miracle of common forbearances, duties, abnegations, but bound together in a *noyade* of passion that left them resisting yet clinging as they went down.

After buying her ticket, Lydia had stood for a moment looking out across the lake; then he saw her seat herself on one of the benches near the landing. He and she, at that moment, were both listening for the same sound: the whistle of the boat as it rounded the nearest promontory. Gannett turned again to glance at the clock: the boat was due now.

Where would she go? What would her life be when she had left him? She had no near relations and few friends. There was money enough . . . but she asked so much of life, in ways so complex and immaterial. He thought of her as walking barefooted through a stony waste. No one would understand her—no one would pity her—and he, who did both, was powerless to come to her aid.

He saw that she had risen from the bench and walked toward the edge of the lake. She stood looking in the direction from which the steamboat was to come; then she turned to the ticket office, doubtless to ask the cause of the delay. After that she went back to the bench and sat down with bent head. What was she thinking of?

The whistle sounded; she started up, and Gannett involuntarily made a movement toward the door. But he turned back and continued to watch her. She stood motionless, her eyes on the trail of smoke that preceded the appearance of the boat. Then the little craft rounded the point, a dead white object on the leaden water: a minute later it was puffing and backing at the wharf.

The few passengers who were waiting—two or three peasants and a snuffy priest—were clustered near the ticket office. Lydia stood apart under the trees.

The boat lay alongside now; the gangplank was run out and the peasants went on board with their baskets of vegetables, followed by the priest. Still Lydia did not move. A bell began to ring querulously; there was a shriek of steam, and someone must have called to her that she would be late, for she started forward, as though in answer to a summons. She moved waveringly, and at the edge of the wharf she paused. Gannett saw a sailor beckon to her; the bell rang again and she stepped upon the gangplank.

Halfway down the short incline to the deck she stopped again; then she turned and ran back to the land. The gangplank was drawn in, the bell ceased to ring, and the boat backed out into the lake. Lydia, with slow steps, was walking toward the garden.

As she approached the hotel she looked up furtively and Gannett drew back into the room. He sat down beside a table; a Bradshaw [a railway timetable] lay at his elbow, and mechanically, without knowing what he did, he began looking out the trains to Paris.

Charlotte Mew

(1869–1928)

Virginia Woolf told Vita Sackville-West that Charlotte Mew was "the greatest living poetess." Other admirers included Siegfried Sassoon, Walter de la Mare, John Masefield, and Thomas Hardy, who considered her "far and away the best living woman poet." Yet when she died, a suicide in a nursing home, Mew and her poetry were well on their way to being forgotten. Her life was full of sorrow. Two siblings were confined to an asylum. Mew and her mother and sister Anna lived within the constraints of poverty after her father's death. A lesbian who dressed in men's clothes, Mew was in love with the writer May Sinclair, who gossiped about her maliciously to Rebecca West. Her poetry expresses the disillusionment, sexual longing, and loneliness of her life, yet the consolations of nature and the beauty of moments and places are there, too, giving her work a haunting complexity. Virago Press reissued her *Collected Poems and Prose* in 1981, and the novelist Penelope Fitzgerald wrote *Charlotte Mew and Her Friends* (1984).

The Changeling

Toll no bell for me, dear Father, dear Mother,
    Waste no sighs;
There are my sisters, there is my little brother
    Who plays in the place called Paradise,
Your children all, your children for ever;
    But I, so wild,
Your disgrace, with the queer brown face, was never,
    Never, I know, but half your child!

In the garden at play, all day, last summer,
　　　Far and away I heard
The sweet "tweet-tweet" of a strange new-comer,
　　　The dearest, clearest call of a bird.
It lived down there in the deep green hollow,
　　　My own old home, and the fairies say
The word of a bird is a thing to follow,
　　　So I was away a night and a day.

One evening, too, by the nursery fire,
　　　We snuggled close and sat round so still,
When suddenly as the wind blew higher,
　　　Something scratched on the window-sill.
A pinched brown face peered in—I shivered;
　　　No one listened or seemed to see;
The arms of it waved and the wings of it quivered,
　　　Whoo—I knew it had come for me;
　　　Some are as bad as bad can be!
All night long they danced in the rain,
Round and round in a dripping chain,
Threw their caps at the window-pane,
　　　Tried to make me scream and shout
　　　And fling the bedclothes all about:
I meant to stay in bed that night,
And if only you had left a light
　　　They would never have got me out.

　　　Sometimes I wouldn't speak, you see,
　　　Or answer when you spoke to me,
Because in the long, still dusks of Spring
You can hear the whole world whispering:
　　　The shy green grasses making love,
　　　The feathers grow on the dear, grey dove,
　　　The tiny heart of the redstart beat,
　　　The patter of the squirrel's feet,
The pebbles pushing in the silver streams,

The rushes talking in their dreams,
　　The swish-swish of the bat's black wings,
　　The wild-wood bluebell's sweet ting-tings,
　　　　Humming and hammering at your ear,
　　　　Everything there is to hear
In the heart of hidden things,
　　But not in the midst of the nursery riot,
　　That's why I wanted to be quiet,
　　　　Couldn't do my sums, or sing,
　　　　Or settle down to anything.
　　And when, for that, I was sent upstairs
　　I *did* kneel down to say my prayers;
But the King who sits on your high church steeple
Has nothing to do with us fairy people!

'Times I pleased you, dear Father, dear Mother,
　　Learned all my lessons and liked to play,
And dearly I loved the little pale brother
　　Whom some other bird must have called away.
Why did They bring me here to make me
　　Not quite bad and not quite good,
Why, unless They're wicked, do They want, in spite, to take me
　　Back to their wet, wild wood?

Now, every night I shall see the windows shining,
　　The gold lamp's glow, and the fire's red gleam,
While the best of us are twining twigs and the rest of us are whining
　　　　In the hollow by the stream.
Black and chill are Their nights on the wold;
　　And They live so long and They feel no pain:
I shall grow up, but never grow old,
I shall always, always be very cold,
　　　　I shall never come back again!

Rooms

I remember rooms that have had their part
In the steady slowing down of the heart.
The room in Paris, the room at Geneva,
The little damp room with the seaweed smell,
And that ceaseless maddening sound of the tide—
    Rooms where for good or for ill—things died.
But there is the room where we (two) lie dead,
Though every morning we seem to wake and might
             just as well seem to sleep again
As we shall somewhere in the other quieter,
        dustier bed
Out there in the sun—in the rain.

Fame

Sometimes in the over-heated house, but not for long,
    Smirking and speaking rather loud,
  I see myself among the crowd,
Where no one fits the singer to his song,
Or sifts the unpainted from the painted faces
Of the people who are always on my stair;
They were not with me when I walked in heavenly places;
    But could I spare
In the blind Earth's great silences and spaces,
  The din, the scuffle, the long stare
  If I went back and it was not there?
Back to the old known things that are the new,
The folded glory of the gorse, the sweet-briar air,
To the larks that cannot praise us, knowing nothing of
    what we do
  And the divine, wise trees that do not care,
Yet, to leave Fame, still with such eyes and that bright hair!
God! If I might! And before I go hence
    Take in her stead

To our tossed bed,
One little dream, no matter how small, how wild.
Just now, I think I found it in a field, under a fence—
A frail, dead, new-born lamb, ghostly and pitiful and
            white,
        A blot upon the night,
        The moon's dropped child!

Exspecto Resurrectionem

Oh! King who hast the key
        Of that dark room
The last which prisons us but held not Thee,
        Thou know'st its gloom.
    Dost Thou a little love this one
        Shut in to-night,
    Young and so piteously alone,
        Cold—out of sight?
    Thou know'st how hard and bare
The pillow of that new-made narrow bed.
        Then leave not there
        So dear a head!

Willa Cather

(1873–1947)

Born of Anglo-Irish parents in the Shenandoah Valley of Virginia, Willa Cather was transplanted at the age of ten to Nebraska, where she grew up riding the prairie and learning how to kill rattlesnakes in the company of new immigrants from Scandinavia, Germany, and Russia. While working her way through the University of Nebraska as a journalist, she discovered her love of music, a life-long passion that gives "A Wagner Matinée" its power. After earning her living as a journalist, editor, and teacher, she finally devoted herself to the full-time writing of fiction on the advice of her friend Sarah Orne Jewett (see page 127). *The Song of the Lark* (1915), *My Ántonia* (1918), *The Professor's House* (1925), *Death Comes for the Archbishop* (1927), and *Lucy Gayheart* (1935), some of her best-known titles, are now classics of American literature. Wallace Stevens remarked in a letter, "We have nothing better than she is." Though her America is often a place of loss and the waste of possibilities, her fiction, according to biographer Sharon O'Brien, is not pessimistic: "Against the forces of pettiness, materialism, and mortality, she places the human desire to make meaning through work, family, religion, art, domestic crafts, and—perhaps most important to Willa Cather—through story telling."

A Wagner Matinée

I received one morning a letter, written in pale ink on glassy, blue-lined note-paper, and bearing the postmark of a little Nebraska village. This communication, worn and rubbed, looking as if it had been carried for some days in a coat pocket that was none too clean, was from my uncle Howard, and informed me that his wife had been left a small legacy by a bachelor relative, and that it would be necessary for her to go to Boston to attend to the settling of the estate. He requested me to meet her at the station and render her whatever services might be necessary. On examining the date indicated as that of her arrival, I found it to be no later than tomorrow. He had characteristically delayed writing until, had I been away from home for a day, I must have missed my aunt altogether.

The name of my Aunt Georgiana opened before me a gulf of recollection so wide and deep that, as the letter dropped from my hand, I felt suddenly a stranger to all the present conditions of my existence, wholly ill at ease and out of place amid the familiar surroundings of my study. I became, in short, the gangling farmer-boy my aunt had known, scourged with chilblains and bashfulness, my hands cracked and sore from the corn husking. I sat again before her parlour organ, fumbling the scales with my stiff, red fingers, while she, beside me, made canvas mittens for the huskers.

The next morning, after preparing my landlady for a visitor, I set out for the station. When the train arrived I had some difficulty finding my aunt. She was the last of the passengers to alight, and it was not until I got her into the carriage that she seemed really to recognize me. She had come all the way in a day coach; her linen duster had become black with soot and her black bonnet grey with dust during her journey. When we arrived at my boarding-house the landlady put her to bed at once and I did not see her again until the next morning.

Whatever shock Mrs. Springer experienced at my aunt's appearance, she considerately concealed. As for myself, I saw my aunt's battered figure with that feeling of awe and respect with which we behold explorers who have left their ears and fingers north of Franz-Joseph-Land, or their health somewhere along the Upper Congo. My Aunt Georgiana had been a music teacher at the Boston Conservatory, somewhere back in the latter sixties. One summer, while visiting in the little village among the Green Mountains where her ancestors had dwelt for generations, she had kindled the callow fancy of my uncle, Howard Carpenter, then an idle, shiftless boy of twenty-one. When she returned to her duties in Boston, Howard followed her, and the upshot of this infatuation was that she eloped with him, eluding the reproaches of her family and the criticism of her friends by going with him to the Nebraska frontier. Carpenter, who, of course, had no money, took up a homestead in Red Willow County, fifty miles from the railroad. There they had measured off their land themselves, driving across the prairie in a wagon, to the wheel of which they had tied a red cotton handkerchief, and counting its revolutions. They built a dug-out in the red hillside, one of those cave dwellings whose inmates so often reverted to primitive conditions. Their water they got from the lagoons where the buffalo drank, and their slender stock of provisions was always at the mercy of bands of roving Indians. For thirty years my aunt had not been farther than fifty miles from the homestead.

I owed to this woman most of the good that ever came my way in my boyhood, and had a reverential affection for her. During the years when I was riding herd for my uncle, my aunt, after cooking the three meals—the first of which was ready at six o'clock in the morning—and putting the six children to bed, would often stand until midnight at her ironing-board, with me at the kitchen table beside her, hearing me recite Latin declensions and conjugations, gently shaking me when my drowsy head sank down over a page of irregular verbs. It was to her, at her ironing or mending, that I read my first Shakespeare, and her old textbook on mythology was the first that ever came into my empty hands. She taught me my scales and exercises on the little parlour organ which her husband had bought her after fifteen years during which she had not so much as seen a musical instrument. She would sit beside me by the hour, darning and counting, while I struggled with the "Joyous Farmer." She seldom talked to me about music, and I understood why. Once when I had been doggedly beating out some easy passages from an old score of *Euryanthe* I had found among her music books, she came up to me and, putting her hands over my eyes, gently drew my head back upon her shoulder, saying tremulously, "Don't love it so well, Clark, or it may be taken from you."

When my aunt appeared on the morning after her arrival in Boston, she was still in a semi-somnambulant state. She seemed not to realize that she was in the city where she had spent her youth, the place longed for hungrily half a lifetime. She had been so wretchedly trainsick throughout the journey that she had no recollection of anything but her discomfort, and, to all intents and purposes, there were but a few hours of nightmare between the farm in Red Willow County and my study on Newbury Street. I had planned a little pleasure for her that afternoon, to repay her for some of the glorious moments she had given me when we used to milk together in the straw-thatched cowshed and she, because I was more than usually tired, or because her husband had spoken sharply to me, would tell me of the splendid performance of the *Huguenots* she had seen in Paris, in her youth.

At two o'clock the Symphony Orchestra was to give a Wagner program, and I intended to take my aunt; though, as I conversed with her, I grew doubtful about her enjoyment of it. I suggested our visiting the Conservatory and the Common before lunch, but she seemed altogether too timid to wish to venture out. She questioned me absently about various changes in the city, but she was chiefly concerned that she had forgotten to leave instructions about feeding half-skimmed milk to a certain weakling calf, "old Maggie's calf, you know, Clark," she explained, evidently having forgotten how long I had been away. She was further troubled because she had neglected to tell her daughter about the freshly-opened kit of mackerel in the cellar, which would spoil if it were not used directly.

I asked her whether she had ever heard any of the Wagnerian operas, and found that she had not, though she was perfectly familiar with their respective situations, and had once possessed the piano score of *The Flying Dutchman.* I began to think it would be best to get her back to Red Willow County without waking her, and regretted having suggested the concert.

From the time we entered the concert hall, however, she was a trifle less passive and inert, and for the first time seemed to perceive her surroundings. I had felt some trepidation lest she might become aware of her queer, country clothes, or might experience some painful embarrassment at stepping suddenly into the world to which she had been dead for a quarter of a century. But, again, I found how superficially I had judged her. She sat looking about her with eyes as impersonal, almost as stony, as those with which the granite Rameses in a museum watches the froth and fret that ebbs and flows about his pedestal. I have seen this same aloofness in old miners who drift into the Brown hotel at Denver, their pockets full of bullion, their linen soiled, their haggard faces unshaven; standing in the thronged corridors as solitary as though they were still in a frozen camp on the Yukon.

The matinée audience was made up chiefly of women. One lost the contour of faces and figures, indeed any effect of line whatever, and there was only the colour of bodices past counting, the shimmer of fabrics soft and firm, silky and sheer; red, mauve, pink, blue, lilac, purple, écru, rose, yellow, cream, and white, all the colours that an impressionist finds in a sunlit landscape, with here and there the dead shadow of a frock coat. My Aunt Georgiana regarded them as though they had been so many daubs of tube-paint on a palette.

When the musicians came out and took their places, she gave a little stir of anticipation, and looked with quickening interest down over the rail at that invariable grouping, perhaps the first wholly familiar thing that had greeted her eye since she had left old Maggie and her weakling calf. I could feel how all those details sank into her soul, for I had not forgotten how they had sunk into mine when I came fresh from ploughing forever and forever between green aisles of corn, where, as in a treadmill, one might walk from daybreak to dusk without perceiving a shadow of change. The clean profiles of the musicians, the gloss of their linen, the dull black of their coats, the beloved shapes of the instruments, the patches of yellow light on the smooth, varnished bellies of the 'cellos and the bass viols in the rear, the restless, wind-tossed forest of fiddle necks and bows—I recalled how, in the first orchestra I ever heard, those long bow-strokes seemed to draw the heart out of me, as a conjurer's stick reels out yards of paper ribbon from a hat.

The first number was the *Tannhäuser* overture. When the horns drew out the first strain of the Pilgrim's chorus, Aunt Georgiana clutched my coat sleeve. Then it was I first realized that for her this broke a silence of thirty years. With the battle between the two motives, with the frenzy of the Venusberg theme and its ripping of strings, there came to me an overwhelming sense of the waste and wear we are so powerless to combat; and I saw again the tall, naked house on the prairie, black and grim as a wooden fortress; the black pond where I had learned to swim, its margin pitted with sun-dried cattle tracks; the rain-gullied clay banks about the naked house, the four dwarf-ash seedlings where the dish-cloths were always hung to dry before the kitchen door. The world there was the flat world of the ancients; to the east, a cornfield that stretched to daybreak; to the west, a corral that reached to sunset; between, the conquests of peace, dearer-bought than those of war.

The overture closed, my aunt released my coat sleeve, but she said nothing. She sat staring dully at the orchestra. What, I wondered, did she get from it? She had been a good pianist in her day, I knew, and her musical education had been broader than that of most music teachers of a quarter of a century ago. She had often told me of Mozart's operas and Meyerbeer's, and I could remember hearing her sing, years ago, certain melodies of Verdi. When I had fallen ill with a fever in her house she used to sit by my cot in the evening— when the cool, night wind blew in through the faded mosquito netting tacked over the window and I lay watching a certain bright star that burned red above the cornfield—and sing "Home to our mountains, O, let us return!" in a way fit to break the heart of a Vermont boy near dead of homesickness already.

I watched her closely through the prelude to *Tristan and Isolde*, trying vainly to conjecture what that seething turmoil of strings and winds might mean to her, but she sat mutely staring at the violin bows that drove obliquely downward, like the pelting streaks of rain in a summer shower. Had this music any message for her? Had she enough left to at all comprehend this power which had kindled the world since she had left it? I was in a fever of curiosity, but Aunt Georgiana sat silent upon her peak in Darien. She preserved this utter immobility throughout the number from *The Flying Dutchman*, though her fingers worked mechanically upon her black dress, as if, of themselves, they were recalling the piano score they had once played. Poor hands! They had been stretched and twisted into mere tentacles to hold and lift and knead with;—on one of them a thin, worn band that had once been a wedding ring. As I pressed and gently quieted one of those groping hands, I remembered with quivering eyelids their services for me in other days.

Soon after the tenor began the "Prize Song," I heard a quick drawn breath and turned to my aunt. Her eyes were closed, but the tears were glistening on her cheeks, and I think, in a moment more, they were in my eyes as well. It never really died, then—the soul which can suffer so excruciatingly and so interminably; it withers to the outward eye only: like that strange moss which can lie on a dusty shelf half a century and yet, if placed in water, grows green again. She wept so throughout the development and elaboration of the melody.

During the intermission before the second half, I questioned my aunt and found that the "Prize Song" was not new to her. Some years before there had drifted to the farm in Red Willow County a young German, a tramp cow-puncher, who had sung in the chorus at Bayreuth when he was a boy, along with the other peasant boys and girls. Of a Sunday morning he used to sit on his gingham-sheeted bed in the hands' bedroom which opened off the kitchen, cleaning the leather of his boots and saddle, singing the "Prize Song," while my aunt went about her work in the kitchen. She had hovered over him until she had prevailed upon him to join the country church, though his sole fitness for this step, in so far as I could gather, lay in his boyish face and his possession of this divine melody. Shortly afterward, he had gone to town on the Fourth of July, been drunk for several days, lost his money at a faro table, ridden a saddled Texas steer on a bet, and disappeared with a fractured collar-bone. All this my aunt told me huskily, wanderingly, as though she were talking in the weak lapses of illness.

"Well, we have come to better things than the old *Trovatore* at any rate, Aunt Georgie?" I queried, with a well-meant effort at jocularity.

Her lip quivered and she hastily put her handkerchief up to her mouth. From behind it she murmured, "And you have been hearing this ever since you left me, Clark?" Her question was the gentlest and saddest of reproaches.

The second half of the program consisted of four numbers from the *Ring*, and closed with Siegfried's funeral march. My aunt wept quietly, but almost continuously, as a shallow vessel overflows in a rain-storm. From time to time her dim eyes looked up at the lights, burning softly under their dull glass globes.

The deluge of sound poured on and on; I never knew what she found in the shining current of it; I never knew how far it bore her, or past what happy islands. From the trembling of her face I could well believe that before the last number she had been carried out where the myriad graves are, into the grey nameless burying grounds of the sea; or into some world of death vaster yet, where, from the beginning of the world, hope has lain down with hope and dream with dream and, renouncing, slept.

The concert was over; the people filed out of the hall chattering and laughing, glad to relax and find the living level again, but my kinswoman made no effort to rise. The harpist slipped the green felt cover over his instrument; the flute-players shook the water from their mouth-pieces; the men of the orchestra went out one by one, leaving the stage to the chairs and music stands, empty as a winter cornfield.

I spoke to my aunt. She burst into tears and sobbed pleadingly. "I don't want to go, Clark, I don't want to go!"

I understood. For her, just outside the concert hall, lay the black pond with the cattle-tracked bluffs; the tall, unpainted house, with weather-curled boards, naked as a tower; the crook-backed ash seedlings where the dish-cloths hung to dry; the gaunt, molting turkeys picking up refuse about the kitchen door.

Gertrude Stein

(1874-1946)

"I wish I had died when I was a little baby and had not any feeling, I would not then have to be always suffering," Gertrude Stein wrote in *The Making of Americans*, a thousand-page volume she described as a history of her family and every sort of American "who ever can or is or was or will be living." After college at Radcliffe and medical school at Johns Hopkins, she went to live in Paris, joined by Alice B. Toklas, who became her lifelong companion and secretary. Their home at 27 rue de Fleurus was the legendary salon of painters, writers, and members of the so-called Lost Generation who lived in Paris after World War I. *The Autobiography of Alice B. Toklas* (1933) evokes that modernist world and the famous characters on the scene. Stein's experimental use of language in her fiction—*Three Lives* (1909), comprising "The Good Anna," "Melanctha," and "The Gentle Lena," is her masterpiece—and in her plays, essays, and autobiography was of the experimental cultural moment. Her use of the continuous present reflects the influence of her former teacher, the psychologist William James, for whom time was not a linear progression but a stream of consciousness, a series of discrete moments. Her style has been described as Cubist, as Steinese (gnomic, repetitive, illogical, sparsely punctuated), as straightforward ("Sentences must not have bad plumbing—they must not leak," in her words to F. Scott Fitzgerald). In recent years her importance within the world of modern art as well as her stance during the Nazi occupation of France after 1940 have become subjects of controversy. According to Elizabeth Hardwick, "Matisse charged she knew nothing about painting"; someone else described her as "a clinical case of megalomania."

FROM *The Making of Americans*

Once an angry man dragged his father along the ground through his own orchard. "Stop!" cried the groaning old man at last, "Stop! I did not drag my father beyond this tree."

It is hard living down the tempers we are born with. We all begin well, for in our youth there is nothing we are more intolerant of than our own sins writ large in others and we fight them fiercely in ourselves; but we grow old and we see that these our sins are of all sins the really harmless ones to own, nay that they give a charm to any character, and so our struggle with them dies away.

I am writing for myself and strangers. This is the only way that I can do it. Everybody is a real one to me, everybody is like some one else too to me. No one of them that I know can want to know it and so I write for myself and strangers.

Every one is always busy with it, no one of them then ever want to know it that every one looks like some one else and they see it. Mostly every one dislikes to hear it. It is very important to me to always know it, to always see it which one looks like others and to tell it. I write for myself and strangers. I do this for my own sake and for the sake of those who know I know it that they look like other ones, that they are separate and yet always repeated. There are some who like it that I know they are like many others and repeat it, there are many who never can really like it.

There are many that I know and they know it. They are all of them repeating and I hear it. I love it and I tell it, I love it and now I will write it. This is now the history of the way some of them are it.

I write for myself and strangers. No one who knows me can like it. At least they mostly do not like it that every one is of a kind of men and women and I see it. I love it and I write it.

I want readers so strangers must do it. Mostly no one knowing me can like it that I love it that every one is a kind of men and women, that always I am looking and comparing and classifying of them, always I am seeing their repeating. Always more and more I love repeating, it may be irritating to hear from them but always more and more I love it of them. More and more I love it of them, the being in them, the mixing in them, the repeating in them, the deciding the kind of them every one is who has human being.

This is now a little of what I love and how I write it. Later there will be much more of it.

There are many ways of making kinds of men and women. Now there will be descriptions of every kind of way every one can be a kind of men and women.

This is now a history of Martha Hersland. This is now a history of Martha and of every one who came to be of her living.

There will then be soon much description of every way one can think of men and women, in their beginning, in their middle living, and their ending.

Every one then is an individual being. Every one then is like many others always living, there are many ways of thinking of every one, this is now a description of all of them. There must then be a whole history of each one of them. There must then now be a description of all repeating. Now I will tell all the meaning to me in repeating, the loving there is in me for repeating.

Every one is one inside them, every one reminds some one of some other one who is or was or will be living. Every one has it to say of each one he is like such a one I see it in him, every one has it to say of each one she is like some one else I can tell by remembering. So it goes on always in living, every one is always remembering some one who is resembling to the one at whom they are then looking. So they go on repeating, every one is themselves inside them and every one is resembling to others, and that is always interesting. There are many ways of making kinds of men and women. In each way of making kinds of them there is a different system of finding them resembling. Sometime there will be here every way there can be of seeing kinds of men and women. Sometime there will be then a complete history of each one. Every one always is repeating the whole of them and so sometime some one who sees them will have a complete history of every one. Sometime some one will know all the ways there are for people to be resembling, some one sometime then will have a completed history of every one.

Soon now there will be a history of the way repeating comes out of them comes out of men and women when they are young, when they are children, they have then their own system of being resembling; this will soon be a description of the men and women in beginning, the being young in them, the being children.

There is then now and here the loving repetition, this is then, now and here, a description of the loving of repetition and then there will be a description of all the kinds of ways there can be seen to be kinds of men and women. Then there will be realised the complete history of every one, the fundamental character of every one, the bottom nature in them, the mixtures in them, the strength and weakness of everything they have inside them, the flavor of them, the meaning in them, the being in them, and then you have a whole history then of each one. Everything then they do in living is clear to the completed understanding, their living, loving, eating, pleasing, smoking, thinking, scolding, drinking, working, dancing, walking, talking, laughing, sleeping, everything in them. There are whole beings then, they are themselves inside them, repeating coming out of them makes a history of each one of them.

Always from the beginning there was to me all living as repeating. This is now a description of my feeling. As I was saying listening to repeating is often irritating, always repeating is all of living, everything in a being is always repeating, more and more listening to repeating gives to me completed understanding. Each one slowly comes to be a whole one to me. Each one slowly comes to be a whole one in me. Soon then it commences to sound through my ears and eyes and feelings the repeating that is always coming out from each one, that is them, that makes then slowly of each one of them a whole one. Repeating then comes slowly then to be to one who has it to have loving repeating as natural being comes to be a full sound telling all the being in each one such a one is ever knowing. Sometimes it takes many years of knowing some one before the repeating that is that one gets to be a steady sounding to the hearing of one who has it as a natural being to love repeating that slowly comes out from every one. Sometimes it takes many years of knowing some one before the repeating in that one comes to be a clear history of such a one. Natures sometimes are so mixed up in some one that steady repeating in them is mixed up with changing. Soon then there will be a completed history of each one. Sometimes it is difficult to know it in some, for what these are saying is repeating in them is not the real repeating of them, is not the complete repeating for them. Sometimes many years of knowing some one pass before repeating of all being in them comes out clearly from them. As I was saying it is often irritating to listen to the repeating they are doing, always then that one that has it as being to love repeating that is the whole history of each one, such a one has it then that this irritation passes over into patient completed understanding. Loving repeating is one way of being. This is now a description of such feeling.

There are many that I know and they know it. They are all of them repeating and I hear it. I love it and I tell it. I love it and now I will write it. This is now a history of my love of it. I hear it and I love it and I write it. They repeat it. They live it and I see it and I hear it. They live it and I hear it and I see it and I love it and now and always I will write it. There are many kinds of men and women and I know it. They repeat it and I hear it and I love it. This is now a history of the way they do it. This is now a history of the way I love it.

Now I will tell of the meaning to me in repeating, of the loving there is in me for repeating.

Sometime every one becomes a whole one to me. Sometime every one has a completed history for me. Slowly each one is a whole one to me, with some, all their living is passing before they are a whole one to me. There is a completed history of them to me then when there is of them a completed understanding of the bottom nature in them of the nature or natures mixed up in them with the bottom nature of them or separated in them. There is then a history of the things they say and do and feel, and happen to them. There is then a history of the living in them. Repeating is always in all of them. Repeating in them comes out of them, slowly making clear to any one that looks closely at them the nature and the natures mixed up in them. This sometime comes to be clear in every one.

Often as I was saying repeating is very irritating to listen to from them and then slowly it settles into a completed history of them. Repeating is a wonderful thing in living being. Sometime then the nature of every one comes to be clear to some one listening to the repeating coming out of each one.

This is then now to be a little description of the loving feeling for understanding of the completed history of each one that comes to one who listens always steadily to all repeating. This is the history then of the loving feeling in me of repeating, the loving feeling in me for completed understanding of the completed history of every one as it slowly comes out in every one as patiently and steadily I hear it and see it as repeating in them. This is now a little a description of this loving feeling. This is now a little history of it from the beginning. . . .

Virginia Woolf

(1882-1941)

As great a writer of fiction as Virginia Woolf is—*Mrs. Dalloway* (1925), *To the Lighthouse* (1927), and *Orlando* (1928) are among her best—it's possible that her nonfiction has made at least as influential a contribution to modern literary history. *A Room of One's Own* (1929), her essay on women and the writing of fiction, is already regarded as the first major contribution to feminist criticism in the English language. In her most radical piece of cultural commentary, *Three Guineas* (1938), the sequel to *A Room of One's Own* that was ridiculed in the press, her point about the connection between private and public politics belongs now to the common wisdom. As Kennedy Fraser puts it in "Ornament and Silence":

> [Woolf] was harsh on patriarchs in general. She thought that the model of the patriarchal family, with men given license to bully and rant while women and children submitted and served, was unwholesome. She went further: such a model in private life, when it was mirrored in the public life of nations, led to Fascism. "The tyrannies and servilities of the one are the tyrannies and servilities of the other," she wrote.

Woolf had in mind, of course, Hitler's Nazis, who were holding mass parades for the Fatherland in the years she was writing *Three Guineas*. Oppression of the psychically weak and helpless is the background dynamic in much of her fiction. Louise DeSalvo's *Virginia Woolf: The Impact of Childhood Sexual Abuse on Her Life and Work* attributes her dark sense of the forces that destroy the self to her experience of sexual molestation by her stepbrothers, which started when she was six. The self-deprecating Mabel Waring in "The New Dress" can be read as a figure of Woolf's intimate knowledge of an obsessive insecurity and alienation.

FROM *A Room of One's Own*

And since a novel has this correspondence to real life, its values are to some extent those of real life. But it is obvious that the values of women differ very often from the values which have been made by the other sex; naturally, this is so. Yet it is the masculine values that prevail. Speaking crudely, football and sport are "important"; the worship of fashion, the buying of clothes "trivial." And these values are inevitably transferred from life to fiction. This is an important book, the critic assumes, because it deals with war. This is an insignificant book because it deals with the feelings of women in a drawing-room. A scene in a battlefield is more important than a scene in a shop—everywhere and much more subtly the difference of value persists. The whole structure, therefore, of the early nineteenth-century novel was raised, if one was a woman, by a mind which was sightly pulled from the straight, and made to alter its clear vision in deference to external authority. One has only to skim those old forgotten novels and listen to the tone of voice in which they are written to divine that the writer was meeting criticism; she was saying this by way of aggression, or that by way of conciliation. She was admitting that she was "only a woman," or protesting that she was "as good as a man." She met that criticism as her temperament dictated, with docility and diffidence, or with anger and emphasis. It does not matter which it was; she was thinking of something other than the thing itself. Down comes her book upon our heads. There was a flaw in the centre of it. And I thought of all the women's novels that lie scattered, like small pock-marked apples in an orchard, about the second-hand book shops of London. It was the flaw in the centre that had rotted them. She had altered her values in deference to the opinion of others.

But how impossible it must have been for them not to budge either to the right or to the left. What genius, what integrity it must have required in face of all that criticism, in the midst of that purely patriarchal society, to hold fast to the thing as they saw it without shrinking. Only Jane Austen did it and Emily Brontë. It is another feather, perhaps the finest, in their caps. They wrote as women write, not as men write. Of all the thousand women who wrote novels then, they alone entirely ignored the perpetual admonitions of the eternal pedagogue—write this, think that. They alone were deaf to that persistent voice, now grumbling, now patronizing, now domineering, now grieved, now shocked, now angry, now avuncular, that voice which cannot let women alone, but must be at them like some too-conscientious governess, adjuring them, like Sir Egerton Brydges, to be refined; dragging even into the criticism of poetry criticism of sex; admonishing them, if they would be good and win, as I suppose, some shiny prize, to keep within certain limits which the gentleman in question thinks suitable—". . . female novelists should only aspire to excellence by courageously acknowledging the limitations of their sex." That puts the matter in a nutshell, and when I tell you, rather to your surprise, that this sentence was written not in August 1828 but in August 1928, you will agree, I think, that however delightful it is to us now, it represents a vast body of opinion—I am not going to stir those old pools; I take only what chance has floated to my feet—that was far more vigorous and far more vocal a century ago. It would have needed a very stalwart young woman in 1828 to disregard all those snubs and chidings and promises of prizes. One must have been something of a firebrand to say to oneself, Oh, but they can't buy literature too. Literature is open to everybody. I refuse to allow you, Beadle though you are, to turn me off the grass. Lock up your libraries if you like; but there is no gate, no lock, no bolt that you can set upon the freedom of my mind.

But whatever effect discouragement and criticism had upon their writing—and I believe that they had a very great effect—that was unimportant compared with the other difficulty which faced them (I was still considering those early nineteenth-century novelists) when they came to set their thoughts on paper—that is that they had no tradition behind them, or one so short and partial that it was of little help. For we think back through our mothers if we are women. It is useless to go to the great men writers for help, however much one may go to them for pleasure. Lamb, Browne, Thackeray, Newman, Sterne, Dickens, De Quincey—whoever it may be—never helped a women yet, though she may have learnt a few tricks of them and adapted them to her use. The weight, the pace, the stride of a man's mind are too unlike her own for her to lift anything substantial from him successfully. The ape is too distant to be sedulous. Perhaps the first thing she would find, setting pen to paper, was that there was no common sentence ready for her use. All the great novelists like Thackeray and Dickens and Balzac have written a natural prose, swift but not slovenly, expressive but not precious, taking their own tint without ceasing to be common property. They have based it on the sentence that was current at the time. The sentence that was current at the beginning of the nineteenth century ran something like this perhaps: "The grandeur of their works was an argument with them, not to stop short, but to proceed. They could have no higher excitement or satisfaction than in the exercise of their art and endless generations of truth and beauty. Success prompts to exertion; and habit facilitates success." That is a man's sentence; behind it one can see Johnson, Gibbon and the rest. It was a sentence that was unsuited for a woman's use. Charlotte Brontë, with all her splendid gift for prose, stumbled and fell with that clumsy weapon in her hands. George Eliot committed atrocities with it that beggar description. Jane Austen looked at it and laughed at it and devised a perfectly natural, shapely sentence proper for her own use and never departed from it. Thus, with less genius for writing than Charlotte Brontë, she got infinitely more said. Indeed, since freedom and fullness of expression are of the essence of the art, such a lack of tradition, such a scarcity and inadequacy of tools, must have told enormously upon the writing of women. Moreover, a book is not made of sentences laid end to end, but of sentences built, if an image helps, into arcades or domes. And this shape too has been made by men out of their own needs for their own uses. There is no reason to think that the form of the epic or of the poetic play suit a woman any more than the sentence suits her. But all the older forms of literature were hardened and set by the time she became a writer. The novel alone was young enough to be soft in her hands—another reason, perhaps, why she wrote novels. Yet who shall say that even now "the novel" (I give it [quotes] to mark my sense of the words' inadequacy), who shall say that even this most pliable of all forms is rightly shaped for her use? No doubt we shall find her knocking that into shape for herself when she has the free use of her limbs; and providing some new vehicle, not necessarily in verse, for the poetry in her. For it is the poetry that is still denied outlet. And I went on to ponder how a woman nowadays would write a poetic tragedy in five acts. Would she use verse?—would she not use prose rather?

But these are difficult questions which lie in the twilight of the future. I must leave them, if only because they stimulate me to wander from my subject into trackless forests where I shall be lost and, very likely, devoured by wild beasts. I do not want, and I am sure that you do not want me, to broach that very dismal subject, the future of fiction, so that I will only pause here one moment to draw your attention to the great part which must be played in that future so far as women are concerned by physical conditions. The book has somehow to be adapted to the body, and at a venture one would say that women's books should be shorter, more concentrated, than those of men, and framed so that they do not need long hours of steady and uninterrupted work. For interruptions there will always be. Again, the nerves that feed the brain would seem to differ in men and women, and if you are going to make them work their best and hardest, you must find out what treatment suits them—whether these hours of lectures, for instance, which the monks devised, presumably, hundreds of years ago, suit them—what alternations of work and rest they need, interpreting rest not as doing nothing but as doing something but something that is different; and what should that difference be? All this should be discussed and discovered; all this is part of the question of women and fiction. And yet, I continued, approaching the bookcase again, where shall I find that elaborate study of the psychology of women by a woman? If through their incapacity to play football women are not going to be allowed to practise medicine—

Happily my thoughts were now given another turn.

The New Dress

Mabel had her first serious suspicion that something was wrong as she took her cloak off and Mrs. Barnet, while handing her the mirror and touching the brushes and thus drawing her attention, perhaps rather markedly, to all the appliances for tidying and improving hair, complexion, clothes, which existed on the dressing table, confirmed the suspicion—that it was not right, not quite right, which growing stronger as she went upstairs and springing at her, with conviction as she greeted Clarissa Dalloway, she went straight to the far end of the room, to a shaded corner where a looking-glass hung and looked. No! It was not *right*. And at once the misery which she always tried to hide, the profound dissatisfaction—the sense she had had, ever since she was a child, of being inferior to other people—set upon her, relentlessly, remorselessly, with an intensity which she could not beat off, as she would when she woke at night at home, by reading Borrow or Scott; for oh these men, oh these women, all were thinking—"What's Mabel wearing? What a fright she looks! What a hideous new dress!"—their eyelids flickering as they came up and then their lids shutting rather tight. It was her own appalling inadequacy; her cowardice; her mean, water-sprinkled blood that depressed her. And at once the whole of the room where, for ever so many hours, she had planned with the little dressmaker how it was to go, seemed sordid, repulsive; and her own drawing-room so shabby, and herself, going out, puffed up with vanity as she touched the letters on the hall table and said: "How dull!" to show off—all this now seemed unutterably silly, paltry, and provincial. All this had been absolutely destroyed, shown up, exploded, the moment she came into Mrs. Dalloway's drawing-room.

What she had thought that evening when, sitting over the teacups, Mrs. Dalloway's invitation came, was that, of course, she could not be fashionable. It was absurd to pretend it even—fashion meant cut, meant style, meant thirty guineas at least—but why not be original? Why not be herself, anyhow? And, getting up, she had taken that old fashion book of her mother's, a Paris fashion book of the time of the Empire, and had thought how much prettier, more dignified, and more womanly they were then, and so set herself—oh, it was foolish—trying to be like them, pluming herself in fact, upon being modest and old-fashioned, and very charming, giving herself up, no doubt about it, to an orgy of self-love, which deserved to be chastised, and so rigged herself out like this.

But she dared not look in the glass. She could not face the whole horror—the pale yellow, idiotically old-fashioned silk dress with its long skirt and its high sleeves and its waist and all the things that looked so charming in the fashion book, but not on her, not among all these ordinary people. She felt like a dressmaker's dummy standing there, for young people to stick pins into.

"But, my dear, it's perfectly charming!" Rose Shaw said, looking her up and down with that little satirical pucker of the lips which she expected—Rose herself being dressed in the height of fashion, precisely like everybody else, always.

We are all like flies trying to crawl over the edge of the saucer, Mabel thought, and repeated the phrase as if she were crossing herself, as if she were trying to find some spell to annul this pain, to make this agony endurable. Tags of Shakespeare, lines from books she had read ages ago, suddenly came to her when she was in agony, and she repeated them over and over again. "Flies trying to crawl," she repeated. If she could say that over often enough and make herself see the flies, she would become numb, chill, frozen, dumb.

Now she could see flies crawling slowly out of a saucer of milk with their wings stuck together; and she strained and strained (standing in front of the looking-glass, listening to Rose Shaw) to make herself see Rose Shaw and all the other people as flies, trying to hoist themselves out of something, or into something, meagre, insignificant, toiling flies. But she could not see them like that, not other people. She saw herself like that—she was a fly, but the others were dragonflies, butterflies, beautiful insects, dancing, fluttering, skimming, while she alone dragged herself up out of the saucer. (Envy and spite, the most detestable of the vices, were her chief faults.)

"I feel like some dowdy, decrepit, horribly dingy old fly," she said, making Robert Haydon stop just to hear her say that, just to reassure herself by furbishing up a poor weak-kneed phrase and so showing how detached she was, how witty, that she did not feel in the least out of anything. And, of course, Robert Haydon answered something, quite polite, quite insincere, which she saw through instantly, and said to herself, directly he went (again from some book), "Lies, lies, lies!" For a party makes things either much more real, or much less real, she thought; she saw in a flash to the bottom of Robert Haydon's heart; she saw through everything. She saw the truth. *This* was true, this drawing-room, this self, and the other false. Miss Milan's little workroom was really terribly hot, stuffy, sordid. It smelt of clothes and cabbage cooking; and yet, when Miss Milan put the glass in her hand, and she looked at herself with the dress on, finished, an extraordinary bliss shot through her heart. Suffused with light, she sprang into existence. Rid of cares and wrinkles, what she had dreamed of herself was there—a beautiful woman. Just for a second (she had not dared looked longer, Miss Milan wanted to know about the length of the skirt), there looked at her, framed in the scrolloping mahogany, a grey-white, mysteriously smiling, charming girl, the core of herself, the soul of herself; and it was not vanity only, not only self-love that made her think it good, tender, and true. Miss Milan said that the skirt could not well be longer; if anything the skirt, said Miss Milan, puckering her forehead, considering with all her wits about her, must be shorter; and she felt, suddenly, honestly, full of love for Miss Milan, much, much fonder of Miss Milan than of any one in the whole world, and could have cried for pity that she should be crawling on the floor with her mouth full of pins, and her face red and her eyes bulging—that one human being should be doing this for another, and she saw them all as human beings merely, and herself going off to her party, and Miss Milan pulling the cover over the canary's cage, or letting him pick a hempseed from between her lips, and the thought of it, of this side of human nature and its patience and its endurance and its being content with such miserable, scanty, sordid, little pleasures filled her eyes with tears.

And now the whole thing had vanished. The dress, the room, the love, the pity, the scrolloping looking-glass, and the canary's cage—all had vanished, and here she was in a corner of Mrs. Dalloway's drawing-room, suffering tortures, woken wide awake to reality.

But it was all so paltry, weak blooded, and petty-minded to care so much at her age with two children, to be still so utterly dependent on people's opinions and not have principles or convictions, not to be able to say as other people did, "There's Shakespeare! There's death! We're all weevils in a captain's biscuit"—or whatever it was that people did say.

She faced herself straight in the glass; she pecked at her left shoulder; she issued out into the room, as if spears were thrown at her yellow dress from all sides. But instead of looking fierce or tragic, as Rose Shaw would have done—Rose would have looked like Boadicea—she looked foolish and self-conscious, and simpered like a schoolgirl and slouched across the room, positively slinking, as if she were a beaten mongrel, and looked at a picture, an engraving. As if one went to a party to look at a picture! Everybody knew why she did it—it was from shame, from humiliation.

"Now the fly's in the saucer," she said to herself, "right in the middle, and can't get out, and the milk," she thought, rigidly staring at the picture, "is sticking its wings together."

"It's so old-fashioned," she said to Charles Burt, making him stop (which by itself he hated) on his way to talk to some one else.

She meant, or she tried to make herself think that she meant, that it was the picture and not her dress, that was old-fashioned. And one word of praise, one word of affection from Charles would have made all the difference to her at the moment. If he had only said, "Mabel, you're looking charming tonight!" it would have changed her life. But then she ought to have been truthful and direct. Charles said nothing of the kind, of course. He was malice itself. He always saw through one, especially if one were feeling particularly mean, paltry, or feeble-minded.

"Mabel's got a new dress!" he said, and the poor fly was absolutely shoved into the middle of the saucer. Really, he would like her to drown, she believed. He had no heart, no fundamental kindness, only a veneer of friendliness. Miss Milan was much more real, much kinder. If only one could feel that and stick to it, always. "Why," she asked herself—replying to Charles much too pertly, letting him see that she was out of temper, or "ruffled" as he called it. ("Rather ruffled?" he said and went on to laugh at her with some woman over there)—"Why," she asked herself, "can't I feel one thing always, feel quite sure that Miss Milan is right, and Charles wrong and stick to it, feel sure about the canary and pity and love and not be whipped all round in a second by coming into a room full of people?" It was her odious, weak, vacillating character again, always giving at the critical moment and not being seriously interested in conchology, etymology, botany, archaeology, cutting up potatoes and watching them fructify like Mary Dennis, like Violet Searle.

Then Mrs. Holman, seeing her standing there, bore down upon her. Of course a thing like a dress was beneath Mrs. Holman's notice, with her family always tumbling downstairs or having the scarlet fever. Could Mabel tell her if Elmthorpe was ever let for August and September? Oh, it was a conversation that bored her unutterably!—it made her furious to be treated like a house agent or a messenger boy, to be made use of. Not to have value, that was it, she thought, trying to grasp something hard, something real, while she tried to answer sensibly about the bathroom and the south aspect and the hot water to the top of the house; and all the time she could see little bits of her yellow dress in the round looking-glass which made them all the size of boot-buttons or tadpoles; and it was amazing to think how much humiliation and agony and self-loathing and effort and passionate ups and downs of feeling were contained in a thing the size of a threepenny bit. And what was still odder, this thing, this Mabel Waring, was separate, quite disconnected: and though Mrs. Holman (the black button) was leaning forward and telling her how her eldest boy had strained his heart running, she could see her, too, quite detached in the looking-glass, and it was impossible that the black dot, leaning forward, gesticulating, should make the yellow dot, sitting solitary, self-centred, feel what the black dot was feeling, yet they pretended.

"So impossible to keep boys quiet"—that was the kind of thing one said.

And Mrs. Holman, who could never get enough sympathy and snatched what little there was greedily, as if it were her right (but she deserved much more for there was her little girl who had come down this morning with a swollen knee-joint), took this miserable offering and looked at it suspiciously, grudgingly, as if it were a half-penny when it ought to have been a pound and put it away in her purse, must put up with it, mean and miserly though it was, times being hard, so very hard; and on she went, creaking, injured Mrs. Holman, about the girl with the swollen joints. Ah, it was tragic, this greed, this clamour of human beings, like a row of cormorants, barking and flapping their wings for sympathy—it was tragic, could one have felt it and not merely pretended to feel it!

But in her yellow dress to-night she could not wring out one drop more; she wanted it all, all for herself. She knew (she kept on looking into the glass, dipping into that dreadfully showing-up blue pool) that she was condemned, despised, left like this in a backwater, because of her being like this a feeble, vacillating creature; and it seemed to her that the yellow dress was a penance which she had deserved, and if she had been dressed like Rose Shaw, in lovely, clinging green with a ruffle of swansdown, she would have deserved that; and she thought that there was no escape for her—none whatever. But it was not her fault altogether, after all. It was being one of a family of ten; never having money enough, always skimping and paring; and her mother carrying great cans, and the linoleum worn on the stair edges, and one sordid little domestic tragedy after another—nothing catastrophic, the sheep farm failing, but not utterly; her eldest brother marrying beneath him but not very much—there was no romance, nothing extreme about them all. They petered out respectably in seaside resorts; every watering-place had one of her aunts even now asleep in some lodging with the front windows not quite facing the sea. That was so like them—they had to squint at things always. And she had done the same—she was just like her aunts. For all her dreams of living in India, married to some hero like Sir Henry Lawrence, some empire builder (still the sight of a native in a turban filled her with romance), she had failed utterly. She had married Hubert, with his safe, permanent underling's job in the Law Courts, and they managed tolerably in a smallish house, without proper maids, and hash when she was alone or just bread and butter, but now and then—Mrs. Holman was off, thinking her the most dried-up, unsympathetic twig she had ever met, absurdly dressed, too, and would tell every one about Mabel's fantastic appearance—now and then, thought Mabel Waring, left alone on the blue sofa, punching the cushion in order to look occupied, for she would not join Charles Burt and Rose Shaw, chattering like magpies and perhaps laughing at her by the fireplace—now and then, there did come to her delicious moments, reading the other night in bed, for instance, or down by the sea on the sand in the sun, at Easter—let her recall it—a great tuft of pale sand-grass standing all twisted like a shock of spears against the sky, which was blue like a smooth china egg, so firm, so hard, and then the melody of the waves—"Hush, hush," they said, and the children's shouts paddling—yes, it was a divine moment, and there she lay, she felt, in the hand of the Goddess who was the world; rather a hard-hearted, but very beautiful Goddess, a little lamb laid on the altar (one did think these silly things, and it didn't matter so long as one never said them). And also with Hubert sometimes she had quite unexpectedly—carving the mutton for Sunday lunch, for no reason, opening a letter, coming into a room—divine moments, when she said to herself (for she would never say this to anybody else), "This is it. This has happened. This is it!" And the other way about it was equally surprising—that is, when everything was arranged—music, weather, holidays, every reason for happiness was there—then nothing happened at all. One wasn't happy. It was flat, just flat, that was all.

Her wretched self again, no doubt! She had always been a fretful, weak, unsatisfactory mother, a wobbly wife, lolling about in a kind of twilight existence with nothing very clear or very bold, or more one thing than another, like all her brothers and sisters, except perhaps Herbert—they were all the same poor water-veined creatures who did nothing. Then in the midst of this creeping, crawling life, suddenly she was on the crest of a wave. That wretched fly—where had she read the story that kept coming into her mind about the fly and the saucer?—struggled out. Yes, she had those moments. But now that she was forty, they might come more and more seldom. By degrees she would cease to struggle any more. But that was deplorable! That was not to be endured! That made her feel ashamed of herself!

She would go to the London Library tomorrow. She would find some wonderful, helpful, astonishing book, quite by chance, a book by a clergyman, by an American no one had ever heard of; or she would walk down the Strand and drop, accidentally, into a hall where a miner was telling about the life in the pit, and suddenly she would become a new person. She would be absolutely transformed. She would wear a uniform; she would be called Sister Somebody; she would never give a thought to clothes again. And for ever after she would be perfectly clear about Charles Burt and Miss Milan and this room and that room; and it would be always, day after day, as if she were lying in the sun or carving the mutton. It would be it!

So she got up from the blue sofa, and the yellow button in the looking-glass got up too, and she waved her hand to Charles and Rose to show them she did not depend on them one scrap, and the yellow button moved out of the looking-glass, and all the spears were gathered into her breast as she walked towards Mrs. Dalloway and said, "Good night."

"But it's too early to go," said Mrs. Dalloway, who was always so charming.

"I'm afraid I must," said Mabel Waring. "But," she added in her weak, wobbly voice which only sounded ridiculous when she tried to strengthen it, "I have enjoyed myself enormously."

"I have enjoyed myself," she said to Mrs. Dalloway, whom she met on the stairs.

"Lies, lies, lies!" she said to herself, going downstairs, and "Right in the saucer!" she said to herself as she thanked Mrs. Barnet for helping her and wrapped herself, round and round and round, in the Chinese cloak she had worn these twenty years.

Marianne Moore

(1887-1972)

To Louise Bogan she was "our most distinguished contemporary American poet." Introducing her *Selected Poems*, T. S. Eliot said they were "part of the body of durable poetry written in our time." Ezra Pound and Elizabeth Bishop were friends and correspondents. *The Collected Poems* (1951) won the Pulitzer Prize, the Bollingen Prize, and the National Book Award. Marianne Moore's poetry, which is not confessional—"compression," she said, is "the first grace of style"—has received little attention from feminist critics. A modest and shy woman who lived with her mother in their native Missouri and after 1918 in New York City, she wrote in the voice of an elegant conversationalist. There's also a tough American pragmatism in her letters and prose—a sample follows here—and beneath the fastidious lines of her poetry. In "In Distrust of Merits," written during World War II, she posits a moral responsibility stemming from her firm religious belief. A passionate baseball fan and Brooklynite, who wore a tricorn hat and a black cape, she was asked one year to throw out the first ball of the Brooklyn Dodgers's baseball season.

FROM *When I Was Sixteen*

My grandfather was a Presbyterian minister and was present during the Battle of Gettysburg. He was a pastor there, and his wife, my grandmother, died of typhoid fever as a result of the battle, since conditions in Gettysburg were very unwholesome.

My brother was born in Massachusetts; I in Missouri. As young children we lived with my aunt and grandfather, my grandfather being a pastor of a Presbyterian church in Kirkwood, Missouri. He had a little white manse with a porch and about five white buildings surrounding it.

There were oak trees and bluejays in the churchyard. An aunt had sent me a little alligator as a pet, and we had numerous kittens. There were flowers along the fence between the yard and the adjoining one, with crimson roses and white clematis along the fence which separated the two yards—in the autumn, chrysanthemums—and there was spatterdock in tubs by the back door.

We children attended a kindergarten and carried a small market basket holding an orange and butter-thin biscuits.

We then went to live in Pennsylvania. My brother attended high school, and I, Metzger Institute. My mother taught English there. She prepared me for Bryn Mawr and spoiled me badly.

I was diffident when I was sixteen, intimidated by sleigh rides, barn dances, and such parties. I was interested in animals and sports, and after school I read books like *Captains Courageous* and *Stories Mother Nature Told Her Children, For Freedom's Cause* and one about Scotland. I was always reading or preparing lessons. I was over-anxious when sixteen. I'd be uncertain whether I'd pass this or that subject. My main thought was to know English and French—I'd read Carlyle. But I couldn't take French at Metzger and I couldn't take English, not elective, that is, so I was badly disappointed. Then later on I wanted very much to go to Bryn Mawr. I did go there. I was one of two girls in the Latin course, the only girl in French.

I also took piano lessons, but I've forgotten it by now. I'm very fond of music. I even took singing lessons—not because I could sing, because I could *not*. I had a very dutiful teacher. She was really a precisionist and did me a lot of good. We had chapel and had to sing "Onward, Christian Soldiers." I used to sing it like this: "Onward, Christian Sold-i-e-rs." My teacher said, "You must never do that. Cut the long note out." I admired that. She was articulate.

I never cared much for poetry then, though I did read the classics—Spenser, Tennyson, the early English poets. I was plagued, of course, by having to master subjects to get into college. There wasn't the pressure of today, but I wanted to. People said to me, "Why don't you go to Dickinson College? It's coeducational, and you and your brother can both go." But I had met some graduates of Bryn Mawr who seemed to me very talented and unusual. I thought I'd like to be like them.

When I got there, the teams of girls were coming up from the athletic field and were far from beautiful. Their hair hung down over their faces, their hockey skirts were dragging. Otherwise we wore velveteen. There were different colors for each class—yellow, blue, darker blue, green and red. The color of my class was red. We made up a song.

> Ruber ruber ruber rex
> DCCCCIX

Later on, I gave a course in Contemporary Poetry there, in 1953, second semester.

My brother went to Yale. He was very self-reliant. I was homesick, very. I'd never been anywhere. Oh, to Boston, and before I was in college my mother took us to Florida, to see historic sites, the Fountain of Eternal Youth, and the compositions of rock and shell walls characteristic of old towns in Florida. I heard about Pizarro and Ponce de León and saw a Spanish dungeon. The prisoners were lowered into the prison through a high window; food was let down to them. They were never released.

I was always reading then. I read Dickens from one end to the other; I was getting ready for college. When I was in college, Kipling and Henry James. But more to the point, *now* I am reading Augustus Buell's *Life of John Paul Jones*, from which I am learning a great deal. He is someone who can write.

Now I regret that I didn't study chemistry and Greek in college. But I didn't. When I was sixteen, I felt as old and decisive as when I was fifty or sixty. Especially when I was fifteen to twenty, I rarely listened to reason. I think you should be open-minded and as grateful to people as you can be. We should judge ourselves by the least that we are, and judge others by the most that they are. Rate other people as high as we can. People ask me, "How do you think of things to write about?" I don't. *They* think of *me*. They become *irresistible*. I was looking at my little book, the one just out:

> Tell me, tell me
> where there might be a refuge for me
> from egocentricity.

I would say, "Don't think about yourself from morning to night." As for egotism, paranoia and putting pressure on others, most people say you have to be inconsiderate or you won't get anywhere. I've always felt that pushiness and pushy people are obnoxious.

To me, growing up means being able to change from a fixed opinion. When you become liberalized in your judgment, then you are growing up. You are grown up when you make a sacrifice on behalf of another person. . . .

Silence

My father used to say,
"Superior people never make long visits,
have to be shown Longfellow's grave
or the glass flowers at Harvard.
Self-reliant like the cat—
that takes its prey to privacy,
the mouse's limp tail hanging like a shoelace from its mouth—
they sometimes enjoy solitude,
and can be robbed of speech
by speech which has delighted them.
The deepest feeling always shows itself in silence;
not in silence, but restraint."
Nor was he insincere in saying, "Make my house your inn."
Inns are not residences.

The Mind Is an Enchanting Thing

is an enchanted thing
    like the glaze on a
katydid-wing
        subdivided by sun
        till the nettings are legion.
Like Gieseking playing Scarlatti;

like the apteryx-awl
    as a beak, or the
kiwi's rain-shawl
        of haired feathers, the mind
        feeling its way as though blind,
walks along with its eyes on the ground.

It has memory's ear
        that can hear without
having to hear.
                Like the gyroscope's fall,
                truly unequivocal
because trued by regnant certainty,

it is a power of
        strong enchantment. It
is like the dove-
                neck animated by
                sun; it is memory's eye;
it's conscientious inconsistency.

It tears off the veil; tears
        the temptation, the
mist the heart wears,
                from its eyes—if the heart
                has a face; it takes apart
dejection. It's fire in the dove-neck's

iridescence; in the
        inconsistencies
of Scarlatti.
                Unconfusion submits
                its confusion to proof; it's
not a Herod's oath that cannot change.

In Distrust of Merits

Strengthened to live, strengthened to die for
        medals and positioned victories?
They're fighting, fighting, fighting the blind
        man who thinks he sees,—
who cannot see that the enslaver is
enslaved; the hater, harmed. O shining O
            firm star, O tumultuous
                ocean lashed till small things go
            as they will, the mountainous
                wave makes us who look, know

depth. Lost at sea before they fought! O
        star of David, star of Bethlehem,
O black imperial lion
        of the Lord—emblem
of a risen world—be joined at last, be
joined. There is hate's crown beneath which all is
            death; there's love's without which none
                is king; the blessed deeds bless
            the halo. As contagion
            of sickness makes sickness,

contagion of trust can make trust. They're
        fighting in deserts and caves, one by
one, in battalions and squadrons;
        they're fighting that I
may yet recover from disease, My
Self; some have it lightly; some will die. "Man's
            wolf to man" and we devour
                ourselves. The enemy could not
            have made a greater breach in our
                defenses. One pilot-
ing a blind man can escape him, but
        Job disheartened by false comfort knew

that nothing can be so defeating
    as a blind man who
can see. O alive who are dead, who are
proud not to see, O small dust of the earth
        that walks so arrogantly,
            trust begets power and faith is
      an affectionate thing. We
        vow, we make this promise

to the fighting—it's a promise—"We'll
    never hate black, white, red, yellow, Jew,
Gentile, Untouchable." We are
    not competent to
make our vows. With set jaw they are fighting,
fighting, fighting,—some we love whom we know,
      some we love but know not—that
        hearts may feel and not be numb.
      It cures me; or am I what
        I can't believe in? Some

in snow, some on crags, some in quicksands,
    little by little, much by much, they
are fighting fighting fighting that where
    there was death there may
be life. "When a man is prey to anger,
he is moved by outside things; when he holds
      his ground in patience patience
        patience, that is action or
      beauty," the soldier's defense
      and hardest armor for

the fight. The world's an orphans' home. Shall
    we never have peace without sorrow?
without pleas of the dying for
    help that won't come? O
quiet form upon the dust, I cannot

look and yet I must. If these great patient
     dyings—all these agonies
        and wound bearings and bloodshed—
    can teach us how to live, these
       dyings were not wasted.

Hate-hardened heart, O heart of iron,
   iron is iron till it is rust.
There never was a war that was
   not inward; I must
fight till I have conquered in myself what
causes war, but I would not believe it.
     I inwardly did nothing.
      O Iscariot-like crime!
     Beauty is everlasting
      and dust is for a time.

Katherine Mansfield

(1888-1923)

Katherine Mansfield was born Kathleen Beauchamp in New Zealand. She was always a "colonial," an outsider, in London, though she was befriended by Virginia Woolf, D. H. Lawrence, and married the critic John Middleton Murry, who edited her letters and journals after her death from tuberculosis at the age of thirty-four. The character of Gudrun in Lawrence's *Women in Love* is based on Mansfield, and Gudrun's lover Gerald is based on Murry; Lawrence and his wife Frieda, and the Murrys lived as a *ménage à quatre* in Cornwall during part of World War I. Frequently compared with Chekhov, Mansfield set her best stories in New Zealand (where in later years she couldn't bear to return or live): "Prelude," "At the Bay," and "The Garden Party" are luminous memories of happy childhood. Virginia Woolf wrote in her diary that Mansfield's was "the only writing I have ever been jealous of."

The Garden Party

And after all the weather was ideal. They could not have had a more perfect day for a garden-party if they had ordered it. Windless, warm, the sky without a cloud. Only the blue was veiled with a haze of light gold, as it is sometimes in early summer. The gardener had been up since dawn, mowing the lawns and sweeping them, until the grass and the dark flat rosettes where the daisy plants had been seemed to shine. As for the roses, you could not help feeling they understood that roses are the only flowers that impress people at garden-parties; the only flowers that everybody is certain of knowing. Hundreds, yes, literally hundreds, had come out in a single night; the green bushes bowed down as though they had been visited by archangels.

Breakfast was not yet over before the men came to put up the marquee.

"Where do you want the marquee put, mother?"

"My dear child, it's no use asking me. I'm determined to leave everything to you children this year. Forget I am your mother. Treat me as an honoured guest."

But Meg could not possibly go and supervise the men. She had washed her hair before breakfast, and she sat drinking coffee in a green turban, with a dark wet curl stamped on each cheek. Jose, the butterfly, always came down in a silk petticoat and kimono jacket.

"You'll have to go, Laura; you're the artistic one."

Away Laura flew, still holding her piece of bread-and-butter. It's so delicious to have an excuse for eating out of doors, and besides, she loved having to arrange things; she always felt she could do it so much better than anybody else.

Four men in their shirt-sleeves stood grouped together on the garden path. They carried staves covered with rolls of canvas, and they had big tool-bags slung on their backs.

They looked impressive. Laura wished now that she had not got the bread-and-butter, but there was nowhere to put it, and she couldn't possibly throw it away. She blushed and tried to look severe and even a little bit short-sighted as she came up to them.

"Good morning," she said, copying her mother's voice. But that sounded so fearfully affected that she was ashamed, and stammered like a little girl, "Oh—er—have you come—is it about the marquee?"

"That's right, miss," said the tallest of the men, a lanky, freckled fellow, and he shifted his tool-bag, knocked back his straw hat and smiled down at her. "That's about it."

His smile was so easy, so friendly that Laura recovered. What nice eyes he had, small, but such a dark blue! And now she looked at the others, they were smiling too. "Cheer up, we won't bite," their smile seemed to say. How very nice workmen were! And what a beautiful morning! She mustn't mention the morning; she must be businesslike. The marquee.

"Well, what about the lily-lawn? Would that do?"

And she pointed to the lily-lawn with the hand that didn't hold the bread-and-butter. They turned, they stared in the direction. A little fat chap thrust out his under-lip, and the tall fellow frowned.

"I don't fancy it," said he. "Not conspicuous enough. You see, with a thing like a marquee," and he turned to Laura in his easy way, "you want to put it somewhere where it'll give you a bang slap in the eye, if you follow me."

Laura's upbringing made her wonder for a moment whether it was quite respectable of a workman to talk to her of bangs slap in the eye. But she did quite follow him.

"A corner of the tennis-court," she suggested. "But the band's going to be in one corner."

"H'm, going to have a band, are you?" said another of the workmen. He was pale. He had a haggard look as his dark eyes scanned the tennis-court. What was he thinking?

"Only a very small band," said Laura gently. Perhaps he wouldn't mind so much if the band was quite small. But the tall fellow interrupted.

"Look here, miss, that's the place. Against those trees, over there. That'll do fine."

Against the karakas. Then the karakas-trees would be hidden. And they were so lovely, with their broad, gleaming leaves, and their clusters of yellow fruit. They were like trees you imagined growing on a desert island, proud, solitary, lifting their leaves and fruits to the sun in a kind of silent splendour. Must they be hidden by a marquee?

They must. Already the men had shouldered their staves and were making for the place. Only the tall fellow was left. He bent down, pinched a sprig of lavender, put his thumb and forefinger to his nose and snuffed up the smell. When Laura saw that gesture she forgot all about the karakas in her wonder at him caring for things like that—caring for the smell of lavender. How many men that she knew would have done such a thing? Oh, how extraordinarily nice workmen were, she thought. Why couldn't she have workmen for friends rather than the silly boys she danced with and who came to Sunday night supper? She would get on much better with men like these.

It's all the fault, she decided, as the tall fellow drew something on the back of an envelope, something that was to be looped up or left to hang, of these absurd class distinctions. Well, for her part, she didn't feel them. Not a bit, not an atom. . . . And now there came the chock-chock of wooden hammers. Some one whistled, some one sang out, "Are you right there, matey?" "Matey!" The friendliness of it, the—the—Just to prove how happy she was, just to show the tall fellow how at home she felt, and how she despised stupid conventions, Laura took a big bite of her bread-and-butter as she stared at the little drawing. She felt just like a work-girl.

"Laura, Laura, where are you? Telephone, Laura!" a voice cried from the house.

"Coming!" Away she skimmed, over the lawn, up the path, up the steps, across the veranda, and into the porch. In the hall her father and Laurie were brushing their hats ready to go to the office.

"I say, Laura," said Laurie very fast, "you might just give a squiz at my coat before this afternoon. See if it wants pressing."

"I will," said she. Suddenly she couldn't stop herself. She ran at Laurie and gave him a small, quick squeeze. "Oh, I do love parties, don't you?" gasped Laura.

"Ra-ther," said Laurie's warm, boyish voice, and he squeezed his sister too, and gave her a gentle push. "Dash off to the telephone, old girl."

The telephone. "Yes, yes; oh yes. Kitty? Good morning, dear. Come to lunch? Do, dear. Delighted of course. It will only be a very scratch meal—just the sandwich crusts and broken meringue-shells and what's left over. Yes, isn't it a perfect morning? Your white? Oh, I certainly should. One moment—hold the line. Mother's calling." And Laura sat back. "What, mother? Can't hear."

Mrs. Sheridan's voice floated down the stairs. "Tell her to wear that sweet hat she had on last Sunday."

"Mother says you're to wear that *sweet* hat you had on last Sunday. Good. One o'clock. Bye-bye."

Laura put back the receiver, flung her arms over her head, took a deep breath, stretched and let them fall. "Huh," she sighed, and the moment after the sigh sat up quickly. She was still, listening. All the doors in the house seemed to be open. The house was alive with soft, quick steps and running voices. The green baize door that led to the kitchen regions swung open and shut with a muffled thud. And now there came a long, chuckling absurd sound. It was the heavy piano being moved on its stiff castors. But the air! If you stopped to notice, was the air always like this? Little faint winds were playing chase, in at the tops of the windows, out at the doors. And there were two tiny spots of sun, one on the inkpot, one on a silver photograph frame, playing too. Darling little spots. Especially the one on the inkpot lid. It was quite warm. A warm little silver star. She could have kissed it.

The front door bell pealed, and there sounded the rustle of Sadie's print skirt on the stairs. A man's voice murmured; Sadie answered, careless, "I'm sure I don't know. Wait. I'll ask Mrs. Sheridan."

"What is it, Sadie?" Laura came into the hall.

"It's the florist, Miss Laura."

It was, indeed. There, just inside the door, stood a wide, shallow tray full of pots of pink lilies. No other kind. Nothing but lilies—canna lilies, big pink flowers, wide open, radiant, almost frighteningly alive on bright crimson stems.

"O-oh, Sadie!" said Laura, and the sound was like a little moan. She crouched down as if to warm herself at that blaze of lilies; she felt they were in her fingers, on her lips, growing in her breast.

"It's some mistake," she said faintly. "Nobody ever ordered so many. Sadie, go and find mother."

But at that moment Mrs. Sheridan joined them.

"It's quite right," she said calmly. "Yes, I ordered them. Aren't they love-ly?" She pressed Laura's arm. "I was passing the shop yesterday, and I saw them in the window. And I suddenly thought for once in my life I shall have enough canna lilies. The garden-party will be a good excuse."

"But I thought you said you didn't mean to interfere," said Laura. Sadie had gone. The florist's man was still outside at his van. She put her arm round her mother's neck and gently, very gently, she bit her mother's ear.

"My darling child, you wouldn't like a logical mother, would you? Don't do that. Here's the man."

He carried more lilies still, another whole tray.

"Bank them up, just inside the door, on both sides of the porch, please," said Mrs. Sheridan. "Don't you agree, Laura?"

"Oh, I *do*, mother."

In the drawing-room Meg, Jose and good little Hans had at last succeeded in moving the piano.

"Now, if we put this chesterfield against the wall and move everything out of the room except the chairs, don't you think?"

"Quite."

"Hans, move these tables into the smoking-room, and bring a sweeper to take these marks off the carpet and—one moment, Hans—" Jose loved giving orders to the servants, and they loved obeying her. She always made them feel they were taking part in some drama. "Tell mother and Miss Laura to come here at once."

"Very good, Miss Jose."

She turned to Meg. "I want to hear what the piano sounds like, just in case I'm asked to sing this afternoon. Let's try over 'This Life is Weary.'"

Pom! Ta-ta-ta *Tee*-ta! The piano burst out so passionately that Jose's face changed. She clasped her hands. She looked mournfully and enigmatically at her mother and Laura as they came in.

> This Life is *Wee*-ary,
> A Tear—A Sigh.
> A Love that Chan-ges,
>   This Life is *Wee*-ary,
> A Tear—a Sigh.
> A Love that *Chan*-ges,
> And then . . . Good-bye!

But at the word "Good-bye," and although the piano sounded more desperate than ever, her face broke into a brilliant, dreadfully unsympathetic smile.

"Aren't I in good voice, mummy?" she beamed.

> This Life is *Wee*-ary,
> Hope comes to Die.
> A Dream—a *Wa*-kening.

But now Sadie interrupted them. "What is it, Sadie?"

"If you please, m'm, cook says have you got the flags for the sandwiches?"

"The flags for the sandwiches, Sadie?" echoed Mrs. Sheridan dreamily. And the children knew by her face that she hadn't got them. "Let me see." And she said to Sadie firmly, "Tell cook I'll let her have them in ten minutes."

Sadie went.

"Now, Laura," said her mother quickly. "Come with me into the smoking-room. I've got the names somewhere on the back of an envelope. You'll have to write them out for me. Meg, go upstairs this minute and take that wet thing off your head. Jose, run and finish dressing this instant. Do you hear me, children, or shall I have to tell your father when he comes home tonight? And—and, Jose, pacify cook if you do go into the kitchen, will you? I'm terrified of her this morning."

The envelope was found at last behind the dining-room clock, though how it had got there Mrs. Sheridan could not imagine.

"One of you children must have stolen it out of my bag, because I remember vividly—cream cheese and lemon-curd. Have you done that?"

"Yes."

"Egg and—" Mrs. Sheridan held the envelope away from her. "It looks like mice. It can't be mice, can it?"

"Olive, pet," said Laura, looking over her shoulder.

"Yes, of course, olive. What a horrible combination it sounds. Egg and olive."

They were finished at last, and Laura took them off to the kitchen. She found Jose there pacifying the cook, who did not look at all terrifying.

"I have never seen such exquisite sandwiches," said Jose's rapturous voice. "How many kinds did you say there were, cook? Fifteen?"

"Fifteen, Miss Jose."

"Well, cook, I congratulate you."

Cook swept up crusts with the long sandwich knife, and smiled broadly.

"Godber's has come," announced Sadie, issuing out of the pantry. She had seen the man pass the window.

That meant the cream puffs had come. Godber's were famous for their cream puffs. Nobody ever thought of making them at home.

"Bring them in and put them on the table, my girl," ordered cook.

Sadie brought them in and went back to the door. Of course Laura and Jose were far too grown-up to really care about such things. All the same, they couldn't help agreeing that the puffs looked very attractive. Very. Cook began arranging them, shaking off the extra icing sugar.

"Don't they carry one back to all one's parties?" said Laura.

"I suppose they do," said practical Jose, who never liked to be carried back. "They look beautifully light and feathery, I must say."

"Have one each, my dears," said cook in her comfortable voice. "Yer ma won't know."

Oh, impossible. Fancy cream puffs so soon after breakfast. The very idea made one shudder. All the same, two minutes later Jose and Laura were licking their fingers with that absorbed inward look that only comes from whipped cream.

"Let's go into the garden, out by the back way," suggested Laura. "I want to see how the men are getting on with the marquee. They're such awfully nice men."

But the back door was blocked by cook, Sadie, Godber's man and Hans.

Something had happened.

"Tuk-tuk-tuk," clucked cook like an agitated hen. Sadie had her hand clapped to her cheek as though she had toothache. Hans's face was screwed up in the effort to understand. Only Godber's man seemed to be enjoying himself; it was his story.

"What's the matter? What's happened?"

"There's been a horrible accident," said cook. "A man killed."

"A man killed! Where? How? When?"

But Godber's man wasn't going to have his story snatched from under his very nose.

"Know those little cottages just below here, miss?" Know them? Of course she knew them. "Well, there's a young chap living there, name of Scott, a carter. His horse shied at a traction-engine, corner of Hawke Street this morning, and he was thrown out on the back of his head. Killed."

"Dead!" Laura stared at Godber's man.

"Dead when they picked him up," said Godber's man with relish. "They were taking the body home as I come up here." And she said to the cook, "He's left a wife and five little ones."

"Jose, come back here." Laura caught hold of her sister's sleeve and dragged her through the kitchen to the other side of the green baize door. There she paused and leaned against it. "Jose!" she said, horrified, "however are we going to stop everything?"

"Stop everything, Laura!" cried Jose in astonishment. "What do you mean?"

"Stop the garden-party, of course." Why did Jose pretend?

But Jose was still more amazed. "Stop the garden-party? My dear Laura, don't be so absurd. Of course we can't do anything of the kind. Nobody expects us to. Don't be so extravagant."

"But we can't possibly have a garden-party with a man dead just outside the front gate."

That really was extravagant, for the little cottages were in a lane to themselves at the very bottom of a steep rise that led up to the house. A broad road ran between. True, they were far too near. They were the greatest possible eyesore, and they had no right to be in that neighbourhood at all. They were little mean dwellings painted a chocolate brown. In the garden patches there was nothing but cabbage stalks, sick hens and tomato cans. The very smoke coming out of their chimneys was poverty-stricken. Little rags and shreds of smoke, so unlike the great silvery plumes that uncurled from the Sheridans' chimneys. Washer-women lived in the lane and sweeps and a cobbler, and a man whose house-front was studded all over with minute bird-cages. Children swarmed. When the Sheridans were little they were forbidden to set foot there because of the revolting language and of what they might catch. But since they were grown up, Laura and Laurie on their prowls sometimes walked through. It was disgusting and sordid. They came out with a shudder. But still one must go everywhere; one must see everything. So through they went.

"And just think of what the band would sound like to that poor woman," said Laura.

"Oh, Laura!" Jose began to be seriously annoyed. "If you're going to stop a band playing every time some one has an accident, you'll lead a very strenuous life. I'm every bit as sorry about it as you. I feel just as sympathetic." Her eyes hardened. She looked at her sister just as she used to when they were little and fighting together. "You won't bring a drunken workman back to life by being sentimental," she said softly.

"Drunk! Who said he was drunk?" Laura turned furiously on Jose. She said, just as they had used to say on those occasions, "I'm going straight up to tell mother."

"Do, dear," cooed Jose.

"Mother, can I come into your room?" Laura turned the big glass doorknob.

"Of course, child. Why, what's the matter? What's given you such a colour?" And Mrs. Sheridan turned round from her dressing-table. She was trying on a new hat.

"Mother, a man's been killed," began Laura.

"*Not* in the garden?" interrupted her mother.

"No, no!"

"Oh, what a fright you gave me!" Mrs. Sheridan sighed with relief, and took off the big hat and held it on her knees.

"But listen, mother," said Laura. Breathless, half-choking, she told the dreadful story. "Of course, we can't have our party, can we?" she pleaded. "The band and everybody arriving. They'd hear us, mother; they're nearly neighbours!"

To Laura's astonishment her mother behaved just like Jose; it was harder to bear because she seemed amused. She refused to take Laura seriously.

"But, my dear child, use your common sense. It's only by accident we've heard of it. If some one had died there normally—and I can't understand how they keep alive in those poky little holes—we should still be having our party, shouldn't we?"

Laura had to say "yes" to that, but she felt it was all wrong. She sat down on her mother's sofa and pinched the cushion frill.

"Mother, isn't it really terribly heartless of us?" she asked.

"Darling!" Mrs. Sheridan got up and came over to her, carrying the hat. Before Laura could stop her she had popped it on. "My child!" said her mother, "the hat is yours. It's made for you. It's much too young for me. I have never seen you look such a picture. Look at yourself!" And she held up her hand-mirror.

"But, mother," Laura began again. She couldn't look at herself; she turned aside.

This time Mrs. Sheridan lost patience just as Jose had done.

"You are being very absurd, Laura," she said coldly. "People like that don't expect sacrifices from us. And it's not very sympathetic to spoil everybody's enjoyment as you're doing now."

"I don't understand," said Laura, and she walked quickly out of the room into her own bedroom. There, quite by chance, the first thing she saw was this charming girl in the mirror, in her black hat trimmed with gold daisies, and a long black velvet ribbon. Never had she imagined she could look like that. Is mother right? she thought. And now she hoped her mother was right. Am I being extravagant? Perhaps it was extravagant. Just for a moment she had another glimpse of that poor woman and those little children, and the body being carried into the house. But it all seemed blurred, unreal, like a picture in the newspaper. I'll remember it again after the party's over, she decided. And somehow that seemed quite the best plan. . . .

Lunch was over by half-past one. By half-past two they were all ready for the fray. The green-coated band had arrived and was established in a corner of the tennis-court.

"My dear!" trilled Kitty Maitland, "aren't they too like frogs for words? You ought to have arranged them round the pond with the conductor in the middle on a leaf."

Laurie arrived and hailed them on his way to dress. At the sight of him Laura remembered the accident again. She wanted to tell him. If Laurie agreed with the others, then it was bound to be all right. And she followed him into the hall.

"Laurie!"

"Hallo!" He was half-way upstairs, but when he turned round and saw Laura he suddenly puffed out his cheeks and goggled his eyes at her. "My word, Laura! You do look stunning," said Laurie. "What an absolutely topping hat!"

Laura said faintly "Is it?" and smiled up at Laurie, and didn't tell him after all.

Soon after that people began coming in streams. The band stuck up; the hired waiters ran from the house to the marquee. Wherever you looked there were couples strolling, bending to the flowers, greeting, moving on over the lawn. They were like bright birds that had alighted in the Sheridans' garden for this one afternoon, on their way to—where? Ah, what happiness it is to be with people who all are happy, to press hands, press cheeks, smile into eyes.

"Darling Laura, how well you look!"

"What a becoming hat, child!"

"Laura, you look quite Spanish. I've never seen you look so striking."

And Laura, glowing, answered softly, "Have you had tea? Won't you have an ice? The passion-fruit ices really are rather special." She ran to her father and begged him. "Daddy darling, can't the band have something to drink?"

And the perfect afternoon slowly ripened, slowly faded, slowly its petals closed.

"Never a more delightful garden-party . . ." "The greatest success . . ." "Quite the most . . ."

Laura helped her mother with the good-byes. They stood side by side in the porch till it was all over.

"All over, all over, thank heaven," said Mrs. Sheridan. "Round up the others, Laura. Let's go and have some fresh coffee. I'm exhausted. Yes, it's been very successful. But oh, these parties, these parties!" And they all of them sat down in the deserted marquee.

"Have a sandwich, daddy dear. I wrote the flag."

"Thanks." Mr. Sheridan took a bite and the sandwich was gone. He took another. "I suppose you didn't hear of a beastly accident that happened to-day?" he said.

"My dear," said Mrs. Sheridan, holding up her hand, "we did. It nearly ruined the party. Laura insisted we should put it off."

"Oh mother!" Laura didn't want to be teased about it.

"It was a horrible affair all the same," said Mr. Sheridan. "The chap was married too. Lived just below in the lane, and leaves a wife and half a dozen kiddies, so they say."

An awkward little silence fell. Mrs. Sheridan fidgeted with her cup. Really, it was very tactless of father . . .

Suddenly she looked up. There on the table were all those sandwiches, cakes, puffs, all uneaten, all going to be wasted. She had one of her brilliant ideas.

"I know," she said. "Let's make up a basket. Let's send that poor creature some of this perfectly good food. At any rate, it will be the greatest treat for the children. Don't you agree? And she's sure to have neighbours calling in and so on. What a point to have it all ready prepared. Laura!" She jumped up. "Get me the big basket out of the stairs cupboard."

"But, mother, do you really think it's a good idea?" said Laura.

Again, how curious, she seemed to be different from them all. To take scraps from their party. Would the poor woman really like that?

"Of course! What's the matter with you to-day? An hour or two ago you were insisting on us being sympathetic, and now—"

Oh, well! Laura ran for the basket. It was filled, it was heaped by her mother.

"Take it yourself, darling," said she. "Run down just as you are. No, wait, take the arum lilies too. People of that class are so impressed by arum lilies."

"The stems will ruin her lace frock," said practical Jose.

So they would. Just in time. "Only the basket, then. And, Laura!"—her mother followed her out of the marquee—"don't on any account—"

"What, mother?"

No, better not put such ideas into the child's head! "Nothing! Run along."

It was just growing dusky as Laura shut their garden gates. A big dog ran by like a shadow. The road gleamed white, and down below in the hollow the little cottages were in deep shade. How quiet it seemed after the afternoon. Here she was going down the hill to somewhere where a man lay dead, and she couldn't realize it. Why couldn't she? She stopped a minute. And it seemed to her that kisses, voices, tinkling spoons, laughter, the smell of crushed grass were somehow inside her. She had no room for anything else. How strange! She looked up at the pale sky, and all she thought was, "Yes, it was the most successful party."

Now the broad road was crossed. The lane began, smoky and dark. Women in shawls and men's tweed caps hurried by. Men hung over the palings; the children played in the doorways. A low hum came from the mean little cottages. In some of them there was a flicker of light, and a shadow, crab-like, moved across the window. Laura bent her head and hurried on. She wished now she had put on a coat. How her frock shone! And the big hat with the velvet streamer—if only it was another hat! Were the people looking at her? They must be. It was a mistake to have come; she knew all along it was a mistake. Should she go back even now?

No, too late. This was the house. It must be. A dark knot of people stood outside. Beside the gate an old, old woman with a crutch sat in a chair, watching. She had her feet on a newspaper. The voices stopped as Laura drew near. The group parted. It was as though she was expected, as though they had known she was coming here.

Laura was terribly nervous. Tossing the velvet ribbon over her shoulder, she said to a woman standing by, "Is this Mrs. Scott's house?" and the woman, smiling queerly, said, "It is, my lass."

Oh, to be away from this! She actually said, "Help me, God," as she walked up the tiny path and knocked. To be away from those staring eyes, or to be covered up in anything, one of those women's shawls even. I'll just leave the basket and go, she decided. I shan't even wait for it to be emptied.

Then the door opened. A little woman in black showed in the gloom.

Laura said, "Are you Mrs. Scott?" But to her horror the woman answered, "Walk in please, miss," and she was shut in the passage.

"No," said Laura, "I don't want to come in. I only want to leave this basket. Mother sent—"

The little woman in the gloomy passage seemed not to have heard her. "Step this way, please, miss," she said in an oily voice, and Laura followed her.

She found herself in a wretched little low kitchen, lighted by a smoky lamp. There was a woman sitting before the fire.

"Em," said the little creature who had let her in. "Em! It's a young lady." She turned to Laura. She said meaningly, "I'm 'er sister, miss. You'll excuse 'er, won't you?"

"Oh, but of course!" said Laura. "Please, please don't disturb her. I—I only want to leave—"

But at that moment the woman at the fire turned round. Her face, puffed up, red, with swollen eyes and swollen lips, looked terrible. She seemed as though she couldn't understand why Laura was there. What did it mean? Why was this stranger standing in the kitchen with a basket? What was it all about? And the poor face puckered up again.

"All right, my dear," said the other. "I'll thenk the young lady."

And again she began, "You'll excuse her, miss, I'm sure," and her face, swollen too, tried an oily smile.

Laura only wanted to get out, to get away. She was back in the passage. The door opened. She walked straight through into the bedroom, where the dead man was lying.

"You'd like a look at 'im, wouldn't you?" said Em's sister, and she brushed past Laura over to the bed. "Don't be afraid, my lass—" and now her voice sounded fond and sly, and fondly she drew down the sheet—" 'e looks a picture. There's nothing to show. Come along, my dear."

Laura came.

There lay a young man, fast asleep—sleeping so soundly, so deeply, that he was far, far away from them both. Oh, so remote, so peaceful. He was dreaming. Never wake him up again. His head was sunk in the pillow, his eyes were closed; they were blind under the closed eyelids. He was given up to his dream. What did garden-parties and baskets and lace frocks matter to him? He was far from all those things. He was wonderful, beautiful. While they were laughing and while the band was playing, this marvel had come to the lane. Happy . . . happy. . . . All is well, said that sleeping face. This is just as it should be. I am content.

But all the same you had to cry, and she couldn't go out of the room without saying something to him. Laura gave a loud childish sob.

"Forgive my hat," she said.

And this time she didn't wait for Em's sister. She found her way out of the door, down the path, past all those dark people. At the corner of the lane she met Laurie.

He stepped out of the shadow. "Is that you, Laura?"

"Yes."

"Mother was getting anxious. Was it all right?"

"Yes, quite. Oh, Laurie!" She took his arm, she pressed up against him.

"I say, you're not crying, are you?" asked her brother.

Laura shook her head. She was.

Laurie put his arm round her shoulder. "Don't cry," he said in his warm, loving voice. "Was it awful?"

"No," sobbed Laura. "It was simply marvellous. But, Laurie—" She stopped, she looked at her brother. "Isn't life—" But what life was she couldn't explain. No matter. He quite understood.

"*Isn't* it, darling?" said Laurie.

Katherine Anne Porter

(1890-1980)

Katherine Anne Porter once said she left the South—she was born and raised in rural Texas—because she thought as a woman writer she'd be made to feel like a "freak." Her biography is a tangled web of myths she promoted about herself—she claimed an old south-ern aristocratic background—and the attempts of critics and biog-raphers to chart the details of her tumultuous life in the pages of her stories. What is incontrovertibly clear in her twenty-seven works of short fiction, published in such well-known collections as *Flowering Judas* (1930), *Pale Horse, Pale Rider* (1939), *The Leaning Tower* (1944), the *Collected Stories* (1965)—winner of the Pulitzer Prize and the National Book Award—is their "bright aesthetic intelligence," to quote Elizabeth Hardwick (who also calls her "a complicated ego-ist"); Robert Penn Warren thought Porter's stories were "unsur-passed in modern fiction." Like another southern woman writer, Flannery O'Connor, Porter wrote out of a profound sense of reli-gious mystery, often focused on society's outcasts. Despite the grand-southern-lady act of her later years, she herself knew many years of poverty in a dirt-poor rural Texas that gives the following story its terrible reality.

He

Life was very hard for the Whipples. It was hard to feed all the hungry mouths, it was hard to keep the children in flannels during the winter, short as it was: "God knows what would become of us if we lived north," they would say: keeping them decently clean was hard. "It looks like our luck won't never let up on us," said Mr. Whipple, but Mrs. Whipple was all for taking what was sent and calling it good, anyhow when the neighbors were in earshot. "Don't ever let a soul hear us complain," she kept saying to her husband. She couldn't stand to be pitied. "No, not if it comes to it that we have to live in a wagon and pick cotton around the country," she said, "nobody's going to get a chance to look down on us."

Mrs. Whipple loved her second son, the simple-minded one, better than she loved the other two children put together. She was forever saying so, and when she talked with certain of her neighbors, she would even throw in her husband and her mother for good measure.

"You needn't keep on saying it around," said Mr. Whipple, "you'll make people think nobody else has any feelings about Him but you."

"It's natural for a mother," Mrs. Whipple would remind him. "You know yourself it's more natural for a mother to be that way. People don't expect so much of fathers, some way."

This didn't keep the neighbors from talking plainly among themselves. "A Lord's pure mercy if He should die," they said. "It's the sins of the fathers," they agreed among themselves. "There's bad blood and bad doings somewhere, you can bet on that." This behind the Whipples' backs. To their faces everybody said, "He's not so bad off. He'll be all right yet. Look how He grows!"

Mrs. Whipple hated to talk about it, she tried to keep her mind off it, but every time anybody set foot in the house, the subject always came up, and she had to talk about Him first, before she could get on to anything else. It seemed to ease her mind. "I wouldn't have anything happen to Him for all the world, but it just looks like I can't keep Him out of mischief. He's so strong and active, He's always into everything; He was like that since He could walk. It's actually funny sometimes, the way He can do anything; it's laughable to see Him up to His tricks. Emly has more accidents; I'm forever tying up her bruises, and Adna can't fall a foot without cracking a bone. But He can do everything and not get a scratch. The preacher said such a nice thing once when he was here. He said, and I'll remember it to my dying day, 'The innocent walk with God—that's why He don't get hurt.'" Whenever Mrs. Whipple repeated these words, she always felt a warm pool spread in her breast, and the tears would fill her eyes, and then she could talk about something else.

He did grow and He never got hurt. A plank blew off the chicken house and struck Him on the head and He never seemed to know it. He had learned a few words, and after this He forgot them. He didn't whine for food as the other children did, but waited until it was given Him; He ate squatting in the corner, smacking and mumbling. Rolls of fat covered Him like an overcoat, and He could carry twice as much wood and water as Adna. Emly had a cold in the head most of the time—"she takes that after me," said Mrs. Whipple—so in bad weather they gave her the extra blanket off His cot. He never seemed to mind the cold.

Just the same, Mrs. Whipple's life was a torment for fear something might happen to Him. He climbed the peach trees much better than Adna and went skittering along the branches like a monkey, just a regular monkey. "Oh, Mrs. Whipple, you hadn't ought to let Him do that. He'll lose His balance sometime. He can't rightly know what He's doing."

Mrs. Whipple almost screamed out at the neighbor. "He *does* know what He's doing! He's as able as any other child! Come down out of there, you!" When He finally reached the ground she could hardly keep her hands off Him for acting like that before people, a grin all over His face and her worried sick about Him all the time.

"It's the neighbors," said Mrs. Whipple to her husband. "Oh, I do mortally wish they would keep out of our business. I can't afford to let Him do anything for fear they'll come nosing around about it. Look at the bees, now. Adna can't handle them, they sting him up so; I haven't got time to do everything, and now I don't dare let Him. But if He gets a sting He don't really mind."

"It's just because He ain't got sense enough to be scared of anything," said Mr. Whipple.

"You ought to be ashamed of yourself," said Mrs. Whipple, "talking that way about your own child. Who's to take up for Him if we don't, I'd like to know? He sees a lot that goes on, He listens to things all the time. And anything I tell Him to do He does it. Don't never let anybody hear you say such things. They'd think you favored the other children over Him."

"Well, now I don't, and you know it, and what's the use of getting all worked up about it? You always think the worst of everything. Just let Him alone, He'll get along somehow. He gets plenty to eat and wear, don't He?" Mr. Whipple suddenly felt tired out. "Anyhow, it can't be helped now."

Mrs. Whipple felt tired too, she complained in a tired voice. "What's done can't never be undone, I know that as good as anybody; but He's my child, and I'm not going to have people say anything. I get sick of people coming around saying things all the time."

In the early fall Mrs. Whipple got a letter from her brother saying he and his wife and two children were coming over for a little visit next Sunday week. "Put the big pot in the little one," he wrote at the end. Mrs. Whipple read this part out loud twice, she was so pleased. Her brother was a great one for saying funny things. "We'll just show him that's no joke," she said, "we'll just butcher one of the sucking pigs."

"It's a waste and I don't hold with waste the way we are now," said Mr. Whipple. "That pig'll be worth money by Christmas."

"It's a shame and a pity we can't have a decent meal's vittles once in a while when my own family comes to see us," said Mrs. Whipple. "I'd hate for his wife to go back and say there wasn't a thing in the house to eat. My God, it's better than buying up a great chance of meat in town. There's where you'd spend the money!"

"All right, do it yourself then," said Mr. Whipple. "Christa-mighty, no wonder we can't get ahead!"

The question was how to get the little pig away from his ma, a great fight-er, worse than a Jersey cow. Adna wouldn't try it: "That sow'd rip my insides out all over the pen." "All right, old fraidy," said Mrs. Whipple, "*He's* not scared. Watch *Him* do it." And she laughed as though it was all a good joke and gave Him a little push towards the pen. He sneaked up and snatched the pig right away from the teat and galloped back and was over the fence with the sow raging at His heels. The little black squirming thing was screeching like a baby in a tantrum, stiffening its back and stretching its mouth to the ears. Mrs. Whipple took the pig with her face stiff and sliced its throat with one stroke. When He saw the blood He gave a great jolting breath and ran away. "But He'll forget and eat plenty, just the same," thought Mrs. Whipple. Whenever she was thinking, her lips moved making words. "He'd eat it all if I didn't stop Him. He'd eat up every mouthful from the other two if I'd let Him."

She felt badly about it. He was ten years old now and a third again as large as Adna, who was going on fourteen. "It's a shame, a shame," she kept saying under her breath, "and Adna with so much brains!"

She kept on feeling badly about all sorts of things. In the first place it was the man's work to butcher; the sight of the pig scraped pink and naked made her sick. He was too fat and soft and pitiful-looking. It was simply a shame the way things had to happen. By the time she had finished it up, she almost wished her brother would stay at home.

Early Sunday morning Mrs. Whipple dropped everything to get Him all cleaned up. In an hour He was dirty again, with crawling under fences after a possum, and straddling along the rafters of the barn looking for eggs in the hayloft. "My Lord, look at you now after all my trying! And here's Adna and Emly staying so quiet. I get tired trying to keep you decent. Get off that shirt and put on another, people will say I don't half dress you!" And she boxed Him on the ears, hard. He blinked and blinked and rubbed His head, and His face hurt Mrs. Whipple's feelings. His knees began to tremble, she had to sit down while she buttoned His shirt. "I'm just all gone before the day starts."

The brother came with his plump healthy wife and two great roaring hungry boys. They had a grand dinner, with the pig roasted to a crackling in the middle of the table, full of dressing, a pickled peach in his mouth and plenty of gravy for the sweet potatoes.

"This looks like prosperity all right," said the brother; "you're going to have to roll me home like I was a barrel when I'm done."

Everybody laughed out loud; it was fine to hear them laughing all at once around the table. Mrs. Whipple felt warm and good about it. "Oh, we've got six more of these; I say it's as little as we can do when you come to see us so seldom."

He wouldn't come into the dining room, and Mrs. Whipple passed it off very well. "He's timider than my other two," she said, "He'll just have to get used to you. There isn't everybody He'll make up with, you know how it is with some children, even cousins." Nobody said anything out of the way.

"Just like my Alty here," said the brother's wife. "I sometimes got to lick him to make him shake hands with his own grandmammy."

So that was over, and Mrs. Whipple loaded up a big plate for Him first, before everybody. "I always say He ain't to be slighted, no matter who else goes without," she said, and carried it to Him herself.

"He can chin Himself on the top of the door," said Emly, helping along.

"That's fine. He's getting along fine," said the brother.

They went away after supper. Mrs. Whipple rounded up the dishes, and sent the children to bed and sat down and unlaced her shoes. "You see?" she said to Mr. Whipple. "That's the way my whole family is. Nice and considerate about everything. No out-of-the-way remarks—they *have* got refinement. I get awfully sick of people's remarks. Wasn't that pig good?"

Mr. Whipple said, "Yes, we're out three hundred pounds of pork, that's all. It's easy to be polite when you come to eat. Who knows what they had in their minds all along?"

"Yes, that's like you," said Mrs. Whipple. "I don't expect anything else from you. You'll be telling me next that my own brother will be saying around that we made Him eat in the kitchen! Oh, my God!" She rocked her head in her hands, a hard pain started in the very middle of her forehead. "Now it's all spoiled, and everything was so nice and easy. All right, you don't like them and you never did—all right, they'll not come here again soon, never you mind! But they *can't* say He wasn't dressed every lick as good as Adna—oh, honest, sometimes I wish I was dead!"

"I wish you'd let up," said Mr. Whipple. "It's bad enough as it is."

It was a hard winter. It seemed to Mrs. Whipple that they hadn't ever known anything but hard times, and now to cap it all a winter like this. The crops were about half of what they had a right to expect; after the cotton was in it didn't do much more than cover the grocery bill. They swapped off one of the plow horses, and got cheated, for the new one died of the heaves. Mrs. Whipple kept thinking all the time it was terrible to have a man you couldn't depend on not to get cheated. They cut down on everything, but Mrs. Whipple kept saying there are things you can't cut down on, and they cost money. It took a lot of warm clothes for Adna and Emly, who walked four miles to school during the three-months session. "He sets around the fire a lot, He won't need so much," said Mr. Whipple. "That's so," said Mrs. Whipple, "and when He does the outdoor chores He can wear your tarpaullion coat. I can't do no better, that's all."

In February He was taken sick, and lay curled up under His blanket looking very blue in the face and acting as if He would choke. Mr. and Mrs. Whipple did everything they could for Him for two days, and then they were scared and sent for the doctor. The doctor told them they must keep Him warm and give Him plenty of milk and eggs. "He isn't as stout as he looks, I'm afraid," said the doctor. "You've got to watch them when they're like that. You must put more cover on to Him, too."

"I just took off His big blanket to wash," said Mrs. Whipple, ashamed. "I can't stand dirt."

"Well, you'd better put it back on the minute it's dry," said the doctor, "or He'll have pneumonia."

Mr. and Mrs. Whipple took a blanket off their own bed and put His cot by the fire. "They can't say we didn't do everything for Him," she said, "even to sleeping cold ourselves on His account."

When the winter broke He seemed to be well again, but He walked as if His feet hurt Him. He was able to run a cotton planter during the season.

"I got it all fixed up with Jim Ferguson about breeding the cow next time," said Mr. Whipple. "I'll pasture the bull this summer and give Jim some fodder in the fall. That's better than paying out money when you haven't got it."

"I hope you didn't say such a thing before Jim Ferguson," said Mrs. Whipple. "You oughtn't to let him know we're so down as all that."

"Godamighty, that ain't saying we're down. A man is got to look ahead sometimes. He can lead the bull over today. I need Adna on the place."

At first Mrs. Whipple felt easy in her mind about sending Him for the bull. Adna was too jumpy and couldn't be trusted. You've got to be steady around animals. After He was gone she started thinking, and after a while she could hardly bear it any longer. She stood in the lane and watched for Him. It was nearly three miles to go and a hot day, but He oughtn't to be so long about it. She shaded her eyes and and stared until colored bubbles floated in her eyeballs. It was just like everything else in life, she must always worry and never know a moment's peace about anything. After a long time she saw Him turn into the side lane, limping. He came on very slowly, leading the big hulk of an animal by a ring in the nose, twirling a little stick in His hand, never looking back or sideways, but coming on like a sleepwalker with His eyes half shut.

Mrs. Whipple was scared sick of bulls; she had heard awful stories about how they followed on quietly enough, and then suddenly pitched on with a bellow and pawed and gored a body to pieces. Any second now that black monster would come down on Him, my God, He'd never have sense enough to run.

She mustn't make a sound nor a move; she mustn't get the bull started. The bull heaved his head aside and horned the air at a fly. Her voice burst out of her in a shriek, and she screamed at Him to come on, for God's sake. He didn't seem to hear her clamor, but kept on twirling His switch and limping on, and the bull lumbered along behind him as gently as a calf. Mrs. Whipple stopped calling and ran towards the house, praying under her breath: "Lord, don't let anything happen to Him. Lord, you *know* people will say we oughtn't to have sent Him. You *know* they'll say we didn't take care of Him. Oh, get

Him home, safe home, safe home, and I'll look out for Him better! Amen."

She watched from the window while He led the beast in, and tied him up in the barn. It was no use trying to keep up, Mrs. Whipple couldn't bear another thing. She sat down and rocked and cried with her apron over her head.

From year to year the Whipples were growing poorer and poorer. The place just seemed to run down of itself, no matter how hard they worked. "We're losing our hold," said Mrs. Whipple. "Why can't we do like other people and watch for our best chances? They'll be calling us poor white trash next."

"When I get to be sixteen I'm going to leave," said Adna. "I'm going to get a job in Powell's grocery store. There's money in that. No more farm for me."

"I'm going to be a schoolteacher," said Emly. "But I've got to finish the eighth grade, anyhow. Then I can live in town. I don't see any chances here."

"Emly takes after my family," said Mrs. Whipple. "Ambitious every last one of them, and they don't take second place for anybody."

When fall came Emly got a chance to wait on table in the railroad eating-house in the town near by, and it seemed such a shame not to take it when the wages were good and she could get her food too, that Mrs. Whipple decided to let her take it, and not bother with school until the next session. "You've got plenty of time," she said. "You're young and smart as a whip."

With Adna gone too, Mr. Whipple tried to run the farm with just Him to help. He seemed to get along fine, doing His work and part of Adna's without noticing it. They did well enough until Christmas time, when one morning He slipped on the ice coming up from the barn. Instead of getting up He thrashed round and round, and when Mr. Whipple got to Him, He was having some sort of fit.

They brought him inside and tried to make Him sit up, but He blubbered and rolled, so they put Him to bed and Mr. Whipple rode to town for the doctor. All the way there and back he worried about where the money was to come from: it sure did look like he had about all the trouble he could carry.

From then on He stayed in bed. His legs swelled up double their size, and the fits kept coming back. After four months, the doctor said, "It's no use, I think you'd better put Him in the County Home for treatment right away. I'll see about it for you. He'll have good care there and be off your hands."

"We don't begrudge Him any care, and I won't let Him out of my sight," said Mrs. Whipple. "I won't have it said I sent my sick child off among strangers."

"I know how you feel," said the doctor. "You can't tell me anything about that, Mrs. Whipple. I've got a boy of my own. But you'd better listen to me. I can't do anything more for Him, that's the truth."

Mr. and Mrs. Whipple talked it over a long time that night after they went to bed. "It's just charity," said Mrs. Whipple, "that's what we've come to, charity! I certainly never looked for this."

"We pay taxes to help support the place just like everybody else," said Mr. Whipple, "and I don't call that taking charity. I think it would be fine to have Him where He'd get the best of everything . . . and besides, I can't keep up with these doctor bills any longer."

"Maybe that's why the doctor wants us to send Him—he's scared he won't get his money," said Mrs. Whipple.

"Don't talk like that," said Mr. Whipple, feeling pretty sick, "or we won't be able to send Him."

"Oh, but we won't keep Him there long," said Mrs. Whipple. "Soon He's better, we'll bring Him right back home."

"The doctor has told you and told you time and again He can't ever get better, and you might as well stop talking," said Mr. Whipple.

"Doctors don't know everything," said Mrs. Whipple, feeling almost happy. "But anyhow, in the summer Emly can come home for a vacation, and Adna can get down for Sundays: we'll all work together and get on our feet again, and the children will feel they've got a place to come to."

All at once she saw it full summer again, with the garden going fine, and new white roller shades up all over the house, and Adna and Emly home, so full of life, all of them happy together. Oh, it could happen, things would ease up on them.

They didn't talk before Him much, but they never knew just how much He understood. Finally the doctor set the day and a neighbor who owned a double-seated carryall offered to drive them over. The hospital would have sent an ambulance, but Mrs. Whipple couldn't stand to see Him going away looking so sick as all that. They wrapped Him in blankets, and the neighbor and Mr. Whipple lifted Him into the back seat of the carryall beside Mrs. Whipple, who had on her black shirt waist. She couldn't stand to go looking like charity.

"You'll be all right, I guess I'll stay behind," said Mr. Whipple. "It don't look like everybody ought to leave the place at once."

"Besides, it ain't as if He was going to stay forever," said Mrs. Whipple to the neighbor. "This is only for a little while."

They started away, Mrs. Whipple holding to the edges of the blankets to keep Him from sagging sideways. He sat there blinking and blinking. He worked His hands out and began rubbing His nose with His knuckles, and then with the end of the blanket. Mrs. Whipple couldn't believe what she saw; He was scrubbing away big tears that rolled out of the corners of His eyes. He sniveled and made a gulping noise. Mrs. Whipple kept saying, "Oh, honey, you don't feel so bad, do you? You don't feel so bad, do you?" for He seemed to be accusing her of something. Maybe He remembered that time she boxed His ears, maybe He had been scared that day with the bull, maybe He had slept cold and couldn't tell her about it; maybe He knew they were sending Him away for good and all because they were too poor to keep Him. Whatever it was, Mrs. Whipple couldn't bear to think about it. She began to cry, frightfully, and wrapped her arms tight around Him. His head rolled on her shoulder: she had loved Him as much as she possibly could, there were Adna and Emly who had to be thought of too, there was nothing she could do to make up to Him for His life. Oh, what a mortal pity He was ever born.

They came in sight of the hospital, with the neighbor driving very fast, not daring to look behind him.

Zora Neale Hurston

(1891–1960)

When Zora Neale Hurston was a child in Florida she was told by her mother to "jump at de sun—and you might at least catch holt to de moon." Her mother died when she was young and she left home to move north, graduating from Barnard, and becoming a professional folklorist and one of the writers of the Harlem Literary Renaissance. She was always a witness to the expressive beauty and courage of African American culture, celebrating it in over one hundred manuscripts—short stories, novels, plays, essays, articles. Her masterpiece, the novel *Their Eyes Were Watching God* (1937), the story of Janie Crawford's rise above racism, sexism, and poverty to a triumphant wisdom, is now a favorite of African American literature. *Dust Tracks on a Road* (1942), one of the century's most popular autobiographies, received the mixed reviews from both white and black critics that dogged Hurston throughout her long career. Her use of black vernacular speech and rituals in her writing was thought to denigrate her people. (Richard Wright accused her of minstrelsy.) She died in poverty and obscurity in Florida. Her unmarked pauper's grave was discovered by Alice Walker during her crusade to reclaim Hurston's writing and reputation, a literary revival published by Walker as *I Love Myself When I Am Laughing: A Zora Neale Hurston Reader* (1977). In Walker's words, Hurston inspires all African American writers as a symbol of "racial health—a sense of black people as complete, complex, undiminished human beings."

How It Feels to Be Colored Me

I am colored but I offer nothing in the way of extenuating circumstances except the fact that I am the only Negro in the United States whose grandfather on the mother's side was *not* an Indian chief.

I remember the very day that I became colored. Up to my thirteenth year

I lived in the little Negro town of Eatonville, Florida. It is exclusively a colored town. The only white people I knew passed through the town going to or coming from Orlando. The native whites rode dusty horses, the Northern tourists chugged down the sandy village road in automobiles. The town knew the Southerners and never stopped cane chewing when they passed. But the Northerners were something else again. They were peered at cautiously from behind curtains by the timid. The more venturesome would come out on the porch to watch them go past and got just as much pleasure out of the tourists as the tourists got out of the village.

The front porch might seem a daring place for the rest of the town, but it was a gallery seat for me. My favorite place was atop the gate-post. Proscenium box for a born first-nighter. Not only did I enjoy the show, but I didn't mind the actors knowing that I liked it. I usually spoke to them in passing. I'd wave at them and when they returned my salute, I would say something like this: "Howdy-do-well-I-thank-you-where-you-goin'?" Usually automobile or the horse paused at this, and after a queer exchange of compliments, I would probably "go a piece of the way" with them, as we say in farthest Florida. If one of my family happened to come to the front in time to see me, of course negotiations would be rudely broken off. But even so, it is clear that I was the first "welcome-to-our-state" Floridian, and I hope the Miami Chamber of Commerce will please take notice.

During this period, white people differed from colored to me only in that they rode through town and never lived there. They liked to hear me "speak pieces" and sing and wanted to see me dance the parse-me-la, and gave me generously of their small silver for doing these things, which seemed strange to me for I wanted to do them so much that I needed bribing to stop. Only they didn't know it. The colored people gave me no dimes. They deplored any joyful tendencies in me, but I was their Zora nevertheless. I belonged to them, to the nearby hotels, to the county—everybody's Zora.

But changes came in the family when I was thirteen, and I was sent to school in Jacksonville. I left Eatonville, the town of the oleanders, as Zora. When I disembarked from the river-boat at Jacksonville, she was no more. It seemed that I had suffered a sea change. I was not Zora of Orange County any more, I was now a little colored girl. I found it out in certain ways. In my heart as well as in the mirror, I became a fast brown—warranted not to rub nor run.

But I am not tragically colored. There is no great sorrow dammed up in my soul, nor lurking behind my eyes. I do not mind at all. I do not belong to the sobbing school of Negrohood who hold that nature somehow has given them a lowdown dirty deal and whose feelings are all hurt about it. Even in the helter-skelter skirmish that is my life, I have seen that the world is to the strong regardless of a little pigmentation more or less. No, I do not weep at the world—I am too busy sharpening my oyster knife.

Someone is always at my elbow reminding me that I am the grand-daughter of slaves. It fails to register depression with me. Slavery is sixty years in the past. The operation was successful and the patient is doing well, thank you. The terrible struggle that made me an American out of a potential slave said "On the line!" The Reconstruction said "Get set!"; and the generation before said "Go!" I am off to a flying start and I must not halt in the stretch to look behind and weep. Slavery is the price I paid for civilization, and the choice was not with me. It is a bully adventure and worth all that I have paid through my ancestors for it. No one on earth ever had a greater chance for glory. The world to be won and nothing to be lost. It is thrilling to think—to know that for any act of mine, I shall get twice as much praise or twice as much blame. It is quite exciting to hold the center of the national stage, with the spectators not knowing whether to laugh or to weep.

The position of my white neighbor is much more difficult. No brown specter pulls up a chair beside me when I sit down to eat. No dark ghost thrusts its leg against mine in bed. The game of keeping what one has is never so exciting as the game of getting.

I do not always feel colored. Even now I often achieve the unconscious Zora of Eatonville before the Hegira. I feel most colored when I am thrown against a sharp white background.

For instance at Barnard. "Beside the waters of the Hudson" I feel my race. Among the thousand white persons, I am a dark rock surged upon, and overswept, but through it all, I remain myself. When covered by the waters, I am; and the ebb but reveals me again.

Sometimes it is the other way around. A white person is set down in our midst, but the contrast is just as sharp for me. For instance, when I sit in the drafty basement that is The New World Cabaret with a white person, my color comes. We enter chatting about any little nothing that we have in common and are seated by the jazz waiters. In the abrupt way that jazz orchestras have, this one plunges into a number. It loses no time in circumlocutions, but gets right down to business. It constricts the thorax and splits the heart with its tempo and narcotic harmonies. This orchestra grows rambunctious, rears on its hind legs and attacks the tonal veil with primitive fury, rending it, clawing it until it breaks through to the jungle beyond. I follow those heathen— follow them exultingly. I dance wildly inside myself; I yell within, I whoop; I shake my assegai [spear] above my head, I hurl it true to the mark *yeeeeoouw*! I am in the jungle and living in the jungle way. My face is painted red and yellow and my body is painted blue. My pulse is throbbing like a war drum. I want to slaughter something—give pain, give death to what, I don't know. But the piece ends. The men of the orchestra wipe their lips and rest their fingers. I creep back slowly to the veneer we call civilization with the last tone and find the white friend sitting motionless in his seat, smoking calmly.

"Good music they have here," he remarks, drumming the table with his fingertips.

Music. The great blobs of purple and red emotion have not touched him. He has only heard what I felt. He is far away and I see him but dimly across the ocean and the continent that have fallen between us. He is so pale with his whiteness then and I am *so* colored.

At certain times I have no race, I am *me*. When I set my hat at a certain angle and saunter down Seventh Avenue, Harlem City, feeling as snooty as the lions in front of the Forty-second Street Library, for instance. So far as my feelings are concerned, Peggy Hopkins Joyce on the Boule Mich with her gorgeous raiment, stately carriage, knees knocking together in a most aristocratic manner, has nothing on me. The cosmic Zora emerges. I belong to no race nor time. I am the eternal feminine with its string of beads.

I have no separate feeling about being an American citizen and colored. I am merely a fragment of the Great Soul that surges within the boundaries. My country, right or wrong.

Sometimes, I feel discriminated against, but it does not make me angry. It merely astonishes me. How *can* any deny themselves the pleasure of my company? It's beyond me.

But in the main, I feel like a brown bag of miscellany propped against a wall. Against a wall in company with other bags, white, red and yellow. Pour out the contents, and there is discovered a jumble of small things priceless and worthless. A first-water diamond, an empty spool, bits of broken glass, lengths of string, a key to a door long since crumbled away, a rusty knife-blade, old shoes saved for a road that never was and never will be, a nail bent under the weight of things too heavy for any nail, a dried flower or two still a little fragrant. In your hand is the brown bag. On the ground before you is the jumble it held—so much like the jumble in the bags, could they be emptied, that all might be dumped in a single heap and the bags refilled without altering the content of any greatly. A bit of colored glass more or less would not matter. Perhaps that is how the Great Stuffer of Bags filled them in the first place—who knows?

Edna St. Vincent Millay

(1892–1950)

Edna St. Vincent Millay grew up in rural Maine, the oldest of three daughters whose father abandoned them and their mother when she was twelve years old. A precocious child poet, she went to Vassar on scholarship and after graduation moved to Greenwich Village, where, in the words of author Dan Jacobson, "she lived like a modernist—sex, alcohol, drugs, feminism, nervous breakdowns, left-wing politics—but wrote like a late Victorian." Critic Edmund Wilson, the most famous of her lovers, who also proposed to her, said she had "an intoxicating effect on people." Red-haired, reckless, beautiful, and gifted, she is the subject of Wilson's novel *I Thought of Daisy*. In 1923 she became the first woman to receive the Pulitzer Prize in poetry for *The Harp-Weaver*. She wrote plays, essays, and poetry prolifically, publishing seventeen volumes of poetry. She was intensely involved in the unsuccessful fight to save the anarchists and immigrants Nicola Sacco and Bartolomeo Vanzetti from execution in 1927, writing a number of poems (*The Buck in the Snow,* 1928) in support of their cause. Because of her use of traditional poetic forms, especially the sonnet, during an experimental age, her work for a time went out of style. Now, however, Millay's poetry, which voices the sexual and emotional freedom she extolled in her politics—especially in her popular *A Few Figs for Thistles* (1920)—is receiving new attention. There is a new Modern Library edition of her early poems as well as two new biographies.

God's World

O world, I cannot hold thee close enough!
    Thy winds, thy wide grey skies!
    Thy mists that roll and rise!
Thy woods, this autumn day, that ache and sag
And all but cry with colour! That giant crag

To crush! To life the lean of that black bluff!
World, World, I cannot get you close enough!

Long have I known a glory in it all,
         But never knew I this;
         Here such a passion is
As stretcheth me apart. Lord I do fear
Thou'st made the world too beautiful this year.
My soul is all but out of me,—let fall
No burning leaf; prithee, let no bird call.

First Fig

My candle burns at both ends;
   It will not last the night;
But ah, my foes, and oh, my friends—
   It gives a lovely light!

What lips my lips have kissed, and where, and why

What lips my lips have kissed, and where, and why,
I have forgotten, and what arms have lain
Under my head till morning; but the rain
Is full of ghosts tonight, that tap and sigh
Upon the glass and listen for reply,
And in my heart there stirs a quiet pain
For unremembered lads that not again
Will turn to me at midnight with a cry.
Thus in the winter stands the lonely tree,
Nor knows what birds have vanished one by one,
Yet knows its boughs more silent than before:
I cannot say what loves have come and gone;
I only know that summer sang in me
A little while, that in me sings no more.

Sonnet XXX

Love is not all; it is not meat nor drink
Nor slumber nor a roof against the rain,
Nor yet a floating spar to men that sink
And rise and sink and rise and sink again;
Love can not fill the thickened lung with breath,
Nor clean the blood, nor set the fractured bone;
Yet many a man is making friends with death
Even as I speak, for lack of love alone.
It well may be that in a difficult hour,
Pinned down by pain and moaning for release,
Or nagged by want past resolution's power,
I might be driven to sell your love for peace,
Or trade the memory of this night for food.
It well may be. I do not think I would.

Sylvia Townsend Warner

(1893-1978)

A central theme of Sylvia Townsend Warner's many novels and the 150 short stories she published in *The New Yorker* is liberation from ideological constraints and the assumptions of privilege. Born at Harrow-on-the-Hill, England, a resident for much of her life in Dorset with her lover, Valentine Ackland, Warner was a poet and musicologist, and a devoted member of the Communist Party, and she has been called one of the mavericks of twentieth-century literature, with a subversive genius that positions her work within a feminist literary tradition anticipating the writing of Angela Carter and Jeanette Winterson. Of her highly acclaimed first novel, *Lolly Willowes* (1926)—the first selection of the Book-of-the-Month Club—Alison Lurie writes in her introduction to a new edition (1999): "The novel was revolutionary. . . . a subtle demand for women's right to privacy and independence from their families, for power over their own lives—even if they had to make a pact with Satan to get it. [It] spoke to single women of all ages." Warner was also an indefatigable writer of witty and forthright letters to many friends. Her forty-year correspondence with novelist and *New Yorker* editor William Maxwell has been collected in *The Element of Lavishness* (2001), a volume that breathes with the happiness the two prose masters had in each other's writing. In Warner's words, "Never mislay a pleasure. I might die in the night, so I will write to William now."

A Widow's Quilt

"Emma loves museums," said Helena, "and I think it's good for her to look at things being still, for a change, instead of that incessant jiggety-jog of television. Not like us when we were young, Charlotte—though you were never so tied to the box as I was."

"I hated watching people breathe."

The sisters were visiting the American Museum at Claverton, in Somerset. It was Charlotte's first visit.

"Do you come here often?"

"Yes. It's an easy run from Bristol, and I enjoy buying fancy jams from their shop. Expensive. But traditional things are always expensive. And Henry likes them. You should take something back to Everard."

"Remind me to."

Emma was staring into a quiescent period parlour. "That clock doesn't strike," she said. "Why doesn't it strike, Mummy? Hasn't it got an inside? Is it too old to be wound up?" Other visitors smiled, murmured, seemed inclined to enter into conversation. "Now I want to see the blue dogs."

They moved on into the quilt room. It was hung with pieced and appliqué quilts, brilliant as an assembly of macaws. Emma ran from one to another, identifying the blue dogs in an appliqué miscellany of rosebuds, hatchets, stars, kites, apples, horsemen, and shawled ladies encircling Abraham Lincoln in a stovepipe hat, quitting them for a geometrical pieced design of lilac and drab.

"Queen Charlotte's Crown—that's for you, Aunt Charlotte. And here's Fox and Geese."

"Darling! Don't touch."

One would always have to be being patient, thought Charlotte. On the whole she was glad she did not have a child. Her attention was caught by a quilt that stood out from the others, dominating their rich vivacity with a statement of dulled black on white. She moved towards it.

"That's a widow's quilt," said Helena. "Narrow, you see, for a single bed. I suppose you made one for yourself, when your husband died. Or your friends made it for you. Rather grisly."

"I think it's a hideous quilt," Emma said.

They descended to the shop, where Charlotte was reminded of the something she must take back to Everard, and chose horehound candies. Then Helena drove her to the station, and she made her platform thanks and farewells. "I particularly enjoyed the quilts," she said. "One doesn't see enough blue dogs."

But between Bath and London Charlotte sat in a dreamlike frenzy, planning the construction of her own black-and-white quilt. Built up from hexagons, and narrow, it would not be more than a winter's work, once she had assembled its materials: half a dozen exact geometrical hexagons; heavy paper, over which she would tack her patches; fine needles for the small stitches; a couple of sheets. The black would not be so easily found—that lustreless soot-black, dead-rook black. Perhaps she might find some second-hand weeds in the Chelsea fantasy boutiques. Or should she qualify the white unanimity of the sheets by using a variety of blacks already available? There were remains of the official blacking-out curtains drawn over the windows at home during the war, kept to come in useful, her mother had said, and still kept in the inherited piece box from which she had pulled fragments of chintz for the patchwork cushion cover started for Great-Aunt Emma but never completed. There was the black shawl bought at Avignon; some black taffeta; some sateen; quantities of black velvet. As she recalled these varieties of black, the design of her widow's quilt shaped itself to her mind's eye. In the centre, a doubled, even a trebled ring of black velvet hexagons massively enclosing the primal hexagon of white wedding-dress brocade. Extending to the four corners of the quilt, long black diagonals, the spaces between interspersed with star-spangled black hexagons conjoined.

Dizzied, she got out of the terminus because everyone else was doing so, and took a wasteful taxi to the usual address without realizing she was going home.

Next morning, as soon as Everard had tapped the barometer, put on the indicated topcoat, and left for his office (he was a partner in a firm that sold rare postage stamps), she chose the pair of sheets and went out to buy the fine needles, going on to F. Wilkens, Electrician and Household Repairs—for during the night it had occurred to her that the basic hexagons would be much more satisfactory if they were exact to measure and cut out of tin. F. Wilkens, oddly calling them templates, knew exactly what she meant, and would have them ready in half an hour. She spent the interval in the Health Food Shop, buying Everard's muesli, then collected the templates and went back to the flat in Perivale Mansions. By the time he returned she had assembled most of the double garland of black velvet round the wedding-dress brocade, folded it away in a pillowcase, and prepared supper.

That night her pleasure in the progress of the black velvet garland was soured by seeing it as so much done already. At this rate, the quilt would be snatched from her hands, no more to the purpose than a daisy chain. Patch after patch would lessen her private entertainment; the last patch in the border of black hexagons would topple her over the edge to drown in the familiar tedium. She did not want to make another quilt, or any other kind of quilt. This was her only, her nonpareil, her one assertion of a life of her own. When Everard left for his office, she hardly dared take out the pillowcase. While stitching in the first white hexagons, she realized the extent of even a single-bed quilt. She need not despair for some time yet.

By midday it was raining steadily. The barometer's counsel of an umbrella was, as usual, justified. The sound of rain was agreeable to work to. It rained. She worked. Between two and three in the afternoon, finding herself extremely hungry, she ravaged the larder for an impromptu meal—unwontedly delicious, since she fed on the tinned delicacies.

The weekend jolted her out of her contentment. Two days of Everard at home she was inured to, but to waste two days without setting a stitch in the quilt was torment. She festered in idleness; she had never hated his company more. And it increased her exasperation that he should be unaware of it.

Yet as time went on, and the quilt enlarged, and weekends fell into the pattern of her existence as though they were recurring hexagons of an unassimilable material which she would presently unpick, her disposition changed; she was complacent, she was even benign. Strange, to think that Everard, whose demands and inroads had compelled her to such an abiding rancour that seeing the widow's quilt had given her a purpose in life, should have supplied this soothing influence. Meanwhile she went on with the quilt, never losing sight of its intimations and in the main preserving her original scheme—though the diagonal had to be revised: the single black line lacked emphasis, and had to be changed to a couple of lines hedging a band of white. This, in turn, involved a reconsideration of the corners. The solution had been found (there was exactly the right amount of the black shawl to supply its hexagons) when Christmas stared her in the face—and Everard. She could not securely hope that his seasonal influenza would keep him coughing in bed and out of her way; but she was on fire to get at the revised corners, and told herself that a little publicity would be the surest safeguard of the secrecy which was an essential ingredient in her pleasure. On Christmas Eve Everard came home to find her with the quilt on her knee. He glanced at it warily, as though it were something that might disagree with him. When it was there next day and the day after, he mentioned its presence.

"What's that, Charlotte—all those bits you're sewing together?"

She displayed it.

"How nicely you've done it. What's it for?"

"In time it will be a quilt."

"Oh. So it's not finished yet."

"No. Not yet."

She stitched in another hexagon.

"Do you make it up as you go along?"

"I saw one like it in the American Museum."

"In a museum. How interesting. Was that black and white too?"

"Yes. It's a traditional pattern. It's called a magpie quilt."

"Magpie? Magpie? Oh, because it's black and white, I suppose. Quite imaginative."

She stitched, Everard pondered.

"I wonder the United States Post Office doesn't use these old designs—now that they go in for so many commemorative stamps."

She thought of the blue dogs, but refrained.

By the New Year Everard's cough was so insistent that he had to give up taking his temperature. She foresaw herself stitching her widow's quilt at his bedside. Instead, his partner brought a Puerto Rican violet for his opinion. Finding it spurious, Everard felt equal to going back to his office.

With the enlarging days the quilt gathered momentum. It outgrew the pillowcase and had to be folded away in a bedspread. Each morning it seemed to have grown in the night; each day it was more responsive, more compliant. The hexagons fitted into place as if drawn by a magnet. It had a rationality now, a character; the differing blacks superimposed a pattern of their own, as well-kept fields do with the various tints of their crops. She was so much at ease with it that she could let her thoughts stray as she worked—not so far as to make a mistake, though. She hated mistakes, even those she could unpick. But looking forward to the time when she would rightfully sleep under it, her mind made excursions to places where she might go as a quiet travelling widow. To Lincolnshire, perhaps, with its "fields of barley and of rye" bordering the river—a sinuous, slow-flowing river with no conversation, effortlessly engulfing the chatter of Tennysonian brooks. Then, on the one hand, a quiet cross-country bus would show her Boston Stump outlined against the pale eastern sky, or, catching a train at Dukeries Junction Station, she would survey the Vale of Beauvoir.

Not since her marriage had she gone beyond the Home Counties, and these had only been visited at licensed holiday seasons; a dab of green at Easter, in August a smear of summer with Everard's cousins in Surrey. Meanwhile, she had travelled a great deal in theory, studying guidebooks and ordnance maps and railway guides, even a list of bus routes in East Anglia which had chanced her way. The row of Methuen's Little Guides in the bookcase on her side of the bed had assured her in detail of the existence of what imagination left visionary: churches (E. E., Perp., restored in 1870), the number of different species of bat in Essex, an almshouse or a gasworks, a disused bridge, a local industry, an extensive prospect of rolling country, a forgotten battlefield, a clay soil, a sandy loam, floodmarks, plantations of conifer, a canal. On the whole, it was the dullish Midlands she preferred; romantic extremities, like Cornwall, could come later.

She was stitching away at Everard's demise—every hexagon brought it a step nearer—when Helena, who was in London to visit her dressmaker, came on to Perivale Mansions. After a momentary gasp, Helena admired the quilt, now three-quarters done.

"And what are you going to stuff it with?"

"Stuff it?"

"It would have to be interlined and stitched through to the backing, you know. Otherwise it wouldn't be a quilt. The one you admired in the museum has harps outlined in stitching—I suppose she felt strongly about Ireland." She talked on about New England quilting bees, and left before Everard was due to return.

There was nothing for it but to swallow the shock, be glad that the quilt could continue into summer, and decide on the stitched design which should complete it. Not harps, anyhow. A speedy crisscross would be about as much as she could manage. For with the added weight of the backing and the interlined padding, the quilt would be too heavy to handle comfortably, could become a drudgery—another marital obligation, almost another Everard.

She began to make mistakes, straying from the order of her design, choosing the black sateen when it should have been the fustier black of the curtain material. Twice she sewed in a hexagon back side uppermost. The thread tangled, slid out of the needle's eye. When she came to re-thread a needle, she had to make shot after shot at it, holding the needle with a grip of iron, poking the thread at it with a shaking hand. Her heart thumped. Her fingers swelled.

If I were sensible, she thought, I would take to my bed. But the voice of reason reminded her of Everard's disconsolate fidgeting, his dependence on her (Where do I find the toaster? Oh dear, the milk has boiled over again! What am I to mop it up with?) when she had rheumatic fever. She was not in a fit state to be an invalid. The widow's quilt, even if at the moment it was thwarting her intentions, was the more enlivening companion.

She was in the last corner row. It was mid-March, and the east wind was howling down the street like the harlot's curse, when the last of her misfortunes, the silliest and most derisive, tripped her: she had no more thread. She shook some of the ache out of her back, put on her thickest coat, eased her swollen hands into gloves, grimaced at the barometer, and went downstairs and out. It was as though the wind had whirled her out of herself. She was loose again, the solitary traveller, and back in Lincolnshire. She took the narrow road across the saltmarsh flats between her and the sea. They stretched on either hand, featureless, limitless. Nothing would gainsay their level till the enormous breakers reared up, one driven forward on another, and fell with a crash and a flump on the beach. The wind streamed through her; she fought it with every step, and was one with it. At the corner of Perivale Street and Sebastopol Terrace a burly holidaymaker off an advertisement was blown overhead, exclaiming "Skegness Is So Bracing!"

She had to struggle for breath before she could ask for thread and civilly agree with the shopwoman that the wind was quite savage, wasn't it. And, indeed, as she walked back she could hardly walk straight. The wind was still roaring in her ears when she stood in the hallway of Perivale Mansions, with the stairs in front of her—three flights, each of seventeen steps. She paused on the first landing. The roaring in her ears had changed and was now loud beats on a gong. Twice seventeen was twice seventeen. She mounted the second flight. The gong beat on, but irregularly—thunder to the flashes of lightning across her eyes. At the foot of the third flight she stumbled and fell. She saw her gloved hands clutch the air. A little paper bag fell from one of them. Two reels of thread escaped from it, rolled along the landing, and went tap-tapping down the stairs. Another of her misfortunes. Her lips tried to grin but had turned to lead. The wind had blown out all the lights, and down in the hallway the sea rose higher and higher. A seventh wave, a master wave, would surge up the stairs she had climbed so painfully, thrust its strength beneath her, carry her away like a wisp of seaweed. She was still vaguely alive when Everard almost tripped over her. He called "Help! Help!" and blew the police whistle he always carried on his key ring.

"There was something wrong with her heart," he said to Helena, who came next morning. "It might have happened at any moment. You can imagine what a shock it was to me. I think I must move." He had not much to say, but he talked incessantly. "At first I thought she had been killed. You can imagine what I felt. There is so much violence about nowadays—no post office is safe. I never felt easy leaving her. But it was something wrong with her heart. She was everything to me, everything, my poor Charlotte. Where do you think I should go?"

Helena had picked up the quilt and began folding it.

"And there's that quilt. What should we do about it? It's not finished, you see. Poor Charlotte, so unfortunate! It's a magpie quilt."

"Magpie?"

"Yes, because it's all black and white—like the birds, she said."

"I see."

"I can't very well take it with me. Yet it would be a pity to throw it away. Could you take charge of it, Helena? It would be a weight off my mind if you would. You'd know how to finish it, and I don't suppose it would take you very long. Not that there's any hurry now. And then you could keep it, to remember her by. I'm sure she'd like you to have it. It meant a great deal to her."

Louise Bogan

(1897–1970)

One of the finest poets of the century, Louise Bogan has been compared with Emily Dickinson, William Blake, and William Butler Yeats; she influenced Sylvia Plath, and in her lifetime other writers praised her work: W. H. Auden admired her wresting "beauty and truth out of dark places"; Theodore Roethke, her lover and friend, called her "one of the true inheritors of the great tradition. [Her] best work will stay in the language as long as the language survives." Bogan grew up poor in Maine, oppressed by the misery of her parents' marriage. "My father had his job . . . My mother had nothing but her temperament, her fantasies, her despairs, her secrets, her subterfuges," Bogan wrote in *Journey Around My Room*, a "mosaic" of autobiographical fragments. After she moved to New York City, she began to publish her poems, becoming poetry editor at *The New Yorker* for thirty-eight years. Throughout her life, she suffered from depression, seeking treatment at the New York Neurological Institute of Columbia Presbyterian Hospital as well as in Europe for the periodic breakdowns she referred to as her "sabbatical six months." Her friends remember her sense of humor, calling her "one of the most amusing people of her time. To be with her was to laugh with her." Her reaction to the many honors that came her way—the Bollingen Prize, membership in the National Institute of Arts and Letters and the Academy of American Poets, a Guggenheim fellowship, poetry consultant to the Library of Congress—was always modest: "Not bad," she'd say, "for an Irish girl from Camden, Maine." Her last volume of poetry, *The Blue Estuaries*, was published a year before she died of a sudden heart attack. Reviewing her posthumously published letters, *What the Woman Lived* (1973), Barbara Grizzuti Harrison described Bogan as "a religious ecstatic with a great deal of good common earthly sense."

Evening in the Sanitarium

The free evening fades, outside the windows fastened with
    decorative iron grilles.
The lamps are lighted; the shades drawn; the nurses are
    watching a little.
It is the hour of the complicated knitting on the safe
    bone needles; of the games of anagrams and bridge;
The deadly game of chess; the book held up like a mask.

The period of the wildest weeping, the fiercest delusion, is over.
The women rest their tired half-healed hearts; they are
    almost well.
Some of them will stay almost well always: the blunt-faced
    woman whose thinking dissolved
Under academic discipline; the manic-depressive girl
Now leveling off; one paranoiac afflicted with jealousy.
Another with persecution. Some alleviation has been possible.

O fortunate bride, who never again will become elated after
    childbirth!
O lucky older wife, who has been cured of feeling unwanted!
To the suburban railway station you will return, return,
To meet forever Jim home on the 5:35.
You will be again as normal and selfish and heartless as
    anybody else.

There is life left: the piano says it with its octave smile.
The soft carpets pad the thump and splinter of the suicide to be.
Everything will be splendid: the grandmother will not drink
    habitually.
The fruit salad will bloom on the plate like a bouquet
And the garden produce the blue-ribbon aquilegia.
The cats will be glad; the fathers feel justified; the
    mothers relieved.

The sons and husbands will no longer need to pay the bills.
Childhoods will be put away, the obscene nightmare abated.

At the ends of the corridors the baths are running.
Mrs. C. again feels the shadow of the obsessive idea.
Miss R. looks at the mantel-piece, which must mean some-
thing.

Cartography

As you lay in sleep
I saw the chart
Of artery and vein
Running from your heart,

Plain as the strength
Marked upon the leaf
Along the length,
Mortal and brief,

Of your gaunt hand.
I saw it clear:
The wiry brand
Of the life we bear

Mapped like the great
Rivers that rise
Beyond our fate
And distant from our eyes.

After the Persian

I

I do not wish to know
The depths of your terrible jungle:
From what nest your leopard leaps
Or what sterile lianas are at once your serpents' disguise
    and home.

I am the dweller on the temperate threshold,
The strip of corn and vine,
Where all is translucence (the light!)
Liquidity, and the sound of water.
Here the days pass under shade
And the nights have the waxing and the waning moon.
Here the moths take flight at evening;
Here at morning the dove whistles and the pigeons coo.
Here, as night comes on, the fireflies wink and snap
Close to the cool ground,
Shining in profusion
Celestial or marine.

Here it is never wholly dark but always wholly green,
And the day stains with what seems to be more than the
    sun
What may be more than my flesh.

II

I have wept with the spring storm;
Burned with the brutal summer.
Now, hearing the wind and the twanging bow-strings,
I know what winter brings.

The hunt sweeps out upon the plain
And the garden darkens.
They will bring the trophies home
To bleed and perish
Beside the trellis and the lattices,
Beside the fountain, still flinging diamond water,
Beside the pool
(Which is eight-sided, like my heart).

III

All has been translated into treasure:
Weightless as amber,
Translucent as the currant on the branch,
Dark as the rose's thorn.

Where is the shimmer of evil?
This is the shell's iridescence
And the wild bird's wing.

IV

Ignorant, I took up my burden in the wilderness.
Wise with great wisdom, I shall lay it down upon flowers.

V

Goodbye, goodbye!
There was so much to love, I could not love it all;
I could not love it enough.

Some things I overlooked, and some I could not find.
Let the crystal clasp them
When you drink your wine, in autumn.

Stevie Smith

(1902-1971)

Florence Margaret Smith spent most of her adult life working as a secretary and taking care of an elderly aunt in their home at Palmers Green, a suburb of North London. Yet throughout the humdrum years she published three novels—*Novel on Yellow Paper* (1936) is the best known—and more than ten volumes of poetry, which is admired for its mordant originality and humor as well as an utter absence of sentimentality. Robert Lowell expressed his admiration of Smith's "unique and cheerfully gruesome voice." In the 1960s her writing was rediscovered after a successful series of public readings created a large audience for Smith on both sides of the Atlantic. She was awarded the Queen's Gold Medal for Poetry in 1969.

Not Waving but Drowning

Nobody heard him, the dead man,
But still he lay moaning:
I was much further out than you thought
And not waving but drowning.

Poor chap, he always loved larking
And now he's dead
It must have been too cold for him his heart gave way,
They said.

Oh, no no no, it was too cold always
(Still the dead one lay moaning)
I was much too far out all my life
And not waving but drowning.

How Cruel Is the Story of Eve

How cruel is the story of Eve
What responsibility
It has in history
For cruelty.

Touch, where the feeling is most vulnerable,
Unblameworthy—ah reckless—desiring children,
Touch there with a touch of pain?
Abominable.

Ah what cruelty,
In history
What misery.

Put up to barter
The tender feelings
Buy her a husband to rule her
Fool her to marry a master
She must or rue it
The Lord said it.

And man, poor man,
Is he fit to rule,
Pushed to it?
How can he carry it, the governance,
And not suffer for it
Insuffisance?
He must make woman lower then

So he can be higher then.
Oh what cruelty,
In history what misery.

Soon woman grows cunning
Masks her wisdom,

How otherwise will he
Bring food and shelter, kill enemies?
If he did not feel superior
It would be worse for her
And for the tender children
Worse for them.

Oh what cruelty,
In history what misery
Of falsity.

It is only a legend
You say? But what
Is the meaning of the legend
If not
To give blame to women most
And most punishment?
This is the meaning of a legend that colours
All human thought; it is not found among animals.

How cruel is the story of Eve,
What responsibility it has
In history
For misery.

Yet there is this to be said still:
Life would be over long ago
If men and women had not loved each other
Naturally, naturally.
Forgetting their mythology
They would have died of it else
Long ago, long ago,
And all would be emptiness now
And silence.

Oh dread Nature, for your purpose,
To have made them love so.

M. F. K. Fisher

(1908-1992)

W. H. Auden considered her "the best prose writer in America." Frank McCourt said, "If I were still teaching high school English, I'd use her books to show how to write simply, how to enjoy food and drink but, most of all, how to enjoy life. Her books and letters are one feast after another." One of the great masters of American English, Mary Frances Kennedy Fisher grew up in California. She wrote sixteen books about family, food, and travel; she also wrote novels, short stories, and memoirs (*Among Friends* and *To Begin Again*). But she is best known for her witty, vigorous, and original writing about food in such books as *Consider the Oyster* (1941), *How to Cook a Wolf* (1942), and the classic *The Art of Eating* (1954). Selections from her writings have been collected in an M. F. K. Fisher Reader, entitled *The Measure of Her Powers* (1999). There is also a new edition of her journals and the superb letters, *M. F. K. Fisher, A Life in Letters: Correspondence 1929–1991* (1997).

How to Be Cheerful Though Starving

> *Obsession by economic issues is as local and transitory*
> *as it is repulsive and disturbing.*
> —The Acquisitive Society, Richard Henry Tawney

When you are really hungry a meal eaten by yourself is not so much an event as the automatic carrying out of a physical function: you must do it to live. [I now disagree completely with this, and could and probably will write a whole book proving my present point, that solitary dining, no matter what the degree of hunger, can be good.] But when you share it with another human or two, or even a respected animal, it becomes dignified. Suddenly it takes on part of the ancient religious solemnity of the Breaking of Bread, the Sharing of Salt. No matter what your hunger nor how fiercely your fingers itch for the warmness of the food, the fact that you are not alone makes flavors clearer and a certain philosophic slowness possible.

And it is well to eat slowly: the food seems to be more plentiful, probably because it lasts longer.

There are many ways to make a little seem like more. They have been followed and changed and reinvented for ten thousand years, with small loss of dignity to mankind. Indeed, sometimes their very following is a thing of admiration, because of the people who are poor and who refuse to be obsessed by that fact until it becomes "repulsive and disturbing."

Of course, it takes a certain amount of native wit to cope gracefully with the problem of having the wolf camp with apparent permanency on your doorstep. That can be a wearing thing, and even the pretense of ignoring his presence has a kind of dangerous monotony about it.

For the average wolf-dodger, good health is probably one of the most important foils. Nothing seems particularly grim if your head is clear and your teeth are clean [Toothpaste now contains chlorophyl. Animals still chew grass.] and your bowels function properly.

Another thing that makes daily, hourly thought about wherewithals endurable is to be able to share it with someone else. That does not mean, and I say it emphatically, sharing the fuss and bother and fretting. It means being companionable with another human who understands, perhaps without any talking at all, what problems of basic nourishment confront you. [This still obtains, as my legal friends say. It is the condition most devoutly to be wished for. However, the years have taught me compromises, as they have all thinking creatures.] Once such a relationship is established, your black thoughts vanish, and how to make a pot of stew last three more meals seems less a nightmare than a form of sensual entertainment.

There was one person, though, who was a part of my education and who refuted all of my tentative rules for fortunate wolf-dodging, and did it with such grace that I often think of her half-doubtingly, as if she were a dream.

Her name was Sue. She was delicate bodily . . . not ill, but never well the way most people are well. She flitted like a night moth through all her days, bemazed by the ardors of sunlight but conducting herself with wary sureness, so that she seldom banged against shut doors or hit her thin bones on sharp table corners.

She was, as far as anyone knew, completely alone. It was impossible to think of her in any more passionate contact with other humans than the occasional suppers she gave for them. The fact that once she must have been young did not change her present remoteness: you could not see her any warmer at seventeen than at seventy.

But her withdrawn impersonal attitude did not make her any less delicately robust. She loved to eat, and she apparently loved, now and then, to eat with other people. Her suppers were legendary. Of course, it depended on who was telling about them: sometimes they were merely strange, or even laughable, and sometimes they sounded like something from a Southern California Twelfth Night, with strange games and witchlike feastings.

Sue lived in a little weatherbeaten house on a big weatherbeaten cliff. At first when you entered it, the house seemed almost empty, but soon you realized that like all dwellings of old lonely people, it was stuffed with a thousand relics of the fuller years. There were incredibly dingy and lump-filled cushions that Whistler had sat on, and a Phyfe chair that had one stormy night been kicked into kindling wood by Oscar Wilde. It was held together with rubber bands, and naturally was not to be used as a chair, but rather as a casually treated but important altar.

When you went to her house, you ate by one candle, no matter whether you were two or eight at table. Of course this seemed intensely romantic to young Americans, but it was because she could afford neither more candles nor electricity.

The walls, covered with third-rate etchings by first-rate men, and a few first-rate ones by the almost unknown Sue, emerged gradually from the dingy darkness. There was an underlying smell, delicate as early death, of age and decay.

The main smell, though, was a good one. It never had the forthright energy of braised meat (although I remember one time, when I may have looked a little peaked, that Sue went against her custom and put a tiny morsel of cooked liver on my plate, and said, "Now, I want you to try to eat *all* of this!" It was no bigger than a dollar, and I made it into at least twelve bites, in a kind of awe).

There was always the exciting, mysterious perfume of bruised herbs, plucked fresh and cool from the tangle of weeds around the shack. Sue put them into a salad.

Then there was usually sage, which she used like a Turk or Armenian in practically everything that went into her pot. She gathered it in the hills, and dried it in bunches above her stove, and in spite of gastronomical scouts who wail now that California sage all has a taste of turpentine, hers never did. She knew only about a hundred kinds, she confessed quietly; someone had told her that the hills behind the village held at least fifty more.

Sue had only a few plates, and no knives. You ate everything from one large Spode soup-plate, when you went there, but it never seemed mussy. And knives were unnecessary, because there was nothing to cut.

As I remember now, her whole cuisine was Oriental. There were the little bowls of chopped fresh and cooked leaves. There were the fresh and dried herbs, which she had gathered from the fields. There was the common bowl of rice (or potatoes that Sue had probably stolen the night before from some patch up the canyon). There was tea, always. There was, occasionally, a fresh egg, which also was stolen, no doubt, and which Sue always put in the teapot to heat through and then broke over the biggest dish of food.

I have never eaten such strange things as there in her dark smelly room, with the waves roaring at the foot of the cliff and Whistler's maroon-taffeta pillow bruising its soft way into the small of my back. People said that Sue robbed garbage pails at night. She did not, of course. But she did flit about, picking leaves from other gardens than her own and wandering like the Lolly Willowes of Laguna along the cliff-tops and the beaches looking in the night light for sea-spinach and pink ice-plant. [For long now the cliffs have been covered with villas, and the wild herbs have vanished. I still taste and smell them in my memory, and feel the close-packed cold beads of the ice-plant's leaves and petals.]

The salads and stews she made from these little shy weeds were indeed peculiar, but she blended and cooked them so skillfully that they never lost their fresh salt crispness. She put them together with thought and gratitude, and never seemed to realize that her cuisine was one of intense romantic strangeness to everyone but herself. I doubt if she spent more than fifty dollars a year on what she and her entranced guests ate, but from the gracious abstracted way she gave you a soup dish full of sliced cactus leaves and lemon-berries and dried crumbled kelp, it might as well have been stuffed ortolans. Moreover, it was good.

I doubt very much if anyone but Sue could make it good. Few other humans know the secret of herbs as she did . . . or if they know them, can use them so nonchalantly.

But anyone in the world, with intelligence and spirit and the knowledge that it must be done, can live with her inspired oblivion to the ugliness of poverty. It is not that she wandered at night hunting for leaves and berries; it is that she cared enough to invite her friends to share them with her, and could serve them, to herself alone or to a dozen guests, with the sureness that she was right.

Sue had neither health nor companionship to comfort her and warm her, but she nourished herself and many other people for many years, with the quiet assumption [this is very important] that man's need for food is not a grim obsession, repulsive, disturbing, but a dignified and even enjoyable function. Her nourishment was of more than the flesh, not because of its strangeness, but because of her own calm. [And this, too, is very important.]

Kathleen Raine

(1908-   )

Poet, memoirist, critic, and translator, Londoner Kathleen Raine sees her writing as the fruit of her Scottish ancestry—"my poetic roots were in wild Northumberland where I lived as a child." She attributes her interest in a specifically women's writing about women's lives to her reading of Virginia Woolf's *A Room of One's Own*. But her poetry—a dozen books of poetry were included in *The Collected Poems: 1935–1980* in 1981—is associated most of all with the antimaterialist, mystical romantic tradition, and with William Blake in particular. Educated at Cambridge in the natural sciences, she was the only woman linked with the Cambridge Poets, a group that included William Empson and Julian Bell. As a critic she wrote four books about Blake as well as studies of Samuel Taylor Coleridge and William Butler Yeats, who was her friend.

Invocation

There is a poem on the way,
there is a poem all round me,
the poem is in the near future,
the poem is in the upper air
above the foggy atmosphere
it hovers, a spirit
that I would make incarnate.
Let my body sweat
let snakes torment my breast
my eyes be blind, ears deaf, hand distraught
mouth parched, uterus cut out,
belly slashed, back lashed,
tongue slivered into thongs of leather
rain stones inserted in my breasts,
head severed,

if only the lips may speak,
if only the god will come.

Storm

God in me is the fury on the bare heath
God in me shakes the interior kingdom of my heaven.
God in me is the fire wherein I burn.

God in me swirling cloud and driving rain
God in me cries a lonely nameless bird
God in me beats my head upon a stone.

God in me the four elements of storm
Raging in the shelterless landscape of the mind
Outside the barred doors of my Goneril heart.

The Unloved

I am pure loneliness
I am empty air
I am drifting cloud.

I have no form
I am boundless
I have no rest.

I have no house
I pass through different places
I am indifferent wind.

I am the white bird
Flying away from land
I am the horizon.

I am a wave
That will never reach the shore.

I am an empty shell
Cast up on the sand.

I am the moonlight
On the cottage with no roof.

I am the forgotten dead
In the broken vault on the hill.

I am the old man
Carrying his water in a pail.

I am light
Travelling in empty space.

I am a diminishing star
Speeding away
Out of the universe.

Heirloom

She gave me childhood's flowers,
Heather and wild thyme,
Eyebright and tormentil,
Lichen's mealy cup
Dry on wind-scored stone,
The corbies on the rock,
The rowan by the burn.

Sea-marvels a child beheld
Out in the fisherman's boat.
Fringed pulsing violet
Medusa, sea-gooseberries,
Starfish on the sea-floor,
Cowries and rainbow-shells
From pools on a rocky shore.

Gave me her memories,
But kept her last treasure:
"When I was a lass," she said,
"Sitting among the heather,
"Suddenly I saw
"That all the moor was alive!
"I have told no one before."

That was my mother's tale.
Seventy years had gone
Since she saw the living skein
Of which the world is woven,
And having seen, knew all;
Through long indifferent years
Treasuring the priceless pearl.

Eudora Welty

(1909-2001)

"I have been told," wrote Eudora Welty in the preface to *The Collected Stories* (1980), "both in approval and in accusation, that I seem to love all my characters. What I do in writing of any character is to try to enter into the mind, heart, and skin of a human being who is not myself. Whether this happens to be a man or a woman, old or young, with skin black or white, the primary challenge lies in making the jump itself. It is the act of a writer's imagination that I set most high." Among the most honored of American writers—every prize in the literary pantheon has gone to her and she was the first living writer to be included in the prestigious Library of America series of works by American literary giants—Welty was born in Jackson, Mississippi, where she spent her life in the house built by her family. Her memoir, *One Writer's Beginnings* (1984), recounts her southern youth and celebrates the region she loves: "It's my source of knowledge. It tells me the important things." What she has searched most consistently through hundreds of short stories and five novels—*The Robber Bridegroom* (1942), *Delta Wedding* (1946), *The Ponder Heart* (1954), *Losing Battles* (1970), *The Optimist's Daughter* (1972)—is the mystery at the heart of human existence and relationship. "Relationship," for Welty, "is a pervading and changing mystery." As she puts it in *Delta Wedding*: "How deep were the complexities of the everyday, of the family, what caves were in the mountains, what blocked chambers and what crystal rivers that had not yet seen light." As a southerner and as a storyteller of hidden inner lives, she finds a similarity between herself and Anton Chekhov: "He's one of us. . . . He loved the singularity in people, the individuality. . . . there's a great love and understanding that prevails . . . and a knowledge and acceptance of each other's idiosyncrasies, a tolerance of them." The first story that follows here, her first published in a commercial magazine—the *Atlantic* took it in 1941 after her agent had sent it out again and again for over a year, getting back rejection after rejection—has become a classic of American literature. The second story was novelist Russell Banks's choice for the anthology *You've Got to Read This: Contemporary American Writers Introduce Stories That Held Them in Awe* (2000). The story left him "spellbound."

A Worn Path

It was December—a bright frozen day in the early morning. Far out in the country there was an old Negro woman with her head tied in a red rag, coming along a path through the pinewoods. Her name was Phoenix Jackson. She was very old and small and she walked slowly in the dark pine shadows, moving a little from side to side in her steps, with the balanced heaviness and lightness of a pendulum in a grandfather clock. She carried a thin, small cane made from an umbrella, and with this she kept tapping the frozen earth in front of her. This made a grave and persistent noise in the still air, that seemed meditative like the chirping of a solitary little bird.

She wore a dark striped dress reaching down to her shoe tops, and an equally long apron of bleached sugar sacks, with a full pocket: all neat and tidy, but every time she took a step she might have fallen over her shoelaces, which dragged from her unlaced shoes. She looked straight ahead. Her eyes were blue with age. Her skin had a pattern all its own of numberless branching wrinkles and as though a whole little tree stood in the middle of her forehead, but a golden color ran underneath, and the two knobs of her cheeks were illumined by a yellow burning under the dark. Under the red rag her hair came down on her neck in the frailest of ringlets, still black, and with an odor like copper.

Now and then there was a quivering in the thicket. Old Phoenix said, "Out of my way, all you foxes, owls, beetles, jack rabbits, coons and wild animals. . . . Keep out from under these feet, little bob-whites. . . . Keep the big wild hogs out of my path. Don't let none of those come running my direction. I got a long way." Under her small black-freckled hand her cane, limber as a buggy whip, would switch at the brush as if to rouse up any hiding things.

On she went. The woods were deep and still. The sun made the pine needles almost too bright to look at, up where the wind rocked. The cones dropped as light as feathers. Down in the hollow was the mourning dove—it was not too late for him.

The path ran up a hill. "Seem like there is chains about my feet, time I get this far," she said, in the voice of argument old people keep to use with themselves. "Something always take a hold of me on this hill—pleads I should stay."

After she got to the top she turned and gave a full, severe look behind her where she had come. "Up through pines," she said at length. "Now down through oaks."

Her eyes opened their widest, and she started down gently. But before she got to the bottom of the hill a bush caught her dress.

Her fingers were busy and intent, but her skirts were full and long, so that before she could pull them free in one place they were caught in another. It was not possible to allow the dress to tear. "I in the thorny bush," she said. "Thorns, you doing your appointed work. Never want to let folks past, no sir. Old eyes thought you were a pretty little *green* bush."

Finally, trembling all over, she stood free, and after a moment dared to stoop for her cane.

"Sun so high!" she cried, leaning back and looking, while the thick tears went over her eyes. "The time getting all gone here."

At the foot of this hill was a place where a log was laid across the creek.

"Now comes the trial," said Phoenix.

Putting her right foot out, she mounted the log and shut her eyes. Lifting her skirt, leveling her cane fiercely before her, like a festival figure in some parade, she began to march across. Then she opened her eyes and she was safe on the other side.

"I wasn't as old as I thought," she said.

But she sat down to rest. She spread her skirts on the bank around her and folded her hands over her knees. Up above her was a tree in a pearly cloud of mistletoe. She did not dare to close her eyes, and when a little boy brought her a plate with a slice of marble-cake on it she spoke to him. "That would be acceptable," she said. But when she went to take it there was just her own hand in the air.

So she left that tree, and had to go through a barbed-wire fence. There she had to creep and crawl, spreading her knees and stretching her fingers like a baby trying to climb the steps. But she talked loudly to herself: she could not let her dress be torn now, so late in the day, and she could not pay for having her arm or her leg sawed off if she got caught fast where she was.

At last she was safe through the fence and risen up out in the clearing. Big dead trees, like black men with one arm, were standing in the purple stalks of the withered cotton field. There sat a buzzard.

"Who you watching?"

In the furrow she made her way along.

"Glad this not the season for bulls," she said, looking sideways, "and the good Lord made his snakes to curl up and sleep in the winter. A pleasure I don't see no two-headed snake coming around that tree, where it come once. It took a while to get by him, back in the summer."

She passed through the old cotton and went into a field of dead corn. It whispered and shook and was taller than her head. "Through the maze now," she said, for there was no path.

Then there was something tall, black, and skinny there, moving before her.

At first she took it for a man. It could have been a man dancing in the field. But she stood still and listened, and it did not make a sound. It was as silent as a ghost.

"Ghost," she said sharply, "who be you the ghost of? For I have heard of nary death close by."

But there was no answer—only the ragged dancing in the wind.

She shut her eyes, reached out her hand, and touched a sleeve. She found a coat and inside that an emptiness, cold as ice.

"You scarecrow," she said. Her face lighted. "I ought to be shut up for good," she said with laughter. "My senses is gone. I too old. I the oldest people I ever know. Dance, old scarecrow," she said, "while I dancing with you."

She kicked her foot over the furrow, and with mouth drawn down, shook her head once or twice in a little strutting way. Some husks blew down and whirled in streamers about her skirts.

Then she went on, parting her way from side to side with the cane, through the whispering field. At last she came to the end, to a wagon track where the silver grass blew between the red ruts. The quail were walking around like pullets, seeming all dainty and unseen.

"Walk pretty," she said. "This the easy place. This the easy going."

She followed the track, swaying through the quiet bare fields, through the little strings of trees silver in their dead leaves, past cabins silver from weather, with the doors and windows boarded shut, all like old women under a spell sitting there. "I walking in their sleep," she said, nodding her head vigorously.

In a ravine she went where a spring was silently flowing through a hollow log. Old Phoenix bent and drank. "Sweet-gum makes the water sweet," she said, and drank more. "Nobody know who made this well, for it was here when I was born."

The track crossed a swampy part where the moss hung as white as lace from every limb. "Sleep on, alligators, and blow your bubbles." Then the track went into the road.

Deep, deep the road went down between the high green-colored banks. Overhead the live-oaks met, and it was as dark as a cave.

A black dog with a lolling tongue came up out of the weeds by the ditch. She was meditating, and not ready, and when he came at her she only hit him a little with her cane. Over she went in the ditch, like a little puff of milk-weed.

Down there, her senses drifted away. A dream visited her, and she reached her hand up, but nothing reached down and gave her a pull. So she lay there and presently went to talking. "Old woman," she said to herself, "that black dog come up out of the weeds to stall you off, and now there he sitting on his fine tail, smiling at you."

A white man finally came along and found her—a hunter, a young man, with his dog on a chain.

"Well, Granny!" he laughed. "What are you doing there?"

"Lying on my back like a June-bug waiting to be turned over, mister," she said, reaching up her hand.

He lifted her up, gave her a swing in the air, and set her down. "Anything broken, Granny?"

"No sir, them old dead weeds is springy enough," said Phoenix, when she had got her breath. "I thank you for your trouble."

"Where do you live, Granny?" he asked, while the two dogs were growling at each other.

"Away back yonder, sir, behind the ridge. You can't even see it from here."

"On your way home?"

"No sir, I going to town."

"Why, that's too far! That's as far as I walk when I come out myself, and I get something for my trouble." He patted the stuffed bag he carried, and there hung down a little closed claw. It was one of the bob-whites, with its beak hooked bitterly to show it was dead. "Now you go on home, Granny!"

"I bound to go to town, mister," said Phoenix. "The time come around."

He gave another laugh, filling the whole landscape. "I know you old colored people! Wouldn't miss going to town to see Santa Claus!"

But something held old Phoenix very still. The deep lines in her face went into a fierce and different radiation. Without warning, she had seen with her own eyes a flashing nickel fall out of the man's pocket onto the ground.

"How old are you, Granny?" he was saying.

"There is no telling, mister," she said, "no telling."

Then she gave a little cry and clapped her hands and said, "Git on away from here, dog! Look! Look at that dog!" She laughed as if in admiration. "He ain't scared of nobody. He a big black dog." She whispered, "Sic him!"

"Watch me get rid of that cur," said the man. "Sic him, Pete! Sic him!"

Phoenix heard the dogs fighting, and heard the man running and throwing sticks. She even heard a gunshot. But she was slowly bending forward by that time, further and further forward, the lids stretched down over her eyes, as if she were doing this in her sleep. Her chin was lowered almost to her knees. The yellow palm of her hand came out from the fold of her apron. Her fingers slid down and along the ground under the piece of money with the grace and care they would have in lifting an egg from under a setting hen. Then she slowly straightened up, she stood erect, and the nickel was in her apron pocket. A bird flew by. Her lips moved. "God watching me the whole time. I come to stealing."

The man came back, and his own dog panted about them. "Well, I scared him off that time," he said, and then he laughed and lifted his gun and pointed it at Phoenix.

She stood straight and faced him.

"Doesn't the gun scare you?" he said, still pointing it.

"No, sir, I seen plenty go off closer by, in my day, and for less than what I done," she said, holding utterly still.

He smiled, and shouldered the gun. "Well, Granny," he said, "you must be a hundred years old, and scared of nothing. I'd give you a dime if I had any money with me. But you take my advice and stay home, and nothing will happen to you."

"I bound to go on my way, mister," said Phoenix. She inclined her head in the red rag. Then they went in different directions, but she could hear the gun shooting again and again over the hill.

She walked on. The shadows hung from the oak trees to the road like curtains. Then she smelled wood-smoke, and smelled the river, and she saw a steeple and the cabins on their steep steps. Dozens of little black children whirled around her. There ahead was Natchez shining. Bells were ringing. She walked on.

In the paved city it was Christmas time. There were red and green electric lights strung and crisscrossed everywhere, and all turned on in the daytime. Old Phoenix would have been lost if she had not distrusted her eyesight and depended on her feet to know where to take her.

She paused quietly on the sidewalk where people were passing by. A lady came along in the crowd, carrying an armful of red-, green- and silver-wrapped presents; she gave off perfume like the red roses in hot summer, and Phoenix stopped her.

"Please, missy, will you lace up my shoe?" She held up her foot.

"What do you want, Grandma?"

"See my shoe," said Phoenix. "Do all right for out in the country, but wouldn't look right to go in a big building."

"Stand still then, Grandma," said the lady. She put her packages down on the sidewalk beside her and laced and tied both shoes tightly.

"Can't lace 'em with a cane," said Phoenix. "Thank you, missy. I doesn't mind asking a nice lady to tie up my shoe, when I gets out on the street."

Moving slowly and from side to side, she went into the big building, and into a tower of steps, where she walked up and around and around until her feet knew to stop.

She entered a door, and there she saw nailed up on the wall the document that had been stamped with the gold seal and framed in the gold frame, which matched the dream that was hung up in her head.

"Here I be," she said. There was a fixed and ceremonial stiffness over her body.

"A charity case, I suppose," said an attendant who sat at the desk before her.

But Phoenix only looked above her head. There was sweat on her face, the wrinkles in her skin shone like a bright net.

"Speak up, Grandma," the woman said. "What's your name? We must have your history, you know. Have you been here before? What seems to be the trouble with you?"

Old Phoenix only gave a twitch to her face as if a fly were bothering her.

"Are you deaf?" cried the attendant.

But then the nurse came in.

"Oh, that's just old Aunt Phoenix," she said. "She doesn't come for herself—she has a little grandson. She makes these trips just as regular as clockwork. She lives away back off the Old Natchez Trace." She bent down. "Well,

Aunt Phoenix, why don't you just take a seat? We won't keep you standing after your long trip." She pointed.

The old woman sat down, bolt upright in the chair.

"Now, how is the boy?" asked the nurse.

Old Phoenix did not speak.

"I said, how is the boy?"

But Phoenix only waited and stared straight ahead, her face very solemn and withdrawn into rigidity.

"Is his throat any better?" asked the nurse. "Aunt Phoenix, don't you hear me? Is your grandson's throat any better since the last time you came for the medicine?"

With her hands on her knees, the old woman waited, silent, erect and motionless, just as if she were in armor.

"You mustn't take up our time this way, Aunt Phoenix," the nurse said. "Tell us quickly about your grandson, and get it over. He isn't dead, is he?"

At last there came a flicker and then a flame of comprehension across her face, and she spoke.

"My grandson. It was my memory had left me. There I sat and forgot why I made my long trip."

"Forgot?" the nurse frowned. "After you came so far?"

Then Phoenix was like an old woman begging a dignified forgiveness for waking up frightened in the night. "I never did go to school, I was too old at the Surrender," she said in a soft voice. "I'm an old woman without an education. It was my memory fail me. My little grandson, he is just the same, and I forgot it in the coming."

"Throat never heals, does it?" said the nurse, speaking in a loud, sure voice to old Phoenix. By now she had a card with something written on it, a little list. "Yes. Swallowed lye. When was it?—January—two, three years ago—"

Phoenix spoke unasked now. "No, missy, he not dead, he just the same. Every little while his throat begin to close up again, and he not able to swallow. He not get his breath. He not able to help himself. So the time come around, and I go on another trip for the soothing medicine."

"All right. The doctor said as long as you came to get it, you could have it," said the nurse. "But it's an obstinate case."

"My little grandson, he sit up there in the house all wrapped up, waiting by himself," Phoenix went on. "We is the only two left in the world. He suffer and it don't seem to put him back at all. He got a sweet look. He going to last. He wear a little patch quilt and peep out holding his mouth open like a little bird. I remembers so plain now. I not going to forget him again, no, the whole enduring time. I could tell him from all the others in creation."

"All right." The nurse was trying to hush her now. She brought her a bottle of medicine. "Charity," she said, making a check mark in a book.

Old Phoenix held the bottle close to her eyes, and then carefully put it into her pocket.

"I thank you," she said.

"It's Christmas time, Grandma," said the attendant. "Could I give you a few pennies out of my purse?"

"Five pennies is a nickel," said Phoenix stiffly.

"Here's a nickel," said the attendant.

Phoenix rose carefully and held out her hand. She received the nickel and then fished the other nickel out of her pocket and laid it beside the new one. She stared at her palm closely, with her head on one side.

Then she gave a tap with her cane on the floor.

"This is what come to me to do," she said. "I going to the store and buy my child a little windmill they sells, made out of paper. He going to find it hard to believe there such a thing in the world. I'll march myself back where he waiting, holding it straight up in this hand."

She lifted her free hand, gave a little nod, turned around, and walked out of the doctor's office. Then her slow step began on the stairs, going down.

No Place for You, My Love

They were strangers to each other, both fairly well strangers to the place, now seated side by side at luncheon—a party combined in a free-and-easy way when the friends he and she were with recognized each other across Galatoire's. The time was a Sunday in summer—those hours of afternoon that seem Time Out in New Orleans.

The moment he saw her little blunt, fair face, he thought that here was a woman who was having an affair. It was one of those odd meetings when such an impact is felt that it has to be translated at once into some sort of speculation.

With a married man, most likely, he supposed, slipping quickly into a groove—he was long married—and feeling more conventional, then, in his curiosity as she sat there, leaning her cheek on her hand, looking no further before her than the flowers on the table, and wearing that hat.

He did not like her hat, any more than he liked tropical flowers. It was the wrong hat for her, thought this Eastern businessman who had no interest whatever in women's clothes and no eye for them; he thought the unaccustomed thing crossly.

It must stick out all over me, she thought, so people think they can love me or hate me just by looking at me. How did it leave us—the old, safe, slow way people used to know of learning how one another feels, and the privilege that went with it of shying away if it seemed best? People in love like me, I suppose, give away the short cuts to everybody's secrets.

Something, though, he decided, had been settled about her predicament—for the time being, anyway; the parties to it were all still alive, no doubt. Nevertheless, her predicament was the only one he felt so sure of here, like the only recognizable shadow in that restaurant, where mirrors and fans were busy agitating the light, as the very local talk drawled across and agitated the peace. The shadow lay between her fingers, between her little square hand and her cheek, like something always best carried about the person. Then suddenly, as she took her hand down, the secret fact was still there—it lighted her. It was a bold and full light, shot up under the brim of that hat, as close to them all as the flowers in the center of the table.

Did he dream of making her disloyal to that hopelessness that he saw very well she'd been cultivating down here? He knew very well that he did not. What they amounted to was two Northerners keeping each other company. She glanced up at the big gold clock on the wall and smiled. He didn't smile back. She had that naïve face that he associated, for no good reason, with the Middle West—because it said "Show me," perhaps. It was a serious, now-watch-out-everybody face, which orphaned her entirely in the company of these Southerners. He guessed her age, as he could not guess theirs: thirty-two. He himself was further along.

Of all human moods, deliberate imperviousness may be the most quickly communicated—it may be the most successful, most fatal signal of all. And two people can indulge in imperviousness as well as in anything else. "You're not very hungry either," he said.

The blades of fan shadows came down over their two heads, as he saw inadvertently in the mirror, with himself smiling at her now like a villain. His remark sounded dominant and rude enough for everybody present to listen back a moment; it even sounded like an answer to a question she might have just asked him. The other women glanced at him. The Southern look— Southern mask—of life-is-a-dream irony, which could turn to pure challenge at the drop of a hat, he could wish well away. He liked naïveté better.

"I find the heat down here depressing," she said, with the heart of Ohio in her voice.

"Well—I'm in somewhat of a temper about it, too," he said.

They looked with grateful dignity at each other.

"I have a car here, just down the street," he said to her as the luncheon party was rising to leave, all the others wanting to get back to their houses and sleep. "If it's all right with— Have you ever driven down south of here?"

Out on Bourbon Street, in the bath of July, she asked at his shoulder, "South of New Orleans? I didn't know there was any south to *here*. Does it just go on and on?" She laughed, and adjusted the exasperating hat to her head in a different way. It was more than frivolous, it was conspicuous, with some sort of glitter or flitter tied in a band around the straw and hanging down.

"That's what I'm going to show you."

"Oh—you've been there?"

"No!"

His voice rang out over the uneven, narrow sidewalk and dropped back from the walls. The flaked-off, colored houses were spotted like the hides of beasts faded and shy, and were hot as a wall of growth that seemed to breathe flowerlike down onto them as they walked to the car parked there.

"It's just that it couldn't be any worse—we'll see."

"All right, then," she said. "We will."

So, their actions reduced to amiability, they settled into the car—a faded-red Ford convertible with a rather threadbare canvas top, which had been standing in the sun for all those lunch hours.

"It's rented," he explained. "I asked to have the top put down, and was told I'd lost my mind."

"It's out of this world. *Degrading* heat," she said and added, "Doesn't matter."

The stranger in New Orleans always sets out to leave it as though following the clue in a maze. They were threading through the narrow and one-way streets, past the pale-violet bloom of tired squares, the brown steeples and statues, the balcony with the live and probably famous black monkey dipping along the railing as over a ballroom floor, past the grille-work and the lattice-work to all the iron swans painted flesh color on the front steps of bungalows outlying.

Driving, he spread his new map and put his finger down on it. At the intersection marked Arabi, where their road led out of the tangle and he took it, a small Negro seated beneath a black umbrella astride a box chalked "Shou Shine" lifted his pink-and-black hand and waved them languidly good-by. She didn't miss it, and waved back.

Below New Orleans there was a raging of insects from both sides of the concrete highway, not quite together, like the playing of separated marching bands. The river and the levee were still on her side, waste and jungle and some occasional settlements on his—poor houses. Families bigger than housefuls thronged the yards. His nodding, driving head would veer from side to side, looking and almost lowering. As time passed and the distance from New Orleans grew, girls ever darker and younger were disposing themselves over the porches and the porch steps, with jet-black hair pulled high, and ragged palm-leaf fans rising and falling like rafts of butterflies. The children running forth were nearly always naked ones.

She watched the road. Crayfish constantly crossed in front of the wheels, looking grim and bonneted, in a great hurry.

"How the Old Woman Got Home," she murmured to herself.

He pointed, as it flew by, at a saucepan full of cut zinnias which stood waiting on the open lid of a mailbox at the roadside, with a little note tied onto the handle.

They rode mostly in silence. The sun bore down. They met fishermen and other men bent on some local pursuits, some in sulphur-colored pants, walking and riding; met wagons, trucks, boats in trucks, autos, boats on top of autos—all coming to meet them, as though something of high moment were doing back where the car came from, and he and she were determined to miss it. There was nearly always a man lying with his shoes off in the bed of any truck otherwise empty—with the raw, red look of a man sleeping in the daytime, being jolted about as he slept. Then there was a sort of dead man's land, where nobody came. He loosened his collar and tie. By rushing through the heat at high speed, they brought themselves the effect of fans turned onto their cheeks. Clearing alternated with jungle and canebrake like something tried, tried again. Little shell roads led off on both sides; now and then a road of planks led into the yellow-green.

"Like a dance floor in there." She pointed.

He informed her, "In there's your oil, I think."

There were thousands, millions of mosquitoes and gnats—a universe of them, and on the increase.

A family of eight or nine people on foot strung along the road in the same direction the car was going, beating themselves with the wild palmettos. Heels, shoulders, knees, breasts, back of the heads, elbows, hands, were touched in turn—like some game, each playing it with himself.

He struck himself on the forehead, and increased their speed. (His wife would not be at her most charitable if he came bringing malaria home to the family.)

More and more crayfish and other shell creatures littered their path, scuttling or dragging. These little samples, little jokes of creation, persisted and sometimes perished, the more of them the deeper down the road went. Terrapins and turtles came up steadily over the horizons of the ditches.

Back there in the margins were worse—crawling hides you could not penetrate with bullets or quite believe, grins that had come down from the primeval mud.

"Wake up." Her Northern nudge was very timely on his arm. They had veered toward the side of the road. Still driving fast, he spread his map.

Like a misplaced sunrise, the light of the river flowed up; they were mounting the levee on a little shell road.

"Shall we cross here?" he asked politely.

He might have been keeping track over years and miles of how long they could keep that tiny ferry waiting. Now skidding down the levee's flank, they were the last-minute car, the last possible car that could squeeze on. Under the sparse shade of one willow tree, the small, amateurish-looking boat slapped the water, as, expertly, he wedged on board.

"Tell him we put him on hub cap!" shouted one of the numerous olive-skinned, dark-eyed young boys standing dressed up in bright shirts at the railing, hugging each other with delight that that last straw was on board.

Another boy drew his affectionate initials in the dust of the door on her side.

She opened the door and stepped out, and, after only a moment's standing at bay, started up a little iron stairway. She appeared above the car, on the tiny bridge beneath the captain's window and the whistle.

From there, while the boat still delayed in what seemed a trance—as if it were too full to attempt the start—she could see the panlike deck below, separated by its rusty rim from the tilting, polished water.

The passengers walking and jostling about there appeared oddly amateurish, too—amateur travelers. They were having such a good time. They all knew each other. Beer was being passed around in cans, bets were being loudly settled and new bets made, about local and special subjects on which they all doted. One red-haired man in a burst of wildness even tried to give away his truckload of shrimp to a man on the other side of the boat—nearly all the trucks were full of shrimp—causing taunts and then protests of "They good! They good!" from the giver. The young boys leaned on each other thinking of what next, rolling their eyes absently.

A radio pricked the air behind her. Looking like a great tomcat just above her head, the captain was digesting the news of a fine stolen automobile.

At last a tremendous explosion burst—the whistle. Everything shuddered in outline from the sound, everybody said something—everybody else.

They started with no perceptible motion, but her hat blew off. It went spiralling to the deck below, where he, thank heaven, sprang out of the car and picked it up. Everybody looked frankly up at her now, holding her hands to her head.

The little willow tree receded as its shade was taken away. The heat was like something falling on her head. She held the hot rail before her. It was like riding a stove. Her shoulders dropping, her hair flying, her skirt buffeted by the sudden strong wind, she stood there, thinking they all must see that with her entire self all she did was wait. Her set hands, with the bag that hung from her wrist and rocked back and forth—all three seemed objects bleaching there, belonging to no one; she could not feel a thing in the skin of her face; perhaps she was crying, and not knowing it. She could look down and see him just below her, his black shadow, her hat, and his black hair. His hair in the wind looked unreasonably long and rippling. Little did he know that from here it had a red undergleam like an animal's. When she looked up and outward, a vortex of light drove through and over the brown waves like a star in the water.

He did after all bring the retrieved hat up the stairs to her. She took it back—useless—and held it to her skirt. What they were saying below was more polite than their searchlight faces.

"Where you think he come from, that man?"

"I bet he come from Lafitte."

"Lafitte? What you bet, eh?"—all crouched in the shade of trucks, squatting and laughing.

Now his shadow fell partly across her; the boat had jolted into some other strand of current. Her shaded arm and shaded hand felt pulled out from the blaze of light and water, and she hoped humbly for more shade for her head. It had seemed so natural to climb up and stand in the sun.

The boys had a surprise—an alligator on board. One of them pulled it by a chain around the deck, between the cars and trucks, like a toy—a hide that could walk. He thought, Well they had to catch one sometime. It's Sunday afternoon. So they have him on board now, riding him across the Mississippi River. . . . The playfulness of it beset everybody on the ferry. The hoarseness of the boat whistle, commenting briefly, seemed part of the general appreciation.

"Who want to rassle him? Who want to, eh?" two boys cried, looking up. A boy with shrimp-colored arms capered from side to side, pretending to have been bitten.

What was there so hilarious about jaws that could bite? And what danger was there once in this repulsiveness—so that the last worldly evidence of some old heroic horror of the dragon had to be paraded in capture before the eyes of country clowns?

He noticed that she looked at the alligator without flinching at all. Her distance was set—the number of feet and inches between herself and it mattered to her.

Perhaps her measuring coolness was to him what his bodily shade was to her, while they stood pat up there riding the river, which felt like the sea and looked like the earth under them—full of the red-brown earth, charged with it. Ahead of the boat it was like an exposed vein of ore. The river seemed to swell in the vast middle with the curve of the earth. The sun rolled under them. As if in memory of the size of things, uprooted trees were drawn across their path, sawing at the air and tumbling one over the other.

When they reached the other side, they felt that they had been racing around an arena in their chariot, among lions. The whistle took and shook the stairs as they went down. The young boys, looking taller, had taken out colored combs and were combing their wet hair back in solemn pompadour above their radiant foreheads. They had been bathing in the river themselves not long before.

The cars and trucks, then the foot passengers and the alligator, waddling like a child to school, all disembarked and wound up the weed-sprung levee.

Both respectable and merciful, their hides, she thought, forcing herself to dwell on the alligator as she looked back. Deliver us all from the naked in heart. (As she had been told.)

When they regained their paved road, he heard her give a little sigh and saw her turn her straw-colored head to look back once more. Now that she rode with her hat in her lap, her earrings were conspicuous too. A little metal ball set with small pale stones danced beside each square, faintly downy cheek.

Had she felt a wish for someone else to be riding with them? He thought it was more likely that she would wish for her husband if she had one (his wife's voice) than for the lover in whom he believed. Whatever people liked to think, situations (if not scenes) were usually three-way—there was some-body else always. The one who didn't—couldn't—understand the two made the formidable third.

He glanced down at the map flapping on the seat between them, up at his wristwatch, out at the road. Out there was the incredible brightness of four o'clock.

On this side of the river, the road ran beneath the brow of the levee and followed it. Here was a heat that ran deeper and brighter and more intense than all the rest—its nerve. The road grew one with the heat as it was one with the unseen river. Dead snakes stretched across the concrete like mark-ers—inlaid mosaic bands, dry as feathers, which their tires licked at intervals that began to seem clocklike.

No, the heat faced them—it was ahead. They could see it waving at them, shaken in the air above the white of the road, always at a certain dis-tance ahead, shimmering finely as a cloth, with running edges of green and gold, fire and azure.

"It's never anything like this in Syracuse," he said.

"Or in Toledo, either," she replied with dry lips.

They were driving through greater waste down here, through fewer and even more insignificant towns. There was water under everything. Even where a screen of jungle had been left to stand, splashes could be heard from under the trees. In the vast open, sometimes boats moved inch by inch through what appeared endless meadows of rubbery flowers.

Her eyes overcome with brightness and size, she felt a panic rise, as sudden as nausea. Just how far below questions and answers, concealment and revelation, they were running now—that was still a new question, with a power of its own, waiting. How dear—how costly—could this ride be?

"It looks to me like your road can't go much further," she remarked cheerfully. "Just over there, it's all water."

"Time out," he said, and with that he turned the car into a sudden road of white shells that rushed at them narrowly out of the left.

They bolted over a cattle guard, where some rayed and crested purple flowers burst out of the vines in the ditch, and rolled onto a long, narrow, green, mowed clearing: a churchyard. A paved track ran between two short rows of raised tombs, all neatly white-washed and now brilliant as faces against the vast flushed sky.

The track was the width of the car with a few inches to spare. He passed between the tombs slowly but in the manner of a feat. Names took their places on the walls slowly at a level with the eye, names as near as the eyes of a person stopping in conversation, and as far away in origin, and in all their music and dead longing, as Spain. At intervals were set packed bouquets of zinnias, oleanders, and some kind of purple flowers, all quite fresh, in fruit jars, like nice welcomes on bureaus.

They moved on into an open plot beyond, of violent-green grass, spread before the green-and-white frame church with worked flower beds around it, flowerless poinsettias growing up to the windowsills. Beyond was a house, and left on the doorstep of the house a fresh-caught catfish the size of a baby—a fish wearing whiskers and bleeding. On a clothesline in the yard, a priest's black gown on a hanger hung airing, swaying at man's height, in a vague, trainlike, ladylike sweep along an evening breath that might otherwise have seemed imaginary from the unseen, felt river.

With the motor cut off, with the raging of the insects about them, they sat looking out at the green and white and black and red and pink as they leaned against the sides of the car.

"What is your wife like?" she asked. His right hand came up and spread—iron, wooden, manicured. She lifted her eyes to his face. He looked at her like that hand.

Then he lit a cigarette, and the portrait, and the right-hand testimonial it made, were blown away. She smiled, herself as unaffected as by some stage performance; and he was annoyed in the cemetery. They did not risk going on to her husband—if she had one.

Under the supporting posts of the priest's house, where a boat was, solid ground ended and palmettos and water hyacinths could not wait to begin; suddenly the rays of the sun, from behind the car, reached that lowness and struck the flowers. The priest came out onto the porch in his underwear, stared at the car a moment as if he wondered what time it was, then collected his robe off the line and his fish off the doorstep and returned inside. Vespers was next, for him.

After backing out between the tombs he drove on still south, in the sunset. They caught up with an old man walking in a sprightly way in their direction, all by himself, wearing a clean bright shirt printed with a pair of palm trees fanning green over his chest. It might better be a big colored woman's shirt, but she didn't have it. He flagged the car with gestures like hoops.

"You're coming to the end of the road," the old man told them. He pointed ahead, tipped his hat to the lady, and pointed again. "End of the road." They didn't understand that he meant, "Take me."

They drove on. "If we do go any further, it'll have to be by water—is that it?" he asked her, hesitating at this odd point.

"You know better than I do," she replied politely.

The road had for some time ceased to be paved; it was made of shells. It was leading into a small, sparse settlement like the others a few miles back, but with even more of the camp about it. On the lip of the clearing, directly before a green willow blaze with the sunset gone behind it, the row of houses and shacks faced out on broad, colored, moving water that stretched to reach the horizon and looked like an arm of the sea. The houses on their shaggy posts, patchily built, some with plank runways instead of steps, were flimsy and alike, and not much bigger than the boats tied up at the landing.

"Venice," she heard him announce, and he dropped the crackling map in her lap.

They coasted down the brief remainder. The end of the road—she could not remember ever seeing a road simply end—was a spoon shape, with a tree stump in the bowl to turn around by.

Around it, he stopped the car, and they stepped out, feeling put down in the midst of a sudden vast pause or subduement that was like a yawn. They made their way on foot toward the water, where at an idle-looking landing men in twos and threes stood with their backs to them.

The nearness of darkness, the still uncut trees, bright water partly under a sheet of flowers, shacks, silence, dark shapes of boats tied up, then the first sounds of people just on the other side of thin walls—all this reached them. Mounds of shells like day-old snow, pink-tinted, lay around a central shack with a beer sign on it. An old man up on the porch there sat holding an open newspaper, with a fat white goose sitting opposite him on the floor. Below, in the now shadowless and sunless open, another old man, with a colored pencil bright under his hat brim, was late mending a sail.

When she looked clear around, thinking they had a fire burning somewhere now, out of the heat had risen the full moon. Just beyond the trees, enormous, tangerine-colored, it was going solidly up. Other lights just striking into view, looking farther distant, showed moss shapes hanging, or slipped and broke matchlike on the water that so encroached upon the rim of ground they were standing on.

There was a touch at her arm—his, accidental.

"We're at the jumping-off place," he said.

She laughed, having thought his hand was a bat, while her eyes rushed downward toward a great pale drift of water hyacinths—still partly open, flushed and yet moonlit, level with her feet—through which paths of water for the boats had been hacked. She drew her hands up to her face under the brim of her hat; her own cheeks felt like the hyacinths to her, all her skin full of too much light and sky, exposed. The harsh vesper bell was ringing.

"I believe there must be something wrong with me, that I came on this excursion to begin with," she said, as if he had already said this and she were merely in hopeful, willing, maddening agreement with him.

He took hold of her arm, and said, "Oh, come on—I see we can get something to drink here, at least."

But there was a beating, muffled sound from over the darkening water. One more boat was coming in, making its way through the tenacious, tough, dark flower traps, by the shaken light of what first appeared to be torches. He and she waited for the boat, as if on each other's patience. As if borne in on a mist of twilight or a breath, a horde of mosquitoes and gnats came singing and striking at them first. The boat bumped, men laughed. Somebody was offering somebody else some shrimp.

Then he might have cocked his dark city head down at her; she did not look up at him, only turned when he did. Now the shell mounds, like the shacks and trees, were solid purple. Lights had appeared in the not-quite-true window squares. A narrow neon sign, the lone sign, had come out in bright blush on the beer shack's roof: "Baba's Place." A light was on on the porch.

The barnlike interior was brightly lit and unpainted, looking not quite finished, with a partition dividing this room from what lay behind. One of the four cardplayers at a table in the middle of the floor was the newspaper reader; the paper was in his pants pocket. Midway along the partition was a bar, in the form of a pass-through to the other room, with a varnished, second-hand fretwork overhang. They crossed the floor and sat, alone there, on wooden stools. An eruption of humorous signs, newspaper cutouts and cartoons, razor-blade cards, and personal messages of significance to the owner or his friends decorated the overhang, framing where Baba should have been but wasn't.

Through there came a smell of garlic and cloves and red pepper, a blast of hot cloud escaped from a cauldron they could see now on a stove at the back of the other room. A massive back, presumably female, with a twist of gray hair on top, stood with a ladle akimbo. A young man joined her and with his fingers stole something out of the pot and ate it. At Baba's they were boiling shrimp.

When he got ready to wait on them, Baba strolled out to the counter, young, black-headed, and in very good humor.

"Coldest beer you've got. And food— What will you have?"

"Nothing for me, thank you," she said. "I'm not sure I could eat, after all."

"Well, I could," he said, shoving his jaw out. Baba smiled. "I want a good solid ham sandwich."

"I could have asked him for some water," she said, after he had gone.

While they sat waiting, it seemed very quiet. The bubbling of the shrimp, the distant laughing of Baba, and the slap of cards, like the beating of moths on the screens, seemed to come in fits and starts. The steady breathing they heard came from a big rough dog asleep in the corner. But it was bright.

Electric lights were strung riotously over the room from a kind of spider web of old wires in the rafters. One of the written messages tacked before them read, "Joe! At the boyy!!" It looked very yellow, older than Baba's Place. Outside, the world was pure dark.

Two little boys, almost alike, almost the same size, and just cleaned up, dived into the room with a double bang of the screen door, and circled around the card game. They ran their hands into the men's pockets.

"Nickel for some pop!"

"Nickel for some pop!"

"Go 'way and let me play, you!"

They circled around and shrieked at the dog, ran under the lid of the counter and raced through the kitchen and back, and hung over the stools at the bar. One child had a live lizard on his shirt, clinging like a breast pin— like lapis lazuli.

Bringing in a strong odor of geranium talcum, some men had come in now—all in bright shirts. They drew near the counter, or stood and watched the game.

When Baba came out bringing the beer and sandwich, "Could I have some water?" she greeted him.

Baba laughed at everybody. She decided the woman back there must be Baba's mother.

Beside her, he was drinking his beer and eating his sandwich—ham, cheese, tomato, pickle, and mustard. Before he finished, one of the men who had come in beckoned from across the room. It was the old man in the palm-tree shirt.

She lifted her head to watch him leave her, and was looked at, from all over the room. As a minute passed, no cards were laid down. In a far-off way, like accepting the light from Arcturus, she accepted it that she was more beautiful or perhaps more fragile than the women they saw every day of their lives. It was just this thought coming into a woman's face, and at this hour, that seemed familiar to them.

Baba was smiling. He had set an opened, frosted brown bottle before her on the counter, and a thick sandwich, and stood looking at her. Baba made her eat some supper, for what she was.

"What the old fellow wanted," said he when he came back at last, "was to have a friend of his apologize. Seems church is just out. Seems the friend made a remark coming in just now. His pals told him there was a lady present."

"I see you bought him a beer," she said.

"Well, the old man looked like he wanted *something*."

All at once the juke box interrupted from back in the corner, with the same old song as anywhere. The half-dozen slot machines along the wall were suddenly all run to like Maypoles, and thrown into action—taken over by further battalions of little boys.

There were three little boys to each slot machine. The local custom appeared to be that one pulled the lever for the friend he was holding up to put the nickel in, while the third covered the pictures with the flat of his hand as they fell into place, so as to surprise them all if anything happened.

The dog lay sleeping on in front of the raging juke box, his ribs working fast as a concertina's. At the side of the room a man with a cap on his white thatch was trying his best to open a side screen door, but it was stuck fast. It was he who had come in with the remark considered ribald; now he was trying to get out the other way. Moths as thick as ingots were trying to get in. The cardplayers broke into shouts of derision, then joy, then tired derision among themselves; they might have been here all afternoon—they were the only ones not cleaned up and shaved. The original pair of little boys ran in once more, with the hyphenated bang. They got nickels this time, then were brushed away from the table like mosquitoes, and they rushed under the counter and on to the cauldron behind, clinging to Baba's mother there. The evening was at the threshold.

They were quite unnoticed now. He was eating another sandwich, and she, having finished part of hers, was fanning her face with her hat. Baba had lifted the flap of the counter and come out into the room. Behind his head there was a sign lettered in orange crayon: "Shrimp Dance Sun. PM." That was tonight, still to be.

And suddenly she made a move to slide down from her stool, maybe wishing to walk out into that nowhere down the front steps to be cool a moment. But he had hold of her hand. He got down from his stool, and, patiently, reversing her hand in his own—just as she had had the look of being about to give up, faint—began moving her, leading her. They were dancing.

"I get to thinking this is what we get—what you and I deserve," she whispered, looking past his shoulder into the room. "And all the time, it's real. It's a real place—away off down here. . . ."

They danced gratefully, formally, to some song carried on in what must be the local patois, while no one paid any attention as long as they were together, and the children poured the family nickels steadily into the slot machines, walloping the handles down with regular crashes and troubling nobody with winning.

She said rapidly, as they began moving together too well, "One of those clippings was an account of a shooting right here. I guess they're proud of it. And that awful knife Baba was carrying . . . I wonder what he called me," she whispered in his ear.

"Who?"

"The one who apologized to you."

If they had ever been going to overstep themselves, it would be now as he held her closer and turned her, when she became aware that he could not help but see the bruise at her temple. It would not be six inches from his eyes. She felt it come out like an evil star. (Let it pay him back, then, for the hand he had stuck in her face when she'd tried once to be sympathetic, when she'd asked about his wife.) They danced on still as the record changed, after standing wordless and motionless, linked together in the middle of the room, for the moment between.

Then, they were like a matched team—like professional Spanish dancers wearing masks—while the slow piece was playing.

Surely even those immune from the world, for the time being, need the touch of one another, or all is lost. Their arms encircling each other, their bodies circling the odorous, just-nailed-down floor, they were, at last, imperviousness in motion. They had found it, and had almost missed it: they had had to dance. They were what their separate hearts desired that day, for themselves and each other.

They were so good together that once she looked up and half smiled. "For whose benefit did we have to show off?"

Like people in love, they had a superstition about themselves almost as soon as they came out on the floor, and dared not think the words "happy" or "unhappy," which might strike them, one or the other, like lightning.

In the thickening heat they danced on while Baba himself sang with the mosquito-voiced singer in the chorus of *"Moi pas l'aimez ça,"* enumerating the *ça*'s with a hot shrimp between his fingers. He was counting over the platters the old woman now set out on the counter, each heaped with shrimp in their shells boiled to iridescence, like mounds of honeysuckle flowers.

The goose wandered in from the back room under the lid of the counter and hitched itself around the floor among the table legs and people's legs, never seeing that it was neatly avoided by two dancers—who nevertheless vaguely thought of this goose as learned, having earlier heard an old man read to it. The children called it Mimi, and lured it away. The old thatched man was again drunkenly trying to get out by the stuck side door; now he gave it a kick, but was prevailed on to remain. The sleeping dog shuddered and snored.

It was left up to the dancers to provide nickels for the juke box; Baba kept a drawerful for every use. They had grown fond of all the selections by now. This was the music you heard out of the distance at night—out of the roadside taverns you fled past, around the late corners in cities half asleep, drifting up from the carnival over the hill, with one odd little strain always managing to repeat itself. This seemed a homey place.

Bathed in sweat, and feeling the false coolness that brings, they stood finally on the porch in the lapping night air for a moment before leaving. The first arrivals of the girls were coming up the steps under the porch light—all flowered fronts, their black pompadours giving out breathlike feelers from sheer abundance. Where they'd resprinkled it since church, the talcum shone like mica on their downy arms. Smelling solidly of geranium, they filed across the porch with short steps and fingers joined, just timed to turn their smiles loose inside the room. He held the door open for them.

"Ready to go?" he asked her.

Going back, the ride was wordless, quiet except for the motor and the insects driving themselves against the car. The windshield was soon blinded. The headlights pulled in two other spinning storms, cones of flying things that, it seemed, might ignite at the last minute. He stopped the car and got out to clean the windshield thoroughly with his brisk, angry motions of driving. Dust lay thick and cratered on the roadside scrub. Under the now ash-white moon, the world traveled through very faint stars—very many slow stars, very high, very low.

It was a strange land, amphibious—and whether water-covered or grown with jungle or robbed entirely of water and trees, as now, it had the same loneliness. He regarded the great sweep—like steppes, like moors, like deserts (all of which were imaginary to him); but more than it was like any likeness, it was South. The vast, thin, wide-thrown, pale, unfocused star-sky, with its veils of lightning adrift, hung over this land as it hung over the open sea. Standing out in the night alone, he was struck as powerfully with recognition of the extremity of this place as if all other bearings had vanished—as if snow had suddenly started to fall.

He climbed back inside and drove. When he moved to slap furiously at his shirtsleeves, she shivered in the hot, licking night wind that their speed was making. Once the car lights picked out two people—a Negro couple, sitting on two facing chairs in the yard outside their lonely cabin—half undressed, each battling for self against the hot night, with long white rags in endless, scarflike motions.

In peopleless open places there were lakes of dust, smudge fires burning at their hearts. Cows stood in untended rings around them, motionless in the heat, in the night—their horns standing up sharp against that glow.

At length, he stopped the car again, and this time he put his arm under her shoulder and kissed her—not knowing ever whether gently or harshly. It was the loss of that distinction that told him this was now. Then their faces touched unkissing, unmoving, dark, for a length of time. The heat came inside the car and wrapped them still, and the mosquitoes had begun to coat their arms and even their eyelids.

Later, crossing a large open distance, he saw at the same time two fires. He had the feeling that they had been riding for a long time across a face—great, wide, and upturned. In its eyes and open mouth were those fires they had had glimpses of, where the cattle had drawn together: a face, a head, far down here in the South—south of South, below it. A whole giant body sprawled downward then, on and on, always, constant as a constellation or an angel. Flaming and perhaps falling, he thought.

She appeared to be sound asleep, lying back flat as a child, with her hat in her lap. He drove on with her profile beside his, behind his, for he bent forward to drive faster. The earrings she wore twinkled with their rushing motion in an almost regular beat. They might have spoken like tongues. He looked straight before him and drove on, at a speed that, for the rented, overheated, not at all new Ford car, was demoniac.

It seemed often now that a barnlike shape flashed by, roof and all outlined in lonely neon—a movie house at a crossroads. The long white flat road itself, since they had followed it to the end and turned around to come back, seemed able, this far up, to pull them home.

A thing is incredible, if ever, only after it is told—returned to the world it came out of. For their different reasons, he thought, neither of them would tell this (unless something was dragged out of them): that, strangers, they had ridden down into a strange land together and were getting safely back—by a slight margin, perhaps, but margin enough. Over the levee wall now, like an aurora borealis, the sky of New Orleans, across the river, was flickering gently. This time they crossed by bridge, high above everything, merging into a long light-stream of cars turned cityward.

For a time afterward he was lost in the streets, turning almost at random with the noisy traffic until he found his bearings. When he stopped the car at the next sign and leaned forward frowning to make it out, she sat up straight on her side. It was Arabi. He turned the car right around.

"We're all right now," he muttered, allowing himself a cigarette.

Something that must have been with them all along suddenly, then, was not. In a moment, tall as panic, it rose, cried like a human, and dropped back.

"I never got my water," she said.

She gave him the name of her hotel, he drove her there, and he said good night on the sidewalk. They shook hands.

"Forgive . . ." For, just in time, he saw she expected it of him.

And that was just what she did, forgive him. Indeed, had she waked in time from a deep sleep, she would have told him her story. She disappeared through the revolving door, with a gesture of smoothing her hair, and he thought a figure in the lobby strolled to meet her. He got back in the car and sat there.

He was not leaving for Syracuse until early in the morning. At length, he recalled the reason; his wife had recommended that he stay where he was this extra day so that she could entertain some old, unmarried college friends without him underfoot.

As he started up the car, he recognized in the smell of exhausted, body-warm air in the streets, in which the flow of drink was an inextricable part, the signal that the New Orleans evening was just beginning. In Dickie Grogan's, as he passed, the well-known Josefina at her organ was charging up and down with *Clair de Lune*. As he drove the little Ford safely to its garage, he remembered for the first time in years when he was young and brash, a student in New York, and the shriek and horror and unholy smother of the subway had its original meaning for him as the lilt and expectation of love.

Elizabeth Bishop

(1911–1979)

An American poet who was highly respected by other poets, Elizabeth Bishop was born in Worcester, Massachusetts, where by the age of five she had lost both her parents, her father to Bright's disease and her mother to mental illness and confinement in a sanitarium. (The day her mother was taken away forever is recounted in her story "In the Village"; her friend Robert Lowell made the narrative into a poem entitled "The Scream.") The year before Bishop graduated from Vassar she met Marianne Moore, who became her lifelong literary mentor and friend. Bishop shared Moore's dislike of confessional poetry. ("You just wish they'd keep some of those things to themselves," she said.) After graduation she became an inveterate traveler, living along the way in Paris, London, Key West, Cape Cod, Petrópolis, San Francisco, Mexico, Boston, Greenwich Village, and Seattle. Between 1951 and 1966 she settled at Ouro Prêto in Brazil, living with her lover, Lota Costellat de Macedo Soares. Their house was named Casa Mariana after the nearby town of Mariana and after Marianne Moore. Bishop's nomadic life is reflected in the titles of her books, which include *North & South* (1946), a winner of the Pulitzer Prize; *Questions of Travel* (1965); *Brazil* (1967); and *Geography III* (1976). Poet and novelist Brad Leithauser points out that Bishop used to tell her students that "dark visions can come too easily to the artist, and it's often a far more arduous struggle to locate the bright tableau of salvation." Her published letters, *One Art* (1994), have, in the words of another poet, the same qualities she admired in poetry: accuracy, spontaneity, and mystery.

Roosters

At four o'clock
in the gun-metal blue dark
we hear the first crow of the first cock

just below
the gun-metal blue window
and immediately there is an echo

off in the distance
then one from the backyard fence,
then one, with horrible insistence,

grates like a wet match
from the broccoli patch,
flares, and all over town begins to catch.

Cries galore
come from the water-closet door,
from the dropping-plastered henhouse floor,

where in the blue blur
their rustling wives admire,
the roosters brace their cruel feet and glare

with stupid eyes
while from their beaks there rise
the uncontrolled, traditional cries.

Deep from protruding chests
in green-gold medals dressed,
planned to command and terrorize the rest,

the many wives
who lead hens' lives
of being courted and despised;

deep from raw throats
a senseless order floats
all over town. A rooster gloats

over our beds
from rusty iron sheds
and fences made from old bedsteads,

over our churches
where the tin rooster perches,
over our little wooden northern houses,

making sallies
from all the muddy alleys,
marking out maps like Rand McNally's:

glass-headed pins,
oil-golds and copper greens,
anthracite blues, alizarins,

each one an active
displacement in perspective;
each screaming, "This is where I live!"

Each screaming
"Get up! Stop dreaming!"
Roosters, what are you projecting?

You, whom the Greeks elected
to shoot at on a post, who struggled
when sacrificed, you whom they labeled

"Very combative . . ."
what right have you to give
commands and tell us how to live,

cry "Here!" and "Here!"
and wake us here where are
unwanted love, conceit and war?

The crown of red
set on your little head
is charged with all your fighting blood.

Yes, that excrescence
makes a most virile presence,
plus all that vulgar beauty of iridescence.

Now in mid-air
by twos they fight each other.
Down comes a first flame-feather,

and one is flying,
with raging heroism defying
even the sensation of dying.

And one has fallen,
but still above the town
his torn-out, bloodied feathers drift down;

and what he sung
no matter. He is flung
on the gray ash-heap, lies in dung

with his dead wives
with open, bloody eyes,
while those metallic feathers oxidize.

St. Peter's sin
was worse than that of Magdalen
whose sin was of the flesh alone;

of spirit, Peter's,
falling, beneath the flares,
among the "servants and officers."

Old holy sculpture
could set it all together
in one small scene, past and future:

Christ stands amazed,
Peter, two fingers raised
to surprised lips, both as if dazed.

But in between
a little cock is seen
carved on a dim column in the travertine,

explained by *gallus canit;*
flet Petrus★ underneath it.
There is inescapable hope, the pivot;

yes, and there's Peter's tears
run down our chanticleer's
sides and gem his spurs.

Tear-encrusted thick
as a medieval relic
he waits. Poor Peter, heart-sick,

still cannot guess
those cock-a-doodles yet might bless,
his dreadful rooster come to mean forgiveness,

a new weathervane
on basilica and barn,
and that outside the Lateran

★ "The cock crows; Peter weeps."

there would always be
a bronze cock on a porphyry
pillar so the people and the Pope might see

that even the Prince
of the Apostles long since
had been forgiven, and to convince

all the assembly
that "Deny deny deny"
is not all the roosters cry.

In the morning
a low light is floating
in the backyard, and gilding

from underneath
the broccoli, leaf by leaf;
how could the night have come to grief?

gilding the tiny
floating swallow's belly
and lines of pink cloud in the sky,

the day's preamble
like wandering lines in marble.
The cocks are now almost inaudible.

The sun climbs in,
following, "to see the end,"
faithful as enemy, or friend.

FROM *Efforts of Affection:*
A Memoir of Marianne Moore

In the first edition of Marianne Moore's *Collected Poems* of 1951 there is a poem originally called "Efforts and Affection." In my copy of this book, Marianne crossed out the "and" and wrote "of" above it. I liked this change very much, and so I am giving the title "Efforts of Affection" to the whole piece.

I first met Marianne Moore in the spring of 1934 when I was a senior at Vassar College, through Miss Fanny Borden, the college librarian. A school friend and the friend's mother, both better read and more sophisticated in their literary tastes than I was, had told me about Marianne Moore's poetry several years earlier. I had already read every poem of Miss Moore's I could find, in back copies of *The Dial*, "little magazines," and anthologies in the college library. I hadn't known poetry could be like that; I took to it immediately, but although I knew there was a volume of hers called *Observations*, it was not in the library and I had never seen it.

Because Miss Borden seems like such an appropriate person to have introduced me to Marianne Moore, I want to say a little about her. She was the niece of the Fall River Lizzie Borden, and at college the rumor was that Lizzie Borden's lurid career had had a permanently subduing effect on Miss Fanny Borden's personality. She was extremely shy and reserved and spoke in such a soft voice it was hard to hear her at all. She was tall and thin; she always dressed in browns and grays, old-fashioned, muted, and distinguished-looking. She also rode a chainless bicycle. I remember watching her ride slowly up to the library, seated very high and straight on this curiosity, which somehow seemed more lady-like than a bicycle with a chain, and park it in the rack. (We didn't padlock bicycles then.) Once, after she had gone inside, I examined the bicycle, which was indeed chainless, to see if I could figure out how it worked. I couldn't. Contact with the librarian was rare; once in a long while, in search of a book, one would be sent to Miss Borden's office, shadowy and cave-like, with books piled everywhere. She weighed down the papers on her desk with smooth, round stones, quite big stones, brought from the seashore, and once when my roommate admired one of these, Miss Borden said in her almost inaudible voice, "Do you like it? You may *have* it," and handed it over, gray, round, and very heavy.

One day I was sent in to Miss Borden's office about a book, I no longer remember what. We continued talking a little, and I finally got up my courage to ask her why there was no copy of *Observations* by that wonderful poet Marianne Moore in the Vassar library. She looked ever so gently taken aback and inquired, "Do you *like* Marianne Moore's poems?" I said I certainly did, the few I'd been able to find. Miss Borden then said calmly, "I've known her since she was a little girl," and followed that with the question that was possibly to influence the whole course of my life: "Would you like to meet her?" I was painfully—no, excruciatingly—shy and I had run away many times rather than face being introduced to adults of much less distinction than Marianne Moore, but I immediately said, "Yes." Miss Borden said that she would write to Miss Moore, who lived in Brooklyn, and also that she would be glad to lend me *her* copy of *Observations*.

Miss Borden's copy of *Observations* was an eye-opener in more ways than one. Poems like "An Octopus," about a glacier, or "Peter," about a cat, or "Marriage," about marriage, struck me, as they still do, as miracles of language and construction. Why had no one ever written about things in this clear and dazzling way before? But at the same time I was astonished to discover that Miss Borden (whom I now knew to be an old family friend of the Moores) obviously didn't share my liking for these poems. Tucked in the back of the book were quite a few reviews that had appeared when *Observations* was published, in 1924, and most of these were highly unfavorable, some simply obtuse. There was even a parody Moore poem by Franklin P. Adams. Even more revealing, Miss Borden hadn't seen fit to place a copy of her friend's book in the college library. (Later that year I found a copy for myself, on a secondhand-book table at Macy's.)

The day came when Miss Borden told me that she had heard from Miss Moore and that Miss Moore was willing to meet me in New York, on a Saturday afternoon. Years later I discovered that Marianne had agreed to do this with reluctance; in the past, it seems, dear Miss Borden had sent several Vassar girls to meet Miss Moore and sometimes her mother as well, and every one had somehow failed to please. This probably accounted for the conditions laid down for our first rendezvous: I was to find Miss Moore seated on the bench at the right of the door leading to the reading room of the New York Public Library. They might have been even more strict. I learned later that if Miss Moore really expected *not* to like would-be acquaintances, she arranged to meet them at the Information Booth in Grand Central

Station—no place to sit down, and, if necessary, an instant getaway was possible. In the meantime, I had been told a little more about her by Miss Borden, who described her as a child, a strange and appealing little creature with bright red hair—playful, and, as might have been expected, fond of calling her family and friends by the names of animals.

I was very frightened, but I put on my new spring suit and took the train to New York. I had never seen a picture of Miss Moore; all I knew was that she had red hair and usually wore a wide-brimmed hat. I expected the hair to be bright red and for her to be tall and intimidating. I was right on time, even a bit early, but she was there before me (no matter how early one arrived, Marianne was always there first) and, I saw at once, not very tall and not in the least intimidating. She was forty-seven, an age that seemed old to me then, and her hair was mixed with white to a faint rust pink, and her rust-pink eyebrows were frosted with white. The large flat black hat was as I'd expected it to be. She wore a blue tweed suit that day and, as she usually did then, a man's "polo shirt," as they were called, with a black bow at the neck. The effect was quaint, vaguely Bryn Mawr 1909, but stylish at the same time. I sat down and she began to talk.

It seems to me that Marianne talked to me steadily for the next thirty-five years, but of course that is nonsensical. I was living far from New York many of those years and saw her at long intervals. She must have been one of the world's greatest talkers: entertaining, enlightening, fascinating, and memorable; her talk, like her poetry, was quite different from anybody else's in the world. I don't know what she talked about at that first meeting; I wish I had kept a diary. Happily ignorant of the poor Vassar girls before me who hadn't passed muster, I began to feel less nervous and even spoke some myself. I had what may have been an inspiration, I don't know—at any rate, I attribute my great good fortune in having known Marianne as a friend in part to it. Ringling Bros. and Barnum & Bailey Circus was making its spring visit to New York and I asked Miss Moore (we called each other "Miss" for over two years) if she would care to go to the circus with me the Saturday after next. I didn't know that she *always* went to the circus, wouldn't have missed it for anything, and when she accepted, I went back to Poughkeepsie in the grimy day coach extremely happy.

The Circus

I got to Madison Square Garden very early—we had settled on the hour because we wanted to see the animals before the show began—but Marianne was there ahead of me. She was loaded down: two blue cloth bags, one on each arm, and two huge brown paper bags, full of something. I was given one of these. They contained, she told me, stale brown bread for the elephants, because stale brown bread was one of the things they liked best to eat. (I later suspected that they might like stale white bread just as much but that Marianne had been thinking about their health.) As we went in and down to the lower level, where we could hear (and smell) the animals, she told me her preliminary plan for the circus. Her brother, Warner, had given her an ele-phant-hair bracelet, of which she was very fond, two or three strands of black hairs held together with gold clasps. One of the elephant hairs had fallen out and been lost. As I probably knew, elephant hairs grow only on the tops of the heads of very young elephants. In her bag, Marianne had a pair of strong nail scissors. I was to divert the adult elephants with the bread, and, if we were lucky, the guards wouldn't observe her at the end of the line where the babies were, and she could take out her scissors and snip a few hairs from a baby's head, to repair her bracelet.

She was quite right; the elephants adored stale brown bread and started trumpeting and pushing up against each other to get it. I stayed at one end of the line, putting slices of bread into the trunks of the older elephants, and Miss Moore went rapidly down to the other end, where the babies were. The large elephants were making such a to-do that a keeper did come up my way, and out of the corner of my eye I saw Miss Moore leaning forward over the rope on tiptoe, scissors in hand. Elephant hairs are tough; I thought she would never finish her hair-cutting. But she did, and triumphantly we hand-ed out the rest of the bread and set off to see the other animals. She opened her bag and showed me three or four coarse, grayish hairs in a piece of Kleenex.

I hate seeing animals in cages, especially small cages, and especially circus animals, but I think that Marianne, while probably feeling the same way, was so passionately interested in them, and knew so much about them, that she could put aside any pain or outrage for the time being. That day I remember that one handsomely patterned snake, writhing about in a glass-walled cage, seemed to raise his head on purpose to look at us. "See, he knows me!" said Miss Moore. "He remembers me from last year." This was a joke, I decided, but perhaps not altogether a joke. Then we went upstairs and the six-ring affair began. The blue bags held our refreshments: thermos jugs of orange juice, hard-boiled eggs (the yolks only), and more brown bread, but fresh this time, and buttered. I also remember of this first visit to the circus (there were to be others) that in front of us sat a father with three young children, two boys and a girl. A big circus goes on for a long time and the children began to grow restless. Marianne leaned over with the abruptness that characterized all her movements and said to the father that if the little girl wanted to go to the bathroom, she'd be glad to take her.

Mary Lavin

(1912-1996)

Born in Massachusetts to Irish parents, at the age of ten Mary Lavin moved back to Ireland, where she became one of the most prominent writers on modern Ireland's literary landscape, publishing twelve volumes of short stories (many originally in *The New Yorker*): *Tales from Bective Bridge* (1942), *The Great Wave* (1961), *In the Middle of the Fields* (1969), *Happiness* (1970), and several prize-winning novels. With her writing and as a farmer in County Meath, she supported her three daughters after an early widowhood—the subject of her story "In A Café" and "Happiness," which follows here. She was well-known for her hospitable support of younger writers. (Nuala O'Faolain remembers Lavin's generous friendship in her memoir *Are You Somebody? An Accidental Memoir of a Dublin Woman*.) The tributes of other writers underscore the achievement of her fiction. "I cannot think of any Irish writer who has gone so profoundly without fear into the Irish heart," said V. S. Pritchett. For William Trevor, she can "make moments timeless [and] illuminate people and places, words and things, by touching them with the magic of the rarely-gifted storyteller." In the words of Alice Munro: "Mary Lavin's stories have always given me a feeling of wonder and security—security because of the way the view keeps opening up, with such ease and authority, and wonder because she is, after all, so intrepid, so original and astonishing."

Happiness

Mother had a lot to say. This does not mean she was always talking but that we children felt the wells she drew upon were deep, deep, deep. Her theme was happiness; what it was, what it was not; where we might find it, where not; and how, if found, it must be guarded. Never must we confound it with pleasure. Nor think sorrow its exact opposite.

"Take Father Hugh," Mother's eyes flashed as she looked at him. "According to him, sorrow is an ingredient of happiness—a *necessary* ingredient, if you please!" And when he tried to protest she put up her hand. "There may be a freakish truth in the theory—for some people. But not for me. And not, I hope, for my children." She looked severely at us three girls. We laughed. None of us had had much experience with sorrow. Bea and I were children and Linda only a year old when our father died suddenly after a short illness that had not at first seemed serious. "I've known people to make sorrow a *substitute* for happiness," Mother said.

Father Hugh protested again. "You're not putting me in that class, I hope?"

Father Hugh, ever since our father died, had been the closest of anyone to us as a family, without being close to anyone in particular—even to Mother. He lived in a monastery near our farm in County Meath, and he had been one of the celebrants at the Requiem High Mass our father's political importance had demanded. He met us that day for the first time, but he took to dropping in to see us, with the idea of filling the crater of loneliness left at our centre. He did not know that there was a cavity in his own life, much less that we would fill it. He and Mother were both young in those days, and perhaps it gave scandal to some that he was so often in our house, staying till late into the night and, indeed, thinking nothing of stopping all night if there was any special reason, such as one of us being sick. He had even on occasion slept there if the night was too wet for tramping home across the fields.

When we girls were young, we were so used to having Father Hugh around that we never stood on ceremony with him but in his presence dried our hair and pared our nails and never minded what garments were strewn about. As for Mother—she thought nothing of running out of the bathroom in her slip, brushing her teeth or combing her hair, if she wanted to tell him something she might otherwise forget. And she brooked no criticism of her behaviour. "Celibacy was never meant to take all the warmth and homeliness out of their lives," she said.

On this point, too, Bea was adamant. Bea, the middle sister, was our oracle. "I'm so glad he *has* Mother," she said, "as well as her having him, because it must be awful the way most women treat them—priests, I mean—as if they were pariahs. Mother treats him like a human being—that's all!"

And when it came to Mother's ears that there had been gossip about her making free with Father Hugh, she opened her eyes wide in astonishment. "But he's only a priest!" she said.

Bea giggled. "It's a good job he didn't hear *that*," she said to me afterwards. "It would undo the good she's done him. You'd think he was a eunuch."

"Bea!" I said. "Do you think he's in love with her?"

"If so, he doesn't know it," Bea said firmly. "It's her soul he's after! Maybe he wants to make sure of her in the next world!"

But thoughts of the world to come never troubled Mother. "If anything ever happens to me, children," she said, "suddenly, I mean, or when you are not near me, or I cannot speak to you, I want you to promise you won't feel bad. There's no need! Just remember that I had a happy life—and that if I had to choose my kind of heaven I'd take it on this earth with you again, no matter how much you might annoy me!"

You see, annoyance and fatigue, according to Mother, and even illness and pain, could coexist with happiness. She had a habit of asking people if they were happy at times and in places that—to say the least of it—seemed to us inappropriate. "But are you happy?" she'd probe us as one lay sick and bathed in sweat, or in the throes of a jumping toothache. And once in our presence she made the inquiry of an old friend as he lay upon his deathbed.

"Why not?" she said when we took her to task for it later. "Isn't it more important than ever to be happy when you're dying? Take my own father! You know what he said in his last moments? On his deathbed, he defied me to name a man who had enjoyed a better life. In spite of dreadful pain, his face *radiated* happiness!" Mother nodded her head comfortably. "Happiness drives out pain, as fire burns out fire."

Having no knowledge of our own to pit against hers, we thirstily drank in her rhetoric. Only Bea was sceptical. "Perhaps you *got* it from him, like spots, or fever," she said. "Or something that could at least be slipped from hand to hand."

"Do you think I'd have taken it if that were the case!" Mother cried. "Then, when he needed it most?"

"Not there and then!" Bea said stubbornly. "I meant as a sort of legacy."

"Don't you think in *that* case," Mother said, exasperated, "he would have felt obliged to leave it to your grandmother?"

Certainly we knew that in spite of his lavish heart our grandfather had failed to provide our grandmother with enduring happiness. He had passed that job on to Mother. And Mother had not made too good a fist of it, even when Father was living and she had him—and, later, us children—to help.

As for Father Hugh, he had given our grandmother up early in the game. "God Almighty couldn't make that woman happy," he said one day, seeing Mother's face, drawn and pale with fatigue, preparing for the nightly run over to see her own mother's flat that would exhaust her utterly.

There were evenings after she came home from the library where she worked when we saw her stand with the car keys in her hand, trying to think which would be worse—to slog over there on foot, or take out the car again. And yet the distance was short. It was Mother's day that had been too long.

"Weren't you over to see her this morning?" Father Hugh demanded.

"No matter!" said Mother. She was no doubt thinking of the forlorn face our grandmother always put on when she was leaving. ("Don't say good night, Vera," Grandmother would plead. "It makes me feel too lonely. And you never can tell—you might slip over again before you go to bed!")

"Do you know the time?" Bea would say impatiently, if she happened to be with Mother. Not indeed that the lateness of the hour counted for any-thing, because in all likelihood Mother *would* go back, if only to pass by under the window and see that the lights were out, or stand and listen and make sure that as far as she could tell all was well.

"I wouldn't mind if she was happy," Mother said.

"And how do you know she's not?" we'd ask.

"When people are happy, I can feel it. Can't you?"

We were not sure. Most people thought our grandmother was a gay crea-ture, a small birdy being who even at a great age laughed like a girl, and—more remarkably—sang like one, as she went about her day. But beak and claw were of steel. She'd think nothing of sending Mother back to shop three times if her errands were not exactly right. "Not sugar like that—that's *too* fine; it's not castor sugar I want. But *not* as coarse as *that*, either. I want an in-between kind."

Provoked one day, my youngest sister, Linda, turned and gave battle. "You're mean!" she cried. "You love ordering people about!"

Grandmother preened, as if Linda had acclaimed an attribute. "I was always hard to please," she said. "As a girl, I used to be called Miss Imperious."

And Miss Imperious she remained as long as she lived, even when she was a great age. Her orders were then given a wry twist by the fact that as she advanced in age she took to calling her daughter Mother, as we did.

There was one great phrase with which our grandmother opened every sentence: "if only." "If only," she'd say, when we came to visit her—"if only you'd come earlier, before I was worn out expecting you!" Or if we were early, then if only it was later, after she'd had a rest and could enjoy us, be *able* for us. And if we brought her flowers, she'd sigh to think that if only we had brought them the previous day she'd have had a visitor to appreciate them, or say it was a pity the stems weren't longer. If only we'd picked a few green leaves, or included some buds, because, she said disparagingly, the poor flowers we'd brought were already wilting. We might just as well not have brought them! As the years went on, Grandmother had a new bead to add to her rosary: if only her friends were not all dead! By their absence, they reduced to nil all *real* enjoyment in anything. Our own father—her son-in-law—was the one person who had ever gone close to pleasing her. But even here there had been a snag. "If only he was my real son!" she used to say, with a sigh.

Mother's mother lived on through our childhood and into our early maturity (though she outlived the money our grandfather left her), and in our minds she was a complicated mixture of valiance and defeat. Courageous and generous within the limits of her own life, her simplest demand was yet enormous in the larger frame of Mother's life, and so we never could see her with the same clarity of vision with which we saw our grandfather, or our own father. Them we saw only through Mother's eyes.

"Take your grandfather!" she'd cry, and instantly we'd see him, his eyes burning upon us—yes, upon *us*, although in his day only one of us had been born: me. At another time, Mother would cry, "Take your own father!" and instantly we'd see *him*—tall, handsome, young, and much more suited to marry one of us than poor bedraggled Mother.

Most fascinating of all were the times Mother would say "Take me!" By magic then, staring down the years, we'd see blazingly clear a small girl with black hair and buttoned boots, who, though plain and pouting, burned bright, like a star. "I was happy, you see," Mother said. And we'd strain hard to try and understand the mystery of the light that still radiated from her. "I used to lean along a tree that grew out over the river," she said, "and look down through the grey leaves at the water flowing past below, and I used to think it was not the stream that flowed but me, spread-eagled over it, who flew through the air! Like a bird! That I'd found the secret!" She made it seem there might *be* such a secret, just waiting to be found. Another time she'd dream that she'd be a great singer.

"We didn't know you sang, Mother!"

She had to laugh. "Like a crow," she said.

Sometimes she used to think she'd swim the Channel.

"Did you swim *that* well, Mother?"

"Oh, not really—just the breast stroke," she said. "And then only by the aid of two pig bladders blown up by my father and tied around my middle. But I used to throb—yes, throb—with happiness."

Behind Mother's back, Bea raised her eyebrows.

What was it, we used to ask ourselves—that quality that she, we felt sure, misnamed? Was it courage? Was it strength, health, or high spirits? Something you could not give or take—a conundrum? A game of catch-as-catch-can?

"I know," cried Bea. "A sham!"

Whatever it was, we knew that Mother would let no wind of violence from within or without tear it from her. Although, one evening when Father Hugh was with us, our astonished ears heard her proclaim that there might be a time when one had to slacken hold on it—let go—to catch at it again with a surer hand. In the way, we supposed, that the high-wire walker up among the painted stars of his canvas sky must wait to fling himself through the air until the bar he catches at has started to sway perversely from him. Oh no, no! That downward drag at our innards we could not bear, the belly swelling to the shape of a pear. Let happiness go by the board. "After all, lots of people seem to make out without it," Bea cried. It was too tricky a business. And might it not be that one had to be born with a flair for it?

"A flair would not be enough," Mother answered. "Take Father Hugh. He, if anyone, had a flair for it—a natural capacity! You've only to look at him when he's off guard, with you children, or helping me in the garden. But he rejects happiness! He casts it from him."

"That is simply not true, Vera," cried Father Hugh, overhearing her. "It's just that I don't place an inordinate value on it like you. I don't think it's enough to carry one all the way. To the end, I mean—and after."

"Oh, don't talk about the end when we're only in the middle," cried

Mother. And, indeed, at that moment her own face shone with such happiness it was hard to believe that her earth was not her heaven. Certainly it was her constant contention that of happiness she had had a lion's share. This, however, we, in private, doubted. Perhaps there were times when she had had a surplus of it—when she was young, say, with her redoubtable father, whose love blazed circles around her, making winter into summer and ice into fire. Perhaps she did have a brimming measure in her early married years. By straining hard, we could find traces left in our minds from those days of milk and honey. Our father, while he lived, had cast a magic over everything, for us as well as for her. He held his love up over us like an umbrella and kept off the troubles that afterwards came down on us, pouring cats and dogs!

But if she did have more than the common lot of happiness in those early days, what use was that when we could remember so clearly how our father's death had ravaged her? And how could we forget the distress it brought on us when, afraid to let her out of our sight, Bea and I stumbled after her everywhere, through the woods and along the bank of the river, where, in the weeks that followed, she tried vainly to find peace.

The summer after Father died, we were invited to France to stay with friends, and when she went walking on the cliffs at Fécamp our fears for her grew frenzied, so that we hung on to her arm and dragged at her skirt, hoping that like leaded weights we'd pin her down if she went too near to the edge. But at night we had to abandon our watch, being forced to follow the conventions of a family still whole—a home still intact—and go to bed at the same time as the other children. It was at that hour, when the coast guard was gone from his rowing boat offshore and the sand was as cold and grey as the sea, that Mother liked to swim. And when she had washed, kissed, and left us, our hearts almost died inside us and we'd creep out of bed again to stand in our bare feet at the mansard and watch as she ran down the shingle, striking out when she reached the water where, far out, wave and sky and mist were one, and the greyness closed over her. If we took our eyes off her for an instant, it was impossible to find her again.

"Oh, make her turn back, God, please!" I prayed out loud one night.

Startled, Bea turned away from the window. "She'll *have* to turn back sometime, won't she? Unless . . . ?"

Locking our damp hands together, we stared out again. "She wouldn't!" I whispered. "It would be a sin!"

Secure in the deterring power of sin, we let out our breath. Then Bea's breath caught again. "What if she went out so far she used up all her strength? She couldn't swim back! It wouldn't be a sin then!"

"It's the intention that counts," I whispered.

A second later, we could see an arm lift heavily up and wearily cleave down, and at last Mother was in the shallows, wading back to shore.

"Don't let her see us!" cried Bea. As if our chattering teeth would not give us away when she looked in at us before she went to her own room on the other side of the corridor, where, later in the night, sometimes the sound of crying would reach us.

What was it worth—a happiness bought that dearly.

Mother had never questioned it. And once she told us, "On a wintry day, I brought my own mother a snowdrop. It was the first one of the year—a bleak bud that had come up stunted before its time—and I meant it for a sign. But do you know what your grandmother said? 'What good are snowdrops to me now?' Such a thing to say! What good is a snowdrop at all if it doesn't hold its value always, and never lose it! Isn't that the whole point of a snowdrop? And that is the whole point of happiness, too! What good would it be if it could be erased without a trace? Take me and those daffodils!" Stooping, she buried her face in a bunch that lay on the table waiting to be put in vases. "If they didn't hold their beauty absolute and inviolable, do you think I could bear the sight of them after what happened when your father was in hospital?"

It was a fair question. When father went to hospital, Mother went with him and stayed in a small hotel across the street so she could be with him all day from early to late. "Because it was so awful for him—being in Dublin!" she said. "You have no idea how he hated it."

That he was dying neither of them realised. How could they know, as it rushed through the sky, that their star was a falling star! But one evening when she'd left him asleep Mother came home for a few hours to see how we were faring, and it broke her heart to see the daffodils out all over the place—in the woods, under the trees, and along the sides of the avenue. There had never been so many, and she thought how awful it was that Father was missing them. "You sent up little bunches to him, you poor dears!" she said. "Sweet little bunches, too—squeezed tight as posies by your little fists! But stuffed into vases they couldn't really make up to him for not being able to see them growing!"

So on the way back to the hospital she stopped her car and pulled a great bunch—the full of her arms. "They took up the whole back seat," she said, "and I was so excited at the thought of walking into his room and dumping them on his bed—you know—just plomping them down so he could smell them, and feel them, and look and look! I didn't mean them to be put in vases, or anything ridiculous like that—it would have taken a rainwater barrel to hold them. Why, I could hardly see over them as I came up the steps; I kept tripping. But when I came into the hall, that nun—I told you about her—that nun came up to me, sprang out of nowhere it seemed, although I know now that she was waiting for me, knowing that somebody had to bring me to my senses. But the way she did it! Reached out and grabbed the flowers, letting lots of them fall—I remember them getting stood on. "Where are you going with those foolish flowers, you foolish woman?" she said. "Don't you know your husband is dying? Your prayers are all you can give him now!"

"She was right. I *was* foolish. But I wasn't cured. Afterwards, it was nothing but foolishness the way I dragged you children after me all over Europe. As if any one place was going to be different from another, any better, any less desolate. But there was great satisfaction in bringing you places your father and I had planned to bring you—although in fairness to him I must say that he would not perhaps have brought you so young. And he would not have had an ulterior motive. But above all, he would not have attempted those trips in such a dilapidated car."

Oh, that car! It was a battered and dilapidated red sports car, so depleted of accessories that when, eventually, we got a new car Mother still stuck out her hand on bends, and in wet weather jumped out to wipe the windscreen with her sleeve. And if fussed, she'd let down the window and shout at people, forgetting she now had a horn. How we had ever fitted into it with all our luggage was a miracle.

"You were never lumpish—any of you!" Mother said proudly. "But you were very healthy and very strong." She turned to me. "Think of how you got that car up the hill in Switzerland!"

"The Alps are not hills, Mother!" I pointed out coldly, as I had done at the time, when, as actually happened, the car failed to make it on one of the inclines. Mother let it run back until it wedged against the rock face, and I

had to get out and push till she got going again in first gear. But when it got
started it couldn't be stopped to pick me up until it got to the top, where they
had to wait for me, and for a very long time.

"Ah, well," she said, sighing wistfully at the thought of those trips. "You
got something out of them, I hope. All that travelling must have helped you
with your geography and your history."

We looked at each other and smiled, and then Mother herself laughed.
"Remember the time," she said, "when we were in Italy, and it was Easter, and
all the shops were chock-full of food? The butchers' shops had poultry and
game hanging up outside the doors, fully feathered, and with their poor heads
dripping blood, and in the windows they had poor little lambs and suckling
pigs and young goats, all skinned and hanging by their hindfeet." Mother
shuddered. "They think so much about food. I found it revolting. I had to
hurry past. But Linda, who must have been only four then, dragged at me and
stared and stared. You know how children are at that age; they have a morbid
fascination for what is cruel and bloody. Her face was flushed and her eyes
were wide. I hurried her back to the hotel. But next morning she crept into
my room. She crept up to me and pressed against me. 'Can't we go back, just
once, and look again at that shop?' she whispered. 'The shop where they have
the little children hanging up for Easter!' It was the young goats, of course, but
I'd said 'kids', I suppose. How we laughed." But her face was grave. "You were
so good on those trips, all of you," she said. "You were really very good children in general. Otherwise I would never have put so much effort into rear-
ing you, because I wasn't a bit maternal. You brought out the best in me! I put
an unnatural effort into you, of course, because I was taking my standards
from your father, forgetting that his might not have remained so inflexible if
he had lived to middle age and was beset by life, like other parents."

"Well, the job is nearly over now, Vera," said Father Hugh. "And you
didn't do so badly."

"That's right, Hugh," said mother, and she straightened up, and put her
hand to her back the way she sometimes did in the garden when she got up
from her knees after weeding. "I didn't go over to the enemy anyway! We
survived!" Then a flash of defiance came into her eyes. "And we were happy.
That's the main thing!"

Father Hugh frowned. "There you go again!" he said.

Mother turned on him. "I don't think you realise the onslaughts that were made upon our happiness! The minute Robert died, they came down on me—cohorts of relatives, friends, even strangers, all draped in black, opening their arms like bats to let me pass into their company. 'Life is a vale of tears,' they said. 'You are privileged to find out so young!' Ugh! After I staggered on to my feet and began to take hold of life once more, they fell back defeated. And the first day I gave a laugh—pouff, they were blown out like candles. They weren't living in a real world at all; they belonged to a ghostly world where life was easy: all one had to do was sit and weep. It takes effort to push back the stone from the mouth of the tomb and walk out."

Effort. Effort. Ah, but that strange-sounding word could invoke little sympathy from those who had not learned yet what it meant. Life must have been hardest for Mother in those years when we older ones were at college—no longer children, and still dependent on her. Indeed, we made more demands on her than ever then, having moved into new areas of activity and emotion. And our friends! Our friends came and went as freely as we did ourselves, so that the house was often like a café—and one where pets were not prohibited but took their places on our chairs and beds, as regardless as the people. And anyway it was hard to have sympathy for someone who got things into such a state as Mother. All over the house there was clutter. Her study was like the returned-letter department of a post-office, with stacks of paper everywhere, bills paid and unpaid, letters answered and unanswered, tax returns, pamphlets, leaflets. If by mistake we left the door open on a windy day, we came back to find papers flapping through the air like frightened birds. Efficient only in that she managed eventually to conclude every task she began, it never seemed possible to outsiders that by Mother's methods anything whatever could be accomplished. In an attempt to keep order elsewhere, she made her own room the clearing house into which the rest of us put everything: things to be given away, things to be mended, things to be stored, things to be treasured, things to be returned—even things to be thrown out! By the end of the year, the room resembled an obsolescence dump. And no one could help her; the chaos of her life was as personal as an act of creation—one might as well try to finish another person's poem.

As the years passed, Mother rushed around more hectically. And although Bea and I had married and were not at home any more, except at holiday time and for occasional weekends, Linda was noisier than the two of us put together had been, and for every follower we had brought home she brought twenty. The house was never still. Now that we were reduced to being visitors, we watched Mother's tension mount to vertigo, knowing that, like a spinning top, she could not rest till she fell. But now at the smallest pretext Father Hugh would call in the doctor and Mother would be put on the mail boat and dispatched for London. For it was essential that she get far enough away to make phoning home every night prohibitively costly.

Unfortunately, the thought of departure often drove a spur into her and she redoubled her effort to achieve order in her affairs. She would be up until the early hours ransacking her desk. To her, as always the shortest parting entailed a preparation as for death. And as if it were her end that was at hand, we would all be summoned, although she had no time to speak a word to us, because five minutes before departure she would still be attempting to reply to letters that were the acquisition of weeks and would have taken whole days to dispatch.

"Don't you know the taxi is at the door, Vera?" Father Hugh would say, running his hand through his grey hair and looking very dishevelled himself. She had him at times as distracted as herself. "You can't do any more. You'll have to leave the rest till you come back."

"I can't, I can't!" Mother would cry. "I'll have to cancel my plans."

One day, Father Hugh opened the lid of her case, which was strapped up in the hall, and with a swipe of his arm he cleared all the papers on the top of the desk pell-mell into the suitcase. "You can sort them on the boat," he said, "or the train to London!"

Thereafter, Mother's luggage always included an empty case to hold the unfinished papers on her desk. And years afterwards a steward on the Irish Mail told us she was a familiar figure, working away at letters and bills nearly all the way from Holyhead to Euston. "She gave it up about Rugby or Crewe," he said. "She'd get talking to someone in the compartment." He smiled. "There was one time coming down the train I was just in time to see her close up the window with a guilty look. I didn't say anything, but I think she'd emptied those papers of hers out the window!"

Quite likely. When we were children, even a few hours away from us gave her composure. And in two weeks or less, when she'd come home, the well of her spirit would be freshened. We'd hardly know her—her step so light, her eye so bright, and her love and patience once more freely flowing. But in no time at all the house would fill up once more with the noise and confusion of too many people and too many animals, and again we'd be fighting our corner with cats and dogs, bats, mice, bees and even wasps. "Don't kill it!" Mother would cry if we raised a hand to an angry wasp. "Just catch it, dear, and put it outside. Open the window and let it fly away!" But even this treatment could at times be deemed too harsh. "Wait a minute. Close the window!" she'd cry. "It's too cold outside. It will die. That's why it came in, I suppose! Oh dear, what will we do?" Life would be going full blast again.

There was only one place Mother found rest. When she was at breaking point and fit to fall, she'd go out into the garden—not to sit or stroll around but to dig, to drag up weeds, to move great clumps of corms or rhizomes, or indeed quite frequently to haul huge rocks from one place to another. She was always laying down a path, building a dry wall, or making compost heaps as high as hills. However jaded she might be going out, when dark forced her in at last her step had the spring of a daisy. So if she did not succeed in defining happiness to our understanding, we could see that whatever it was, she possessed it to the full when she was in her garden.

One of us said as much one Sunday when Bea and I had dropped round for the afternoon. Father Hugh was with us again. "It's an unthinking happiness, though," he cavilled. We were standing at the drawing-room window, looking out to where in the fading light we could see Mother on her knees weeding, in the long border that stretched from the house right down to the woods. "I wonder how she'd take it if she were stricken down and had to give up that heavy work!" he said. Was he perhaps a little jealous of how she could stoop and bend? He himself had begun to use a stick. I was often a little jealous of her myself, because although I was married and had children of my own, I had married young and felt the weight of living as heavy as a weight of years. "She doesn't take enough care of herself," Father Hugh said sadly. "Look at her out there with nothing under her knees to protect her from the damp ground." It was almost too dim for us to see her, but even in the drawing room it was chilly. "She should not be let to stay out there after the sun goes down."

"Just you try to get her in then!" said Linda, who had come into the room in time to hear him. "Don't you know by now anyway that what would kill another person only seems to make Mother thrive?"

Father Hugh shook his head again. "You seem to forget it's not younger she's getting!" He fidgeted and fussed, and several times went to the window to stare out apprehensively. He was really getting quite elderly.

"Come and sit down, Father Hugh," Bea said, and to take his mind off Mother she turned on the light and blotted out the garden. Instead of seeing through the window, we saw into it as into a mirror, and there between the flower-laden tables and the lamps it was ourselves we saw moving vaguely. Like Father Hugh, we, too, were waiting for her to come in before we called an end to the day.

"Oh, this is ridiculous!" Father Hugh cried at last. "She'll have to listen to reason." And going back to the window he threw it open. "Vera!" he called. "Vera!"—sternly, so sternly that, more intimate than an endearment, his tone shocked us. "She didn't hear me," he said, turning back blinking at us in the lighted room. "I'm going out to get her." And in a minute he was gone from the room. As he ran down the garden path, we stared at each other, astonished; his step, like his voice, was the step of a lover. "I'm coming, Vera!" he cried.

Although she was never stubborn except in things that mattered, Mother had not moved. In the wholehearted way she did everything, she was bent down close to the ground. It wasn't the light only that was dimming; her eyesight also was failing, I thought, as instinctively I followed Father Hugh.

But halfway down the path I stopped. I had seen something he had not: Mother's hand that appeared to support itself in a forked branch of an old tree peony she had planted as a bride was not in fact gripping it but impaled upon it. And the hand that appeared to be grubbing in the clay in fact was sunk into the soft mould. "Mother!" I screamed, and I ran forward, but when I reached her I covered my face with my hands. "Oh Father Hugh!" I cried. "Is she dead?"

It was Bea who answered, hysterical. "She is! She is!" she cried, and she began to pound Father Hugh on the back with her fists, as if his pessimistic words had made this happen.

But Mother was not dead. And at first the doctor even offered hope of her pulling through. But from the moment Father Hugh lifted her up to carry her into the house we ourselves had no hope, seeing how effortlessly he, who was not strong, could carry her. When he put her down on her bed, her head hardly creased the pillow. Mother lived for four more hours.

Like the days of her life, those four hours that Mother lived were packed tight with concern and anxiety. Partly conscious, partly delirious, she seemed to think the counterpane was her desk, and she scrabbled her fingers upon it as if trying to sort out a muddle of bills and correspondence. No longer indifferent now, we listened, anguished, to the distracted cries that had for all our lifetime been so familiar to us. "Oh, where is it? Where is it? I had it a minute ago! Where on earth did I put it?"

"Vera, Vera, stop worrying," Father Hugh pleaded, but she waved him away and went on sifting through the sheets as if they were sheets of paper. "Oh, Vera!" he begged. "Listen to me. Do you not know—"

Bea pushed between them. "You're not to tell her!" she commanded. "Why frighten her?"

"But it ought not to frighten her," said Father Hugh. "This is what I was always afraid would happen—that she'd be frightened when it came to the end."

At that moment, as if to vindicate him, Mother's hands fell idle on the coverlet, palm upward and empty. And turning her head she stared at each of us in turn, beseechingly, "I cannot face it," she whispered. "I can't! I can't! I can't!"

"Oh, my God!" Bea said, and she started to cry.

"Vera. For God's sake listen to me," Father Hugh cried, and pressing his face to hers, as close as a kiss, he kept whispering to her, trying to cast into the dark tunnel before her the light of his own faith.

But it seemed to us that Mother must already be looking into God's exigent eyes. "I can't!" she cried. "I can't!"

Then her mind came back from the stark world of the spirit to the world where her body was still detained, but even that world was now a whirling kaleidoscope of things which only she could see. Suddenly her eyes focussed, and, catching at Father Hugh, she pulled herself up a little and pointed to something we could not see. "What will be done with them?" Her voice was anxious. "They ought to be put in water anyway," she said, and, leaning over the edge of the bed, she pointed to the floor. "Don't step on that one!" she said sharply. Then, more sharply still, she addressed us all. "Have them sent to the public ward," she said peremptorily. "Don't let that nun take them; she'll only put them on the altar. And God doesn't want them! He made them for *us*—not for Himself!"

It was the familiar rhetoric that all her life had characterised her utterances. For a moment we were mystified. Then Bea gasped. "The daffodils!"

she cried. "The day Father died!" And over her face came the light that had so often blazed over Mother's. Leaning across the bed, she pushed Father Hugh aside. And, putting out her hands, she held Mother's face between her palms as tenderly as if it were the face of a child. "It's all right, Mother. You don't *have* to face it! It's over!" Then she who had so fiercely forbade Father Hugh to do so blurted out the truth. "You've finished with this world, Mother," she said, and, confident that her tidings were joyous, her voice was strong.

Mother made the last effort of her life and grasped at Bea's meaning. She let out a sigh, and, closing her eyes, she sank back, and this time her head sank so deep into the pillow that it would have been dented had it been a pillow of stone.

Tillie Olsen

(1913-   )

Human beings hobbled by circumstance, in particular the poverty she knew growing up as the child of Russian Jewish immigrants in Nebraska, have been the focus of Tillie Olsen's life and work. A labor activist in Nebraska, Kansas City, and then in San Francisco, where she raised her four children with Jack Olsen, she went to jail twice for public resistance of economic and political injustice. (In 1981, May 18 was proclaimed "Tillie Olsen Day" in San Francisco.) Acting as the founding godmother to the literary awakening of the 1960s women's movement, she has inspired individual writers and institutions (curriculum committees of universities—she taught the first "women in literature" class at Stanford—as well as publishing houses) to make room for more women at the feast of literature. (*Silences*, [1962], a work of nonfiction, explores the ways in which circumstances of "class, color, sex" have thwarted the creativity of women who would write.) Her fiction is internationally renowned (translated into thirteen languages) for the voice she has created for the world's voiceless. The novel *Yonnondio: From the Thirties*, a casualty of her own difficult circumstances during and after the depression (the first chapter appeared in 1934), was published in 1974. But it was in 1961, when the title story of the four-story collection *Tell Me a Riddle* won the O. Henry Award as the best American story of the year, that readers and critics discovered her. "When she wrote *Tell Me a Riddle*," said John Leonard, "Tillie Olsen, like William Blake, covered paper with words for the angels to read."

I Stand Here Ironing

I stand here ironing, and what you asked me moves tormented back and forth with the iron.

"I wish you would manage the time to come in and talk with me about your daughter. I'm sure you can help me understand her. She's a youngster who needs help and whom I'm deeply interested in helping."

"Who needs help.". . . Even if I came, what good would it do? You think because I am her mother I have a key, or that in some way you could use me as a key? She has lived for nineteen years. There is all that life that has happened outside of me, beyond me.

And when is there time to remember, to sift, to weigh, to estimate, to total? I will start and there will be an interruption and I will have to gather it all together again. Or I will become engulfed with all I did or did not do, with what should have been and what cannot be helped.

She was a beautiful baby. The first and only one of our five that was beautiful at birth. You do not guess how new and uneasy her tenancy in her now-loveliness. You did not know her all those years she was thought homely, or see her poring over her baby pictures, making me tell her over and over how beautiful she had been—and would be, I would tell her—and was now, to the seeing eye. But the seeing eyes were few or non-existent. Including mine.

I nursed her. They feel that's important nowadays. I nursed all the children, but with her, with all the fierce rigidity of first motherhood, I did like the books then said. Though her cries battered me to trembling and my breasts ached with swollenness, I waited till the clock decreed.

Why do I put that first? I do not even know if it matters, or if it explains anything.

She was a beautiful baby. She blew shining bubbles of sound. She loved motion, loved light, loved color and music and textures. She would lie on the floor in her blue overalls patting the surface so hard in ecstasy her hands and feet would blur. She was a miracle to me, but when she was eight months old I had to leave her daytimes with the woman downstairs to whom she was no miracle at all, for I worked or looked for work and for Emily's father, who "could no longer endure" (he wrote in his good-bye note) "sharing want with us."

I was nineteen. It was the pre-relief, pre-WPA world of the depression. I would start running as soon as I got off the streetcar, running up the stairs, the place smelling sour, and awake or asleep to startle awake, when she saw me she would break into a clogged weeping that could not be comforted, a weeping I can hear yet.

After a while I found a job hashing at night so I could be with her days, and it was better. But it came to where I had to bring her to his family and leave her.

It took a long time to raise the money for her fare back. Then she got chicken pox and I had to wait longer. When she finally came, I hardly knew her, walking quick and nervous like her father, looking like her father, thin, and dressed in a shoddy red that yellowed her skin and glared at the pockmarks. All the baby loveliness gone.

She was two. Old enough for nursery school they said, and I did not know then what I know now—the fatigue of the long day, and the lacerations of group life in the kinds of nurseries that are only parking places for children.

Except that it would have made no difference if I had known. It was the only place there was. It was the only way we could be together, the only way I could hold a job.

And even without knowing, I knew. I knew the teacher that was evil because all these years it has curdled into my memory, the little boy hunched in the corner, her rasp, "why aren't you outside, because Alvin hits you? that's no reason, go out scaredy." I knew Emily hated it even if she did not clutch and implore "don't go Mommy" like the other children, mornings.

She always had a reason why we should stay home. Momma, you look sick, Momma. I feel sick. Momma, the teachers aren't there today, they're sick. Momma, we can't go, there was a fire there last night. Momma, it's a holiday today, no school, they told me.

But never a direct protest, never rebellion. I think of our others in their three-, four-year-oldness—the explosions, the tempers, the denunciations, the demands—and I feel suddenly ill. I put the iron down. What in me demanded that goodness in her? And what was the cost, the cost to her of such goodness?

The old man living in the back once said in his gentle way: "You should smile at Emily more when you look at her." What *was* in my face when I looked at her? I loved her. There were all the acts of love.

It was only with the others I remembered what he said, and it was the face of joy, and not of care or tightness or worry I turned to them—too late for Emily. She does not smile easily, let alone almost always as her brothers and sisters do. Her face is closed and sombre, but when she wants, how fluid. You must have seen it in her pantomimes, you spoke of her rare gift for comedy on the stage that rouses a laughter out of the audience so dear they applaud and applaud and do not want to let her go.

Where does it come from, that comedy? There was none of it in her when she came back to me that second time, after I had had to send her away again. She had a new daddy now to learn to love, and I think perhaps it was a better time.

Except when we left her alone nights, telling ourselves she was old enough.

"Can't you go some other time, Mommy, like tomorrow?" she would ask. "Will it be just a little while you'll be gone? Do you promise?"

The time we came back, the front door open, the clock on the floor in the hall. She rigid awake. "It wasn't just a little while. I didn't cry. Three times I called you, just three times, and then I ran downstairs to open the door so you could come faster. The clock talked loud. I threw it away, it scared me what it talked."

She said the clock talked loud again that night I went to the hospital to have Susan. She was delirious with the fever that comes before red measles, but she was fully conscious all the week I was gone and the week after we were home when she could not come near the new baby or me.

She did not get well. She stayed skeleton thin, not wanting to eat, and night after night she had nightmares. She would call for me, and I would rouse from exhaustion to sleepily call back: "You're all right, darling, go to sleep, it's just a dream," and if she still called, in a sterner voice, "now go to sleep, Emily, there's nothing to hurt you." Twice, only twice, when I had to get up for Susan anyhow, I went in to sit with her.

Now when it is too late (as if she would let me hold and comfort her like I do the others) I get up and go to her at once at her moan or restless stirring. "Are you awake, Emily? Can I get you something?" And the answer is always the same: "No, I'm all right, go back to sleep, Mother."

They persuaded me at the clinic to send her away to a convalescent home in the country where "she can have the kind of food and care you can't manage for her, and you'll be free to concentrate on the new baby." They still send children to that place. I see pictures on the society page of sleek young women planning affairs to raise money for it, or dancing at the affairs, or decorating Easter eggs or filling Christmas stockings for the children.

They never have a picture of the children so I do not know if the girls still wear those gigantic red bows and the ravaged looks on the every other Sunday when parents can come to visit "unless otherwise notified"—as we were notified the first six weeks.

Oh it is a handsome place, green lawns and tall trees and fluted flower beds. High up on the balconies of each cottage the children stand, the girls in their red bows and white dresses, the boys in white suits and giant red ties. The parents stand below shrieking up to be heard and the children shriek down to be heard, and between them and the invisible wall "Not To Be Contaminated by Parental Germs or Physical Affection."

There was a tiny girl who always stood hand in hand with Emily. Her parents never came. One visit she was gone. "They moved her to Rose Cottage" Emily shouted in explanation. "They don't like you to love anybody here."

She wrote once a week, the labored writing of a seven-year-old. "I am fine. How is the baby. If I write my leter nicly I will have a star. Love." There never was a star. We wrote every other day, letters she could never hold or keep but only hear read—once. "We simply do not have room for children to keep any personal possessions," they patiently explained when we pieced one Sunday's shrieking together to plead how much it would mean to Emily, who loved so to keep things, to be allowed to keep her letters and cards.

Each visit she looked frailer. "She isn't eating," they told us.

(They had runny eggs for breakfast or mush with lumps, Emily said later, I'd hold it in my mouth and not swallow. Nothing ever tasted good, just when they had chicken.)

It took us eight months to get her released home, and only the fact that she gained back so little of her seven lost pounds convinced the social worker.

I used to try to hold and love her after she came back, but her body would stay stiff, and after a while she'd push away. She ate little. Food sickened her, and I think much of life too. Oh she had physical lightness and brightness, twinkling by on skates, bouncing like a ball up and down up and down over the jump rope, skimming over the hill; but these were momentary.

She fretted about her appearance, thin and dark and foreign-looking at a time when every little girl was supposed to look or thought she should look a chubby blonde replica of Shirley Temple. The doorbell sometimes rang for her, but no one seemed to come and play in the house or be a best friend. Maybe because we moved so much.

There was a boy she loved painfully through two school semesters. Months later she told me how she had taken pennies from my purse to buy him candy. "Licorice was his favorite and I brought him some every day, but he still liked Jennifer better'n me. Why, Mommy?" The kind of question for which there is no answer.

School was a worry to her. She was not glib or quick in a world where glibness and quickness were easily confused with ability to learn. To her overworked and exasperated teachers she was an overconscientious "slow learner" who kept trying to catch up and was absent entirely too often.

I let her be absent, though sometimes the illness was imaginary. How different from my now-strictness about attendance with the others. I wasn't working. We had a new baby, I was home anyhow. Sometimes, after Susan grew old enough, I would keep her home from school, too, to have them all together.

Mostly Emily had asthma, and her breathing, harsh and labored, would fill the house with a curiously tranquil sound. I would bring the two old dresser mirrors and her boxes of collections to her bed. She would select beads and single earrings, bottle tops and shells, dried flowers and pebbles, old postcards and scraps, all sorts of oddments; then she and Susan would play Kingdom, setting up landscapes and furniture, peopling them with action.

Those were the only times of peaceful companionship between her and Susan. I have edged away from it, that poisonous feeling between them, that terrible balancing of hurts and needs I had to do between the two, and did so badly, those earlier years.

Oh there are conflicts between the others too, each one human, needing, demanding, hurting, taking—but only between Emily and Susan, no, Emily toward Susan, that corroding resentment. It seems so obvious on the surface, yet it is not obvious. Susan, the second child, Susan, golden- and curly-haired and chubby, quick and articulate and assured, everything in appearance and manner Emily was not; Susan, not able to resist Emily's precious things, losing or sometimes clumsily breaking them; Susan telling jokes and riddles to company for applause while Emily sat silent (to say to me later: that was *my* riddle, Mother, I told it to Susan); Susan, who for all the five years' difference in age was just a year behind Emily in developing physically.

I am glad for that slow physical development that widened the difference between her and her contemporaries, though she suffered over it. She was too vulnerable for that terrible world of youthful competition, of preening and parading, of constant measuring of yourself against every other, of envy,

"If I had that copper hair," "If I had that skin. . . ." She tormented herself enough about not looking like the others, there was enough of the unsureness, the having to be conscious of words before you speak, the constant caring—what are they thinking of me? without having it all magnified by the merciless physical drives.

Ronnie is calling. He is wet and I change him. It is rare there is such a cry now. That time of motherhood is almost behind me when the ear is not one's own but must always be racked and listening for the child cry, the child call. We sit for a while and I hold him, looking out over the city spread in charcoal with its soft aisles of light. "*Shoogily*," he breathes and curls closer. I carry him back to bed, asleep. *Shoogily*. A funny word, a family word, inherited from Emily, invented by her to say: *comfort*.

In this and other ways she leaves her seal, I say aloud. And startle at my saying it. What do I mean? What did I start to gather together, to try and make coherent? I was at the terrible, growing years. War years. I do not remember them well. I was working, there were four smaller ones now, there was not time for her. She had to help be a mother, and housekeeper, and shopper. She had to set her seal. Mornings of crisis and near hysteria trying to get lunches packed, hair combed, coats and shoes found, everyone to school or Child Care on time, the baby ready for transportation. And always the paper scribbled on by a smaller one, the book looked at by Susan then mislaid, the homework not done. Running out to that huge school where she was one, she was lost, she was a drop; suffering over her unpreparedness, stammering and unsure in her classes.

There was so little time left at night after the kids were bedded down. She would struggle over books, always eating (it was in those years she developed her enormous appetite that is legendary in our family) and I would be ironing, or preparing food for the next day, or writing V-mail to Bill, or tending the baby. Sometimes, to make me laugh, or out of her despair, she would imitate happenings or types at school.

I think I said once: "Why don't you do something like this in the school amateur show?" One morning she phoned me at work, hardly understandable through the weeping: "Mother, I did it. I won, I won: they gave me first prize; they clapped and clapped and wouldn't let me go."

Now suddenly she was Somebody, and as imprisoned in her difference as she had been in her anonymity.

She began to be asked to perform at other high schools, even in colleges, then at city and statewide affairs. The first one we went to, I only recognized her that first moment when thin, shy, she almost drowned herself into the curtains. Then: Was this Emily? The control, the command, the convulsing and deadly clowning, the spell, then the roaring, stamping audience, unwilling to let this rare and precious laughter out of their lives.

Afterwards: You ought to do something about her with a gift like that— but without money or knowing how, what does one do? We have left it all to her, and the gift has as often eddied inside, clogged and clotted, as been used and growing.

She is coming. She runs up the stairs two at a time with her light graceful step, and I know she is happy tonight. Whatever it was that occasioned your call did not happen today.

"Aren't you ever going to finish the ironing, Mother? Whistler painted his mother in a rocker. I'd have to paint mine standing over an ironing board." This is one of her communicative nights and she tells me everything and nothing as she fixes herself a plate of food out of the icebox.

She is so lovely. Why did you want me to come in at all? Why were you concerned? She will find her way.

She starts up the stairs to bed. "Don't get me up with the rest in the morning." "But I thought you were having midterms." "Oh, those," she comes back in, kisses me, and says quite lightly, "in a couple of years when we'll all be atom-dead they won't matter a bit."

She has said it before. She *believes* it. But because I have been dredging the past, and all that compounds a human being is so heavy and meaningful in me, I cannot endure it tonight.

I will never total it all. I will never come in to say: She was a child seldom smiled at. Her father left me before she was a year old. I had to work her first six years when there was work, or I sent her home and to his relatives. There were years she had care she hated. She was dark and thin and foreign-looking in a world where the prestige went to blondness and curly hair and dimples, she was slow where glibness was prized. She was a child of anxious, not proud, love. We were poor and could not afford for her the soil of easy growth. I was a young mother, I was a distracted mother. There were the other children pushing up, demanding. Her younger sister seemed all that she was not. There were years she did not let me touch her. She kept too much in herself, her life was such she had to keep too much in herself. My wisdom came too late. She has much to her and probably little will come of it. She is a child of her age, of depression, of war, of fear.

Let her be. So all that is in her will not bloom—but in how many does it? There is still enough left to live by. Only help her to know—help make it so there is cause for her to know—that she is more than this dress on the ironing board, helpless before the iron.

Muriel Rukeyser

(1913-1980)

Muriel Rukeyser grew up as a rich girl in New York City but spent her adult life distancing herself from her privileged background. As a writer and an activist, she was a tireless advocate of political and social justice. In twelve volumes of poetry—*The Collected Poems* were published in 1979—she criticized the destructiveness of a materialist and violent America. She attended the 1933 trial of the Scottsboro Boys in Alabama; with Denise Levertov and Mary McCarthy she traveled to Hanoi in 1972 to protest the war in Vietnam; in 1975 as president of the PEN American Center, she demonstrated against the imprisonment of poet Kim Chi-ha in South Korea. She also acted as literary godmother to such younger writers as Anne Sexton, Marge Piercy, Alice Walker, and Sharon Olds, all of whom have acknowledged the importance of her influence. In *The Life of Poetry* (1949), her prose meditation on the liberating effect of poetry on an oppressive social order, she expresses the expansive and optimistic vision that has led to comparisons of Rukeyser with Walt Whitman. As a lesbian who was also a single mother, she wanted to change the world. In her own words, "No more masks, no more mythologies!"

More of a Corpse Than a Woman

Give them my regards when you go to the school reunion;
and at the marriage-supper, say that I'm thinking about them.
They'll remember my name; I went to the movies with that one,
feeling the weight of their death where she sat at my elbow;
    she never said a word,
    but all of them were heard.

all of them alike, expensive girls, the leaden friends:
one used to play the piano, one of them once wrote a sonnet,
one even seemed awakened enough to photograph wheatfields—
the dull girls with the educated minds and technical passions—
> pure love was their employment,
> they tried it for enjoyment.

Meet them at the boat: they've brought the souvenirs of boredom,
a seashell from the faltering monarchy;
the nose of a marble saint; and from the battlefield,
an empty shell divulged from a flower-bed.
> The lady's wealthy breath
> perfumes the air with death.

The leaden lady faces the fine, voluptuous woman,
faces a rising world bearing its gifts in its hands.
Kisses her casual dreams upon the lips she kisses,
risen, she moves away; takes others; moves away.
> Inadequate to love,
> supposes she's enough.

Give my regards to the well-protected woman,
I knew the ice-cream girl, we went to school together.
There's something to bury, people, when you begin to bury.
When your women are ready and rich in their wish for the world,
> destroy the leaden heart,
> we've a new race to start.

Maeve Brennan

(1917–1993)

Maeve Brennan came from Dublin to New York when she was seventeen and never went back home. In 1949 she joined the staff of *The New Yorker*, where she published the short stories that were later collected in *In and Out of Never-Never Land* (1969) and *Christmas Eve* (1974). She also wrote the sketches for the magazine's "The Talk of the Town" that were collected in *The Long-Winded Lady* (1969). According to novelist William Maxwell, who was her editor for twenty years, the title story of the most recent edition of Brennan's stories, *The Springs of Affection* (1997)—which follows here—"belongs with the great short stories of this century." It is told in the voice of the deceased Delia Bagot's sister-in-law Min, an old woman, in Maxwell's words, "[who] is the embodiment of that side of the Irish temperament that delights in mockery and rejoices in the downfall of those whom life has smiled on." Most of Brennan's stories are set in Ireland. As Maxwell puts it, "I don't know whether in Ireland she is considered an Irish writer or an American. In fact, she is both, and both countries ought to be proud to claim her." At the end of her life, she suffered from psychotic episodes, becoming a familiar bag lady in the area around Times Square. The reputation of her fiction is of the highest order: "controlled, wise, and fearless," said the *Nation*. "Not many writers go this deep or far from home."

The Springs of Affection

Delia Bagot died suddenly and quietly, alone in her bed, with the door shut, and six years later, after eight months of being bedridden, Martin, her husband, died, attended by a nursing nun and his eighty-seven-year-old twin sister, Min. And at last Min was released from the duty she had imposed on herself, to remain with him as long as he needed her. She could go home now, back to her flat in Wexford, and settle into the peace and quiet she had enjoyed before

Delia's death summoned her to the suburbs of Dublin. To the suburbs of Dublin and the freedom of that house where she had wandered so often in her fancy. For fifty years she had wandered in their private lives, ever since Delia appeared out of the blue and fascinated Martin, the born bachelor, into marrying her. Min wasn't likely to forget that wedding day, the misery of it, the anguish of it, the abomination of deprivation as she and her mother stood together and looked at him, the happy bridegroom, standing there grinning his head off as though he had ascended into Heaven. She and her mother and her two sisters, all three of them gone now, and Martin, too, gone. Min thought of the neat graves, one by one—a sister's grave, a sister's grave, a mother's grave, a brother's grave—all gone, all present, like medals on the earth. And she thought it was fitting that she should be the one to remain alive, because out of them all she was the one who was always faithful to the family. She was the only one of the lot of them who hadn't gone off and got married. She had never wanted to assert herself like that, never needed to. She had wondered at their lack of shame as they exhibited themselves, Clare and Polly with their husbands, and Martin with poor Delia, the poor thing. They didn't seem to care what anybody thought of them when they got caught up in that excitement, like animals. It was disgusting, and they seemed to know it, the way they pretended their only concern was with the new clothes they'd have and the flowers they'd grow in their very own gardens. And now it was over for them, and they might just as well have controlled themselves, for all the good they had of it. And she, standing alone as always, had lived to sum them all up. It was a great satisfaction to see finality rising up like the sun. Min thought not many people knew that satisfaction. To watch the end of all was not much different from watching the beginning of things, and if you weren't ever going to take part anyway, then to watch the end was far and away better. You could be jealous of people who were starting out, but you could hardly be jealous of the dead.

Not that I was ever jealous, Min thought. God forbid that I should encourage small thoughts in myself, but I couldn't help but despise Delia that day, the way she stood looking up at Martin as though she was ready to fall down on her knees before him. She made a show of herself that day. We were late getting out for the wedding. We were late getting started, and then we were all late getting there and they were all waiting for us. And after it was over and they were married and we were all in the garden, she came running up to my mother and she said, "Oh, I was afraid you weren't coming. I began to imagine Martin had changed his mind about me. I thought I would burst with impatience and longing. I had such a longing to see his face, and then, when I saw you driving up, I still had a great fear something might come between us. I'll never forget how impatient I was—I see it would be easy to go mad with love." She said that to my mother. "Mad with love," she said. My mother just looked at her, and when she flew off, all full of herself as she was that day, my mother turned and looked at me, and said to me, "Min, I am an old woman, but never in my life have I spoken like that. Never in my life have I said the like of that. All the years I've lived, and I've never, never allowed myself to feel like that about anybody, let alone be that open about it. That girl has something the matter with her. My heart goes out to Martin, I can tell you. There's something lacking in her."

Min remembered that Martin's wedding day was a very long day, with many different views and scenes, country roads, country lanes, gardens and orchards and fields and streams, and a house with rooms that multiplied in recollection, because she visited them only that one time, and they attracted her very much—dim, old rooms that maintained an air of simple, implacable formality. She envied the way the rooms were able to remain unknown even when you were standing in them. It was the same with the people out there in the country—even when they were most friendly and open they kept a lot of themselves hidden. Min thought they were like a strange tribe that only shows up in force on festival days.

The days before the wedding were a great strain, and Min always said she never understood how they got themselves out of the house the morning of the wedding. If it had not been that Markey was standing outside with the horse and car they had hired, they might all have stayed in the house and let Martin find his way out to Oylegate as best he could. He might have changed his mind then, and remained at home where he belonged. Driving out of the town of Wexford, they crossed the bridge at Ferrycarrig, and there was the Slaney pouring away under them, flowing straight for the harbor as unconcernedly as though it were any old day. And then the long drive out to Oylegate. And when they got to Oylegate the chapel yard was waiting for them, looking more like an arena than a religious place. And the chapel itself, all solemn and hedged in with flowers so full in bloom that they seemed to be overflowing their petals, color flowing freely through the air. Min drew deep breaths, filling her lungs with fright. The fright built up inside her chest—she could feel it beginning to smother her. There was no air in the place. She said to her mother later, "I nearly got a headache in the chapel. I thought I might have to walk outside. It was too close in there. I began to feel weak. I thought we'd never get away out of the place." Polly was listening. Polly always seemed to be listening in time to turn your own words against you.

Polly said, "You always tell everybody you never had a headache in your life. You always say you never had time to have a headache. You leave the headaches to the rest of us. Clare and Polly have time for all that kind of nonsense, imagining themselves to be delicate—that's what you always say. And then in the next breath, every time anything goes against you, you tell us you *almost* got a headache. If you almost got a headache it would show on your face. You're overcome by your own bad humor—that's all that's the matter with you."

"In the name of God," their mother said, "this is not the time for the two of you to start fighting. Do you want to make a show of us all, have them all laughing at us more than they're laughing already?"

They were walking through the chapel yard after the wedding, and Min went ahead, looking hurried, as though she had left something outside in the road and wanted to look for it. In Polly's voice she heard the enmity that had been oppressing her all day, enmity that came at her out of the streets of the town as they started to drive out here, distant, incomprehensible enmity that rose up at her from the bridge at Ferrycarrig, and from the road itself, and from the fields and trees and cottages they passed, and even from the sky itself, blue and white and summery though it was. Even the faraway sky looked satisfied to see her in the condition she was in. Min didn't know what condition she was in. She knew that she couldn't say a word without being misunderstood. She knew that something had happened that deprived her of an approbation so natural that she had always taken it for granted. She only noticed it now that she missed it—it was as though the whole world had turned against her. Polly must have rehearsed that speech—Polly was very spiteful. But where had Polly found that tone of voice, so hard and condescending? She's very sure of herself all of a sudden, Min thought. I must have given myself away, somehow. But what was there to give away—Min knew she had done nothing to earn that tone of contempt from a younger sister. She had an awful feeling of being in disgrace with somebody she had never seen and who had never liked her very much, never, not even when she was a little mite trying to help her mother with the younger children. No, wherever it came from, this impersonal dislike had been lying in wait for her all her life. And it was clear from the way people were looking at her that everybody knew about it. She couldn't even say a word to her mother about a headache without being attacked as though she were a scoundrel. All the good marks she had won at school were forgotten. Nothing was known about her now except that she had presumed to a place far above her station in life. She had believed she could fly sky-high, with her brains for wings. Nobody notices me as I am, Min thought; all they can see is the failure. I was done out of my right, but they'd rather say, She got too big for her boots, and Pride must have a fall. She had to face up to it. There was nothing else she could say in her own defense, and she condemned herself if she remained silent. It is impossible to prove you are not a disappointed old maid.

Min remembered Martin's wedding day as the day when everything changed in their lives at home. My mother was never the same after Martin married, she thought, and it was then, too, that Clare and Polly became restless and hard to get along with, and stopped joining in the conversation we always had about the family fortunes and talked instead about what they were going to do with their own lives. *Their* lives—and what about sticking together as a family, as we had been brought up to do? They got very selfish all of a sudden, and the house seemed very empty, as though Martin had died. After the wedding he never came back again except as a visitor. They lived only around the corner, but it wasn't the same, knowing he was not sleeping in his own bed.

There was eight years between Delia and Martin, and then, since he lived six years after her, there was fourteen years between them, and now that they were both gone, none of it mattered at all. They might have been born hundreds of years apart, Min thought with satisfaction. But it was not likely that Martin would ever have belonged to any family except his own, or that he would ever have had sisters who were not Min and Clare and Polly, or that he would ever have had another woman for his mother than their own mother, who had sacrificed everything for them and asked in return only that they stick together as a family, and build themselves up, and make a wall around themselves that nobody could see through, let alone climb. What she had in mind was a fort, a fortress, where they could build themselves up in private and strengthen their hold on the earth, because in the long run that is what matters—a firm foothold and a roof over your head. But all that hope ended and all their hard work was mocked when Delia Kelly walked into their lives. She smashed us up, Min thought, and got us all out into the open where blood didn't count anymore, and where blood wasn't thicker than water, and where the only mystery was, what did he see in her. It was like the end of the world, knowing he was at the mercy of somebody outside the family. A farmer's daughter is all she was, even if she had attended the Loreto convent and owned certificates to show what a good education she had.

Min sat beside her own gas fire in her own flat in Wexford and considered life and crime and punishment according to the laws of arithmetic. She counted up and down the years, and added and subtracted the questions and answers, and found that she came out with a very tidy balance in her favor. She glanced over to the old brown chest that now held those certificates, still in the big brown paper envelope that Delia had kept them in. Min intended to do away with the certificates, but not yet. She liked looking at them—especially at the one given for violin playing. It was strange that in spite of her good memory she had quite forgotten that Delia had a little reputation as a musician when she first met Martin. A very little reputation, and she came by it easily, because she had been given every chance. All the chances in Min's own family had gone to Martin, because he was the boy, and he took all their chances with him when he left. And spoiled his own chances for good, because he did nothing for the rest of his life, tied down as he was, slaving to support a wife and children, turning himself into a nobody. After all that promise and all that talk and all those plans, he made nothing of himself. A few pounds in the bank, a few sticks of furniture, a few books, and a garden that still bloomed although it had gone untended for six years—that was the sum of his life, all he had to show for himself. He would have done better to think of his mother, and stay at home, and benefit from the encouragement of his own family, all of them pushing for him in everything he did. With his ability and his brains and the nice way he had about him, he could have done anything. He could have risen to any height, a natural leader like him, able to be at ease anywhere with anybody. As it was, he died friendless. How could he have friends when he was ashamed to invite anybody to the house? He was ashamed of Delia and ashamed of the house, and more than anything else, he was unwilling to let people know of his unhappiness. He was like all of us in that, Min thought, proud and sensitive and fond of our privacy. Delia came from another class of people altogether. They were a different breed, more coarse-grained than we are, country people, accustomed to being out in all weathers, plowing, and gathering in the hay, and dealing with animals. They had no thoughts in their heads beyond saving the corn. They tried to be friendly; Min gave them that much. She wanted to be fair. But she didn't trust them, and in any case they were rejoicing over herself and her mother, because Martin made himself such an easy catch. Min didn't like to see her mother being made a fool of, and Martin too being made a fool of, because he didn't know what he was doing when he turned around and got married. He went out of his head about that girl, mad with longing, all decency gone. He was like somebody in a delirium. Min couldn't help feeling a bit contemptuous of him, to see him so helpless. And then the same thing overcame Clare and Polly, Clare marrying a dirty shabby fellow nearly old enough to be her father, and Polly marrying a commercial traveler and having one child after another until she nearly had her mother and Min out in the street with the expense she put on them. But Martin started it all, vanishing out of their lives as casually as though he had never been more than a lodger in the house.

It was a shame, what happened, all their plans gone for nothing. By that time they were all out working—Polly in the knitting factory, Clare in the news agent's, Martin in the county surveyor's office, and Min in the dressmaking business. She was a dressmaker from the beginning, through no choice of her own, and she made a good job of it. Everybody said she was very reliable and that she had good style. As soon as she could manage it she moved the sewing machine out of her mother's front parlor and into the rooms on Main Street, where she now lived. One way and another, she had had a title to these rooms for almost sixty years. The house changed owners, but Min remained on. She had no intention of giving up her flat, especially since her rent included the three little atticky rooms on the third floor, the top floor of the house. She showed great foresight when she had those top-floor rooms included in her original arrangement, all those many years ago. Now she had made the top floor into a little flat, makeshift but very nice. She found young couples liked it for the first years or so of their married lives. And she still had the lease of the little house at the corner of Georges Street and Oliver Plunkett Street, where her mother had taken them all to live when they were still babies. That little house Min had turned, in her informal way, into two flats, and she had the rent from them. And she had her old-age pension, and something in the bank—nobody knew how much, although there were many guesses. Some said she was too clever, too sharp altogether. The butcher downstairs under her flat hated her. She didn't care. She had the last laugh. He could stand in the doorway of his shop and watch her coming up the street, and give her all the black looks he liked—she didn't care. She couldn't help laughing when she thought of how sure he was when he bought the house that he would be able to get rid of her simply by telling her she wasn't wanted, and that he needed the whole house for his growing family. She wasn't going to die to suit him and she didn't care whether he wanted her or not. It was presumptuous of him to imagine she would care whether he wanted her there or didn't want her there. He even had the impertinence to tell her that he and his wife had the greatest respect for her. Min didn't know the wife but she knew the people the wife came from. No need to see people of that class to know what they were, and what their "respect" was worth. She told the butcher to his face that he might as well leave her alone. She wasn't going to budge. Of course, it would be very nice and convenient for him only to have to walk upstairs to his tea at night after he shut up the shop, but he was going to have to wait for his convenience. A narrow gate alongside his shop entrance led into a covered passage, and there was her downstairs front door at the side of the house, as private as you please. She was very well off there. The place was nicely fixed up. She liked being there in the flat alone, with the downstairs door locked and the door of her flat locked and the fire going and the electric reading lamp at her shoulder and an interesting book to read and the day's paper to hand, in case she felt like going over it again. And she had Delia's little footstool to keep her feet off the floor. She thought it was like a miracle the way things had evened out in the end. She had gone around and around and up and down for all those years, doing her duty and observing the rules of life as far as she knew them, and her feet had stopped walking on the exact spot where her road ended—here in this room, with everything gathered around her, and everything in its right place. Her mother had always said that Min was the one who would keep the flag flying no matter what. Min had never in her life been content to sit down and do nothing, but now she was quite content to sit idle. What she saw about her in the room was a job well done. She had not known until now that a job well done creates an eminence that you can rest on.

The room where she sat beside the fire, and where she spent nearly all of her time, had been her workroom in the old days. It was the front room, running the whole width of the narrow old house, and it had a high ceiling and three tall windows. The windows were curtained in thin blue stuff that showed gaps of darkness outside when she pulled them together at night. Min didn't care. Often she didn't bother to pull them but just left them open. The house opposite was all given over to offices, dead at night, and in any case, she told herself, she had nothing to hide . . . It was only a manner of speaking with her, that she had nothing to hide: she meant that she wasn't afraid to be alone at night with the windows wide open to the night.

There were three doors in the wall that faced the three windows. Two of the doors led into the two smaller rooms of the flat, and the middle door led out into the hall. One of the smaller rooms used to be her fitting room, and the tall gilt mirror was still attached to the wall there. It was Min's bedroom now, although more and more she slept on the narrow studio couch against the wall in her big room. The gas fire was on so much, the big room was always warm. She craved the warmth. She believed the climate in Wexford to be warmer than in Dublin, and she blamed the six years she had spent living with her brother for the colds that plagued her life now. She wore two cardigans and sometimes a shawl as well, over her woolen pullover. She buttoned only the top button of the outer cardigan. The inner cardigan she buttoned from top to bottom. Her pullover had long sleeves, and so she appeared with thick stuffed arms that ended at the wrist in three worn edges—green of the pullover, beige of the inner cardigan, and mottled brown of the outer cardigan, which was of very heavy wool, an Aran knit, Min called it. Her hands were mottled too, brown on pink, and she had very small yellow nails that were always cut short. She was very small and thin, and only a little stooped, and in the street she walked quickly, with no hesitation. She went out every day to buy a newspaper, and she bought food. Bread, milk, sometimes a slice of cooked ham or a tomato. She liked hardboiled eggs. She nodded to very few people as she went along, and very few people spoke to her. She was a tiny old woman, dressed in black, wearing a scrap of a hat that she had made herself and decorated with an eye veil.

She read a good deal, leaning attentively back toward the weak light given by the lamp she had taken from Delia's bedside table. Before getting the lamp she had relied on a naked bulb screwed into a socket in the middle of the ceiling. She was very saving in her ways—she had never lost the habit of rigid economy, and in fact she enjoyed pinching her pennies. She hadn't amassed a great fortune, but it was the amassing she enjoyed as she watched her wealth grow. She looked at people with calculation not for what she might get from them but for what they might rake from her if she gave them their chance. She wasn't inclined to gossip. She admitted to disliking or hating people only to the degree in which they reminded her of a certain type of class. "Oh, I *hate* that class of person," she would say, or "Oh, that's not a nice class of person at all." Grimaces, winks, nods, and gestures indicating mock alarm, mock shyness, mock anger, and mock piety were her repertoire, together with a collection of sarcastic or humorous phrases she had found useful in her youth. But she saw few people.

In the days when this was her workroom, the furniture had been sewing machines, ironing boards, storage shelves, and, down the center of the room, the huge cutting table that was always having to be cleared of its litter of fashion books and paper patterns, and cups of tea, and scissors, and scraps and ribbons of cloth. Underfoot there was always a field of thread and straight pins. Mountains of color and acres of texture were submerged in that room under the flat, tideless peace of Min's old age. The gas fire glowed red and orange—it was her only extravagance. On the floor was a flowered carpet that had once been the pride of Delia's front sitting room in Dublin, and the room was furnished with Min's souvenirs—Delia's books, Martin's books, Delia's low chair, Martin's armchair. She had Delia's sewing basket and Martin's framed map of Dublin. On the fourth finger of her left hand she wore Martin's wedding ring. She had slipped it from his dead hand. She told herself she wanted to save it from the grave robbers.

If she lifted her eyes from her book she could see, down a length of narrow side street, the sky over the harbor, and if she stood up and walked to the window she could see the water. Below her windows there was the Main Street. The streets in Wexford are very narrow, and crooked rather than winding. At some points the Main Street is only wide enough to allow one car to pass, and the side path for pedestrians shrinks to the width of a plank. There are always children bobbing along with one foot in the street and one on the path, and children dodging and running, making intricacies among the slowly moving bicycles and cars. It is a small, worn, angular town with plain unmatched houses that are dried into color by the sun and washed into color by the rain. There is nothing dark about Wexford. The sun comes up very close to the town and sometimes seems to be rising from among the houses. The wind scatters seeds against the walls and along the edges of the roofs, so that you can look up and see marigolds blooming between you and the sky.

Min's father had been a good deal older than her mother, Bridget, and he could neither read nor write. He was silent with his vivacious, quick-tempered wife, who read Dickens and Scott and Maria Edgeworth with her children, and he worked at odd jobs, when he could get them. It was the dream of his life to make money exporting pigs to the English market, and to everyone's surprise he succeeded on one occasion in getting hold of enough money to buy a few pigs and rent a pen to keep them in. He discovered at once that possession of the pigs brought him automatically into the company of a little crowd of amateurs like himself, who gathered together in serious discussion of their animals, their ambitions, their hopes, and their chances. The pigs were young and trim and pink and healthy, and they were very greedy. He found he very much enjoyed giving them their food and that he didn't mind cleaning up after them. He began talking about how clean they were, and how well mannered, and how friendly. He marveled at the way they opened and shut their mouths, and he thought their big round nostrils were very natural-looking, not piglike at all. He liked to see them lift their heads and look up at him with their tiny, blind-looking eyes. He said a lot of lies had been told about pigs. He interpreted their grunts and squeals as words of affection for him, and after a day or two Bridget told the children their father had gone off to live with the pigs. "He likes the pigs better than he likes his own children," she said. He did like the pigs. He liked having a place of his own to go to, outside the house. He liked being a man of affairs. He began smiling around at his children, as though he were keeping a little secret from them. Martin kept his accounts for him, writing down the number of pigs, the price he had paid for them, and the price he expected to get for them. Once Martin visited the pen and saw the pigs. He was forbidden to go a second time. Bridget said that one lunatic in the family was enough. Martin cried and said he wanted a dog of his own. He knew better than that. There was never a dog or a cat in that house. Bridget said she had enough to do, keeping their own mouths fed.

The great day dawned when the pigs were to be sold. Their father was gone before any of them were awake, and he didn't come home until long after the hour when they were supposed to be in bed. They weren't in bed. They all waited up for him. When he came in they were all sitting around the stove in the kitchen waiting for him. They heard him coming along the passage from the door at the Georges Street side of the house and, as their mother had instructed them to do, they remained very quiet, so that he thought there was nobody up. At the doorway he saw them all, and he looked surprised and not very pleased. Then he put his hand in his top pocket and took out the money, which he had wrapped in brown paper, and he walked over to the kitchen table and put it down.

"There's the money," he said to Bridget. "Blood money."

He looked very cold, but instead of getting near the stove to warm himself he sat down at the table and put his elbows on the table and his head in his hands.

"What sort of acting is this?" Bridget asked. "What ails you now, talking about blood money in front of the children. Will you answer me?"

"I'm no better than a murderer," he said. "I'll never forget the look in their eyes till the day I die. I shouldn't have sold them. I lay awake all last night thinking of ways to keep them, and all day today after I sold them I kept thinking of ways I could have kept them in hiding someplace where nobody would know about them—I got that fond of them. They knew me when they saw me."

Bridget stood up and walked to the table and picked up the money and put it into her apron pocket. She was a very small, stout, vigorous woman with round blue eyes and straight black hair, and she was proud of the reputation she had for speaking her mind. She was proud, cunning, suspicious, and resourceful, and where her slow, stumbling husband was concerned she was pitiless. She didn't want the children to grow up to be like him. She didn't want them to be seen with him. She told them she didn't want them dragging around after him. She had long ago grown tired of trying to understand what it was that was holding him back, and so impeding them all. But tonight, for once, it was clear to her that he was going to make an excuse of the pigs for doing nothing at all about anything for weeks or even months to come. It would be laughable if it weren't for the bad effect his laziness might have on the children. But he was useful to her around the house, as a bad example. The children were half afraid of him, because they were afraid of being drawn into his bad luck. They were ashamed of him. Min thought anybody could tell by the way her father spoke that he couldn't read or write. Maybe that was the great attraction between him and the pigs. He always seemed to be begging for time until his speech could catch up with his memory, and he never seemed to have come to any kind of an understanding with himself. He always seemed to be looking around as though somebody might arrange that understanding for him, and tell him about it.

On the night he came back so late after having sold the pigs, he was so distressed that he forgot to take off his hat. It was a hat he had worn as long as any of the children could remember, and Bridget told them he had been wearing it the first time she ever set eyes on him. She said she was so impressed by the hat that she hardly noticed him at first. It was a big, wide-brimmed black hat, a very distinguished-looking hat, although it was conspicuous now for its shabbiness. It was green with age, and the greenness showed up very much in the lamplight that night as he sat by the table with his face in his hands, grieving for his pigs. He never went out without first putting his hat on. He was never without it. He depended on it, and the children depended on being able to spot it in time to avoid meeting him outside on the street someplace. When the money was safe in Bridget's deep pocket she reached out and snatched the hat off her husband's head. "Haven't I told you never to wear that hat in the house?" she said.

He looked up at her in bewilderment and then he stood up and reached out his hand for the hat. "Give me back my hat," he said, looking at her as though he were ready to smile.

Min hated her father's weak, foolish smile. Sometimes Martin smiled like that, when he was trying to prove he understood something he couldn't understand. She thought Martin and her father were both like cowards alongside her mother. She wished her mother would throw the hat in her father's face and make him go away. She wished everything could be different—no pigs, no old hat, no struggling and scheming. She wished her mother hadn't snatched the hat off her father's head. She didn't like it when her mother started fighting, and sometimes it seemed she was always fighting. She even went out of the house sometimes and went into the house of somebody who had annoyed her and started fighting there. Then she would come home and tell the children what she'd said and what had been said to her.

One time Bridget's sister Mary came storming into the house. Bridget
and Mary hated each other. They began fighting, and then they began hitting
each other. Bridget hit the hardest, and Mary ran out of the house with her
children screaming at her heels. Martin and Min saw it all, and they told their
mother she was very brave, but they were frightened. Afterward, when
Bridget told the story of the battle, she always ended up saying, "And there
was my sister Mary with her precious blood running down her face." Min
despised her father, but she hoped her mother wouldn't hit him. She didn't
want to see his precious blood running down his face. She began to cry, and
when Clare and Polly saw their formidable older sister crying they began crying along with her. Martin stood up and begged, "Give him the hat, Mam,
give him his hat!" And then he began crying and lifting his feet up and down
as though he was getting ready to run a race.

"You'll frighten the wits out of the children," their father said, and for
once in his life he sounded as though he knew what he was saying. "Give me
that hat this minute. I'm going out. I'm getting out of here." And he made a
grab for the hat, which Bridget was holding behind her back.

She struck out at him. "Don't defy me, I'm warning you!" she screamed.
But he dodged her hand and reached behind her to snatch the hat away, and
then he hurried out of the kitchen, and they heard the Georges Street door
bang after him.

He didn't come home again that night, but he was there in the morning, sitting at the kitchen table, and Bridget gave him his tea as usual. The
children looked around for the hat. It was in its usual place, where he always
left it, on top of a cupboard that stood to one side of the door that led out
into the yard. He used to lift the hat from his head and toss it up on top of
the cupboard in one gesture. Always, when he walked in from outside, he
threw the hat up, as though he were saluting the wall of the house. And
when he was going out, in one gesture he lifted his arm to reach the hat and
put it on his head, often without even looking at it. One afternoon, when
they were all in the kitchen after school, Bridget decided to play a little trick
on their father, a joke. She said he needed a new hat anyway, and that a cap
would suit him better. A cap would be better for keeping out the rain—a
nice dark blue or dark gray cap. He looked a sketch in the old hat, and it was
time he got rid of it. Once he was rid of it, he would be glad, and he would
thank them all, but there was no use trying to persuade him to get rid of it

himself—he would only say no. He could feel loyalty for anything, even an old hat. Look at the way he had gone on about those pigs. He wasn't able to deal with his own feelings, that was his weakness. There are only certain things a person can be true to, but he didn't know that. Once the hat was gone he'd soon forget about it, and it was a shame to see him going around with that monstrosity on his head. She had an idea. They would take the hat down and cut the crown away from the brim and then put the whole hat back on the top of the cupboard and see what happened when he lifted it down the next time he was going out. They got the hat down and Bridget cut the brim away, but she left a thin strip of the velours—hardly more than a thread—to hold the two parts of the hat together when their father lifted it down onto his head. It all happened just as they expected—the brim tumbled down around their father's face and hung around his neck. He put his hands up and felt around his face and neck to see what happened, and then he took the hat off and looked at it.

"Which of you did this?" he said.

"We all did it," Bridget said.

He held the hat up and looked at it. "It's done for," he said, but he didn't seem angry—just puzzled. Then he went out, carrying the hat in his hand, and they heard no more about it.

Not long after that, Bridget went to see a man she knew who worked in Vernon's on the Main Street, and he arranged for her to buy a sewing machine on the installment plan, and she set about teaching herself to make dresses. Min was the one who helped her mother, so Min was sentenced to a lifetime of sewing, when she had her heart set on going to a college and becoming a teacher. Min wanted to teach. She wanted to have a dignified position in the town, to be appointed secretary to different committees, to meet important people who came to Wexford, and to have numbers of mothers and fathers deferring to her because she had their children under her thumb. But she learned to cut a pattern and run a sewing machine, and the only committee she ever sat on was the Committee of One she established in her own place on the Main Street. She always thought if her father had gone ahead with the pigs, and learned to control his feelings, and if he had cared anything about her, she would have had a better chance. But all the chances in the family had to go to Martin, because he was the boy, and because he had the best brains, and because he was the only hope they had of struggling up out of the poverty they lived in. He was doing very well and turning out to have a good business head when he threw it all away to get married. The best part of their lives ended the day Martin met Delia. Min remembered the nights they all used to sit around talking, sometimes till past midnight. They were happy in those years, when they were all out working, and at night they had so much to talk about they didn't know where to start or when to stop. Clare used to bring all the new books and papers and weeklies home from the news agent's on the sly for them to read. Polly and Martin had joined the Amateur Dramatics, and they were always off at rehearsals and recitations, and they began to talk knowledgeably about scenery and costumes and dialogue and backgrounds. They talked about nothing but plays and acting, and they knew everything that was going to happen—they had all the information about concerts and performances and competitions that were coming off, not merely in Wexford but in Dublin. Min thought the future was much more interesting when you knew at least a few of the things that were going to happen. There was something going on every minute, and it was really very nice being in the swim. People went out of their way to say hello to the Bagots in the street. They had a piano now, secondhand but very good. It was the same shape as their tiny parlor and it took up half the space there. They took turns picking out tunes, but Clare had the advantage over all, because she had had a few lessons from the daughter of a German family that lived in the street for a short time. The Germans knew their music—you had to admit that. Clare felt that with a few more lessons she might have made a good accompanist. They all liked to sing—they got that from Bridget. Martin went off by himself to Dublin once in a while, just for the night, and he always brought back something new—a song sheet, or a book. He always went to a concert, or a play, or to hear a lecture.

Martin and Polly liked to act out scenes, and Min used to get behind them and imitate their gestures until her mother said that she'd rather watch Min than the real thing any day. Min was glad she had found a way to join in the fun. She hadn't as much voice as the others, and serious acting was beyond her.

In one way it was a pity their father wasn't there to witness their prosperity, but in another way it was just as well, because he would have done something to spoil things—not meaning any harm but because he couldn't help himself. Min remembered how irritating it used to be to have him hanging around, like a skeleton at the feast. And he got on their mother's nerves, because they all knew he didn't understand a word of what they talked about. And he had a peaceful death. He must have been glad to go. He was never more than a burden to himself and to everybody else.

Min always remembered how stalwart and kind Martin was, comforting her mother after their father's death, and she never could understand how he could be so thoughtful, and make the promises he made, and pretend the way he did, and then run off and leave them all the first chance he got. She always said, "I can get along without the menfolk. They are more trouble and annoyance than they're worth." But she had liked very much having Martin in her life. She liked it very much when he crept upstairs to her workroom in the Main Street and stood outside the door and called out, "There's a man in the house. Will you let me in, Min?" And he would stand outside making jokes while all the women scurried about pretending to be alarmed and making themselves decent. The women used to tease her about having such a handsome brother, and ask her if she wasn't afraid some girl would steal him away. And Min always replied that Martin thought far too much of his mother ever to leave home.

"He's devoted to my mother," she always said, lowering her eyes to her work in a way that showed Martin's devotion to be of such magnitude that it was almost sacred, so that the mere mention of it made her want silence in the room. Silence or an end to that kind of careless meddlesome talk.

"Martin has no time to spend gadding around," she said to a customer who teased her too pointedly.

"Oh, Min, you're a real old maid," the customer said. "Martin's going to surprise you all one of these days. Some girl will come along and sweep him off his feet. Wait and see."

Min told her mother about that remark. "Pay no attention to her, Min," Bridget said. "Martin's no fool. He knows when he's well off. He's too comfortable ever to want to leave home. He's as set in his ways as a man of forty. Martin's a born bachelor."

And of course, the next thing they knew, Martin was married and gone. And then Polly ran off with the commercial traveler, a Protestant, and it turned out he was tired of traveling and wanted to settle down. Being settled didn't suit him either; he was never able to make a go of anything. And Clare married another Protestant, an old fellow who made a sort of living catching rabbits, and he used to walk into the house as if he owned it, with the rabbits hanging from his hand, dripping blood all over Bridget's clean floor.

Min never understood how things could come to an end so fast and so quietly. It was as though a bad trick had been played on them all. There was an end to order and thrift and books and singing, and the house seemed to fill up with detestable confusion and noise. Everywhere you turned, there was Clare's husband or Polly's children, he with his dead rabbits and his smelly pipe and the children always wanting a bag of sweets or wanting to go to the lavatory or falling down and having to be picked up screaming. She couldn't stick any of them, couldn't stand the sight of them. And then Martin moved off to Dublin in anger, telling them that his mother wouldn't let Delia have a minute's peace, that Delia had no life at all in this place, and that there was no future in Wexford anyway. Bridget always said that Delia had ruined Martin's life, and Min agreed with her, except that Min said Delia ruined all their lives. They were a good team before Delia arrived on the scene. The saying was that when a couple got married they went off by themselves and closed the door on the world, but Min thought that in her family what they did was to get married and let the whole world into the house so that there wasn't a quiet minute or a sensible thought left in this life for anybody. Such a din those marriages made, such racket and confusion and expense and quarreling. She thought it was awful that brothers and sisters could shape your whole life with doings that had nothing at all to do with you. She felt they were all tugging at her, and that her mother was on their side.

When Min got back to Wexford after Martin's death, and got her flat all cleared out and arranged with her new acquisitions—Delia's things, Martin's things, their set of wedding furniture, and their books and pictures and lamps—she suddenly realized that she was at home for good. There was nobody left who mattered to her, nobody to disturb her. The family circle was closed. She was the only one left of them. She could only think of them as the crowd in the kitchen at home long ago, and she felt it was they who had finally died, not the men and women they had turned into, who had been such an aggravation to her. She dismissed Delia. Delia was just a long interlude that had separated Martin from his twin, but the twins were joined at the end as they had been at the beginning. Min was Martin's family now.

It was hard to believe that only nine years had elapsed between her father's death and Martin's marriage. Those were the best years. She remembered the day her father died, giving them all a great fright. None of them really missed him. It was a relief not to have to worry about him—an old man not able to write his name, going around looking for work, or pretending to look for work. He couldn't stay in the house. He was gone before any of them got up in the morning, but he was always there to spoil their dinnertime, and to spoil their teatime. And often in the evening he was there listening to them, although they all knew he couldn't understand a word they said. What was most annoying to Min was that he took it for granted he had a right to come in and join them and sit down in the corner and settle himself as though he had something to offer. He had nothing to offer except his restlessness. He always seemed to be on the point of leaving. He even interrupted their conversations to describe long journeys he might take, but he never went anywhere in particular. He just wandered. The restlessness that brought him to Wexford afflicted him till the day he died.

Maybe if he'd learned to read he would have been more content. He could have learned if he'd wanted to. Bridget would have taught him to read when they were first married, but he said no, he'd wait till the children were big enough and then learn when they were learning. But the children weren't pleased to have him sit down with them when they were doing their homework, and he said himself that he felt in the way. Bridget felt that he was indeed in the way, and that he was depriving the children of a part of something they needed a good deal more than he needed it. Bridget was surprised at how strongly she felt that he should not look into their books. She was afraid he might hold the children back. She despised him, the way he went on talking about his dream of being a sailor, when everybody knew he was afraid of water. Oh, he was a great trial to them all, and toward the end of his life people got to be a bit fearful of him, and even the children seemed to know there was something not quite right about him.

It was probably the same restlessness that made their father queer that drove Martin to go off and get married on impulse the way he did. He made up his mind in two seconds, and there was no arguing with him. Min would never forget that wedding day, the struggle they had to get Bridget dressed. She was dressed in black from head to toe, as though she were going to a funeral. She generally wore black, very suitable for a middle-aged woman who was a widow, but that day the black seemed blacker than usual. Min made her a new bonnet for the wedding, of black satin with jet beads, and a shoulder cape of black satin, with jet beads around the neck. It made a very fetching outfit, but Bridget spoiled the effect by carrying her old prayer book stuffed with holy pictures and leaflets and memory cards, and she wound her black rosary beads around the prayer book so that the big metal crucifix dangled free. She looked very smart, quite the Parisienne, until she got the prayer book in her hand. Her iron gray hair was pulled up into a tight knot on top of her head, the same as every day, and the bonnet, skewered with long hatpins, crowned the knot and gave her a few more inches extra height. Min and her sisters wore stiff-brimmed white hats and white blouses with their gray costumes, and Min felt they gave the country wedding a cosmopolitan touch. But of course Clare had to spoil it all by saying to anybody who would listen to her, "We're Martin's sisters. We have the name of being short on beauty but long on brains." Clare always said the wrong thing at the wrong time. It was her way of trying to get on the right side of people. It didn't matter whether she liked a person or not, Clare had to curry favor. She couldn't help herself. You could trust her to make a fool not only of herself but of you. And Polly got fed up and said, "Oh, it's well known that Martin's the beauty of the family." And naturally there was no one at the wedding but friends and relatives of Delia and her family; Bridget invited nobody, because it wasn't all certain, she said, that Martin would go through with it.

It was true that Martin, with his glossy black curls and his bright blue eyes, was the beauty of the family. On him the features that were angular in Clare and lumpy in Polly and pinched in Min became regular and harmonious. Before he got married, when they all used to go around together, the three girls took luster from Martin's face, and that was fair enough, because their faces reflected his so faithfully that one could say, "He shows what they really look like." But after he left them, the likeness between them became one they did not want attention for. Instead of being reflections of Martin they became copies of one another, or three not very fortunate copies of a face that was gone. It was as though Martin was the family silver. They all went down in value when he went out of their lives.

Martin's wedding day always opened up in Min's memory as though it had started as an explosion. It was because they had been so full of dread driving out in the car they'd hired, and then, when they arrived in Oylegate, there was everybody ready and waiting, the priests and all the strangers, and candles and flowers, and the terrible sense of being caught up in the ceremony and of having to go on and on and on, knowing all the time that you had no voice in the matter and that it didn't matter what you did now. That was a terrible drive out to Oylegate that day. When they finally succeeded in getting their mother out of the house and into the car, she closed her eyes and kept them closed until she got out at the chapel gates. Up to the last minute she had been hoping Martin would change his mind.

"Martin, I'm asking you for your own good," she said. "Couldn't you put it off till tomorrow? I'll never get used to losing my little son, but I might feel stronger tomorrow." She even offered Martin the fare to go to Dublin and start up on his own, away from all of them, at least until any fuss there was blew over.

"Ah, what's the use of this, Mother?" Min said. "Come on now, and we'll all go out together with big smiles on our faces, not to let everybody in the town know how cut up you are."

Min was angling for a grateful look from Martin, and she got it. She thought how easily swayed he was, for all his brains. Oh, she could have kept him and given me his chances, she thought. But Min could not really have been accused of holding a grudge against Martin. She could be angry with him, but she couldn't hate him or even dislike him. He was her twin. There should have been only one of us, she thought, in despair, and saw Delia Kelly making free with a part of Min Bagot, who had known more about hard work when she was ten years old than Delia Kelly could ever know. She wondered what Delia really saw when she looked at Martin. She wondered what Delia saw and how much she noticed with those queer, cloud green eyes. All the Bagots had bright blue eyes, very keen eyes, and they all had coal black hair, but only Martin's was curly. The Kellys were much fairer in coloring; they didn't look Irish at all, Bridget said. And except for Delia they were all bigger than the Bagots, big and strong-looking, country people. Min felt defeated by them, and she didn't know why. She felt that what mattered to her could never matter a bit to them, and she didn't know what mattered to them. They were friendly enough, and why wouldn't they be, with Martin taking one of the girls off their hands. They're not our sort at all, she thought. East is East and West is West. In a way, it was worse than if Martin had married a girl from a foreign country.

On the way out to the wedding Bridget made Markey go slow. They jogged along, and they were late already; they were late leaving the house. The horse kept flicking his tail as though he were impatient with them. Markey was irritated, because he'd had such a long wait outside the house, but he tried to put a good face on it with philosophical chat about weddings and marriages and young men, and on and on. Bridget lost patience with him and asked him whether he charged extra for the conversational accompaniment. Markey was so insulted he started to stand up, which shook the car and made the horse try to turn his head to look back at them, and Polly squealed with fear and asked her mother if she was out to have them all killed with a runaway horse. Bridget replied, "I wouldn't mind."

It was an inside car, and they sat three one each seat, Markey and Clare on one side with Min in between, and, facing them, Bridget and Polly with Martin in the middle. Markey looked at Polly when she spoke, and then he winked at her and sat down without saying a word, and they continued on at the same slow rate until they got to the chapel gate.

Entering Oylegate, they passed the top of the lane that led with ups and downs and various curves to the house where Delia lived. The lane was on their left, and on their right there was a prosperous-looking grocery with a public house attached to it. There was a gap between the grocery and a row of whitewashed cottages with thatched roofs. Outside one of these an old white-haired woman sat crouched on a short wooden bench. The narrow door of her cottage stood open behind her, showing how much darkness can gather in a small room on a bright day in June. She had a piece of sacking tied around her waist for an apron, and on her head she wore a man's cloth cap. She smoked a clay pipe and regarded the carful of Bagots with an amusement that was as empty of malice as it was of innocence. Markey touched his hat to her and said, "Fine day, Ma'am." The others didn't notice her—their eyes were ahead to the little knot of people at the chapel gate. Min knew Delia must be waiting, and she thought, One good thing, we've given her a few anxious minutes. Martin looked as if he had felt a twinge of doubt about what he was doing. He said, "I feel like a great stranger all of a sudden."

"There's time yet, Martin," Min said. "We can hurry the horse and go on past them all and go to Enniscorthy and take the train back to Wexford and never see any of them again."

Bridget turned her head and opened her eyes and looked at Martin.

"Come on home with us, darling," she said, "and you'll never hear another word about it."

Markey pulled the horse up and said to Martin, "Here you are, now."

Martin stood up, making the little car suddenly flimsy, and he pushed his way between their skirts and jumped out onto the road. It was at that moment, when she heard his feet land on the ground, that the day began whirling in Min's memory. She had known perfectly well that the day would be hateful, but she had not known that it would all be so unnatural, or that she herself would feel worn and dry and unable to manage, because the only thing she wanted was to escape from it all, and she couldn't leave her mother's side. Min had never felt trapped before that day. She felt like a prisoner. She longed to be back in her workroom, where she was monarch of all she surveyed. She didn't like the voices of the people out here in the country. They were hard to understand. She knew they were discussing her behind her back, and she tried to let them know she was on to them by the knowing way she looked at them. Martin behaved as though he had forgotten she was alive. She thought it was strange that the world lit up in moments of joy, but that everything remained exactly the same when disaster struck. Martin turned into a different person when he jumped out of the car at the chapel gate. From now on there would be nothing more between her and him than running into each other in the street once in a while.

After the wedding ceremony was over, they all drove out a very long way along the road to Enniscorthy, and then off that road onto a rough country road that took them to the Slaney River. Delia's mother's family, her old brother and her three old sisters, lived by the Slaney in a very big farmhouse, whitewashed, with a towering thatched roof. The size of the house and the prosperous appearance of the place impressed Min. Delia's aunts and her uncle were all unmarried, and they all had been born here. Min heard the house was very old, and that the family had been in this lovely spot beside the Slaney for centuries. She and her mother were amazed by the furniture they saw in the parlor and in the rooms beyond the parlor. It was grandeur to have furniture like this.

"This house must have a great upstairs," Bridget whispered to Min, and Min felt very sorry for her mother. The best her mother had been able to do was to struggle out of a district where the people were down and out and into a street where the poor lived—self-respecting people, but poor. And here

they were, at Martin's wedding, surrounded by women who were mistresses of farms, some of them owning more than one house, all of them in possession of so many acres, and even the least of them with a firm hold on the
house she lived in, even if it was only a cottage, or even a half acre.

Min glanced about. These people out here in the country all belonged to
one another, and they were related to one another from the distant past.
These families went a long way back in time, and they remembered marriages that had taken place a hundred years before. They didn't talk, as Min
understood talk. Here in the country they wove webs with names and dates
and places. The dead were mentioned in the same voice with the living, so
that fathers and sisters and cousins who had been gone for decades could
have trooped through the house and through the orchards and gardens and
found themselves at home, the same as always, and they could even have
counted on finding their own names and their own faces registered faithfully somewhere among the generations that had succeeded them. Min thought
of all the dead who had been familiar here, and she wished her name could
have been woven into talk somehow. She noticed there were no children in
sight—they must have been sent off to play by themselves. There was plenty
of room for children here—the farm was big, a hundred acres.

She thought many acres seemed to have been given to the orchard—there
was no end to it, and from where she stood, the view was more like a forest
than like a field of fruit trees, which is what she understood an orchard to be.
The ground was uneven, for one thing, slanting this way and that. In her reading, she had always imagined an orchard to be a geometrical place, square or
oblong, with the trees spaced evenly. This orchard was wild and looked
unknown, as though it had been laid out and cultivated long ago and then forgotten until this wedding day. Min thought of the town of Wexford, of the
trees and houses and shops, and she thought of the harbor. Even in the dead
of night when people were asleep, the town remained alive and occupied,
waiting to be reclaimed in the morning, and the harbor was always restless.
The town was always the same, very old and always on the go, with people
around every corner, and no matter who they were, you knew you had as
much right there as they had. Min knew every inch of Wexford and every lift
of the water in the harbor, and she thought that even if everybody belonging
to her was dead and gone she would never feel lost or out of place as long as
she could walk about in the streets she had known all her life. Out here in

the country, things were different. You had to own your place—not merely the house but some of the land. And the houses were miles apart from one another, and the families lived according to laws of succession that were known only to them, and people had to depend for recognition on a loose web of relationships, a complicated genealogy that they kept in their heads and reinforced by repetition on days like today when they were all gathered together. Min thought it would be pleasant to walk around the orchard once in a while when the weather was fine, but for a nice interesting walk she would take the streets of Wexford any time.

Min stood on a narrow path that led from the orchard's entrance to nowhere—it seemed to pause and fade under grass somewhere among the trees. There were rounded grassy banks on either side of the path, but they disappeared into high ground beyond the point where the path gave out. Near the edge of the bank, which was not very high, Min's mother sat talking with two of Delia's aunts—Aunt Mag and Aunt Annie. Some of the lads had carried out three kitchen chairs so that the ladies could rest themselves while they looked at the orchard. The ladies talked comfortably, all of them glad to have something to divert them from the marriage that had brought them together. Bridget lost something of her edginess and made complimentary remarks about the house, and said it was a treat to get out into the country on a day like this. The day grew in beauty, coming in like the tide, minute by minute. There were a lot of butterflies. Min saw a bronze-and-gold one she would have liked for a dress, except that she was not likely to have occasion to wear such colors, and it would be hard to find a design like that anyway, even in the best silk.

"Oh, Min has good sense. She is a born old maid. I can always depend on Min," she heard her mother say, but she kept her eyes on the ground as though she were deep in thought. She didn't care what they said, and she wasn't going to be drawn into their talk. She thought of wandering off toward the garden. Most of the younger people were there, and she supposed Martin was there too, with Delia at his side. She wondered when Martin and Delia would be leaving for the station. They were taking the train to Dublin. They were going to a hotel there. Well, she wasn't going to the station to see them off. She would get out of that little demonstration, even if it meant she had to walk back to Wexford. She would go on toward the garden now, not to have to listen to her mother talking nonsense to these strangers. There were times when her mother was as bad as Clare.

There was a stone wall around the garden, and inside the wall a rich green box hedge that grew very tall and was clipped into a round arch over the narrow gate at the garden entrance. A similar green box arch showed the way into the orchard, but the orchard had no gate. When Min and her mother walked into the orchard earlier, Min had the impression, just for a second, that she was coming out of a dark tunnel, the green box was so thick at her sides and over her head—so dense, you might say—and that they were walking into an unfamiliar, brilliantly illuminated place full of shadows and green caves and a floor of broken sunlight that seemed to undulate before their dazzled eyes. The boys who carried the chairs out from the kitchen were going to put them in an open space where the ground dipped—a very suitable-looking grassy sward, Min thought it. But Delia's Aunt Mag wanted to sit close to a particular tree she said was her favorite, and that is where her chair was placed, with the two other chairs nearby. The boys couldn't get the chair close enough to the tree to suit Delia's Aunt Mag, and when she sat down she moved her body sideways in a very adroit quick way, and then she put her arm around the tree and her face up against the trunk as though she were cuddling it. "I love my old tree," she said. She looked up into the tree, stretching her head back, and she began laughing. "The best parts of the sky show through this tree. Now you know my secret." Min thought she was a bit queer.

She told them the tree bore cooking apples that were as big as your head and too sour to eat. Delia's Aunt Mag and her three sisters, including Delia's mother, all wore long-sleeved, high-necked black dresses cut to show the rigidity of their busts and waists, and the straightness of their backs. They were big woman, and the sweeping motion of their long heavy skirts gave them the appearance of nuns. Yes, they looked like women belonging to a religious order. Min thought them very forbidding, all four of them, and she was surprised at the change in Aunt Mag once she got her arm around the tree. Her face got much younger and she looked a bit mischievous. She was a strange, wayward old woman, and Min wondered if Delia took after her. There was something dreamy about Delia that Min didn't really trust.

Thirty years later, when Min was obliged to have Clare locked up in the Enniscorthy lunatic asylum, she remembered Delia's Aunt Mag, and she wondered how many people were abroad in the world who should by rights be locked up out of harm's way. By then, of course, Bridget was dead. Bridget had always said that their father would have ended up in the poorhouse if he had been left to himself. Min thought he might have been very well off in the poorhouse. Maybe that was where his place was. There were people who couldn't manage in the world. But Bridget would never have let Clare go into the lunatic asylum. She always said, "Poor Clare, she takes after her father." Min couldn't see that at all. Their father had been very silent. But Clare never shut up, and all she did was pray for them all. It got on Min's nerves to hear the rosary going day and night. Clare's rabbit-chasing husband was no help at all. He just laughed, probably pleased in his heart to hear the prayers mocked. Min finally lost patience when she found out that Clare had given away every piece but one of the blue-and-white German china their mother had treasured. Only the soup tureen remained, with its heavy lid. Min never got over the loss of that china. She would have gone and demanded it back, but Clare wouldn't tell her who had it. It was gone for good, no hope of ever seeing it again. Clare claimed the china was hers, and that where it went was none of Min's business. Min knew otherwise. Clare didn't live many years after being shut up, and Min brought her body back to Wexford and buried her there where they would all be buried. All but Martin. Martin and Delia were buried together in St. Jerome's in Dublin.

During the years she lived with him after Delia died, Min found Martin very changed. Fifty years with Delia had left their mark on him. He wasn't the brother she remembered. She had seen other men like that—so buried in habit that their lives were worth nothing to them when the wife was gone. Martin would begin to read, and then his hand would sink down, with the book in it, and he would stare over to the side of his chair, as though he were trying to remember something. More likely he was trying to understand something, Min thought. He had had a habit like that when he was young, of staring away at the wall, or at nothing, when things were going against him. He didn't want her in the house with him—that was obvious—but he had to put up with her. She didn't care. She was being loyal to their mother, that was the main thing. He continued to take his walk every day till his legs gave out. He never went out in the garden, never, but every once in a while he would go to the big window that looked out on the garden and he would stand there staring and always turn away saying, "The garden misses her."

Min got tired of that, and one day she burst out, "Oh, she was a good gardener. That is what she had a talent for. She was good at gardening." He turned from the window and he said to her, "What did you say? What was that you said?" She repeated what she had said. She wasn't afraid of him. "I said, she was a good gardener. That is what she was good at, I said." Min was shocked at what he said to her then. "And what were you ever good at, may we ask?" he said. Martin of all people ought to know she had always been good at anything she chose to put her hand to. All the times she came here to visit them, he used to hold her up as an example to Delia. He used to tell Delia that Min could have done wonders if she hadn't been tied to the sewing machine. Martin ought to be ashamed of himself, but she said nothing to defend herself now. He was an old man, wandering in his mind like their father.

Martin was restless too, and the more feeble he became, the less he wanted to stay in the house. He said he wanted to see the water again. He wanted to go to the sea. He wanted to walk on the strand. He even talked about paying a last visit to the west of Ireland. He wanted to walk by the Atlantic Ocean once again. He said the air there would put new life into him. Once he began talking about Connemara and Kerry, there was no stopping him. He liked to recall the adventures he'd had on the holidays he used to take by himself in Connemara and Kerry long ago. He used to go on long walking tours by himself. He'd stay away for a week at a time. He liked to recall those days when he was on his own. He seemed proud of having gone off on his own, away from this house and from Delia and the children, away from all he knew. He sounded like a conjurer describing some magical rope trick when he talked about how he left the house at such and such an hour, and what So-and-So had said to him on the train, and how he carried nothing with him but his knapsack and his blackthorn stick. Min didn't like hearing about it. She knew his adventures, and she had no sympathy with him. If he was all that anxious to have a change from Delia—and nobody could blame him for that—why hadn't he come to Wexford to see his mother, and to see his sisters, and to go about the town and have a word with all the old crowd? Most of them were still there at the time.

He could have taken a walk about the town with me, Min thought. It would have set me up, in those days, to be seen with him, show off a bit. Many a time he could have come down to see us, but no, he was off to Connemara, or to Kerry, to enjoy another holiday by himself with the Atlantic Ocean. The Irish Sea wasn't good enough for him anymore, and

Wexford Harbor was nothing compared with the beauties of Galway Bay. He talked about the wild Mayo coast as though wildness were a sort of virtue, and one you didn't find in the scenery in Wexford. She reminded him that he had once been in love with their own strand at Rosslare, and she described to him how he used to spend half his life out there, riding out on his bicycle every chance he got. Every free minute he could get he spent at Rosslare. He listened to her, but as though he was being patient with her. "I'd be very glad to see Rosslare again," he said when she had finished talking.

Then he gave up talking about Connemara and Kerry, and he began to wish for a day out at Dun Laoghaire. And he said he'd like to have a day at Greystones. And he wanted to go out to Killiney for a day. Which would Min like best? Maybe they could manage it. Min didn't see how they were going to manage it. A whole day out of the house, and no guarantee of what the weather might be like. They might not be able to find shelter so easily in case of a sudden shower. If he got his feet wet there'd be the devil to pay. They had no car, even if they could drive, and it was an awful drag out to Killiney and back on the bus, or on the train, if they took the train. It would be foolish to go to the expense of hiring a car. She didn't see how they were going to do it.

He seemed to let go of the idea, and then one day he said, "Min, do you remember the lovely view of the Slaney from the garden that day? Do you remember how the Slaney looked that day, flowing past us into Wexford? And we all stood looking at it? I thought of the passage of time. I stood there, and I thought for a minute that the garden was moving along with the river. And then later on when Delia and I were at Edermine station waiting for the train to Dublin, there were all the flowers in the station, and the stationmaster laughing at us and talking to us, and the white stones spelling out the name of the station. Delia said an expert gardener must have planted the bed of flowers beside the station house, and the stationmaster said he'd done it all himself, getting the place ready for her. But the garden they had there by the Slaney—that was magnificent. Wasn't it, Min?"

Min remembered standing in the garden, surrounded by roses with big heavy heads, and hearing her mother say that she would like very much to have a bunch of flowers to take back to Wexford with her. They all got bunches of flowers to take home. And there was a bunch of flowers for Markey to take to his wife. The car was filled with flowers, and still the garden looked as though it hadn't been touched.

"That was a grand place they had there," Min said, and she was glad to know that the garden was in ruins now, and that the house stood empty with the roof falling in and that the door there stood open to display the vacant rooms and the cold hearth in the kitchen. "It's all gone now," she said.

"It was a marvelous day," Martin said. "I never forgot what Delia's Aunt Mag said to me. Do you remember—she said the air was like mother o' pearl. Wasn't that a funny thing for an old country woman to say? I wonder what put a thought like that in her head. 'The air is like mother o' pearl today," she said, looking at me as though we were the same age and had known each other all our lives."

"She didn't look at me that way," Min said. "But I remember her saying that. She was a bit affected, I think—inclined to talk above herself. I didn't care for her. Something about her made me very uneasy."

"Ah, no," Martin said. "Delia was very fond of her."

"Oh, Delia," Min said impatiently. "Delia said the first thing that came into her head. You told her so often enough, to her face, with me sitting here in this room listening to you barging at her. She couldn't open her mouth to suit you. There was no harm in Delia, but she never knew what she said. Half the time she made no sense. There was nothing to Delia."

The minute she finished speaking, she was sorry. She didn't want to start a row. But Martin was silent, and then he said, "Nothing to Delia. That's true. I never thought that. But as Shakespeare says, It's true. It's true, it's a pity, and pity 'tis it's true. Nothing to Delia. Shakespeare was right that time."

"Shakespeare didn't say it. I said it," Min cried furiously.

"You or Shakespeare, what matter now. It's true, there was nothing to Delia. Wasn't she a lovely girl, though."

"Are you making a song out of it?" Min said. "What's got into you, Martin?"

She looked at him sitting across the hearth from her. His snow white curls floated on his head. His narrow face was the same shape as her own face. His blue eyes watched her through his rimless spectacles, and he smiled easily, as though they were discussing something pleasant from the past. She thought of Clare singing "You stick to the boats, lads . . ." that morning when she was being driven off in the car that took her to the asylum. They told Min later that Clare stopped singing quick enough when she saw where she was going. Min wondered if the queer strain that was in Clare had touched

Martin, and she was glad that she herself was free of it. Martin seemed to follow her thoughts.

"You put poor Clare into the asylum," he said gently.

"She was off her head, driving us all to distraction, trying to give the house away!" Min said indignantly. "What help were you, up here in Dublin, away from all the unpleasantness?"

"Clare was mad," Martin said. "There was nothing to Delia. That's a weight off my mind. I know where I am now. I always knew where I was with her, even though I didn't know what she was, and now I still don't know what she was, and God knows I don't know where I am without her. But there was nothing to her."

"My mother said Delia didn't amount to much," Min said spitefully. "Right from the beginning, she said that."

"Nothing to her. You said it yourself," Martin said. "I'll show you a picture of her, taken when she was sixteen years old."

He pulled himself slowly to his feet, and made his way across the room to the cupboard, which had glass doors on top and solid wooden doors underneath. Behind the glass doors Delia's Waterford glass bowls and her Waterford glass jug shimmered dimly. They had a shelf to themselves. Another shelf held her good Arklow china. Martin bent painfully to open the lower doors, and when they were open wide he reached in and took out a large brown envelope. He pushed the doors shut and made his way back to where Min sat in Delia's chair on Delia's side of the fire. He unfastened the envelope and slid the photograph out carefully, holding it as though it were thin glass. His hands are trembling more these days, Min thought. When the photograph was free, he held it up for Min to see.

"There she is," he said. "That's what she looked like. Look at the hair she had. Who ever had hair like that, that color? Nobody else in that family had hair like that. They said she took after her father. He died young. Look at that, Min."

"That photograph glorifies her," Min said.

"She was very good," Martin said. "I remember that day we got married, I was standing off to myself, looking at the Slaney. I was lost in admiration. I was looking through a gap in the hedge—one of the children had pulled open a place there, to look through. The river seemed very close up to the garden, under my feet. It was very close. Even then the water was eating in under the garden, and the little strand they told me they had there at one time was gone, or nearly gone. I remember I was there by myself—the water was dazzling. I didn't know where I was. I was inside a dream, and everything was safe, I know. The Slaney was very broad that day, and powerful, sure and strong— you know the way it used to be. An Irish river of great importance, the inspector said the day he visited the school. But I felt grand, looking at the Slaney that day. To know it was my own native river and was so, long before I was born. I was standing there like that, when Delia's Aunt Mag came up alongside me. "I was looking for you," she said. My God, how well I remember her voice, as if it was five minutes ago. We might still be there. "I was looking for you," she said. She saw the break in the hedge. "Ah, you found a spy hole," she said. And do you know what she did? She put her arm around my shoulders. She was taller than me—they were big women in that family—and she stuck her face out past me so that she could see what I was looking at. I started to move to the side, to give her room, but she held on to me. "Stay where you are," she said. I said, "I'm in your way." "You're not in my way, child," she said. "Haven't you more right to stand here than anybody? I only want to have a little look before Willie comes along and finds this hole and starts to patch it up. "The lads have been up to mischief again"—that's what Willie will say. He says they're tearing down the hedge, helping the garden into the river. The river is eating up the garden, you know—if it wasn't for Willie always on guard, we'd be swallowed up." I said, "It's great to see the Slaney like this." "I have a great fondness for the water," she said. "I couldn't be content any place but here where I was born and brought up. I've never spent a night away from this house in my life, do you know that? It's a blessing the day turned out so grand. And nobody was sick or anything. Everybody was able to come see Delia married. The Slaney is in full flood, and the springs of affection are rising around us." She spoke the truth. The Slaney was in full flood that day."

"That's sheer nonsense," Min said. "How could the Slaney be in full flood on a fine day in June? The Slaney was the same as any other day."

Martin went to his own chair and sat down. "My legs aren't getting any better," he said. "I can't stand on my own feet these days."

"You've tired yourself out making speeches," Min said.

Martin still held the photograph of Delia. He lifted it to see it better. He's trembling too much, Min thought. She wondered if she could get him to go to his room and lie down. "You're wearing yourself out," she said.

Martin gazed at the shaking photograph. "It's very like her," he said. Then he fitted it back into its envelope, pressing his lips together and frowning, like a foolish old man making an effort to do something that was beyond him.

"I'll do that for you," she said, getting ready to stand up and go over to him.

"You stay where you are," he said, and when he had the photograph safe he placed the envelope on the low shelf under his table. "I shouldn't have stood up so long," he said, and then he took his book from the table and began reading, but after a minute he got up and went out of the room, carrying the book with him. "I'm going to my room," he said without looking at her. "I might lie down for a bit."

Min was glad to see him go. There would be peace now, for a while. She didn't like to see him getting into these states where he talked so much. All that raking up of the past was a bad sign. She would have asked the priest to come in and talk to him, but she knew Martin would fight the priest's coming until he could fight no more. Martin didn't want the priest in the house. His mind was made up to that, and there was no use arguing with him. Min only hoped she would be able to get the priest in time, when the time came. She didn't want her brother dying without the Last Sacraments. She didn't understand Martin's bitter attitude toward the Church. Polly went very much the same way, of course. Min would never forget Polly's blasphemous language when the third-eldest child died, the little one they called Mary. Min was trying to comfort Polly by telling her the baby would be well taken care of in Heaven, when Polly burst out laughing and crying and saying she could take care of her own child better than God and His Blessed Mother and all the saints and angels put together. "They might have left poor little Mary with her own Mammy!" Polly said. "They must have seen the way she was holding on to my hand, wanting to stay with me. They have very hard hearts up there, if you ask me." Martin had never gone that far in his talk against the Church. At least, as far as Min knew he'd never gone that far, but she knew she was going to have to do a bit of scheming to get the priest into the house. "The springs of affection are rising." She didn't like to hear him talking like that. What Min remembered of that day in the garden by the Slaney was that she felt worn out and dried up, and trapped, crushed in by people who were determined to see only the bright surface of the occasion. They could call it a wedding or anything they liked, but she knew it was a holocaust and that she was the victim, although nobody would ever admit that.

She thought they were all very clumsy. It wasn't that she wanted to be noticed. But she knew that any notice she got was pity or derision. Nothing she could say was right. She was out of it, and nothing could convince those people that she wanted to be out of it. She would ten times rather have been back in Wexford working as usual, but she had to go to the wedding or cause a scandal. Now here they were. Bridget was giving every evidence of enjoying herself, and so were Polly and Clare, and in Min's opinion they were letting the side down. She had been dragged out here like a victim of war at the back of a chariot, and all to bolster Martin up, and he didn't need bolstering up.

She stood outside the garden gate. The children had all vanished, and she imagined they had gone to play somewhere by themselves, but suddenly the place was full of children running around, and she thought they must have been having their dinner. Children always had to be fed, no matter what. These children were a healthy-looking lot, fair-haired or red-headed, most of them. Min remembered how black she and Martin had been as children, Martin with his black curls and she with her straight black plait. They were a skinny pair, very different from these children. A little boy ran up to her so suddenly that she thought he was going to crash into her, but he stopped just in time and stared up at her. He was about five years old, a very solid-looking little fellow. His eyes were so blue that it was like two flowers looking at you, and he had a very short nose, and there was sweat on his forehead. His hair was nearly white. He wore a little suit of clothes, a little coat and trousers and a white shirt, and black stockings pulled up on his legs under the trousers. He opened his mouth, but he said nothing, just stared at her. Min gave him no encouragement. She didn't dislike children, but she had no great fondness for them, and she didn't want a whole crowd of them trooping along after him and asking her questions and making her conspicuous. He turned red, and he threw his arm up over his eyes, and peered up at her from under his sleeve, and began to smile. She smiled at him. He was a nice little fellow. She ought to say something to him.

"Are you a good boy?" she asked him. He turned and ran off, flapping his arms at his sides like a farmyard bird, and when he was a little distance away he turned and looked back to see if she was watching him. Then he ran off out of the garden. She didn't see him again.

The next thing she remembered was a moment of terrible unhappiness—it gave her a shock. What happened was that Martin and one of Delia's brothers and a woman she didn't even know came up to her and began talking about the train. They kept saying that it wouldn't do for Delia and Martin to miss the train. Min never knew the woman's name, but she remembered that she made a great fuss, as though she imagined that the day depended on her. There were always people like that everywhere, trying to boss things. She wanted to tell that woman to mind her own business. All these strangers were taking Martin over. They thought they owned him now.

"The springs of affection are rising." It would be those people who would say a thing like that, including everybody in their inspirations, everybody, even people who didn't want to be included. Min thought of that garden. She thought of the green box hedge and the monkey-puzzle tree and the pink and white roses and all the big dark and white star-shaped flowers, and she thought of Delia's Aunt Mag on the kitchen chair under the cooking-apple tree, and she remembered Delia's brothers and sister and Delia's mother, and the white-haired child. She had forgotten nothing of that glittering day, and she saw it all enclosed in a radiant fountain that rushed up through a rain of sunlight to meet with and rejoice with whatever was up there—Heaven, God the Father, the Good Shepherd, everything everybody ever wanted, wonderful prizes, happiness.

Min knew it was only the transfiguration of memory. She was no fool, and she was not likely to mistake herself for a visionary. The lovely fountain was like a mirage, except that in a mirage people saw what they wanted and were starving for, and in the fountain Min saw what she did not want and never had wanted. Why was it nobody ever believed her when she told them she wanted nothing to do with all that hullabaloo? The fortunes of war condemned her to a silence that misrepresented her as thoroughly as the words she was too proud to speak would have done, and she knew all that. Martin's lightmindedness had changed the course of her life, and there wasn't one single thing she could do about it. He turned all their lives around. He cared no more about his mother and sisters and what happened to them than if he had been a stranger passing through the house on his way to a far better place, where the people were more interesting.

He made his mother cry. For a wedding present, Bridget wanted to give Martin the good dining-room set that she had paid for penny by penny at a time when she couldn't afford it. A big round mahogany table and four matching chairs that must have had pride of place in some great house at one time. She kept that furniture up to the nines, polished and waxed till you could see to do your hair in it. But Martin turned up his nose at it. No secondhand stuff for him and Delia, and the mahogany was too big and heavy anyway. He didn't want it. He and Delia went and ordered furniture made just for them; new furniture, all walnut—a bed, a chest of drawers, a wardrobe, a washstand, and two sitting-room chairs so that Delia could hold court in style when they had visitors. Those were Martin's very words. "Now Delia can hold court in style," he said, and never noticed the look on his mother's face. Min noticed the bed had vanished out of the house in Dublin, and she was never able to find out what happened to it. But the other things were still there. Above all, the two sitting-room chairs were still there—Martin sat in his own, and she sat in Delia's. She would take the whole lot back to Wexford when the time came. She would bring the furniture back where it belonged. It was never too late to make things right.

In Wexford, in her own flat, she sat in Delia's chair, and sometimes for a change sat propped up with pillows in Martin's big chair, his armchair. It was nice to have the two chairs. The wardrobe and the chest of drawers went into her bedroom, and the washstand into the room she used for a kitchen. Delia's old sitting-room carpet was threadbare, but the colors held up well, and it looked nice on the floor, almost like an antique carpet. And the hearthrug from the house in Dublin looked very suitable in front of Min's old fireplace, where so many girls and ladies had warmed themselves when they came in to be measured for a dress, or to have a fitting.

Against the end wall, facing down the room to the fireplace, Delia's bookshelves were ranged along, filled with Delia's books, and with some of Martin's books. Some of Martin's books Min wouldn't have in the house, and she had sold them. She was glad now that she had never spent money on books; these had been waiting for her. The room looked very distinguished, very literary. It was what she should always have had. She wished they could all see it. There was room for them, and a welcome. There was even a deep, dim corner there between the end wall and the far window where her father could steal in and sit down and listen to them with his silence, as he used to do. There was a place here for all of them—a place for Polly, a place for poor Clare. A place in the middle for Bridget. A place for Martin in his own chair. They could come in anytime and feel right at home although the room was warmer and the furniture a bit better than anything they had been used to in the old days.

Muriel Spark

(1918-   )

Born in Edinburgh—the setting of her best-known novel, *The Prime of Miss Jean Brodie* (1961)—Muriel Spark lived for a number of years in Rhodesia (now Zimbabwe) and on her return to Britain in 1944 worked in the Foreign Office on anti-Nazi propaganda. In the 1950s she wrote biographies of Mary Shelley, the Brontës, and edited the letters of John Henry Cardinal Newman. In 1954 she converted to Catholicism. A great satirist, in an address to the American Academy of Arts and Letters in 1970 she called for a literature of savage ridicule as "the only honorable weapon we have left." Some reviewers have praised her short stories more highly than her many novels, which include *Memento Mori* (1959), *The Girls of Slender Means* (1963), *The Mandelbaum Gate* (1965), *The Abbess of Crewe* (1974), and *Territorial Rights* (1979). "[She's] one of the few writers of the language on either side of the Atlantic with enough resources, daring, and stamina to be altering, as well as feeding, the fiction machine," wrote John Updike.

The First Year of My Life

I was born on the first day of the second month of the last year of the First World War, a Friday. Testimony abounds that during the first year of my life I never smiled. I was known as the baby whom nothing and no one could make smile. Everyone who knew me then has told me so. They tried very hard, singing and bouncing me up and down, jumping around, pulling faces. Many times I was told this later by my family and their friends; but, anyway, I knew it at the time.

You will shortly be hearing of that new school of psychology, or maybe you have heard of it already, which, after long and far-adventuring research and experiment, has established that all of the young of the human species are born omniscient. Babies, in their waking hours, know everything that is going on everywhere in the world; they can tune in to any conversation they choose, switch on to any scene. We have all experienced this power. It is only after the first year that it was brainwashed out of us; for it is demanded of us by our immediate environment that we grow to be of use to it in a practical way. Gradually, our know-all brain-cells are blacked out, although traces remain in some individuals in the form of E.S.P., and in the adults of some primitive tribes.

It is not a new theory. Poets and philosophers, as usual, have been there first. But scientific proof is now ready and to hand. Perhaps the final touches are being put to the new manifesto in some cell at Harvard University. Any day now it will be given to the world, and the world will be convinced.

Let me therefore get my word in first, because I feel pretty sure, now, about the authenticity of my remembrance of things past. My autobiography, as I very well perceive at the time, started in the very worst year that the world had ever seen so far. Apart from being born bedridden and toothless, unable to raise myself on the pillow or utter anything but farmyard squawks or police-siren wails, my bladder and my bowels totally out of control, I was further depressed by the curious behavior of the two-legged mammals around me. There were those black-dressed people, females of the species to which I appeared to belong, saying they had lost their sons. I slept a great deal. Let them go and find their sons. It was like the special pin for my nappies which my mother or some other hoverer dedicated to my care was always losing. These careless women in black lost their husbands and their brothers. Then they came to visit my mother and clucked and crowed over my cradle. I was not amused.

"Babies never really smile till they're three months old," said my mother. "They're not *supposed* to smile till they're three months old."

My brother, aged six, marched up and down with a toy rifle over his shoulder.

> The grand old Duke of York
> He had ten thousand men;
> He marched them up to the top of the hill
> And he marches them down again.
>
> And when they were up, they were up.
> And when they were down, they were down.
> And when they were neither down nor up
> They were neither up nor down.

"Just listen to him!"

"Look at him with his rifle!"

I was about ten days old when Russia stopped fighting. I tuned in to the Czar, a prisoner, with the rest of his family, since evidently the country had put him off his throne and there had been a revolution not long before I was born. Everyone was talking about it. I tuned in to the Czar. "Nothing would ever induce me to sign the treaty of Brest-Litovsk," he said to his wife. Anyway, nobody had asked him to.

At this point I was sleeping twenty hours a day to get my strength up. And from what I discerned in the other four hours of the day I knew I was going to need it. The Western Front on my frequency was sheer blood, mud, dismembered bodies, blistering crashes, hectic flashes of light in the night skies, explosions, total terror. Since it was plain I had been born into a bad moment in the history of the world, the future bothered me, unable as I was to raise my head from the pillow and as yet only twenty inches long. "I truly wish I were a fox or a bird," D. H. Lawrence was writing to somebody. Dreary old creeping Jesus. I fell asleep.

Red sheets of flame shot across the sky. It was 21 March, the fiftieth day of my life, and the German Spring Offensive had started before my morning feed. Infinite slaughter. I scowled at the scene, and made an effort to kick out. But the attempt was feeble. Furious, and impatient for some strength, I wailed for my feed. After which I stopped wailing but continued to scowl.

> The grand old Duke of York
> He had ten thousand men . . .

They rocked the cradle. I never heard a sillier song. Over in Berlin and Vienna the people were starving, freezing, striking, rioting and yelling in the streets. In London everyone was bustling to work and muttering that it was time the whole damn business was over.

The big people around me bared their teeth; that meant a smile, it meant they were pleased or amused. They spoke of ration cards for meat and sugar and butter.

"Where will it all end?"

I went to sleep. I woke and tuned in to Bernard Shaw who was telling someone to shut up. I switched over to Joseph Conrad who, strangely enough, was saying precisely the same thing. I still didn't think it worth a smile, although it was expected of me any day now. I got on to Turkey. Women draped in black huddled and chattered in their harems; yak-yak-yak. This was boring, so I came back to home base.

In and out came and went the women in British black. My mother's brother, dressed in his uniform, came coughing. He had been poison-gassed in the trenches. *"Tout le monde à la bataille!"* declaimed Marshal Foch the old swine. He was now Commander-in-Chief of the Allied Forces. My uncle coughed from deep within his lungs, never to recover but destined to return to the Front. His brass buttons gleamed in the firelight. I weighed twelve pounds by now; I stretched and kicked for exercise, seeing that I had a lifetime before me, coping with this crowd. I took six feeds a day and kept most of them down by the time the *Vindictive* was sunk in Ostend harbour, on which day I kicked with special vigour in my bath.

In France the conscripted soldiers leapfrogged over the dead on the advance and littered the fields with limbs and hands, or drowned in the mud. The strongest men on all fronts were dead before I was born. Now the sentries used bodies for barricades and the fighting men were unhealthy from the start. I checked my toes and my fingers, knowing I was going to need them. *The Playboy of the Western World* was playing at the Court Theatre in London, but occasionally I beamed over to the House of Commons which made me drop off gently to sleep. Generally, I preferred the Western Front where one got the true state of affairs. It was essential to know the worst, blood and explosions and all, for one had to be prepared, as the boy scouts said. Virginia Woolf yawned and reached for her diary. Really, I preferred the Western Front.

In the fifth month of my life I could raise my head from my pillow and hold it up. I could grasp the objects that were held out to me. Some of these things rattled and squawked. I gnawed on them to get my teeth started. "She hasn't smiled yet?" said the dreary old aunties. My mother, on the defensive, said I was probably one of those late smilers. On my wavelength Pablo Picasso was getting married and early in that month of July the Silver Wedding of King George V and Queen Mary was celebrated in joyous pomp at St. Paul's Cathedral. They drove through the streets of London with their children. Twenty-five years of domestic happiness. A lot of fuss and ceremonial handing over of swords went on at the Guildhall where the King and Queen received a cheque for £53,000 to dispose of for charity as they thought fit. *Tout le monde à la bataille!* Income tax in England had reached six shillings in the pound. Everyone was talking about the Silver Wedding; yak-yak-yak, and ten days later the Czar and his family, now in Siberia, were invited to descend to a little room in the basement. Crack, crack, went the guns; screams and blood all over the place, and that was the end of the Romanoffs. I flexed my muscles. "A fine healthy baby," said the doctor; which gave me much satisfaction.

Tout le monde à la bataille! That included my gassed uncle. My health had improved to the point where I was able to crawl in my playpen. Bertrand Russell was still cheerily in prison for writing something seditious about pacifism. Tuning in as usual to the Front Lines it looked as if the Germans were winning all the battles yet losing the war. And so it was. The upper-income people were upset about the income tax at six shillings to the pound. But all women over thirty got the vote. "It seems a long time to wait," said one of my drab old aunts, aged twenty-two. The speeches in the House of Commons always sent me to sleep which was why I missed, at the actual time, a certain oration by Mr. Asquith following the armistice on 11 November. Mr. Asquith was a greatly esteemed former prime minister later to be an Earl, and had been ousted by Mr. Lloyd George. I clearly heard Asquith, in private, refer to Lloyd George as "that damned Welsh goat."

The armistice was signed and I was awake for that. I pulled myself on to my feet with the aid of the bars of my cot. My teeth were coming through very nicely in my opinion, and well worth all the trouble I was put to in bringing them forth. I weighed twenty pounds. On all the world's fighting fronts the men killed in action or dead of wounds numbered 8,538,315 and the warriors wounded and maimed were 21,219,452. With these figures in my mind I sat up in my high chair and banged my spoon on the table. One of my mother's black-draped friends recited:

> I have a rendezvous with Death
> At some disputed barricade,
> When spring comes back with rustling shade
> And apple blossoms fill the air—
> I have a rendezvous with Death.

Most of the poets, they said, had been killed. The poetry made them dab their eyes with clean white handkerchiefs.

Next February on my first birthday, there was a birthday cake with one candle. Lots of children and their elders. The war had been over two months and twenty-one days. "Why doesn't she smile?" My brother was to blow out the candle. The elders were talking about the war and the political situation. Lloyd George and Asquith, Asquith and Lloyd George. I remembered recently having switched on to Mr. Asquith at a private party where he had been drinking a lot. He was playing cards and when he came to cut the cards he tried to cut a large box of matches by mistake. On another occasion I had seen him putting his arm around a lady's shoulder in a Daimler motor car, and generally behaving towards her in a very friendly fashion. Strangely enough she said, "If you don't stop this nonsense immediately I'll order the chauffeur to stop and I'll get out." Mr. Asquith replied, "And pray, what reason will you give?" Well anyway it was my feeding time.

The guests arrived for my birthday. It was so sad, said one of the black widows, so sad about Wilfred Owen who was killed so late in the war, and she quoted from a poem of his:

> What passing-bells for these who die as cattle?
> Only the monstrous anger of the guns.

The children were squealing and toddling around. One was sick and another wet the floor and stood with his legs apart gaping at the puddle. All was mopped up. I banged my spoon on the table of my high chair.

> But I've a rendezvous with Death
> At midnight in some flaming town;
> When spring trips north again this year,
> And I to my pledged word am true,
> I shall not fail that rendezvous.

More parents and children arrived. One stout man who was warming his behind at the fire, said, "I always think those words of Asquith's after the armistice were so apt. . . ."

They brought the cake close to my high chair for me to see, with the candle shining and flickering above the pink icing. "A pity she never smiles."

"She'll smile in time," my mother said, obviously upset.

"What Asquith told the House of Commons just after the war," said that stout gentleman with his backside to the fire, "—so apt, what Asquith said. He said that the war has cleansed and purged the world, by God! I recall his actual words: 'All things have become new. In this great cleansing and purging it has been the privilege of our country to play her part. . . .'"

That did it. I broke into a decided smile and everyone noticed it, convinced that it was provoked by the fact that my brother had blown out the candle on the cake. "She smiled!" my mother exclaimed. And everyone was clucking away about how I was smiling. For good measure I crowed like a demented raven. "My baby's smiling," said my mother.

"It was the candle on her cake," they said.

The cake be damned. Since that time I have grown to smile naturally, like any other healthy and house-trained person, but when I really mean a smile, deeply felt from the core, then to all intents and purposes it comes in response to the words uttered in the House of Commons after the First World War by the distinguished, the immaculately dressed and the late Mr. Asquith.

Doris Lessing

(1919-   )

Doris Lessing grew up on a poor maize farm in Southern Rhodesia, the only child of British parents; she left Africa (and her marriage and children) in 1949 for the London her mother had never stopped longing for. A committed activist, Lessing has worked her political interests, especially feminism and a socialist critique of the inequalities of capitalism, into her fiction. *The Golden Notebook* (1962) is probably her most famous book, but in addition to many novels she has published more than fifty short stories, a form to which she says she is addicted. Though she has experimented with various styles—science fiction, fantasy, feminist bildungsroman, political realism—she still rereads her first teachers in fiction—Tolstoy, Dostoevsky, Turgenev, Balzac, Stendhal—for their humanity: their fierce love of people that makes their novels statements of belief in individual human beings. Because she dislikes the "English attitude towards women," she has never felt close to the English novelists, except for the Brontës, Thomas Hardy, and Charles Dickens, despite "the nonsense he writes about women."

An Old Woman and Her Cat

Her name was Hetty, and she was born with the twentieth century. She was seventy when she died of cold and malnutrition. She had been alone for a long time, since her husband had died of pneumonia in a bad winter soon after the Second World War. He had not been more than middle-aged. Her four children were now middle-aged, with grown children. Of these descendants one daughter sent her Christmas cards, but otherwise she did not exist for them. For they were all respectable people, with homes and good jobs and cars. And Hetty was not respectable. She had always been a bit strange, these people said, when mentioning her at all.

When Fred Pennefather, her husband, was alive, and the children just growing up, they all lived much too close and uncomfortable in a Council flat in that part of London which is like an estuary, with tides of people flooding in and out: they were not half a mile from the great stations of Euston, St. Pancras and King's Cross. The blocks of flats were pioneers in that area, standing up grim, grey, hideous, among many acres of little houses and gardens, all soon to be demolished so that they could be replaced by more tall grey blocks. The Pennefathers were good tenants, paying their rent, keeping out of debt; he was a building worker, "steady," and proud of it. There was no evidence then of Hetty's future dislocation from the normal, unless it was that she very often slipped down for an hour or so to the platforms where the locomotives drew in and ground out again. She liked the smell of it all, she said. She liked to see people moving about, "coming and going from all those foreign places." She meant Scotland, Ireland, the North of England. These visits into the din, the smoke, the massed swirling people, were for her a drug, like other people's drinking or gambling. Her husband teased her, calling her a gipsy. She was in fact part-gipsy, for her mother had been one, but had chosen to leave her people and marry a man who lived in a house. Fred Pennefather liked his wife for being different from the run of the women he knew, and had married her because of it; but her children were fearful that her gipsy blood might show itself in worse ways than haunting railway stations. She was a tall woman with a lot of glossy black hair, a skin that tanned easily, and dark strong eyes. She wore bright colours, and enjoyed quick tempers and sudden reconciliations. In her prime she attracted attention, was proud and handsome. All this made it inevitable that the people in those streets should refer to her as "that gipsy woman." When she heard them, she shouted back that she was none the worse for that.

After her husband died and the children married and left, the Council moved her to a small flat in the same building. She got a job selling food in a local store, but found it boring. There seem to be traditional occupations for middle-aged women living alone, the busy and responsible part of their lives being over. Drink. Gambling. Looking for another husband. A wistful affair or two. That's about it. Hetty went through a period of, as it were, testing out all these, like hobbies, but tired of them. While still earning her small wage as a saleswoman, she began a trade in buying and selling second-hand clothes. She did not have a shop of her own, but bought or begged clothes from householders, and sold these to stalls and the second-hand shops. She adored doing this. It was a passion. She gave up her respectable job and forgot all about her love of trains and travellers. Her room was always full of bright bits of cloth, a dress that had a pattern she fancied and did not want to sell, strips of beading, old furs, embroidery, lace. There were street traders among the people in the flats, but there was something in the way Hetty went about it that lost her friends. Neighbours of twenty or thirty years' standing said she had gone queer, and wished to know her no longer. But she did not mind. She was enjoying herself too much, particularly the moving about the streets with her old perambulator, in which she crammed what she was buying or selling. She liked the gossiping, the bargaining, the wheedling from householders. It was this last which—and she knew this quite well of course—the neighbours objected to. It was the thin edge of the wedge. It was begging. Decent people did not beg. She was no longer decent.

Lonely in her tiny flat, she was there as little as possible, always preferring the lively streets. But she had after all to spend some time in her room, and one day she saw a kitten lost and trembling in a dirty corner, and brought it home to the block of flats. She was on a fifth floor. While the kitten was growing into a large strong tom, he ranged about that conglomeration of staircases and lifts and many dozens of flats, as if the building were a town. Pets were not actively persecuted by the authorities, only forbidden and then tolerated. Hetty's life from the coming of the cat became more sociable, for the beast was always making friends with somebody in the cliff that was the block of flats across the court, or not coming home for nights at a time so that she had to go and look for him and knock on doors and ask, or returning home kicked and limping, or bleeding after a fight with his kind. She made scenes with the kickers, or the owners of the enemy cats, exchanged cat lore with cat-lovers, was always having to bandage and nurse her poor Tibby. The cat was soon a scarred warrior with fleas, a torn ear, and a ragged look to him. He was a multicoloured cat and his eyes were small and yellow. He was a long way down the scale from the delicately coloured, elegantly shaped pedigree cats. But he was independent, and often caught himself pigeons when he could no longer stand the tinned cat food, or the bread and packet gravy Hetty fed him, and he purred and nestled when she grabbed him to her bosom at those times she suffered loneliness. This happened less and less. Once she had realized that her children were hoping that she would leave them alone because the old rag-trader was an embarrassment to them, she accepted it, and a bitterness that always had wild humour in it welled up only at times like Christmas. She sang or chanted to the cat: "You nasty old beast, filthy old cat, nobody wants you, do they Tibby, no, you're just an alley tom, just an old stealing cat, hey Tibs, Tibs, Tibs."

The building teemed with cats. There were even a couple of dogs. They all fought up and down the grey cement corridors. There were sometimes dog and cat messes which someone had to clear up, but which might be left for days and weeks as part of neighbourly wars and feuds. There were many complaints. Finally an official came from the Council to say that the ruling about keeping animals was going to be enforced. Hetty, like the others, would have to have her cat destroyed. This crisis coincided with a time of bad luck for her. She had had flu; had not been able to earn money; had found it hard to get out for her pension; had run into debt. She owed a lot of back rent, too. A television set she had hired and was not paying for attracted the visits of a television representative. The neighbours were gossiping that Hetty had "gone savage." This was because the cat had brought up the stairs and along the passageways a pigeon he had caught, shedding feathers and blood all the way; a woman coming in to complain found Hetty plucking the pigeon to stew it, as she had done with others, sharing the meal with Tibby.

"You're filthy," she would say to him, setting the stew down to cool in his dish. "Filthy old thing. Eating that dirty old pigeon. What do you think you are, a wild cat? Decent cats don't eat dirty birds. Only those old gipsies eat wild birds."

One night she begged help from a neighbour who had a car, and put into the car herself, the television set, the cat, bundles of clothes and the pram. She was driven across London to a room in a street that was a slum because it was waiting to be done up. The neighbour made a second trip to bring her bed and her mattress, which were tied to the roof of the car, a chest of drawers, an old trunk, saucepans. It was in this way that she left the streets in which she had lived for thirty years, nearly half her life.

She set up house again in one room. She was frightened to go near "them" to re-establish pension rights and her identity, because of the arrears of rent she had left behind, and because of the stolen television set. She started trading again, and the little room was soon spread, like her last, with a rainbow of colours and textures and lace and sequins. She cooked on a single gas ring and washed in the sink. There was no hot water unless it was boiled in saucepans. There were several old ladies and a family of five children in the house, which was condemned.

She was in the ground-floor back, with a window which opened on to a derelict garden, and her cat was happy in a hunting ground that was a mile around this house where his mistress was so splendidly living. A canal ran close by, and in the dirty city-water were islands which a cat could reach by leaping from moored boat to boat. On the islands were rats and birds. There were pavements full of fat London pigeons. The cat was a fine hunter. He soon had his place in the hierarchies of the local cat population and did not have to fight much to keep it. He was a strong male cat, and fathered many litters of kittens.

In the place Hetty and he lived five happy years. She was trading well, for there were rich people close by to shed what the poor needed to buy cheaply. She was not lonely for she made a quarrelling but satisfying friendship with a woman on the top floor, a widow like herself who did not see her children either. Hetty was sharp with the five children, complaining about their noise and mess, but she slipped them bits of money and sweets after telling their mother that "she was a fool to put herself out for them, because they wouldn't appreciate it." She was living well, even without her pension. She sold the television set and gave herself and her friend upstairs some day-trips to the coast, and bought a small radio. She never read books or magazines. The truth was that she could not write or read, or only so badly it was no pleasure to her. Her cat was all reward and no cost, for he fed himself, and continued to bring in pigeons for her to cook and eat, for which in return he claimed milk.

"Greedy Tibby, you greedy *thing*, don't think I don't know, oh yes I do, you'll get sick eating those old pigeons, I do keep telling you that, don't I?"

At last the street was being done up. No longer a uniform, long, disgraceful slum, houses were being bought by the middle-class people. While this meant more good warm clothes for trading—or begging, for she still could not resist the attraction of getting something for nothing by the use of her plaintive inventive tongue, her still flashing handsome eyes—Hetty knew, like her neighbours, that soon this house with its cargo of poor people would be bought for improvement.

In the week Hetty was seventy years old came the notice that was the end of this little community. They had four weeks to find somewhere else to live.

Usually, the shortage of housing being what it is in London—and every-where else in the world, of course—these people would have had to scatter, fending for themselves. But the fate of this particular street was attracting attention, because a municipal election was pending. Homelessness among the poor was finding a focus in this street which was a perfect symbol of the whole area, and indeed the whole city, half of it being fine, converted, taste-ful houses, full of people who spent a lot of money, and half being dying houses tenanted by people like Hetty.

As a result of speeches by councillors and churchmen, local authorities found themselves unable to ignore the victims of this redevelopment. The peo-ple in the house Hetty was in were visited by a team consisting of an unem-ployment officer, a social worker and a rehousing officer. Hetty, a strong gaunt old woman wearing a scarlet wool suit she had found among her cast-offs that week, a black knitted tea-cosy on her head, and black-buttoned Edwardian boots too big for her, so that she had to shuffle, invited them into her room. But although all were well used to the extremes of poverty, none wished to enter the place, but stood in the doorway and made her this offer: that she should be aided to get her pension—why had she not claimed it long ago?—and that she, together with the four other old ladies in the houses should move to a Home run by the Council out in the northern suburbs. All these women were used to, and enjoyed, lively London, and while they had no alternative but to agree, they fell into a saddened and sullen state. Hetty agreed too. The last two winters had set her bones aching badly, and a cough was never far away. And while perhaps she was more of an urban soul even than the others, since she had walked up and down so many streets with her old perambulator loaded with rags and laces, and since she knew so intimately London's texture and taste, she minded least of all the idea of a new home "among green fields." There were, in fact, no fields near the promised Home, but for some reason all the old ladies had chosen to bring out this old song of a phrase, as if it belonged to their situation, that of old women not far off death. "It will be nice to be near green fields again," they said to each other over cups of tea.

The housing officer came to make final arrangements. Hetty Pennefather was to move with the others in two weeks' time. The young man, sitting on the very edge of the only chair in the crammed room, because it was greasy and he suspected it had fleas or worse in it, breathed as lightly as he could because of the appalling stink: there was a lavatory in the house, but it had been out of order for three days, and it was just the other side of a thin wall. The whole house smelled.

The young man, who knew only too well the extent of the misery due to lack of housing, who knew how many old people abandoned by their children did not get the offer to spend their days being looked after by the authorities, could not help feeling that this wreck of a human being could count herself lucky to get a place in his Home, even if it was—and he knew and deplored the fact—an institution in which the old were treated like naughty and dim-witted children until they had the good fortune to die.

But just as he was telling Hetty that a van would be coming to take her effects and those of the other four old ladies, and that she need not take anything more with her than her clothes "and perhaps a few photographs," he saw what he had thought was a heap of multicoloured rags get up and put its ragged gingery-black paws on the old woman's skirt. Which today was a cretonne curtain covered with pink and red roses that Hetty had pinned around her because she liked the pattern.

"You can't take that cat with you," he said automatically. It was something he had to say often, and knowing what misery the statement caused, he usually softened it down. But he had been taken by surprise.

Tibby now looked like a mass of old wool that had been matting together in dust and rain. One eye was permanently half-closed, because a muscle had been ripped in a fight. One ear was vestigial. And down a flank was a hairless slope with a thick scar on it. A cat-hating man had treated Tibby as he treated all cats, to a pellet from his airgun. The resulting wound had taken two years to heal. And Tibby smelled.

No worse, however, than his mistress, who sat stiffly still, bright-eyed with suspicion, hostile, watching the well-brushed tidy young man from the Council.

"How old is that beast?"

"Ten years, no, only eight years, he's a young cat about five years old," said Hetty, desperate.

"It looks as if you'd do him a favour to put him out of his misery," said the young man.

When the official left, Hetty had agreed to everything. She was the only one of the old women with a cat. The others had budgerigars or nothing. Budgies were allowed in the Home.

She made her plans, confided in the others, and when the van came for them and their clothes and photographs and budgies, she was not there, and they told lies for her. "Oh, we don't know where she can have gone, dear," the old women repeated again and again to the indifferent van-driver. "She was here last night, but she did say something about going to her daughter in Manchester." And off they went to die in the Home.

Hetty knew that when houses have been emptied for re-development they may stay empty for months, even years. She intended to go on living in this one until the builders moved in.

It was a warm autumn. For the first time in her life she lived like a gipsy forbear, and did not go to bed in a room in a house like respectable people. She spent several nights, with Tibby, sitting crouched in a doorway of an empty house two doors from her own. She knew exactly when the police would come around, and where to hide herself in the bushes of the over-grown shrubbery garden.

As she had expected, nothing happened in the house, and she moved back in. She smashed a back window-pane so that Tibby could move in and out without her having to unlock the front door for him, and without leaving a window suspiciously open. She moved to the top back room and left it every morning early, to spend the day in the streets with her pram and her rags. At night she kept a candle glimmering low down on the floor. The lavatory was still out of order, so she used a pail on the first floor instead, and secretly emptied it at night into the canal which in the day was full of pleasure boats and people fishing.

Tibby brought her several pigeons during that time.

"Oh, you are a clever puss, Tibby, Tibby! Oh, you're clever, you are. You know how things are, don't you, you know how to get around and about."

The weather turned very cold; Christmas came and went. Hetty's cough came back, and she spent most of her time under piles of blankets and old clothes, dozing. At night she watched the shadows of the candle flame on floor and ceiling—the window-frames fitted badly, and there was a draught. Twice tramps spent the night in the bottom of the house and she heard them being moved on by the police. She had to go down to make sure the police had not blocked up the broken window the cat used, but they had not. A blackbird had flown in and had battered itself to death trying to get out. She plucked it, and roasted it over a fire made with bits of floorboard in a bakingpan: the gas of course had been cut off. She had never eaten very much, and was not frightened that some dry bread and a bit of cheese was all that she had eaten during her sojourn under the heap of clothes. She was cold, but did not think about that much. Outside there was slushy brown snow everywhere. She went back to her nest, thinking that soon the cold spell would be over and she could get back to her trading. Tibby sometimes got into the pile with her, and she clutched the warmth of him to her. "Oh, you clever cat, you clever old thing, looking after yourself, aren't you? That's right, my ducky, that's right, my lovely."

And then, just as she was moving about again, with snow gone off the ground for a time but winter only just begun, in January, she saw a builder's van draw up outside, a couple of men unloading their gear. They did not come into the house: they were to start work next day. By then Hetty, her cat, her pram piled with clothes and her two blankets, were gone. She also took a box of matches, a candle, an old saucepan and a fork and spoon, a tin-opener and a rat-trap. She had a horror of rats.

About two miles way, among the homes and gardens of amiable Hampstead, where live so many of the rich, the intelligent and the famous, stood three empty, very large houses. She had seen them on an occasion, a couple of years before, when she had taken a bus. This was a rare thing for her, because of the remarks and curious looks provoked by her mad clothes, and by her being able to appear at the same time such a tough battling old thing, and a naughty child. For the older she got, this disreputable tramp, the more there strengthened in her a quality of fierce, demanding childishness. It was all too much of a mixture; she was uncomfortable to have near.

She was afraid that "they" might have rebuilt the houses, but there they still stood, too tumbledown and dangerous to be of much use to tramps, let alone the armies of London's homeless. There was no glass left anywhere. The flooring at ground level was mostly gone, leaving small platforms and juts of planking over basements full of water. The ceilings were crumbling. The roofs were going. The houses were like bombed buildings.

But in the cold dark of a late afternoon she pulled the pram up the broken stairs and moved cautiously around the frail boards of a second-floor room that had a great hole in it right down to the bottom of the house. Looking into it was like looking into a well. She held a candle to examine the state of the walls, here more or less whole, and saw that rain and wind blowing in from the window would leave one corner dry. Here she made her home. A sycamore tree screened the gaping window from the main road twenty yards away. Tibby, who was cramped after making the journey under the clothes piled in the pram, bounded down and out and vanished into neglected undergrowth to catch his supper. He returned fed and pleased, and seemed happy to stay clutched in her hard thin old arms. She had come to watch for his return after hunting trips, because the warm purring bundle of bones and fur did seem to allay, for a while, the permanent ache of cold in her bones.

Next day she sold her Edwardian boots for a few shillings—they were fashionable again—and bought a loaf and some bacon scraps. In a corner of the ruins well away from the one she had made her own, she pulled up some floorboards, built a fire, and toasted bread and the bacon scraps. Tibby had brought in a pigeon, and she roasted that, but not very efficiently. She was afraid of the fire catching and the whole mass going up in flames; she was afraid too, of the smoke showing and attracting the police. She had to keep damping down the fire, and so the bird was bloody and unappetizing and in the end Tibby got most of it. She felt confused, and discouraged, but thought it was because of the long stretch of winter still ahead of her before spring could come. In fact, she was ill. She made a couple of attempts to trade and earn money to feed herself before she acknowledged she was ill. She knew she was not yet dangerously ill, for she had been that in her life, and would have been able to recognize the cold listless indifference of a real last-ditch illness. But all her bones ached, and her head ached, and she coughed more than she ever had. Yet she still did not think of herself as suffering particularly from the cold, even in that sleety January weather. She had never, in all her life, lived in a properly heated place, had never known a really warm home, not even when she lived in the Council flats. Those flats had electric fires, and the family had never used them, for the sake of economy, except in very bad spells of cold. They piled clothes on to themselves, or went to bed early. But she did know that to keep herself from dying now she could not treat the cold with her usual indifference. She knew she must eat. In the comparatively dry corner of the windy room, away from the gaping window through which snow and sleet were drifting, she made another nest—her last. She had found a piece of polythene sheeting in the rubble, and she laid that down first, so that the damp would not strike up. Then she spread her two blankets over that. Over them were heaped the mass of old clothes. She wished she had another piece of polythene to put on top, but she used sheets of newspaper instead. She heaved herself into the middle of this, with a loaf of bread near to her hand. She dozed, and waited, and nibbled bits of bread, and watched the snow drifting softly in. Tibby sat close to the old blue face that poked out of the pile and put up a paw to touch it. He miaowed and was restless, and then went out into the frosty morning and brought in a pigeon. This the cat put, still struggling and fluttering a little, close to the old woman. But she was afraid to get out of the pile in which the heat was being made and kept with such difficulty. She really could not climb out long enough to pull up more splinters of plank from the floors, to make a fire, to pluck the pigeon, to roast it. She put out a cold hand to stroke the cat.

"Tibby, you old thing, you brought it for me, then, did you? You did, did you? Come here, come in here . . ." But he did not want to get in with her. He miaowed again, pushed the bird closer to her. It was now limp and dead.

"You have it, then. You eat it. I'm not hungry, thank you, Tibby."

But the carcass did not interest him. He had eaten a pigeon before bringing this one up to Hetty. He fed himself well. In spite of his matted fur, and his scars and his half-closed yellow eye, he was a strong, healthy cat.

At about four the next morning there were steps and voices downstairs. Hetty shot out of the pile and crouched behind a fallen heap of plaster and beams, now covered with snow, at the end of the room near the window. She could see through the hole in the floorboards down to the first floor, which had collapsed entirely, and through it to the ground floor. She saw a man in a thick overcoat and muffler and leather gloves holding a strong torch to illuminate a thin bundle of clothes lying on the floor. She saw that this bundle was a sleeping man or woman. She was afraid because she had not been aware of this other tenant of the ruin. Had he, or she, heard her talking to the cat? And where was the cat? If he wasn't careful he could be caught, and that would be the end of him! The man with a torch went off and came back with a second man. In the thick dark far below Hetty, was a small cave of strong light, which was the torchlight. In this space of light two men bent to lift the bundle, which was the corpse of a man or a woman like Hetty. They carried it across the danger-traps of fallen and rotting boards that made gangplanks over the water-filled basement. One man was holding the torch in the hand that supported the dead person's feet, and the light jogged and lurched over trees and grasses: the corpse was being taken through the shrubberies to a car.

There are men in London who, between the hours of two and five in the morning, when the real citizens are asleep, who should not be disturbed by such unpleasantness as the corpses of the poor, make the rounds of all the empty, rotting houses they know about, to collect the dead, and to warn the living that they ought not to be there at all, inviting them to one of the official Homes or lodgings for the homeless.

Hetty was too frightened to get back into her warm heap. She sat with the blankets pulled around her, and looked through gaps in the fabric of the house, making out shapes and boundaries and holes and puddles and mounds of rubble, as her eyes, like her cat's, became accustomed to the dark.

She heard scuffling sounds and they were rats. She had meant to set the trap, but the thought of her friend Tibby, who might catch his paw, had stopped her. She sat up until the morning light came in grey and cold, after nine. Now she did know herself to be very ill and in danger, for she had lost all the warmth she had huddled into her bones under the rags. She shivered violently. She was shaking herself apart with shivering. In between spasms she drooped limp and exhausted. Through the ceiling above her—but it was not a ceiling, only a cobweb of slats and planks—she could see into a dark cave which had been a garret, and through the roof above that, the grey sky, teeming with incipient rain. The cat came back from where he had been hiding, and sat crouched on her knees, keeping her stomach warm, while she thought out her position. These were her last clear thoughts. She told herself that she would not last out until spring unless she allowed "them" to find her, and take her to hospital. After that, she would be taken to a Home.

But what would happen to Tibby, her poor cat? She rubbed the old beast's scruffy head with the ball of her thumb and muttered: "Tibby, Tibby, they won't get you, no, you'll be all right, yes, I'll look after you."

Towards midday, the sun oozed yellow through miles of greasy grey cloud, and she staggered down the rotting stairs, to the shops. Even in those London Streets, where the extraordinary had become usual, people turned to stare at a tall gaunt woman, with a white face that had flaming red patches on it, and blue compressed lips, and restless black eyes. She wore a tightly buttoned man's overcoat, torn brown woollen mittens, and an old fur hood. She pushed a pram loaded with old dresses and scraps of embroidery and torn jerseys and shoes, all stirred into a tight tangle, and she kept pushing this pram up against people as they stood in queues, or gossiped, or stared into windows, and she muttered: "Give me your old clothes, darling, give me your old pretties, give Hetty something, poor Hetty's hungry." A woman gave her a handful of small change, and Hetty bought a roll filled with tomato and lettuce. She did not dare go into a café, for even in her confused state she knew she would offend, and would probably be asked to leave. But she begged a cup of tea at a street stall, and when the hot sweet liquid flooded through her she felt she might survive the winter. She bought a carton of milk and pushed the pram back through the slushy snowy street to the ruins.

Tibby was not there. She urinated down through the hole in the boards, muttering, "A nuisance, that old tea," and wrapped herself in a blanket and waited for the dark to come.

Tibby came in later. He had blood on his foreleg. She had heard scuffling and she knew that he had fought a rat, or several, and had been bitten. She poured the milk into the tilted saucepan and Tibby drank it all.

She spent the night with the animal held against her chilly bosom. They did not sleep, but dozed off and on. Tibby would normally be hunting, the night was his time, but he had stayed with the old woman now for three nights.

Early next morning they again heard the corpse-removers among the rubble on the ground floor, and saw the beams of the torch moving on wet walls and collapsed beams. For a moment the torchlight was almost straight on Hetty, but no one came up: who could believe that a person could be desperate enough to climb those dangerous stairs, to trust those crumbling splintery floors, and in the middle of winter?

Hetty had now stopped thinking of herself as ill, of the degrees of her illness, of her danger—of the impossibility of her surviving. She had cancelled out in her mind the presence of winter and its lethal weather, and it was as if spring were nearly here. She knew that if it had been spring when she had had to leave the other house, she and the cat could have lived here for months and months, quite safely and comfortable. Because it seemed to her an impossible and even a silly thing that her life, or, rather, her death, could depend on something so arbitrary as builders starting work on a house in January rather than in April, she could not believe it: the fact would not stay in her mind. The day before she had been quite clear-headed. But today her thoughts were cloudy, and she talked and laughed aloud. Once she scrambled up and rummaged in her rags for an old Christmas card she had got four years before from her good daughter. In a hard harsh angry grumbling voice she said to her four children that she needed a room of her own now that she was getting on. "I've been a good mother to you," she shouted to them before invisible witnesses—former neighbours, welfare workers, a doctor. "I never let you want for anything, never! When you were little you always had the best of everything! You can ask anybody, go on, ask them then!"

She was restless and made such a noise that Tibby left her and bounded on to the pram and crouched watching her. He was limping, and his foreleg was rusty with blood. The rat had bitten deep. When the daylight came, he left Hetty in a kind of a sleep, and went down into the garden where he saw a pigeon feeding on the edge of the pavement. The cat pounced on the bird, dragged it into the bushes, and ate it all, without taking it up to his mistress. After he had finished eating, he stayed hidden, watching the passing people. He stared at them intently with his blazing yellow eye, as if he were thinking, or planning. He did not go into the old ruin and up the crumbling wet stairs until late—it was as if he knew it was not worth while going at all.

He found Hetty, apparently asleep, wrapped loosely in a blanket, propped sitting in a corner. Her head had fallen on her chest, and her quantities of white hair had escaped from a scarlet woollen cap, and concealed a face that was flushed a deceptive pink—the flush of coma from cold. She was not yet dead, but she died that night. The rats came up the walls and along the planks and the cat fled down and away from them, limping still, into the bushes.

Hetty was not found for a couple of weeks. The weather changed to warm, and the man whose job it was to look for corpses was led up the dangerous stairs by the smell. There was something left of her, but not much.

As for the cat, he lingered for two or three days in the thick shrubberies, watching the passing people and beyond them, the thundering traffic of the main road. Once a couple stopped to talk on the pavement, and the cat, seeing two pairs of legs, moved out and rubbed himself against one of the legs. A hand came down and he was stroked and patted for a little. Then the people went away.

The cat saw he would not find another home, and he moved off, nosing and feeling his way from one garden to another, through empty houses finally into an old churchyard. This graveyard already had a couple of stray cats in it, and he joined them. It was the beginning of a community of stray cats

going wild. They killed birds, and the field mice that lived among the grasses, and they drank from puddles. Before winter had ended the cats had had a
hard time of it from thirst, during the two long spells when the ground froze
and there was snow and no puddles and the birds were hard to catch because
the cats were so easy to see against the clean white. But on the whole they
managed quite well. One of the cats was a female, and soon there were a
swarm of wild cats, as wild as if they did not live in the middle of a city surrounded by streets and houses. This was just one of half a dozen communities of wild cats living in that square mile of London.

Then an official came to trap the cats and take them away. Some of them
escaped, hiding till it was safe to come back again. But Tibby was caught. Not
only was he getting old and stiff—he still limped from the rat's bite—but he
was friendly, and did not run away from the man, who had only to pick him
up in his arms.

"You're an old soldier, aren't you?" said the man. "A real tough one, a real
old tramp."

It is possible that the cat even thought that he might be finding another
human friend and a home.

But it was not so. The haul of wild cats that week numbered hundreds,
and while if Tibby had been younger a home might have been found for him,
since he was amiable, and wished to be liked by the human race, he was really too old, and smelly and battered. So they gave him an injection and, as we
say, "put him to sleep."

Grace Paley

(1922-   )

Like Cynthia Ozick, Kate Simon, and Vivian Gornick, Grace Paley is a child of the Bronx, where she grew up in a socialist family of Jewish immigrants from Russia. A lifelong political activist on behalf of peace and justice, Paley has lived true to her roots. Her belief that politics, morality, and religion cannot be separated calls to mind the voice of the Hebrew Bible's prophets as well as Jonathan Swift's, though Paley's indignation about injustice never comes across as savage. Her short stories, *The Little Disturbances of Man* (1959), *Enormous Changes at the Last Minute* (1974), *Later the Same Day* (1985), and her nonfiction, *Just as I Thought* (1988), from which "Traveling" is taken, reflect the moral foundation of her vision. In her own words, "I don't see any reason in being in this world actually if you can't in some way be better, repair it somehow . . . to be like all the other nations seems to me a waste of . . . energy, and a waste of life." In *The End of the Novel of Love*, Vivian Gornick articulates the effect of Paley's generous art: "All over the would, in languages you never heard of, she is read as a master storyteller in the great tradition: people love life more because of her writing."

Samuel

Some boys are very tough. They're afraid of nothing. They are the ones who climb a wall and take a bow at the top. Not only are they brave on the roof, but they make a lot of noise in the darkest part of the cellar where even the super hates to go. They also jiggle and hop on the platform between the locked doors of the subway cars.

Four boys are jiggling on the swaying platform. Their names are Alfred, Calvin, Samuel, and Tom. The men and the women in the cars on either side watch them. They don't like them to jiggle or jump but don't want to interfere. Of course some of the men in the cars were once brave boys like these. One of them had ridden the tail of a speeding truck from New York to Rockaway Beach without getting off, without his sore fingers losing hold. Nothing happened to him then or later. He had made a compact with other boys who preferred to watch: Starting at Eighth Avenue and Fifteenth Street, he would get to some specified place, maybe Twenty-third and the river, by hopping the tops of the moving trucks. This was hard to do when one truck turned a corner in the wrong direction and the nearest truck was a couple of feet too high. He made three or four starts before succeeding. He had gotten this idea from a film at school called *The Romance of Logging.* He had finished high school, married a good friend, was in a responsible job and going to night school.

These two men and others looked at the four boys jumping and jiggling on the platform and thought, It must be fun to ride that way, especially now the weather is nice and we're out of the tunnel and way high over the Bronx. Then they thought, These kids do seem to be acting sort of stupid. They *are* little. Then they thought of some of the brave things they had done when they were boys and jiggling didn't seem so risky.

The ladies in the car became very angry when they looked at the four boys. Most of them brought their brows together and hoped the boys could see their extreme disapproval. One of the ladies wanted to get up and say, Be careful you dumb kids, get off that platform or I'll call a cop. But three of the boys were Negroes and the fourth was something else she couldn't tell for sure. She was afraid they'd be fresh and laugh at her and embarrass her. She wasn't afraid they'd hit her, but she was afraid of embarrassment. Another lady thought, Their mothers never know where they are. It wasn't true in this particular case. Their mothers knew that they had gone to see the missile exhibit on Fourteenth Street.

Out on the platform, whenever the train accelerated, the boys would raise their hands and point them up to the sky to act like rockets going off, then they rat-rat-tatted the shatterproof glass pane like machine guns, although no machine guns had been exhibited.

For some reason known only to the motorman, the train began a sudden slowdown. The lady who was afraid of embarrassment saw the boys jerk forward and backward and grab the swinging guard chains. She had her own boy at home. She stood up with determination and went to the door. She slid it open and said, "You boys will be hurt. You'll be killed. I'm going to call the conductor if you don't just go into the next car and sit down and be quiet."

Two of the boys said, "Yes'm," and acted as though they were about to go. Two of them blinked their eyes a couple of times and pressed their lips together. The train resumed its speed. The door slid shut, parting the lady and the boys. She leaned against the side door because she had to get off at the next stop.

The boys opened their eyes wide at each other and laughed. The lady blushed. The boys looked at her and laughed harder. They began to pound each other's back. Samuel laughed the hardest and pounded Alfred's back until Alfred coughed and the tears came. Alfred held tight to the chain hook. Samuel pounded him even harder when he saw the tears. He said, "Why you bawling? You a baby, huh?" and laughed. One of the men whose boyhood had been more watchful than brave became angry. He stood up straight and looked at the boys for a couple of seconds. Then he walked in a citizenly way to the end of the car, where he pulled the emergency cord. Almost at once, with a terrible hiss, the pressure of air abandoned the brakes and the wheels were caught and held.

People standing in the most secure places fell forward, then backward. Samuel had let go of his hold on the chain so he could pound Tom as well as Alfred. All the passengers in the cars whipped back and forth, but he pitched only forward and fell head first to be crushed and killed between the cars.

The train had stopped hard, halfway into the station, and the conductor called at once for the trainmen who knew about this kind of death and how to take the body from the wheels and brakes. There was silence except for passengers from other cars who asked, What happened! What happened! The ladies waited around wondering if he might be an only child. The men recalled other afternoons with very bad endings. The little boys stayed close to each other, leaning and touching shoulders and arms and legs.

When the policeman knocked at the door and told her about it, Samuel's mother began to scream. She screamed all day and moaned all night, though the doctors tried to quiet her with pills.

Oh, oh, she hopelessly cried. She did not know how she could ever find another boy like that one. However, she was a young woman and she became pregnant. Then for a few months she was hopeful. The child born to her was a boy. They brought him to be seen and nursed. She smiled. But immediately she saw that this baby wasn't Samuel. She and her husband together have had other children, but never again will a boy exactly like Samuel be known.

—

Traveling

My mother and sister were traveling south. The year was 1927. They had begun their journey in New York. They were going to visit my brother, who was studying in the South Medical College of Virginia. Their bus was an express and had stopped only in Philadelphia, Wilmington, and now Washington. Here, the darker people who had gotten on in Philadelphia or New York rose from their seats, put their bags and boxes together, and moved to the back of the bus. People who boarded in Washington knew where to seat themselves. My mother had heard that something like this would happen. My sister had heard of it, too. They had not lived in it. This reorganization of passengers by color happened in silence. My mother and sister remained in their seats, which were about three-quarters of the way back.

When everyone was settled, the bus driver began to collect tickets. My sister saw him coming. She pinched my mother: Ma! Look! Of course, my mother saw him, too. What frightened my sister was the quietness. The white people in front, the black people in back—silent.

The driver sighed, said, You can't sit here, ma'am. It's for them, waving over his shoulder at the Negroes, among whom they were now sitting. Move, please.

My mother said, No.

He said, You don't understand, ma'am. It's against the law. You have to move to the front.

My mother said, No.

When I first tried to write this scene, I imagined my mother saying, That's all right, mister, we're comfortable. I can't change my seat every minute. I read this invention to my sister. She said it was nothing like that. My mother did not try to be friendly or pretend innocence. While my sister trembled in the silence, my mother said, for the third time, quietly, No.

Somehow finally, they were in Richmond. There was my brother in school among so many American boys. After hugs and my mother's anxious looks at her young son, my sister said, Vic, you know what Mama did?

My brother remembers thinking, What? Oh! She wouldn't move? He had a classmate, a Jewish boy like himself, but from Virginia, who had had a public confrontation with a Negro man. He had punched that man hard, knocked him down. My brother couldn't believe it. He was stunned. He couldn't imagine a Jewish boy wanting to knock anyone down. He had never wanted to. But he thought, looking back, that he had been set down to work and study in a nearly foreign place and had to get used to it. Then he told me about the Second World War, when the disgrace of black soldiers being forced to sit behind white German POWs shook him. Shamed him.

About fifteen years later, in 1943, in early summer, I rode the bus for about three days from New York to Miami Beach, where my husband in sweaty fatigues, along with hundreds of other boys, was trudging up and down the streets and beaches to prepare themselves for war.

By late afternoon of the second long day, we were well into the South, beyond Richmond, maybe South Carolina or Georgia. My excitement about travel in the wide world was damaged a little by a sudden fear that I might not recognize Jess or he, me. We hadn't seen each other for two months. I took a photograph out of my pocket; yes, I would know him.

I had been sleeping walking reading writing dozing waking. So many hours, the movement of the passengers was something like a tide that sometimes ebbed and now seemed to be noisily rising. I opened my eyes to the sound of new people brushing past my aisle seat. And looked up to see a colored woman holding a large sleeping baby, who, with the heaviness of sleep, his arms so tight around her neck, seemed to be pulling her head down. I looked around and noticed that I was in the last white row. The press of travelers had made it impossible for her to move farther back. She seemed so tired and I had been sitting and sitting for a day and a half at least. Not thinking, or maybe refusing to think, I offered her my seat.

She looked to the right and left as well as she could. Softly she said, Oh no. I became fully awake. A white man was standing right beside her, but on the other side of the invisible absolute racial border. Of course, she couldn't accept my seat. Her sleeping child hung mercilessly from her neck. She shifted a little to balance the burden. She whispered to herself, Oh, I just don't know. So I said, Well, at least give me the baby. First, she turned, barely looking at the man beside her. He made no move. So, to my surprise, but obviously out of sheer exhaustion, she disengaged the child from her body and placed him on my lap. He was deep in child-sleep. He stirred, but not enough to bother himself or me. I liked holding him, aligning him along my twenty-year-old young woman's shape. I thought ahead to that holding, that breathing together that would happen in my life if this war would ever end.

I was so comfortable under his nice weight. I closed my eyes for a couple of minutes, but suddenly opened them to look up into the face of a white man talking. In a long voice he addressed me: Lady, I wouldn't of touched that thing with a meat hook.

I thought, Oh, this world will end in ice. I could do nothing but look straight into his eyes. I did not look away from him. Then I held that boy a little tighter, kissed his curly head, pressed him even closer so that he began to squirm. So sleepy, he reshaped himself inside my arms. His mother tried to narrow herself away from that dangerous border, too frightened at first to move at all. After a couple of minutes, she leaned forward a little, placed her hand on the baby's head, and held it there until the next stop. I couldn't look up into her mother face.

I write this remembrance more than fifty years later. I look back at that mother and child. How young she is. Her hand on his head is quite small, though she tries by spreading her fingers wide to hide him from the white man. But the child I'm holding, his little face as he turns toward me, is the brown face of my own grandson, my daughter's boy, the open mouth of the sleeper, the full lips, the thick little body of a child who runs wildly from one end of the yard to the other, leaps from dangerous heights with certain experienced caution, muscling his body, his mind, for coming realities.

Of course, when my mother and sister returned from Richmond, the family at home wanted to know: How was Vic doing in school among all those gentiles? Was the long bus ride hard, was the anti-Semitism really bad or just normal? What happened on the bus? I was probably present at that supper, the attentive listener and total forgetter of information that immediately started to form me.

Then last year, my sister, casting the net of old age (through which recent experience easily slips), brought up that old story. First I was angry. How come you never told me about your bus ride with Mama? I mean, really, so many years ago.

I don't know, she said, anyway you were only about four years old, and besides, maybe I did.

I asked my brother why we'd never talked about that day. He said he thought now that it had had a great effect on him; he had tried unraveling its meaning for years—then life family work happened. So I imagined him, a youngster really, a kid from the Bronx in Virginia in 1927; why, he was a stranger there himself.

In the next couple of weeks, we continued to talk about our mother, the way she was principled, adamant, and at the same time so shy. What else could we remember . . . Well, I said, I have a story about those buses, too. Then I told it to them: How it happened on just such a journey, when I was still quite young, that I first knew my grandson, first held him close, but could protect him for only about twenty minutes fifty years ago.

Marie Ponsot

(1922-   )

When at the age of seventy-seven Marie Ponsot won the National Book Critics Circle Award in poetry for her latest collection, *The Bird Catcher*, questions were raised about why recognition had taken so long to come her way. *True Minds*, the first of her four volumes of poetry, was published by City Lights Books in San Francisco in 1957 by her friend Lawrence Ferlinghetti. What transpired between this debut and her next book, *Admit Impediment* (1981), was the birth of her seven children, whom she supported (she was divorced in 1970) as a teacher at various universities, a translator of thirty-seven books from French to English, and a writer of radio and television scripts (though she didn't have a TV). Born and raised in Queens, New York City, she grew up in a Catholic family. Catholicism, she says, "is sort of like a club you can't resign from, but anyone can get in." Her poetry has received numerous awards and praise from other poets: Carolyn Kizer calls her a poet of "elegance, not only of thought and craft but spiritual elegance as well." Writing about *The Bird Catcher*, from which the following poems are taken, Irish poet Eavan Boland notes its "delicate ambition and powerful insistence. . . . but the central preoccupation of this book . . . is the life of feeling."

One Is One

Heart, you bully, you punk, I'm wrecked, I'm shocked
stiff. You? you still try to rule the world—though
I've got you: identified, starving, locked
in a cage you will not leave alive, no
matter how you hate it, pound its walls,
& thrill its corridors with messages.

Brute. Spy. I trusted you. Now you reel & brawl
in your cell but I'm deaf to your rages,
your greed to go solo, your eloquent
threats of worse things you (knowing me) could do.
You scare me, bragging you're a double agent

since jailers are prisoners' prisoners too.
Think! Reform! Make us one. Join the rest of us,
and joy may come, and make its test of us.

The Story After the Story

In bubbles to the elbow, on my knees,
I am washing children. You are laughing,
pleased to observe me at my mysteries.

Antoine & Will giggle as I sluice their backs.
My knees soaked by local tidal splashes
creak as I stand and towel two relaxed

bed-ready boys. I crib them, warm in their
soft shirts, & sit to eat a bruised sweet apple
as I nurse Chris and float on mild air

a story for everyone; Monique & Denis
settle on child-chairs; we are a tangle,
bitch and pups, in the oldest comity.

You like that less, leave us for the kitchen
to finish the fruit and cheese. The ample
story falls short on me. My mind itches.

Sighing & smiling Antoine drops to sleep.
Will lies awake, only his eyes active.
Monique trusts the story somehow to keep

mapping new ways home through more & more world.
Chris drowses. Will's eyelids lift up, lapse back.
Denis' fists lie in his lap, loosely curled.

Foreign Correspondent

(For Margaret Fuller, drowned in a shipwreck just off Fire Island, July 1850)

Margaret, always at Fire Island
I swim with you in mind,

you afraid of the sea
you ended in and as—
your neckbones chalk,
the lime of your kneecap
gone to the lobsterclaw,
and in the buoyant embrace
of saltwater, your blent chemistry.
When sandbars shift on the seafloor
they disturb your locked seachest,
its lumpy key, the victory medals
of your husband whose luck
fell just short of this shore.

Gothic at fifteen, I liked to pretend
I might find your lockbox
and dove and dove to explore
off the beach where storm-force sank you
and the bubble of your hope broke free
drowning your politics in metaphor.

I still pretend to sense you here, no ghost,
my elbows & nose out in the air of your urgency.

As the undertow makes itself felt I gulp breath
and swim harder against your destiny
riding the slipstream of your working changes
groping for the good inshore current,
my thoughts flawed but full of your prose
eager angry speculative.

A kickturn, & I check the beach-line
you likely saw flare-lit. Now
the summer waves are soft
as your lake-summer days
with Indian women, you gesturing
toward the amity common among them,
holding a baby, a shawl,
your account of this long out of print,
your histories drowned in their only versions.

I peel myself upright
out of your warm element
and walk the sand where Thoreau
all that next day went rushing
scouring the seawrack for signs,
your reticule, the sea-chest
of manuscripts, a word
from any who'd seen you.

Staring without finding, he began
to be able to think what to do,
could do nothing, gave up, and
crossed back to the mainland
over the water
glittering in the windwash
transcendent with afterstorm.

Nadine Gordimer

(1923-   )

South African writer Nadine Gordimer, the daughter of a British mother and Jewish father, grew up outside Johannesburg, the setting of her first novel, *The Lying Days* (1953). Though her eight novels, including *A Guest of Honour* (1970), *The Conservationist* (1974), *Burger's Daughter* (1979), and *July's People* (1981), have received more attention than her seven volumes of short stories, she is considered "certainly one of the half-dozen best story writers in English today," according to the *Observer*. Set mostly in South Africa, much of her fiction represents an unsentimental dissection of the personal and political devastation caused by apartheid, the system that denied native Africans their civil and human rights. For their incisive indictment of the moral failure inherent in this system, many of her books were banned in her native country. Elizabeth Hardwick praised the body of Gordimer's work as "one of the major artistic achievements of our time." Respected in her homeland for the professional help she has given to black writers, Gordimer is a founding member of the Congress of South African Writers as well as a member of the African National Congress. She was awarded the Nobel Prize for literature in 1991.

Something for the Time Being

He thought of it as discussing things with her, but the truth was that she did not help him out at all. She said nothing, while she ran her hand up the ridge of bone behind the rim of her child-sized yellow-brown ear, and raked her fingers tenderly into her hairline along the back of her neck as if feeling out some symptom in herself. Yet her listening was very demanding; when he stopped at the end of a supposition or a suggestion, her silence made the stop inconclusive. He had to take up again what he had said, carry it—where?

"Ve vant to give you a tsance, but you von't let us," he mimicked; and made a loud glottal click, half-angry, resentfully amused. He knew it wasn't because Kalzin Brothers were Jews that he had lost his job at last, but just because he had lost it, Mr. Solly's accent suddenly presented to him the irresistibly vulnerable. He had come out of prison nine days before, after spending three months as an awaiting-trial prisoner in a political case that had just been quashed—he was one of those who would not accept bail. He had been in prison three or four times since 1952; his wife Ella and the Kalzin Brothers were used to it. Until now, his employers had always given him his job back when he came out. They were importers of China and glass and he was head packer in a team of black men who ran the dispatch department. "Well, what the hell, I'll get something else," he said. "Hey?"

She stopped the self-absorbed examination of the surface of her skin for a slow moment and shrugged, looking at him.

He smiled.

Her gaze loosened hold like hands falling away from grasp. The ends of her nails pressed at small imperfections in the skin of her neck. He drank his tea and tore off pieces of bread to dip in it; then he noticed the tin of sardines she had opened and sopped up the pale matrix of oil in which ragged flecks of silver were suspended. She offered him more tea, without speaking.

They lived in one room of a decent, three-roomed house belonging to someone else; it was better for her that way, since he was often likely to have to be away for long stretches. She worked in a factory that made knitted socks; there was no one at home to look after their one child, a girl, and the child lived with a grandmother in a dusty, peaceful village a day's train-journey from the city.

He said, dismissing it as of no importance, "I wonder what chance they meant? You can imagine. I don't suppose they were going to give me an office with my name on it." He spoke as if she would appreciate the joke. She had known when she married him that he was a political man; she had been proud of him because he didn't merely want something for himself, like the other young men she knew, but everything, and for *the people*. It had excited her, under his influence, to change her awareness of herself as a young black girl to awareness of herself as belonging to the people. She knew that everything wasn't like something—a hand-out, a wangled privilege, a trinket you could hold. She would never get something from him.

Her hand went on searching over her skin as if it must come soon, come anxiously, to the flaw, the sickness, the evidence of what was wrong with her; for on this Saturday afternoon all these things that she knew had deserted her. She had lost her wits. All that she could understand was the one room, the child growing up far away in the mud house, and the fact that you couldn't keep a job if you kept being away from work for weeks at a time.

"I think I'd better look up Flora Donaldson," he said. Flora Donaldson was a white woman who had set up an office to help political prisoners. "Sooner the better. Perhaps she'll dig up something for me by Monday. It's the beginning of the month."

He got on all right with those people. Ella had met Flora Donaldson once; she was a pretty white woman who looked just like any white woman who would automatically send a black face round to the back door, but she didn't seem to know that she was white and you were black.

He pulled the curtain that hung across one corner of the room and took out his suit. It was a thin suit, of the kind associated with holidaymakers in American clothing advertisements, and when he was dressed in it, with a sharp-brimmed grey hat tilted slightly back on his small head, he looked a wiry, boyish figure, rather like one of those boy-men who sing and shake before a microphone, and whose clothes admirers try to touch as a talisman.

He kissed her good-bye, obliging her to put down, the lowering of a defence, the piece of sewing she held. She had cleared away the dishes from the table and set up the sewing-machine, and he saw that the shapes of cut material that lay on the table were the parts of a small girl's dress.

She spoke suddenly. "And when the next lot gets tired of you?"

"When that lot gets tired of me, I'll get another job again, that's all."

She nodded, very slowly, and her hand crept back to her neck.

"Who was that?" Madge Chadders asked.

Her husband had been out into the hall to answer the telephone.

"Flora Donaldson. I wish you'd explain to these people exactly what sort of factory I've got. It's so embarrassing. She's trying to find a job for some chap, he's a skilled packer. There's no skilled packing done in my workshop, no skilled jobs at all done by black men. What on earth can I offer the fellow? She says he's desperate and anything will do."

Madge had the broken pieces of a bowl on a newspaper spread on the Persian carpet. "Mind the glue, darling! There, just next to your foot. Well, anything is better than nothing. I suppose it's someone who was in the Soganiland sedition case. Three months awaiting trial taken out of their lives, and now they're chucked back to fend for themselves."

William Chadders had not had any black friends or mixed with coloured people on any but master-servant terms until he married Madge, but his views on the immorality and absurdity of the colour bar were sound; sounder, she often felt, than her own, for they were backed by the impersonal authority of a familiarity with the views of great thinkers, saints and philosophers, with history, political economy, sociology and anthropology. She knew only what she felt. And she always did something, at once, to express what she felt. She never measured the smallness of her personal protest against the establishment she opposed; she marched with Flora and eight hundred black women in a demonstration against African woman being forced to carry passes; outside the university where she had once been a student, she stood between sandwich-boards bearing messages of mourning because a Bill had been passed closing the university, for the future, to all but white students; she had living in the house for three months a young African who wanted to write and hadn't the peace or space to get on with it in a location. She did not stop to consider the varying degrees of usefulness of the things she did, and if others pointed this out to her and suggested that she might make up her mind to throw her weight on the side either of politics or philanthropy, she was not resentful but answered candidly that there was so little it was possible to do that she simply took any and every chance to get off her chest her disgust at the colour bar. When she had married William Chadders, her friends had thought that her protestant activities would stop; they underestimated not only Madge, but also William, who, although he was a wealthy businessman, subscribed to the view of absolute personal freedom as strictly as any bohemian. Besides he was not fool enough to want to change in any way the person who had enchanted him just as she was.

She reacted upon him, rather than he upon her; she, of course, would not hesitate to go ahead and change anybody. (But why not? she would have said, astonished. If it's to the good?) The attitude she sought to change would occur to her as something of independent existence, she would not see it as a cell in the organism of personality, whose whole structure would have to regroup itself round the change. She had the boldness of being unaware of these consequences.

William did not carry a banner in the streets, of course; he worked up there, among his first principles and historical precedents and economic necessities, but now they were translated from theory to practice of an anonymous, large-scale and behind-the-scenes sort—he was the brains and part of the money in a scheme to get Africans some economic power besides consumer power, through the setting up of an all-African trust company and investment corporation. A number of Madge's political friends, both white and black (like her activities, her friends were mixed, some political, some do-gooders), thought this was putting the middle-class cart before the proletarian horse, but most of the African leaders welcomed the attempt as an essential backing to popular movements on other levels—something to count on outside the unpredictability of mobs. Sometimes it amused Madge to think that William, making a point at a meeting in a boardroom, fifteen floors above life in the streets, might achieve in five minutes something of more value than she did in all her days of turning her hand to anything—from sorting old clothes to roneo-ing a manifesto or driving people during a bus boycott. Yet this did not knock the meaning out of her own life, for her; she knew that she had to see, touch and talk to people in order to care about them, that's all there was to it.

Before she and her husband dressed to go out that evening she finished sticking together the broken Chinese bowl and showed it to him with satisfaction. To her, it was whole again. But it was one of a set, that had belonged together, and whose unity had illustrated certain philosophical concepts. William had bought them long ago, in London; for him, the whole set was damaged for ever.

He said nothing to her, but he was thinking of the bowls when she said to him as they drove off, "Will you see that chap, on Monday, yourself?"

He changed gear deliberately, attempting to follow her out of his preoccupation. But she said, "The man Flora's sending. What was his name?"

He opened his hand on the steering wheel, indicating that the name escaped him.

"See him yourself?"

"I'll have to leave it to the works manager to find something for him to do," he said.

"Yes, I know. But see him yourself, too?"

Her anxious voice made him feel very fond of her. He turned and smiled at her suspiciously. "Why?"

She was embarrassed at his indulgent manner. She said, frank and wheedling, "Just to show him. You know. That you know about him and it's not much of a job."

"All right," he said. "I'll see him myself."

He met her in town straight from the office on Monday and they went to the opening of an exhibition of paintings and on to dinner and to see a play, with friends. He had not been home at all, until they returned after midnight. It was a summer night and they sat for a few minutes on their terrace, where it was still mild with the warmth of the day's sun coming from the walls in the darkness, and drank lime juice and water to quench the thirst that wine and the stuffy theatre had given them. Madge made gasps and groans of pleasure at the release from the pressures of company and noise. Then she lay quiet for a while, her voice lifting now and then in fragments of unrelated comment on the evening—the occasional chirp of a bird that has already put its head under its wing for the night.

By the time they went in, they were free of the evening. Her black dress, her ear-rings and her bracelets felt like fancy-dress; she shed the character and sat on the bedroom carpet, and, passing her, he said, "Oh—that chap of Flora's came today, but I don't think he'll last. I explained to him that I didn't have the sort of job he was looking for."

"Well, that's all right, then," she said enquiringly. "What more could you do?"

"Yes," he said, deprecating. "But I could see he didn't like the idea much. It's a cleaner's job; nothing for him. He's an intelligent chap. I didn't like having to offer it to him."

She was moving about her dressing table, piling out upon it the contents of her handbag. "Then I'm sure he'll understand. It'll give him something for the time being, anyway, darling. You can't help it if you don't need the sort of work he does."

"Huh, he won't last. I could see that. He accepted it, but only with his head. He'll get fed up. Probably won't turn up tomorrow. I had to speak to him about his Congress button, too. The works manager came to me."

"What about his Congress button?" she said.

He was unbuttoning his shirt and his eyes were on the unread evening paper that lay folded on the bed. "He was wearing one," he said inattentively.

"I know, but what did you have to speak to him about it for?"

"He was wearing it in the workshop all day."

"Well, what about it?" She was sitting at her dressing-table, legs spread, as if she had sat heavily and suddenly. She was not looking at him, but at her own face.

He gave the paper a push and drew his pyjamas from under the pillow. Vulnerable and naked, he said authoritatively, "You can't wear a button like that among the men in the workshop."

"Good heavens," she said, almost in relief, laughing, backing away from the edge of tension, chivvying him out of a piece of stuffiness. "And why can't you?"

"You can't have someone clearly representing a political organization like Congress."

"But he's not there *representing* anything, he's there as a workman?" Her mouth was still twitching with something between amusement and nerves.

"Exactly."

"Then why can't he wear a button that signifies his allegiance to an organization in his private life outside the workshop? There's no rule about not wearing tie-pins or club buttons or anything, in the workshop, is there?"

"No, there isn't, but that's not quite the same thing."

"My dear William," she said, "it is exactly the same. It's nothing to do with the works manager whether the man wears a Rotary button, or an Elvis Presley button, or an African National Congress button. It's damn all his business."

"No, Madge, I'm sorry," William said, patient, "but it's not the same. I can give the man a job because I feel sympathetic towards the struggle he's in, but I can't put him in the workshop as a Congress man. I mean that wouldn't be fair to Fowler. That I can't do to Fowler." He was smiling as he went towards the bathroom, but his profile, as he turned into the doorway, was incisive.

She sat on at her dressing-table, pulling a comb through her hair, dragging it down through knots. Then she rested her face on her palms, caught sight of herself and became aware, against her fingers, of the curving shelf of bone, like the lip of a strong shell, under each eye. Everyone had his own intimations of mortality. For her, the feel of the bone beneath the face, in any living creature, brought her the message of the skull. Once hollowed out of this, outside the world, too. For what it's worth. It's worth a lot, the world, she affirmed, as she always did, life rising at once in her as a fish opens its jaws to a fly. It's worth a lot; and she sighed and got up with the sigh.

She went into the bathroom and sat down on the edge of the bath. He was lying there in the water, his chin relaxed on his chest, and he smiled at her. She said, "You mean you don't want Fowler to know."

"Oh," he said, seeing where they were again. "What is it I don't want Fowler to know?"

"You don't want your partner to know that you slip black men with political ideas into your workshop. Cheeky kaffir agitators. Specially a man who's been in jail for getting people to defy the government!—What was his name; you never said?"

"Daniel something. I don't know. Mongoma or Ngoma. Something like that."

A line like a cut appeared between her eyebrows. "Why can't you remember his name?" Then she went on at once, "You don't want Fowler to know what you think, do you? That's it? You want to pretend you're like him, you don't mind the native in his place. You want to pretend that to please Fowler. You don't want Fowler to think you're cracked or Communist or whatever it is that good-natured, kind, jolly rich people like old Fowler think about people like us."

"I couldn't have less interest in what Fowler thinks outside our boardroom. And inside it, he never thinks about anything but how to sell more earth-moving gear."

"I don't mind the native in his place. You want him to think you go along with all that." She spoke aloud, but she seemed to be telling herself rather than him.

"Fowler and I run a factory. Our only common interest is the efficient running of that factory. Our *only* one. The factory depends on a stable, satisfied black labour-force, and that we've got. Right, you and I know that the whole black wage standard is too low, right, we know that the conditions they live under make it impossible for them really to be stable. All that. But the fact is, so far as accepted standards go in this crazy country, they're a stable, satisfied labour-force with better working conditions than most. So long as I'm a partner in a business that lives by them, I can't officially admit an element that represents dissatisfaction with their lot."

"A green badge with a map of Africa on it," she said.

"If you make up your mind not to understand, you don't, and there it is," he said indulgently.

"You give him a job but you make him hide his Congress button."

He began to soap himself. She wanted everything to stop while she inquired into things, she could not go on while a remark was unexplained or a problem unsettled, but he represented a principle she subscribed to but found so hard to follow, that life must go on, trivially, commonplace, the trailing hem of the only power worth clinging to. She smoothed the film of her nightgown over the shape of her knees, over and over, and presently she said, in exactly the flat tone of statement that she had used before, the flat tone that was the height of belligerence in her, "He can say and do what he likes, he can call for strikes and boycotts and anything he likes, outside the factory, but he mustn't wear his Congress button at work."

He was standing up, washing his body that was full of scars; she knew them all, from the place on his left breast where a piece of shrapnel had gone in, all the way back to the place under his arm where he had torn himself on barbed wire as a child. "Yes, of course, anything he likes."

"Anything except his self-respect," she grumbled to herself. "Pretend, pretend. Pretend he doesn't belong to a political organization. Pretend he doesn't want to be a man. Pretend he hasn't been to prison for what he believes." Suddenly she spoke to her husband: "You'll let him have anything except the one thing worth giving."

They stood in uncomfortable proximity to each other, in the smallness of the bathroom. They were at once aware of each other as people who live in intimacy are only when hostility returns each to the confines of himself. He felt himself naked before her, where he had stepped out onto the towelling mat, and he took a towel and slowly covered himself, pushing the free end in round his waist. She felt herself an intrusion and, in silence, went out.

Her hands were tingling as if she were coming round from a faint. She walked up and down the bedroom floor like someone waiting to be summoned, called to account. I'll forget about it, she kept thinking, very fast, I'll forget about it again. Take a sip of water. Read another chapter. Don't call a halt. Let things flow, cover up, go on.

But when he came into the room with his wet hair combed and his stranger's face, and he said, "You're angry," it came from her lips, a black bird in the room, before she could understand what she had released—"I'm not angry. I'm beginning to get to know you."

Ella Mngoma knew he was going to a meeting that evening and didn't expect him home early. She put the paraffin lamp on the table so that she could see to finish the child's dress. It was done, buttons and all, by the time he came in at half past ten.

"Well, now we'll see what happens. I've got them to accept, *in principle*, that in future we won't take bail. You should have seen Ben Tsolo's face when I said that we lent the government our money interest-free when we paid bail. That really hit him. That was language he understood." He laughed, and did not seem to want to sit down, the heat of the meeting still upon him. "*In principle.* Yes, it's easy to accept in principle. We'll see."

She pumped the primus and set a pot of stew to warm up for him. "Ah, that's nice." He saw the dress. "Finished already?" And she nodded vociferously in pleasure; but at once she noticed his forefinger run lightly along the braid round the neck, and the traces of failure that were always at the bottom of her cup tasted on her tongue again. Probably he was not even aware of it, or perhaps his instinct for what was true—the plumb line, the coin with the right ring—led him absently to it, but the fact was that she had botched the neck.

She had an almost Oriental delicacy about not badgering him and she waited until he had washed and sat down to eat before she asked, "How did the job go?"

"Oh that," he said. "It went." He was eating quickly, moving his tongue strongly round his mouth to marshal the bits of meat that escaped his teeth. She was sitting with him, feeling, in spite of herself, the rest of satisfaction in her evening's work. "Didn't you get it?"

"It got *me*. But I got loose again, all right."

She watched his face to see what he meant. "They don't want you to come back tomorrow?"

He shook his head, no, no, no, to stem the irritation of her suppositions. He finished his mouthful and said, "Everything very nice. Boss takes me into his office, apologizes for the pay, he knows it's not the sort of job I should have and so forth. So I go off and clean up in the assembly shop. Then at lunchtime he calls me into the office again; they don't want me to wear my

A.N.C. badge at work. Flora Donaldson's sympathetic white man, who's going to do me the great favour of paying me three pounds a week." He laughed. "Well, there you are."

She kept on looking at him. Her eyes widened and her mouth tightened; she was trying to prime herself to speak, or was trying not to cry. The idea of tears exasperated him and he held her with a firm, almost belligerently inquiring gaze. Her hand went up round the back of her neck under her collar, anxiously exploratory. "Don't do that!" he said. "You're like a monkey catching lice."

She took her hand down swiftly and broke into trembling, like a sweat. She began to breathe hysterically. "You couldn't put it in your pocket, for the day," she said wildly, grimacing at the bitterness of malice towards him.

He jumped up from the table. "Christ! I knew you'd say it! I've been waiting for you to say it. You've been wanting to say it for five years. Well, now it's out. Out with it. Spit it out!" She began to scream softly as if he were hitting her. The impulse to cruelty left him and he sat down before his dirty plate, where the battered spoon lay among bits of gristle and potato-eyes. Presently he spoke. "You come out and you think there's everybody waiting for you. The truth is, there isn't anybody. You think straight in prison because you've got nothing to lose. Nobody thinks straight, outside. They don't want to hear you. What are you all going to do with me, Ella? Send me back to prison as quickly as possible? Perhaps I'll get a banishment order next time. That'd do. That's what you've got for me. I must keep myself busy with that kind of thing."

He went over to her and said, in a kindly voice, kneading her shoulder with spread fingers, "Don't cry. Don't cry. You're just like any other woman."

Denise Levertov

(1923-1997)

Born in England, the daughter of a Welsh mother and Russian Jewish father who became an Anglican priest, Denise Levertov was already a published poet (*The Double Image* [1946]) when she moved to the United States after World War II. Though early on she declared herself a disciple of the American poet William Carlos Williams—"He made available to us the whole range of the language, he showed us the rhythms of speech as poetry"—she remains a poet who defies categorization. There is, however, a recurring evocation of a mystical presence in the world that runs through her many volumes of poetry, which include *With Eyes at the Back of Our Heads* (1960), *The Sorrow Dance* (1967), *The Freeing of the Dust* (1975), *Breathing the Water* (1987), and *The Door in the Hive* (1989). The spirit that enlivens and joins together all the forms of creation imposes, in her words, "the obligation of social conscience." In her own life she has performed acts of resistance to war, nuclear arms, and injustice in Latin America. "The tragic and fearful character of our times is not something from which we can detach ourselves; we are in it, as fish are in the sea." One of the most important poets of the second half of the twentieth century, Levertov was the recipient of many awards and honors, served as poetry editor of the *Nation* and *Mother Jones*, and taught at MIT, Stanford, and Berkeley. She also published three collections of essays, *The Poet in the World* (1973), *Light Up the Cave* (1981), and *New and Selected Essays* (1992), which includes pieces about religious belief and her late conversion to Catholicism.

What Were They Like?

1) Did the people of Viet Nam
   use lanterns of stone?

2) Did they hold ceremonies
   to reverence the opening of buds?
3) Were they inclined to quiet laughter?
4) Did they use bone and ivory,
   jade and silver, for ornament?
5) Had they an epic poem?
6) Did they distinguish between speech and singing?

1) Sir, their light hearts turned to stone.
   It is not remembered whether in gardens
   stone lanterns illumined pleasant ways.
2) Perhaps they gathered once to delight in blossom,
   but after the children were killed
   there were no more buds.
3) Sir, laughter is bitter to the burned mouth.
4) A dream ago, perhaps. Ornament is for joy.
   All the bones were charred.
5) It is not remembered. Remember,
   most were peasants; their life
   was in rice and bamboo.
   When peaceful clouds were reflected in the paddies
   and the water buffalo stepped surely along terraces,
   maybe fathers told their sons old tales.
   When bombs smashed those mirrors
   there was time only to scream.
6) There is an echo yet
   of their speech which was like a song.
   It was reported their singing resembled
   the flight of moths in moonlight.
   Who can say? It is silent now.

Love Poem

"We are good for each other."
                                   —X

What you give me is

the extraordinary sun
splashing its light
                        into astonished trees.

A branch
of berries, swaying

under the feet of a bird.

I know
other joys—they taste
bitter, distilled as they are
from roots, yet I thirst for them.

But you—
you give me

the flash of golden daylight
in the body's
midnight,
warmth of the fall noonday
between the sheets in the dark.

Wedding-Ring

My wedding-ring lies in a basket
as if at the bottom of a well.
Nothing will come to fish it back up
and onto my finger again.
                        It lies
among keys to abandoned houses,
nails waiting to be needed and hammered
into some wall,
telephone numbers with no names attached,
idle paperclips.
                It can't be given away
for fear of bringing ill-luck.
                It can't be sold
for the marriage was good in its own
time, though that time is gone.
                Could some artificer
beat into it bright stones, transform it
into a dazzling circlet no one could take
for solemn betrothal or to make promises
living will not let them keep? Change it
into a simple gift I could give in friendship?

Contraband

The tree of knowledge was the tree of reason.
That's why the taste of it
drove us from Eden. That fruit
was meant to be dried and milled to a fine powder
for use a pinch at a time, a condiment.
God had probably planned to tell us later
about this new pleasure.
                                We stuffed our mouths full of it,
gorged on *but* and *if* and *how* and again
but, knowing no better.
It's toxic in large quantities; fumes
swirled in our heads and around us
to form a dense cloud that hardened to steel,
a wall between us and God, Who was paradise.
Not that God is unreasonable—but reason
in such excess was tyranny
and locked us into its own limits, a polished cell
reflecting our own faces. God lives
on the other side of that mirror,
but through the slit where the barrier doesn't
quite touch ground, manages still
to squeeze in—as filtered light,
splinters of fire, a strain of music heard
then lost, then heard again.

Flannery O'Connor

(1925–1964)

A native Georgian whose paternal ancestors came from Tipperary in Ireland—and, like her father, a victim of fatal lupus—Flannery O'Connor named her major influences as "being a Catholic, and a Southerner, and a writer." The author of two novels, *Wise Blood* (1952) and *The Violent Bear It Away* (1960), and three collections of short stories, *A Good Man Is Hard to Find,* (1955), *Everything That Rises Must Converge* (1965), and the posthumously published *Collected Stories,* which won the National Book Award for fiction in 1971, she said she wrote "because I'm good at it." Her nonfiction appears in *Mystery and Manners* (1969); her collected letters, edited by Sally Fitzgerald, are entitled *The Habits of Being* (1979). Her fiction casts a cold, comic, and original eye on the grotesque and eccentric characters who were her friends and neighbors in the Protestant Bible Belt. She is said to be the twentieth-century American woman writer who each year receives the most critical attention from scholars.

A Late Encounter with the Enemy

General Sash was a hundred and four years old. He lived with his grand-daughter, Sally Poker Sash, who was sixty-two years old and who prayed every night on her knees that he would live until her graduation from college. The General didn't give two slaps for her graduation but he never doubted he would live for it. Living had got to be such a habit with him that he couldn't conceive of any other condition. A graduation exercise was not exactly his idea of a good time, even if, as she said, he would be expected to sit on the stage in his uniform. She said there would be a long procession of teachers and students in their robes but that there wouldn't be anything to equal *him* in his uniform. He knew this well enough without her telling him, and as for the damn procession, it could march to hell and back and not cause him a quiver.

He liked parades with floats full of Miss Americas and Miss Daytona Beaches and Miss Queen Cotton Products. He didn't have any use for processions and a procession full of schoolteachers was about as deadly as the River Styx to his way of thinking. However, he was willing to sit on the stage in his uniform so that they could see him.

Sally Poker was not as sure as he was that he would live until her graduation. There had not been any perceptible change in him for the last five years, but she had the sense that she might be cheated out of her triumph because she so often was. She had been going to summer school every year for the past twenty because when she started teaching, there were no such things as degrees. In those times, she said, everything was normal but nothing had been normal since she was sixteen, and for the past twenty summers, when she should have been resting, she had had to take a trunk in the burning heat to the state teacher's college; and though when she returned in the fall, she always taught in the exact way she had been taught not to teach, this was a mild revenge that didn't satisfy her sense of justice. She wanted the General at her graduation because she wanted to show what she stood for, or, as she said, "what all was behind her," and was not behind them. This *them* was not anybody in particular. It was just all the upstarts who had turned the world on its head and unsettled the ways of decent living.

She meant to stand on that platform in August with the General sitting in his wheel chair on the stage behind her and she meant to hold her head very high as if she were saying, "See him! See him! My kin, all you upstarts! Glorious upright old man standing for the old traditions! Dignity! Honor! Courage! See him!" One night in her sleep she screamed, "See him! See him!" and turned her head and found him sitting in his wheel chair behind her with a terrible expression on his face and with all his clothes off except the general's hat and she had waked up and had not dared to go back to sleep again that night.

For his part, the General would not have consented even to attend her graduation if she had not promised to see to it that he sit on the stage. He liked to sit on any stage. He considered that he was still a very handsome man. When he had been able to stand up, he had measured five feet four inches of pure game cock. He had white hair that reached to his shoulders behind and he would not wear teeth because he thought his profile was more striking without them. When he put on his full-dress general's uniform, he knew well enough that there was nothing to match him anywhere.

This was the not the same uniform he had worn in the War between the States. He had not actually been a general in that war. He had probably been a foot soldier; he didn't remember what he had been; in fact, he didn't remember that war at all. It was like his feet, which hung down now shriveled at the very end of him, without feeling, covered with a blue-gray afghan that Sally Poker had crocheted when she was a little girl. He didn't remember the Spanish-American War in which he had lost a son; he didn't even remember the son. He didn't have any use for history because he never expected to meet it again. To his mind, history was connected with processions and life with parades and he liked parades. People were always asking him if he remembered this or that—a dreary black procession of questions about the past. There was only one event in the past that had any significance for him and that he cared to talk about; that was twelve years ago when he had received the general's uniform and had been in the premiere.

"I was in that preemy they had in Atlanta," he would tell visitors sitting on his front porch. "Surrounded by beautiful guls. It wasn't a thing local about it. It was nothing local about it. Listen here. It was a nashnul event and they had me in it—up onto the stage. There was no bob-tails at it. Every person at it had paid ten dollars to get in and had to wear his tuxseeder. I was in this uniform. A beautiful gul presented me with it that afternoon in a hotel room."

"It was in a suite in the hotel and I was in it too, Papa," Sally Poker would say, winking at the visitors. "You weren't alone with any young lady in a hotel room."

"Was, I'd a known what to do," the old General would say with a sharp look and the visitors would scream with laughter. "This was a Hollywood, California, gul," he'd continue. "She was from Hollywood, California, and didn't have any part in the pitcher. Out there they have so many beautiful guls that they don't need that they call them a extra and they don't use them for nothing but presenting people with things and having their pitchers taken. They took my pitcher with her. No, it was two of them. One on either side and me in the middle with my arms around each of them's waist and their waist ain't any bigger than a half a dollar."

Sally Poker would interrupt again. "It was Mr. Govisky that gave you the uniform, Papa, and he gave me the most exquisite corsage. Really, I wish you could have seen it. It was made with gladiola petals taken off and painted gold and put back together to look like a rose. It was exquisite. I wish you could have seen it, it was . . ."

"It was a big as her head," the General would snarl. "I was tellin it. They gimme this soward and they say, "Now General, we don't want you to start a war on us. All we want you to do is march right up on that stage when you're innerduced tonight and answer a few questions. Think you can do that?" "Think I can do it!" I say. "Listen here. I was doing things before you were born," and they hollered."

"He was the hit of the show," Sally Poker would say, but she didn't much like to remember the premiere on account of what had happened to her feet at it. She had bought a new dress for the occasion—a long black crepe dinner dress with a rhinestone buckle and a bolero—and a pair of silver slippers to wear with it, because she was supposed to go up on the stage with him to keep him from falling. Everything was arranged for them. A real limousine came at ten minutes to eight and took them to the theater. It drew up under the marquee at exactly the right time, after the big stars and the director and the author and the governor and the mayor and some less important stars. The police kept traffic from jamming and there were ropes to keep the people off who wouldn't go. All the people who couldn't go watched them step out of the limousine into the lights. Then they walked down the red and gold foyer and an usherette in a Confederate cap and little short skirt conducted them to their special seats. The audience was already there and a group of UDC members began to clap when they saw the General in his uniform and that started everybody to clap. A few more celebrities came after them and then the doors closed and the lights went down.

A young man with blond wavy hair who said he represented the motion-picture industry came out and began to introduce everybody and each one who was introduced walked up on the stage and said how really happy he was to be here for this great event. The General and his granddaughter were introduced sixteenth on the program. He was introduced as General Tennessee Flintrock Sash of the Confederacy, though Sally Poker had told Mr. Govisky that his name was George Poker Sash and that he had only been a major. She helped him up from his seat but her heart was beating so fast she didn't know whether she'd make it herself.

The old man walked up the aisle slowly with his fierce white head high and his hat held over his heart. The orchestra began to play the Confederate

Battle Hymn very softly and the UDC members rose as a group and did not sit down again until the General was on the stage. When he reached the center of the stage with Sally Poker just behind him guiding his elbow, the orchestra burst out in a loud rendition of the Battle Hymn and the old man, with real stage presence, gave a vigorous trembling salute and stood at attention until the last blast had died away. Two of the usherettes in Confederate caps and short skirts held a Confederate and a Union flag crossed behind them.

The General stood in the exact center of the spotlight and it caught a weird moon-shaped slice of Sally Poker—the corsage, the rhinestone buckle and one hand clenched around a white glove and handkerchief. The young man with the blond wavy hair inserted himself into the circle of light and said he was *really* happy to have here tonight for this great event, one, he said, who had fought and bled in the battles they would soon see daringly reenacted on the screen, and "Tell me, General," he asked, "how old are you?"

"Niiiiiinnttty-two!" the General screamed.

The young man looked as if this were just about the most impressive thing that had been said all evening. "Ladies and gentlemen," he said, "let's give the General the biggest hand we've got!" and there was applause immediately and the young man indicated Sally Poker with a motion of his thumb that she could take the old man back to his seat now so that the next person could be introduced; but the General had not finished. He stood immovable in the exact center of the spotlight, his neck thrust forward, his mouth slightly open, and his voracious gray eyes drinking in the glare and the applause. He elbowed his granddaughter roughly away. "How I keep so young," he screeched, "I kiss all the pretty guls!"

This was met with a great din of spontaneous applause and it was at just that instant that Sally Poker looked down at her feet and discovered that in the excitement of getting ready she had forgotten to change her shoes: two brown Girl Scout oxfords protruded from the bottom of her dress. She gave the General a yank and almost ran with him off the stage. He was very angry that he had not got to say how glad he was to be here for this event and on the way back to his seat, he kept saying as loud as he could, "I'm glad to be here at this preemy with all these beautiful guls!" but there was another celebrity going up the other aisle and nobody paid any attention to him. He slept through the picture, muttering fiercely every now and then in his sleep.

Since then, his life had not been very interesting. His feet were completely dead now, his knees worked like old hinges, his kidneys functioned when they would, but his heart persisted doggedly to beat. The past and the future were the same thing to him, one forgotten and the other not remembered; he had no more notion of dying than a cat. Every year on Confederate Memorial Day, he was bundled up and lent to the Capitol City Museum where he was displayed from one to four in a musty room full of old photographs, old uniforms, old artillery, and historic documents. All these were carefully preserved in glass cases so that children would not put their hands on them. He wore his general's uniform from the premiere and sat, with a fixed scowl, inside a small roped area. There was nothing about him to indicate that he was alive except an occasional movement in his milky gray eyes, but once when a bold child touched his sword, his arm shot forward and slapped the hand off in an instant. In the spring when the old homes were opened for pilgrimages, he was invited to wear his uniform and sit in some conspicuous spot and lend atmosphere to the scene. Some of these times he only snarled at the visitors but sometimes he told about the premiere and the beautiful girls.

If he had died before Sally Poker's graduation, she thought she would have died herself. At the beginning of the summer term, even before she knew if she would pass, she told the Dean that her grandfather, General Tennessee Flintrock Sash of the Confederacy, would attend her graduation and that he was a hundred and four years old and that his mind was still as clear as a bell. Distinguished visitors were always welcome and could sit on the stage and be introduced. She made arrangements with her nephew, John Wesley Poker Sash, a Boy Scout, to come wheel the General's chair. She thought how sweet it would be to see the old man in his courageous gray and the young boy in his clean khaki—the old and the new, she thought appropriately—they would be behind her on the stage when she received her degree.

Everything went almost exactly as she had planned. In the summer while she was away at school, the General stayed with other relatives and they brought him and John Wesley, the Boy Scout, down to the graduation. A reporter came to the hotel where they stayed and took the General's picture with Sally Poker on one side of him and John Wesley on the other. The General, who had had his picture taken with beautiful girls, didn't think much of this. He had forgotten precisely what kind of event this was he was going to attend but he remembered that he was to wear his uniform and carry the sword.

On the morning of the graduation, Sally Poker had to line up in the academic procession with the B.S.'s in Elementary Education and she couldn't see to getting him on the stage herself—but John Wesley, a fat blond boy of ten with an executive expression, guaranteed to take care of everything. She came in her academic gown to the hotel and dressed the old man in his uniform. He was as frail as a dried spider. "Aren't you just thrilled, Papa?" she asked. "I'm just thrilled to death!"

"Put the sword across my lap, damn you," the old man said, "where it'll shine."

She put it there and then stood back looking at him. "You look just grand," she said.

"God damn it," the old man said in a slow monotonous certain tone as if he were saying it to the beating of his heart. "God damn every goddam thing to hell."

"Now, now," she said and left happily to join the procession.

The graduates were lined up behind the Science building and she found her place just as the line started to move. She had not slept much the night before and when she had, she had dreamed of the exercises, murmuring, "See him, see him?" in her sleep but waking up every time just before she turned her head to look at him behind her. The graduates had to walk three blocks in the hot sun in their black wool robes and as she plodded stolidly along she thought that if anyone considered this academic procession something impressive to behold, they need only wait until they saw that old General in his courageous gray and that clean young Boy Scout stoutly wheeling his chair across the stage with the sunlight catching the sword. She imagined that John Wesley had the old man ready now behind the stage.

The black procession wound its way up the two blocks and started on the main walk leading to the auditorium. The visitors stood on the grass, picking out their graduates. Men were pushing back their hats and wiping their foreheads and women were lifting their dresses slightly from the shoulders to keep them from sticking to their backs. The graduates in their heavy robes looked as if the last beads of ignorance were being sweated out of them. The sun blazed off the fenders of automobiles and beat from the columns of the buildings and pulled the eye from one spot of glare to another. It pulled Sally Poker's toward the big red Coca-Cola machine that had been set up by the side of the auditorium. Here she saw the General parked, scowling and hatless in his chair in the blazing sun while John Wesley, his blouse loose behind, his hip and cheek pressed to the red machine, was drinking a Coca-Cola. She broke from the line and galloped to them and snatched the bottle away. She shook the boy and thrust in his blouse and put the hat on the old man's head. "Now get him in there!" she said, pointing one rigid finger to the side door of the building.

For his part the General felt as if there were a little hole beginning to widen in the top of his head. The boy wheeled him rapidly down a walk and up a ramp and into a building and bumped him over the stage entrance and into position where he had been told and the General glared in front of him at heads that all seemed to flow together and eyes that moved from one face to another. Several figures in black robes came and picked up his hand and shook it. A black procession was flowing up each aisle and forming to stately music in a pool in front of him. The music seemed to be entering his head through the little hole and he thought for a second that the procession would try to enter it too.

He didn't know what procession this was but there was something familiar about it. It must be familiar to him since it had come to meet him, but he didn't like a black procession. Any procession that came to meet him, he thought irritably, ought to have floats with beautiful guls on them like the floats before the preemy. It must be something connected with history like they were always having. He had no use for any of it. What happened then wasn't anything to a man living now and he was living now.

When all the procession had flowed into the black pool, a black figure began orating in front of it. The figure was telling something about history and the General made up his mind he wouldn't listen, but the words kept seeping in through the little hole in his head. He heard his own name mentioned and his chair was shuttled forward roughly and the Boy Scout took a big bow. They called his name and the fat brat bowed. Goddam you, the old man tried to say, get out of my way, I can stand up!—but he was jerked back again before he could get up and take the bow. He supposed the noise they made was for him. If he was over, he didn't intend to listen to any more of it. If it hadn't been for the little hole in the top of his head, none of the words would have got to him. He thought of putting his finger up there into the hole to block them but the hole was a little wider than his finger and it felt as if it were getting deeper.

Another black robe had taken the place of the first one and was talking now and he heard his name mentioned again but they were not talking about him, they were still talking about history. "If we forget our past," the speaker was saying, "we won't remember our future and it will be as well for we won't have one." The General heard some of these words gradually. He had forgotten history and he didn't intend to remember it again. He had forgotten the name and face of his wife and the names and faces of his children or even if he had a wife and children, and he had forgotten the names of places and the places themselves and what had happened at them.

He was considerably irked by the hole in his head. He had not expected to have a hole in his head at this event. It was the slow black music that had put it there and though most of the music had stopped outside, there was still a little of it in the hole, going deeper and moving around in his thoughts, letting the words he heard into the dark places of his brain. He heard the words, Chickamauga, Shiloh, Johnston, Lee, and he knew he was inspiring all these words that meant nothing to him. He wondered if he had been a general at Chickamauga or at Lee. Then he tried to see himself and the horse mounted in the middle of a float full of beautiful girls, being driven slowly through downtown Atlanta. Instead, the old words began to stir in his head as if they were trying to wrench themselves out of place and come to life.

The speaker was through with that war and had gone on to the next one and now he was approaching another and all his words, like the black procession, were vaguely familiar and irritating. There was a long finger of music in the General's head, probing various spots that were words, letting in a little light on the words and helping them to live. The words began to come toward him and he said, Dammit! I ain't going to have it! and he started edging backwards to get out of the way. Then he saw the figure in the black robe sit down and there was a noise and the black pool in front of him began to rumble and to flow toward him from either side to the black slow music, and he said, Stop dammit! I can't do but one thing at a time! He couldn't protect himself from the words and attend to the procession too and the words were coming at him fast. He felt that he was running backwards and the words were coming at him like musket fire, just escaping him but getting nearer and nearer. He turned around and began to run as fast as he could but he found himself running toward the words. He was running into a regular volley of them and meeting them with quick curses. As the music swelled toward him,

the entire past opened up on him out of nowhere and he felt his body rid-
dled in a hundred places with sharp stabs of pain and he fell down, returning
a curse for every hit. He saw his wife's narrow face looking at him critically
through her round gold-rimmed glasses; he saw one of his squinting bald-
headed sons; and his mother ran toward him with an anxious look; then a
succession of places—Chickamauga, Shiloh, Marthasville—rushed at him as
if the past were the only future now and he had to endure it. Then suddenly he saw that the black procession was almost on him. He recognized it, for
it had been dogging all his days. He made such a desperate effort to see over
it and find out what comes after the past that his hand clenched the sword
until the blade touched the bone.

The graduates were crossing the stage in a long file to receive their scrolls
and shake the president's hand. As Sally Poker, who was near the end,
crossed, she glanced at the General and saw him sitting fixed and fierce, his
eyes wide open, and she turned her head forward again and held it a perceptible degree higher and received her scroll. Once it was all over and she was
out of the auditorium in the sun again, she located her kin and they waited
together on a bench in the shade for John Wesley to wheel the old man out.
That crafty scout had bumped him out the back way and rolled him at high
speed down a flagstone path and was waiting now, with the corpse, in the
long line at the Coca-Cola machine.

Anne Sexton

(1928-1974)

A survivor of several mental breakdowns and hospitalizations, New Englander Anne Sexton began writing poetry on the advice of her psychiatrist. She found her life-line, if only temporarily, as a poet. She made friends with the poet Sylvia Plath, her fellow student in a class taught by Robert Lowell at Boston University. The teacher and his two most famous students are now recognized as three of the great "confessional poets" of the postwar period: each tells the secrets of their personal history, showing where their private hells reverberate as public nightmare. Sexton's first book of poetry, *To Bedlam and Part Way Back* (1960), recounts her mental breakdown and recovery. Subsequent volumes include *All My Pretty Ones* (1962), *Live or Die* (1966)—which won the Pulitzer Prize—*Love Poems* (1969), *Transformations* (1971), *The Book of Folly* (1972), and *The Death Notebooks* (1974). Because Sexton ignored the tradition of silence about women's sexuality—she writes about her uterus, about menstruation, about masturbation and incest—her work was controversial. As her critics poured scorn, her admirers provided large audiences for her readings and awarded her many literary prizes. Obsessed for many years with the desire for self-destruction, Sexton committed suicide in 1974. Her elder daughter, Linda Gray Sexton, edited her letters: *Anne Sexton: A Self Portrait in Letters* (1977).

Ringing the Bells

And this is the way they ring
the bells in Bedlam
and this is the bell-lady
who comes each Tuesday morning
to give us a music lesson
and because the attendants make you go

and because we mind by instinct,
like bees caught in the wrong hive,
we are the circle of the crazy ladies
who sit in the lounge of the mental house
and smile at the smiling woman
who passes us each a bell,
who points at my hand
that holds my bell, E flat,
and this is the gray dress next to me
who grumbles as if it were special
to be old, to be old,
and this is the small hunched squirrel girl
on the other side of me
who picks at the hairs over her lip,
who picks at the hairs over her lip all day,
and this is how the bells really sound,
as untroubled and clean
as a workable kitchen,
and this is always my bell responding
to my hand that responds to the lady
who points at me, E flat;
and although we are no better for it,
they tell you to go. And you do.

In Celebration of My Uterus

Everyone in me is a bird.
I am beating all my wings.
They wanted to cut you out
but they will not.
They said you were immeasurably empty
but you are not.
They said you were sick unto dying
but they were wrong.
You are singing like a school girl.
You are not torn.

Sweet weight,
in celebration of the woman I am
and of the soul of the woman I am
and of the central creature and its delight
I sing for you. I dare to live.
Hello, spirit. Hello, cup.
Fasten, cover. Cover that does contain.
Hello to the soil of the fields.
Welcome, roots.

Each cell has a life.
There is enough here to please a nation.
It is enough that the populace own these goods.
Any person, any commonwealth would say of it,
"It is good this year that we may plant again
and think forward to a harvest.
A blight had been forecast and has been cast out."
Many women are singing together of this:
one is in a shoe factory cursing the machine,
one is at the aquarium tending a seal,
one is dull at the wheel of her Ford,
one is at the toll gate collecting,
one is tying the cord of a calf in Arizona,
one is straddling a cello in Russia,
one is shifting pots on the stove in Egypt,
one is painting her bedroom walls moon color,
one is dying but remembering a breakfast,
one is stretching on her mat in Thailand,
one is wiping the ass of her child,
one is staring out the window of a train
in the middle of Wyoming and one is
anywhere and some are everywhere and all
seem to be singing, although some can not
sing a note.

Sweet weight,
in celebration of the woman I am
let me carry a ten-foot scarf,
let me drum for the nineteen-year-olds,
let me carry bowls for the offering
(if that is my part).
Let me study the cardiovascular tissue,
let me examine the angular distance of meteors,
let me suck on the stems of flowers
(if that is my part).
Let me make certain tribal figures
(if that is my part).
For this thing the body needs
let me sing
for the supper,
for the kissing,
for the correct
yes.

Housewife

Some women marry houses.
It's another kind of skin; it has a heart,
a mouth, a liver and bowel movements.
The walls are permanent and pink.
See how she sits on her knees all day,
faithfully washing herself down.
Men enter by force, drawn back like Jonah
into their fleshy mothers.
A woman *is* her mother.
That's the main thing.

The Abortion

Somebody who should have been born
is gone.

Just as the earth puckered its mouth,
each bud puffing out from its knot,
I changed my shoes, and then drove south.

Up past the Blue Mountains, where
Pennsylvania humps on endlessly,
wearing, like a crayoned cat, its green hair,

its road sunken in like a gray washboard;
where, in truth, the ground cracks evilly,
a dark socket from which the coal has poured,

Somebody who should have been born
is gone.

the grass as bristly and stout as chives,
and me wondering when the ground would break,
and me wondering how anything fragile survives;

up in Pennsylvania, I met a little man,
not Rumpelstiltskin, at all, at all . . .
he took the fullness that love began.

Returning north, even the sky grew thin
like a high window looking nowhere.
The road was as flat as a sheet of tin.

Somebody who should have been born
is gone.

Yes, woman, such logic will lead
to loss without death. Or say what you meant,
you coward . . . this baby that I bleed.

Maya Angelou

(1928-   )

Born Marguerite Annie Johnson in St. Louis, at the age of three
Maya Angelou was sent with her older brother Bailey to live with
their beloved grandmother, Ann Henderson, in Stamps, Arkansas.
Her first volume of autobiography, *I Know Why the Caged Bird Sings*
(1970), recounts the four years in Stamps and then the move back
to her mother's house in St. Louis, where she was raped by her
mother's boyfriend. For the next five years Maya Angelou was
mute. But she listened intently, ultimately finding deliverance in
language. "For a long time I would think of myself, of my whole
body, as an ear. . . . Language. I loved it. I never did find a voice I
didn't find wonderful and beautiful. Because I really like the way
we talk. I find it wonderful." A prolific and joyful poet (and the first
since Robert Frost to be invited to read her work—"On the Pulse
of Morning"—at a presidential inauguration), she is best known for
the five volumes of her autobiography, which include *Gather
Together in My Name* (1974), *Singin' & Swingin' & Gettin' Merry Like
Christmas* (1976), *The Heart of a Woman* (1981), and *All God's
Children Need Traveling Shoes* (1986).

FROM *Shades and Slashes of Light*

*". . . We are a tongued folk. A race of singers. Our lips shape words and rhythms which elevate our
spirits and quicken our blood. . . . I have spent over fifty years listening to my people."*

I write for the Black voice and any ear which can hear it. As a composer writes
for musical instruments and a choreographer creates for the body, I search for
sound, tempos, and rhythms to ride through the vocal cord over the tongue,
and out of the lips of Black people. I love the shades and slashes of light. Its
rumblings and passages of magical lyricism. I accept the glory of stridencies and
purrings, trumpetings and sombre sonorities.

Having said that, I must now talk about content. I have noted most carefully for the past twenty years our speech patterns, the ambiguities, contradictions, the moans and laughter, and am even more enchanted at this time than I was when I began eavesdropping.

After, and during pestilential assaults of frustration, hate, demeanings, and murders, our language continues to expand and mature. Our lives, made inadequate and estranged by the experience of malice, loathing, and hostility, are enriched by the words we use to, and with, each other. By our intonations, our modulations, our shouts and hollers.

I write because I am a Black woman, listening attentively to her talking people.

When I turn my conscious mind to writing (my unconscious or subconscious is always busy recording images, phrases, sound, colors, and scents) I follow a fairly rigid habit. I rise early, around 5:30 or 6 A.M., wash, pray, put on coffee, and arrange my mind in writing order. That is, I tell myself how lucky I am that this morning is new, a day never seen before, that ideas will come to me which I have never consciously known. I have coffee and allow the work of the day before to flood my mind. The characters and situations take over the chambers of my existence until they are all I see and hear. Then I go to my writing room, most times a little cubicle I have rented in a cheap but clean hotel; rarely but sometimes it is a room in my own home.

I keep in my writing room a Bible, a dictionary, Roget's Thesaurus, a bottle of sherry, cigarettes, an ashtray, and three or four decks of playing cards. During the five hours I spend there I use every object, but I play solitaire more than I actually write. It seems to me that when my hands and small mind (a Southern Black phrase) are engaged in placing the reds on the blacks and blacks on the reds, my working mind arranges and rearranges the characters and the plot. Finally when they are in a plausible order, I simply have to write down where they are and what they say.

Later, after I have returned home or if I have worked at home, when I have left my writing room, I bathe and change clothes. This seems to signal my total mind that it may now stop working for the writer and begin to think for the woman, the wife, the friend, and the cook.

I begin thinking about dinner midafternoon. I love to cook and find it both creative and relaxing. After I have planned dinner and possibly begun a dish which demands long stewing, I take the morning's work to my dining room table and polish it, straighten out the grammar, clear up the syntax, and try to eliminate repetitions and contradictions. By dinnertime, I am ready to join my family or friends (although truthfully, when I'm working on a book I am never totally away from it). I know that they are aware that they and their concerns are not of great importance to me during the creative period (as long as a year, sometimes less), but we all pretend. The discipline I use to be in company stands me in good stead on the following morning when I must go alone into my small writing room and face a host of new ideas and headstrong characters, yet keep myself open so that they can interact, grow, and become real.

I also wear a hat or a very tightly pulled head tie when I write. I suppose I hope by doing that I will keep my brains from seeping out of my scalp and running in great gray blobs down my neck, into my ears, and over my face.

Still I Rise

You may write me down in history
With your bitter, twisted lies,
You may trod me in the very dirt
But still, like dust, I rise.

Does my sassiness upset you?
Why are you beset with gloom?
'Cause I walk like I've got oil wells
Pumping in my living room.

Just like moons and like suns,
With the certainty of tides,
Just like hopes springing high,
Still I'll rise.

Did you want to see me broken?
Bowed head and lowered eyes?
Shoulders falling down like teardrops,
Weakened by my soulful cries.

Does my haughtiness offend you?
Don't you take it awful hard
'Cause I laugh like I've got gold mines
Diggin' in my own back yard.

You may shoot me with your words,
You may cut me with your eyes,
You may kill me with your hatefulness,
But still, like air, I'll rise.

Does my sexiness upset you?
Does it come as a surprise
That I dance like I've got diamonds
At the meeting of my thighs?

Out of the huts of history's shame
I rise
Up from a past that's rooted in pain
I rise
I'm a black ocean, leaping and wide,
Welling and swelling I bear in the tide.
Leaving behind nights of terror and fear
I rise
Into a daybreak that's wondrously clear

I rise
Bringing the gifts that my ancestors gave,
I am the dream and the hope of the slave.
I rise
I rise
I rise.

Cynthia Ozick

(1928-   )

Born and bred in the Bronx, which she has brought to vivid life in her novels, including *Trust* (1966) and *The Cannibal Galaxy* (1983), essays—*Art & Ardor* (1983), from which "A Drugstore in Winter" is taken, is one collection—and volumes of short stories—*The Pagan Rabbi* (1971), *Bloodshed* (1976), and *Levitation* (1982)—Cynthia Ozick was described by novelist/editor William Abrahams as "one of the three greatest living American writers of short fiction" when her story "Rosa" won first prize in the 1984 O. Henry Prize Story Awards. (She has won four O. Henry first prizes.) Her artistic strength, according to novelist Edmund White, "derives from her moral energy, for Miss Ozick is not an esthete. Judaism has given to her what Catholicism gave to Flannery O'Connor—authority, penetration and indignation." "The Shawl," which follows here, first appeared in *The New Yorker*. The volume entitled *The Shawl* consists of this story and the novella *Rosa*, in which the heroine of "The Shawl" is imagined living in poverty and isolation many years later in Florida.

The Shawl

Stella, cold, cold, the coldness of hell. How they walked on the roads together, Rosa with Magda curled up between sore breasts, Magda wound up in the shawl. Sometimes Stella carried Magda. But she was jealous of Magda. A thin girl of fourteen, too small, with thin breasts of her own, Stella wanted to be wrapped in a shawl, hidden away, asleep, rocked by the march, a baby, a round infant in arms. Magda took Rosa's nipple, and Rosa never stopped walking, a walking cradle. There was not enough milk; sometimes Magda sucked air; then she screamed. Stella was ravenous. Her knees were tumors on sticks, her elbows chicken bones.

Rosa did not feel hunger; she felt light, not like someone walking but like

someone in a faint, in trance, arrested in a fit, someone who is already a floating angel, alert and seeing everything, but in the air, not there, not touching
the road. As if teetering on the tips of her fingernails. She looked into
Magda's face through a gap in the shawl: a squirrel in a nest, safe, no one
could reach her inside the little house of a shawl's windings. The face, very
round, a pocket mirror of a face: but it was not Rosa's bleak complexion, dark
like cholera, it was another kind of face altogether, eyes blue as air, smooth
feathers of hair nearly as yellow as the Star sewn into Rosa's coat. You could
think she was one of *their* babies.

Rosa, floating, dreamed of giving Magda away in one of the villages. She
could leave the line for a minute and push Magda into the hands of any
woman on the side of the road. But if she moved out of line they might
shoot. And even if she fled the line for half a second and pushed the shawl-
bundle at a stranger, would the woman take it? She might be surprised, or
afraid; she might drop the shawl, and Magda would fall out and strike her
head and die. The little round head. Such a good child, she gave up screaming, and sucked now only for the taste of the drying nipple itself. The neat
grip of the tiny gums. One mite of a tooth tip sticking up in the bottom gum,
how shining, an elfin tombstone of white marble gleaming there. Without
complaining, Magda relinquished Rosa's teats, first the left, then the right;
both were cracked, not a sniff of milk. The duct-crevice extinct, a dead vol-
cano, blind eye, chill hole, so Magda took the corner of the shawl and milked
it instead. She sucked and sucked, flooding the threads with wetness. The
shawl's good flavor, milk of linen.

It was a magic shawl, it could nourish an infant for three days and three
nights. Magda did not die, she stayed alive, although very quiet. A peculiar
smell, of cinnamon and almonds, lifted out of her mouth. She held her eyes
open every moment, forgetting how to blink or nap, and Rosa and sometimes Stella studied their blueness. On the road they raised one burden of a
leg after another and studied Magda's face. "Aryan," Stella said, in a voice
grown as thin as a string; and Rosa thought how Stella gazed at Magda like a
young cannibal. And the time that Stella said "Aryan," it sounded to Rosa as
if Stella had really said "Let us devour her."

But Magda lived to walk. She lived that long, but she did not walk very
well, partly because she was only fifteen months old, and partly because the
spindle of her legs could not hold up her fat belly. It was fat with air, full and

round. Rosa gave almost all her food to Magda, Stella gave nothing; Stella was ravenous, a growing child herself, but not growing much. Stella did not menstruate. Rosa did not menstruate. Rosa was ravenous, but also not; she learned from Magda how to drink the taste of a finger in one's mouth. They were in a place without pity, all pity was annihilated in Rosa, she looked at Stella's bones without pity. She was sure that Stella was waiting for Magda to die so she could put her teeth into the little thighs.

Rosa knew Magda was going to die very soon; she should have been dead already, but she had been buried away deep inside the magic shawl, mistaken there for the shivering mound of Rosa's breasts; Rosa clung to the shawl as if it covered only herself. No one took it away from her. Magda was mute. She never cried. Rosa hid her in the barracks, under the shawl, but she knew that one day someone would inform; or one day someone, not even Stella, would steal Magda to eat her. When Magda began to walk, Rosa knew that Magda was going to die very soon, something would happen. She was afraid to fall asleep; she slept with the weight of her thigh on Magda's body; she was afraid she would smother Magda under her thigh. The weight of Rosa was becoming less and less; Rosa and Stella were slowly turning into air.

Magda was quiet, but her eyes were horribly alive, like blue tigers. She watched. Sometimes she laughed—it seemed a laugh, but how could it be? Magda had never seen anyone laugh. Still, Magda laughed at her shawl when the wind blew its corners, the bad wind with pieces of black in it, that made Stella's and Rosa's eyes tear. Magda's eyes were always clear and tearless. She watched like a tiger. She guarded her shawl. No one could touch it; only Rosa could touch it. Stella was not allowed. The shawl was Magda's own baby, her pet, her little sister. She tangled herself up in it and sucked on one of the corners when she wanted to be very still.

Then Stella took the shawl away and made Magda die.

Afterward Stella said: "I was cold."

And afterward she was always cold, always. The cold went into her heart: Rosa saw that Stella's heart was cold. Magda flopped onward with her little pencil legs scribbling this way and that, in search of the shawl; the pencils faltered at the barracks opening, where the light began. Rosa saw and pursued. But already Magda was in the square outside the barracks, in the jolly light. It was the roll-call arena. Every morning Rosa had to conceal Magda under the shawl against a wall of the barracks and go out and stand in the arena with Stella and hundreds of others, sometimes for hours, and Magda, deserted, was quiet under the shawl, sucking on her corner. Every day Magda was silent, and so she did not die. Rosa saw that today Magda was going to die, and at the same time a fearful joy ran in Rosa's two palms, her fingers were on fire, she was astonished, febrile: Magda, in the sunlight, swaying on her pencil legs, was howling. Ever since the drying up of Rosa's nipples, ever since Magda's last scream on the road, Magda had been devoid of any syllable; Magda was a mute. Rosa believed that something had gone wrong with her vocal cords, with her windpipe, with the cave of her larynx; Magda was defective, without a voice; perhaps she was deaf; there might be something amiss with her intelligence; Magda was dumb. Even the laugh that came when the ash-stippled wind made a clown out of Magda's shawl was only the air-blown showing of her teeth. Even when the lice, head lice and body lice, crazed her so that she became as wild as one of the big rats that plundered the barracks at daybreak looking for carrion, she rubbed and scratched and kicked and bit and rolled without a whimper. But now Magda's mouth was spilling a long viscous rope of clamor.

"Maaaa—"

It was the first noise Magda had ever sent out from her throat since the drying up of Rosa's nipples.

"Maaaa . . . aaa!"

Again! Magda was wavering in the perilous sunlight of the arena, scribbling on such pitiful little bent shins. Rosa saw. She saw that Magda was grieving for the loss of her shawl, she saw that Magda was going to die. A tide of commands hammered in Rosa's nipples: Fetch, get, bring! But she did not know what to go after first, Magda or the shawl. If she jumped out into the arena to snatch Magda up, the howling would not stop, because Magda would still not have the shawl; but if she ran back into the barracks to find the shawl, and if she found it, and if she came after Magda holding it and shaking it, then she would get Magda back, Magda would put the shawl in her mouth and turn dumb again.

Rosa entered the dark. It was easy to discover the shawl. Stella was heaped under it, asleep in her thin bones. Rosa tore the shawl free and flew— she could fly, she was only air—into the arena. The sunheat murmured of another life, of butterflies in summer. The light was placid, mellow. On the other side of the steel fence, far away, there were green meadows speckled with dandelions and deep-colored violets; beyond them, even farther, innocent tiger lilies, tall, lifting their orange bonnets. In the barracks they spoke of "flowers," of "rain": excrement, thick turd-braids, and the slow stinking maroon waterfall that slunk down from the upper bunks, the stink mixed with a bitter fatty floating smoke that greased Rosa's skin. She stood for an instant at the margin of the arena. Sometimes the electricity inside the fence would seem to hum; even Stella said it was only an imagining, but Rosa heard real sounds in the wire: grainy sad voices. The farther she was from the fence, the more clearly the voices crowded at her. The lamenting voices strummed so convincingly, so passionately, it was impossible to suspect them of being phantoms. The voice told her to hold up the shawl, high; the voices told her to shake it, to whip with it, to unfurl it like a flag. Rosa lifted, shook, whipped, unfurled. Far off, very far, Magda leaned across her air-fed belly, reaching out with the rods of her arms. She was high up, elevated, riding someone's shoulder. But the shoulder that carried Magda was not coming toward Rosa and the shawl, it was drifting away, the speck of Magda was moving more and more into the smoky distance. Above the shoulder a helmet glinted. The light tapped the helmet and sparkled it into a goblet. Below the helmet a black body like a domino and a pair of black boots hurled themselves in the direction of the electrified fence. The electric voices began to chatter wildly. "Maamaa, maaamaaa," they all hummed together. How far Magda was from Rosa now, across the whole square, past a dozen barracks, all the way on the other side! She was no bigger than a moth.

All at once Magda was swimming through the air. The whole of Magda traveled through loftiness. She looked like a butterfly touching a silver vine. And the moment Magda's feathered round head and her pencil legs and balloonish belly and zigzag arms splashed against the fence, the steel voices went mad in their growling, urging Rosa to run and run to the spot where Magda had fallen from her flight against the electrified fence; but of course Rosa did not obey them. She only stood, because if she ran they would shoot, and if she tried to pick up the sticks of Magda's body they would shoot, and if she let the wolf's screech ascending now through the ladder of her skeleton break out, they would shoot; so she took Magda's shawl and filled her own mouth with it, stuffed it in and stuffed it in, until she was swallowing up the wolf's screech and tasting the cinnamon and almond depth of Magda's saliva; and Rosa drank Magda's shawl until it dried.

A Drugstore in Winter

This is about reading; a drugstore in winter; the gold leaf on the dome of the Boston State House; also loss, panic, and dread.

First, the gold leaf. (This part is a little like a turn-of-the-century pulp tale, though only a little. The ending is a surprise, but there is no plot.) Thirty years ago I burrowed in the Boston Public Library one whole afternoon, to find out—not out of curiosity—how the State House got its gold roof. The answer, like the answer to most Bostonian questions, was Paul Revere. So I put Paul Revere's gold dome into an "article," and took it (though I was just as scared by recklessness then as I am now) to the Boston Globe, on Washington Street. The Features Editor had a bare severe head, a closed parenthesis mouth, and silver Dickensian spectacles. He made me wait, standing, at the side of his desk while he read; there was no bone in me that did not rattle. Then he opened a drawer and handed me fifteen dollars. Ah, joy of Homer, joy of Milton! Grub Street bliss!

The very next Sunday, Paul Revere's gold dome saw print. Appetite for more led me to a top-floor chamber in Filene's department store: Window Dressing. But no one was the least bit dressed—it was a dumbstruck nudist colony up there, a mob of naked frozen enigmatic manikins, tall enameled skinny ladies with bald breasts and skulls, and legs and wrists and necks that horribly unscrewed. Paul Revere's dome paled beside this gold mine! A sight—mute numb Walpurgisnacht—easily worth another fifteen dollars. I had a Master's degree (thesis topic: "Parable in the Later Novels of Henry James") and a job as an advertising copywriter (9 A.M. to 6 P.M. six days a week, forty dollars per week; if you were male and had no degree at all, sixty dollars). Filene's Sale Days—Crib Bolsters! Lulla-Buys! Jonnie-Mops! Maternity Skirts with Expanding Invisible Trick Waist! And a company show; gold watches to mark the retirement of elderly Irish salesladies; for me the chance to write song lyrics (to the tune of "On Top of Old Smoky") honoring our Store. But "Mute Numb Walpurgisnacht in Secret Downtown Chamber" never reached the *Globe*. Melancholy and meaning business, the Advertising Director forbade it. Grub Street was bad form, and I had to promise never again to sink to another article. Thus ended my life in journalism.

Next: reading, and certain drugstore winter dusks. These come together. It is an aeon before Filene's, years and years before the Later Novels of Henry James. I am scrunched on my knees at a round glass table near a plate glass door on which is inscribed, in gold leaf Paul Revere never put there, letters that must be read backward: YCAMRAHP WEIV KRAP There is an evening smell of late coffee from the fountain, and all the librarians are lined up in a row on the tall stools, sipping and chattering. They have just stepped in from the cold of the Traveling Library, and so have I. The Traveling Library is a big green truck that stops, once every two weeks, on the corner of Continental Avenue, just a little way in from Westchester Avenue, not far from a house that keeps a pig. Other houses fly pigeons from their roofs, other yards have chickens, and down on Mayflower there is even a goat. This is Pelham Bay, the Bronx, in the middle of the Depression, all cattails and weeds, such a lovely place and tender hour! Even though my mother takes me on the subway far, far down-town to buy my winter coat in the frenzy of Klein's on Fourteenth Street, and even though I can recognize the heavy power of a quarter, I don't know it's the Depression. On the trolley on the way to Westchester Square I see the children who live in the boxcar strangely set down in an empty lot some dis-tance from Spy Oak (where a Revolutionary traitor was hanged—served him right for siding with redcoats); the lucky boxcar children dangle their stick-legs from their train-house maw and wave; how I envy them! I envy the orphans of the Gould Foundation, who have their own private swings and seesaws. Sometimes I imagine I am an orphan, and my father is an impostor pretending to be my father.

My father writes in his prescription book: *#59330 Dr. O'Flaherty Pow .60/ #59331 Dr. Mulligan Gtt .65/ #59332 Dr. Thron Tab .90.* Ninety cents! A ter-rifically expensive medicine; someone is really sick. When I deliver a pre-scription around the corner or down the block, I am offered a nickel tip. I always refuse, out of conscience; I am, after all, the Park View Pharmacy's own daughter, and it wouldn't be seemly. My father grinds and mixes powders, weighs them out in tiny snowy heaps on an apothecary scale, folds them into delicate translucent papers or meticulously drops them into gelatin capsules.

In the big front window of the Park View Pharmacy there is a startling display—goldfish bowls, balanced one on the other in amazing pyramids. A German lady enters, one of my father's cronies—his cronies are both women and men. My quiet father's eyes are water-color blue, he wears his small skeptical quiet smile and receives the neighborhood's life-secrets. My father is discreet and inscrutable. The German lady pokes a punchboard with a pin, pushes up a bit of rolled paper, and cries out—she has just won a goldfish bowl, with two swimming goldfish in it! Mr. Jaffe, the salesman from McKesson & Robbins, arrives, trailing two mists: winter steaminess and the animal fog of his cigar,★ which melts into the coffee smell, the tarpaper smell, the eerie honeyed tangled drugstore smell. Mr. Jaffe and my mother and father are intimates by now, but because it is the 1930s, so long ago, and the old manners still survive, they address one another gravely as Mr. Jaffe, Mrs. Ozick, Mr. Ozick. My mother calls my father Mr. O, even at home, as in a Victorian novel. In the street my father tips his hat to ladies. In the winter his hat is a regular fedora; in the summer it is a straw boater with a black ribbon and a jot of blue feather.

What am I doing at this round glass table, both listening and not listening to my mother and father tell Mr. Jaffe about their struggle with "Tessie," the lion-eyed landlady who has just raised, threefold, in the middle of that Depression I have never heard of, the Park View Pharmacy's devouring rent? My mother, not yet forty, wears bandages on her ankles, covering oozing varicose veins; back and forth she strides, dashes, runs, climbing cellar stairs or ladders; she unpacks cartons, she toils behind drug counters and fountain counters. Like my father, she is on her feet until one in the morning, the Park View's closing hour. My mother and father are in trouble, and I don't know it. I am too happy. I feel the secret center of eternity, nothing will ever alter, no one will ever die. Through the window, past the lit goldfish, the gray oval sky deepens over our neighborhood wood, where all the dirt paths lead down to seagull-specked water. I am familiar with every frog-haunted monument: Pelham Bay Park is thronged with WPA art—statuary, fountains, immense rococo staircases cascading down a hillside, Bacchus-faced stelae—stone Roman glories afterward mysteriously razed by an avenging Robert Moses. One year—how distant it seems now, as if even the climate is past returning—the bay froze so hard that whole families, mine among them, crossed back and forth to City Island, strangers saluting and calling out in ecstasy of the bright trudge over such a sudden wilderness of ice.

★ Mr. Matthew Bruccoli, another Bronx drugstore child, has written to say he remembers with certainty that Mr. Jaffe did not smoke. In my memory the cigar is somehow there, so I leave it.

In the Park View Pharmacy, in the winter dusk, the heart in my body is revolving like the goldfish fleet-finned in their clear bowls. The librarians are still warming up over their coffee. They do not recognize me, though only half an hour ago I was scrabbling in the mud around the two heavy boxes from the Traveling Library—oafish crates tossed with a thump to the ground. One box contains magazines—*Boy's Life*, *The American Girl*, *Popular Mechanix*. But the other, the other! The other transforms me. It is tumbled with storybooks, with clandestine intimations and transfigurations. In school I am a luckless goosegirl, friendless and forlorn. In P.S. 71 I carry, weighty as a cloak, the ineradicable knowledge of my scandal—I am cross-eyed, dumb, an imbecile at arithmetic; in P.S. 71 I am publicly shamed in Assembly because I am caught not singing Christmas carols; in P.S. 71 I am repeatedly accused of deicide. But in the Park View Pharmacy, in the winter dusk, branches blackening in the park across the road, I am driving in rapture through the Violet Fairy Book and the Yellow Fairy Book, insubstantial chariots snatched from the box in the mud. I have never been *inside* the Traveling Library; only grownups are allowed. The boxes are for the children. No more than two books may be borrowed, so I have picked the fattest ones, to last. All the same, the Violet and the Yellow are melting away. Their pages dwindle. I sit at the round glass table, dreaming, dreaming. Mr. Jaffe is murmuring advice. He tells a joke about Wrong-Way Corrigan. The librarians are buttoning up their coats. A princess, captive of an ogre, receives a letter from her swain and hides it in her bosom. I can visualize her bosom exactly—she clutches it against her chest. It is a tall and shapely vase, with a hand-painted flower on it, like the vase on the secondhand piano at home.

I am incognito. No one knows who I truly am. The teachers in P.S. 71 don't know. Rabbi Meskin, my *cheder* teacher, doesn't know. Tessie the lion-eyed landlady doesn't know. Even Hymie the fountain clerk can't know—though he understands other things better than anyone: how to tighten roller skates with a skatekey, for instance, and how to ride a horse. On Friday afternoons, when the new issue is out, Hymie and my brother fight hard over who gets to see *Life* magazine first. My brother is older than I am, and doesn't like me; he builds radios in his bedroom, he is already W2LOM, and operates his transmitter (*da-di-da-dit, da-da-di-da*) so penetratingly on Sunday mornings that Mrs. Eva Brady, across the way, complains. Mrs. Eva Brady has a subscription to *The Writer*; I fill a closet with her old copies. How to Find a

Plot. Narrative and Character, the Writer's Tools. Because my brother has his ham license, I say, "I have a license too." What kind of license?" my brother asks, falling into the trap. "Poetic license," I reply; my brother hates me, but anyhow his birthday presents are transporting: one year *Alice in Wonderland*, *Pinocchio* the next, then *Tom Sawyer*. I go after Mark Twain, and find *Joan of Arc* and my first satire, *Christian Science*. My mother surprises me with *Pollyanna*, the admiration of her Lower East Side childhood, along with *The Lady of the Lake*. Mrs. Eva Brady's daughter Jeannie has outgrown her Nancy Drew and Judy Boltons, so on rainy afternoons I cross the street and borrow them, trying not to march away with too many—the child of immigrants, I worry that the Bradys, true and virtuous Americans, will judge me greedy or careless. I wrap the Nancy Drews in paper covers to protect them. Old Mrs. Brady, Jeannie's grandmother, invites me back for more. I am so timid I can hardly speak a word, but I love her dark parlor; I love its black bookcases. Old Mrs. Brady sees me off, embracing books under an umbrella; perhaps she divines who I truly am. My brother doesn't care. My father doesn't notice. I think my mother knows. My mother reads the *Saturday Evening Post* and the *Woman's Home Companion*; sometimes the *Ladies' Home Journal*, but never *Good Housekeeping*. I read all my mother's magazines. My father reads *Drug Topics* and *Der Tog*, the Yiddish daily. In Louie Davidowitz's house (waiting our turn for the rabbi's lesson, he teaches me chess in *cheder*) there is a piece of furniture I am in awe of: a shining circular table that is also a revolving bookshelf holding a complete set of Charles Dickens. I borrow *Oliver Twist*. My cousins turn up with *Gulliver's Travels, Just So Stories, Don Quixote,* Oscar Wilde's *Fairy Tales*, uncannily different from the usual kind. Blindfolded, I reach into a Thanksgiving grabbag and pull out *Mrs. Leicester's School,* Mary Lamb's desolate stories of rejected children. Books spill out of rumor, exchange, miracle. In the Park View Pharmacy's lending library I discover, among the nurse romances, a browning, brittle miracle: *Jane Eyre*. Uncle Morris comes to visit (*his* drugstore is on the other side of the Bronx) and leaves behind, just like that, a three-volume Shakespeare. Peggy and Betty Provan, Scottish sisters around the corner, lend me their *Swiss Family Robinson*. Norma Foti, a whole year older, transmits a rumor about Louisa May Alcott; afterward I read *Little Women* a thousand times. Ten thousand! I am no longer incognito, not even to myself. I am Jo in her "vortex"; not Jo exactly, but some Jo-of-the-future. I am under an enchantment: who I truly am must be deferred, waited for and waited for. My father, silently filling capsules, is grieving over his mother in Moscow. I write letters in Yiddish to my Moscow grandmother, whom I will never know. I will never know my Russian aunts, uncles, cousins. In Moscow there is suffering, deprivation, poverty. My mother, threadbare, goes without a new winter coat so that packages can be sent to Moscow. Her fiery justice-eyes are semaphores I cannot decipher.

Some day, when I am free of P.S 71, I will write stories; meanwhile, in winter dusk, in the Park View, in the secret bliss of the Violet Fairy Book, I both see and do not see how these grains of life will stay forever, papa and mama will live forever, Hymie will always turn my skatekey.

Hymie, after Italy, after the Battle of the Bulge, comes back from the war with a present: *From Here to Eternity*. Then he dies, young. Mama reads *Pride and Prejudice* and every single word of Willa Cather. Papa reads, in Yiddish, all of Sholem Aleichem and Peretz. He reads Malamud's *The Assistant* when I ask him to.

Papa and mama, in Staten Island, are under the ground. Some other family sits transfixed in the sun parlor where I read *Jane Eyre* and *Little Women* and, long afterward, *Middlemarch*. The Park View Pharmacy is dismantled, turned into a Hallmark card shop. It doesn't matter! I close my eyes, or else only stare, and everything is in its place again, and everyone.

A writer is dreamed and transfigured into being by spells, wishes, goldfish, silhouettes of trees, boxes of fairy tales dropped in the mud, uncles' and cousins' books, tablets and capsules and powders, papa's Moscow ache, his drugstore jacket with his special fountain pen in the pocket, his beautiful Hebrew paragraphs, his Talmudist's rationalism, his Russian-Gymnasium Latin and German, mama's furnace-heart, her masses of memoirs, her paintings of autumn walks down to the sunny water, her braveries, her reveries, her old, old school hurts.

A writer is buffeted into being by school hurts—Orwell, Forster, Mann!—but after a while other ambushes begin: sorrows, deaths, disappointments, subtle diseases, delays, guilts, the spite of the private haters of the poetry side of life, the snubs of the glamorous, the bitterness of those for whom resentment is a daily gruel, and so on and so on; and then one day you find yourself leaning here, writing at that selfsame round glass table salvaged from the Park View Pharmacy—writing this, an impossibility, a summary of how you came to be where you are now, and where, God knows, is that? Your hair is whitening, you are a well of tears, what you meant to do (beauty and justice) you have not done, papa and mama are under the earth, you live in panic and dread, the future shrinks and darkens, stories are only vapor, your inmost craving is for nothing but an old scarred pen, and what, God knows, is that?

Adrienne Rich

(1929–   )

"Both the victimization and the anger experienced by women are real, and have real sources, everywhere in the environment, built into society, language, the structures of thought. They will go on being tapped and explored by poets, among others. We can neither deny them, nor will rest there," writes Adrienne Rich in the essay "When We Dead Awaken: Writing as Re-vision" (1971). Rich began as a formalist poet, her work praised by W. H. Auden; then as her life and politics changed (she left her marriage, becoming an activist for peace, civil rights, the liberation of women, and the rights of gays and lesbians), she worked in more experimental forms, using such cinematic techniques as jump cuts and collage. Her consistent focus has been the cultural oppression of women, in particular their erasure from the story of Western civilization. In fifteen volumes of poetry, including *Snapshots of a Daughter-in-Law* (1963), *Diving into the Wreck* (1973), *An Atlas of the Difficult World* (1991), *Dark Fields of the Republic* (1995), and *Fox* (2001), and five of prose, including *Of Woman Born: Motherhood as Experience and Institution* (1976) and *Arts of the Possible: Essays and Conversations* (2001), she has fused her politics of moral indignation with her poetic vision, determined "to write directly and overtly as a woman, out of a woman's body and experience."

Prospective Immigrants Please Note

Either you will
go through this door
or you will not go through.

If you go through
there is always the risk
of remembering your name.

Things look at you doubly
and you must look back
and let them happen.

If you do not go through
it is possible
to live worthily

to maintain your attitudes
to hold your position
to die bravely

but much will blind you,
much will evade you,
at what cost who knows?

The door itself
makes no promises.
It is only a door.

Snapshots of a Daughter-in-Law

1. You, once a belle in Shreveport,
   with henna-colored hair, skin like a peachbud,
   still have your dresses copied from that time,
   and play a Chopin prelude
   called by Cortot: *"Delicious recollections
   float like perfume through the memory."*

   Your mind now, mouldering like wedding-cake,
   heavy with useless experience, rich
   with suspicion, rumor, fantasy,
   crumbling to pieces under the knife-edge
   of mere fact. In the prime of your life.

Nervy, glowering, your daughter
wipes the teaspoons, grows another way.

2. Banging the coffee-pot into the sink
she hears the angels chiding, and looks out
past the raked gardens to the sloppy sky.
Only a week since They said: *Have no patience.*

The next time it was: *Be insatiable.*
Then: *Save yourself; others you cannot save.*
Sometimes she's let the tapstream scald her arm,
a match burn to her thumbnail,

or held her hand above the kettle's snout
right in the woolly steam. They are probably angels,
since nothing hurts her any more, except
each morning's grit blowing into her eyes.

3. A thinking woman sleeps with monsters.
The beak that grips her, she becomes. And Nature,
that sprung-lidded, still commodious
steamer-trunk of *tempora* and *mores*
gets stuffed with it all: the mildewed orange-flowers,
the female pills, the terrible breasts
of Boadicea beneath flat foxes' heads and orchids.

Two handsome women, gripped in argument,
each proud, acute, subtle, I hear scream
across the cut glass and majolica
like Furies cornered from their prey:
The argument *ad feminam*, all the old knives
that have rusted in my back, I drive in yours,
ma semblable, ma soeur!

4. Knowing themselves too well in one another;
    their gifts no pure fruition, but a thorn,
    the prick filed sharp against a hint of scorn . . .
    Reading while waiting
    for the iron to heat,
    writing, *My life had stood—a Loaded Gun—*
    in that Amherst pantry while the jellies boil and scum,
    or, more often,
    iron-eyed and beaked and purposed as a bird,
    dusting everything on the whatnot every day of life.

5. *Dulce ridens, dulce loquens,*★
    she shaves her legs until they gleam
    like petrified mammoth-tusk.

6. When to her lute Corinna sings
    neither words nor music are her own;
    only the long hair dipping
    over her cheek, only the song
    of silk against her knees
    and these
    adjusted in reflections of an eye.

    Poised, trembling and unsatisfied, before
    an unlocked door, that cage of cages,
    tell us, you bird, you tragical machine—
    is this *fertilisante douleur?*★★ Pinned down
    by love, for you the only natural action,
    are you edged more keen
    to prise the secrets of the vault? has Nature shown
    her household books to you, daughter-in-law,
    that her sons never saw?

★ "Sweet laughter, sweet talk."
★★ Enriching pain

7. *"To have in this uncertain world some stay*
   which cannot be undermined, is
   of the utmost consequence."★

                    Thus wrote
   a woman, partly brave and partly good,
   who fought with what she partly understood.
   Few men about her would or could do more,
   hence she was labelled harpy, shrew and whore.

8. "You all die at fifteen," said Diderot,
   and turn part legend, part convention.
   Still, eyes inaccurately dream
   behind closed windows blankening with steam.
   Deliciously, all that we might have been,
   all that we were—fire, tears,
   wit, taste, martyred ambition—
   stirs like the memory of refused adultery
   the drained and flagging bosom of our middle years.

9. *Not that it is done well, but*
   that it is done at all?★★ Yes, think
   of the odds! or shrug them off forever.
   This luxury of the precocious child,
   Time's precious chronic invalid,—
   would we, darlings, resign it if we could?
   Our blight has been our sinecure:
   mere talent was enough for us—
   glitter in fragments and rough drafts.

★ The words of Mary Wollstonecraft (see page 33).
★★ Reference to Samuel Johnson's comment: "A woman's preaching is like a dog's walking on his hinder legs. It is not done well, but you are surprised to find it done at all."

Sigh no more, ladies.
                                        Time is male
and in his cups drinks to the fair.
Bemused by gallantry, we hear
our mediocrities over-praised,
indolence read as abnegation,
slattern thought styled intuition,
every lapse forgiven, our crime
only to cast too bold a shadow
or smash the mould straight off.

For that, solitary confinement,
tear gas, attrition shelling.
Few applicants for that honor.

10.   Well,
    she's long about her coming, who must be
    more merciless to herself than history.
    Her mind full to the wind, I see her plunge
    breasted and glancing through the currents,
    taking the light upon her
    at least as beautiful as any boy
    or helicopter,
                    poised, still coming,
    her fine blades making the air wince

    but her cargo
    no promise then:
    delivered
    palpable
    ours.

Toni Morrison

(1931-   )

Toni Morrison, one of the most celebrated of living American writ-ers, was born Chloe Anthony Wofford in Ohio, which is the setting of three of her six novels, *The Bluest Eye* (1970), *Sula* (1973), and *Beloved* (1987); the others are *Song of Solomon* (1977), *Tar Baby* (1981), and *Jazz* (1992). In *Imagining Characters*, British novelist A. S. Byatt describes the imaginative power of Morrison's writings as "Tolstoyan": "she gives you no option but to inhabit her world." When she became the first African American writer to be awarded the Nobel Prize for literature in 1993, Henry Louis Gates com-mented that the award would have been deserved had Morrison written only *Beloved*, a winner of the Pulitzer Prize, which many consider her masterpiece. A professor at Princeton University, Morrison wrote that fiction "should be beautiful and powerful, but it should also work. It should have something in it that enlightens; something in it that opens the door and points the way. Something in it that suggests what the conflicts are, what the problems are. But it need not solve those problems because it is not a case study, it is not a recipe."

Nobel Lecture, 7 December 1993

Members of the Swedish Academy, Ladies and Gentlemen:

Narrative has never been merely entertainment for me. It is, I believe, one of the principal ways in which we absorb knowledge. I hope you will understand, then, why I begin these remarks with the opening phrase of what must be the oldest sentence in the world, and the earliest one we remember from childhood: "Once upon a time . . ."

"Once upon a time there was an old woman. Blind but wise." Or was it an old man? A guru, perhaps. Or a *griot*★ soothing restless children. I have

★ A storyteller in western Africa.

heard this story, or one exactly like it, in the lore of several cultures.

"Once upon a time there was an old woman. Blind. Wise."

In the version I know the woman is the daughter of slaves, black, American, and lives alone in a small house outside of town. Her reputation for wisdom is without peer and without question. Among her people she is both the law and its transgression. The honor she is paid and the awe in which she is held reach beyond her neighborhood to places far away; to the city where the intelligence of rural prophets is the source of much amusement.

One day the woman is visited by some young people who seem to be bent on disproving her clairvoyance and showing her up for the fraud they believe she is. Their plan is simple: they enter her house and ask the one question the answer to which rides solely on her difference from them, a difference they regard as a profound disability: her blindness. They stand before her, and one of them says,

"Old woman, I hold in my hand a bird. Tell me whether it is living or dead."

She does not answer, and the question is repeated. "Is the bird I am holding living or dead?"

Still she does not answer. She is blind and cannot see her visitors, let alone what is in their hands. She does not know their color, gender, or homeland. She knows only their motive.

The old woman's silence is so long, the young people have trouble holding their laughter.

Finally she speaks, and her voice is soft but stern. "I don't know," she says. "I don't know whether the bird you are holding is dead or alive, but what I do know is that it is in your hands. It is in your hands."

Her answer can be taken to mean: if it is dead, you have either found it that way or you have killed it. If it is alive, you can still kill it. Whether it is to stay alive is your decision. Whatever the case, it is your responsibility.

For parading their power and her helplessness, the young visitors are reprimanded, and told they are responsible not only for the act of mockery but also for the small bundle of life sacrificed to achieve its aims. The blind woman shifts attention away from assertions of power to the instrument through which that power is exercised.

Speculation on what (other than its own frail body) that bird in the hand might signify has always been attractive to me, but especially so now, thinking as I have been about the work I do that has brought me to this company. So I choose to read the bird as language and the woman as a practiced writer.

She is worried about how the language she dreams in, given to her at birth, is handled, put into service, even withheld from her for certain nefarious purposes. Being a writer, she thinks of language partly as a system, partly as a living thing over which one has control, but mostly as agency—as an act with consequences. So the question the children put to her, "Is it living or dead?," is not unreal, because she thinks of language as susceptible to death, erasure; certainly imperiled and salvageable only by an effort of the will. She believes that if the bird in the hands of her visitors is dead, the custodians are responsible for the corpse. For her a dead language is not only one no longer spoken or written, it is unyielding language content to admire its own paralysis. Like statist language, censored and censoring. Ruthless in its policing duties, it has no desire or purpose other than to maintain the free range of its own narcotic narcissism, its own exclusivity and dominance. However, moribund, it is not without effect, for it actively thwarts the intellect, stalls conscience, suppresses human potential. Unreceptive to interrogation, it cannot form or tolerate new ideas, shape other thoughts, tell another story, fill baffling silences. Official language smitheried to sanction ignorance and preserve privilege is a suit of armor, polished to shocking glitter, a husk from which the knight departed long ago. Yet there it is; dumb, predatory, sentimental. Exciting reverence in schoolchildren, providing shelter for despots, summoning false memories of stability, harmony among the public.

She is convinced that when language dies, out of carelessness, disuse, indifference, and absence of esteem, or killed by fiat, not only she herself but all users and makers are accountable for its demise. In her country children have bitten their tongues off and use bullets instead to iterate the void of speechlessness, of disabled and disabling language, of language adults have abandoned altogether as a device for grappling with meaning, providing guidance, or expressing love. But she knows tongue-suicide is not only the choice of children. It is common among the infantile heads of state and power merchants whose evacuated language leaves them with no access to what is left of their human instincts, for they speak only to those who obey, or in order to force obedience.

The systematic looting of language can be recognized by the tendency of its users to forgo its nuanced, complex, midwifery properties, replacing them with menace and subjugation. Oppressive language does more than represent violence; it is violence; does more than represent the limits of knowledge; it limits knowledge. Whether it is obscuring state language or the faux language of mindless media; whether it is the proud but calcified language of the academy or the commodity-driven language of science; whether it is the malign language of law-without-ethics, or language designed for the estrangement of minorities, hiding its racist plunder in its literary cheek—it must be rejected, altered, and exposed. It is the language that drinks blood, laps vulnerabilities, tucks its fascist boots under crinolines of respectability and patriotism as it moves relentlessly toward the bottom line and the bottomed-out mind. Sexist language, racist language, theistic language—all are typical of the policing languages of mastery, and cannot, do not, permit new knowledge or encourage the mutual exchange of ideas.

The old woman is keenly aware that no intellectual mercenary or insatiable dictator, no paid-for politician or demagogue, no counterfeit journalist would be persuaded by her thoughts. There is and will be rousing language to keep citizens armed and arming; slaughtered and slaughtering in the malls, courthouses, post offices, playgrounds, bedrooms, and boulevards; stirring, memorializing language to mask the pity and waste of needless death. There will be more diplomatic language to countenance rape, torture, assassination. There is and will be more seductive, mutant language designed to throttle women, to pack their throats like pâté-producing geese with their own unsayable, transgressive words; there will be more of the language of surveillance disguised as research; of politics and history calculated to render the suffering of millions mute; language glamorized to thrill the dissatisfied and bereft into assaulting their neighbors; arrogant pseudo-empirical language crafted to lock creative people into cages of inferiority and hopelessness.

Underneath the eloquence, the glamour, the scholarly associations, however stirring or seductive, the heart of such language is languishing, or perhaps not beating at all—if the bird is already dead.

She has thought about what could have been the intellectual history of any discipline if it had not insisted upon, or been forced into, the waste of time and life that rationalizations for and representations of dominance required—lethal discourses of exclusion blocking access to cognition for both the excluder and the excluded.

The conventional wisdom of the Tower of Babel story is that the collapse was a misfortune. That it was the distraction or the weight of many languages that precipitated the tower's failed architecture. That one monolithic language would have expedited the building, and heaven would have been reached. Whose heaven, she wonders? And what kind? Perhaps the achievement of Paradise was premature, a little hasty if no one could take the time to understand other languages, other views, other narratives. Had they, the heaven they imagined might have been found at their feet. Complicated, demanding, yes, but a view of heaven as life; not heaven as post-life.

She would not want to leave her young visitors with the impression that language should be forced to stay alive merely to be. The vitality of language lies in its ability to limn the actual, imagined, and possible lives of its speakers, readers, writers. Although its poise is sometimes in displacing experience, it is not a substitute for it. It arcs toward the place where meaning may lie. When a president of the United States thought about the graveyard his country had become, and said, "The world will little note nor long remember what we say here. But it will never forget what they did here," his simple words were exhilarating in their life-sustaining properties because they refused to encapsulate the reality of 600,000 dead men in a cataclysmic race war. Refusing to monumentalize, disdaining the "final word," the precise "summing up," acknowledging their "poor power to add or detract," his words signal deference to the uncapturability of the life it mourns. It is the deference that moves her, that recognition that language can never live up to life once and for all. Nor should it. Language can never "pin down" slavery, genocide, war. Nor should it yearn for the arrogance to be able to do so. Its force, its felicity, is in its reach toward the ineffable.

Be it grand or slender, burrowing, blasting or refusing to sanctify; whether it laughs out loud or is a cry without an alphabet, the choice word or the chosen silence, unmolested language surges toward knowledge, not its destruction. But who does not know of literature banned because it is interrogative; discredited because it is critical; erased because alternate? And how many are outraged by the thought of a self-ravaged tongue?

Word-work is sublime, she thinks, because it is generative; it makes meaning that secures our difference, our human difference—the way in which we are like no other life.

We die. That may be the meaning of life. But we *do* language. That may be the measure of our lives.

"Once upon a time . . ." Visitors ask an old woman a question. Who are they, these children? What did they make of that encounter? What did they hear in those final words: "The bird is in your hands"? A sentence that gestures toward possibility, or one that drops a latch? Perhaps what the children heard was, "It's not my problem. I am old, female, black, blind. What wisdom I have now is in knowing I cannot help you. The future of language is yours."

They stand there. Suppose nothing was in their hands. Suppose the visit was only a ruse, a trick to get to be spoken to, taken seriously as they have not been before. A chance to interrupt, to violate the adult world, its miasma of discourse about them. Urgent questions are at stake, including the one they have asked: "Is it the bird we are holding living or dead?" Perhaps the question meant: "Could someone tell us what is life? What is death?" No trick at all; no silliness. A straightforward question worthy of the attention of a wise one. An old one. And if the old and wise who have lived life and faced death cannot describe either, who can?

But she does not; she keeps her secret, her good opinion of herself, her gnomic pronouncements, her art without commitment. She keeps her distance, enforces it and retreats into the singularity of isolation, in sophisticated, privileged space.

Nothing, no word follows her declaration of transfer. That silence is deep, deeper than the meaning available in the words she has spoken. It shivers, this silence, and the children, annoyed, fill it with language invented on the spot.

"Is there no speech," they ask her, "no words you can give us that help us break through your dossier of failures? through the education you have just given us that is no education at all because we are paying close attention to what you have done as well as to what you have said? to the barrier you have erected between generosity and wisdom?

"We have no bird in our hands, living or dead. We have only you and our important question. Is the nothing in our hands something you could not bear to contemplate, to even guess? Don't you remember being young, when language was magic without meaning? When what you could say, could not mean? When the invisible was what imagination strove to see? When questions and demands for answers burned so brightly you trembled with fury at not knowing?

"Do we have to begin consciousness with a battle heroes and heroines like you have already fought and lost, leaving us with nothing in our hands except what you have imagined is there? Your answer is artful, but its artfulness embarrasses us and ought to embarrass you. Your answer is indecent in its self-congratulation. A made-for-television script that makes no sense if there is nothing in our hands.

"Why didn't you reach out, touch us with your soft fingers, delay the sound bite, the lesson, until you knew who we were? Did you so despise our trick, our modus operandi, that you could not see that we were baffled about how to get your attention? We are young. Unripe. We have heard all our short lives that we have to be responsible. What could that possibly mean in the catastrophe this world has become; where, as a poet said, 'nothing needs to be exposed since it is already barefaced'? Our inheritance is an affront. You want us to have your old, blank eyes and see only cruelty and mediocrity. Do you think we are stupid enough to perjure ourselves again and again with the fiction of nationhood? How dare you talk to us of duty when we stand waist deep in the toxin of your past?

"You trivialize us and trivialize the bird that is not in our hands. Is there no context for our lives? No song, no literature, no poem full of vitamins, no history connected to experience that you can pass along to help us start strong? You are an adult. The old one, the wise one. Stop thinking about saving your face. Think of our lives and tell us your particularized world. Make up a story. Narrative is radical, creating us at the very moment it is being created. We will not blame you if your reach exceeds your grasp; if love so ignites your words that they go down in flames and nothing is left but their scald. Or if, with the reticence of a surgeon's hands, your words suture only the places where blood might flow. We know you can never do it properly—once and for all. Passion is never enough; neither is skill. But try. For our sake and yours forget your name in the street; tell us what the world has been to you in the dark places and in the light. Don't tell us what to believe, what to fear. Show us belief's wide skirt and the stitch that unravels fear's caul. You, old woman, blessed with blindness, can speak the language that tells us what only language can: how to see without pictures. Language alone protects us from the scariness of things with no names. Language alone is meditation.

"Tell us what it is to be a woman so that we may know what it is to be a man. What moves at the margin. What it is to have no home in this place. To be set adrift from the one you knew. What it is to live at the edge of towns that cannot bear your company.

"Tell us about ships turned away from shorelines at Easter, placenta in a field. Tell us about a wagonload of slaves, how they sang so softly their breath was indistinguishable from the falling snow. How they knew from the hunch of the nearest shoulder that the next stop would be their last. How, with hands prayered in their sex, they thought of heat, then sun. Lifting their faces as though it was there for the taking. Turning as though there for the taking. They stop at an inn. The driver and his mate go in with the lamp, leaving them humming in the dark. The horse's void steams into the snow beneath its hooves and the hiss and melt are the envy of the freezing slaves.

"The inn door opens: a girl and a boy step away from its light. They climb into the wagon bed. The boy will have a gun in three years, but now he carries a lamp and a jug of warm cider. They pass it from mouth to mouth. The girl offers bread, pieces of meat, and something more: a glance into the eyes of the one she serves. One helping for each man, two for each woman. And a look. They look back. The next stop will be their last. But not this one. This one is warmed."

It's quiet again when the children finish speaking, until the woman breaks into the silence.

"Finally," she says. "I trust you now. I trust you with the bird that is not in your hands because you have truly caught it. Look. How lovely it is, this thing we have done—together."

Alice Munro

(1931–   )

For Cynthia Ozick, Alice Munro is "our Chekhov." Declaring herself humbled by the comparison, Munro acknowledges other literary influences who are closer to her native place—southern Ontario—and her generation: starting out, she admired Eudora Welty, Carson McCullers, Katherine Anne Porter, Flannery O'Connor, James Agee; later came John Updike, John Cheever, Joyce Carol Oates, Peter Taylor—and "especially and forever" William Maxwell—then William Trevor, Edna O'Brien, and Richard Ford. On the basis of her eight volumes of short stories, including *The Beggar Maid* (1980), *The Moons of Jupiter* (1982), *The Progress of Love* (1986), *Friend of My Youth* (1990), and one novel, *Lives of Girls and Women* (1971), she's been called one of the best short-story writers in the English language. A moralist who is never judgmental, she sees always the ambiguity of every situation and choice. Her 1998 collection, *The Love of a Good Woman*, from which the following story comes, was described by one reviewer as amounting to "a portrait of a generation: a generation [of women] that came to adulthood with one set of rules and then found it could live with another."

The Children Stay

Thirty years ago, a family was spending a holiday together on the east coast of Vancouver Island. A young father and mother, their two small daughters, and an older couple, the husband's parents.

What perfect weather. Every morning, every morning it's like this, the first pure sunlight falling through the high branches, burning away the mist over the still water of Georgia Strait.

If it weren't for the tide, it would be hard to remember that this is the sea. You look across the water to the mountains on the mainland, the ranges that are the western wall of the continent of North America. These humps and peaks coming clear now through the mist are of interest to the grandfather and to his son, Brian. The two men are continually trying to decide which of these shapes are actual continental mountains and which are improbable heights of the islands that ride in front of the shore.

There is a map, set up under glass, between the cottages and the beach. You can stand there looking at the map, then looking at what's in front of you and back at the map again, until you get things sorted out. The grandfather and Brian usually get into an argument—though you'd think there would not be much room for disagreement with the map right there.

Brian's mother won't look at the map. She says it boggles her mind. Her concern is always about whether anybody is hungry yet, or thirsty, whether the children have their sun hats on and have been rubbed with protective lotion. She makes her husband wear a floppy cotton hat and thinks that Brian should wear one, too—she reminds him of how sick he got from the sun that summer they went to the Okanagan, when he was a child. Sometimes Brian says to her, "Oh, dry up, Mother." His tone is mostly affectionate, but his father may ask him if that's the way he thinks he can talk to his mother nowadays.

"She doesn't mind," says Brian.

"How do you know?" says his father.

"Oh, for Pete's sake," says his mother.

Pauline, the young mother, slides out of bed as soon as she's awake every morning, slides out of reach of Brian's long, sleepily searching arms and legs. What wakes her is the first squeaks and mutters of the baby, Mara, in the children's room, then the creak of the crib as Mara—sixteen months old now, getting to the end of babyhood—pulls herself up to stand hanging on to the railing. She continues her soft amiable talk as Pauline lifts her out—Caitlin, nearly five, shifting about but not waking, in her nearby bed—and as she is carried into the kitchen to be changed, on the floor. Then she is settled into her stroller, with a biscuit and a bottle of apple juice, while Pauline gets into her sundress and sandals, goes to the bathroom, combs out her hair—all as quickly and quietly as possible. They leave the cottage and head for the bumpy unpaved road that runs behind the cottages, a mile or so north till it stops at the bank of the little river that runs into the sea. The road is still mostly in deep morning shadow, the floor of a tunnel under fir and cedar trees.

The grandfather, also an early riser, sees them from the porch of his cottage, and Pauline sees him. But all that is necessary is a wave. He and Pauline never have much to say to each other (though sometimes there's an affinity they feel, in the midst of some long-drawn-out antics of Brian's or some apologetic but insistent fuss made by the grandmother, there's an awareness of not looking at each other, lest their look reveal a bleakness that would discredit others).

On this holiday Pauline steals time to be by herself—being with Mara is still almost the same thing as being by herself. Early morning walks, the late morning hour when she washes and hangs out the diapers. She could have had another hour or so in the afternoons, while Mara is napping. But Brian has fixed up a shelter on the beach, and he carries the playpen down every day, so that Mara can nap there and Pauline won't have to absent herself. He says his parents might be offended if she's always sneaking off. He agrees, though, that she does need some time to go over her lines for the play she's going to be in, back in Victoria, this September.

Pauline is not an actress. This is an amateur production, and she didn't even try out for the role. She was asked if she would like to be in this play by a man she met at a barbecue, in June. The people there were mostly teachers, and their wives or husbands—it was held at the house of the principal of the high school where Brian taught. The woman who taught French was a widow—she had brought her grown son, who was staying for the summer with her and working as a night clerk in a downtown hotel. She told everybody that he had got a job teaching at a college in western Washington State and would be going there in the fall.

Jeffrey Toom was his name. "Without the 'b,'" he said, as if the staleness of the joke wounded him.

What was he going to teach?

"Dram-ah," he said, drawing the word out in a mocking way.

He spoke of his present job disparagingly as well.

"It's a pretty sordid place," he said. "Maybe you heard—a hooker was killed there last February. And then we get the usual losers checking in to O.D. or bump themselves off."

People did not quite know what to make of this way of talking and drifted away from him. Except for Pauline.

"I'm thinking about putting on a play," he said. He asked her if she had ever heard of *Eurydice*.

Pauline said, "You mean Anouilh's?" and he was unflatteringly surprised. He immediately said he didn't know if it would ever work out. "I just thought it might be interesting to see if you could do something different here in the land of Noël Coward."

Pauline did not remember when there had been a play by Noël Coward put on in Victoria, though she supposed there had been several. She said, "We saw *The Duchess of Malfi* last winter at the college."

"Yeah. Well," he said, flushing. She had thought he was older than she was, at least as old as Brian—who was thirty, though people were apt to say he didn't act it—but as soon as he started talking to her, in this offhand, dismissive way, never quite meeting her eyes, she suspected that he was younger than he'd like to appear. Now, with that flush, she was sure of it.

As it turned out, he was a year younger than she was. Twenty-five.

She said that she couldn't be Eurydice—she couldn't act. But Brian came over to see what the conversation was about and said at once that she must try it.

"She just needs a kick in the behind," Brian said to Jeffrey. "She's like a little mule—it's hard to get her started. No, seriously, she's too self-effacing. I tell her that all the time. She's very smart. She's actually a lot smarter than I am."

At that Jeffrey did look directly into Pauline's eyes—impertinently and searchingly—and she was the one who was flushing.

He had chosen her immediately as his Eurydice because of the way she looked. But it was not because she was beautiful. "I'd never put a beautiful girl in that part," he said. "I don't know if I'd ever put a beautiful girl onstage in anything. It's distracting."

So what did he mean about the way she looked? He said it was her hair, which was long and dark and rather bushy (not in style at that time), and her pale skin ("Stay out of the sun this summer") and, most of all, her eyebrows.

"I never liked them," said Pauline, not quite sincerely. Her eyebrows were level, dark, luxuriant. They dominated her face. Like her hair, they were not in style. But if she had really disliked them, wouldn't she have plucked them?

Jeffrey seemed not to have heard her. "They give you a sulky look and that's disturbing," he said. "Also your jaw's a little heavy and that's sort of Greek. It would be better in a movie, where I could get you close up. The routine thing for Eurydice would be a girl who looked ethereal. I don't want ethereal."

As she walked Mara along the road, Pauline did work at the lines. There was a long speech at the end that was giving her trouble. She bumped the stroller along and repeated to herself, "You are terrible, you know, you are terrible like the angels. You think everybody's going forward, as brave and bright as you are—oh, don't look at me, please, darling, don't look at me— Perhaps I'm not what you wish I was, but I'm here, and I'm warm, I'm kind, and I love you. I'll give you all the happiness I can. Don't look at me. Don't look. Let me live."

She had left something out. "Perhaps I'm not what you wish I was, but you feel me here, don't you? I'm warm and I'm kind—"

She had told Jeffrey that she thought the play was beautiful.

He said, "Really?" What she'd said didn't please or surprise him—he seemed to feel it was predictable, superfluous. He would never describe a play in that way. He spoke of it more as a hurdle to be got over. Also a challenge to be flung at various enemies. At the academic snots, as he called them, who had done *The Duchess of Malfi*. And at the social twits, as he called them, in the little theatre. He saw himself as an outsider heaving his weight against these people, putting on his play—he called it his—in the teeth of their contempt and opposition. In the beginning Pauline thought that this must be all in his imagination. Then something would happen that could be, but might not be, a coincidence—repairs to be done on the church hall where the play was to be performed, making it unobtainable, an unexpected increase in the cost of printing advertising posters—and she found herself seeing it his way. If you were going to be around him much, you almost had to see it his way— arguing was dangerous and exhausting.

"Sons of bitches," said Jeffrey between his teeth, but with some satisfaction. "I'm not surprised. I'm going to get to the bottom of this."

The rehearsals were held upstairs in an old building on Fisgard Street. Sunday afternoon was the only time that everybody could get there, though there were fragmentary rehearsals during the week. Pauline had to depend on sometimes undependable high-school babysitters—for the first six weeks of the summer Brian was busy teaching summer school. And Jeffrey himself had to be at his hotel job by eight o'clock in the evening. But on Sunday afternoons they were all there, laboring in the dusty high-ceilinged room on Fisgard Street. The windows were rounded at the top as in some plain and dignified church, and propped open in the heat with whatever objects could be found—ledger books from the nineteen-twenties, belonging to the hat shop that had once operated downstairs, pieces of wood left over from the picture frames made by the artist whose canvases were now stacked against one wall and apparently abandoned. The glass was grimy, but outside the sunlight bounced off the sidewalks, the empty gravelled parking lots, the low stuccoed buildings, with what seemed a special Sunday brightness. Hardly anybody moved through these downtown streets. Nothing was open except the occasional hole-in-the-wall coffee shop or lackadaisical, flyspecked convenience store.

Pauline was the one who went out at the break to get soft drinks and coffee. She was the one who had the least to say about the play and the way it was going—even though she was the only one who had read it before—because she alone had never done any acting. So it seemed proper for her to volunteer. She enjoyed her short walk in the empty streets—she felt as if she had become an urban person, someone detached and solitary, who lived in the glare of an important dream. Sometimes she thought of Brian at home, working in the garden and keeping an eye on the children. Or perhaps he had taken them to Dallas Road—she recalled a promise—to sail boats on the pond. That life seemed ragged and tedious compared to what went on in the rehearsal room—the hours of effort, the concentration, the sharp exchanges, the sweating and tension. Even the taste of the coffee, its scalding bitterness, and the fact that it was chosen by nearly everybody in preference to a fresher-tasting and maybe more healthful drink out of the cooler, seemed satisfying to her.

—

When she said that she had to go away for the two-week holiday, Jeffrey looked thunderstruck, as if he had never imagined that things like holidays could come into her life. Then he turned grim and slightly satirical, as if this were just another blow that he might have expected. Pauline explained that she would miss only the one Sunday—the one in the middle of the two weeks—because she and Brian were driving up the Island on a Monday and coming back on a Sunday morning. She promised to get back in time for rehearsal. Privately she wondered how she would do this—it always took so much longer than you expected to pack up and get away. She wondered if she could possibly come back by herself, on the morning bus. That would probably be too much to ask for. She didn't mention it.

She couldn't ask him if it was only the play he was thinking about, only her absence from a rehearsal that caused the thundercloud. At the moment, it very likely was. When he spoke to her at rehearsals there was never any suggestion that he ever spoke to her in any other way. The only difference in his treatment of her was that perhaps he expected less of her, of her acting, than he did of the others. And that would be understandable to anybody. She was the only one chosen out of the blue, for the way she looked—the others had all shown up at the audition he had advertised on signs put up in cafés and bookstores around town.

Yet she thought they all knew what was going on, in spite of Jeffrey's offhand and abrupt and none too civil ways. They knew that after every one of them had straggled off home he would walk across the room and bolt the staircase door. (At first Pauline had pretended to leave with the rest and had even got into her car and circled the block, but later such a trick had come to seem insulting, not just to herself and Jeffrey but to the others, whom she was sure would never betray her, bound as they all were under the temporary but potent spell of the play.)

Jeffrey crossed the room and bolted the door. Every time, this was like a new decision that he had to make. Until it was done, she wouldn't look at him. The sound of the bolt being pushed into place, the ominous or fatalistic sound of metal hitting metal, gave her a localized shock of capitulation. But she didn't make a move, she waited for him to come back to her with the whole story of the afternoon's labor draining out of his face, the expression of matter-of-fact and customary disappointment cleared away, replaced by the live energy she always found surprising.

"So. Tell us what this play of yours is about," Brian's father said. "Is it one of those ones where they take their clothes off on the stage?"

"Now, don't tease her," said Brian's mother.

Brian and Pauline had put the children to bed and walked over to his parents' cottage for an evening drink. The sunset was behind them, behind the forests of Vancouver Island, but the mountains in front of them, all clear now and hard cut against the sky, shone in its pink light. Some high inland mountains were capped with pink summer snow.

"The story of Orpheus and Eurydice is that Eurydice died," Pauline said.

"And Orpheus goes down to the underworld to try to get her back. And his wish is granted, but only if he promises not to look at her. Not to look back at her. She's walking behind him—"

"Twelve paces," said Brian. "As is only right."

"It's a Greek story, but it's set in modern times," said Pauline. "At least this version is. More or less modern. Orpheus is a musician travelling around with his father—they're both musicians—and Eurydice is an actress. This is in France."

"Translated?" Brian's father said.

"No," said Brian. "But don't worry, it's not in French. It was written in Transylvanian."

"It's so hard to make sense of anything," Brian's mother said with a worried laugh. "It's so hard, with Brian around."

"It's in English," Pauline said.

"And you're what's-her-name?"

She said, "I'm Eurydice."

"He get you back O.K.?"

"No," she said. "He looks back at me and then I have to stay dead."

"Oh, an unhappy ending," Brian's mother said.

"You're so gorgeous?" said Brian's father skeptically. "He can't stop himself from looking back?"

"It's not that," said Pauline. But at this point she felt that something had been achieved by her father-in-law, he had done what he meant to do, which was the same thing that he nearly always meant to do, in any conversation she had with him. And that was to break through the careful structure of some explanation he had asked her for, and she had unwillingly but patiently given, and with a seemingly negligent kick knock it into rubble. He had been dangerous to her for a long time in this way, though he wasn't particularly so tonight.

But Brian did not know that. Brian was still figuring out how to come to her rescue.

"Pauline is gorgeous," Brian said.

"Yes indeed," said his mother.

"Maybe if she'd go to the hairdresser," his father said. But Pauline's long hair was such an old objection of his that it had become a family joke. Even Pauline laughed. She said, "I can't afford to till we get the veranda roof fixed."

And Brian laughed boisterously, full of relief that she was able to take all this as a joke. It was what he had always told her to do.

"Just kid him back. It's the only way to handle him."

"Yeah, well, if you'd got yourselves a decent house," said his father. But this, like Pauline's hair, was such a familiar sore point that it couldn't rouse anybody. Brian and Pauline had bought a handsome house in bad repair on a street in Victoria where old mansions were being turned into ill-used apartment buildings. The house, the street, the messy old Garry oaks, the fact that no basement had been blasted out under the house, was all a horror to Brian's father. So what he said now about a decent house might be some kind of peace signal. Or could be taken so.

Brian was an only son. He was a math teacher. His father was a civil engineer, and part owner of a contracting company. If he had hoped that he would have a son who was an engineer and might come into the company, there was never any mention of it. Pauline had asked Brian whether he thought the carping about their house, and her hair, and the books she read, might be a cover for this larger disappointment, but Brian had said, "Nope. In our family we complain about just whatever we want to complain about. We ain't subtle, Ma'am."

Pauline still wondered, when she heard his mother talking about how teachers ought to be the most honored people in the world and they did not get half the credit they deserved and that she didn't know how Brian managed it, day after day. Then his father might say, "That's right," or "I sure wouldn't want to do it, I can tell you that. They couldn't pay me to do it."

And Brian would turn that into a joke, as he turned nearly everything into a joke.

"Don't worry, Dad. They don't pay you much."

Brian in his everyday life was a much more dramatic person than Jeffrey. He dominated his classes by keeping up a parade of jokes and antics, extending the role that he had always played, Pauline believed, with his mother and father. He acted dumb, he bounced back from pretended humiliations, he traded insults. He was a bully in a good cause—a chivying, cheerful, indestructible bully.

"Your boy has certainly made his mark with us," the principal said to Pauline. "He has not just survived, which is something in itself. He has made his mark."

Your boy.

He called his students boneheads. His tone was affectionate, fatalistic. He said that his father was the King of the Philistines, a pure and natural barbarian. And that his mother was a dishrag, good-natured and worn out. But however he dismissed such people, he could not be long without them. He took his students on camping trips. And he could not imagine a summer without this shared holiday. He was mortally afraid, every year, that Pauline would refuse to go along. Or that, having agreed to go, she was going to be miserable, take offense at something his father said, complain about how much time she had to spend with his mother, sulk because there was no way they could do anything by themselves. She might decide to spend all day in their own cottage, reading, and pretending to have a sunburn.

All those things had happened, on previous holidays. But this year she was easing up. He told her he could see that, and he was grateful to her.

"I know it's an effort," he said. "It's different for me. They're my parents and I'm used to not taking them seriously."

Pauline came from a family that took things so seriously that her parents had got a divorce. Her mother was not dead. She had a distant, though cordial, relationship with her father and her two much older sisters. She said that they had nothing in common. She knew Brian could not understand how that could be a reason. She saw what comfort it gave him, this year, to see things going so well. She had thought it was laziness or cowardice that kept him from breaking the arrangement, but now she saw that it was something far more positive. He needed to have his wife and his parents and his children bound together like this, he needed to involve Pauline in his life with his parents and to bring his parents to some recognition of her—though the recognition, from his father, would always be muffled and contrary, and from his mother too profuse, too easily come by, to mean much. Also he wanted Pauline to be connected—and the children, too—to his own childhood. He wanted these holidays to be linked to the holidays of his youth with their lucky or unlucky weather, car troubles, boating scares, bee stings, marathon Monopoly games, to all the things that he told his mother he was bored to death hearing about. He wanted pictures from this summer to be taken, and fitted into his mother's album, a continuation of all the other pictures that he groaned at the mention of.

The only time they could talk to each other was in bed, late at night. But they did talk then, more than was usual with them at home, where Brian was so tired that often he fell immediately asleep. And in ordinary daylight it was hard to talk to him because of his jokes. She could see the joke brightening his eyes. (His coloring was very like hers—dark hair and pale skin and gray eyes—but her eyes were cloudy and his were light, like clear water over stones.) She could see it pulling at the corners of his mouth as he foraged among your words to catch a pun or the start of a rhyme—anything that could take the conversation away, into absurdity. His whole body, tall and loosely joined together and still almost as skinny as a teenager's, twitched with comic propensity. Before she married him, Pauline had a friend named Gracie, a rather grumpy-looking girl, subversive about men. Brian had thought her a girl whose spirits needed a boost, and so he made even more than the usual effort. And Gracie said to Pauline, "How can you stand the non-stop show?"

"That's not the real Brian," Pauline had said. "He's different when we're alone." But, looking back, she wondered how true that had ever been. Had she said it simply to defend her choice, as you did when you had made up your mind to get married?

Even in the cottage, with the window open on the unfamiliar darkness and stillness of the night, he teased a little. He had to speak of Jeffrey as Monsieur le Directeur, which made the play, or the fact that it was a French play, slightly ridiculous. Or perhaps it was Jeffrey himself, Jeffrey's serious-ness about the play, that had to be called into question.

Pauline didn't care. It was such a pleasure and a relief to her to mention Jeffrey's name.

Though most of the time she didn't mention him, she circled around that pleasure. She described all the others instead. The hairdresser and the harbor pilot and the busboy and the old man who claimed to have once acted on the radio. He played Orphée's father, and gave Jeffrey the most trouble, because he had the stubbornest notions of his own about acting.

The middle-aged impresario, M. Dulac, was played by a twenty-four-year-old travel agent. And Mathias, who was Eurydice's former boyfriend, presumably around her own age, was played by the manager of a shoe store, who was married and a father.

"Why didn't Monsieur le Directeur cast those two the other way round?" said Brian.

"That's the way he does things," Pauline said. "What he see in us is some-thing different from the obvious."

For instance, she said, the busboy was a difficult Orphée.

"He's only nineteen, he's terribly shy, but he's determined to be an actor. Even if it's like making love to his grandmother. Jeffrey has to keep at him. 'Keep your arms around her a little longer, stroke her a little—'"

"He might get to like it," Brian said. "Maybe I should come around and keep an eye on him."

At this Pauline snorted. When she had started to quote Jeffrey she had felt a giving-way in her womb or the bottom of her stomach, a shock that had travelled oddly upward and hit her vocal cords. She had to cover up this quaking by growling in a way that was supposed to be an imitation (though Jeffrey never growled or ranted or carried on in any theatrical way at all).

Stroke her a little.

"But there's a point about him being so innocent," she said hurriedly. "Being not so physical. Being awkward." She began to talk about Orphée in the play, not the busboy—Orphée's problems with love and reality. Orphée will not put up with anything less than perfection. He wants a love that is outside of ordinary life. He wants a perfect Eurydice.

"Eurydice is more realistic. She's carried on with Mathias and with M. Dulac. She's been around her mother and her mother's lover. She knows what people are like. But she loves Orphée. She loves him better, in a way, than he loves her. She loves him better because she's not such a fool. She loves him like a human person."

"She's slept with those other guys?"

"Well, with M. Dulac she had to, she couldn't get out of it. She didn't want to, but probably after a while she enjoyed it, because after a certain point she couldn't help enjoying it. Just because she's slept with those men doesn't mean she's corrupt," Pauline said. "She wasn't in love then. She hadn't met Orphée. There's one speech where he tells her that everything she's done is sticking to her, and it's disgusting. Lies she's told him. The other men. It's all sticking to her forever. And then of course M. Henri plays up to that. He tells Orphée that he'll be just as bad and that one day he'll walk down the street with Eurydice and he'll look like a man with a dog he's trying to lose."

Brian laughed. He said, "That could be true."

"But not inevitably," said Pauline. "That's what's silly. It's not inevitable at all."

So Orphée is at fault, Pauline said decidedly. He looks back at Eurydice on purpose to kill her and get rid of her because she isn't perfect. Because of him she has to die a second time.

Brian, on his back and with his eyes wide open (she knew that because of the tone of his voice), said, "But doesn't he die, too?"

"Yes. He chooses to."

"So then they're together?"

"Yes. Like Romeo and Juliet. Orphée is with Eurydice at last. That's what M. Henri says. That's the last line of the play. That's the end." Pauline rolled over onto her side and touched her cheek to Brian's shoulder—not to start anything but to emphasize what she said next. "It's a beautiful play in one way but in another it's so silly. And it isn't really like *Romeo and Juliet*, because it isn't bad luck or circumstances. It's on purpose. So they don't have to go on with life and get married and have kids and buy an old house and fix it up and—"

"And have affairs," said Brian. "After all, they're French."

Then he said, "And be like my parents."

Pauline laughed. "Do they have affairs? I can't imagine."

"Oh, sure," said Brian. "I meant their life."

"Oh."

"Logically I can see killing yourself so you won't turn into your parents. I just don't believe anybody would do it."

They went on speculating, and comfortably arguing, in a way that was not usual, but not altogether unfamiliar to them. They had done this before, at long intervals in their married life—talked half the night about God or fear of death or how children should be educated or whether money was important. At last they admitted to being too tired to make sense any longer, and arranged themselves in a comradely cuddle and went to sleep.

Finally a rainy day. Brian and his parents were driving into Campbell River to get groceries, and gin, and to take Brian's father's car to a garage. Brian had to go along, with his car, just in case the other car had to be left in the garage overnight. Pauline said that she had to stay home because of Mara's nap.

She persuaded Caitlin to lie down, too—allowing her to take her music box to bed with her if she played it under the covers. Then Pauline spread the script on the kitchen table, and drank coffee and went over the scene in which Orphée says that it's intolerable, at last, to stay in two skins, two envelopes with their own blood and oxygen sealed up in their solitude, and Eurydice tells him to be quiet.

"Don't talk. Don't think. Just let your hand wander, let it be happy on its own."

Your hand is my happiness, says Eurydice. Accept that. Accept your happiness.

Of course he says he cannot.

Caitlin called out frequently to ask what time it was, and Pauline could hear the music box. She hurried to the bedroom door and hissed at her to turn it off, not to wake Mara.

"If you play it like that again I'll take it away from you. O.K.?"

But Mara was already rustling around in her crib and in the next few minutes there were sounds of soft, encouraging conversation from Caitlin, designed to get her sister wide awake. Then of Mara rattling the crib railing, pulling herself up, throwing her bottle out onto the floor, and starting the bird cries that would grow more and more desolate until they brought her mother.

"I didn't wake her," Caitlin said. "She was awake all by herself. It's not raining anymore. Can we go down to the beach?"

She was right. It wasn't raining. Pauline changed Mara, told Caitlin to get her bathing suit on and find her sand pail. She got into her own bathing suit and put on her shorts on top of it, in case the rest of the family arrived home while she was down there. ("Dad doesn't like the way some women just go right out of their cottages in their bathing suits," Brian's mother had said to her. "I guess he and I just grew up in other times.") She picked up the script to take it along, then laid it down. She was afraid that she would get too absorbed in it and take her eye off the children for a moment too long.

The thoughts that came to her, of Jeffrey, were not really thoughts at all—they were more like alterations in her body. This could happen when she was sitting on the beach (trying to stay in the half shade of a bush and so preserve her pallor, as Jeffrey had ordered). Or when she was wringing out diapers, or when she and Brian were visiting his parents. In the middle of Monopoly games, Scrabble games, card games. She went right on talking, listening, working, keeping track of the children, while some memory of her secret life disturbed her like a radiant explosion. Then a warm weight settled, reassurance filling up all her hollows. But it didn't last, this comfort leaked away, and she was like a miser whose windfall has vanished and who is convinced such luck can never strike again. Longing buckled her up and drove her to the discipline of counting days. Sometimes she even cut the days into fractions to figure out more exactly how much time had gone.

She thought of going in to Campbell River, making some excuse, so that she could get to a phone booth and call him. The cottages had no phones—the only public phone was in the hall of the Lodge, across from the entrance to the dining room. But she did not have the number of the hotel where Jeffrey worked. And, besides that, she could never get away to Campbell River in the evening. She was afraid that if she called him at home in the daytime his mother the French teacher might answer. He said she hardly ever left the house in the summer. Just once, she had taken the ferry to Vancouver for the day. Jeffrey had phoned Pauline to ask her to come over. Brian was teaching and Caitlin was at her play group.

Pauline said, "I can't. I have Mara."

"Couldn't you bring her along?" he asked.

She said no.

"Why not? Couldn't you bring some things for her to play with?"

No, said Pauline. "I couldn't," she said. "I just couldn't." It seemed too dangerous to her, to trundle her baby along on such a guilty expedition. To a house where cleaning fluids would not be bestowed on high shelves and all pills and cough syrups and cigarettes and buttons put safely out of reach. And even if she escaped poisoning or choking, Mara might be storing up time bombs—memories of a strange house where she was strangely disregarded, of a closed door, noises on the other side of it.

"I just wanted you," Jeffrey said. "I just wanted you in my bed."

She said again, weakly, "No."

Those words of his kept coming back to her. I wanted you in my bed. A half-joking urgency in his voice but also a determination, a practicality, as if "in my bed" meant something more, the bed he spoke of taking on larger, less material dimensions.

Had she made a great mistake, with that refusal? With that reminder of how fenced in she was, in what anybody would call her real life?

The beach was nearly empty—people had got used to its being a rainy day.

The sand was too heavy for Caitlin to make a castle or dig an irrigation system—projects she would undertake only with her father, anyway, because she sensed that his interest in them was wholehearted, and Pauline's was not. She wandered a bit forlornly at the edge of the water, missing the presence of other children, the nameless instant friends and occasional stone-throwing, water-kicking enemies, the shrieking and splashing and falling about. A boy a little bigger than she was and apparently all by himself stood knee deep in the water farther down the beach. If these two could get together it might be all right, the whole beach experience might be retrieved. Pauline couldn't tell if Caitlin was now making those little splashy runs into the water for his benefit, or whether he was watching her with interest or scorn.

Mara didn't need company, at least for now. She stumbled toward the water, felt it touch her feet and changed her mind, stopped, looked around, and spotted Pauline. "Paw. Paw," she said, in happy recognition. "Paw" was what she said for "Pauline," instead of "Mother" or "Mommy." Looking around overbalanced her; she sat down half on the sand and half in the water, made a squawk of surprise which turned into an announcement, and then, by some determined ungraceful maneuvers that involved putting her weight on her hands, rose to her feet, wavering and triumphant. She had been walking for half a year, but getting around on the sand was still a challenge. Now she came back toward Pauline, making some reasonable casual remarks in her own language.

"Sand," said Pauline, holding up a clot of it. "Look. Mara. Sand."

Mara corrected her, calling it something else—it sounded like "whap." Her thick diaper under her plastic pants and her terry-cloth playsuit gave her a fat bottom, and that, along with her plump cheeks and shoulders and her sidelong important expression, made her look like a roguish matron.

Pauline became aware of someone calling her name. It had been called two or three times, but because the voice was unfamiliar she had not recognized it. She stood up and waved. It was the woman who worked in the store at the Lodge. She was leaning over the porch rail and calling, "Mrs. Keating. Mrs. Keating? Telephone, Mrs. Keating."

Pauline hoisted Mara onto her hip and summoned Caitlin. She and the little boy were aware of each other now: they were both picking up stones from the bottom and flinging them out into the water. At first she didn't hear Pauline, or pretended not to hear.

"Store," called Pauline. "Caitlin. Store." When she was sure Caitlin would follow—it was the word "store" that had done it, the reminder of the tiny store in the Lodge where you could buy ice cream and candy—she began the trek across the sand and up the flight of wooden steps. Halfway up she stopped, said, "Mara, you weigh a ton," and shifted the baby to her other hip. Caitlin followed, banging a stick against the railing.

"Can I have a Fudgsicle? Mother? Can I?"

"We'll see."

The public phone was beside a bulletin board on the other side of the main hall and across from the door to the dining room. A bingo game had been set up in there, because of the rain.

"Hope he's still hanging on," the woman who worked in the store called out. She was unseen now behind her counter.

Pauline, still holding Mara, picked up the dangling receiver and said breathlessly, "Hello?" She was expecting to hear Brian telling her about some delay in Campbell River or asking her what it was she had wanted him to get at the drugstore. It was just the one thing—calamine lotion—so he had not written it down.

"Pauline," said Jeffrey. "It's me."

Mara was bumping and scrambling along Pauline's side, eager to get down. Caitlin came along the hall and went into the store, leaving wet sandy footprints. Pauline said, "Just a minute, just a minute." She let Mara slide down and hurried to close the door that let to the steps. She did not remember telling Jeffrey the name of this place, though she had told him roughly where it was. She heard the woman in the store speaking to Caitlin in a sharper voice than she would use to children whose parents were beside them.

"Did you forget to put your feet under the tap?"

"I'm here," said Jeffrey. "I didn't get along so well without you. I didn't get along at all."

Mara made for the dining room, as if the male voice calling out "Under the N" were a direct invitation to her.

"Here. Where?" said Pauline.

She read the signs that were tacked up on the bulletin board beside the phone:

No Person Under Fourteen Years of Age Not Accompanied
by Adult Allowed in Boats or Canoes.

Fishing Derby.

Bake and Craft Sale, St. Bartholomew's Church.

Your life is in your hands. Palms and Cards read.
Reasonable and Accurate. Call Claire.

"In a motel. In Campbell River."

Pauline knows where she is before she opens her eyes. Nothing surprises her.
She has slept, but not deeply enough to let go of anything.

She had waiting for Brian in the parking area of the Lodge, with the children in tow, and then she had asked for the keys. She told him in front of his
parents that there was something else she needed, from Campbell River. He
asked what was it? And did she have any money?

"Just something," she said, so he would think that it was tampons or
birth-control supplies, something that she didn't want to mention.

"Sure. O.K., but you'll have to put some gas in," he said.

Later she had to speak to him on the phone. Jeffrey said she had to do it.

"Because he won't take it from me. He'll think I kidnapped you or something. He won't believe it."

But the strangest thing of all the things that day was that Brian did seem,
immediately, to believe it. Standing where she had stood not so long before,
in the public hallway of the Lodge—the bingo game over now, but people
going past, she could hear them, people on their way out of the dining room
after dinner—Brian had said, "Oh. Oh. Oh. O.K.," in a voice that would have
to be quickly controlled but that seemed to draw on a supply of fatalism or
foreknowledge that went far beyond that necessity.

"O.K.," he said. "What about the car?"

He said something else, something impossible, and then hung up, and
she came out of the phone booth beside a row of gas pumps in Campbell
River.

"That was quick," Jeffrey said. "Easier than you expected?"

Pauline said, "I don't know."

"He may have known it subconsciously. People do know."

She shook her head, to tell him not to say any more, and he said, "Sorry." They walked along the street not touching or talking.

Now, looking around at leisure—the first real leisure or freedom she's had since she came into that room—Pauline sees that there isn't much of anything in it. Just a junky dresser, the bed without a headboard, an armless upholstered chair. On the window a Venetian blind with a broken slat. Also a noisy air-conditioner—Jeffrey turned it off in the night and left the door open on the chain, since the window was sealed. The door is shut now. He must have got up in the night and shut it.

This is all she has. Her connection with the cottage where Brian lies now asleep or not asleep is broken. Also her connection with the house that has been an expression of her life with Brian, of the way they wanted to live. She has cut herself off from all the large solid acquisitions, like the washer and dryer and the oak table and the refinished wardrobe and the chandelier that is a copy of the one in a painting by Vermeer. And just as much from those things that were particularly hers—the press-glass tumblers that she had been collecting and the prayer rug that was probably not authentic, but beautiful. Especially from those things. The skirt and blouse and sandals she put on for the trip to Campbell River might as well be all she has now to her name. She would never go back to lay claim to anything. If Brian got in touch with her to ask what was to be done with things, she would tell him to do what he liked—throw everything into garbage bags and take it to the dump, if that was what he liked. (In fact she knows that he will probably pack up a trunk, which he does, sending on, scrupulously, not only her winter coat and boots but things like the waist cincher she wore at her wedding and never since, with the prayer rug draped on top of everything like a final statement of his generosity, either natural or calculated.)

She believes that she will never again care about what sort of rooms she lives in or what sort of clothes she puts on. She will not be looking for that sort of help to give anybody an idea of who she is, what she is like. Not even to give herself an idea. What she has done will be enough, it will be the whole thing.

What she has done will be what she has heard about and read about. It will be what Anna Karenina did and what Mme. Bovary wanted to do. And what a teacher at Brian's school did, with the school secretary. He ran off with her. That was what it was called. Running off with. Taking off with. It was spoken of disparagingly, humorously, enviously. It was adultery taken one step further. The people who did it had almost certainly been having an affair already, committing adultery for quite some time before they became desperate or courageous enough to take this step. Once in a long while a couple might claim their love was unconsummated and technically pure, but these people would be thought of—if anybody believed them—as being not only very serious and high-minded but almost devastatingly foolish, almost in a class with those who gave up everything to go and work in some poor and dangerous country.

The others, the adulterers, were seen as irresponsible, immature, selfish, or even cruel. Also lucky. They were lucky because the sex they had been having in parked cars or the long grass or in each other's sullied marriage beds or most likely in motels like this one must surely have been splendid. Otherwise they would never have got such a yearning for each other's company at all costs or such a faith that their shared future would be altogether better and different in kind from what they had in the past.

Different in kind. That is what Pauline must believe now—that there is this major difference in lives or in marriages or unions between people. That some of them have a necessity, a fatefulness about them, which others do not have. Of course she would have said the same thing a year ago. People did say that, they seemed to believe that, and to believe that their own cases were all of the first, the special kind, even when anybody could see that they were not.

It is too warm in the room. Jeffrey's body is too warm. Conviction and contentiousness seem to radiate from it, even in sleep. His torso is thicker than Brian's, he is pudgier around the waist. More flesh on the bones, yet not so slack to the touch. Not so good-looking in general—she is sure most people would say that. And not so fastidious. Brian in bed smells of nothing. Jeffrey's skin, every time she's been with him, has had a baked-in, slightly oily or nutty smell. He didn't wash last night—but, then, neither did she. There wasn't time. Did he even have a toothbrush with him? She didn't, but she had not known she was staying.

When she met Jeffrey here it was still in the back of her mind that she had to concoct some colossal lie to serve her when she got home. And she—they—had to hurry. When Jeffrey said to her that he had decided that they must stay together, that she would come with him to Washington State, that they would have to drop the play because things would be too difficult for them in Victoria, she had looked at him just in the blank way you'd look at somebody the moment that an earthquake started. She was ready to tell him all the reasons why this was not possible, she still thought she was going to tell him that, but her life was coming adrift in that moment. To go back would be like tying a sack over her head.

All she said was "Are you sure?"

He said, "Sure." He said sincerely, "I'll never leave you."

That did not seem the sort of thing that he would say. Then she realized he was quoting—maybe ironically—from the play. It was what Orphée says to Eurydice within a few moments of their first meeting in the station buffet.

So her life was falling forward, she was becoming one of those people who ran away. A woman who shockingly and incomprehensibly gave everything up. For love, observers would say wryly. Meaning, for sex. None of this would happen if it weren't for sex.

And yet what's the great difference there? It's not such a variable procedure, in spite of what you're told. Skins, motions, contact, results. Pauline isn't a woman from whom it's difficult to get results. Brian got them. Probably anybody would, who wasn't wildly inept or morally disgusting.

But nothing's the same, really. With Brian—especially with Brian, to whom she had dedicated a selfish sort of good will, with whom she's lived in married complicity—there can never be this stripping away, the inevitable flight, the feelings she doesn't have to strive for but only to give in to like breathing or dying. That she believes can only come when the skin is on Jeffrey, the motions made by Jeffrey, and the weight that bears down on her has Jeffrey's heart in it, also his habits, thought, peculiarities, his ambition and loneliness (that for all she knows may have mostly to do with his youth).

For all she knows. There's a lot she doesn't know. She hardly knows anything about what he likes to eat or what music he likes to listen to or what role his mother plays in his life (no doubt a mysterious but important one, like the role of Brian's parents). One thing she's pretty sure of: whatever preferences or prohibitions he has will be definite. Plates in his armor.

She slides out from under Jeffrey's hand and from under the top sheet, which has a harsh smell of bleach, slips down to the floor where the bedspread is lying and wraps herself quickly in that rag of greenish-yellow chenille. She doesn't want him to open his eyes and see her from behind and note the droop of her buttocks. He's seen her naked before, but generally in a more forgiving moment.

She rinses her mouth and washes herself, using the bar of soap that is about the size of two thin squares of chocolate and firm as stone. She's hard used between the legs, swollen and stinking. Urinating takes an effort and it seems she's constipated. Last night when they went out and got hamburgers she found she could not eat. Presumably she'll learn to do all these things again, they'll resume their natural importance in her life. At the moment it's as if she can't quite spare the attention.

She has some money in her purse. She has to go out and buy a tooth-brush, toothpaste, deodorant, shampoo. Also vaginal jelly. Last night they used condoms the first two times but nothing the third time.

She didn't bring her watch and Jeffrey doesn't wear one. There's no clock in the room, of course. She thinks it's early—there's still an early look to the light in spite of the heat. The stores probably won't be open, but there'll be someplace where she can get coffee.

Jeffrey has turned on his other side. She must have wakened him, just for a moment.

They'll have a bedroom. A kitchen, an address. He'll go to work. She'll go to the laundromat. Maybe she'll go to work, too. Selling things, waiting on tables, tutoring students. She knows French and Latin—do they teach French and Latin in American high schools? Can you get a job if you're not an American? Jeffrey isn't.

She leaves him the key, She'll have to wake him to get back in. There's nothing to write a note with, or on.

It is early. The motel is on the highway at the north end of town, beside the bridge. There's no traffic yet. She scuffs back and forth under the cotton-wood trees at the edge of the lot for quite a while before a vehicle of any kind rumbles over the bridge—though the traffic on it shook their bed regularly late into the night.

Something is coming now. A truck. But not just a truck—there's a large bleak fact coming at her. And it has not arrived out of nowhere—it's been waiting, cruelly nudging at her ever since she woke up or even all night.

Caitlin and Mara.

Last night on the phone, after speaking in such a flat and controlled and almost agreeable voice—as if he prided himself on not being shocked, not objecting or pleading—Brian cracked open. He said with contempt and fury and no concern for whoever might hear him, "Well, then—what about the kids?"

The receiver began to shake against Pauline's ear.

She said, "We'll talk—" but he did not seem to hear her.

"The children," he said, in this same shivering and vindictive voice. Changing the word "kids" to "children" was like slamming a board down on her—a heavy, formal, righteous threat.

"The children stay," Brian said. "Pauline. Did you hear me?"

"No," said Pauline. "Yes. I heard you, but—"

"All right. You heard me. Remember. The children stay."

It was all he could do. To make her see what she was doing, what she was ending, and to punish her if she did so. Nobody would blame him. There might be finagling, there might be bargaining, there would certainly be humbling of herself, but there it was, like a round cold stone in her gullet, like a cannonball. And it would remain there unless she changed her mind entirely. The children stay.

Their car—hers and Brian's—is still sitting in the motel parking lot. Brian will have to ask his father or his mother to drive him up here today to get it. She has the keys in her purse. There are spare keys—he will surely bring them. She unlocks the car door and throws her keys on the seat, then locks the door from the inside and shuts it.

Now she can't go back. She can't get into the car and drive back and say that she'd been insane. If she did that he would forgive her but he'd never get over it and neither would she. They'd go on, though, as people did.

She walks out of the parking lot, she walks along the sidewalk, into town.

The weight of Mara on her hip yesterday. The sight of Caitlin's footprints on the floor.

Paw. Paw.

She doesn't need the keys to get back to them, she doesn't need the car. She could beg a ride on the highway. Give in, give in, get back to them any way at all—how can she not do that?

A sack over her head.

This is acute pain. It will become chronic. Chronic means that it will be permanent but perhaps not constant. It may also mean that you won't die of it. You won't get free of it but you won't die of it. You won't feel it every minute but you won't spend many days without it, either. And you'll learn some tricks to dull it or banish it or else you'll end up destroying what you've got. What you incurred this pain to get. It isn't his fault. He's still an innocent or a savage, who doesn't know there's a pain so durable in the world. Say to yourself, You lose them anyway. They grow up. For a mother there's always waiting this private, slightly ridiculous desolation. They'll forget this time, in one way or another they'll disown you. Or hang around till you don't know what to do about them, the way Brian has.

And, still, what pain. To carry along and get used to until it's only the past you're grieving for and no longer any possible present.

Her children have grown up. They don't hate her. For going away or staying away. They don't forgive her, either. Perhaps they wouldn't have forgiven her anyway, but it would have been about something different.

Caitlin remembers a little about the summer at the Lodge, Mara nothing. Caitlin calls it "that place Grandma and Grandpa stayed at."

"The place we were at when you went away," she says. "Only we didn't know you went away with the man who was Orphée."

Pauline has told them about the play.

Pauline says, "It wasn't Orphée."

"It wasn't Orphée? Oh, well. I thought it was."

"No."

"Who was it, then?"

"Just a man connected," says Pauline. "It wasn't him."

Edna O'Brien

(1932–   )

Edna O'Brien, "the most gifted woman now writing fiction in English," according to Philip Roth, grew up on a farm in the west of Ireland but exiled herself to England in 1959 a year before the publication of her first novel, *The Country Girls*, banned as "a smear on Irish womanhood," in the words of the censor, and burned by the parish priest on the grounds of her village church. ("Banning is only the tip of the iceberg," O'Brien commented. "Keeping our psyches closed is the real bogey.") In 1995 she was awarded the European Prize for Literature in recognition of her life's work: eighteen works of fiction of which the best known is *The Country Girls Trilogy,* including the first novel; *The Lonely Girl (*1962; reprinted as *The Girl with Green Eyes*); and *Girls in Their Married Bliss* (1963). Other novels include *A Pagan Place* (1970), *House of Splendid Isolation* (1994), *Down by the River* (1996), and *Wild Decembers* (1999). The short-story collections *The Love Object* (1968), *A Fanatic Heart* (1984), and *Lantern Slides* (1990) received numerous literary prizes. An honorary member of the American Institute of Arts and Letters, O'Brien, in the words of a London critic, has "the soul of Molly Bloom and the gifts of Virginia Woolf." Her memoir, *Mother Ireland* (1976)—"Edna O'Brien at her best," to quote novelist William Trevor—is an autobiographical tapestry of the country that is at the center of every story this Irish exile has ever written.

FROM *Mother Ireland*

ESCAPE TO ENGLAND

Leaving Ireland was no wrench at all. I took the mail boat, like most others, sat up all night, watched the drinking, the spilling, walked the deck, remembered how Mr. Thackeray and Mr. Heinrich Böll had come in by boat to write leisurely about it, remembered the myriad others, natives, who had gone out to forget. Euston Station was a jungle, grim and impersonal, the very pigeons looked factory-made, and when I saw the faces of the English I thought not of the long catalogue of blood-letting history, but of murder stories I had read in the Sunday papers and of that swarthy visiting English woman from long ago who brought corn caps and a powder puff stitched into her hanky.

This was to be home. It had nothing to recommend it. Unhealthy, unfriendly, mortarish and to my ignorant eye morbid because I kept seeing wreaths and did not know that there was such a thing in England as Remembrance Sunday.

But I had got away. That was my victory. The real quarrel with Ireland began to burgeon in me then; I had thought of how it had warped me, and those around me, and their parents before them, all stooped by a variety of fears—fear of church, fear of gombeenism, fear of phantoms, fear of ridicule, fear of hunger, fear of annihilation, and fear of their own deeply ingrained aggression that can only strike a blow at each other, not having the innate authority to strike at those who are higher. Pity arose too, pity for a land so often denuded, pity for a people reluctant to admit that there is anything wrong. That is why we leave. Because we beg to differ. Because we dread the psychological choke. But leaving is only conditional. The person you are is anathema to the person you would like to be.

But time changes everything including our attitude to a place. There is no such thing as a perpetual hatred no more than there are unambiguous states of earthly love. Hour after hour I can think of Ireland, I can imagine without going far wrong what is happening in any one of the little towns by day or by night, can see the tillage and the walled garden, see the spilt porter foam along the counters, I can hear argument and ballads, hear the elevation bell and the prayers for the dead. I can almost tell what any one of my friends might be doing at an hour so steadfast is the rhythm of life there. I open a book, a school book maybe, or a book of superstition, or a book of place names, and I have only to see the names of Ballyhooly or Raheen★ to be plunged into that world from which I have derived such a richness and an unquenchable grief. The tinkers at Rathkeale★ will be driving back to their settlement by now I say, and the woman who tells fortunes in her caravan will

★ Townlands in O'Brien's native County Clare in the west of Ireland.

be sending her child down for the tenth loaf of sliced bread, while a mile or two away in her domain Lady so-and-so will tell the groomsman how yet again she got her horse into a lather, and on some door in a town a little black crêpe scarf dangling from a knocker will have on it a handwritten black-edged card stating at what time the remains will be removed, while the hideous bald bungalows will be mushrooming along the main roadsides. The men will be trying as always to distance their fate either through drink, or dirty stories, and the older women will be filled with the knowledge of how crushing their burdens are, while young girls will be gabbling, to invent diversion for themselves.

It is true that a country encapsulates our childhood and those lanes, byres, fields, flowers, insects, suns, moons and stars are forever re-occurring and tantalizing me with a possibility of a golden key which would lead beyond birth to the roots of one's lineage. Irish? In truth I would not want to be anything else. It is a state of mind as well as an actual country. It is being at odds with other nationalities, having quite different philosophy about pleasure, about punishment, about life, and about death. At least it does not leave one pusillanimous.

Ireland for me is moments of its history, and its geography, a few people who embody its strange quality, the features of a face, a holler, a line from a Synge play, the whiff of night air, but Ireland insubstantial like the goddesses poets dream of, who lead them down into strange circles. I live out of Ireland because something in me warns me that I might stop if I lived there, that I might cease to feel what it has meant to have such a heritage, might grow placid when in fact I want yet again and for indefinable reasons to trace that same route, that trenchant childhood route, in the hope of finding some clue that will, or would, or could, make possible the leap that would restore one to one's original place and state of consciousness, to the radical innocence of the moment just before birth.

Sylvia Plath

(1932-1963)

"I have this demon who wants me to run away screaming if I am going to be flawed, fallible. It wants me to think I'm so good I must be perfect. Or nothing. . . . Not being perfect hurts. . . . Brief note: to self. Time to take myself in hand . . . to build into myself, to give myself backbone, however much I fail. . . . Salvation in work. What if my work is lousy? . . ." These excerpts from the diary Sylvia Plath kept in 1957-58 while teaching Freshman English at Smith College offer glimpses into an interior life where demons of depression and perfectionism battled with Plath's yearning to achieve "not perfection," "but an acceptance of myself as having a right to live on my own human, fallible terms." Eventually the demons triumphed. Overwhelmed by personal circumstances—a broken marriage, single motherhood—Plath committed suicide at the age of thirty. The posthumously published poems collected in *Ariel* (1965) established her reputation as one of the most important American poets of the twentieth century.

Kindness

Kindness glides about my house.
Dame Kindness, she is so nice!
The blue and red jewels of her rings smoke
In the windows, the mirrors
Are filling with smiles.

What is so real as the cry of a child?
A rabbit's cry may be wilder
But it has no soul.
Sugar can cure everything, so Kindness says.
Sugar is a necessary fluid,

Its crystals a little poultice.
O kindness, kindness
Sweetly picking up pieces!
My Japanese silks, desperate butterflies,
May be pinned any minute, anesthetized.

And here you come, with a cup of tea
Wreathed in steam.
The blood jet is poetry,
There is no stopping it.
You hand me two children, two roses.

The Moon and the Yew Tree

This is the light of the mind, cold and planetary.
The trees of the mind are black. The light is blue.
The grasses unload their griefs on my feet as if I were God,
Prickling my ankles and murmuring of their humility.
Fumy, spiritous mists inhabit this place
Separated from my house by a row of headstones.
I simply cannot see where there is to get to.

The moon is no door. It is a face in its own right,
White as a knuckle and terribly upset.
It drags the sea after it like a dark crime; it is quiet
With the O-gape of complete despair. I live here.
Twice on Sunday, the bells startle the sky—
Eight great tongues affirming the Resurrection.
At the end, they soberly bong out their names.

The yew tree points up. It has a Gothic shape.
The eyes lift after it and find the moon.
The moon is my mother. She is not sweet like Mary.
Her garments unloose small bats and owls.
How I would like to believe in tenderness—
The face of the effigy, gentled by candles,
Bending, on me in particular, its mild eyes.

I have fallen a long way. Clouds are flowering
Blue and mystical over the face of the stars.
Inside the church, the saints will be all blue,
Floating on their delicate feet over the cold pews,
Their hands and faces stiff with holiness.
The moon sees nothing of this. She is bald and wild.
And the message of the yew tree is blackness—
                                        blackness and silence.

Mary Oliver

(1935-   )

"Poetry," writes Mary Oliver, "is a life-cherishing force. . . . Poems are not words, after all, but fires for the cold, ropes let down to the lost, something as necessary as bread in the pockets of the hungry." She started out in Cleveland, Ohio, and settled on Cape Cod in Massachusetts, where she has lived for more than thirty years. From Oliver's first collection, *No Voyage and Other Poems* (1963), the New England landscape and Oliver's attention to the natural world are at the heart of her celebratory and deeply religious poetry. "There is no complaint in Ms. Oliver's poetry, no whining," said Stephen Dobyns. "But neither is there the sense that life is in any way easy. . . . Although few poets have fewer human beings in their poems than Mary Oliver, it is ironic that few poets also go so far to help us forward." The author of ten books of poetry—she won the Pulitzer Prize for *American Primitive* in 1984 and a National Book Award for *New and Selected Poems* in 1992—and several of prose about the writing of poetry, including *Blue Pastures* (1995) and *A Poetry Handbook* (1994), she has taught at a number of colleges and universities, most recently at Bennington College in Vermont.

Wild Geese

You do not have to be good.
You do not have to walk on your knees
for a hundred miles through the desert, repenting.
You only have to let the soft animal of your body
    love what it loves.
Tell me about despair, yours, and I will tell you mine.
Meanwhile the world goes on.
Meanwhile the sun and the clear pebbles of the rain

are moving across the landscapes,
over the prairies and the deep trees,
the mountains and the rivers.
Meanwhile the wild geese, high in the clean blue air,
are heading home again.
Whoever you are, no matter how lonely,
the world offers itself to your imagination,
calls to you like the wild geese, harsh and exciting—
over and over announcing your place
in the family of things.

When Death Comes

When death comes
like the hungry bear in autumn;
when death comes and takes all the bright coins from his purse

to buy me, and snaps the purse shut;
when death comes
like the measle-pox;

when death comes
like an iceberg between the shoulder blades,

I want to step through the door full of curiosity, wondering:
what is it going to be like, that cottage of darkness?

And therefore I look upon everything
as a brotherhood and a sisterhood,
and I look upon time as no more than an idea,
and I consider eternity as another possibility,

and I think of each life as a flower, as common
as a field daisy, and as singular,

and each name a comfortable music in the mouth,
tending, as all music does, toward silence,

and each body a lion of courage, and something
precious to the earth.

When it's over, I want to say: all my life
I was a bride married to amazement.
I was the bridegroom, taking the world into my arms.

When it's over, I don't want to wonder
if I have made of my life something particular, and real.
I don't want to find myself sighing and frightened,
or full of argument.

I don't want to end up simply having visited this world.

Lucille Clifton

(1936-   )

Poet Lucille Clifton's focus is the deep vein of spiritual strength in the African American experience. From her first volume of poems, *Good Times* (1969), to her most recent, *Blessing the Boats* (2000), which won the Pulitzer Prize, as well as in her memoir, *Generations* (1976), she celebrates the resilient love of life that has survived in the black community in spite of centuries of oppression. She often imagines the trials and dignity of her own ancestors, a line that goes back to her great-great-grandmother, born in West Africa in 1822 and kidnapped by slave traders. Clifton's great-grandmother Lucille, who murdered the white father of her only son, was the first black woman to be hanged in Virginia. A mother of six children, Clifton claims her family as a source of creativity and hope. In her memoir she expresses her vision of the saving power of love in an unjust world: "Things don't fall apart. Things hold. Lines connect in thin ways made out of pictures and words just kept."

song at midnight

> *. . . do not*
> *send me out*
> *among strangers*
>
> —Sonia Sanchez

brothers,
this big woman
carries much sweetness
in the folds of her flesh.
her hair
is white with wonderful.

she is
rounder than the moon
and far more faithful.
brothers,
who will hold her,
who will find her beautiful
if you do not?

won't you celebrate with me

won't you celebrate with me
what i have shaped into
a kind of life? i had no model.
born in babylon
both nonwhite and woman
what did i see to be except myself?
i made it up
here on this bridge between
starshine and clay,
my one hand holding tight
my other hand; come celebrate
with me that everyday
something has tried to kill me
and has failed.

mary

this kiss
as soft as cotton

over my breasts
all shiny bright

something is in this night
oh Lord have mercy on me

i feel a garden
in my mouth

between my legs
i see a tree

miss rosie

when i watch you
wrapped up like garbage
sitting, surrounded by the smell
of too old potato peels
or
when i watch you
in your old man's shoes
with the little toe cut out
sitting, waiting for your mind
like next week's grocery
i say
when i watch you
you wet brown bag of a woman
who used to be the best looking gal in georgia
used to be called the Georgia Rose
i stand up
through your destruction
i stand up

June Jordan

(1936-   )

June Jordan brings to the teaching and writing of poetry the same creative fire that drives her political activism. "And I/ invent the mother of the courage I require not to quit," she writes in "War and Memory." As a professor of African American Studies and Women's Studies at the University of California, Berkeley, and director of Berkeley's Poetry for the People project, she bears witness to the power of language to redeem the world from ignorance and injustice. This idealistic vision is articulated in over twenty books. Her collections of poetry include *Things That I Do in the Dark* (1977), *Naming Our Destiny* (1989), *Haruko/Love Poems* (1994), and *Kissing God Goodbye: Poems 1991–1997*; collections of essays are *Civil Wars* (1981), *Technical Difficulties* (1994), and *Affirmative Acts* (1998). A memoir, *Soldier: A Poet's Childhood* (2000), recounts her youth in Harlem, where she was born, and Bedford-Stuyvesant in Brooklyn, New York, where she grew up, the daughter of an abusive father and a mother who eventually committed suicide. Adrienne Rich calls Jordan "one of the most lyrically gifted poets of the late twentieth century. Her poems are extraordinarily tonal, sensuous, capturing . . . ways of being which might make love . . . more possible, more revolution-directed."

The Reception

Doretha wore the short blue lace last night
and William watched her drinking so she fight
with him in flying collar slim-jim orange
tie and alligator belt below the navel pants uptight

"I flirt. You hear me? Yes I flirt.
Been on my pretty knees all week
to clean the rich white downtown dirt
the greedy garbage money reek.

I flirt. Damned right. You look at me."
But William watched her carefully
his mustache shaky she could see
him jealous, "which is how he always be
at parties." Clementine and Wilhelmina
looked at trouble in the light blue lace
and held to George while Roosevelt Senior
circled by the yella high and bitterly light blue face

He liked because she worked
the crowded room like clay like molding men
from dust to muscle jerked
the arms and shoulders moving when
she moved.

The Lord Almighty Seagrams
bless

Doretha in her short blue dress
and Roosevelt waiting for his chance:
a true gut-funky blues to make her really dance.

In Memoriam: Poem for Mrs. Fannie Lou Hamer

You used to say, "June?
Honey when you come down here you
supposed to stay with me. Where
else?"
Meanin home
against the beer the shotguns and the

point of view of whitemen don'
never see Black anybodies without
some violent itch start up.
                        The ones who
said, "No Nigga's Votin in This Town . . .

less'n it be feet first to the booth"
Then jailed you
beat you brutal
bloody/battered/beat
you blue beyond the feeling
of the terrible
And failed to stop you.
Only God could but He
wouldn't stop
you
fortress from self-
pity
Humble as a woman anywhere
I remember finding you inside the

        laundromat
in Ruleville
                    lion spine relaxed/hell
                    what's the point to courage
                    when you washin clothes?

But that took courage

            just to sit there/target
            to the killers lookin
            for your singin face
            perspirey through the rinse
            and spin

and later
you stood mighty in the door on James Street
loud callin:

> "BULLETS OR NO BULLETS!
> THE FOOD IS COOKED
> AN' GETTIN COLD!"

We ate
A family tremulous but fortified
by turnips/okra/handpicked
like the lilies

filled to the very living
full
one solid gospel

> *(sanctified)*

one gospel

> *(peace)*

one full Black lily
luminescent
in a homemade field

of love

Marge Piercy

(1936-   )

Marge Piercy found her inspiration as a poet and novelist in the 1960s when she worked in the anti-Vietnam War movement and the women's movement. Her poetry, in particular, reflects both her politics and her origins in a working-class Jewish family in Detroit, Michigan. The voice is plain and polemical, at times uncompromisingly harsh and darkly comic; the rhythms are of ordinary speech; the focus is often on the varieties of cultural oppression produced by political and social injustice. A prolific writer—there are more than twelve volumes of poetry, including *Living in the Open* (1976), *The Moon Is Always Female* (1980), *Stone, Paper, Knife* (1983), *Available Light* (1988), *What Are Big Girls Made Of?* (1997), and six novels, including *Small Changes* (1973), *Woman on the Edge of Time* (1976), *Braided Lives* (1982), *Gone to Soldiers* (1987)—Piercy has been poetry editor of *Tikkun* magazine, the recipient of numerous awards, and a voice in support of ecological awareness and activism. The influence of Muriel Rukeyser ("No more masks, no more mythologies!") shows up in Piercy's advocacy of cultural reinvention: "The myths we are living shape our choices; what we use we must remake."

Barbie Doll

This girlchild was born as usual
and presented dolls that did pee-pee
and miniature GE stoves and irons
and wee lipsticks the color of cherry candy.
Then in the magic of puberty, a classmate said:
You have a great big nose and fat legs.

She was healthy, tested intelligent,
possessed strong arms and back,
abundant sexual drive and manual dexterity.
She went to and fro apologizing.
Everyone saw a fat nose on thick legs.

She was advised to play coy,
exhorted to come on hearty,
exercise, diet, smile and wheedle.
Her good nature wore out
like a fan belt.
So she cut off her nose and her legs
and offered them up.

In the casket displayed on satin she lay
with the undertaker's cosmetics painted on,
a turned-up putty nose,
dressed in a pink and white nightie.
Doesn't she look pretty? everyone said.
Consummation at last.
To every woman a happy ending.

to be of use

The people I love the best
jump into work head first
without dallying in the shadows
and swim off with sure strokes almost out of sight.
They seem to become natives of that element,
the black sleek heads of seals
bouncing like half-submerged balls.

I love people who harness themselves, an ox to a heavy cart,
who pull like water buffalo, with massive patience,
who strain in the mud and the muck to move things forward,
who do what has to be done, again and again.

I want to be with people who submerge
in the task, who go into the fields to harvest
and work in a row and pass the bags along,
who stand in the line and haul in their places,
who are not parlor generals and field deserters
but move in a common rhythm
when the food must come in or the fire be put out.

The work of the world is common as mud.
Botched, it smears the hands, crumbles to dust.
But the thing worth doing well done
has a shape that satisfies, clean and evident.
Greek amphoras for wine or oil,
Hopi vases that held corn, are put in museums,
but you know they were made to be used.
The pitcher cries for water to carry
and a person for work that is real.

Joyce Carol Oates

(1938-   )

The amazingly prolific Joyce Carol Oates—she's published more than seventy-five volumes of fiction, plays, poems, and essays—grew up near Buffalo, New York, in an Irish Catholic working-class family. A major contemporary writer who is also a professor at Princeton University, she has made the violence of families and the random and sexual aggression of teenagers a central theme of her fiction. Within this sinister and loveless culture she plots the odyssey of the self: what she calls "the phantasmagoria of personality" trouble the lives of her characters, who are often the uncomprehending victims of unlucky circumstances. Though many scholars and critics pay more attention to her novels—*them* (1969), *Because It Is Bitter and Because It Is My Heart* (1990), *Foxfire: Confessions of a Girl Gang* (1993), than to her short stories, Oates won so many O. Henry Awards for best short story of the year that the O. Henry award committee gave her a special prize for continuing achievement.

Christmas Night 1962

Come on then! he said. Goddamn you I'll take you.

My mother was in the back bedroom crying. Christmas night, you wouldn't think it could still be the same day. She'd been crying seeing the raggedy doll thrown across the room. She'd been drinking too except with her, unlike the men, it made the freckles come out in her face, and the skin beneath like skim milk. It made her walk strange like the floor was tilted and laugh when nothing was funny and rub her knuckles into her eyes like she was trying to wake up and not succeeding. Her hair red-frizzed like mine except it was coarser than mine which was so fine I'd squirm and whimper when she ran the hairbrush through, then the steel comb. Frantic to get every last one of the snarls out she said, damn you hush! don't be a baby.

It started after we got home from Grandpa's. He was on the sofa watching the same TV football they'd had on at the other house then he said something making her laugh that sharp laugh like scraping your finger on a blackboard and that was the mistake. For always there was a mistake you could point to. First he slapped her with his open hand and she screamed and turned over the table where some of the presents were from that morning, and his beer, and somehow it happened the raggedy doll that was Grandma's present for me went flying across the room hitting the doorframe banging its head *crack!*

She'd tried to stop him but she'd run into his fist—more than his fist. When it happens it happens fast. Like the boxing he took us to in Port Oriskany, the men up in the ring in the lights coming at each other slow and wary so you think nothing's going to happen you could shut your eyes seeing something far away but suddenly people are yelling and it's happening faster than you can see so you have to invent what it was to account for one of the boxers down on the canvas, blood leaking from his mouth. Just like that, that fast, in the living room with the TV on high and the Christmas tree in the corner knocked now on its side and some of the glass bulbs shattered.

I cried, I wasn't to blame. I knew I would be blamed.

The red-swirled glass bulbs shaped like pears, that Grandma gave us, the ones that were so beautiful. And the frosted white ones with the glitter dust. Home by myself I'd drag the cardboard box of ornaments out of the closet just to look through them, touch them. The tinsel for looping over the tree branches, the colored lights in the shape of candles, the angel for the top of the tree with her pretty painted-on face and gold halo like the statue of the Blessed Virgin Mary in church. Where the tree was fallen over, the angel hung upside down like something in a cartoon.

Come on Honey, he said, wiping his mouth, squatting over where the raggedy doll was broken on the floor. You know you're okay.

If you'd stop that goddamn fucking crying, he said. His face going white like the blood was being squeezed out of it.

My mother came out of the back bedroom running with towels and a blanket and she screamed at him to get away, she was going to take me to Yewville to the hospital and he shoved at her saying she was too pissed to drive and she screamed *he* was too pissed, *he* was the crazy one, if he took me out of the house she'd call the police. He said, You call the police and I'll rip you apart, go for that phone to call anybody you'll wish you were never born, nor her either. She was trying to wrap the towel around my head where I was bleeding and they both pulled at me, *he* was going to take me he said, he guessed my leg might be broken, and my mother ran back into the bedroom then returned with the gun waving it at him, holding it in both hands waving it at him, You think I won't? You bastard, you think I won't?

This pistol he'd brought home last summer, he'd won playing poker. My mother was scared to have it in the house but later on, back in the woods, he'd target practice shooting bottles and got my mother to try it too, giggling and nervous and I'd crouch behind them pressing my hands against my ears as he held her with his right arm around her to steady her, helping her aim, pull the trigger, absorb the kick. And her hiding her face in his neck afterward, breathless from what she'd done.

Now my mother in a velour shirt the color of crushed strawberries ripped off the shoulder from where he'd grabbed her and her black slacks glistening with blood holding that pistol trembling in her hands. Screaming and waving it her eyes wild so he backed off on his haunches, Okay Anna, okay just don't pull that trigger, you're crazy enough to do it, and she said, That's right! I am! Just try me, mister, I *am*!

So she lifted me and wrapped me in the blanket holding him off with the gun. The blood soaked into the gray wool making it wet. I was crying, I couldn't stop, like hiccups when you can't stop. She was sobbing too saying, Don't fight me, Honey, you're going to be all right but it hurt so when she lifted me I had to scream.

That Christmas night. Snow blowing gritty as sand. She had to carry me, I couldn't walk where the bone was cracked. My left leg below the knee where I'd hit against the doorframe, and my forehead bleeding and swollen already to the size of a hen's egg. And my mouth, there was something wrong with my mouth Mommy was trying to hold the towel against slipping and sliding out to the car. Oh! oh! oh! our breaths were steaming, she'd grabbed her coat but hadn't time to put on boots. Saying, Honey don't cry Mommy has you safe now okay? trying to fit me in the front seat but I screamed with the pain so she had to put me in the back laying me out flat wrapped in the blanket. I screamed and held onto her not wanting to let go.

Christmas night, and the morning so long ago. Snowdrifts up to the windows, taller than a man by the garage, giant icicles glittering like knife blades hanging down from the roof's edge frozen solid in the minus-ten-degree-fahrenheit cold. That morning the windows were blinding with snow-light and now it was dark, snowflakes swirling in the car headlights like something you could stare and stare into and lose your way not remembering who you are.

I can't tell this. I don't have the words. I remember everything but I don't have the words. Even when I say them, the words are not the right ones.

The raggedy doll sewed by my grandmother, it was big enough for me to need both arms to carry it. A floppy head with shiny black button eyes and a button nose and a smile and orange-red pigtails braided out of yarn. Her top was cotton printed in tiny flowers and her bottom was cotton printed in bright yellow checks and her legs which had no bones were white wool stockings and she was stuffed with something soft like cotton batting. Every year for all the years I could remember Grandma sewed me a Christmas doll, and things to wear.

I loved Grandma so much. She was his mother so she had to take his side. My other grandmother wasn't here they said and when I asked where was she they said with God in Heaven. But I knew what that was—buried in the cemetery that's just a hilly field behind the church.

That morning my mother dressed me for Christmas before she dressed herself. Only a few times a year we'd go to church and Christmas morning was one but *he* didn't go. Mommy brushed my hair wetting and shaping the curls into corkscrew-curls around her fingers then tickling blowing in my ear, Pretty girl! who's my pretty girl! Mommy loves you so. She pulled on over my head the new jumper Grandma had sewed for me for Christmas, soft velour to match Mommy's shirt she'd sewed too with a big patch pocket green like a strawberry leaf. White woolly socks, black patent-leather shoes but the same old scuffed boots to fit over them.

A little velour bow too in my hair. A row of bobby pins, barrettes. Corkscrew curls to my shoulders so I'd turn my head and feel them moving, tickling. Before Mommy and I went to church he squatted down in front of me staring at me. Cupped my face in his hands looking at me for a long time his eyes like that kind of marble with a glaze to them so the colors inside look cracked. That way I knew he wasn't seeing me though he said, Merry Christmas, sweetheart! The big day's here, eh?

Mommy said in her careful voice, Don't scare her. You scare her looking at her like that.

Like what? he said. Now straightening up, and taking Mommy's chin in his hand, holding her so she had to look at him. Like this?

He used to be Daddy but says not to call him that anymore but sometimes I forget. But after Christmas night I won't forget.

It was at my grandparents' place the drinking started. The big old farmhouse, the long table for Christmas dinner. So much food at two in the afternoon, your stomach isn't ready for it. The men were playing poker and they
were loud and laughing and my father was loud winning a hand but louder
losing, red-faced and squinting up his eyes laughing like it was a joke only he
got. Uncle Dwight who's married to Aunt Helen, Uncle Marcus who's married to Auntie Irene, Uncle Bud who used to be married but isn't now and
you're not to ask why, you never ask *why* of adults. Grandpa and Uncle
Dwight worked in the gypsum plant on the Jamestown Road where my
father did except they were laid off through January. How long after that
nobody knew. They'd been laid off, the factory gates chained shut, since
before the first snow.

Who can you believe, they said. What any one of them tells you, or you
read in the paper, if it's somebody in a suit and tie for sure he's lying to you
because he makes his money off you. And if it's a politician he's already lied
to get where he is. So fuck it.

Once when I was real little I said that word. My cousins whispered it in
my ear and afterward when I said it some people laughed except not
Grandma, and not Mommy. Mommy scolded saying that's not a nice word,
nice little girls don't say that word. I giggled saying Yes they do! yes they do!
and said the word again running around the table where she couldn't catch
me. Except this time the way she looked at me I was sorry so I didn't say it
ever again, that Mommy could hear.

My mother was driving our old 1957 Chevy along the Canal Road trying to
keep the car's tires in the ruts in the snow made by other cars. The snow plow
had come by in the morning and all day it had been snowing and now in the
night the narrow road was drifting over and she was praying Holy Mary
Mother of God! Holy Mary Mother of God! and in the back seat the limp
sobbing raggedy doll. Leg cracked below the knee, bleeding from a swelling
cut above her eye. And vomit, and the stink of vomit, on the gray blanket. No
other cars were on the road. The headlights swung and lurched, snowflakes
rushed at the windshield, the car's stops and starts and skids and jolts were

stabs of pain Oh! oh! oh! At the steep ramp to the Yewville bridge the drifts are so high the car's front wheels get stuck. Back up, go forward, back up, go forward rocking the car until momentum carries it onto the ramp.

Honey, are you all right?—Honey?—your Mommy's going to take care of you. Don't cry! Don't cry!

Then scared and angry-sounding as the car moves slowly so slowly not five miles an hour across the high windblown shaky plank-floored bridge, Holy Mary Mother of God have mercy on us!

The water tower at the top of Church Street. The steep drop to Memorial Avenue, the ice-slick pavement where the car skids, begins to slide. The front tire jolting against the curb Oh! oh! Seneca Street, Ontario, Locust. The redbrick Episcopal Church with the high tower, the big stained-glass window. Bell Telephone Co. where my mother worked as an operator before she fell in love with and married the man who would be my father. Before she came to live in the country nine miles north of Yewville where I was born, where she became a woman who was a mother and where her life changed and could never return to what it was. And now at Locust near Main there are cars moving with painstaking slowness in the blizzard and my mother has no choice but to follow behind them sobbing Holy Mary help us! help us! God help us! like it was a curse.

At Providence Hospital on Locust and Van Buren there's a Christmas tree blinking red lights over the front entrance and the parking lot is two-thirds empty, drifted over in snow but my mother parks the car and carries me through the snow stinging gritty as sand in our faces and into the brightly lit reception area where there's only a single nurse behind the counter whose eyes swing onto us startled and disapproving. My mother begins to speak and the nurse cuts her off saying there's no emergency room in this hospital you'll have to go to Yewville General don't you know this isn't that kind of hospital, and my mother says, My little girl's hurt, she fell and hurt herself and I think her leg is broken, I think she's hurt her head bad, please can we see a doctor? please is there a doctor? I'll pay—and another nurse comes out and says in a loud voice like my mother might be hard of hearing, Ma'am? would you like us to call ahead to Yewville General? would you like us to call an ambulance to take you there? the two nurses staring at us, keeping their distance. My young mother with her windblown red-frizzed hair, her white skin splotched with freckles like tiny rust-stains, a purplish bruise swelling the right side of her face. Shivering, swaying with the weight of the child in her arms, a girl of about four years of age, wrapped in a blanket stained with blood and vomit. And my mother asks again for a doctor raising her voice and again the nurses raising their voices say you'll have to go to Yewville General, there's no doctor on duty here tonight and there are no emergency room facilities in this hospital and my mother says begging will you look at her, then? please help us will you please help us? coming forward so the nurses speak more sharply saying Sorry ma'am, sorry you'll have to go to Yewville General, we have no emergency room facilities in this hospital ma'am, and my mother begins to shout, Aren't you nurses? what the hell are you if you aren't nurses? my little girl's hurt, my little girl's in pain Goddamn you! and the older nurse says angrily, Ma'am, we'll have to ask you to leave these premises, picks up a telephone receiver threatening to call the police. So my mother backs off, sobbing and cursing carrying me back outside to the car where the headlights are on, the back door's wide open, the back seat already filling up with snow.

Driving then along Van Buren skidding through a red light then stuck behind a sanding truck moving at five miles an hour all the way to East Avenue where the big hospital Yewville General is. Where Auntie Irene was for her surgery and I was brought to visit one Sunday but we don't go to the front entrance, my mother drives around to the rear where the parking lot is filled with snow and almost empty of cars too and she parks at the curb and carries me half-staggering into another bright-lit reception area larger than the other but there's no one in the waiting room and just one woman at the desk saying Yes? What is it? How can we help you? and Mommy says, quick and scared like she knows she's going to be turned away, It's my little girl, she's hurt, I need to see a doctor!—coming forward past the desk toward the double swinging doors NO ADMITTANCE EMERGENCY and the woman calls out, Ma'am! Stop! and a young man in a white uniform appears to block her way and Mommy is saying, We need a doctor, please help us, my little girl is hurt bad, her head! her leg! I think her leg is broken please help us! her voice shrill and her eyes wild like she's been drinking. There's a nurse too saying, You'll have to check in at reception first, ma'am, ma'am?—you have to check in at reception first. My mother is pleading with the young man, Doctor? help us please, will you examine my little girl? she hit her head running, she fell down and I think her leg is broken, please Doctor? her voice rising as if to prevent the young man from interrupting saying he isn't a doctor, he isn't in charge.

Mommy is a thin woman, you wouldn't think she'd be strong enough to carry me, to hold me like this in her arms. The tight hard muscles tensing in her upper arms and shoulders like it's lifting from the bone.

And everybody in this bright lit place staring at the limp raggedy doll, bleeding from a cut about the left eye. Wrapped in a filthy blanket. Frizzy red corkscrew curls messy as a rat's nest.

The strong smell pierces my nostrils like the dentist's office to make me gag. Mommy hugs me, whispering Honey it's all right, Honey you're safe now, but there's a woman's voice running on and on repeating no patients can be treated at Yewville General Hospital without first filling out the proper forms at reception, yes and you need insurance identification, this is hospital policy, this is New York State law. There's an artificial silver-tinsel Christmas tree, three feet high, on a table, glittery sequin-snow sprinkled onto the green cloth beneath. And brightly wrapped Christmas presents, the kind of presents that if you lift them are just empty boxes. At the reception desk there's a radio playing "Rudolph the Red-Nosed Reindeer." My mother is saying, pleading, I don't know about our insurance, I don't know the name of the insurance, I came out without my wallet and I.D. speaking fast so they can't interrupt, then angry, saying, You're going to take this child! this is a hurt child, an injured child, Goddamn you! And a nurse, an older woman with peach-colored hair and a little fringe of bangs says making her voice steely calm, Ma'am, this is a private hospital and we are not obliged to accept any patient not adequately covered by hospital and medical insurance so if you will please cooperate—, and my mother says screaming, I told you! I don't have my wallet! There isn't time! This is an emergency! Her arms are weakening and give way and she almost drops me on the floor carrying me to a couch in the waiting room, now the voices are louder, there are more of them and more disapproving and Mommy is saying, furious, You think we're trash, is that it, we're white trash is that it! We're poor, we're from the country, we don't count, we're shit on your shoes is that it! Now there's another, older man wearing a white coat, a doctor this time asking what's going on here, and the nurse tells him, and my mother interrupts, You're not going to let my daughter die, Goddamn you, you sons of bitches you're not going to let my daughter die, taking the pistol out of her coat pocket and waving it in their faces her hand trembling and her eyes wild and frightened as everybody goes Oh! oh! shrinking back in astonishment and the quick terror of animals you see in their eyes in a car's headlights at night but my mother lets the pistol fall, she's sobbing Goddamn you, Goddamn you, letting it fall clattering onto the floor and for a long moment there's no sound except over the radio the tinkly jingly "Rudolph the Red-Nosed Reindeer" coming to an end.

Then the older man, the doctor, stoops quickly to pick up the pistol. He hands it to the young man saying call the police, please.

And Mommy is standing there panting like she's been running, turning her head from side to side like she's trying to clear it, to wake up. And the doctor says, Yes, I will examine your little girl but you'll remain out here until the police arrive. Do you understand, ma'am?—you will remain out here. And Mommy says her lips moving slow, Yes Doctor.

There's a stretcher brought out to where I'm lying and they lift me onto it and Mommy wants to help but they make her stand back. Staring at me seeing the ugly bruised cut on my forehead, the slack wet mouth and the bloody root of a missing front tooth, the blanket falls open showing the surprise of the strawberry-red velour jumper sewed by Grandma who loves me. White woolly socks and shiny patent-leather shoes and the skinny leg hanging limp, swelling below the knee like a giant bee had stung it.

On the radio, a woman's happy voice singing "Walking in the Winter Wonder-land."

This woman who's my mother stands watching as I'm carried into the emergency room of Yewville General Hospital, Yewville, New York, 9:25 P.M. of Christmas night 1962. Standing clenching her fingers into fists her head slightly lowered as if to hide her own injuries and her lips moving and she begins to cry giving herself up to hoarse racking angry sobs, helpless sobs as if, now she's got what she has wanted, now she sees her child taken from her by strangers, now these strangers have yielded as if by magic to her desperate will, bearing me through the doors below NO ADMITTANCE EMERGENCY, she's surrendered me forever. It's over.

Angela Carter

(1940-1992)

A brilliant essayist and critic, best known for her boldly original novels—*The Infernal Desire Machines of Doctor Hoffman* (1972), *The Passion of New Eve* (1977), *Nights at the Circus* (1984), *Saints and Strangers* (1987), and *Wise Children* (1991), and the collection of stories *The Bloody Chamber* (1979)—Angela Carter was called by her former student, novelist Rick Moody, "one of the most important thinkers of twentieth-century world literature and one of its most pungent voices." Grace Paley, commenting on the collection from which the following autobiographical piece is taken—*Shaking a Leg: Collected Writings* (1997)—remembers the company of "that real, intelligent tough writing woman." Carter is British feminism's quickest wit. Coming at a subject from many different and new angles, she makes the act of reading proof of her argument that "reading is just as creative an activity as writing and most intellectual development depends upon new readings of old texts." Her own new readings—and writing—overturn old ideas, especially as they thwart a liberated sexual politics.

Sugar Daddy

I would say my father did not prepare me well for patriarchy; himself confronted, on his marriage with my mother, with a mother-in-law who was the living embodiment of peasant matriarchy, he had no choice but to capitulate, and did so. Further, I was the child of his mid-forties, when he was just the age to be knocked sideways by the arrival of a baby daughter. He was putty in my hands throughout my childhood and still claims to be so, although now I am middle-aged myself while he, not though you'd notice, is somewhat older than the present century.

I was born in 1940, the week that Dunkirk fell. I think neither of my parents was immune to the symbolism of this, of bringing a little girl-child into the world at a time when the Nazi invasion of England seemed imminent, into the midst of death and approaching dark. Perhaps I seemed particularly vulnerable and precious and that helps to explain the overprotectiveness they felt about me, later on. But that as it may, no child, however inauspicious the circumstances, could have been made more welcome. I did not get a birthday card from him a couple of years ago; when I querulously rang him up about it, he said: "I'd never forget the day you came ashore." (The card came in the second post.) His turn of phrase went straight to my heart, an organ which has inherited much of his Highland sentimentality.

He is a Highland man, the perhaps atypical product of an underdeveloped, colonialised country in the last years of Queen Victoria, of oatcakes, tatties and the Church of Scotland, of four years' active service in the First World War, of the hurly-burly of Fleet Street in the 1920s. His siblings, who never left the native village, were weird beyond belief. To that native village he competently removed himself ten years ago.

He has done, I realise, what every Sicilian in New York, what every Cypriot in Camden Town wants to do, to complete the immigrant's journey, to accomplish the perfect symmetry, from A to B and back again. Just his luck, when he returned, that all was as it had been before and he could, in a manner of speaking, take up his life where it left off when he moved south seventy years ago. He went south; and made a career; and married an Englishwoman; and lived in London; and fathered children, in an enormous parenthesis of which he retains only sunny memories. He has "gone home," as immigrants do; he established, in his seventh decade, that "home" has an existential significance for him which is not part of the story of his children's independent lives. My father lives now in his granite house filled with the souvenirs of a long and, I think, happy life. (Some of them bizarre; that framed certificate from an American tramp, naming my father a "Knight of the Road," for example.)

He has a curious, quite unEnglish, ability to live life in, as it were, the *third person*, to see his life objectively, as a not unfortunate one, and to live up to that notion. Those granite townships on the edge of the steel-grey North Sea forge a flinty sense of self. Don't think, from all this, he isn't a volatile man. He laughs easily, cries easily, and to his example I attribute my conviction that tears, in a man, are a sign of inner strength.

He is still capable of surprising me. He recently prepared an electric bed for my boyfriend, which is the sort of thing a doting father in a Scots ballad might have done had the technology been available at the time. We knew he'd put us in separate rooms—my father is a Victorian, by birth—but not that he'd plug the metal base of Mark's bed into the electric-light fitment. Mark noticed how the bed throbbed when he put his hand on it and disconnected every plug in sight. We ate breakfast, next morning, as if nothing untoward had happened, and I should say, in the context of my father's house, it had not. He is an enthusiastic handyman, with a special fascination with electricity, whose work my mother once described as combining the theory of Heath Robinson with the practice of Mr. Pooter.

All the same, the Freudian overtones are inescapable. However, unconsciously, as if *that* were an excuse, he'd prepared a potentially lethal bed for his daughter's lover. But let me not dot the i's and cross the t's. His final act of low, emotional cunning (another Highland characteristic) is to have lived so long that everything is forgiven, even his habit of referring to the present incumbent by my first husband's name, enough to give anybody a temporary feeling.

He is a man of immense, nay, imposing physical presence, yet I tend to remember him in undignified circumstances.

One of my first memories is how I bust his nose. (I was, perhaps, three years old. Maybe four.) It was on a set of swings in a public park. He'd climbed up Pooterishly to adjust the chains from which the swings hung. I thought he was taking too long and set the swing on which I sat in motion. He wasn't badly hurt but there was a lot of blood. I was not punished for my part in this accident. They were a bit put out because I wanted to stay and play when they went home to wash off the blood.

They. That is my father and my mother. Impossible for me to summon one up out of the past without the other.

Shortly after this, he nearly drowned me, or so my mother claimed. He took me for a walk one autumn afternoon and stopped by the pond on Wandsworth Common and I played a game of throwing leaves into the water until I forgot to let go of one. He was in after me in a flash, in spite of the peril to his gents' natty suiting (ever the dandy, my old man) and wheeled me dripping in my pushchair home to the terrible but short-lived recriminations of my mother. Short-lived because both guilt and remorse are emotions alien to my father. Therefore the just apportioning of blame is not one of his specialities, and though my mother tried it on from time to time, he always thought he could buy us off with treats and so he could and that is why my brother and I don't sulk, much. Whereas she—

She has been dead for more than a decade, now, and I've had ample time to appreciate my father's individual flavour, which is a fine and gamy one, but, as parents, they were far more than the sum of their individual parts. I'm not sure they understood their instinctive solidarity against us, because my mother often tried to make us take sides. Us. As their child, the product of their parenting, I cannot dissociate myself from my brother, although we did not share a childhood for he is twelve years older than I and was sent off, with his gas mask, his packed lunch and his name tag, as an evacuee, a little hostage to fortune, at about the time they must have realised another one was on the way.

I can only think of my parents as a peculiarly complex unit in which neither bulks larger than the other, although they were very different kinds of people and I often used to wonder how they got on, since they seemed to have so little in common, until I realised that was *why* they got on, that not having much in common means you've always got something interesting to talk about. And their children, far from being the *raison d'être* of their marriage, of their ongoing argument, of that endless, quietly murmuring conversation I used to hear, at night, softly, dreamily, the other side of the bedroom wall, were, in some sense, a sideshow. Source of pleasure, source of grief; not the glue that held them together. And neither of us more important than the other, either.

Not that I suspected this when I was growing up. My transition from little girl to ravaged anorexic took them by surprise and I thought they wanted my blood. I didn't know what they wanted of me, nor did I know what I wanted for myself. In those years of ludicrously overprotected adolescence, I often had the feeling of being "pawns in their game" . . . in *their* game, note . . . and perhaps I indeed served an instrumental function, at that time, rather than being loved for myself.

All this is so much water under the bridge. Yet those were the only years I can remember when my mother would try to invoke my father's wrath against me, threaten me with his fury for coming home late and so on. Though, as far as the "and so on" was concerned, chance would have been a fine thing. My adolescent rebellion was considerably hampered by the fact that I could find nobody to rebel with. I now recall this period with intense embarrassment, because my parents' concern to protect me from predatory boys was only equalled by the enthusiasm with which the boys I did indeed occasionally meet protected themselves against me.

It was a difficult time, terminated, inevitably, by my early marriage as soon as I finally bumped into somebody who would go to Godard movies with me and on CND marches and even have sexual intercourse with me, although he insisted we should be engaged first. Neither of my parents were exactly overjoyed when I got married, although they grudgingly did all the necessary. My father was particularly pissed off because he'd marked me out for a career on Fleet Street. It took me twenty years more of living, and an involvement with the women's movement, to appreciate he was unusual in wanting this for his baby girl. Although he was a journalist himself, I don't think he was projecting his own ambitions on me, either, even if to be a child is to be, to some degree, the projective fantasy of its parents. No. I suspect that, if he ever had any projective fantasies about me, I sufficiently fulfilled them by being born. All he'd wanted for me was a steady, enjoyable job that, perhaps, guaranteed me sufficient income to ensure I wouldn't too hastily marry some nitwit (a favourite word of his) who would displace him altogether from my affections. So, since from a child I'd been good with words, he apprenticed me to a suburban weekly newspaper when I was eighteen, intending me to make my traditional way up from there. From all this, given my natural perversity, it must be obvious why I was so hell-bent on getting married—not, and both my parents were utterly adamant about this, that getting married meant I'd give up my job.

In fact, it *did* mean that because soon my new husband moved away from London. "I suppose you'll have to go with him," said my mother doubtfully. Anxious to end my status as their child, there was no other option and so I changed direction although, as it turns out, I *am* a journalist, at least some of the time.

As far as projective fantasies go, sometimes it seems the old man is only concerned that I don't end up in the workhouse. Apart from that, anything goes. My brother and I remain, I think, his most constant source of pleasure—always, perhaps, a more positive joy to our father than to our mother, who, a more introspective person, got less pure entertainment value from us, partly, like all mothers, for reasons within her own not untroubled soul. As for my father, few souls are less troubled. He can be simply pleased with us, pleased that we exist, and, from the vantage point of his wondrously serene and hale old age, he contemplates our lives almost as if they were books he can dip into whenever he wants.

As for the books I write myself, my "dirty books," he said the other day: "I was a wee bitty shocked, at first, but I soon got used to it." He introduces me in the third person. "This young woman . . ." In his culture, it is, of course, a matter of principle to express pride in one's children. It occurs to me that this, too, is not a particularly English sentiment.

Himself, he is a rich source of anecdote. He has partitioned off a little room in the attic of his house, constructed the walls out of cardboard boxes, and there he lies, on a camp-bed, listening to the World Service on a portable radio with his cap on. When he lived in London, he used to wear a trilby to bed but, a formal man, he exchanged it for a cap as soon as he moved. There are two perfectly good bedrooms in his house, with electric blankets and everything, as I well know, but these bedrooms always used to belong to his siblings, now deceased. He moves downstairs into one of these when the temperature in the attic drops too low for even his iron constitution, but he always shifts back up again, to his own place, when the ice melts. He has a ferocious enthusiasm for his own private space. My mother attributed this to a youth spent in the trenches, where no privacy was to be had. His war was the war to end wars. He was too old for conscription in the one after that.

When he leaves the house for any length of time, he fixes up a whole lot of burglar traps, basins of water balanced on the tops of doors, tripwires, bags of flour suspended by strings, so that we worry in case he forgets where he's left what and ends up hoist with his own petard.

He has a special relationship with cats. He talks to them in a soft chirruping language they find irresistible. When we all lived in London and he worked on the night news desk of a press agency, he would come home on the last tube and walk, chirruping, down the street, accompanied by an ever-increasing procession of cats, to whom he would say good night at the front door. On those rare occasions, in my late teens, when I'd managed to persuade a man to walk me home, the arrival of my father and his cats always caused consternation, not least because my father was immensely tall and strong.

He is the stuff of which sitcoms are made.

His everyday discourse, which is conducted in the stately prose of a 1930s *Times* leader, is enlivened with a number of stock phrases of a slightly eccentric, period quality. For example. On a wild night: "Pity the troops on a night like this." On a cold day:

> Cold, bleak, gloomy and glum,
> Cold as the hairs on a polar bear's—

The last word of the couplet is supposed to be drowned by the cries of outrage. My mother always turned up trumps on this one, interposing: "Father!" on an ascending scale.

At random: "Thank God for the Navy, who guard our shores." On entering a room: "Enter the fairy, singing and dancing." Sometimes, in a particularly cheerful mood, he'll add to this formula: "Enter the fairy, singing and dancing and waving her wooden leg."

Infinitely endearing, infinitely irritating, irascible, comic, tough, sentimental, ribald old man, with his face of a borderline eagle and his bearing of a Scots guard, who, in my imagination as when I was a child, drips chocolate from his pockets as, a cat dancing in front of him, he strides down the road bowed down with gifts, crying: "Here comes the Marquess of Carrabus!" The very words, "my father," always make me smile.

But why, when he was so devilish handsome—oh, that photograph in battledress!—did he never marry until his middle thirties? Until he saw my mother, playing tennis with a girlfriend on Clapham Common, and that was it. The die was cast. He gave her his card, proof of his honourable intentions. She took him home to meet her mother. Then he must have felt as though he were going over the top, again.

In 1967 or 1968, forty years on, my mother wrote to me: "He really loves me (I think)." At that time, she was a semi-invalid and he tended her, with more dash than efficiency, and yet remorselessly, cooking, washing up, washing her smalls, hoovering, as if that is just what he'd retired from work to do, up to his elbows in soapsuds after a lifetime of telephones and anxiety. He'd bring her dinner on a tray with always a slightly soiled tray-cloth. She thought the dirty cloth spoiled the entire gesture. And yet, and yet . . . was she, after all those years, still keeping him on the hook? For herself, she always applauded his ability to spirit taxis up as from the air at crowded railway stations and also the dexterous way he'd kick his own backside, a feat he continued to perform until well into his eighties.

Now, very little of all this has to do with the stern, fearful face of the Father in patriarchy, although the Calvinist north is virtually synonymous with that ideology. Indeed, a short-tempered man, his rages were phenomenal; but they were over in the lightning flash they resembled, and then we all had ice-cream. And there was no fear. So that, now, for me, when fear steps in the door, then love and respect fly out of the window.

I do not think my father has ever asked awkward questions about life, or the world, or anything much, except when he was a boy reporter and asking awkward questions was part of the job. He would regard himself as a law-and-order man, a law-abiding man, a man with a due sense of respect for authority. So far, so in tune with his background and his sense of decorum. And yet somewhere behind all this lurks a strangely free, anarchic spirit. Doorknobs fall from doors the minute he puts his hand on them. Things fall apart. There is a sense that anything might happen. He is a law-and-order man helplessly tuned in to misrule.

And somewhere in all this must lie an ambivalent attitude to the authority to which he claims to defer. Now, my father is not, I repeat, an introspective man. Nor one prone to intellectual analysis; he's always got by on his wits so never felt the need of the latter. But he has his version of the famous story, about one of the Christmas truces during the First World War, which was *his* war, although, when he talks about it, I do not recognise Vera Brittain's war, or Siegfried Sassoon's war, or anything but a nightmarish adventure, for, as I say, he feels no fear. The soldiers, bored with fighting, remembering happier times, put up white flags, moved slowly forward, showed photographs, exchanged gifts—a packet of cigarettes for a little brown loaf . . . and then, he says, "Some fool of a first lieutenant fired a shot."

When he tells his story, he doesn't know what it *means*, he doesn't know what the story shows he really felt about the bloody officers, nor why I'm proud of him for feeling that; nor why I'm proud of him for giving the German private his cigarettes and remembering so warmly the little loaf of bread, and proud of him for his still undiminished anger at the nitwit of a boy whom they were all forced to obey just when the ranks were in a mood to pack it in and go home.

Of course, the old man thinks that, if the rank and file *had* packed it in and gone home in 1915, the Tsar would still rule Russia and the Kaiser Germany, and the sun would never have set on the British Empire. He is a man of great simplicities. He still grieves over my mother's "leftish" views; indeed, he grieves over mine, though not enough to spoil his dinner. He seems, rather, to regard them as, in some way, genetically linked. I have inherited her nose, after all; so why not my mother's voting patterns?

She never forgave him for believing Chamberlain. She'd often bring it up, at moments of stress, as proof of his gullibility. "And what's more, you came home from the office and said: 'There ain't gonna be a war.'"

See how she has crept into the narrative, again. He wrote to me last year: "Your mammy was not only very beautiful but also very clever." (Always in dialect, always "mammy.") Not that she did anything with it. Another husband might have encouraged her to work, or study, although in the 1930s that would have been exceptional enough in this first-generation middle-class family to have projected us into another dimension of existence altogether. As it was, he, born a Victorian and a sentimentalist, was content to adore, and that, in itself, is sufficiently exceptional, dammit, although it was not good for her moral fibre. She, similarly, trapped by historic circumstances, did not even know, I think, that her own vague discontent, manifested by sick headaches and complicated later on by genuine ill-health, might have had something to do with being a "wife," a role for which she was in some respects ill suited, as my father's tribute ought to indicate, since beauty and cleverness are usually more valued in mistresses than they are in wives. For her sixtieth birthday, he gave her a huge bottle of Chanel No. 5.

For what it's worth, I've never been in the least attracted to older men— nor they to me, for that matter. Why *is* that? Possibly something in my manner hints I will expect, nay, demand, behaviour I deem appropriate to a father figure, that is, that he kicks his own backside from time to time, and brings me tea in bed, and weeps at the inevitability of loss; and these are usually young men's talents.

Don't think, from all this, it's been all roses. We've had our ups and downs, the old man and I, for he was born a Victorian. Though it occurs to me his unstated but self-evident idea that I should earn my own living, have a career, in fact, may have originated in his experience of the first wave of feminism, that hit in his teens and twenties, with some of whose products he worked, by one of whose products we were doctored. (Our family doctor, Helen Gray, was eighty when she retired twenty years ago, and must have been one of the first women doctors.)

Nevertheless, his Victorianness, for want of a better word, means he feels duty bound to become the heavy father, from time to time, always with a histrionic overemphasis: "You just watch out for yourself, that's all." "Watching out for yourself" has some obscure kind of sexual meaning, which he hesitates to spell out. If advice he gave me when I was a girl (I could paraphrase this advice as "Kneecap them"), if this advice would be more or less what I'd arm my own daughters with now, it ill accorded with the mood of the sixties. Nor was it much help in those days when almost the entire male sex seemed in a conspiracy to deprive me of the opportunity to get within sufficient distance. The old man dowered me with too much self-esteem.

But how can a girl have *too much* self-esteem?

Nevertheless, not all roses. He is, you see, a foreigner; what is more, a Highland man, who struck further into the heartland of England than Charles Edward Stuart's army ever did, and then buggered off, leaving his children behind to carve niches in the alien soil. Oh, he'd hotly deny this version of his life; it is my own romantic interpretation of his life, obviously. He's all for the Act of Union. He sees no difference at all between the English and the Scots, except, once my mother was gone, he saw no reason to remain among the English. And his always unacknowledged foreignness, the extroversion of his manners, the stateliness of his demeanour, his fearlessness, guiltlessness, his inability to feel embarrassment, the formality of his discourse, above all, his utter ignorance of and complete estrangement from the English system of social class, make him a being I puzzle over and wonder at.

It is that last thing—for, in England, he seemed genuinely classless—that may have helped me always feel a stranger, here, myself. He is of perfectly good petty-bourgeois stock; my grandfather owned a shoe shop although, in those days, that meant being able to make the things as well as sell them, and repair them, too, so my grandfather was either a shopkeeper or a cobbler, depending on how you looked at it. The distinction between entrepreneur and skilled artisan may have appeared less fine, in those days, in that town beside the North Sea which still looks as if it could provide a good turnout for a witchburning.

There are all manner of stories about my paternal grandfather, whom I never met; he was the village atheist, who left a fiver in his will to every minister in the place, just in case. I never met my Gaelic-speaking grandmother, either. (She died, as it happens of toothache, shortly before I was born.) From all these stories I know they both possessed in full measure that peculiar Highland ability, much perplexing to early tourists, which means that the meanest, grubbing crofter can, if necessary, draw himself up to his full height and welcome a visitor into his stinking hovel as if its miserable tenant were a prince inviting a foreign potentate into a palace. This is the courtly grace of the authentic savage. The women do it with especially sly elegance. Lowering a steaming bowl on to a filthy tablecloth, my father's sister used to say: "Now, take some delicious kale soup." And it was the water in which the cabbage had been boiled.

It's possible to suspect they're having you on, and so they may be; yet this formality always puts the visitor, no matter what his or her status, in the role of supplicant. Your humiliation is what spares you. When a Highlander grovels, then, oh, then is the time to keep your hand on your wallet. One learns to fear an apology most.

These are the strategies of underdevelopment and they are worlds away from those which my mother's family learned to use to contend with the savage urban class struggle in Battersea, in the 1900s. Some of my mother's family learned to manipulate cynically the English class system and helped me and my brother out. All of them knew, how can I put it, that a good table with clean linen meant self-respect and to love Shakespeare was a kind of class revenge. (Perhaps that is why those soiled tray-cloths upset my mother so; she had no quarrel with his taste in literature.) For my father, the grand gesture was the thing. He entered Harrods like a Jacobite army invading Manchester. He would arrive at my school to "sort things out" like the wrath of God.

This effortless sense of natural dignity, or his own unquestioned worth, is of his essence; there are noble savages in his heredity and I look at him, sometimes, to quote Mayakovsky, "like an Eskimo looking at a train."

For I know so little about him, although I know so much. Much of his life was conducted in my absence, on terms of which I am necessarily ignorant, for he was older than I am now when I was born, although his life has shaped my life. This is the curious abyss that divides the closest kin, that the tender curiosity appropriate to lovers is inappropriate, here, where the bond is involuntary, so that the most important things stay undiscovered. If I am short-tempered, volatile as he is, there is enough of my mother's troubled soul in me to render his very transparency, his psychic good health, endlessly mysterious. He is my father and I love him as Cordelia did, "according to my natural bond." What the nature of that "natural bond" might be, I do not know, and, besides, I have a theoretical objection to the notion of a "natural bond."

But, at the end of *King Lear*, one has a very fair notion of the strength of that bond, whatever it is, whether it is the construct of culture rather than nature, even if we might all be better off without it. And I do think my father gives me far more joy than Cordelia ever got from Lear.

Sharon Olds

(1942-   )

Poet Alicia Ostriker notes the "sacralizing of the sexual and procreative body" in the poetry of Sharon Olds. It's "pure fire in the hands," in the words of novelist Michael Ondaatje: "I love the roughness and humor and brag and tenderness and completion in her work as she carries her reader through rooms of passion and loss." Poet Galway Kinnell compares her to Emily Dickinson, a poet for whom "inner experience is primary. In a very direct way [Olds] is using herself as subject matter. She seems to speak where others are silent." Born in San Francisco, Olds grew up in Berkeley, the daughter of an alcoholic father in a family that practiced, in her words, a "hellfire Episcopalianism." After graduate school at Columbia, where she protested the Vietnam War and the nuclear arms race while writing a doctoral dissertation about Ralph Waldo Emerson, she devoted herself to writing poetry full-time. Her six volumes of poetry—which include *Satan Says* (1980), *The Dead and the Living* (1983), *The Gold Cell* (1987), *The Father* (1992), *The Wellspring* (1997), and *Blood, Tin, Straw* (1999)—have won many awards and sold well; her readings are SROs; she is highly regarded not only as a poet but as a teacher at New York University's graduate school of creative writing and as founder of the poetry workshop at Goldwater Hospital for the severely disabled on Roosevelt Island in New York City. "Everybody is a poet," she told an interviewer. "Or could be. A vein of art courses through all of us." She would put a poet in every elementary and high school, in every hospital and hospice, in every prison. "I think people don't imagine what others' lives are like. That's what the arts are for. We as a species seem to be in need of imagining each other."

I Go Back to May 1937

I see them standing at the formal gates of their colleges,
I see my father strolling out
under the ochre sandstone arch, the
red tiles glinting like bent
plates of blood behind his head, I
see my mother with a few light books at her hip
standing at the pillar made of tiny bricks with the
wrought-iron gate still open behind her, its
sword-tips black in the May air,
they are about to graduate, they are about to get married,
they are kids, they are dumb, all they know is they are
innocent, they would never hurt anybody.
I want to go up to them and say Stop,
don't do it—she's the wrong woman,
he's the wrong man, you are going to do things
you cannot imagine you would ever do,
you are going to do bad things to children,
you are going to suffer in ways you never heard of,
you are going to want to die. I want to go
up to them there in the late May sunlight and say it,
her hungry pretty blank face turning to me,
her pitiful beautiful untouched body,
his arrogant handsome blind face turning to me,
his pitiful beautiful untouched body,
but I don't do it. I want to live. I
take them up like the male and female
paper dolls and bang them together
at the hips like chips of flint as if to
strike sparks from them, I say
Do what you are going to do, and I will tell about it.

Topography

After we flew across the country we
got in bed, laid our bodies
delicately together, like maps laid
face to face, East to West, my
San Francisco against your New York, your
Fire Island against my Sonoma, my
New Orleans deep in your Texas, your Idaho
bright on my Great Lakes, my Kansas
burning against your Kansas your Kansas
burning against my Kansas, your Eastern
Standard Time pressing into my
Pacific Time, my Mountain Time
beating against your Central Time, your
sun rising swiftly from the right my
sun rising swiftly from the left your
moon rising slowly from the left my
moon rising slowly from the right until
all four bodies of the sky
burn above us, sealing us together,
all our cities twin cities,
all our states united, one
nation, indivisible, with liberty and justice for all.

Bathing the New Born

I love with a fearful love to remember the
first baths I gave this boy—
my second child, so my hands knew what to do,
I laid the tiny torso along my
left forearm, nape of the noodle
neck in the crook of my elbow, hips
tiny as a bird's hips against my wrist, and the
thigh the thickness of a thick pencil held

loosely in the loop of my thumb and forefinger, the
sign that means perfect. I'd soap him slowly, the
long thin cold feet, the
scrotum tight and wrinkled as a rosy
shell so new it was flexible yet, the
miniature underweight athlete's chest, the
gummy furze of the scalp. If I got him too
soapy he'd get so slippery he'd
slide in my grip like an armful of white
buttered noodles, but I'd hold him not too tight,
I knew I was so good for him, and I'd
talk to him the whole time, I'd
tell him about his wonderful body
and the wonderful soap, the whole world made of love,
and he'd look up at me, one week old,
his eyes still wide and apprehensive of his
new life. I love that time
when you croon and croon to them, you can see the
calm slowly entering them, you can
feel it in your anchoring hand, the
small necklace of the spine against the
muscle of your forearm, you feel the fear
leaving their bodies, he lay in the blue
oval plastic baby tub and
looked at me in wonder and began to
move his silky limbs at will in the water.

The Race

When I got to the airport I rushed up to the desk,
bought a ticket, ten minutes later
they told me the flight was cancelled, the doctors
had said my father would not live through the night
and the flight was cancelled. A young man
with a dark blonde moustache told me
another airline had a non-stop
leaving in seven minutes. See that
elevator over there, well go
down to the first floor, make a right, you'll
see a yellow bus, get off at the
second Pan Am terminal, I
ran, I who have no sense of direction
raced exactly where he'd told me, a fish
slipping upstream deftly against
the flow of the river. I jumped off that bus with those
bags I had thrown everything into
in five minutes, and ran, the bags
wagged me from side to side as if
to prove I was under the claims of the material,
I ran up to a man with a white flower on his breast,
I who always go to the end of the line, I said
Help me. He looked at my ticket, he said
Make a left and then a right, go up the moving stairs and
then
run. I lumbered up the moving stairs,
at the top I saw the corridor,
and then I took a deep breath, I said
Goodbye to my body, goodbye to comfort,
I used my legs and heart as if I would
gladly use them up for this,
to touch him again in this life. I ran, and the
bags banged me, wheeled and coursed
in skewed orbits, I have seen pictures of

women running, their belongings tied
in scarves grasped in their fists, I blessed my
long legs he gave me, my strong
heart I abandoned to its own purpose,
I ran to Gate 17 and they were
just lifting the thick white
lozenge of the door to fit it into
the socket of the plane. Like the one who is not
too rich, I turned sideways and
slipped through the needle's eye, and then
I walked down the aisle toward my father. The jet
was full, and people's hair was shining, they were
smiling, the interior of the plane was filled with a
mist of gold endorphin light,
I wept as people weep when they enter heaven,
in massive relief. We lifted up
gently from one tip of the continent
and did not stop until we set down lightly on the
other edge, I walked into his room
and watched his chest rise slowly
and sink again, all night
I watched him breathe.

Alice Walker

(1944-   )

The eighth child of sharecroppers, Alice Walker grew up in Eatonton, Georgia, won a scholarship to Spelman College in Atlanta, and later transferred to Sarah Lawrence in New York, where the poet Muriel Rukeyser recognized her literary gifts and helped her find a publisher. Through the many volumes of poetry, of prize-winning fiction—especially *The Color Purple* (1982) and *In Love and Trouble: Stories of Black Women* (1973)—and of essays that have appeared since 1965, she has probed the lives of southern African American women. Her mother, who was known for her beautiful gardens, inspired the classic essay "In Search of Our Mothers' Gardens: The Legacy of Southern Black Women" (1974). (Appropriately, Walker entitled her 1975 essay about her reclamation of the legacy of Zora Neale Hurston—see page 235—"In Search of Zora Neale Hurston.") The piece that follows here, an early one in Walker's bibliography, won first prize in the 1966 essay contest of the *American Scholar*. It has at its center an old woman, wrapped in silence, excluded from her country's bounty (as she'd been from the canon of American literature) before the revolution led by Martin Luther King, Jr. Walker knew the territory of the civil rights movement. During the 1960s, she was active in the campaign for voter registration in Georgia and for welfare rights in Mississippi. She now lives in the San Francisco area.

The Civil Rights Movement: What Good Was It?

I wrote the following essay in the winter of 1966–67 while sharing one room above Washington Square Park in New York with a struggling young Jewish law student who became my husband. It was my first published essay and won the three-hundred-dollar first prize in the annual American Scholar *essay contest. The money was almost magically reassuring to us in those days of disaffected parents, outraged friends, and one-item meals, and kept us in tulips, peonies, daisies, and lamb chops for several months.*

Someone said recently to an old black lady from Mississippi, whose legs had been badly mangled by local police who arrested her for "disturbing the peace," that the Civil Rights Movement was dead, and asked, since it was dead, what she thought about it. The old lady replied, hobbling out of his presence on her cane, that the Civil Rights Movement was like herself, "if it's dead, it shore ain't ready to lay down!"

This old lady is a legendary freedom fighter in her small town in the Delta. She has been severely mistreated for insisting on her rights as an American citizen. She has been beaten for singing Movement songs, placed in solitary confinement in prisons for talking about freedom, and placed on bread and water for praying aloud to God for her jailers' deliverance. For such a woman the Civil Rights Movement will never be over as long as her skin is black. It also will never be over for twenty million others with the same "affliction," for whom the Movement can never "lay down," no matter how it is killed by the press and made dead and buried by the white American public. As long as one black American survives, the struggle for equality with other Americans must also survive. This is a debt we owe to those blameless hostages we leave to the future, our children.

Still, white liberals and deserting Civil Rights sponsors are quick to justify their disaffection from the Movement by claiming that it is all over. "And since it is over," they will ask, "would someone kindly tell me what has been gained by it?" They then list statistics supposedly showing how much more advanced segregation is now than ten years ago—in schools, housing, jobs. They point to a gain in conservative politicians during the last few years. They speak of ghetto riots and of the survey that shows that most policemen are admittedly too anti-Negro to do their jobs in ghetto areas fairly and effectively. They speak of every area that has been touched by the Civil Rights Movement as somehow or other going to pieces.

They rarely talk, however, about human attitudes among Negroes that have undergone terrific changes just during the past seven to ten years (not to mention all those years when there was a Movement and only the Negroes knew about it). They seldom speak of changes in personal lives because of the influence of people in the Movement. They see general failure and few, if any, individual gains.

They do not understand what it is that keeps the Movement from "laying down" and Negroes from reverting to their former *silent* second-class status. They have apparently never stopped to wonder why it is always the white man—on his radio and in his newspaper and on his television—who says that the Movement is dead. If a Negro were audacious enough to make such a claim, his fellows might hanker to see him shot. The Movement is dead to the white man because it no longer interests him. And it no longer interests him because he can afford to be uninterested: he does not have to live by it, with it, or for it, as Negroes must. He can take a rest from the news of beatings, killings, and arrests that reach him from North and South—if his skin is white. Negroes cannot now and will never be able to take a rest from the injustices that plague them, for they—not the white man—are the target.

Perhaps it is naïve to be thankful that the Movement "saved" a large number of individuals and gave them something to live for, even if it did not provide them with everything they wanted. (Materially, it provided them with precious little that they wanted.) When a movement awakens people to the possibilities of life, it seems unfair to frustrate them by then denying what they had thought was offered. But what was offered? What was promised? What was it all about? What good did it do? Would it have been better, as some have suggested, to leave the Negro people as they were, unawakened, unallied with one another, unhopeful about what to expect for their children in some future world?

I do not think so. If knowledge of my condition is all the freedom I get from a "freedom movement," it is better than unawareness, forgottenness, and hopelessness, the existence that is like the existence of a beast. Man only truly lives by knowing; otherwise he simply performs, copying the daily habits of others, but conceiving nothing of his creative possibilities as a man, and accepting someone else's superiority and his own misery.

When we are children, growing up in our parents' care, we await the spark from the outside world. Sometimes our parents provide it—if we are lucky—sometimes it comes from another source far from home. We sit, paralyzed, surrounded by our anxiety and dread, hoping we will not have to grow up into the narrow world and ways we see about us. We are hungry for a life that turns us on; we yearn for a knowledge of living that will save us from our innocuous lives that resemble death. We look for signs in every strange event; we search for heroes in every unknown face.

It was just six years ago that I began to be alive. I had, of course, been living before—for I am now twenty-three—but I did not really know it. And I did not know it because nobody told me that I—a pensive, yearning, typical high-school senior, but Negro—existed in the minds of others as I existed in my own. Until that time my mind was locked apart from the outer contours and complexion of my body as if it and the body were strangers. The mind possessed both thought and spirit—I wanted to be an author or a scientist—which the color of the body denied. I had never seen myself and existed as a statistic exists, or as a phantom. In the white world I walked, less real to them than a shadow; and being young and well hidden among the slums, among people who also did not exist—either in books or in films or in the government of their own lives—I waited to be called to life. And, by a miracle, I was called.

There was a commotion in our house that night in 1960. We had managed to buy our first television set. It was battered and overpriced, but my mother had gotten used to watching the afternoon soap operas at the house where she worked as maid, and nothing could satisfy her on days when she did not work but a continuation of her "stories." So she pinched pennies and bought a set.

I remained listless throughout her "stories," tales of pregnancy, abortion, hypocrisy, infidelity, and alcoholism. All these men and women were white and lived in houses with servants, long staircases that they floated down, patios where liquor was served four times a day to "relax" them. But my mother, with her swollen feet eased out of her shoes, her heavy body relaxed in our only comfortable chair, watched each movement of the smartly coiffed women, heard each word, pounced upon each innuendo and inflection, and for the duration of these "stories" she saw herself as one of them. She placed herself in every scene she saw, with her braided hair turned blond, her two hundred pounds compressed into a sleek size-seven dress, her rough dark skin smooth and *white*. Her husband became "dark and handsome," talented, witty, urbane, charming. And when she turned to look at my father sitting near her in his sweat shirt with his smelly feet raised on the bed to "air," there was always a tragic look of surprise on her face. Then she would sigh and go out to the kitchen looking lost and unsure of herself. My mother, a truly great woman who raised eight children of her own and half a dozen of the neighbors' without a single complaint, was convinced that she did not exist compared to "them." She subordinated her soul to theirs and became a faithful and timid supporter of the "Beautiful White People." Once she asked me, in a moment of vicarious pride and despair, if I didn't think that "they" were "jest naturally smarter, prettier, better." My mother asked this: a woman who never got rid of any of her children, never cheated on my father, was never a hypocrite if she could help it, and never even tasted liquor. She could not even bring herself to blame "them" for making her believe what they wanted her to believe: that if she did not look like them, think like them, be sophisticated and corrupt-for-comfort's-sake like them, she was a nobody. Black was not a color on my mother; it was a shield that made her invisible.

Of course, the people who wrote the soap-opera scripts always made the Negro maids in them steadfast, trusty, and wise in a home-remedial sort of way; but my mother, a maid for nearly forty years, never once identified herself with the scarcely glimpsed black servant's face beneath the ruffled cap. Like everyone else, in her daydreams at least, she thought she was free.

Six years ago, after half-heartedly watching my mother's soap operas and wondering whether there wasn't something more to be asked of life, the Civil Rights Movement came into my life. Like a good omen for the future, the face of Dr. Martin Luther King, Jr., was the first black face I saw on our new television screen. And, as in a fairy tale, my soul was stirred by the meaning for me of his mission—at the time he was being rather ignominiously dumped into a police van for having led a protest march in Alabama—and I fell in love with the sober and determined face of the Movement. The singing of "We Shall Overcome"—that song betrayed by nonbelievers in it—rang for the first time in my ears. The influence that my mother's soap operas might have had on me became impossible. The life of Dr. King, seeming bigger and more miraculous than the man himself, because of all he had done and suffered, offered a pattern of strength and sincerity I felt I could trust. He had suffered much because of his simple belief in nonviolence, love, and brotherhood. Perhaps the majority of men could not be reached through these beliefs, but because Dr. King kept trying to reach them in spite of danger to himself and his family, I saw in him the hero for whom I had waited so long.

What Dr. King promised was not a ranch-style house and an acre of manicured lawn for every black man, but jail and finally freedom. He did not promise two cars for every family, but the courage one day for all families everywhere to walk without shame and unafraid on their own feet. He did

not say that one day it will be us chasing prospective buyers out of our prosperous well-kept neighborhoods, or in other ways exhibiting our snobbery
and ignorance as all other ethnic groups before us have done; what he said
was that we had a right to live anywhere in this country we chose, and a right
to a meaningful well-paying job to provide us with the upkeep of our homes.
He did not say we had to become carbon copies of the white American middle class; but he did say we had the right to become whatever we wanted to
become.

Because of the Movement, because of an awakened faith in the newness
and imagination of the human spirit, because of "black and white together"—
for the first time in our history in some human relationship on and off TV—
because of the beatings, the arrests, the hell of battle during the past years, I
have fought harder for my life and for a chance to be myself, to be something
more than a shadow or a number, than I had ever done before in my life.
Before, there had seemed to be no real reason for struggling beyond the effort
for daily bread. Now there was a chance at that other that Jesus meant when
He said we could not live by bread alone.

I have fought and kicked and fasted and prayed and cursed and cried
myself to the point of existing. It has been like being born again, literally. Just
"knowing" has meant everything to me. Knowing has pushed me out into
the world, into college, into places, into people.

Part of what existence means to me is knowing the difference between
what I am now and what I was then. It is being capable of looking after myself
intellectually as well as financially. It is being able to tell when I am being
wronged and by whom. It means being awake to protect myself and the ones
I love. It means being a part of the world community, and being *alert* to which
part it is that I have joined, and knowing how to change to another part if that
part does not suit me. To know is to exist: to exist is to be involved, to move
about, to see the world with my own eyes. This, at least, the Movement has
given me.

The hippies and other nihilists would have me believe that it is all the
same whether the people in Mississippi have a movement behind them or
not. Once they have their rights, they say, they will run all over themselves
trying to be just like everybody else. They will be well fed, complacent about
things of the spirit, emotionless, and without that marvelous humanity and
"soul" that the Movement has seen them practice time and time again. "What

has the Movement done," they ask, "with the few people it has supposedly helped?" "Got them white-collar jobs, moved them into standardized ranch houses in white neighborhoods, given them nondescript gray flannel suits?" "What are these people now?" they ask. And then they answer themselves, "Nothings!"

I would find this reasoning—which I have heard many, many times from hippies and nonhippies alike—amusing if I did not also consider it serious. For I think it is a delusion, a cop-out, an excuse to disassociate themselves from a world in which they feel too little has been changed or gained. The real question, however, it appears to me, is not whether poor people will adopt the middle-class mentality once they are well fed; rather, it is whether they will ever be well fed enough to be able to choose whatever mentality they think will suit them. The lack of a movement did not keep my mother from *wishing* herself bourgeois in her daydreams.

There is widespread starvation in Mississippi. In my own state of Georgia there are more hungry families than Lester Maddox would like to admit—or even see fed. I went to school with children who ate red dirt. The Movement has prodded and pushed some liberal senators into pressuring the government for food so that the hungry may eat. Food stamps that were two dollars and out of the reach of many families not long ago have been reduced to fifty cents. The price is still out of the reach of some families, and the government, it seems to a lot of people, could spare enough free food to feed its own people. It angers people in the Movement that it does not; they point to the billions in wheat we send free each year to countries abroad. Their government's slowness while people are hungry, its unwillingness to believe that there are Americans starving, its stingy cutting of the price of food stamps, make many Civil Rights workers throw up their hands in disgust. But they do not give up. They do not withdraw into the world of psychedelia. They apply what pressure they can to make the government give away food to hungry people. They do not plan so far ahead in their disillusionment with society that they can see these starving families buying identical ranch-style houses and sending their snobbish children to Bryn Mawr and Yale. They take first things first and try to get them fed.

They do not consider it their business, in any case, to say what kind of life the people they help must lead. How one lives is, after all, one of the rights left to the individual—when and if he has opportunity to choose. It is not the prerogative of the middle class to determine what is worthy of aspiration. There is also every possibility that the middle-class people of tomorrow will turn out ever so much better than those of today. I even know some middle-class people of today who are not *all* bad.

I think there are so few Negro hippies because middle-class Negroes, although well fed, are not careless. They are required by the treacherous world they live in to be clearly aware of whoever or whatever might be trying to do them in. They are middle class in money and position, but they cannot afford to be middle class in complacency. They distrust the hippie movement because they know that it can do nothing for Negroes as a group but "love" them, which is what all paternalists claim to do. And since the only way Negroes can survive (which they cannot do, unfortunately, on love alone) is with the support of the group, they are wisely wary and stay away.

A white writer tried recently to explain that the reason for the relatively few Negro hippies is that Negroes have built up a "super-cool" that cracks under LSD and makes them have a "bad trip." What this writer doesn't guess at is that Negroes are needing drugs less than ever these days for any kind of trip. While hippies are "tripping," Negroes are going after power, which is so much more important to their survival and their children's survival than LSD and pot.

Everyone would be surprised if the Israelis ignored the Arabs and took up "tripping" and pot smoking. In this country we are the Israelis. Everybody who can do so would like to forget this, of course. But for us to forget it for a minute would be fatal. "We Shall Overcome" is just a song to most Americans, *but we must do it*. Or die.

What good was the Civil Rights Movement? If it had just given this country Dr. King, a leader of conscience, for once in our lifetime, it would have been enough. If it had just taken black eyes off white television stories, it would have been enough. If it had fed one starving child, it would have been enough.

If the Civil Rights Movement is "dead," and if it gave us nothing else, it gave us each other forever. It gave some of us bread, some of us shelter, some of us knowledge and pride, all of us comfort. It gave us our children, our husbands, our brothers, our fathers, as men reborn and with a purpose for living. It broke the pattern of black servitude in this country. It shattered the phony "promise" of white soap operas that sucked away so many pitiful lives.

It gave us history and men far greater than Presidents. It gave us heroes, self-less men of courage and strength, for our little boys and girls to follow. It gave us hope for tomorrow. It called us to life.

Because we live, it can never die.

Ann Beattie

(1947-   )

Ann Beattie has published seven collections of short stories—
Distortions (1976), *Secrets and Surprises* (1979), *The Burning House*
(1982), *Where You'll Find Me* (1986), *What Was Mine* (1991), *Park City*
(1998), and *Perfect Recall* (2001)—and seven novels, including *Chilly
Scenes of Winter* (1976), *Falling in Place* (1980), *Love Always* (1985),
Picturing Will (1989), *My Life, Starring Dara Falcon* (1997), and *The
Doctor's House* (2002). Often called the chronicler of her generation—the edgy narcissistic 1970s—Beattie has received the highest
praise from other writers, including Margaret Atwood, John
Updike, and Lorrie Moore. Reviewing Beattie's collection *Park City*,
from which the following story is taken, Moore finds it "a reminder
of Beattie's unshakably intelligent, deep-hearted . . . devotion to the
form. . . . It is [her] ear that gives her stories their sharp life, muscle
and surprise. . . . [And] Beattie's forgiving affection for her charming, neurotic men . . . suggests a largeness of authorial sympathy."

The Four-Night Fight

The four-night fight began on Father's Day, June 20, but had nothing to do
with the day. Her father had been dead for almost fifteen years; his father had
left his mother and moved to Santa Barbara to spend his remaining years—
so far, twelve had passed—golfing. Henry was not himself a father.

It had been a beautiful, sunny day. Lavender geraniums were in bloom,
bordering the back porch. Inside the porch, yellow and red begonias blos-
somed, their flowers as large as their leaves. In one of the pots, a plastic par-
rot's one moving wing rotated as the wind blew. The summer before, Henry
had gotten the other wing going, but this year he'd done nothing. Neither
had he brought home plants for the porch, nor helped weed the geranium
bed, to which he had added, against her objections, a dozen blue-black tulips,
planting the bulbs the previous fall as she slept. First he refused to enlarge the

flower bed. Then, when she did that, he "borrowed" bricks from the border to brace a rickety book shelf. Then he ordered red tulips, was sent the bruise-colored ones instead, shrugged, ignored her dismay, and planted them while she was asleep. None of these things had anything to do with the fight.

The fight began in early evening, so that properly speaking, it was a four-night, three-day fight. The fight reminded her of hotel package deals: four nights, five days, in sunny Bermuda—but after you struggled to the hotel the pleasure of the first day would inevitably be shot: plane late; luggage delayed; rainstorm slowing the car to the hotel; a long line for check-in. They had taken a trip to Bermuda in October, to celebrate their anniversary. She had wanted to stay in a small hotel, he had insisted on staying at a sprawling resort. Like his father, he loved to golf. She had gone around on her moped alone, while he golfed, and though that might have made her feel bad, it had not, so why pretend to hold a grudge when actually she had quite enjoyed her freedom? She didn't pretend to hold a grudge. Nothing that happened in Bermuda had anything to do with the fight.

In fact, the reason the fight was so bad was that it snuck up on her. In the seconds preceding the fight, she had been perfectly happy, scooping the center out of a cantaloupe. Henry had become diabetic, so they no longer had cookies for dessert, only fruit. She kept a package of Chips Ahoy hidden behind boxes of Tide in the laundry room, but she'd lost her taste for sweets, suddenly. Or maybe not so suddenly; she'd lost it when the cookies somehow absorbed, like a sponge, the smell of Tide. When she was a child, her mother had put milk of magnesia in chocolate milk to disguise the taste, but all it had done was make her cringe at the thought of plain chocolate milk, and also chocolate ice cream, or chocolate milkshakes. She was even wary of chocolate cake, and sniffed skeptically at Hershey bars. No matter: cookies and chocolate could easily be done without, and a person would be healthier because of it. So there she had been, scooping out the melon, looking forward to a made-for-TV movie the listing had said would be good, when suddenly Henry was standing in the kitchen doorway, looking at her in a peculiar way, contributing nothing toward fixing their dessert, having said not a word about the dinner she had just served. . . . Well: the thing was, the fight, in his mind, had already begun, but she had been slow to understand his sulking, mistaking it for simple fatigue, since before dinner he'd hauled out the trash and sprayed the lid with Clorox so that during the night the raccoon couldn't simply saunter up to the can and with a swipe of its paw crash the top of the trash can to the ground. Also, he had sawed off the broken limb of the lilac and dragged it into the woods, then gone inside and called his mother to give her some information she needed to pay her taxes. His mother was not the world's most pleasant person. Also, since it was Father's Day, she was in a bleaker mood than usual, despising Henry's father for leaving her and spending his retirement golfing in California. Maybe his mother's bad mood was contagious. Maybe Henry had done one too many chores. Maybe he harbored a grudge that she had made him spray the trash can with Clorox, which he continued to call "ridiculous," though it was the one thing that had ever deterred the tenacious, fat, garbage-can-toppling raccoon.

Standing in the kitchen doorway, he had said to her: "Sometimes I think this is all a huge fucking joke. Sometimes I think we're ants, and here in our anthill we scurry around, moving the dirt, building the anthill higher, eating our food, shitting it out, doing out humble chores for the fucking Queen Ant, foraging and accumulating, bringing things in, piling things up, moving the piles around, and all the while, in our little specks of ant brain, we hope a big rainstorm doesn't come and pound the whole fucking anthill into the ground, that we don't get washed down the hill, that we don't drown in the flood, but what would it matter if we did? What the fuck would it matter?"

It was so unexpected. So typical of Henry, though, who while having finally admitted, one night in Bermuda, as the sky was brightening from rose to crimson, that his obsessing about the deterioration of the ozone layer was really a way of not focusing on more immediate, personal problems that he might do something about . . . well: going on with this line of thought would give the mistaken impression that she had been assessing the situation, seeing in it the seeds of similar situations—Christ! Did he think she'd gone to college to scoop the insides of melons into a garbage disposal? Could he really have thought that she would appreciate such a barrage of adolescent, ridiculous despair . . . had he been standing in the doorway with his weight thrown on one hip, in his loafers with their mashed-down backs, and his thumb hooked through a belt loop . . . was this miserable sight, this person she'd for some unfathomable reason married, so stupid as to think she'd appreciate being compared to an ant as she stood scooping pulp and seeds and fiber into the sink so that his diabetes wouldn't rage out of control . . . had they had what they agreed would be their last discussion of the ozone layer only to have him recast everything in terms of their pointless life inside an anthill?

"You're really insane," she said.

"I'm insane?" he said. And then he said something she didn't get—something about the Clorox. That didn't surprise her at all, because whenever she gave him a helpful hint he derided her or ignored it. The use of Clorox as a repellent hadn't been her own epiphany, by the way: it was something she'd read flipping through a tabloid in the supermarket, which was where she spent half her life, half of her pointless ant life, gathering food for Henry, because maybe Henry himself was the Ant King? After all, who was standing in the doorway, the picture of casualness, while her hair had fallen from her barrette to tickle her nose as she peered down into the messy abortion of melon pulp in the sink. . . .

She had apparently thrown the phone book at him. She saw that she had, because his hands flew up to protect his head, and certainly the phone book had not just animated itself to join in the fracas, surely she must have thrown it, accelerating the fight, which by that time had been going on for perhaps five minutes, of screaming and accusations, suspended only for troubled sleep, to resume the next morning.

The day after the fight he did not go to work, which did trouble her. If he had called to say he would not be at work, he would have had to do it while she slept—he didn't mind planting ugly tulips while she slept, for all she knew he had a complete private life. He told her about deficiencies in her character as he toasted an English muffin—one only; none for her—blaming her for trying to infantilize him with her air of superiority, banging his fist on the kitchen island and sending the nondairy creamer crashing to the floor, whatever he was saying about Clorox drowned out by the crashing glass. Then, insanely, completely insanely, as the muffin lodged in the toaster and began to burn, though it would be a cold day in hell if she ever again rescued any of his food, let him forage for it himself, ant that he was . . . Henry began to pick up the shards of glass and throw them, claiming the bits of glass were ants, or like ants—whatever he was saying. He was saying that he was scattering the anthill. Really, he was just a bully, uncivilized and out of control, wanting to lash out at who knew what, who could know who the designated Queen Ant was that morning, in his paranoia and rage. Black smoke poured from the toaster, and again the telephone book was animated, sailing through the air, smeared with cantaloupe juice, crashing way off course into the wall. She had wanted to paint the kitchen walls green; Henry had wanted them yellow. They had compromised on peach, which was good, considering the melon juice that was now smeared on the wall, though she resolutely did not care about that, did not care if the whole toaster erupted, did not care what he did with the rest of his day, did not care if he stood forever making analogies between broken glass and anthills, because he was cynical and unbalanced, she was not, she was—he was saying again—superior. Then he kicked the phone book as if he were making a final goal and looked around crazily, as if she represented a whole team who would cheer him. Looking over his shoulder, he asked if she ever had a kind thought about his mother in her life. It did not deserve an answer.

The next day, he was gone when she woke up, but he was so agitated that he had left a message—a rant, really—on the answering machine. At the beginning, he taunted her by daring her to listen to the message all the way through, which she did intend to do, sitting at the kitchen counter, the air still redolent with the smell of burned bread, bits of glass scattered underfoot. "I did what the raccoon couldn't do," he screamed on the tape. "I turned over your fucking garbage can that the fucking garbage truck neglected to empty because they do not give a flying fuck if the whole world festers and deteriorates, if they can shorten their working day by ignoring the cans on the route. I turned it over and I was within one second, one millionth of an inch, of taking the lid and ramming it through the side window of your car. . . ."

At this, she got slowly off the stool and went out to the driveway, his voice fading in the background. She walked as if in a trance, but she was not really in a trance, she was just practicing being in a trance. What if he had really traumatized her, so that she had become a zombie? What if at this moment she was a zombie, looking at chicken bones, food-stained newspapers, all the detritus of their lives scattered in the street—not by the raccoon, but by the wild beast that was her husband? No: she would not let him drive her crazy. It was reasonable to be superior, and not a zombie. She could shuffle along, traumatized, and become what he would like her to become, but it was better simply to sidestep his expectations, just as she sidestepped the garbage. That night, a neighbor's boy would stuff most of it back in the can. She would see that from the bathroom window, getting up from the closed toilet seat where she was reading a mystery, preferring to be locked in the bathroom

rather than downstairs, where Henry was silently watching the long-ago res-
ignation of Richard Nixon on TV. It was not true that all teenagers were
destructive and self-absorbed. The boy picked up almost everything, including soup cans with jagged edges and soggy coffee filters, then put the lid firmly on the trash can again. He could have been Sir Lancelot, he shone so in her
imagination as what a man could be. Downstairs, she heard gunshots, and for
a horrifying second she was so on edge that she had rewritten history and
imagined Nixon being shot, then realized that Henry must have begun
shooting at the teenager! Henry having a gun. Did he have a gun? Of course
he didn't have a gun. And if he did have a gun, then she hoped he would use
it on himself.

No, she didn't. She tried thinking that, to see how it would feel. It felt
wrong. She was afraid she was beginning to forgive him. In saying she wanted him shot when she did not want him shot, she had begun to forgive him.
And she might have, too, if he hadn't glared at her so coldly before pulling
off the comforter and going to sleep on the sofa. Such histrionics, when there
was a guest room. He was really out of control. Maybe he was actually cracking up. She tossed in bed half the night, and when she went down in the
morning he was still there, the cover over the top of his body, including his
head, his bare legs sticking out, one on the sofa arm, one on the floor. It was
like finding the Elephant Man in a casual moment. She stood in the doorway,
so fatigued she decided to forgive him, to try to get things back on track. If
nothing else, he would certainly have to go back to his job soon. Perhaps he
hadn't gone back yesterday. Perhaps she had assumed, incorrectly, that the
hysterical message of the day before had been left from work—but how likely was that? He had probably not sat at his desk and simply raged, spitting his
irrational thoughts into a telephone. He had probably called from . . .
"Henry," she said, trying to keep her voice calm, "were you at work yesterday
when you left that ridiculous message?"

He jumped up, tossing off the comforter with such force that she
jumped back. He stood there, glowering at her, the comforter puddled
around him like a collapsed parachute, His wild eyes made her think of
someone who had just crashed into dangerous jungle. He might have been
wondering: Could this native be friendly? She tried to look friendlier by
smiling, but the attempt to alter the expression of her mouth, she could tell,
was only resulting in narrowed eyes. She could not smile. She did manage to

unknot the frown that creased between her eyes. They stood there that way, gazing at each other, she barefoot in her long nightgown patterned with blue morning glories, he wearing a white sleeveless undershirt and nothing else, his knock-knees pathetic, his penis curved like a tiny fountain spout, and— she had been blocking it out because she really did not want to focus on it— on his arm, on his biceps, a terrible bruise, a terrible swelling: from doing battle with the trash can? From . . . God, it was a tattoo. It was a tattoo, and he saw that she saw it. Even the fountain spout seemed to recoil in dismay. Henry was standing there, staring at her with the We Are Ants expression on his face, and on his upper arm, the part of his arm she had clasped so many times as they made love, was MOM in red-inked script, and a circle inscribing it, a circle, she saw, upon closer inspection, that was not a conglomerate of ants, but swirls of small hearts and flowers, interspersed with skin puckered into scabs, an outer rim of flesh around the circle swollen and flecked with what seemed to be broken veins.

"Hurts," he said.

"Hurts?" she echoed. She was becoming the zombie whose role she had tried on for size. Numb. Unblinking. Who could blink looking at such a thing?

"I went drinking with Jim Cavalli, made a bet, guy couldn't pay up, we went to his tattoo studio, I got to choose from the fifty-dollar possibilities."

"Henry," she said, "what is this about your mother?"

"Cavalli chose."

"Cavalli had your arm tattooed MOM?"

"Cavalli wanted to beat him up. I was the one who agreed to settle on a tattoo."

"Cavalli . . . ," she said, searching her mind for a visual image of the man. The new, gawky kid from Princeton? Pink shirt, drank a lot of Dos Equis at the company picnic? Though she was not aware she'd been speaking, Henry began to respond to her sharpening mental image of Cavalli. "Went off the wagon himself because his Princeton girlfriend left him for her analyst," Henry said.

"So . . . what?" she said. "You and Cavalli went to a bar, and he told you his girlfriend had left him, you told him the human race, or you and I, how should I know? You told him we were ants, and then some guy who worked at a tattoo parlor sat down and you bet him . . . you bet what?"

"That the guy would miss the shot."

"You bet that a guy on TV would miss a shot, he said the guy would make it, the guy missed, and you ended up with MOM in majesty on your arm?"

"Hurts," he said quietly.

"Well, Jesus," she said. "I think we should go to the doctor and see if he can treat it, because I think your arm is infected." A headache came up inside her like rolling thunderclouds spreading across the sky. By the time she finished her sentence, electricity was crackling through her brain, a tooth-chattering wind had begun.

It was as if her pain made her transparent. Suddenly he looked at her as if he could see the rain clouds inside. The pain piercings sinking into her jaw like lightning. "Your name is Angelina," he said. Her head hurt so much that she didn't mind this simple, neutral observation at all. Indeed she was Angelina. So true. He continued: "While I admit I hated you in that moment, it did occur to me that if I hadn't been angry, if I hadn't been angry when I was getting the tattoo, I could have had a tattoo of my wife's name, except only three letters could be had for fifty dollars, because Cavalli was insisting on scrollwork. The part around the word is called scrolling. It's generic hearts and flowers and stuff."

This was too much to take in. Her head was pounding.

"They do it the way people doodle on a notepad when they're on the telephone, I guess." He had sunk into the sofa, pulling the comforter over himself. He looked like an ill, miserable child. He looked at her expectantly.

"I think we should go to the doctor," she said. She had begun to worry about the tattooist's needles. Why would Henry have done such a thing, when everyone was so worried about AIDS? How could he have been sure the needles were clean? Needles—Jesus Christ. He had let someone take needles and scratch dye into his flesh. He had gone with some self-pitying moron named Cavalli. And yet, she was on the sofa beside him, snuggled under his good arm, the comforter around them both feeling soft and sheltering. At that moment, the last thing she was thinking about was the fight. He had become, in her mind, a victim. Someone who had received far worse punishment then he deserved. Someone who needed medical attention, understanding, forgiveness. She envisioned herself driving him to the doctor's office—never mind that the doctor was sure to be horrified—going there, getting a prescription for antibiotics, perhaps topical creams, perhaps . . . perhaps the doctor would see that Henry was unbalanced and think of something to do. Though the more she thought about it, the more she disbelieved it. Unless she could walk right into the doctor's office with him, he would probably present it as regrettable, drunken madness. She would have to go in and be a Greek chorus: *No, no, he was comparing life to being in an anthill; he's never cared if flowers are atrocious colors, he just plants them anyway, like flowers that would bloom in hell; his mother upsets him, complaining about his father; our fight began on Father's Day, which can't be insignificant—either it's resentment of his own father spilling over into our life, or he's angry that people are procreating: he sees all these things as a personal affront, whether it's the holes in the ozone layer or clear-cutting the forest or people giving birth to a child. He's in a state of madness and despair, I tell you. He doesn't go to work anymore. Come to think of it, for days I haven't seen him eat.* She would have to say those things; no sitting in the waiting room reading *Good Housekeeping.* No information, today, about Kathie Lee's thoughts on how to parent. Cheese dips be damned.

The fight began again when, to her complete surprise, he refused to see the doctor. It was feeling better already, he suddenly said. He thought he had a bit of a fever, though, so he would—if she did not mind—nap for a bit.

"You're going to the doctor," she said.

"No," he said. "I am not."

Thus began a new day of fighting, which she had not been prepared for at all, having begun to forgive him. And, like anyone dragged into something unexpectedly, her reactions were not the best. Instead of focusing on his obviously infected arm, she found herself demanding an explanation of how, exactly, he would keep the raccoon out of the trash if he did not want to use her method. She twisted up her mouth and marched like a martinet, imitating his expression and his quick exit from the living room when the phone rang. The phone: news from the outside world. The doctor, by telepathic message having realized he should call? When she picked it up, it was Cavalli. The nerve! What did he want, she asked: to know if Henry would meet him for more drinks and then go out to a whorehouse? "No," Cavalli said evenly. "To know if he's coming to work." She hung up on him. Then the fight really swung into full gear. She was emasculating him again, it appeared. Again, he threatened her car windows. Couldn't he think of anything more original then that? Or, at the very least, admit that he wanted to hit *her?* "You'd like that, wouldn't you?" he said. It was not until three in the afternoon that she looked out and realized that neither of them had brought in the paper.

That night, he ate nothing. He sat with the remote control, flipping through channels, sentence fragments and incomplete sounds no doubt echoing the chaos of his brain. Once, he ran out the front door with the still-rolled newspaper, threatening a cat digging near a bush. He could have been heard miles away. If he did become violent, no one in the neighborhood would be surprised. Yes, they'd say, that guy was really nuts. Nuts but wounded. She couldn't get the image of his infected arm out of her mind. It was as if the pain throbbed in her own head. Of course, it was next to impossible to sleep. And when she was at last almost asleep, what did he do but tear off in the car, going who knew where, dressed—as she later found out—in the only clothes he could find downstairs: a pair of madras bermudas with a ripped zipper he'd taken from her sewing room and his flip-flops with the thongs he'd glued back together in the basement, and her blouse. The nice navy-blue blouse she'd ironed before the fight began and never taken upstairs. He had left after cramming his body into her navy-blue blouse.

She went downstairs and turned off the answering machine because she did not want to hear whatever vicious message he might leave. She did though, make sure the ringer on the phone was on, so that if he—or the police, God forbid—needed to reach her, they could. The only phone call came from his mother, who had no sense of time, wanting him to install a new bathroom sink for her at what she called "your convenience." Wait until she saw the MOM tattoo. Let the two of them discuss that.

Was he, in fact, headed for his mother's—and should she have warned the woman that might be the case? Or to Cavalli's? Back to the bar? Who knew where. Who knew how this was going to end, if it ever did end. It was the longest fight she had ever been involved in, and it was exhausting her and making her feel crazy herself. She took aspirin and went back to bed.

In the morning, when she awoke, he was lying next to her. It was not a dream, he was really there. The blue blouse was on the floor, the madras bermudas discarded amid the thongs, his eyes squeezed shut so tightly she wondered if he was only pretending to sleep. At first, barely distinguishable in the tangle of white sheets, she didn't realize there was a large gauze bandage on his arm. It was a thick pad of gauze, wrapped entirely around his arm, and near the top were black stitches—no: there was writing. On the gauze bandage, he had written, as best he could, left-handed, because the tattoo was on his right arm, the scratchy letters S O R R Y. There it was: the white flag of surrender, and an added apology lest she mistake it. Propped on one elbow, she frowned as she considered it: the wobbly O like a bubble being blown from a bubble wand; the Y like a sprouting seed. It seemed to her the sweetest thing he had ever done. Though he had done so many sweet things in the time they'd been together. The four-night fight must have been worse for him than for her; because he hated to carry a grudge. "Let him golf. Forget him if you can't forgive him," he always said to his mother. "Buy more flowers if that's what you want, honey," he had said to her when the garden bloomed that spring with its strange blossoms. She stared at the bandage. It was professionally done. He must have gone to the emergency room. On the night table she saw a glass of water and a bottle of medicine. It seemed to her a real salvation: the antibiotics that would cure the wound's infection, protecting his precious arm, that arm that had curled around her so many times, guiding her through crowds, protectively placed when he introduced her to a stranger. She stayed there, propped up, observing him, the way a person will look out a window and study the land after a storm, everything seeming greener, lighter, suddenly distinct. The familiar landscape was all there: from chin stubble to chest hair, from navel to knee, it was Henry, slumbering after the great storm. Henry, simply, no scrollwork needed to establish his importance, because when she saw him small hearts and flowers invisibly surrounded him always, an embellished border around the valentine of affection that was her love. What couple does not occasionally fight?

Leslie Marmon Silko

(1948-   )

Leslie Marmon Silko, whose background is Mexican, Laguna Pueblo, and white, was born in Albuquerque, New Mexico, and grew up on the Laguna Pueblo Reservation. The stories and legends she heard about the Native American past from the women in her family seed the novels, poetry, and short stories that have made her reputation as, in the words of a *New York Times* reviewer, "without question the most accomplished Indian writer of her generation." It was her novel *Ceremony* (1977), the story of a Native American of mixed ancestry who is a veteran of World War II, that won her a large audience, at once popular and academic, and, a few years later, a MacArthur "genius award." Her stories are widely anthologized, and her more recent books, *Storyteller* (1981) and *Almanac of the Dead* (1991), bend traditional genre boundaries to combine family history, stories, Native American myths, and, in the story that follows, a song as timeless as the firmament.

Lullaby

The sun had gone down but the snow in the wind gave off its own light. It came in thick tufts like new wool—washed before the weaver spins it. Ayah reached out for it like her own babies had, and she smiled when she remembered how she had laughed at them. She was an old woman now, and her life had become memories. She sat down with her back against the wide cottonwood tree, feeling the rough bark on her back bones; she faced east and listened to the wind and snow sing a high-pitched Yeibechei song. Out of the wind she felt warmer, and she could watch the wide fluffy snow fill in her tracks, steadily, until the direction she had come from was gone. By the light of the snow she could see the dark outline of the big arroyo a few feet away. She was sitting on the edge of Cebolleta Creek, where in the springtime the thin cows would graze on grass already chewed flat to the ground. In the wide deep creek bed where only a trickle of water flowed in the summer, the skinny cows would wander, looking for new grass along winding paths splashed with manure.

Ayah pulled the old Army blanket over her head like a shawl. Jimmie's blanket—the one he had sent to her. That was a long time ago and the green wool was faded, and it was unraveling on the edges. She did not want to think about Jimmie. So she thought about the weaving and the way her mother had done it. On the tall wooden loom set into the sand under a tamarack tree for shade. She could see it clearly. She had been only a little girl when her grandma gave her the wooden combs to pull the twigs and burrs from the raw, freshly washed wool. And while she combed the wool, her grandma sat beside her, spinning a silvery strand of yarn around the smooth cedar spindle. Her mother worked at the loom with yarns dyed bright yellow and red and gold. She watched them dye the yarn in boiling black pots full of beeweed petals, juniper berries, and sage. The blankets her mother made were soft and woven so tight that rain rolled off them like birds' feathers. Ayah remembered sleeping warm on cold windy nights, wrapped in her mother's blankets on the hogan's sandy floor.

The snow drifted now, with the northwest wind hurling it in gusts. It drifted up around her black overshoes—old ones with little metal buckles. She smiled at the snow which was trying to cover her little by little. She could remember when they had no black rubber overshoes; only the high buckskin leggings that they wrapped over their elkhide moccasins. If the snow was dry or frozen, a person could walk all day and not get wet; and in the evenings the beams of the ceiling would hang with lengths of pale buckskin leggings, drying out slowly.

She felt peaceful remembering. She didn't feel cold any more. Jimmie's blanket seemed warmer than it had ever been. And she could remember the morning he was born. She could remember whispering to her mother, who was sleeping on the other side of the hogan, to tell her it was time now. She did not want to wake the others. The second time she called to her, her mother stood up and pulled on her shoes; she knew. They walked to the old stone hogan together, Ayah walking a step behind her mother. She waited alone, learning the rhythms of the pains while her mother went to call the old woman to help them. The morning was already warm even before dawn and Ayah smelled the bee flowers blooming and the young willow growing at the springs. She could remember that so clearly, but his birth merged into the births of the other children and to her it became all the same birth. They named him for the summer morning and in English they called him Jimmie.

It wasn't like Jimmie died. He just never came back, and one day a dark blue sedan with white writing on its doors pulled up in front of the boxcar shack where the rancher let the Indians live. A man in a khaki uniform trimmed in gold gave them a yellow piece of paper and told them that Jimmie was dead. He said the Army would try to get the body back and then it would be shipped to them; but it wasn't likely because the helicopter had burned after it crashed. All of this was told to Chato because he could understand English. She stood inside the doorway holding the baby while Chato listened. Chato spoke English like a white man and he spoke Spanish too. He was taller than the white man and he stood straighter too. Chato didn't explain why; he just told the military man they could keep the body if they found it. The white man looked bewildered; he nodded his head and he left. Then Chato looked at her and shook his head, and then he told her, "Jimmie isn't coming home anymore," and when he spoke, he used the words to speak of the dead. She didn't cry then, but she hurt inside with anger. And she mourned him as the years passed, when a horse fell with Chato and broke his leg, and the white rancher told them he wouldn't pay Chato until he could work again. She mourned Jimmie because he would have worked for his father then; he would have saddled the big bag horse and ridden the fence lines each day, with wire cutters and heavy gloves, fixing the breaks in the barbed wire and putting the stray cattle back inside again.

She mourned him after the white doctors came to take Danny and Ella away. She was at the shack alone that day they came. It was back in the days before they hired Navajo women to go with them as interpreters. She recognized one of the doctors. She had seen him at the children's clinic at Cañoncito about a month ago. They were wearing khaki uniforms and they waved papers at her and a black ball-point pen, trying to make her understand their English words. She was frightened by the way they looked at the children, like the lizard watches the fly. Danny was swinging on the tire swing on the elm tree behind the rancher's house, and Ella was toddling around the front door, dragging the broomstick horse Chato made for her. Ayah could see they wanted her to sign the papers, and Chato had taught her to sign her name. It was something she was proud of. She only wanted them to go, and to take their eyes away from her children.

She took the pen from the man without looking at his face and she signed the papers in three different places he pointed to. She stared at the ground by their feet and waited for them to leave. But they stood there and began to point and gesture at the children. Danny stopped swinging. Ayah could see his fear. She moved suddenly and grabbed Ella into her arms; the child squirmed, trying to get back to her toys. Ayah ran with the baby toward Danny; she screamed for him to run and then she grabbed him around his chest and carried him too. She ran south into the foothills of juniper trees and black lava rock. Behind her she heard the doctors running, but they had been taken by surprise, and as the hills became steeper and the cholla cactus were thicker, they stopped. When she reached the top of the hill, she stopped to listen in case they were circling around her. But in a few minutes she heard a car engine start and they drove away. The children had been too surprised to cry while she ran with them. Danny was shaking and Ella's little fingers were gripping Ayah's blouse.

She stayed up in the hills for the rest of the day, sitting on a black lava boulder in the sunshine where she could see for miles all around her. The sky was light blue and cloudless, and it was warm for late April. The sun warmth relaxed her and took the fear and anger away. She lay back on the rock and watched the sky. It seemed to her that she could walk into the sky, stepping through clouds endlessly. Danny played with little pebbles and stones, pretending they were birds eggs and then little rabbits. Ella sat at her feet and dropped fistfuls of dirt into the breeze, watching the dust and particles of sand intently. Ayah watched a hawk soar high above them, dark wings gliding; hunting or only watching, she did not know. The hawk was patient and he circled all afternoon before he disappeared around the high volcanic peak the Mexicans called Guadalupe.

Late in the afternoon, Ayah looked down at the gray boxcar shack with the paint all peeled from the wood; the stove pipe on the roof was rusted and crooked. The fire she had built that morning in the oil drum stove had burned out. Ella was asleep in her lap now and Danny sat close to her, complaining that he was hungry; he asked when they would go to the house. "We will stay up here until your father comes," she told him, "because those white men were chasing us." The boy remembered then and he nodded at her silently.

If Jimmie had been there he could have read those papers and explained to her what they said. Ayah would have known then, never to sign them. The doctors came back the next day and they brought a BIA policeman with them. They told Chato they had her signature and that was all they needed. Except for the kids. She listened to Chato sullenly; she hated him when he told her it was the old woman who died in the winter, spitting blood; it was her old grandma who had given the children this disease. "They don't spit blood," she said coldly. "The whites lie." She held Ella and Danny close to her, ready to run to the hills again. "I want a medicine man first," she said to Chato, not looking at him. He shook his head. "It's too late now. The policeman is with them. You signed the paper." His voice was gentle.

It was worse than if they had died: to lose the children and to know that somewhere, in a place called Colorado, in a place full of sick and dying strangers, her children were without her. There had been babies that died soon after they were born, and one that died before he could walk. She had carried them herself, up to the boulders and great pieces of the cliff that long ago crashed down from Long Mesa; she laid them in the crevices of sandstone and buried them in fine brown sand with round quartz pebbles that washed down the hills in the rain. She had endured it because they had been with her. But she could not bear this pain. She did not sleep for a long time after they took her children. She stayed on the hill where they had fled the first time, and she slept rolled up in the blanket Jimmie had sent her. She carried the pain in her belly and it was fed by everything she saw: the blue sky of their last day together and the dust and pebbles they played with; the swing in the elm tree and broomstick horse choked life from her. The pain filled her stomach and there was no room for food or for her lungs to fill with air. The air and the food would have been theirs.

She hated Chato, not because he let the policeman and doctors put the screaming children in the government car, but because he had taught her to sign her name. Because it was like the old ones always told her about learning their language or any of their ways: it endangered you. She slept alone on the hill until the middle of November when the first snows came. Then she made a bed for herself where the children had slept. She did not lie down beside Chato again until many years later, when he was sick and shivering and only her body could keep him warm. The illness came after the white rancher told Chato he was too old to work for him anymore, and Chato and his old woman should be out of the shack by the next afternoon because the rancher had hired new people to work there. That had satisfied her. To see how the white man repaid Chato's years of loyalty and work. All of Chato's fine-sounding English talk didn't change things.

It snowed steadily and the luminous light from the snow gradually diminished into the darkness. Somewhere in Cebolleta a dog barked and other village dogs joined with it. Ayah looked in the direction she had come, from the bar where Chato was buying the wine. Sometimes he told her to go on ahead and wait; and then he never came. And when she finally went back looking for him, she would find him passed out at the bottom of the wooden steps to Azzie's Bar. All the wine would be gone and most of the money too, from the pale blue check that came to them once a month in a government envelope. It was then that she would look at his face and his hands, scarred by ropes and the barbed wire of all those years, and she would think, this man is a stranger; for forty years she had smiled at him and cooked his food, but he remained a stranger. She stood up again, with the snow almost to her knees, and she walked back to find Chato.

It was hard to walk in the deep snow and she felt the air burn in her lungs. She stopped a short distance from the bar to rest and readjust the blanket. But this time he wasn't waiting for her on the bottom step with his old Stetson hat pulled down and his shoulders hunched up in his long wool overcoat.

She was careful not to slip on the wooden steps. When she pushed the door open, warm air and cigarette smoke hit her face. She looked around slowly and deliberately, in every corner, in every dark place that the old man might find to sleep. The bar owner didn't like Indians in there, especially Navajos, but he let Chato come in because he could talk Spanish like he was one of them. The men at the bar stared at her, and the bartender saw that she left the door open wide. Snowflakes were flying inside like moths and melting into a puddle on the oiled wood floor. He motioned to her to close the door, but she did not see him. She held herself straight and walked across the room slowly, searching the room with every step. The snow in her hair melted and she could feel it on her forehead. At the far corner of the room, she saw red flames at the mica window of the old stove door; she looked behind the stove just to make sure. The bar got quiet except for the Spanish polka music playing on the jukebox. She stood by the stove and shook the snow from her blanket and held it near the stove to dry. The wet wool smell reminded her of new-born goats in early March, brought inside to warm near the fire. She felt calm.

In past years they would have told her to get out. But her hair was white now and her face was wrinkled. They looked at her like she was a spider crawling slowly across the room. They were afraid; she could feel the fear. She looked at their faces steadily. They reminded her of the first time the white people brought her children back to her that winter. Danny had been shy and hid behind the thin white woman who brought them. And the baby had not known her until Ayah took her into her arms, and then Ella had nuzzled close to her as she had when she was nursing. The blonde woman was nervous and kept looking at a dainty gold watch on her wrist. She sat on the bench near the small window and watched the dark snow clouds gather around the mountains; she was worrying about the unpaved road. She was frightened by what she saw inside too: the strips of venison drying on a rope across the ceiling and the children jabbering excitedly in a language she did not know. So they stayed for only a few hours. Ayah watched the government car disappear down the road and she knew they were already being weaned from these lava hills and from this sky. The last time they came was in early June, and Ella stared at her the way the men in the bar were now staring. Ayah did not try to pick her up; she smiled at her instead and spoke cheerfully to Danny. When he tried to answer her, he could not seem to remember and he spoke English words with the Navajo. But he gave her a scrap of paper that he had found somewhere and carried in his pocket; it was folded in half, and he shyly looked up at her and said it was a bird. She asked Chato if they were home for good this time. He spoke to the white woman and she shook her head. "How much longer?" he asked, and she said she didn't know; but Chato saw how she stared at the boxcar shack. Ayah turned away then. She did not say good-bye.

She felt satisfied that the men in the bar feared her. Maybe it was her face and the way she held her mouth with teeth clenched tight, like there was nothing anyone could do to her now. She walked north down the road, searching for the old man. She did this because she had the blanket, and there would be no place for him except with her and the blanket in the old adobe barn near the arroyo. They always slept there when they came to Cebolleta. If the money and the wine were gone, she would be relieved because then they could go home again; back to the old hogan with a dirt roof and rock walls where she herself had been born. And the next day the old man could go back to the few sheep they still had, to follow along behind them, guiding them, into dry sandy arroyos where sparse grass grew. She knew he did not like walking behind old ewes when for so many years he rode big quarter horses and worked with cattle. But she wasn't sorry for him; he should have known all along what would happen.

There had not been enough rain for their garden in five years; and that was when Chato finally hitched a ride into the town and brought back brown boxes of rice and sugar and big tin cans of welfare peaches. After that, at the first of the month they went to Cebolleta to ask the postmaster for the check; and then Chato would go to the bar and cash it. They did this as they planted the garden every May, not because anything would survive the summer dust, but because it was time to do this. The journey passed the days that smelled silent and dry like the caves above the canyon with yellow painted buffaloes on their walls.

He was walking along the pavement when she found him. He did not stop or turn around when he heard her behind him. She walked beside him and she noticed how slowly he moved now. He smelled strong of woodsmoke and urine. Lately he had been forgetting. Sometimes he called her by his sister's name and she had been gone for a long time. Once she had found him wandering on the road to the white man's ranch, and she asked him why he was going that way; he laughed at her and said, "You know they can't run that ranch without me," and he walked on determined, limping on the leg that had been crushed many years before. Now he looked at her curiously, as if for the first time, but he kept shuffling along, moving slowly along the side of the highway. His gray hair had grown long and spread out on the shoulders of the long overcoat. He wore the old felt hat pulled down over his ears. His boots were worn out at the toes and he had stuffed pieces of an old red shirt in the holes. The rags made his feet look like little animals up to their ears in snow. She laughed at his feet; the snow muffled the sound of her laugh. He stopped and looked at her again. The wind had quit blowing and the snow was falling straight down; the southeast sky was beginning to clear and Ayah could see a star.

"Let's rest awhile," she said to him. They walked away from the road and up the slope to the giant boulders that had tumbled down from the red sandrock mesa throughout the centuries of rainstorms and earth tremors. In a place where the boulders shut out the wind, they sat down with their backs against the rock. She offered half of the blanket to him and they sat wrapped together.

The storm passed swiftly. The clouds moved east. They were massive and full, crowding together across the sky. She watched them with the feeling of horses—steely blue-gray horses startled across the sky. The powerful haunches pushed into the distances and the tail hairs streamed white mist behind them. The sky cleared. Ayah saw that there was nothing between her and the stars. The light was crystalline. There was no shimmer, no distortion through earth haze. She breathed the clarity of the night sky; she smelled the purity of the half moon and the stars. He was lying on his side with his knees pulled up near his belly for warmth. His eyes were closed now, and in the light from the stars and the moon, he looked young again.

She could see it descend out of the night sky: an icy stillness from the edge of the thin moon. She recognized the freezing. It came gradually, sinking snowflake by snowflake until the crust was heavy and deep. It had the strength of the stars in Orion, and its journey was endless. Ayah knew that with the wine he would sleep. He would not feel it. She tucked the blanket around him, remembering how it was when Ella had been with her; and she felt the rush so big inside her heart for the babies. And she sang the only song she knew to sing for babies. She could not remember if she had ever sung it to her children, but she knew that her grandmother had sung it and her mother had sung it:

> The earth is your mother,
> she holds you.
> The sky is your father,
> he protects you.
> Sleep,
> sleep.
> Rainbow is your sister,
> she loves you.
> The winds are your brothers,
> they sing to you.
> Sleep,
> sleep.
> We are together always
> We are together always
> There never was a time
> when this
> was not so.

Rita Dove

(1952-   )

The first African American to become a poet laureate of the United States (1993–95), Rita Dove possesses an independence of mind that shows up in the originality of her poetry. Considering herself an artist before all else, she resists using language to serve the interests of propaganda. In her words: "As an artist, I shun political considerations and racial and gender partiality; for example I would find it a breach of my integrity as a writer to create a character for didactic . . . purposes, . . . a strong black heroine, . . . just to promote a positive image." Her work does reflect a concern with the injustice her ancestors suffered: *Thomas and Beulah* (1986), which won the Pulitzer Prize—and the source of the poems that follow—is a lyrical portrait of the lives of her maternal grandparents, who survived their suffering to pass on values of dignity and imagination to their descendants. Dove's five volumes of poetry, which include *The Yellow House on the Corner* (1980), *Museum* (1983), *Grace Notes* (1989), and *Mother Love* (1995), achieve their effects through the use of vivid concrete details expressed in the confident voice of a visionary. In the words of critic Helen Vendler, "Dove has planed away unnecessary matter: pure shapes, her poems exhibit the thrift that Yeats called the sign of a perfected manner."

Gospel

Swing low so I
can step inside—
a humming ship of voices
big with all

the wrongs done
done them.
No sound this generous
could fail:

ride joy until
it cracks like an egg,
make sorrow
seethe and whisper.

From a fortress
of animal misery
soars the chill voice
of the tenor, enraptured

with sacrifice.
What do I see,
he complains, notes
brightly rising

towards a sky
blank with promise.
Yet how healthy
the single contralto

settling deeper
into her watery furs!
Carry me home,
she cajoles, bearing

down. Candelabras
brim. But he slips
through God's net and swims
heavenward, warbling.

Weathering Out

She liked mornings the best—Thomas gone
to look for work, her coffee flushed with milk,

outside autumn trees blowsy and dripping.
Past the seventh month she couldn't see her feet

so she floated from room to room, houseshoes flapping,
navigating corners in wonder. When she leaned

against a door jamb to yawn, she disappeared entirely.

Last week they had taken a bus at dawn
to the new airdock. The hangar slid open in segments

and the zeppelin nosed forward in its silver envelope.
The men walked it out gingerly, like a poodle,

then tied it to a mast and went back inside.
Beulah felt just that large and placid, a lake;

she glistened from cocoa butter smoothed in
when Thomas returned every evening nearly

in tears. He'd lean an ear on her belly
and say: *Little fellow's really talking,*

though to her it was more the *pok-pok-pok*
of a fingernail tapping a thick cream lampshade.

Sometimes during the night she woke and found him
asleep there and the child sleeping, too.

The coffee was good but too little. Outside
everything shivered in tinfoil—only the clover

between the cobblestones hung stubbornly on,
green as an afterthought. . . .

Motherhood

She dreams the baby's so small she keeps
misplacing it—it rolls from the hutch
and the mouse carries it home, it disappears
with his shirt in the wash.
Then she drops it and it explodes
like a watermelon, eyes spitting.

Finally they get to the countryside;
Thomas has it in a sling.
He's strewing rice along the road
while the trees chitter with tiny birds.
In the meadow to their right three men
are playing rough with a white wolf. She calls

warning but the wolf breaks free
and she runs, the rattle
rolls into the gully, then she's
there and tossing the baby behind her,
listening for its cry as she straddles
the wolf and circles its throat, counting
until her thumbs push through to the earth.
White fur seeps red. She is hardly breathing.
The small wild eyes
go opaque with confusion and shame, like a child's.

Sandra Cisneros

(1954-   )

A spokeswoman for Latina writers, Sandra Cisneros was born in Chicago to a Mexican father and Chicana mother, the only girl in a family of six boys. In her poetry and in two volumes of short stories, *The House on Mango Street* (1984) and *Woman Hollering Creek* (1991), her focus is the Latina community, especially the experience of Chicanas within a male-dominated culture. The title story of her second book of stories—which follows here—has been called by one critic "a story good enough to take its place in any anthology of American short stories." "I write the kind of stories I didn't get growing up," Cisneros has said. "Stories about people I knew and loved, but never saw in the pages of the books I borrowed from the Chicago Public Library. Now that I live in the southwest I'm even more appalled by the absence of brown people in mainstream literature and more committed than ever to populating . . . the American literary landscape with stories about Mexicanos, Chicanos, and Latinos."

Woman Hollering Creek

The day Don Serafín gave Juan Pedro Martínez Sánchez permission to take Cleófilas Enriqueta DeLeón Hernández as his bride, across her father's threshold, over several miles of dirt road and several miles of paved, over one border and beyond to a town *en el otro lado*—on the other side—already did he divine the morning his daughter would raise her hand over her eyes, look south, and dream of returning to the chores that never ended, six good-for-nothing brothers, and one old man's complaints.

He had said, after all, in the hubbub of parting: I am your father, I will never abandon you. He *had* said that, hadn't he, when he hugged and then let her go. But at the moment Cleófilas was busy looking for Chela, her maid of honor, to fulfill their bouquet conspiracy. She would not remember her father's parting words until later. *I am your father, I will never abandon you.*

Only now as a mother did she remember. Now, when she and Juan Pedrito sat by the creek's edge. How when a man and a woman love each other, sometimes that love sours. But a parent's love for a child, a child's for its parents, is another thing entirely.

This is what Cleófilas thought evenings when Juan Pedro did not come home, and she lay on her side of the bed listening to the hollow roar of the interstate, a distant dog barking, the pecan trees rustling like ladies in stiff petticoats—*shh-shh-shh, shh-shh-shh*—soothing her to sleep.

In the town where she grew up, there isn't very much to do except accompany the aunts and godmothers to the house of one or the other to play cards. Or walk to the cinema to see this week's film again, speckled and with one hair quivering annoyingly on the screen. Or to the center of town to order a milk shake that will appear in a day and a half as a pimple on her backside. Or to the girlfriend's house to watch the latest *telenovela* episode and try to copy the way the women comb their hair, wear their makeup.

But what Cleófilas has been waiting for, has been whispering and sighing and giggling for, has been anticipating since she was old enough to lean against the window displays of gauze and butterflies and lace, is passion. Not the kind on the cover of the *¡Alarma!* magazines, mind you, where the lover is photographed with the bloody fork she used to salvage her good name. But passion in its purest crystalline essence. The kind the books and songs and *telenovelas* describe when one finds, finally, the great love of one's life, and does whatever one can, must do, at whatever the cost.

Tú o Nadie. "You or No One." The title of the current favorite *telenovela.* The beautiful Lucía Méndez having to put up with all kinds of hardships of the heart, separation and betrayal, and loving, always loving no matter what, because *that* is the most important thing, and did you see Lucía Méndez on the Bayer aspirin commercials—wasn't she lovely? Does she dye her hair do you think? Cleófilas is going to go to the *farmacía* and buy a hair rinse; her girlfriend Chela will apply it—it's not that difficult at all.

Because you didn't watch last night's episode when Lucía confessed she loved him more than anyone in her life. In her life! And she sings the song "You or No One" in the beginning and end of the show. *Tú o Nadie.* Somehow one ought to live one's life like that, don't you think? You or no one. Because to suffer for love is good. The pain all sweet somehow. In the end.

Seguin. She had liked the sound of it. Far away and lovely. Not like *Monclova. Coahuia.* Ugly.

Seguin, Tejas. A nice sterling ring to it. The tinkle of money. She would get to wear outfits like the women on the *tele,* like Lucía Méndez. And have a lovely house, and wouldn't Chela be jealous.

And yes, they will drive all the way to Laredo to get her wedding dress. That's what they say. Because Juan Pedro wants to get married right away, without a long engagement since he can't take off too much time from work. He has a very important position in Seguin with, with . . . a beer company, I think. Or was it tires? Yes, he has to be back. So they will get married in the spring when he can take off work, and then they will drive off in his new pickup—did you see it?—to their new home in Seguin. Well, not exactly new, but they're going to repaint the house. You know newlyweds. New paint and new furniture. Why not? He can afford it. And later on add maybe a room or two for the children. May they be blessed with many.

Well, you'll see. Cleófilas has always been so good with her sewing machine. A little *rrr, rrr, rrr* of the machine and *izas!* Miracles. She's always been so clever, that girl. Poor thing. And without even a mama to advise her on things like her wedding night. Well, may God help her. What with a father with a head like a burro, and those six clumsy brothers. Well, what do you think! Yes, I'm going to the wedding. Of course! The dress I want to wear just needs to be altered a teensy bit to bring it up to date. See, I saw a new style last night that I thought would suit me. Did you watch last night's episode of *The Rich Also Cry?* Well, did you notice the dress the mother was wearing?

La Gritona. Such a funny name for such a lovely *arroyo.* But that's what they called the creek that ran behind the house. Though no one could say whether the woman had hollered from anger or pain. The natives only knew the *arroyo* one crossed on the way to San Antonio, and then once again on the way back, was called Woman Hollering, a name no one from these parts questioned, little less understood. *Pues, allá de los indios, quién sabe*—who knows, the townspeople shrugged, because it was of no concern to their lives how this trickle of water received its curious name.

"What do you want to know for?" Trini the laundromat attendant asked in the same gruff Spanish she always used whenever she gave Cleófilas change or yelled at her for something. First for putting too much soap in the machines. Later, for sitting on a washer. And still later, after Juan Pedrito was born, for not understanding that in this country you cannot let your baby walk around with no diaper and his pee-pee hanging out, it wasn't nice, ¿entiendes? Pues.

How could Cleófilas explain to a woman like this why the name Woman Hollering fascinated her. Well, there was no sense talking to Trini.

On the other hand there were the neighbor ladies, one on either side of the house they rented near the *arroyo*. The woman Soledad on the left, the woman Dolores on the right.

The neighbor lady Soledad liked to call herself a widow, though how she came to be one was a mystery. Her husband had either died, or run away with an ice-house floozie, or simply gone out for cigarettes one afternoon and never came back. It was hard to say which since Soledad, as a rule, didn't mention him.

In the other house lived *la señora* Dolores, kind and very sweet, but her house smelled too much of incense and candles from the altars that burned continuously in memory of two sons who had died in the last war and one husband who had died shortly after from grief. The neighbor lady Dolores divided her time between the memory of these men and her garden, famous for its sunflowers—so tall they had to be supported with broom handles and old boards; red red cockscombs, fringed and bleeding a thick menstrual color; and, especially, roses whose sad scent reminded Cleófilas of the dead. Each Sunday *la señora* Dolores clipped the most beautiful of these flowers and arranged them on three modest headstones at the Seguin cemetery.

The neighbor ladies, Soledad, Dolores, they might've known once the name of the *arroyo* before it turned English but they did not know now. They were too busy remembering the men who had left through either choice or circumstance and would never come back.

Pain or rage, Cleófilas wondered when she drove over the bridge the first time as a newlywed and Juan Pedro had pointed it out. *La Gritona*, he had said, and she had laughed. Such a funny name for a creek so pretty and full of happily every after.

The first time she had been so surprised she didn't cry out or try to defend herself. She had always said she would strike back if a man, any man, were to strike her.

But when the moment came, and he slapped her once, and then again, and again; until the lip split and bled an orchid of blood, she didn't fight back, she didn't break into tears, she didn't run away as she imagined she might when she saw such things in the *telenovelas*.

In her own home her parents had never raised a hand to each other or to their children. Although she admitted she may have been brought up a little leniently as an only daughter—*la consentida*, the princess—there were some things she would never tolerate. Ever.

Instead, when it happened the first time, when they were barely man and wife, she had been so stunned, it left her speechless, motionless, numb. She had done nothing but reach up to the heat on her mouth and stare at the blood on her hand as if even then she didn't understand.

She could think of nothing to say, said nothing. Just stroked the dark curls of the man who wept and would weep like a child, his tears of repentance and shame, this time and each.

The men at the ice house. From what she can tell, from the times during her first year when still a newlywed she is invited and accompanies her husband, sits mute beside their conversation, waits and sips a beer until it grows warm, twists a paper napkin into a knot, then another into a fan, one into a rose, nods her head, smiles, yawns, politely grins, laughs at the appropriate moments, leans against her husband's sleeve, tugs at his elbow, and finally becomes good at predicting where the talk will lead, from this Cleófilas concludes each is nightly trying to find the truth lying at the bottom of the bottle like a gold doubloon on the sea floor.

They want to tell each other what they want to tell themselves. But what is bumping like a helium balloon at the ceiling of the brain never finds its way out. It bubbles and rises, it gurgles in the throat, it rolls across the surface of the tongue, and erupts from the lips—a belch.

If they are lucky, there are tears at the end of the long night. At any given moment, the fists try to speak. They are dogs chasing their own tails before lying down to sleep, trying to find a way, a route, an out, and—finally—get some peace.

In the morning sometimes before he opens his eyes. Or after they have finished loving. Or at times when he is simply across from her at the table
putting pieces of food into his mouth and chewing. Cleófilas thinks, This is
the man I have waited my whole life for.

Not that he isn't a good man. She has to remind herself why she loves
him when she changes the baby's Pampers, or when she mops the bathroom
floor, or tries to make the curtains for the doorways without doors, or whiten
the linen. Or wonder a little when he kicks the refrigerator and says he hates
this shitty house and is going out where he won't be bothered with the baby's
howling and her suspicious questions, and her requests to fix this and this
and this because if she had any brains in her head she'd realize he's been up
before the rooster earning his living to pay for the food in her belly and the
roof over her head and would have to wake up again early the next day so
why can't you just leave me in peace, woman.

He is not very tall, no, and he doesn't look like the men on the *telenovelas*. His face still scarred from acne. And he has a bit of a belly from all the
beer he drinks. Well, he's always been husky.

This man who farts and belches and snores as well as laughs and kisses
and holds her. Somehow this husband whose whiskers she finds each morning in the sink, whose shoes she must air each evening on the porch, this
husband who cuts his fingernails in public, laughs loudly, curses like a man,
and demands each course of dinner be served on a separate plate like at his
mother's, as soon as he gets home, on time or late, and who doesn't care at
all for music or *telenovelas* or romance or roses or the moon floating pearly
over the *arroyo*, or through the bedroom window for that matter, shut the
blinds and go back to sleep, this man, this father, this rival, this keeper, this
lord, this master, this husband till kingdom come.

A doubt. Slender as a hair. A washed cup set back on the shelf wrong-side-
up. Her lipstick, and body talc, and hairbrush all arranged in the bathroom a
different way.

No. Her imagination. The house the same as always. Nothing.

Coming home from the hospital with her new son, her husband.
Something comforting in discovering her house slippers beneath the bed,
the faded housecoat where she left it on the bathroom hook. Her pillow.
Their bed.

Sweet sweet homecoming. Sweet as the scent of face powder in the air, jasmine, sticky liquor.

Smudged fingerprint on the door. Crushed cigarette in a glass. Wrinkle in the brain crumpling to a crease.

Sometimes she thinks of her father's house. But how could she go back there? What a disgrace. What would the neighbors say? Coming home like that with one baby on her hip and one in the oven. Where's your husband?

The town of gossips. The town of dust and despair. Which she has traded for this town of gossips. This town of dust, despair. Houses farther apart perhaps, though no more privacy because of it. No leafy *zócalo* in the center of the town, though the murmur of talk is clear enough all the same. No huddled whispering on the church steps each Sunday. Because here the whispering begins at sunset at the ice house instead.

This town with its silly pride for a bronze pecan the size of a baby carriage in front of the city hall. TV repair shop, drugstore, hardware, dry cleaner's, chiropractor's, liquor store, bail bonds, empty storefront, and nothing, nothing, nothing of interest. Nothing one could walk to, at any rate. Because the towns here are built so that you have to depend on husbands. Or you stay home. Or you drive. If you're rich enough to own, allowed to drive, your own car.

There is no place to go. Unless one counts the neighbor ladies. Soledad on one side. Dolores on the other. Or the creek.

Don't go out there after dark, *mi'jita*. Stay near the house. *No es bueno para la salud. Mala suerte.* Bad luck. *Mal aire.* You'll get sick and the baby too. You'll catch a fright wandering about in the dark, and then you'll see how right we were.

The stream sometimes only a muddy puddle in the summer, though now in the springtime, because of the rains, a good-size alive thing, a thing with a voice all its own, all day and all night calling in its high, silver voice. Is it La Llorona, the weeping woman? La Llorona, who drowned her own children. Perhaps La Llorona is the one they named the creek after, she thinks, remembering all the stories she learned as a child.

La Llorona calling to her. She is sure of it. Cleófilas sets the baby's Donald Duck blanket on the grass. Listens. The day sky turning to night. The baby pulling up fistfuls of grass and laughing. La Llorona. Wonders if something as quiet as this drives a woman to the darkness under the trees.

What she needs is . . . and made a gesture as if to yank a woman's buttocks to his groin. Maximiliano, the foul-smelling fool from across the road, said this and set the men laughing, but Cleófilas just muttered. *Grosera*, and went on washing dishes.

She knew he said it not because it was true, but more because it was he who needed to sleep with a woman, instead of drinking each night at the ice house and stumbling home alone.

Maximiliano who was said to have killed his wife in an ice-house brawl when she came at him with a mop. I had to shoot, he had said—she was armed.

Their laughter outside the kitchen window. Her husband's, his friends'. Manolo, Beto, Efraín, el Perico. Maximiliano.

Was Cleófilas just exaggerating as her husband always said? It seemed the newspapers were full of such stories. This woman found on the side of the interstate. This one pushed from a moving car. This one's cadaver, this one unconscious, this one beaten blue. Her ex-husband, her husband, her lover, her father, her brother, her uncle, her friend, her co-worker. Always. The same grisly news in the pages of the dailies. She dunked a glass under the soapy water for a moment—shivered.

He had thrown a book. Hers. From across the room. A hot welt across the cheek. She could forgive that. But what stung more was the fact it was *her* book, a love story by Corín Tellado, what she loved most now that she lived in the U.S., without a television set, without the *telenovelas*.

Except now and again when her husband was away and she could manage it, the few episodes glimpsed at the neighbor lady Soledad's house because Dolores didn't care for that sort of thing, though Soledad was often kind enough to retell what had happened on what episode of *María de Nadie*, the poor Argentine country girl who had the ill fortune of falling in love with the beautiful son of the Arrocha family, the very family she worked for, whose roof she slept under and whose floors she vacuumed, while in that same house, with the dust brooms and floor cleaners as witnesses, the square-jawed Juan Carlos Arrocha had uttered words of love, I love you, María, listen to me, *mi querida*, but it was she who had to say No, no, we are not of the same class, and remind him it was not his place nor hers to fall in love, while all the while her heart was breaking, can you imagine.

Cleófilas thought her life would have to be like that, like a *telenovela*, only now the episodes got sadder and sadder. And there were no commercials in between for comic relief. And no happy ending in sight. She thought this when she sat with the baby out by the creek behind the house. Cleófilas de . . . ? But somehow she would have to change her name to Topazio, or Yesenia, Cristal, Adriana, Stefania, Andrea, something more poetic than Cleófilas. Everything happened to women with names like jewels. But what happened to Cleófilas? Nothing. But a crack in the face.

Because the doctor has said so. She has to go. To make sure the new baby is all right, so there won't be any problems when he's born, and the appointment card says next Tuesday. Could he please take her. And that's all.

No, she won't mention it. She promises. If the doctor asks she can say she fell down the front steps or slipped when she was out in the backyard, slipped out back, she could tell him that. She has to go back next Tuesday, Juan Pedro, please, for the new baby. For their child.

She could write to her father and ask maybe for money, just a loan, for the new baby's medical expenses. Well then if he'd rather she didn't. All right, she won't. Please don't anymore. Please don't. She knows it's difficult saving money with all the bills they have, but how else are they going to get out of debt with the truck payments? And after the rent and the food and the electricity and the gas and the water and the who-knows-what, well, there's hardly anything left. But please, at least for the doctor visit. She won't ask for anything else. She has to. Why is she so anxious? Because.

Because she is going to make sure the baby is not turned around backward this time to split her down the center. Yes. Next Tuesday at five-thirty. I'll have Juan Pedrito dressed and ready. But those are the only shoes he has. I'll polish them, and we'll be ready. As soon as you come from work. We won't make you ashamed.

Felice? It's me, Graciela.

No, I can't talk louder. I'm at work.

Look, I need kind of a favor. There's a patient, a lady here who's got a problem.

Well, wait a minute. Are you listening to me or what?

I can't talk real loud 'cause her husband's in the next room.

Well, would you just listen?

I was going to do this sonogram on her—she's pregnant, right?—and she just starts crying on me. *Híjole*, Felice! This poor lady's got black-and-blue marks all over. I'm not kidding.

From her husband. Who else? Another one of those brides from across the border. And her family's all in Mexico.

Shit. You think they're going to help her? Give me a break. This lady doesn't even speak English. She hasn't been allowed to call home or write or nothing. That's why I'm calling you.

She needs a ride.

Not to Mexico, you goof. Just to the Greyhound. In San Anto.

No, just a ride. She's got her own money. All you have to do is drop her off in San Antonio on your way home. Come on, Felice. Please? If we don't help her, who will? I'd drive her myself, but she needs to be on that bus before her husband gets home from work. What do you say?

I don't know. Wait.

Right away, tomorrow even.

Well, if tomorrow's no good for you . . .

It's a date, Felice. Thursday. At the Cash N Carry off I-10. Noon. She'll be ready.

Oh, and her name's Cleófilas.

I don't know. One of those Mexican saints, I guess. A martyr or something.

Cleófilas. C-L-E-O-F-I-L-A-S. Cle. O. Fi. Las. Write it down.

Thanks, Felice. When her kid's born she'll have to name her after us, right?

Yeah, you got it. A regular soap opera sometimes. *Qué vida, comadre. Bueno* bye.

All morning that flutter of half-fear, half-doubt. At any moment Juan Pedro might appear in the doorway. On the street. At the Cash N Carry. Like in the dreams she dreamed.

There was that to think about, yes, until the woman in the pickup drove up. Then there wasn't time to think about anything but the pickup pointed toward San Antonio. Put your bags in the back and get in.

But when they drove across the *arroyo*, the driver opened her mouth and let out a yell as loud as any mariachi. Which startled not only Cleófilas, but Juan Pedrito as well.

Pues, look how cute. I scared you two, right? Sorry. Should've warned you. Every time I cross that bridge I do that. Because of the name, you know. Woman Hollering. *Pues*, I holler. She said this in a Spanish pocked with English and laughed. Did you ever notice, Felice continued, how nothing around here is named after a woman? Really. Unless she's the Virgin. I guess you're only famous if you're a virgin. She was laughing again.

That's why I like the name of that *arroyo*. Makes you want to holler like Tarzan, right?

Everything about this woman, this Felice, amazed Cleófilas. The fact that she drove a pickup. A pickup, mind you, but when Cleófilas asked if it was her husband's, she said she didn't have a husband. The pickup was hers. She herself had chosen it. She herself was paying for it.

I used to have a Pontiac Sunbird. But those cars are for *viejas*. Pussy cars. Now this here is a *real* car.

What kind of talk was that coming from a woman? Cleófilas thought. But then again, Felice was like no woman she'd ever met. Can you imagine, when we crossed the *arroyo* she just started yelling like a crazy, she would say later to her father and brothers. Just like that. Who would've thought?

Who would've? Pain or rage, perhaps, but not a hoot like the one Felice had just let go. Makes you want to holler like Tarzan, Felice had said.

Then Felice began laughing again, but it wasn't Felice laughing. It was gurgling out of her own throat, a long ribbon of laughter, like water.

Gish Jen

(1956-   )

There are few words of praise that have not been used about Gish Jen's fiction. A sampler includes "tender and funny and vibrant and courageous and biting and insightful and wonderful and engaging." She writes about the Chinese American community and the efforts of the first generation of immigrants to assimilate; she looks, too, satirically and compassionately, at their children, the compromises and losses that both generations suffer. A child of immigrants herself, she grew up on Long Island and in Scarsdale, New York, went to Harvard, and now lives in Massachusetts. Her short stories have won many prizes and appeared in *The New Yorker*, the *Atlantic Monthly*, and *The Best American Short Stories of the Century* (1999), edited by John Updike. Her novels, *Typical American* (1991) and *Mona in the Promised Land* (1996), like the short stories, make the sociological phenomenon of multiculturalism an ebullient and sometimes painful drama of contemporary American life. Ann Beattie notes the luminous quality of Jen's work that you can miss on a first reading—the wit is so utterly engaging. "Gish Jen's stories are keenly observed moments in time," writes Beattie, "in which the characters' foibles predominate just long enough for an odd equilibrium to be established between their yearning and their movement toward small, unexpected moments of grace."

Who's Irish?

In China, people say mixed children are supposed to be smart, and definitely my granddaughter Sophie is smart. But Sophie is wild, Sophie is not like my daughter Natalie, or like me. I am work hard my whole life, and fierce besides. My husband always used to say he is afraid of me, and in our restaurant, busboys and cooks all afraid of me too. Even the gang members come for protection money, they try to talk to my husband. When I am there, they stay away. If they come by mistake, they pretend they are come to eat. They hide behind the menu, they order a lot of food. They talk about their mothers. Oh, my mother have some arthritis, need to take herbal medicine, they say. Oh, my mother getting old, her hair all white now.

I say, Your mother's hair used to be white, but since she dye it, it become black again. Why don't you go home once in a while and take a look? I tell them, Confucius say a filial son knows what color his mother's hair is.

My daughter is fierce too, she is vice president in the bank now. Her new house is big enough for everybody to have their own room, including me. But Sophie take after Natalie's husband's family, their name is Shea. Irish. I always thought Irish people are like Chinese people, work so hard on the railroad, but now I know why the Chinese beat the Irish. Of course, not all Irish are like the Shea family, of course not. My daughter tell me I should not say Irish this, Irish that.

How do you like it when people say the Chinese this, the Chinese that, she say.

You know, the British call the Irish heathen, just like they call the Chinese, she say.

You think the Opium War was bad, how would you like to live right next door to the British, she say.

And that is that. My daughter have a funny habit when she win an argument, she take a sip of something and look away, so the other person is not embarrassed. So I am not embarrassed. I do not call anybody anything either. I just happen to mention about the Shea family, an interesting fact: four brothers in the family, and not one of them work. The mother, Bess, have a job before she got sick, she was executive secretary in a big company. She is handle everything for a big shot, you would be surprised how complicated her job is, not just type this, type that. Now she is a nice woman with a clean house. But her boys, every one of them is on welfare, or so-called severance pay, or so-called disability pay. Something. They say they cannot find work, this is not the economy of the fifties, but I say, Even the black people doing better these days, some of them live so fancy, you'd be surprised. Why the Shea family have so much trouble? They are white people, they speak English. When I come to this country, I have no money and do not speak English. But my husband and I own our restaurant before he die. Free and clear, no mortgage. Of course, I understand I am just lucky, come from a country where the food is popular all over the world. I understand it is not the Shea family's fault they come from a country where everything is boiled. Still, I say.

She's right, we should broaden our horizons, say one brother, Jim, at Thanksgiving. Forget about the car business. Think about egg rolls.

Pad thai, say another brother, Mike. I'm going to make my fortune in pad thai. It's going to be the new pizza.

I say, You people too picky about what you sell. Selling egg rolls not good enough for you, but at least my husband and I can say, We made it. What can you say? Tell me. What can you say?

Everybody chew their tough turkey.

I especially cannot understand my daughter's husband John, who has no job but cannot take care of Sophie either. Because he is a man, he say, and that's the end of the sentence.

Plain boiled food, plain boiled thinking. Even his name is plain boiled: John. Maybe I grew up with black bean sauce and hoisin sauce and garlic sauce, I always feel something is missing when my son-in-law talk.

But, okay: so my son-in-law can be man, I am baby-sitter. Six hours a day, same as the old sitter, crazy Amy, who quit. This is not so easy, now that I am sixty-eight, Chinese age almost seventy. Still, I try. In China, daughter take care of mother. Here it is the other way around. Mother help daughter, mother ask, Anything else I can do? Otherwise daughter complain mother is not supportive. I tell daughter, we do not have this word in Chinese, *supportive*. But my daughter too busy to listen, she has to go to meeting, she has to write memo while her husband go to the gym to be a man. My daughter say otherwise he will be depressed. Seems like all his life he has this trouble, depression.

No one wants to hire someone who is depressed, she say. It is important for him to keep his spirits up.

Beautiful wife, beautiful daughter, beautiful house, oven can clean itself automatically. No money left over, because only one income, but lucky enough, got the baby-sitter for free. If John lived in China, he would be very happy. But he is not happy. Even at the gym things go wrong. One day, he pull a muscle. Another day, weight room too crowded. Always something.

Until finally, hooray, he has a job. Then he feel pressure.

I need to concentrate, he say. I need to focus.

He is going to work for insurance company. Salesman job. A paycheck, he say, and at least he will wear clothes instead of gym shorts. My daughter buy him some special candy bars from the health-food store. They say

THINK! on them, and are supposed to help John think.

John is a good-looking boy, you have to say that, especially now that he shave so you can see his face.

I am an old man in a young man's game, say John.

I will need a new suit, say John.

This time I am not going to shoot myself in the foot, say John.

Good, I say.

She means to be supportive, my daughter say. Don't start the send her back to China thing, because we can't.

Sophie is three years old American age, but already I see her nice Chinese side swallowed up by her wild Shea side. She looks like mostly Chinese. Beautiful black hair, beautiful black eyes. Nose perfect size, not so flat looks like something fell down, not so large looks like some big deal got stuck in wrong face. Everything just right, only her skin is a brown surprise to John's family. So brown, they say. Even John say it. She never goes in the sun, still she is that color, he say. Brown. They say, Nothing the matter with brown. They are just surprised. So brown. Nattie is not that brown, they say. They say, It seems like Sophie should be a color in between Nattie and John. Seems funny, a girl named Sophie Shea be brown. But she is brown, maybe her name should be Sophie Brown. She never go in the sun, still she is that color, they say. Nothing the matter with brown. They are just surprised.

The Shea family talk is like this sometimes, going around and around like a Christmas-tree train.

Maybe John is not her father, I say one day, to stop the train. And sure enough, train wreck. None of the brothers ever say the word *brown* to me again.

Instead, John's mother, Bess, say, I hope you are not offended.

She say, I did my best on those boys. But raising four boys with no father is no picnic.

You have a beautiful family, I say.

I'm getting old, she say.

You deserve a rest, I say. Too many boys make you old.

I never had a daughter, she say. You have a daughter.

I have a daughter, I say. Chinese people don't think a daughter is so great, but you're right. I have a daughter.

I was never against the marriage, you know, she say. I never thought John was marrying down. I always thought Nattie was just as good as white.

I was never against the marriage either, I say. I just wonder if they look at the whole problem.

Of course you pointed out the problem, you are a mother, she say. And now we both have a granddaughter. A little brown granddaughter, she is so precious to me.

I laugh. A little brown granddaughter, I say. To tell you the truth, I don't know how she came out so brown.

We laugh some more. These days Bess need a walker to walk. She take so many pills, she need two glasses of water to get them all down. Her favorite TV show is about bloopers, and she love her bird feeder. All day long, she can watch that bird feeder, like a cat.

I can't wait for her to grow up, Bess say. I could use some female company.

Too many boys, I say.

Boys are fine, she say. But they do surround you after a while.

You should take a break, come live with us, I say. Lots of girls at our house.

Be careful what you offer, say Bess with a wink. Where I come from, people mean for you to move in when they say a thing like that.

Nothing the matter with Sophie's outside, that's the truth. It is inside that she is like not any Chinese girl I ever see. We go to the park, and this is what she does. She stand up in the stroller. She take off all her clothes and throw them in the fountain.

Sophie! I say. Stop!

But she just laugh like a crazy person. Before I take over as baby-sitter, Sophie has that crazy-person sitter, Amy the guitar player. My daughter thought this Amy very creative—another word we do not talk about in China. In China, we talk about whether we have difficulty or no difficulty. We talk about whether life is bitter or not bitter. In America, all day long, people talk about creative. Never mind that I cannot even look at this Amy, with her shirt so short that her belly button showing. This Amy think Sophie should love her body. So when Sophie take off her diaper, Amy laugh. When Sophie run around naked, Amy say she wouldn't want to wear a diaper either. When Sophie go *shu-shu* in her lap, Amy laugh and say there are no germs in pee. When Sophie take off her shoes, Amy say bare feet is best, even the pediatrician say so. That is why Sophie now walk around with no shoes like a beggar child. Also why Sophie love to take off her clothes.

Turn around! say the boys in the park. Let's see that ass!

Of course, Sophie does not understand. Sophie clap her hands, I am the only one to say, No! This is not a game.

It has nothing to do with John's family, my daughter say. Amy was too permissive, that's all.

But I think if Sophie was not wild inside, she would not take off her shoes and clothes to begin with.

You never take off your clothes when you were little, I say. All my Chinese friends had babies, I never saw one of them act wild like that.

Look, my daughter say. I have a big presentation tomorrow.

John and my daughter agree Sophie is a problem, but they don't know what to do.

You spank her, she'll stop, I say another day.

But they say, Oh no.

In America, parents not supposed to spank their child.

It gives them low self-esteem, my daughter say. And that leads to problems later, as I happen to know.

My daughter never have big presentation the next day when the subject of spanking come up.

I don't you want to touch Sophie, she say. No spanking, period.

Don't tell me what to do, I say.

I'm not telling you what to do, say my daughter. I'm telling you how I feel.

I am not your servant, I say. Don't you dare talk to me like that.

My daughter have another funny habit when she lose an argument. She spread out all her fingers and look at them, as if she like to make sure they are still there.

My daughter is fierce like me, but she and John think it is better to explain to Sophie that clothes are a good idea. This is not so hard in the cold weather. In the warm weather, it is very hard.

Use your words, my daughter say. That's what we tell Sophie. How about if you set a good example.

As if good example mean anything to Sophie. I am so fierce, the gang members who used to come to the restaurant all afraid of me, but Sophie is not afraid.

I say, Sophie, if you take off your clothes, no snack.

I say, Sophie, if you take off your clothes, no lunch.

I say, Sophie, if you take off your clothes, no park.

Pretty soon we are stay home all day, and by the end of six hours she still did not have one thing to eat. You never saw a child stubborn like that.

I'm hungry! she cry when my daughter come home.

What's the matter, doesn't your grandmother feed you? My daughter laugh.

No! Sophie say. She doesn't feed me anything!

My daughter laugh again. Here you go, she say.

She say to John, Sophie must be growing.

Growing like a weed, I say.

Still Sophie take off her clothes, until one day I spank her. Not too hard, but she cry and cry, and when I tell her if she doesn't put her clothes back on I'll spank her again, she put her clothes back on. Then I tell her she is good girl, and give her some food to eat. The next day we go to the park and, like a nice Chinese girl, she does not take off her clothes.

She stop taking off her clothes, I report. Finally!

How did you do it? my daughter ask.

After twenty-eight years experience with you, I guess I learn something, I say.

It must have been a phase, John say, and his voice is suddenly like an expert.

His voice is like an expert about everything these days, now that he carry a leather briefcase, and wear shiny shoes, and can go shopping for a new car. On the company, he say. The company will pay for it, but he will be able to drive it whenever he want.

A free car, he say. How do you like that.

It's good to see you in the saddle again, my daughter say. Some of your family patterns are scary.

At least I don't drink, he say. He say, And I'm not the only one with scary family patterns.

That's for sure, say my daughter.

Everyone is happy. Even I am happy, because there is more trouble with Sophie, but now I think I can help her Chinese side fight against her wild side. I teach her to eat food with fork or spoon or chopsticks, she cannot just grab into the middle of a bowl of noodles. I teach her not to play with garbage cans. Sometimes I spank her, but not too often, not too hard.

Still, there are problems. Sophie like to climb everything. If there is a railing, she is never next to it. Always she is on top of it. Also, Sophie like to hit the mommies of her friends. She learned this from her playground best friend, Sinbad, who is four. Sinbad wear army clothes every day and like to ambush his mommy. He is the one who dug a big hole under the play structure, a foxhole he call it, all by himself. Very hardworking. Now he wait in the foxhole with a shovel full of wet sand. When his mommy come, he throw it right at her.

Oh, it's all right, his mommy say. You can't get rid of war games, it's part of their imaginative play. All the boys go through it.

Also, he like to kick his mommy, and one day he tell Sophie to kick his mommy too.

I wish this story is not true.

Kick her, kick her! Sinbad say.

Sophie kick her. A little kick, as if she just so happened was swinging her little leg and didn't realize that big mommy leg was in the way. Still I spank Sophie and make Sophie say sorry, and what does the mommy say?

Really, it's all right, she say. It didn't hurt.

After that, Sophie learn she can attack mommies in the playground, and some will say, Stop, but others will say, Oh, she didn't mean it, especially if they realize Sophie will be punished.

This is how, one day, bigger trouble come. The bigger trouble start when Sophie hide in the foxhole with that shovel full of sand. She wait, and when I come look for her, she throw it at me. All over my nice clean clothes.

Did you ever see a Chinese girl act this way?

Sophie! I say. Come out of there, say you're sorry.

But she does not come out. Instead, she laugh. Naaah, naah-na, naaa-naaa, she say.

I am not exaggerate: millions of children in China, not one act like this.

Sophie! I say. Now! Come out now!

But she know she is in big trouble. She know if she come out, what will happen next. So she does not come out. I am sixty-eight, Chinese age almost seventy, how can I crawl under there to catch her? Impossible. So I yell, yell, yell, and what happen? Nothing. A Chinese mother would help, but American mothers, they look at you, they shake their head, they go home. And, of course, a Chinese child would give up, but not Sophie.

I hate you! she yell. I hate you, Meanie!

Meanie is my new name these days.

Long time goes on, long long time. The foxhole is deep, you cannot see too much, you don't know where is the bottom. You cannot hear too much either. If she does not yell, you cannot even know she is still there or not. After a while, getting cold out, getting dark out. No one left in the playground, only us.

Sophie, I say. How did you become stubborn like this? I am go home without you now.

I try to use a stick, chase her out of there, and once or twice I hit her, but still she does not come out. So finally I leave. I go outside the gate.

Bye-bye! I say. I'm go home now.

But still she does not come out and does not come out. Now it is dinnertime, the sky is black. I think I should maybe go get help, but how can I leave a little girl by herself in the playground? A bad man could come. A rat could come. I go back in to see what is happen to Sophie. What if she have a shovel and is making a tunnel to escape?

Sophie! I say.

No answer.

Sophie!

I don't know if she is alive. I don't know if she is fall asleep down there. If she is crying, I cannot hear her.

So I take the stick and poke.

Sophie! I say. I promise I no hit you. If you come out, I give you a lollipop.

No answer. By now I worried. What to do, what to do, what to do? I poke some more, even harder, so that I am poking and poking when my daughter and John suddenly appear.

What are you doing? What's going on? say my daughter.

Put down that stick! say my daughter.

You are crazy! say my daughter.

John wiggle under the structure, into the foxhole, to rescue Sophie.

She fell asleep, say John the expert. She's okay. That is one big hole.

Now Sophie is crying and crying.

Sophia, my daughter say, hugging her. Are you okay, peanut? Are you okay?

She's just scared, say John.

Are you okay? I say too. I don't know what happen, I say.

She's okay, say John. He is not like my daughter, full of questions. He is full of answers until we get home and can see by the lamplight.

Will you look at her? he yell then. What the hell happened?

Bruises all over her brown skin, and a swollen-up eye.

You are crazy! say my daughter. Look at what you did! You are crazy!

I try very hard, I say.

How could you use a stick? I told you to use your words!

She is hard to handle, I say.

She's three years old! You cannot use a stick! say my daughter.

She is not like any Chinese girl I ever saw, I say.

I brush some sand off my clothes. Sophie's clothes are dirty too, but at least she has her clothes on.

Has she done this before? ask my daughter. Has she hit you before?

She hits me all the time, Sophie say, eating ice cream.

Your family, say John.

Believe me, say my daughter.

A daughter I have, a beautiful daughter. I took care of her when she could not hold her head up. I took care of her before she could argue with me, when she was a little girl with two pigtails, one of them always crooked. I took care of her when we have to escape from China, I took care of her when suddenly we live in a country with cars everywhere, if you are not careful your little girl get run over. When my husband die, I promise him I will keep the family together, even though it was just two of us, hardly a family at all.

But now my daughter take me around to look at apartments. After all, I can cook, I can clean, there's no reason I cannot live by myself, all I need is a telephone. Of course, she is sorry. Sometimes she cry, I am the one to say everything will be okay. She say she have no choice, she doesn't want to end up divorced. I say divorce is terrible, I don't know who invented this terrible idea. Instead of live with a telephone, though, surprise, I come to live with

Bess. Imagine that. Bess make an offer and sure enough, where she come from, people mean for you to move in when they say things like that. A crazy idea, go to live with someone else's family, but she like to have some female company, not like my daughter, who does not believe in company. These days when my daughter visit, she does not bring Sophie. Bess say we should give Nattie time, we will see Sophie again soon. But seems like my daughter have more presentation than ever before, every time she come she have to leave.

I have a family to support, she say, and her voice is heavy, as if soaking wet. I have a young daughter and a depressed husband and no one to turn to.

When she say no one to turn to, she mean me.

These days my beautiful daughter is so tired she can just sit there in a chair and fall asleep. John lost his job again, already, but still they rather hire a baby-sitter than ask me to help, even they can't afford it. Of course, the new baby-sitter is much younger, can run around. I don't know if Sophie these days is wild or not wild. She call me Meanie, but she like to kiss me too, sometimes. I remember that every time I see a child on TV. Sophie like to grab my hair, a fistful in each hand, and then kiss me smack on the nose. I never see any other child kiss that way.

The satellite TV has so many channels, more channels than I can count, including a Chinese channel from the Mainland and a Chinese channel from Taiwan, but most of the time I watch bloopers with Bess. Also, I watch the bird feeder—so many, many kinds of birds come. The Shea sons hang around all the time, asking when I will go home, but Bess tell them, Get lost.

She's a permanent resident, say Bess. She isn't going anywhere.

Then she wink at me, and switch the channel with the remote control.

Of course, I shouldn't say Irish this, Irish that, especially now I am become honorary Irish myself, according to Bess. Me! Who's Irish? I say, and she laugh. All the same, if I could mention one thing about some of the Irish, not all of them of course, I like to mention this: Their talk just stick. I don't know how Bess Shea learn to use her words, but sometimes I hear what she say a long time later. *Permanent resident. Not going anywhere.* Over and over I hear it, the voice of Bess.

Lorrie Moore

(1957–   )

In response to the question, What can a short story do that a novel can't, Lorrie Moore, considered by many critics the most gifted fiction writer of her generation, quipped, "Be over with fast." Then she added, "But I think the short story is one of the most beautiful, limber, and rewarding art forms there is . . . presenting the most emotionally enduring and dramatic aspects of a particular encounter or situation. [It's] a very emotional enterprise, like a song. It can be a single emotion pursued and interrogated, and in that way have a sustained intensity. Such a song within a novel would just be a strand, and would get lost. But as a story it is given its very own architecture." A native of Glens Falls, New York, who now lives in Madison, Wisconsin, and teaches at the University of Wisconsin, she has published three story collections, *Self-Help* (1985), *Like Life* (1990), and *Birds of America* (1998), a National Book Award nominee and winner of the 1999 Irish Times Literature Prize in International Fiction. The story that follows was included in *The Best American Short Stories of the Century,* edited by John Updike. Her two novels are *Anagrams* (1986) and *Who Will Run the Frog Hospital?* (1994). The humor that gives her work such energy is part of her strategy: "People being funny with each other is also a kind of generosity between people. And I'm interested in that, those little moments of generosity."

You're Ugly, Too

You had to get out of them occasionally, those Illinois towns with the funny names: Paris, Oblong, Normal. Once, when the Dow-Jones dipped two hundred points, the Paris paper boasted a banner headline: NORMAL MAN MARRIES OBLONG WOMAN. They knew what was important. They did! But you had to get out once in a while, even if it was just across the border to Terre Haute, for a movie.

Outside of Paris, in the middle of a large field, was a scatter of brick buildings, a small liberal arts college with the improbable name of Hilldale-Versailles. Zoë Hendricks had been teaching American History there for three years. She taught "The Revolution and Beyond" to freshmen and sophomores, and every third semester she had the Senior Seminar for Majors, and although her student evaluations had been slipping in the last year and a half—*Professor Hendricks is often late for class and usually arrives with a cup of hot chocolate, which she offers the class sips of*—generally, the department of nine men was pleased to have her. They felt she added some needed feminine touch to the corridors—the faint trace of Obsession and sweat, the light, fast clicking of heels. Plus they had had a sex-discrimination suit, and the dean had said, well, it was time.

The situation was not easy for her, they knew. Once, at the start of last semester, she had skipped into her lecture hall singing "Getting to Know You"—both verses. At the request of the dean, the chairman had called her into his office, but did not ask her for an explanation, not really. He asked her how she was and then smiled in an avuncular way. She said, "Fine," and he studied the way she said it, her front teeth catching on the inside of her lower lip. She was almost pretty, but her face showed the strain and ambition of always having been close but not quite. There was too much effort with the eyeliner, and her earrings, worn no doubt for the drama her features lacked, were a little frightening, jutting out from the side of her head like antennae.

"I'm going out of my mind," said Zoë to her younger sister, Evan, in Manhattan. *Professor Hendricks seems to know the entire sound track to* The King and I. *Is this history?* Zoë phoned her every Tuesday.

"You always say that," said Evan, "but then you go on your trips and vacations and then you settle back into things and then you're quiet for a while and then you say you're fine, you're busy, and then after a while you say you're going crazy again, and you start all over." Evan was a part-time food designer for photo shoots. She cooked vegetables in green dye. She propped up beef stew with a bed of marbles and shopped for new kinds of silicone sprays and plastic ice cubes. She thought her life was "OK." She was living with her boyfriend of many years, who was independently wealthy and had an amusing little job in book publishing. They were five years out of college, and they lived in a luxury midtown high-rise with a balcony and access to a pool. "It's not the same as having your own pool," Evan was always sighing, as if to let Zoë know that, as with Zoë, there were still things she, Evan, had to do without.

"Illinois. It makes me sarcastic to be here," said Zoë on the phone. She used to insist it was irony, something gently layered and sophisticated, something alien to the Midwest, but her students kept calling it sarcasm, something they felt qualified to recognize, and now she had to agree. It wasn't irony. *What is your perfume?* a student once asked her. *Room freshener*, she said. She smiled, but he looked at her, unnerved.

Her students were by and large good Midwesterners, spacey with estrogen from large quantities of meat and cheese. They shared their parents' suburban values; their parents had given them things, things, things. They were complacent. They had been purchased. They were armed with a healthy vagueness about anything historical or geographic. They seemed actually to know very little about anything, but they were extremely good-natured about it. "All those states in the East are so tiny and jagged and bunched up," complained one of her undergraduates the week she was lecturing on "The Turning Point of Independence: The Battle at Saratoga." "Professor Hendricks, you're from Delaware originally, right?" the student asked her.

"Maryland," corrected Zoë.

"Aw," he said, waving his hand dismissively. "New England."

Her articles—chapters toward a book called *Hearing the One About: Uses of Humor in the American Presidency*—were generally well received, though they came slowly for her. She liked her pieces to have something from every time of day in them—she didn't trust things written in the morning only—so she reread and rewrote painstakingly. No part of a day, its moods, its light, was allowed to dominate. She hung on to a piece for over a year sometimes, revising at all hours, until the entirety of a day had registered there.

The job she'd had before the one at Hilldale-Versailles had been at a small college in New Geneva, Minnesota, Land of the Dying Shopping Mall. Everyone was so blonde there that brunettes were often presumed to be from foreign countries. *Just because Professor Hendricks is from Spain doesn't give her the right to be so negative about our country.* There was a general emphasis on cheerfulness. In New Geneva you weren't supposed to be critical or complain. You weren't supposed to notice that the town had overextended and that its shopping malls were raggedy and going under. You were never to say you weren't fine thank you and yourself. You were supposed to be Heidi. You were supposed to lug goat milk up the hills and not think twice. Heidi did not complain. Heidi did not do things like stand in front of the new IBM photocopier, saying, "If this fucking Xerox machine breaks on me one more time, I'm going to slit my wrists."

But now, in her second job, in her fourth year of teaching in the Midwest, Zoë was discovering something she never suspected she had: a crusty edge, brittle and pointed. Once she had pampered her students, singing them songs, letting them call her at home, even, and ask personal questions. Now she was losing sympathy. They were beginning to seem different. They were beginning to seem demanding and spoiled.

"You act," said one of her Senior Seminar students at a scheduled conference, "like your opinion is worth more than everybody else's in the class."

Zoë's eyes widened. "I *am* the teacher," she said. "I *do* get paid to act like that." She narrowed her gaze at the student, who was wearing a big leather bow in her hair, like a cowgirl in a TV ranch show. "I mean, otherwise *everybody* in the class would have little offices and office hours." *Sometimes Professor Hendricks will take up the class's time just talking about movies she's seen.* She stared at the student some more, then added, "I bet you'd like that."

"Maybe I sound whiny to you," said the girl, "but I simply want my history major to mean something."

"Well, there's your problem," said Zoë, and with a smile, she showed the student to the door. "I like your bow," she added.

Zoë lived for the mail, for the postman, that handsome blue jay, and when she got a real letter, with a real full-price stamp, from someplace else, she took it to bed with her and read it over and over. She also watched television until all hours and had her set in the bedroom, a bad sign. *Professor Hendricks has said critical things about Fawn Hall, the Catholic religion, and the whole state of Illinois. It is unbelievable.* At Christmastime she gave twenty-dollar tips to the mailman and to Jerry, the only cabbie in town, whom she had gotten to know from all her rides to and from the Terre Haute airport, and who, since he realized such rides were an extravagance, often gave her cut rates.

"I'm flying in to visit you this weekend," announced Zoë.

"I was hoping you would," said Evan. "Charlie and I are having a party for Halloween. It'll be fun."

"I have a costume already. It's a bonehead. It's this thing that looks like a giant bone going through your head."

"Great," said Evan.

"It is, it's great."

"Alls I have is my moon mask from last year and the year before. I'll probably end up getting married in it."

"Are you and Charlie getting *married*?" Foreboding filled her voice.

"Hmmmmmmnnno, not immediately."

"Don't get married."

"Why?"

"Just not yet. You're too young."

"You're only saying that because you're five years older than I am and *you're* not married."

"*I'm* not married? Oh, my God," said Zoë. "I forgot to get married."

Zoë had been out with three men since she'd come to Hilldale-Versailles. One of them was a man in the Paris municipal bureaucracy who had fixed a parking ticket she'd brought in to protest and who then asked her to coffee. At first she thought he was amazing—at last, someone who did not want Heidi! But soon she came to realize that all men, deep down, wanted Heidi. Heidi with cleavage. Heidi with outfits. The parking ticket bureaucrat soon became tired and intermittent. One cool fall day, in his snazzy, impractical convertible, when she asked him what was wrong, he said, "You would not be ill-served by new clothes, you know." She wore a lot of gray-green corduroy. She had been under the impression that it brought out her eyes, those shy stars. She flicked an ant from her sleeve.

"Did you have to brush that off in the car?" he said, driving. He glanced down at his own pectorals, giving first the left, then the right, a quick survey. He was wearing a tight shirt.

"Excuse me?"

He slowed down at a yellow light and frowned. "Couldn't you have picked it up and thrown it outside?"

"The ant? It might have bitten me. I mean, what difference does it make?"

"It might have bitten you! Ha! How ridiculous! Now it's going to lay eggs in my car!"

The second guy was sweeter, lunkier, though not insensitive to certain paintings and songs, but too often, too, things he'd do or say would startle her. Once, in a restaurant, he stole the garnishes off her dinner plate and waited for her to notice. When she didn't, he finally thrust his fist across the table and said, "Look," and when he opened it, there was her parsley sprig and her orange slice, crumpled to a wad. Another time he described to her his recent trip to the Louvre. "And there I was in front of Géricault's *Raft of the Medusa*, and everyone else had wandered off, so I had my own private audience with it, all those painted, drowning bodies splayed in every direction, and there's this motion in that painting that starts at the bottom left, swirling and building, and building, and building, and going up to the right-hand corner, where there's this guy waving a flag, and on the horizon in the distance you could see this teeny tiny boat. . . ." He was breathless in the telling. She found this touching and smiled in encouragement. "A painting like that," he said, shaking his head. "It just makes you shit."

"I have to ask you something," said Evan. "I know every woman complains about not meeting men, but really, on my shoots, I meet a lot of men. And they're not all gay, either." She paused. "Not anymore."

"What are you asking?"

The third guy was a political science professor named Murray Peterson, who liked to go out on double dates with colleagues whose wives he was attracted to. Usually the wives would consent to flirt with him. Under the table sometimes there was footsie, and once there was even kneesie. Zoë and the husband would be left to their food, staring into their water glasses, chewing like goats. "Oh, Murray," said one wife, who had never finished her master's in physical therapy and wore great clothes. "You know, I know everything about you: your birthday, your license plate number. I have everything memorized. But then that's the kind of mind I have. Once at a dinner party I amazed the host by getting up and saying good-bye to every single person there, first *and* last names."

"I knew a dog who could do that," said Zoë, with her mouth full. Murray and the wife looked at her with vexed and rebuking expressions, but the husband seemed suddenly twinkling and amused. Zoë swallowed. "It was a Talking Lab, and after about ten minutes of listening to the dinner conversation this dog knew everyone's name. You could say, 'Bring this knife to Murray Peterson,' and it would."

"Really," said the wife, frowning, and Murray Peterson never called again.

"Are you seeing anyone?" said Evan. "I'm asking for a particular reason, I'm not just being like mom."

"I'm seeing my house. I'm tending to it when it wets, when it cries, when it throws up." Zoë had bought a mint-green ranch house near campus, though now she was thinking that maybe she shouldn't have. It was hard to live in a house. She kept wandering in and out of the rooms, wondering where she had put things. She went downstairs into the basement for no reason at all except that it amused her to own a basement. It also amused her to own a tree. The day she moved in, she had tacked to her tree a small paper sign that said *Zoë's Tree*.

Her parents, in Maryland, had been very pleased that one of their children had at last been able to afford real estate, and when she closed on the house they sent her flowers with a Congratulations card. Her mother had even UPS'd a box of old decorating magazines saved over the years, photographs of beautiful rooms her mother used to moon over, since there never had been any money to redecorate. It was like getting her mother's pornography, that box, inheriting her drooled-upon fantasies, the endless wish and tease that had been her life. But to her mother it was a rite of passage that pleased her. "Maybe you will get some ideas from these," she had written. And when Zoë looked at the photographs, at the bold and beautiful living rooms, she was filled with longing. Ideas and ideas of longing.

Right now Zoë's house was rather empty. The previous owner had wall-papered around the furniture, leaving strange gaps and silhouettes on the walls, and Zoë hadn't done much about that yet. She had bought furniture, then taken it back, furnishing and unfurnishing, preparing and shedding, like a womb. She had bought several plain pine chests to use as love seats or boot boxes, but they came to look to her more and more like children's coffins, so she returned them. And she had recently bought an Oriental rug for the living room, with Chinese symbols on it she didn't understand. The salesgirl had kept saying she was sure they meant *Peace* and *Eternal Life*, but when Zoë got the rug home, she worried. What if they didn't mean *Peace* and *Eternal Life*? What if they meant, say, *Bruce Springsteen*. And the more she thought about it, the more she became convinced she had a rug that said *Bruce Springsteen*, and so she returned that, too.

She had also bought a little baroque mirror for the front entryway, which she had been told, by Murray Peterson, would keep away evil spirits. The mirror, however, tended to frighten *her*, startling her with an image of a woman she never recognized. Sometimes she looked puffier and plainer than she remembered. Sometimes shifty and dark. Most times she just looked vague. *You look like someone I know*, she had been told twice in the last year by strangers in restaurants in Terre Haute. In fact, sometimes she seemed not to have a look of her own, or any look whatsoever, and it began to amaze her that her students and colleagues were able to recognize her at all. How did they know? When she walked into a room, how did she look so that they knew it was her? Like this? Did she look like this? And so she returned the mirror.

"The reason I'm asking is that I know a man I think you should meet," said Evan. "He's fun. He's straight. He's single. That's all I'm going to say."

"I think I'm too old for fun," said Zoë. She had a dark bristly hair in her chin, and she could feel it now with her finger. Perhaps when you had been without the opposite sex for too long, you began to resemble them. In an act of desperate invention, you began to grow your own. "I just want to come, wear my bonehead, visit with Charlie's tropical fish, ask you about your food shoots."

She thought about all the papers on "Our Constitution: How It Affects Us" she was going to have to correct. She thought about how she was going in for ultrasound tests on Friday, because, according to her doctor and her doctor's assistant, she had a large, mysterious growth in her abdomen. Gallbladder, they kept saying. Or ovaries or colon. "You guys practice medicine?" asked Zoë, aloud, after they had left the room. Once, as a girl, she brought her dog to a vet, who had told her, "Well, either your dog has worms or cancer or else it was hit by a car."

She was looking forward to New York.

"Well, whatever. We'll just play it cool. I can't wait to see you, hon. Don't forget your bonehead," said Evan.

"A bonehead you don't forget," said Zoë.

"I suppose," said Evan.

The ultrasound Zoë was keeping a secret, even from Evan. "I feel like I'm dying," Zoë had hinted just once on the phone.

"You're not dying," said Evan. "You're just annoyed."

"Ultrasound," Zoë now said jokingly to the technician who put the cold jelly on her bare stomach. "Does that sound like a really great stereo system, or what?" She had not had anyone make this much fuss over her bare stomach since her boyfriend in graduate school, who had hovered over her whenever she felt ill, waved his arms, pressed his hands upon her navel, and drawled evangelically, "Heal! Heal for thy Baby Jesus' sake!" Zoë would laugh and they would make love, both secretly hoping she would get pregnant. Later they would worry together, and he would sink a cheek to her belly and ask whether she was late, was she late, was she sure, she might be late, and when after two years she had not gotten pregnant, they took to quarreling and drifted apart.

"OK," said the technician absently.

The monitor was in place, and Zoë's insides came on the screen in all their gray and ribbony hollowness. They were marbled in the finest gradations of black and white, like stone in an old church or a picture of the moon. "Do you suppose," she babbled at the technician, "that the rise in infertility among so many couples in this country is due to completely different species trying to reproduce?" The technician moved the scanner around and took more pictures. On one view in particular, on Zoë's right side, the technician became suddenly alert, the machine he was operating clicking away.

Zoë stared at the screen. "That must be the growth you found there," suggested Zoë.

"I can't tell you anything," said the technician rigidly. "Your doctor will get the radiologist's report this afternoon and will phone you then."

"I'll be out of town," said Zoë.

"I'm sorry," said the technician.

Driving home, Zoë looked in the rearview mirror and decided she looked—well, how would one describe it? A little wan. She thought of the joke about the guy who visits his doctor and the doctor says, "Well, I'm sorry to say you've got six weeks to live."

"I want a second opinion," says the guy. *You act like your opinion is worth more than everyone else's in the class.*

"You want a second opinion? OK," says the doctor. "You're ugly, too." She liked that joke. She thought it was terribly, terribly funny.

She took a cab to the airport, Jerry the cabbie happy to see her.

"Have fun in New York," he said, getting her bag out of the trunk. He liked her, or at least he always acted as if he did. She called him "Jare."

"Thanks, Jare."

"You know, I'll tell you a secret: I've never been to New York. I'll tell you two secrets: I've never been on a plane." And he waved at her sadly as she pushed her way through the terminal door. "Or an escalator!" he shouted.

The trick to flying safe, Zoë always said, was never to buy a discount ticket and to tell yourself you had nothing to live for anyway, so that when the plane crashed it was no big deal. Then, when it didn't crash, when you had succeeded in keeping it aloft with your own worthlessness, all you had to do was stagger off, locate your luggage, and, by the time a cab arrived, come up with a persuasive reason to go on living.

"You're here!" shrieked Evan over the doorbell, before she even opened the door. Then she opened it wide. Zoë set her bags on the hall floor and hugged Evan hard. When she was little, Evan had always been affectionate and devoted. Zoë had always taken care of her, advising, reassuring, until recently, when it seemed Evan had started advising and reassuring *her*. It startled Zoë. She suspected it had something to do with Zoë's being alone. It made people uncomfortable. "How *are* you?"

"I threw up on the plane. Besides that, I'm OK."

"Can I get you something? Here, let me take your suitcase. Sick on the plane. Eeeyew."

"It was into one of those sickness bags," said Zoë, just in case Evan thought she'd lost it in the aisle. "I was very quiet."

The apartment was spacious and bright, with a view all the way downtown along the East Side. There was a balcony and sliding glass doors. "I keep forgetting how nice this apartment is. Twentieth floor, doorman . . ." Zoë could work her whole life and never have an apartment like this. So could Evan. It was Charlie's apartment. He and Evan lived in it like two kids in a dorm, beer cans and clothes strewn around. Evan put Zoë's bag away from the mess, over by the fish tank. "I'm so glad you're here," she said. "Now what can I get you?"

Evan made them a snack—soup from a can, and saltines.

"I don't know about Charlie," she said, after they had finished. "I feel like we've gone all sexless and middle-aged already."

"Hmmm," said Zoë. She leaned back into Evan's sofa and stared out the window at the dark tops of the buildings. It seemed a little unnatural to live up in the sky like this, like birds that out of some wrongheaded derring-do had nested too high. She nodded toward the lighted fish tanks and giggled. "I feel like a bird," she said, "with my own personal supply of fish."

Evan sighed. "He comes home and just sacks out on the sofa, watching fuzzy football. He's wearing the psychic cold cream and curlers, if you know what I mean."

Zoë sat up, readjusted the sofa cushions. "What's fuzzy football?"

"We haven't gotten cable yet. Everything comes in fuzzy. Charlie just watches it that way."

"Hmmm, yeah, that's a little depressing," Zoë said. She looked at her hands. "Especially the part about not having cable."

"This is how he gets into bed at night." Evan stood up to demonstrate. "He whips all his clothes off, and when he gets to his underwear, he lets it drop to one ankle. Then he kicks up his leg and flips the underwear in the air and catches it. I, of course, watch from the bed. There's nothing else. There's just that."

"Maybe you should just get it over with and get married."

"Really?"

"Yeah. I mean, you guys probably think living together like this is the best of both worlds, but . . ." Zoë tried to sound like an older sister; an older sister was supposed to be the parent you could never have, the hip, cool mom. ". . . I've always found that as soon as you think you've got the best of both worlds"—she thought now of herself, alone in her house; of the toad-faced cicadas that flew around like little caped men at night, landing on her screens, staring; of the size fourteen shoes she placed at the doorstep, to scare off intruders; of the ridiculous inflatable blow-up doll someone had told her to keep propped up at the breakfast table—"it can suddenly twist and become the worst of both worlds."

"Really?" Evan was beaming. "Oh, Zoë. I have something to tell you. Charlie and I *are* getting married."

"Really." Zoë felt confused.

"I didn't know how to tell you."

"Yes, well, I guess the part about fuzzy football misled me a little."

"I was hoping you'd be my maid of honor," said Evan, waiting. "Aren't you happy for me?"

"Yes," said Zoë, and she began to tell Evan a story about an award-winning violinist at Hilldale-Versailles, how the violinist had come home from a competition in Europe and taken up with a local man, who made her go to all his summer softball games, made her cheer for him from the stands, with the wives, until she later killed herself. But when she got halfway through, to the part about cheering at the softball games, Zoë stopped.

"What?" said Evan. "So what happened?"

"Actually, nothing," said Zoë lightly. "She just really got into softball. I mean, really. You should have seen her."

Zoë decided to go to a late-afternoon movie, leaving Evan to chores she needed to do before the party—*I have to do them alone*, she'd said, a little tense after the violinist story. Zoë thought about going to an art museum, but women alone in art museums had to look good. They always did. Chic and serious, moving languidly, with a great handbag. Instead, she walked over and down through Kips Bay, past an earring boutique called Stick It in Your Ear, past a beauty salon called Dorian Gray's. That was the funny thing about *beauty*, thought Zoë. Look it up in the yellow pages, and you found a hundred entries, hostile with wit, cutesy with warning. But look up *truth*—ha! There was nothing at all.

Zoë thought about Evan getting married. Would Evan turn into Peter Pumpkin Eater's wife? Mrs. Eater? At the wedding would she make Zoë wear some flouncy lavender dress, identical with the other maids'? Zoë hated uniforms, had even, in the first grade, refused to join Elf Girls, because she didn't want to wear the same dress as everyone else. Now she might have to. But maybe she could distinguish it. Hitch it up on one side with a clothespin. Wear surgical gauze at the waist. Clip to her bodice one of those pins that said in loud letters, SHIT HAPPENS.

At the movie—*Death by Number*—she bought strands of red licorice to tug and chew. She took a seat off to one side in the theater. She felt strangely self-conscious sitting alone and hoped for the place to darken fast. When it did, and the coming attractions came on, she reached inside her purse for her glasses. They were in a Baggie. Her Kleenex was also in a Baggie. So were her pen and her aspirin and her mints. Everything was in Baggies. This was what she'd become: *a woman alone at the movies and everything in a Baggie.*

At the Halloween party, there were about two dozen people. There were people with ape heads and large hairy hands. There was someone dressed as a leprechaun. There was someone dressed as a frozen dinner. Some man had brought his two small daughters: a ballerina and a ballerina's sister, also dressed as a ballerina. There was a gaggle of sexy witches—women dressed entirely in black, beautifully made up and jeweled. "I hate those sexy witch-es. It's not in the spirit of Halloween," said Evan. Evan had abandoned the moon mask and dolled herself up as a hausfrau, in curlers and an apron, a decision she now regretted. Charlie, because he liked fish, because he owned fish, collected fish, had decided to go as a fish. He had fins and eyes on the side of his head. "Zoë! How are you! I'm sorry I wasn't here when you first arrived!" He spent the rest of his time chatting up the sexy witches.

"Isn't there something I can help you with here?" Zoë asked her sister. "You've been running yourself ragged." She rubbed her sister's arm, gently, as if she wished they were alone.

"Oh, God, not at all," said Evan, arranging stuffed mushrooms on a plate. The timer went off, and she pulled another sheetful out of the oven. "Actually, you know what you can do?"

"What?" Zoë put on her bonehead.

"Meet Earl. He's the guy I had in mind for you. When he gets here, just talk to him a little. He's nice. He's fun. He's going through a divorce."

"I'll try." Zoë groaned. "OK? I'll try." She looked at her watch.

When Earl arrived, he was dressed as a naked woman, steel wool glued strategically to a body stocking, and large rubber breasts protruding like hams.

"Zoë, this is Earl," said Evan.

"Good to meet you," said Earl, circling Evan to shake Zoë's hand. He stared at the top of Zoë's head. "Great bone."

Zoë nodded. "Great tits," she said. She looked past him, out the window at the city thrown glitteringly up against the sky; people were saying the usual things: how it looked like jewels, like bracelets and necklaces unstrung. You could see Grand Central station, the clock of the Con Ed building, the red-and-gold-capped Empire State, the Chrysler like a rocket ship dreamed up in a depression. Far west you could glimpse the Astor Plaza, its flying white roof like a nun's habit. "There's beer out on the balcony, Earl—can I get you one?" Zoë asked.

"Sure, uh, I'll come along. Hey, Charlie, how's it going?"

Charlie grinned and whistled. People turned to look. "Hey, Earl," some-one called, from across the room. "Va-va-va-voom."

They squeezed their way past the other guests, past the apes and the sexy witches. The suction of the sliding door gave way in a whoosh, and Zoë and Earl stepped out onto the balcony, a bonehead and a naked woman, the night air roaring and smoky cool. Another couple was out here, too, murmuring privately. They were not wearing costumes. They smiled at Zoë and Earl. "Hi," said Zoë. She found the plastic-foam cooler, dug into it, and retrieved two beers.

"Thanks," said Earl. His rubber breasts folded inward, dimpled and dented, as he twisted open the bottle.

"Well," sighed Zoë anxiously. She had to learn not to be afraid of a man, the way, in your childhood, you learned not to be afraid of an earthworm or a bug. Often, when she spoke to men at parties, she rushed things in her mind. As the man politely blathered on, she would fall in love, marry, then find herself in a bitter custody battle with him for the kids and hoping for a reconciliation, so that despite all his betrayals she might no longer despise him, and in the few minutes remaining, learn, perhaps, what his last name was and what he did for a living, though probably there was already too much history between them. She would nod, blush, turn away.

"Evan tells me you're a professor. Where do you teach?"

"Just over the Indiana border into Illinois."

He looked a little shocked. "I guess Evan didn't tell me that part."

"She didn't?"

"No."

"Well, that's Evan for you. When we were kids we both had speech impediments."

"That can be tough," said Earl. One of his breasts was hidden behind his drinking arm, but the other shone low and pink, full as a strawberry moon.

"Yes, well, it wasn't a total loss. We used to go to what we called peach pearapy. For about ten years of my life I had to map out every sentence in my mind, way ahead, before I said it. That was the only way I could get a coherent sentence out."

Earl drank from his beer. "How did you do that? I mean, how did you get through?"

"I told a lot of jokes. Jokes you know the lines to already—you can just say them. I love jokes. Jokes and songs."

Earl smiled. He had on lipstick, a deep shade of red, but it was wearing off from the beer. "What's your favorite joke?"

"Uh, my favorite joke is probably . . . OK, all right. This guy goes into a doctor's office and—"

"I think I know this one," interrupted Earl, eagerly. He wanted to tell it himself. "A guy goes into a doctor's office, and the doctor tells him he's got some good news and some bad news—that one, right?"

"I'm not sure," said Zoë. "This might be a different version."

"So the guy says, 'Give me the bad news first,' and the doctor says, 'OK. You've got three weeks to live.' And the guy cries, 'Three weeks to live! Doctor, what is the good news?' And the doctor says, 'Did you see that secretary out front? I finally fucked her.'"

Zoë frowned.

"That's not the one you were thinking of?"

"No." There was accusation in her voice. "Mine was different."

"Oh," said Earl. He looked away and then back again. "You teach history, right? What kind of history do you teach?"

"I teach American, mostly—eighteenth and nineteenth century." In graduate school, at bars, the pickup line was always: "So what's your century?"

"Occasionally I teach a special theme course," she added, "say, 'Humor and Personality in the White House.' That's what my book's on." She thought of something someone once told her about bowerbirds, how they build elaborate structures before mating.

"Your book's on *humor*?"

"Yeah, and, well, when I teach a theme course like that, I do all the centuries." *So what's your century?*

"All three of them."

"Pardon?" The breeze glistened her eyes. Traffic revved beneath them. She felt high and puny, like someone lifted into heaven by mistake and then spurned.

"Three. There's only three."

"Well, four, really." She was thinking of Jamestown, and of the pilgrims coming here with buckles and witch hats to say their prayers.

"I'm a photographer," said Earl. His face was starting to gleam, his rouge smearing in a sunset beneath his eyes.

"Do you like that?"

"Well, actually I'm starting to feel it's a little dangerous."

"Really?"

"Spending all your time in a darkroom with that red light and all those chemicals. There's links with Parkinson's, you know."

"No, I didn't."

"I suppose I should wear rubber gloves, but I don't like to. Unless I'm touching it directly, I don't think of it as real."

"Hmmm," said Zoë. Alarm buzzed through her, mildly, like a tea.

"Sometimes, when I have a cut or something, I feel the sting and think, *Shit*. I wash constantly and just hope. I don't like rubber over the skin like that."

"Really."

"I mean, the physical contact. That's what you want, or why bother?"

"I guess," said Zoë. She wished she could think of a joke, something slow and deliberate, with the end in sight. She thought of gorillas, how when they had been kept too long alone in cages, they would smack each other in the head instead of mating.

"Are you . . . in a relationship?" Earl suddenly blurted.

"Now? As we speak?"

"Well, I mean, I'm sure you have a relationship to your *work*." A smile, a weird one, nestled in his mouth like an egg. She thought of zoos in parks, how when the cities were under siege, during world wars, people ate the animals. "But I mean, with a *man*."

"No, I'm not in a relationship with a *man*." She rubbed her chin with her hand and could feel the one bristly hair there. "But my last relationship was with a very sweet man," she said. She made something up. "From Switzerland. He was a botanist—a weed expert. His name was Jerry. I called him 'Jare.' He was so funny. You'd go to the movies with him and all he would notice were the plants. He would never pay any attention to the plot. Once, in a jungle movie, he started rattling off all these Latin names, out loud. It was very exciting for him." She paused, caught her breath. "Eventually he went back to Europe to, uh, study the edelweiss." She looked at Earl. "Are you involved in a relationship? With a *woman*?"

Earl shifted his weight, and the creases in his body stocking changed, splintering outward like something broken. His pubic hair slid over to one hip, like a corsage on a saloon girl. "No," he said, clearing his throat. The steel wool in his underarms was inching toward his biceps. "I've just gotten out of a marriage that was full of bad dialogue, like 'You want more *space*? I'll give you more space!' *Clonk*. Your basic Three Stooges."

Zoë looked at him sympathetically. "I suppose it's hard for love to recover after that."

His eyes lit up. He wanted to talk about love. "But *I* keep thinking love should be like a tree. You look at trees and they've got bumps and scars from tumors, infestations, what have you, but they're still growing. Despite the bumps and bruises, they're . . . straight."

"Yeah, well," said Zoë, "where I'm from, they're all married or gay. Did you see that movie *Death by Number*?"

Earl looked at her, a little lost. She was getting away from him. "No," he said.

One of his breasts had slipped under his arm, tucked there like a baguette. She kept thinking of trees, of gorillas and parks, of people in wartime eating the zebras. She felt a stabbing pain in her abdomen.

"Want some hors d'oeuvres?" Evan came pushing through the sliding door. She was smiling, though her curlers were coming out, hanging bedraggled at the ends of her hair like Christmas decorations, like food put out for the birds. She thrust forward a plate of stuffed mushrooms.

"Are you asking for donations or giving them away," said Earl, wittily. He liked Evan, and he put his arm around her.

"You know, I'll be right back." said Zoë.

"Oh," said Evan, looking concerned.

"Right back. I promise."

Zoë hurried inside, across the living room, into the bedroom, to the adjoining bath. It was empty; most of the guests were using the half bath near the kitchen. She flicked on the light and closed the door. The pain had stopped and she didn't really have to go to the bathroom, but she stayed there anyway, resting. In the mirror above the sink she looked haggard beneath her bonehead, violet grays showing under the skin like a plucked and pocky bird. She leaned closer, raising her chin a little to find the bristly hair. It was there, at the end of the jaw, sharp and dark as a wire. She opened the medicine cabinet, pawed through it until she found some tweezers. She lifted her head again and poked at her face with the metal tips, grasping and pinching and missing. Outside the door she could hear two people talking low. They had come into the bedroom and were discussing something. They were sitting on the bed. One of them giggled in a false way. She stabbed again at her chin, and it started to bleed a little. She pulled the skin tight along the jawbone, gripped the tweezers hard around what she hoped was the hair, and tugged. A tiny square of skin came away with it, but the hair remained, blood bright at the root of it. Zoë clenched her teeth, "Come on," she whispered. The couple outside in the bedroom were now telling stories, softly, and laughing. There was a bounce and squeak of mattress, and the sound of a chair being moved out of the way. Zoë aimed the tweezers carefully, pinched, then pulled gently away, and this time the hair came, too, with a slight twinge of pain and then a great flood of relief. "Yeah!" breathed Zoë. She grabbed some toilet paper and dabbed at her chin. It came away spotted with blood, and so she tore off some more and pressed hard until it stopped. Then she turned off the light and opened the door, to return to the party. "Excuse me," she said to the couple in the bedroom. They were the couple from the balcony, and they looked at her, a bit surprised. They had their arms around each other, and they were eating candy bars.

Earl was still out on the balcony, alone, and Zoë rejoined him there.

"Hi," she said. He turned around and smiled. He had straightened his costume out a bit, though all the secondary sex characteristics seemed slightly doomed, destined to shift and flip and zip around again any moment.

"Are you OK?" he asked. He had opened another beer and was chugging.

"Oh, yeah. I just had to go to the bathroom." She paused. "Actually I have been going to a lot of doctors recently."

"What's wrong?" asked Earl.

"Oh, probably nothing. But they're putting me through tests." She sighed. "I've had sonograms. I've had mammograms. Next week I'm going in for a candygram." He looked at her worriedly. "I've had too many gram words," she said.

"Here, I saved you these." He held out a napkin with two stuffed mushroom caps. They were cold and leaving oil marks on the napkin.

"Thanks," said Zoë, and pushed them both in her mouth. "Watch, " she said, with her mouth full. "With my luck, it'll be a gallbladder operation."

Earl made a face. "So your sister's getting married," he said, changing the subject. "Tell me, really, what you think about love."

"*Love?*" Hadn't they done this already? "I don't know." She chewed thoughtfully and swallowed. "All right. I'll tell you what I think about love. Here is a love story. This friend of mine—"

"You've got something on your chin," said Earl, and he reached over to touch it.

"*What?*" said Zoë, stepping back. She turned her face away and grabbed at her chin. A piece of toilet paper peeled off it, like tape. "It's nothing," she said. "It's just—it's nothing."

Earl stared at her.

"At any rate," she continued, "this friend of mine was this award-winning violinist. She traveled all over Europe and won competitions; she made records, she gave concerts, she got famous. But she had no social life. So one day she threw herself at the feet of this conductor she had a terrible crush on. He picked her up, scolded her gently, and sent her back to her hotel room. After that she came home from Europe. She went back to her old hometown, stopped playing the violin, and took up with a local boy. This was in Illinois. He took her to some Big Ten bar every night to drink with his buddies from the team. He used to say things like 'Katrina here likes to play the violin,' and then he'd pinch her cheek. When she once suggested that they go home, he said, "What, you think you're too famous for a place like this? Well, let me tell you something. You may think you're famous, but you're not *famous* famous.' Two famouses. 'No one here's ever heard of you.' Then he went up and bought a round of drinks for everyone but her. She got her coat, went home, and shot a gun through her head."

Earl was silent.

"That's the end of my love story," said Zoë.

"You're not at all like your sister," said Earl.

"Ho, really," said Zoë. The air had gotten colder, the wind singing minor and thick as a dirge.

"No." He didn't want to talk about love anymore. "You know, you should wear a lot of blue—blue and white—around your face. It would bring out your coloring." He reached an arm out to show her how the blue bracelet he was wearing might look against her skin, but she swatted it away.

"Tell me, Earl. Does the word *fag* mean anything to you?"

He stepped back, away from her. He shook his head in disbelief. "You know, I just shouldn't try to go out with career women. You're all stricken. A guy can really tell what life has done to you. I do better with women who have part-time jobs."

"Oh, yes?" said Zoë. She had once read an article entitled "Professional Women and the Demographics of Grief." Or no, it was a poem: *If there were a lake, the moonlight would dance across it in conniptions.* She remembered that line. But perhaps the title was "The Empty House: Aesthetics of Barrenness."

Or maybe "Space Gypsies: Girls in Academe." She had forgotten.

Earl turned and leaned on the railing of the balcony. It was getting late. Inside, the party guests were beginning to leave. The sexy witches were already gone. "Live and learn," Earl murmured.

"Live and get dumb," replied Zoë. Beneath them on Lexington there were no cars, just the gold rush of an occasional cab. He leaned hard on his elbows, brooding.

"Look at those few people down there," he said. "They look like bugs. You know how bugs are kept under control? They're sprayed with bug hormones, female bug hormones. The male bugs get so crazy in the presence of this hormone, they're screwing everything in sight: trees, rocks—everything but female bugs. Population control. That's what's happening in this country," he said drunkenly. "Hormones sprayed around, and now men are screwing rocks. Rocks!"

In the back the Magic Marker line of his buttocks spread wide, a sketchy black on pink like a funnies page. Zoë came up, slow, from behind and gave him a shove. His arms slipped forward, off the railing, out over the city below. Beer spilled out of his bottle, raining twenty stories down to the street.

"Hey, what are you doing?!" he said, whipping around. He stood straight and readied and moved away from the railing, sidestepping Zoë. "What the *hell* are you doing?"

"Just kidding," she said. "I was just kidding." But he gazed at her, appalled and frightened, his Magic Marker buttocks turned away now toward all of downtown, a naked pseudo-woman with a blue bracelet at the wrist, trapped out on a balcony with—with *what*? "*Really, I was just kidding!*" Zoë shouted. The wind lifted the hair up off her head, skyward in spines behind the bone. If there were a lake, the moonlight would dance across it in conniptions. She smiled at him, and wondered how she looked.

Acknowledgments

"Shades and Slashes of Light" by Maya Angelou from *Black Women Writers* by Mari Evans, copyright © 1983 by Mari Evans. Used by permission of Doubleday, a division of Random House, Inc.

"Still I Rise" by Maya Angelou from *And Still I Rise* by Maya Angelou, copyright © 1978 by Maya Angelou. Used by permission of Random House, Inc.

"The Four-Night Fight" from *Park City: New and Selected Stories* by Ann Beattie, copyright © 1998 by Irony & Pity, Inc. Used by permission of Alfred A. Knopf, a division of Random House, Inc.

"Rooster" from *The Complete Poems 1927-1979* by Elizabeth Bishop. Copyright © 1979, 1983 by Alice Helen Methfessel. "Efforts of Affection: A Memoir of Marianne Moore" from *The Collected Prose* by Elizabeth Bishop. Copyright © 1984 by Alice Helen Methfessel. Reprinted by permission of Farrar, Straus and Giroux, LLC.

"After the Persian," "Cartography," and "Evening in the Sanitarium" from *The Blue Estuaries* by Louise Bogan. Copyright © 1968 by Louise Bogan. Copyright renewed 1996 by Ruth Limmer. Reprinted by permission of Farrar, Straus and Giroux, LLC.

"The Springs of Affection" from *The Springs of Affection: Stories of Dublin* by Maeve Brennan. Copyright © 1997 by the Estate of Maeve Brennan. Reprinted by permission of Houghton Mifflin Company. All rights reserved.

Excerpt from *The Letters of Charlotte Brontë, Volume I: 1829-1847*, edited by Margaret Smith, copyright © 1995 by Margaret Smith. Reprinted by permission of Oxford University Press.

"Sugar Daddy" by Angela Carter, copyright © 1983 by Angela Carter. Reprinted by permission of the Estate of Angela Carter, c/o Rogers, Coleridge & White Ltd., 20 Powis Mews, London W11 1JN, England.

"Woman Hollering Creek" from *Woman Hollering Creek*, copyright © 1991 by Sandra Cisneros. Published by Vintage Books, a division of Random House, Inc., New York, and originally in hardcover by Random House, Inc. Reprinted by permission of Susan Bergholz Literary Services, New York. All rights reserved.

"song at midnight" and "won't you celebrate with me" by Lucille Clifton, from *The Book of Light*. Copyright © 1993 by Lucille Clifton. Reprinted with the permission of Copper Canyon Press, P.O. Box 271, Port Townsend, WA 98368-0271.

"mary" and "miss rosie" from *Good Woman: Poems and a Memoir 1969-1980*. Copyright © 1987 by Lucille Clifton. Reprinted with the permission of BOA Editions, Ltd.

Poems 292, 479, and 613 by Emily Dickinson reprinted by permission of the publishers and the Trustees of Amherst College from *The Poems of Emily Dickinson*, Thomas H. Johnson, ed., Cambridge, Mass.: The Belknap Press of Harvard University Press, copyright © 1951, 1955, 1979 by the President and Fellows of Harvard College.

"Gospel," "Weathering Out," and "Motherhood" from *Thomas and Beulah*, Carnegie-Mellon University Press, copyright © 1986 by Rita Dove. Reprinted by permission of the author.

Moore. Copyright 1935 by Marianne Moore, copyright © renewed 1963 by Marianne Moore and T. S. Eliot. Reprinted with the permission of Scribner, a division of Simon & Schuster, Inc.

Nobel Prize speech of Toni Morrison reprinted by permission of International Creative Management, Inc. Copyright © 1993 by Toni Morrison.

"The Children Stay" from *The Love of a Good Woman* by Alice Munro, copyright © 1998 by Alice Munro. Used by permission of Alfred A. Knopf, a division of Random House, Inc.

"Christmas Night 1962" by Joyce Carol Oates, copyright © 1996 by Ontario Review Press. Reprinted by permission of John Hawkins & Associates, Inc.

"Escape to England" from *Mother Ireland* by Edna O'Brien, copyright © 1976 by Edna O'Brien. Used by permission of Dutton Signet, a division of Penguin Putnam Inc.

"A Late Encounter with the Enemy" from *A Good Man Is Hard to Find and Other Stories*, copyright © 1953 by Flannery O'Connor and renewed 1981 by Regina O'Connor, reprinted by permission of Harcourt, Inc.

"Bathing the New Born" from *The Wellspring* by Sharon Olds, copyright © 1996 by Sharon Olds. "I Go Back to May 1937" and "Topography" from *The Gold Cell* by Sharon Olds, copyright © 1987 by Sharon Olds. "The Race" from *The Father* by Sharon Olds, copyright © 1992 by Sharon Olds. Used by permission of Alfred A. Knopf, a division of Random House, Inc.

"When Death Comes" from *New and Selected Poems* by Mary Oliver. Copyright © 1992 by Mary Oliver. Reprinted by permission of Beacon Press, Boston.

"Wild Geese" from *Dream Work* by Mary Oliver. Copyright © 1986 by Mary Oliver. Reprinted by permission of Grove/Atlantic, Inc.

"I Stand Here Ironing" copyright © 1956, 1957, 1960, 1961 by Tillie Olsen, from *Tell Me a Riddle* by Tillie Olsen, introduction by John Leonard. Used by permission of Dell Publishing, a division of Random House, Inc.

"A Drugstore in Winter" from *Art and Ardor* by Cynthia Ozick, copyright © 1983 by Cynthia Ozick. "The Shawl" from *The Shawl* by Cynthia Ozick, copyright © 1980, 1983 by Cynthia Ozick. Used by permission of Alfred A. Knopf, a division of Random House, Inc.

"Samuel" from *The Collected Stories* by Grace Paley. Copyright © 1994 by Grace Paley. "Traveling" from *Just As I Thought* by Grace Paley. Copyright © 1998 by Grace Paley. Reprinted by permission of Farrar, Straus and Giroux, LLC.

"Barbie Doll" and "to be of use" from *Circles on the Water* by Marge Piercy, copyright © 1982 by Marge Piercy. Used by permission of Alfred A. Knopf, a division of Random House, Inc.

"Kindness" and "The Moon and the Yew Tree" from *The Collected Poems of Sylvia Plath*, edited by Ted Hughes. Copyright © 1960, 1965, 1971, 1981 by the Estate of Sylvia Plath. Editorial material copyright © 1981 by Ted Hughes. Reprinted by permission of HarperCollins Publishers, Inc.

"One Is One," "The Story After the Story," and "Foreign Correspondent" from *The Bird Catcher* by Marie Ponsot, copyright © 1998 by Marie Ponsot. Used by permission of Alfred A. Knopf, a division of Random House, Inc.